THE
CHINGRI KHAL
CHRONICLES

Dorothy Hobbs
in the 1920s – at about the time
of her long journey.

THE
CHINGRI KHAL
CHRONICLES

A partial family history

MARTIN TUCKER

CK
PUBLICATIONS
WINCHESTER

This edition published in the UK in 2005 by
CK PUBLICATIONS
Chingri Khal, Sleepers Hill, Winchester, SO22 4NB

ISBN 10 : 0-9552049-0-9

ISBN 13 : 978-0-9552049-0-6

Produced and printed by members of
THE GUILD OF MASTER CRAFTSMEN

Book design and typesetting by Cecil Smith
Typeset in Minion

Printed and bound in Great Britain by
RPM PRINT & DESIGN
2-3 Spur Road, Quarry Lane, Chichester, West Sussex PO19 8PR

FOR SHEILA

With all my love and thanks
for making the fourth
Chingri Khal
an even happier home
than were the first three.

CHINGRI KHAL

Chin as in 'chink.'
Gri as in 'grip.'
Khal to rhyme with 'cull.'

CONTENTS

ACKNOWLEDGEMENTS

I AM VERY GRATEFUL indeed to the many people who have given me help and encouragement, whether in the course of their everyday work, or personally. I hope I have remembered them all. I apologise to anyone left out: it has been an accidental and not a deliberate omission.

All custodians of records and archives have been very kind and helpful, including: the staff at the Central Register Office, and those at Winchester, Bournemouth, Poole, Exeter and Croydon Register Offices; the Central and Winchester Probate Offices; the Manager of the Information Centre for Guy's Hospital; the Registration Officer at the General Dental Council; the Archivist at Girton College, Cambridge; the Records Department of the Law Society. The Indian authorities were equally co-operative, if a trifle slower, particularly the Registrar at Calcutta who was prepared to accept a Scottish one pound note to pay a Rs.10 fee (worth a little less than 15 new pence.) Father John, at St. Thomas's Catholic Church, Calcutta was kindness and speedy efficiency personified. The Head of Archive & Library at the National Portrait Gallery gave me much interesting information about Philip Tennyson Cole and his portrait of Harry Hobbs. The Senior Assistant Editor of the Oxford English Dictionary was of great help in dealing with a little linguistic problem and putting me on to *Sahibs, Nabobs and Boxwallahs* by Ivor Lewis which was invaluable in compiling my short Glossary.

I am very grateful for generous permission given by the publishers of *The Daily Mail* to reproduce one of Ian Coster's columns in *The Daily Mail* and by the publishers of *The North Devon Journal* for similar permission relating to their account of life saving at Woolacombe in July, 1901.

The 2nd City of London Regiment (Royal Fusiliers) sadly no longer exists. However the Archivist of the Royal Fusiliers Museum in the Tower of London very kindly encouraged me to reproduce extracts from *The 2nd City of London Regiment (Royal Fusiliers) in the Great War (1914-19)* by Major W. E. Grey, as being well out of copyright. Thacker Spink Publishers, of Calcutta, who published two of Harry Hobbs's books, namely *The Piano in India* and *It was like this!* ceased trading many years ago and I have found no one to ask if they claimed any copyright in either book. The same applies to illustrations on pages 105 (Top) and 240 taken from *Recollections of Calcutta* by Montague Massey (1918) and therein credited to Johnston & Hoffmann. I should have liked also to ask for permission from three Calcutta newspapers or journals, *Capital, The Calcutta Municipal Gazette and Monthly Review* to reproduce obituaries of Harry Hobbs. None are still published and likewise I have found no one from whom to seek permission.

The illustrations of ships on pages 286 and 287 come from various sources. Those of *SS Rawalpindi* and *SS Ruahine* are from *Great Passenger Ships of the World*, Vols. 1 and 3, by Arnold Kludas and are reproduced by kind permission of Patrick Stephens Ltd., an imprint of Haynes Publishing, Sparkford, Yeovil, BA22 7JJ. Those of *SS Arankola* and *SS Marama* (Nos. 28 and 30) come from *Merchant Fleets* by Duncan Haws and are reproduced by kind permission of Shield Publications Ltd. of Low Fell, Gateshead, NE9 7YS. That of *SS Houtman* is reproduced by courtesy of the National Maritime Museum. The photograph of the Danguar Jhar bungalow was provided by Joan Scott. The photograph of Downside Abbey Church is taken from a post card and is reproduced by kind permission of the Prior of Downside. All the other photographs are from my personal collection.

On the professional side I have been very fortunate in having the help of Cecil Smith and of many at RPM Print and Design. Their great skill and expertise has transformed my bare manuscript into a most attractive book. It has always been a great pleasure to work with them, whether in being gently restrained from error, or enthusiastically encouraged to make progress. I have much to thank them for.

All my family have been simply marvellous. Eddie Tyson started me off with an extract from a Census of 1881. My cousin Harry Hobbs in Canada gave me much information and copy documents, as well as putting me on to getting our grandfather's first book. My 'Breaks cousins', Phyllida (Clark), Elizabeth (van den Brul) and James all gave memories and documents which have been extremely helpful. It is a great sadness that James died before publication was possible. Mary Hibbs kindly read the chapter concerning my father's early life and corrected my errors. Joan Scott, a family member to all intents and purposes, gave me much help with her own memories and knowledge of India and of life at the third Chingri Khal. Her undiluted enthusiasm for the project has always been a great tonic.

My own children have been wonderful in rallying round, reading most of the text and giving useful criticism and advice. Adrian researched much shipping for me and has used all his considerable professional skill in preparing the splendid maps which will surely add greatly to the enjoyment of the reader. Catharine undertook a lot of early typing, until my computer arrived, when they all, with sons-in-law as well, helped to set it up and thereafter were all too often the recipients of panic 'phone calls when I found I had done something stupid and was about to throw a brick through the screen.

Finally, my wife, Sheila, has been a tower of strength. She put up with my retiring to my desk and living in the past. She read each chapter as it came out of the computer and talked it over with me. She has been a source of wise advice throughout the whole project and so helping me immeasurably. As with everything else, without her none of this would have happened.

My grateful thanks to them all.

MARTIN TUCKER
December 2005

ILLUSTRATIONS

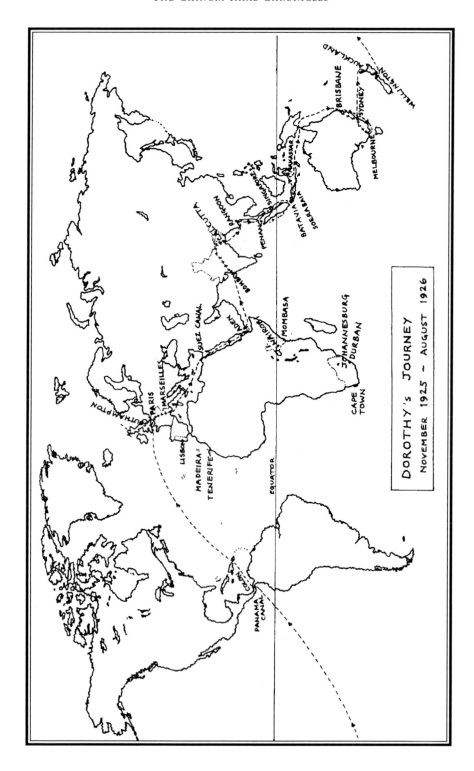

DOROTHY's JOURNEY
NOVEMBER 1925 ~ AUGUST 1926

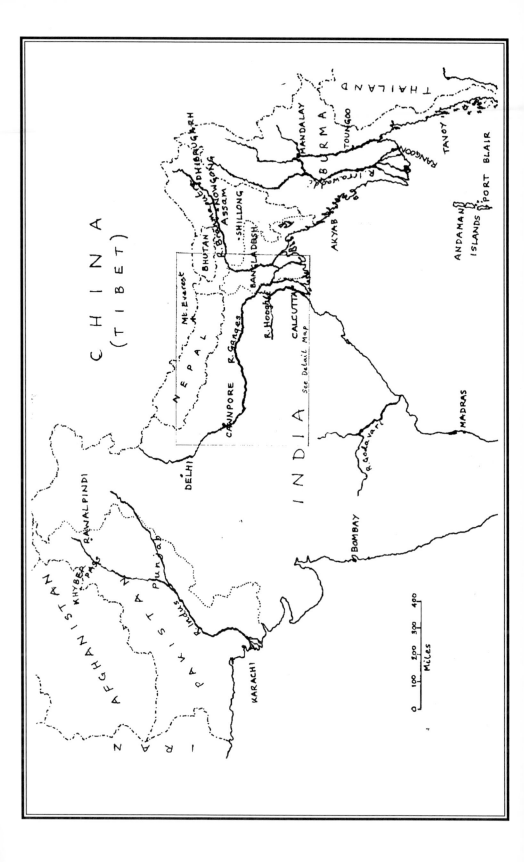

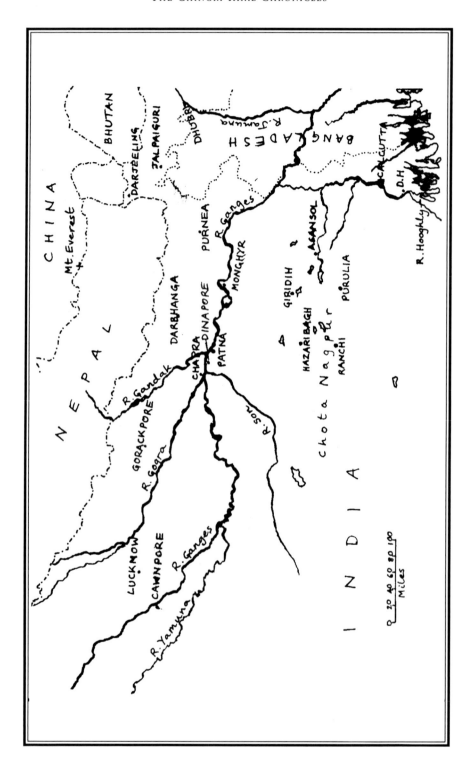

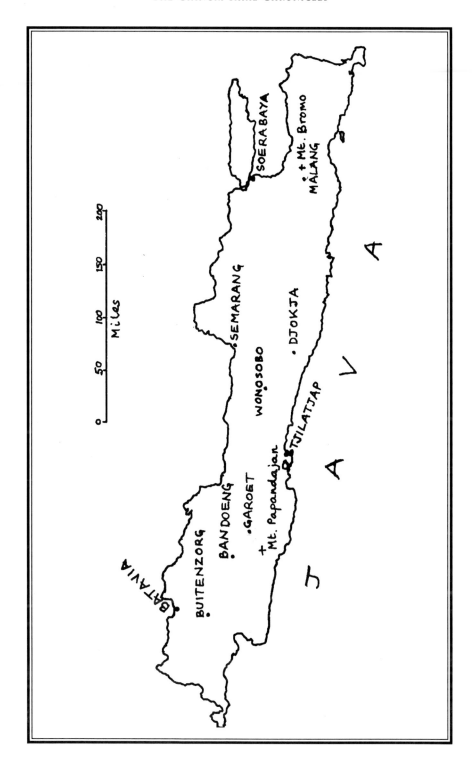

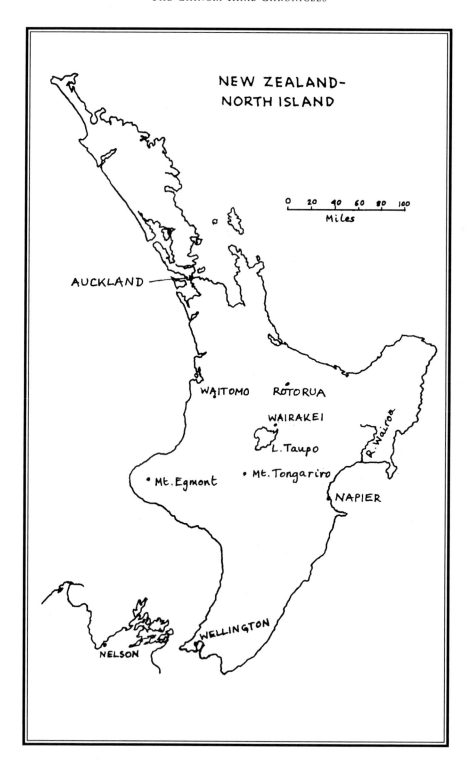

NEW ZEALAND–
NORTH ISLAND

0 20 40 60 80 100
Miles

AUCKLAND

WAITOMO   ROTORUA

WAIRAKEI

L. Taupo

• Mt. Egmont   • Mt. Tongariro

R. Wairoa

NAPIER

WELLINGTON

NELSON

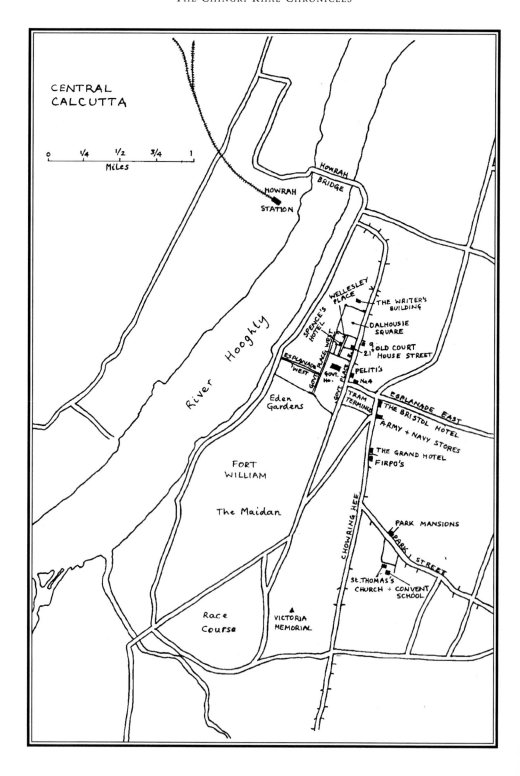

CENTRAL
CALCUTTA

0   1/4   1/2   3/4   1
Miles

HOWRAH
BRIDGE

HOWRAH
STATION

River Hooghly

WELLESLEY
PLACE

THE WRITER'S
BUILDING

SPENCE'S
HOTEL

DALHOUSIE
SQUARE

9
21 OLD COURT
HOUSE STREET

ESPLANADE
WEST

GOVT PLACE WEST

GOVT PLACE EAST

GOVT.
No.1

PELITI's

No.4

ESPLANADE EAST

Eden
Gardens

TRAM
TERMINUS

THE BRISTOL HOTEL

ARMY + NAVY STORES

THE GRAND HOTEL

FIRPO's

FORT
WILLIAM

The Maidan

CHOWRINGHEE

PARK MANSIONS

PARK STREET

St. THOMAS'S
CHURCH + CONVENT
SCHOOL

Race
Course

VICTORIA
MEMORIAL

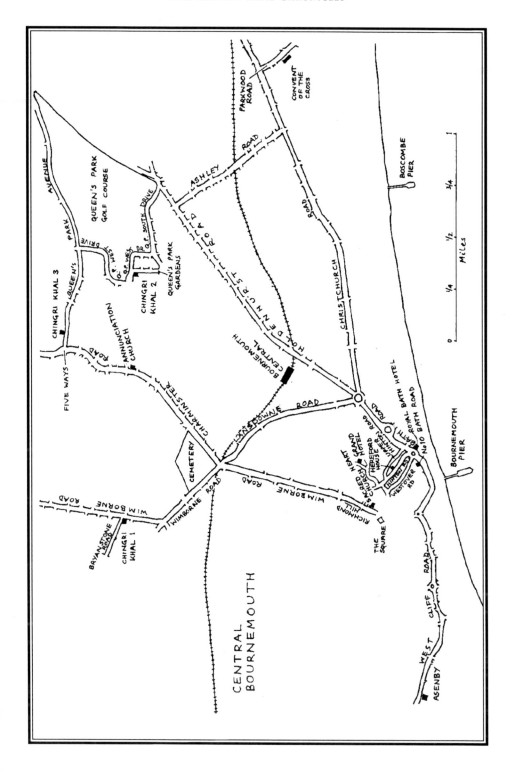

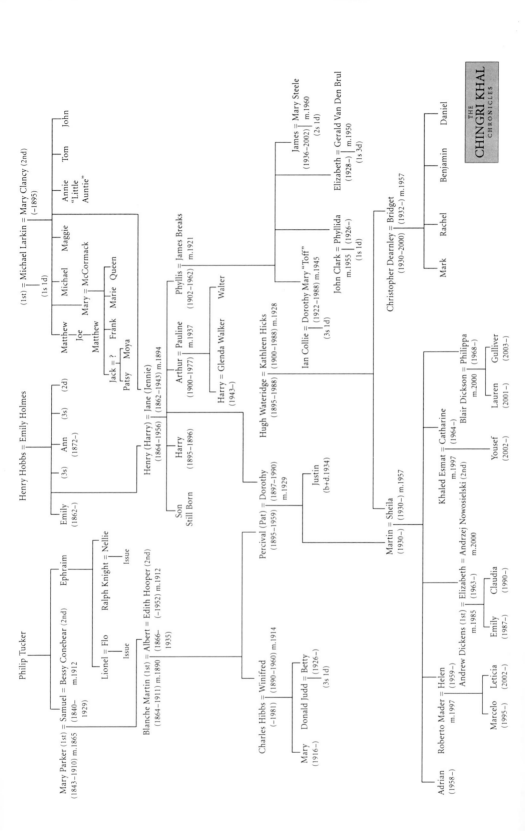

THE
CHINGRI KHAL
CHRONICLES

INTRODUCTION

I T IS PROBABLY TRUE TO SAY that the first germ of an idea for this book came into being in 1943. That was the year in which my maternal grandmother Jennie Hobbs died at her home in Bournemouth. Her husband, my grandfather Harry Hobbs, was in India. He had lived in Calcutta for most of his life. Consequently the task of going through Jennie's effects had to be undertaken by her daughters, and that largely fell to my mother, her eldest daughter, Dorothy. Jennie had lived for over 30 years in Chingri Khal, the house in Bournemouth in which she had died. The task, therefore, was a considerable one. This was not surprising. It did, however, surprise Dorothy to find that Jennie had kept virtually every letter and other personal communication ever written to her by any member of her family. In many families that might not amount to much, but Harry was a most prolific writer. Letters and diaries poured from him in considerable quantities. The volume of paper with which Dorothy was confronted was huge.

Boxes and boxes of correspondence were brought to our home, also in Bournemouth, and Dorothy went through them. On many an evening she read out to my father and to me extracts from the letters from Harry to Jennie. They all began: *My dearest Jennie* and concluded: *Your loving, Husband,* or sometimes *Your loving Husband, H. Hobbs.* In between there was a riotous mixture of daily reporting, political diatribe, caustic comment – often highly condemnatory – on the activities of politicians, civil servants, generals and admirals, bishops and clergymen and religion generally and on family friends, both in India and England and, all too often, personal vindictive vitriol directed towards Jennie herself.

At the time of their receipt many of Harry's letters to Jennie would have caused a lot of tears to flow at Chingri Khal. Despite everything

Jennie never lost her love for Harry, a fact which doubtless made it all the harder for her to bear the comments he directed at her. Dorothy always asserted that the barbs he hurled at Jennie were not in the least true – that she was a drunk, a spendthrift, a gambler, a hypocrite were among the more commonly expressed views. There was always a tiny basis for them. She did like an occasional brandy or whiskey (Irish, of course) in the evening. She liked a new hat or dress. She would occasionally put a few shillings on a horse. She was a very devout Catholic who tried to follow the Church's teaching to the letter. But nothing which could remotely justify Harry's invective.

Dorothy usually chose to read aloud those passages where Harry was commenting, in a letter written many years before, on family friends who by then were middle-aged and mature. To the thirteen-year-old that I was they seemed as old as the hills. To hear them described in lurid language as potentially dangerous corrupters of Harry's family back in England reduced the three of us at times to helpless laughter with tears running down our cheeks. I said to Dorothy that she should write a book about all this. It would be very funny. She could call it *Your Loving Husband*.

Dorothy did not dismiss the idea out of hand. She seemed to agree that there might well be a book there. But in fact nothing came of it. I can understand why. It was the middle of the war. Dorothy was already kept very busy running her home and helping to run the local branch of the Catholic Women's League; space at Hereford House – her home in Hinton Road in Bournemouth – was limited both for storage and concentrated writing. And most of all, I suspect, Harry was still very much alive, as were many folk who might have thought that he had libelled them

So the letters and other documents were disposed of. Whether into the dustbin or burnt in the grate I do not know. I was not a witness to the event. It probably took place when I was out of the house at school. Little was said about them afterwards, although we did remember them at times with a bit of a chuckle. They had gone and that was that.

But not all of them. Many years later Dorothy came to live at another Chingri Khal, the home of myself and my wife Sheila. It was quite an upheaval. Dorothy's bureau, which contained all her personal papers and documents, was carried out of one house and then into the other as one unit, nothing having been emptied from any of its drawers. Even after the removals men had done their necessary and expected unpacking there remained sixty-five packing cases stacked high in our garage. By the time these had all been dealt with and their contents put away – about three months – all I knew of any surviving letters was an occasional glimpse, when having a reason to go to the bureau for her, of a promising looking box or two lying in one of the drawers.

It was not until after Dorothy had died that I got out these boxes and had a proper look to see what they contained. They were closely packed with letters. Many of them carefully tied together with white ribbon. They were letters which Dorothy had written to Jennie between November 1925 and July 1926 while she was on an extended visit to Harry in India. After which the two of them returned to England the long way – that is through the Dutch East Indies (as they were then called) to Australia, New Zealand and then across the Pacific and through the Panama Canal. I had always known of this journey and Dorothy may even have mentioned to me that she had this correspondence. But she had never got it out and I had never seen it before.

I had a quick read through most of the letters. It was somewhat superficial, partly because, although obviously preserved with a good deal of tender care, they were not all in chronological order. There were many to read, written in Dorothy's very clear hand, using most of the page and both sides of the paper. When eventually photocopied in preparation for writing this book there were over five hundred pages relating to the 1925-26 journey alone. Most of Jennie's letters in reply were in another box. Dorothy's letters, I thought, would make a splendid travelogue and could be a substitute for the long-abandoned *Your Loving Husband*. But I knew that I had no hope of doing anything towards making this thought a reality until after I had retired. The letters were put back in their boxes and the boxes back in their drawer, and there they remained until after my retirement.

And so it came about that from late 1999 I began looking with rather more care at the contemporary documents which were available to me. Dorothy was intelligent, observant and sensitive, all of which causes me to be a little surprised that her very detailed letters home contain so little about the state of the British Raj at the time she was out there. But there are very few references to anything political in India – indeed few references to anything specifically Indian. This happened to be a time of relative quiet on the Indian political scene. The Amritsar affair of 1919 with its unsettled aftermath was well in the past and the unrest had subsided. The Indian National Congress was in a period of internal dispute and it was not until 1928 that it issued its next demand for British withdrawal from India. Thus it might well be that the Indian scene appeared to Dorothy to be one of stability and continuity, and indeed of normality, which called for little or no comment. What her letters do paint very clearly is the lifestyle enjoyed by a young Englishwoman in India at that time. Once she and Harry depart from Calcutta we do get from her pen more about the people and places through which she was to travel. However I became more convinced that the interest of the correspondence lay at least as much in the portraying of Dorothy's relationships with other people, especially with her father, as in her descriptions of her travels.

For the human development to be properly understood it seemed necessary to put into context the lengthy letters of 1925-26. A few earlier letters had survived, whether deliberately chosen to be spared the general clearout of 1943 or whether by chance having been tucked away at that time in some cubby-hole I have no means of knowing. I have made use of them to a considerable extent.

Also included in the main box were letters of a very different sort. Plainly kept carefully by the recipient in the first instance, they are all the letters and telegrams written by Dorothy to my father between their meeting and their wedding. They are mostly quite short, always affectionate and at times extremely passionate. Can I really make use of these, I wondered? All of them, without doubt, were written very much for your eyes only, whereas the vast majority of everything else I had in mind to use was written almost for public consumption. But even among the earlier material there are some very private letters and passages, and so I came to the conclusion that these love letters – as in reality they are – could also be used.

There was another source of documents from Harry. I know very little about Lieutenant-Colonel James Wyness. He had been a civil engineer in charge of public health works in Calcutta. He had been a colleague of Harry's in the Calcutta Port Defence Corps, both being retired from the Corps on the same day in early 1918 and ordered soon afterwards always to use their rank as a title (in Harry's case it was Major). It seems that Colonel Wyness retired altogether from service in India and returned with his wife to England some time in the early 1920s. There began a lengthy and fairly regular correspondence between the two of them which continued until Colonel Wyness died. After his death in the early 1950s his widow sent to Dorothy her late husband's collection of letters received from Harry and of the diaries enclosed. Not much of this contains material relevant to this book but there are a few passages I have been glad to use.

A word about Harry's diaries. He began his diaries in 1918 and they continued into the 1950s. Usually he wrote them every week, sometimes more often. Others who know much more about these things than I do have said that the diaries could be of great value to future historians. I am no historian, and I have to confess that I find them very difficult to follow. Closely typed and on very thin paper, often with very narrow margins and few paragraphs, they are rather like his letters only more so. Except, that is, for references to his family, which are almost completely absent. They are not just a record of the day's or week's events but are also a highly spiced account of his views about various politicians, officers in the civil and military services, religion, indeed most aspects of life in India and elsewhere. I have only used a very few extracts from them.

In addition to his diaries, Harry wrote a number of books. A complete list will be found in Appendix 1. I do regret that I do not find them an easier read. They are well produced (good paper, clear printing) but he does jump about a great deal in his thought processes. Two of them – *It Was Like This!* and *Scraps from my Diaries* – almost his first and last, are intended to be largely autobiographical. Others contain accounts of some of his personal adventures and experiences, selected and put together in a rather haphazard way, but virtually nothing about his family life. I have, for instance, not found anything in any of his writings to help me with how he came to meet Jennie, where it was, or how their relationship developed. He was very capable of writing an extremely clear, even vivid account of events he had witnessed and of his feelings in the past – as can be seen in some of what follows. It is sad that he did not leave us a fuller, more coherent account of what must have been a most interesting, as well as a very unusual, life.

Although it is a pity that so much was disposed of in 1943, I am glad that Dorothy kept many letters written to her by Harry from the mid-1930s through to his death, including quite a few letters to me, starting when I was very young, and continuing almost to the end of his life.

A few other letters and documents from family and friends complete what I might call my primary sources. I have to rely a good deal – much more than I would have liked – on my memory of what my mother told me she remembered of events many years before. Accuracy cannot be guaranteed. Time and time again since I started serious reading of her letters have I said to myself how I wish I could ask Dorothy what this means, or why that happened. It is, for instance, a little strange that she calls him Henry at the time of her long journey – a name I never heard applied to him by her or by anyone else.

I have subtitled the book a partial family history. It is partial in two senses. Families spread their wings very far in a very few generations. Harry had, surviving beyond infancy, three children, six grandchildren and eighteen great-grandchildren. It is not possible to explore each line in one book. The history is in part only.

It is also partial in the sense of not being impartial. I expect it is nearly inevitable that the only son and only child of a mother who is a powerful character would either have an extremely close and loving relationship with her or – probably less likely – something approaching the opposite. In my case it was the former. Without being blind to her faults – and of course she had faults as we all have – I have always known that she inspired a great deal of respect, admiration and, indeed, love in a great number of people. Many have told me so, both before and after her death. My instinctive feeling that I had the good fortune to be blest with a mother who was a rather special person was thereby frequently being confirmed by others. So if what follows appears to be somewhat biased or doting I hope the reader will understand and forgive.

BOOK ONE

A PIANO TUNER
IN INDIA

Piano moving – Indian style.

CHAPTER 1

FROM LONDON TO CALCUTTA

A S WE ENTER INTO the third millennium the concept of empire is in disfavour. Associated in the thinking of many with mindless military madness and oppression of native peoples, the British Empire is said by some to be a source of shame rather than of pride. But in the second half of the 19th century few British people would have questioned the glory of the Empire, which had reached its high noon with the proclamation of Queen Victoria as Empress of India in 1876. Although he had had some attraction to soldiering it does not look as if either military madness or the oppression of anyone was in the mind of Harry Hobbs when he set off for India in 1883. A wish to get away from an uncongenial home, perhaps; a thirst for adventure, certainly; even possibly an element of fleeing from the long arm of the law; all may have played their part.

Of his ancestry he wrote in a letter in 1935:

> Our family history must be a naval one. My great grandmother on my father's side was a Bonham Carter – a very good name indeed. My mother's name was Holmes – she hailed from Sudbury in Suffolk.

He had been born on 22nd July, 1864. He was the second child and eldest son of Henry and Emily Hobbs, who by the 1881 census had 11 children, being seven sons and four daughters whose ages then ranged from 18 years to 6 months. They were all living at that time at 93, Offord Road, Islington in London. The first two children were named after their mother and father respectively – perhaps Harry (christened Henry) was so called to distinguish him from his father. On Harry's birth certificate his father's occupation is given as pianoforte tuner. He was also a chorister of the Chapel Royal and – sad though it is to say so – a drunk. Probably on that account Harry, although in no sense a teetotaller, had a lifelong dislike of, and indeed contempt for insobriety of any kind.

As the family grew in number, keeping them all housed and fed and clothed must have been a doubly difficult task with the father's predilection for alcohol to be satisfied. I do not believe it was at all a happy household. When I celebrated my 21st birthday, Harry wrote to me to congratulate me and to wish me long life. Unaccountably his letter, which I know I kept for years, has gone astray; but I confidently recall a typically robust passage which ran in these terms: "You should have every chance of a long life. I have not done so badly* and both my parents lived to a great age – although why they should have wanted to do so I have no idea, except that even a mangy dog likes a whole skin."

Early in his life Harry showed himself to be highly intelligent, quick-witted, an avid reader, musical with a very accurate ear and a high achiever at school. At the age of twelve he won an essay prize in a competition open to all the elementary schoolchildren in London.

In *Scraps from my Diaries*, written when he was over ninety, Harry recalled his early life. It is a tantalisingly brief account, only slightly expanded by a diary entry:

> As far back as I remember I always wanted to go to India and read all I could about it. Not only was I for my age a great reader but I had a fine memory. At the age of eleven I learnt by heart the whole of Byron's *Siege of Corinth* and recited it, or most of it, to some musical friends of the family. The old man gave me a shilling for that. I don't think he ever gave me anything else. What is remarkable is that I can still recite whole slabs of it…
>
> …Put to the piano trade (which I hated), my father having been apprenticed to my mother's father who also made pianos (what my old man used to say about his father-in-law wouldn't look nice here) – my birth certificate states my connection with pianos, with which I had been familiar almost from birth – I naturally knew most of my job before I left home…
>
> …Ten days after my thirteenth birthday – that is in August 1876†

* He was then just on eighty-seven
† Either date or age must be wrong. I was always told he was taken away from school at the age of twelve. I therefore believe the date to be right.

– I started to work at a piano factory in Kentish Town, which meant that I had to walk nearly three miles there and three miles back, for which I was paid half-a-crown a week. The schoolmaster begged my father to give me more education, but as he said he started at the same age it wouldn't do me any harm. I put in about a year, when I got a job nearer home but on the same pay while I could also walk home for dinner.

At Parfitt & Denhams there were more than a dozen apprentices and I was duly apprenticed when fourteen for seven years. Boys were badly treated by the men, and as I had read Marryat, Walter Scott, Mayne Reid, Fennimore Cooper and all the tales of adventure I could get hold of, I had more romance in me than most of the other boys. None-the-less I was knocked about and resented it. [1]

In his diary for 23rd February, 1937, Harry records the holding of a Boy Scout jamboree at Delhi, which he described as "a great occasion if a mixed success". It was presided over by Baden-Powell, for whom Harry had enormous admiration, in particular for what he had done for young boys. This prompted Harry into a brief recollection of his own young days – a reference very rare indeed in the diary pages.

…My boyish recollections were such that I grew up a savage owing to the injustice with which men treated me. I have mighty little sympathy with the working man of my young days. He used his superior strength, and his slightly superior knowledge, to oppress, maltreat, bully and make fools of small boys – or boys up to twenty-one. In the piano factory I played the devil with them in return for the oppression. Quicker-witted than the ordinary man I scored in the end unless it was a matter of a thrashing when, of course, I fared badly. But it was considered clever to get the best side of a boy's belief in others. To hurt them so that they were laughed at was real sport…

Harry continues in *Scraps from my Diaries.*

When I was sixteen I was drawing six shillings a week and the boss threatened to kick my backside over something. I threatened to kick back and was goaded into hitting the old man "with a wooden piece of wood" which I was told sent him to hospital. For a time I disappeared; had I stayed, there would have been a certain three months hard labour for me also the penalty for being a deserting apprentice. One of the boys was clouted by a workman to whom he threw a small block of wood, which knocked the man out. Young Jim got three months hard labour for that. Mercy formed no part of human nature in those Christian days. [2]

Such a display of personal physical violence is distinctly out of character, and may reflect the extent of the provocation. Harry developed strong views about many matters and never hesitated to put them forward on any occasion which he thought might give them a worthwhile airing, from complaining about the major decisions of a leading politician to protesting in a restaurant about the quality of a steak with which he had been served. Verbal lashings, often accompanied by furious loss of temper, were very much part of the Harry Hobbs scene. But not physical beatings.

That is not to say he could not look after himself. As will become apparent, life in India could be tough, and he had probably many an occasion to defend himself or others from attack by those ranging from robber to drunken friend. He was young, strong and kept himself as fit as he could. But in an argument his tongue was his most effective weapon.

The only other instance I have found where he admitted to physical as opposed to verbal comment on a political matter occurred when he was even younger and much nearer home. In his book *Talkeetalkeewallahs and Others*, published in 1938, Harry sets out his views on some seven notable characters from the Indian scene of the previous twenty years or so, most, but not all, politicians or churchmen. One chapter deals more with politics generally and linked to business and commercial probity. He comments that if he published all he had collected about merchants:

…it would be pretty startling, although hardly so complete and spectacular as my first shot in the political arena.

When I was a lad of about fifteen, much credit was given me for a feat of political marksmanship outside the Agricultural Hall, Islington.

I was a Nationalist – the narrator something else. He was getting on quite well, speaking from the tailboard of a van, when I threw a penny bag of flour over the heads of the crowd and scored a direct hit.

Flour in those days was retailed in thin paper bags, which burst easily. As a result, the Liberal fell back into the van, blind and speechless, spending the rest of the time coughing out clouds of dust. Well, a lad who can, at political meetings, be a dead shot with a dead cat is an asset to any party.

Since then I have had various successes in India tackling my own countrymen for activities against their own people, but none proved so devastating to the other side as that bag of flour. [3]

His apparent self-satisfaction at what he calls his political marksmanship must have been more than a little tongue in cheek. Had he continued to deal with opinions or actions with which he disagreed in the same manner when an adult he would surely have landed himself in real trouble with the law and his life may have been very different. He clearly learnt early that the pen is safer than the sword, and probably more effective.

These extracts from his writings, dating as they do from long after the events described, leave many questions unanswered. He claims to have known most of his job before he left home. What did that entail? How well did he play the piano? Had he ever had formal teaching? If so from whom? Did they have a piano in the house in Offord Road? He certainly developed the piano tuner's accurate ear, and would say that he could detect five sounds or frequencies which would pass as being in tune, but of which to him only the middle one was properly in tune. Whether this accuracy of ear also gave him perfect pitch I do not know. He also developed a considerable ability as a sight-reader and he could transpose at sight. One would expect such skills to come only after much practice and probably good teaching. He does not explain how he found the time for the one or the source for the other.

Then there is his encounter with the boss. He says he disappeared 'for a time', but not how long that time was. Nor, perhaps of even more interest, how he came back, or to which factory he returned.

His musical abilities extended to playing some brass instruments and also the organ. The former would have been useful to him in his other field of interest, the military. A one sentence reference in a book he wrote in 1933 states: "More than fifty years ago I was in the North Middlesex Rifles who drilled in Albany Street Barracks." [4] On what sort of engagement he does not say, but it can hardly have been more than as a part-time volunteer. The context suggests that he may have been in that organisation at the time of the assault on his boss. If so, that period of volunteer soldiering would have come to an abrupt end when 'for a time' he 'disappeared.'

Evidently he returned from his self-imposed exile, even to working in a piano factory. It can hardly have been the same establishment and he may have felt he was at some risk of his past misdeeds catching up with him. He was very keen to get away from home, and indeed from England. If his original apprenticeship was still running until he was twenty-one years old it may well have been essential for him to leave England. If there was also Police interest in his whereabouts it may even have been quite urgent for him to get out of the Country. One form of disciplined service or another was the most likely means of securing that end, but that would involve some delay, and he was in a hurry. He tells us briefly how he came to leave, in accounts written many years after the event.

> Before I was 18 I tried to join the Natal Frontier Mounted Police, but couldn't raise the £10 demanded for the passage. Luckily I dodged that.
>
> Having returned to working in a piano factory I was also a bandsman in the 1st London Engineers, a volunteer corps. I played the cornet. The bandmaster said: "You want to go to India? Well, the 7th Dragoon Guards are going out in February* and are offering a bounty of £20 to a man who will enlist and be able to play the organ in church."
>
> The adjutant had a look at me, told the regimental bandmaster to take me over to the church, found I could play a bit, read at sight and extemporise, so he approved. Then came the snag: "You will join the band?" asked the adjutant. "I want to be a soldier, not a bandsman," said I. Taking my name and address I was told to await a letter.
>
> In the train I read an advertisement for a man used to piano repairs who could tune, willing to go to India. I applied and was tested. Samuel Harraden, who had started in India in the 1840s as organist of St John's Cathedral and founded among other businesses the music firm of Harold & Co, engaged me and advanced two pounds as expenses for the voyage. That was

* 1884

14

deducted in two instalments from my pay later but was thankfully accepted then; workers had few rights; they never thought of them, as there were no Trades Unions to tell them they had.

I was on board ship bound for Calcutta four days later. So keen was I to go that I never asked about the pay. [5]

In 1883 I sailed from the Royal Albert Docks for Calcutta on board the British India steamer the *Eldorado*. I have often described that morning as the happiest in my life. Certainly I have never felt so pleased with myself when leaving home as I did then, but I was full of the spirit of adventure and looked forward to the novelty of the voyage.

Second saloon on the BI steamers was very different then from the fine accommodation of today*. The deck was choked with sheep-pens, fowl-houses, rabbit hutches and lumber, so that there was hardly sufficient room for two passengers to walk abreast.

On board the steamer was Harry Norton, who afterwards became the wealthy proprietor of the firm of J. B. Norton & Sons. He was a chubby-faced boy of 16 and spoke with a rich Yorkshire burr. He told me he was going out to the 'ploomering' as his father had a business in Calcutta.

Among the first saloon passengers was Mr Samuel Plimsoll MP, who will be remembered for his efforts to save the lives of sailors. His Plimsoll mark will be found on British ships all over the world. Mr Plimsoll was of a religious turn of mind. On Sundays he used to come aft with his daughter to hold a short service on deck, while I led the singing with my cornet, as there was no piano at our end of the ship. [6]

During the evening of the second day we struck a terrific storm and, although since I have spent nearly three years on the ocean, I have never seen anything like it. As my experiences include three or four cyclones, one resulting in the loss of about 60 deck passengers, I conclude that we must have had a pretty bad time then. [7]

At Malta I went ashore and tremendously enjoyed a fresh meal and the sights of this most ancient place. One of the passengers lowered some whisky to some soldiers who had pulled alongside in a small boat. They knocked the neck off the bottle and the first man cut his mouth dreadfully with the broken glass. One man was apparently a teetotaller, but the others drank the liquor, and when it was finished they had a fight and upset the boat. A good many facts

* 1917

were told to the donor of the whisky bottle, who did not feel altogether pleased with him self about it. [8]

One of the passengers was a jailer named Powell who was employed in Ceylon. He used to entertain us with an old canteen song of many verses about a trooper who eloped with the colonel's daughter. He also used to make Harry Norton say his prayers and would kneel and pray loudly with him for quarter of an hour every night. Harry Norton didn't like to hurt his feelings by telling him he didn't enjoy praying so often. At Port Said, Powell went ashore and got frightfully tight and wanted to fight everybody, while his language was not at all redolent of the Mission room, so Harry Norton was thenceforth able to dodge all religious services held by Mr Powell. [9]

At Colombo, which I thought was the most beautiful spot in the world, the grand way people seemed to walk also took my eye. (In the days before physical culture the only people in England who walked properly were soldiers.) Powell, poor but hospitable, took two of us to a cheap hotel where I tasted mulligatawny soup for the first time and formed a remarkably high opinion of it, which I still hold*. The dinner was not probably the best obtainable but I can still remember even now the delights of the change in food, and that meal stands out in my memory as one of the banquets of my life. [10]

There wasn't much of my travelling expenses left by the time we reached Calcutta; even then I was better off than on my return from leave in 1889 when I started back with eight pence and I half starved for weeks to save that. What is more I was better off than some of the others. A party of 12 nuns bound for Arakan accompanied by a priest had one shilling between them. [11]

Steaming slowly up the Hooghly when a vulture with outspread wings sailing a human body ashore was pointed out, I thought myself no end of a traveller. I saw the immense number of pigeons flying over the King of Oudh's palace, then the forest of masts belonging to tiers of sailing ships, berthed four deep between Hastings and Chandpal Ghat. This was a sight that impressed me deeply and I felt that I had never seen anything to equal it. [12]

All too soon the 45-day voyage came to an end. I would have liked to stay where I was for the whole of my five-year agreement, mainly because I felt impending the divine curse: "By the sweat of

---

* In 1954.

they brow shalt thou earn thy bread." However, as the Germans say, all things have an end except a sausage which has two – and at number four jetty I was soon off the ship and in INDIA! [13]

Harry's hesitation at the prospect of starting work may be understandable; it is also uncharacteristic. He was never a man to be afraid of hard work – nor of hardship. He had plenty of both to come. One can still sense his feeling of delight at having arrived in India. He had been born and brought up in England. He always referred to England as 'home.' Once he had his wife and his children living in their own house in England, then England was even more obviously home. He regarded himself throughout his life as a patriotic Englishman. But, despite all that, from this moment on, for all practical purposes India was to be his home for nearly 73 years.

CHAPTER 2

THE FIRST FIVE YEARS

I T WAS, IN FACT, nearer five and a half years. Harry had signed on to work for Samuel Harraden for five years. He began work on 14th November 1883 and embarked from Calcutta for his first leave in England on 3rd April, 1889. That there was a considerable demand for the services of someone with his skills in both tuning pianos and repairing them cannot be doubted. As he put it: "In those days people without a piano were hardly entitled to consider themselves civilised, and poor men would exalt themselves when boasting that 'my daughter is learning the piano'. And what pianos!"[1] Whether the instrument had been a good one or an indifferent one when made, the effect of the Indian climate with its extremes of heat and humidity would call for more, often much more, than mere tuning to be done to it on the visits by the piano tuner. The first of his published books, *The piano in India: how to keep it in order*, was published in 1899 to help those having to deal with the tropical conditions. A second edition ('profusely illustrated') came out in 1914. It is very largely technical, but Harry included some personal recollections connected with his work.

It would have been interesting to have had from Harry some idea of his employment details. There must have been at least some central office to direct him and any other employed tuners to the various clients. I have found little reference to such a place, where it might have been, how often he attended there, whether there was also a workshop attached. From early in the year following his arrival he was to embark on much travel. He does not say so in terms, but I believe that that travel was to the clients of his employer, who must have been far flung across the northern and particularly north eastern part of the sub-continent. If we lack much information about his work, we can glean from his writings a great deal about life in India, especially life for the impecunious young Englishman. Hardships and even danger were there aplenty. Creature comforts were almost non-existent. None of these features troubled Harry. He may have been used to the same sort of thing at home in London. He boasted – truthfully – that he had never complained about the country from the moment of his arrival in India. We have his first impressions from very soon after he first set foot on jetty number four.

> Taken to No. 5 Crooked Lane (since pulled down) I was given a room without a window (it had a door), which I didn't mind. I remember walking in, throwing my Port Said topee on the bed, and in a feeling of profound contentment saying: "This is all right!"
>
> It was rented by three other Englishmen, two of whom were country-born so knew their way about. Decent fellows, they fed well, drank little and treated me well. I wish I had treated them as kindly as they did me. If a newcomer to India doesn't make himself disliked it must be his own fault. [2]

I have to admit to not understanding the last two sentences. There is nothing to show any unkindness shown by Harry to his colleagues, if anything the reverse, and I wonder if the final sentence is a misprint.

> In the chummery we managed to live on about Rs. 75 per month. There were others where Europeans managed on less. Our principal food was potato chops, brain cutlets, beef curry and banana fritters. The two country-born brothers, fluent in the adjective language of the bazaar, managed the books. They had one accomplishment that took my eye – marksmanship with bread pellets. I have seen them knock a bluebottle off the butter with the greatest ease.
>
> Landing in the cold weather made me naturally inclined to scoff at the talk about India being hot. Those who had been out a year or more resented this. "You wait until the hot weather. It kills the young 'uns," I was told. There was no need to wait and although sleeping in a room without a window or *punkah* was a bit trying, I stuck it out nearly as well as they did. I did a bit of scoffing then. "Wait until the rains! Nothing can keep it out, no matter how well built the house is."
>
> Having been incredulous about the heat I wasn't going to be taken in about the rain, but the first burst of the monsoon came

with a roar. It had been very trying for many days beforehand, and I had not slept well, but with the first cool puff I went off like the dead. I awoke with a start. Water dripped on me; no matter where I dragged the bed, it was obvious that the roof was leaking like a basket. The other fellows were right after all. At breakfast I candidly admitted that they had been quite right about the rain – I was wrong. After a bit of leg pulling I found that they had placed a lump of ice on top of the mosquito net [to drive] out all my disbelief. Loud laughter in which I didn't join. [3]

Harry goes on to comment on the low wages paid at that time to employees brought out from England to India, but for some reason does not disclose what his wage was. He says that the 80s were the meanest days of British rule in India. "Men started on smaller pay than they were earning at home. If they paid their way and kept off extravagances they could save nothing during the first two years. There was no margin."

Harry's attitude to women may account for some of the later family problems. We get a glimpse of it in his account of a rather curious custom.

In two or three firms, the *Burra Mem*, economical by instinct, moth-eaten with long, long Indian days, anxious to keep an eye on new arrivals, took them on as boarders, offering them social comforts such as a suspect would get from the Russian police. The result was always the same. A drunken fellow on the stairs after midnight unbottling in polo language months of exasperation while criticising his hostess and her husband.

Where women rule the devil governs. Few who started life as a paying guest in the house of their boss, wasted much time on the straight and narrow.

Old Europeans, married in the country and more or less prisoners at large for the rest of their lives, tried the spider and fly touch on a few of us. They pitched a tale about Eurasian girls with an income of several hundred a month who were out to marry young and good-looking Europeans. Most inexperienced youngsters believe all dark people must be rich and eager to give their money away, so the introductions sounded attractive.

Being naturally inquisitive I thought I would like a look-see so went to an At Home where the samples were paraded. They were listless women with snaggle teeth and receding chins, sentimentally as dry as a pinch of snuff, with complexions which looked as though someone had thrown a stone while they were drinking a cup of coffee. I must have created a bad impression for I was never invited again. [4]

Just as well, perhaps, that a billet had been found for him in an independent 'chummery' with congenial, if boisterous companions.

Harry tells us more about one of the decent fellows in his first billet. In a chapter entitled *Our Grief Champion* he describes "the oldest man in our chummery was Frederick Shirley Slaide...in an unobtrusive way he good-humouredly controlled our small crowd of five in the cheap flat in Crooked Lane." Slaide was an engineer who preferred the life of a social outcast. His firm was a new one and did not keep him very busy. The result was he drank more than was good for him – but as Harry puts it:

There was nothing particularly attractive about life in Calcutta 50 years ago. The drinking water was unpleasant and unwholesome. The air of the city was permeated with a disgusting odour. Side streets were sodden with the filth of generations and stank like hospital ship clothing packed in the Red Sea...Amusements were few. Drink was cheap and whatever drawbacks it possessed it contained little that was likely to bring on cholera or dysentery. It is hardly to be wondered at that men went to hotel bars for recreation.

One nice bright summer's day Slaide turned up as pleased as a dog with two tin tails. A draft had come on account of one of his patents which gave him enough money to pay his fare home. Not that he was intending leaving, but he was determined to save that. A little cash in hand makes one so independent.

As so often happened, fortune changed within the week. He came home tiffin time with a mourning envelope and his chin almost touching his waistbelt. Trembling with emotion he told us: "I have just heard from home. My poor dear old dad is dead. We didn't write often – that's what makes it so bad – but we were such good pals. He was the only one I looked forward to seeing when I got home again. And now he's dead! Why ever did I come to this rotten country? He didn't want me to. Poor dear old dad."

He lost little time in getting into deep mourning for his poor dear old dad. In spite of the heat he never went out unless clothed from head to foot in heavy black broadcloth with an expansive chest protector, black tie and a pair of black kid gloves in his hand. His gold chain with its wealth of pendants, studs and links were put aside for those of black jet. In those days solar topees were huge, certainly twice the size of those in fashion today *, so Slaide had his swathed in black crepe with two six-inch tails hanging down behind. To wipe his eyes and mop up the perspiration from the back of his neck he laid in a stock of sable-bordered handkerchiefs. Black-bordered visiting cards were pushed on to him when he ordered heavy glazed notepaper and envelopes with a three-quarter inch black border. The few letters he wrote had to be sealed with a blob of black sealing wax. Nothing was omitted. Slaide was in mourning for the world to see; every detail was correct down to black-headed pins.

Thus attired and equipped Slaide took more and more to the consolations of alcohol. He told all who would listen that "only those who had a poor dear old dad like his could understand his feelings, and even they couldn't". He agonised about the funeral; he agonised about the interment. "As one of his sympathisers put it: 'He'd be the life and soul of that funeral! It's a pity he can't be there.'" His firm sent a doctor to see him as he was neglecting his work and a passage home was suggested which resulted in dispute. But…

…He sunk from bad to worse, a pathetic figure dripping with perspiration, half boiled in his deep mourning but a treasure to loafers and those who spend their lives in a spirited protest against the errors and extravagances of industry or total abstinence.

At some time or other he must have been out in the rain for the dye came out of the crepe on his topee leaving a broad black mark right round his head which made him look as if he had washed his face with his hat on. No man could have grieved more thoroughly

* 1937

than he did for the loss of a dear old dad; even his face had a mourning band on it.

He must have accepted a passage home for his firm wrote to ask if we would see him safely on board. About eight one morning we took him to the jetties, helped him up the accommodation ladder and saw him into his cabin. Nothing would stop him from seeing us off. On deck we asked him if he remembered the number of his berth. He shook his head but said he knew the cabin all right.

"How do you know it?"

"There's a country boat outside the window."

After that he walked to the far side of the ship and feebly waved his handkerchief to holy mother Ganga. We left him at it.

Some time later we had a letter.

"You never heard such a wonderful coincidence in all your life. When I reached London I went straight to my girl's house. She was being married that very day, but not to me.

"And who do you think I met there? My poor dear old dad! You see it was my girl who wrote to tell me that her father was dead, but I was so upset I didn't read the letter properly. Funny, wasn't it?" [5]

Harry had always rather hankered after being a soldier, so it is not surprising that the next best thing – membership of a volunteer body – came his way very soon after his arrival in the east. He does not give a precise date, but it seems to have started before even he had his first trip up country; and once started it was to play an important part in his life for thirty-five years.

Almost as soon as I had landed I was roped in to join F, the European Company in the Calcutta Volunteer Rifles, then commanded by Henry Elworthy who seemed to me to be completely ignorant of knowledge of drill. Yet how conceited he seemed to be! On the first parade I attended he walked backwards halfway down the Red Road facing a few men and waving his drawn sword while shouting, "Left, right." Unfortunately I happened to say it was worse than the Salvation Army, which was repeated to him, making me his enemy for life. Fifteen years later he admitted he always had it in for me, and standing six feet four inches and weighing 17 stone naturally permitted him to do and say what he liked.

Whitehead, on the *Indian Daily News,* who held a commission in the Liverpool Volunteers, came out and was posted for duty with the CVR. Keen on rifle shooting we attracted one another; he taught me quite a lot and also suggested that I took up journalism as, he said, I saw things as they were. Poor Whitehead died in hospital from dysentery. Domestic worry with his wife in England led him to say: "I am not trying to get better."

For ordinary men there were practically no inexpensive amusements so a day or half a day in the open air on the rifle range with plenty of company had many attractions. Life ran smoothly. Politics had not started to corrupt our minds; Indians were honest and friendly, precautions undreamed of – I generally had a box of ammunition in my room. Even when things began to tighten up any Volunteer could buy a packet of cartridges for three *annas,* while picking up expended cartridge cases was unthought of.

Like other boys I was intrigued over the feat of William Tell who shot the apple on his son's head. Whether boyish interest would have been so keen had the target been a potato may be open to doubt, but the story aroused admiration for marksmanship. [6]

Volunteering was in the main a poor man's pastime as men who were fairly keen as soldiers were practically lost to the Force as soon as they could afford other amusements such as tennis or golf. The Saturday half holiday was obtained in Calcutta under the promise that the drills would take place then, but, as soon as the concession was granted, sports clubs were formed and matches arranged right through the season so that many men became slack and were as good as lost to the Force.

The advantages gained from a keen interest in volunteering were great and valuable, as a man made many friends and scores of acquaintances. When the cost of advertising is realised the opportunity of knowing a few hundred men is of value to any young businessman.

Then as a non-commissioned officer he would have to handle his section or company and get work out of them by what I once heard a ship captain describe as 'tack and instink', and would acquire a knowledge of human nature difficult to obtain elsewhere. The ability to manage men is as great a gift as that of poetry, painting or music, although one seldom sees that quality detailed on certificates. A group of average non-commissioned officers in a

Volunteer Corps would always be found to possess men of character, and in this respect they were perhaps superior to the army NCOs as it has to be admitted that there were always individuals in the regulars who had no right to be in authority over anybody. In the Volunteers the corporals and sergeants were generally elected, and they were thought mighty little of if they didn't play the game. Certainly as a businessman I feel I owe much to my connection with the Force as I benefited thereby both directly and indirectly. To young men starting life I strongly recommend the advantages of taking up this work keenly and I am sure that time spent with numbers of other men is never wasted.

It was often far more difficult to attain the rank of sergeant in F Company First CVR than to obtain an appointment as a field officer in a battalion, as the NCO had to be more or less efficient – a condition not by any means always necessary with the higher ranks.[7]

Despite its evident importance to Harry, service in the Volunteers had to take second place to the demands of his employer. From very soon after his first Christmas in India – the nature of which he does not describe anywhere – he was sent on many journeys, often of considerable length, and none, it would seem, without involving hazards and hardships.

Once Christmas was passed I went travelling, working in almost every station between the Khyber and Tavoy in Burma. Talk about rough going! Possibly Assam before the railway was the most arduous. All night in a dugout, turned back by elephants or chased by a buffalo, and all the work done by myself. Neither servant nor *mistri* went with me. In the hot weather I almost invariably had to work without a *punkah*; if the *sahib* was out there was no *punkahwallah*. If the *memsahib* was in she had him. [8]

He calls his first experience a 'short trip' despite the distance involved, which was over 300 miles each way and over 400 miles if he went all the way he could by river. Perhaps he meant that he was not a long time at his destination. His accounts of this and other journeys, with their adventures and encounters, need no embellishment. I believe what follows took place in the 1880s, but chronological order cannot be guaranteed.

> In January 1884 I was sent to Darbhanga. At the *Rajbari* I was paid some 3,000 rupees in silver and took it to the *dak* bungalow at Darbhanga. It was there I had my only experience with *dacoits*. About midnight I was sitting up reading when half a dozen men rushed into the room. Knowing nothing whatever I was perfectly unperturbed and, in English, asked what they wanted. Very startled to find me awake they went out without further ado. It never dawned on me at the time that they were robbers. I was perfectly ignorant of the ways of the country, full of that racial exaltation which believed Englishmen to be the salt of the earth, so I was quite calm, thinking they had made a mistake. Perhaps it was lucky a revolver was on the table. It was of pre-mutiny date and so rusty that it could not be fired. I didn't know that and neither did the *dacoits*, but it served its purpose. [9]

Harry probably was very fortunate indeed that he did not fare worse on that occasion. In another place he mentions the activities of the gangs of *dacoits* who were without scruple or mercy, and he quotes from a newspaper entry which he recalled:

> Some poor cultivators, living in an obscure valley, wrote to the editor of an Indian paper about a gang of *dacoits* who "rob and beat us and violate our women which is very irritating, particularly in the daytime." They enclosed a half-anna stamp for a reply. The editor published the letter and added a footnote – "It looks as if, before long, these *dacoits* will go too far." [10]

When a man is sent to a district where he has never been before, with little more than a list of names of the people he must call on, once he is a couple of miles from railway station or steamer *ghat* anything can happen to him.

After my short trip to Darbhanga I went to Hazaribagh, Ranchi, Purulia and Asanol – a sort of round tour through Chota Nagpur.

From Giridih the journey was by push-push, a primitive conveyance drawn and pushed by coolies. Primitive though they were, there were first and second class push-pushes. The former were four-wheelers. The second were two-wheelers, resembling the old type of London bakers' barrows. I went second. The passenger's head was lower than his heels. It was so uncomfortable that I walked quite half the distance: 73 miles.

From Hazaribagh to Ranchi, 65 miles, palanquins (*palkis*) were the cheapest thing to take you about but the swinging movement made me quite seasick. During the night the bearers said a tiger was about so they dropped the *palki* in the jungle leaving me there until morning. My only means of defence was a box of matches which I thought might be used if the tiger snuffled at the door, but nothing happened. From Ranchi to Purulia and thence to Asanol was all by *palki*. Three years later I walked the 73 miles from Hazaribagh to Giridih in the month of May just to see if I could do it. [11]

In June 1884 I went to Burma and during the next eight years I knocked about between the Punjab and Burma, seldom more than six weeks in one place. The charm of such a life is the liberty it brings. The man who has to abide by fixed hours and do a fixed amount of work is a slave as near as makes no odds. If my evenings were dull beyond words, and the next meal was an uncertainty, there was no obligation to answer your name in the morning. Most of my time I was a free agent, and independence counted for more than hardships.

All my hot weathers were spent on the road and it was a common sight to see half a dozen Indians pulled out of the wretched, double-decked third class carriages, victims of the heat. Yet, although I have been at least 30 times through the Red Sea, sweltered off the Gold Coast and been fried in the sun in the Punjab, all those thousands of scorching days and nights, unless other circumstances tattooed them on my memory, have left no impressions. They are clean forgotten.

On a summer's day in England I have tried to visualise what a really hot tropical day is really like, but never succeeded. Every time I pass through the Red Sea on my return journey, even if the passage is by no means a bad one, the heat strikes me by surprise. I find myself saying – I never knew it could be so hot. [12]

One of my hot weather tours was to cross the Ganges at Monghyr and work the indigo factories right up to Ruxaul, then through Sewan, Chapra, Gorackpore to Fyzabad. Most of the indigo concerns were done by horse or pony and as no sensible man would lend a good animal to a stranger, I had a lot of experience with troublesome mounts. Hard as nails, I came off many times – once wiped off by the branch of a tree. When I recovered I didn't know which way I had come by or where to go. *Biharis* were not always friendly and at some places they would not give me permission to take water from the village well.

A keen smoker of Burma cheroots, when travelling I used to smoke after *chota hazri* and one morning, outside the *dak* bungalow I saw a small crowd of villagers with a pony in charge of a *syce*. It looked a real good animal so I asked the *syce* what sort of a *ghora* it was. "Hoohooho," said he, "*coop janiwala.*" He warned that I could not mount from the ground; better from the plinth of the bungalow. With my cheroot well alight, I lowered my chinstrap and got into the saddle. The circus started. My topee came off, knocked the cheroot out of my mouth. The cheroot fell between my backside and the saddle. Didn't I shout! But once clear of the bungalow compound I had a fine ride despite a few burns. After that I never smoked "when on the top of the back of the European horse," as our Babu friends used to say. [13]

Not all the problems encountered by the tuner in India were due to the climate or to ill-intentioned or disagreeable fellow humans. Insects could be very destructive too.

The borer (*ptinus pectinicornis*) appears to be rapidly increasing in numbers and destructiveness…[It] incubates from an egg, laid in the grain or a joint of the timber, and eventually forms a white maggot shaped like a screw and about an inch long…and has been known to reduce a piano leg to powder…

When I first visited Burma in the early 80s I found that no professional tuner had visited that country for a long time. The

28

result was that many pianos had been unused for years and one, a grand, was among the first that I put in tune and in order, much to the satisfaction of the family of young ladies to whom the instrument belonged. The first evening it was used, someone who must have been fond of music leaned on the piano while it was being played; suddenly one of the legs gave way and the piano fell over. Almost by a miracle no one was injured, and after a very unpleasant letter had been written to me grumbling at my bad tuning it was found that the leg had been practically destroyed by borers and only needed a touch to cause it to collapse. There is, therefore, an element of danger about the borer worm, as the hard sweet wood of a piano leg seems to offer a great attraction to this insect. [14]

One of my hot days, 'when the sword melts in the scabbard' was a hungry one too. I fetched up in Purnea around 2:30pm having eaten nothing since dawn. Not a *gharry* was to be seen. A west wind almost made our eyes sizzle, but there was nothing for it. A tramp through three miles of dust to the *dak* bungalow.

Arriving there, all doors and windows were shut. They seemed to be bolted also. While pulling at one it suddenly opened and a naked man armed with a sword made a full swipe at me. Luckily I stepped back as the point caught the door. Never a fast runner, I certainly was quicker than the tramp in the last stages of destitution who walked into a swagger New York Hotel and ordered a banquet. He went out so quick he met himself coming in. As an old writer put it, I felt that the bungalow was not an asylum for a tranquil person.

Clearing the cactus hedge like a goat, I made for a police outpost some 200 yards away, the naked stranger behind yelling like a fiend. Some old-fashioned muskets with triangular bayonets were piled on the plinth of the *thannah* and the clatter they made when I grabbed one aroused the sleeping *parawalas*. Not wishing to bayonet him I stood on guard until a policeman crept behind him, grabbed his feet and brought him down. Little time was lost in binding him head and foot and locking him up.

Walking back to the bungalow I ordered tea, shook the ants out of the sugar after they had evidently gone through it three times, and with a gladsome mind revelled in the peace of a shady verandah. It was good to be alive and, at any rate, the night would be kinder than the day.

The next day the swordsman's brother drove in from some distant indigo factory. We went together to the *thannah*. The unfortunate fellow had been bound from head to foot with *charpoy* string which grid-ironed him all over. As soon as he was released he made a desperate rush at the *parawalas* who scattered like crows, but his brother had little difficulty in persuading him to put on some clothes. With the exception of occasionally sweeping away something that wasn't there, he seemed sane enough. When they drove off neither expressed the least regret for the inconvenience they would have put me to if that first bit of sword exercise caught me. There were excuses. He had lost his job, was wretched to the last degree and had been trying to kill a healthy thirst with kindness. [15]

It didn't take long after my second visit to Hazaribagh before I was off to Rangoon. What a voyage – a dreadful experience. The *Purulia* was a small ship and the seas were the biggest I ever saw. Numbers of deck passengers were washed overboard. In my cabin was a young 2nd Lieutenant, Royal Artillery, who never spoke a word to me.

As soon as I landed I went to the post office for letters, finding one asking me to proceed without delay to Toungu or Begu, so off I went. Walking into the *dak* bungalow I found some men taking away the body of the young officer, my cabin mate. I did not know how he died nor did I know anyone I may ask, but I felt I was really seeing something about life in the east. [16]

My first visit to Akyab was made under rather dramatic circumstances. A cyclone was blowing at the time – this was in October 1884 – the second during that monsoon. The kindly skipper of the B.I. steamer tried all he could to persuade me to stay on board until the morning, but I thought I ought to get ashore.

There was no end of excitement getting ashore – five or six sampans were capsized almost alongside and I was too busy looking after myself to ascertain what became of the occupants, but was told the next day that several boatmen were drowned. We just managed to reach the jetty, soaked to the skin. After some trouble a *gharry* was secured and I drove to the place described as the hotel.

Pushing open the door I saw an act of brutality which astonished me. A man was half-suspended from the ceiling by two lines tied round his thumbs. A little fat fellow was punching him and what with the cries of the unfortunate servant and the curses of the half-drunk European, there was a good deal of noise. I interfered and released the man having a bit of a struggle with his assailant before I could effect this. The fat little blackguard turned out to be the landlord of the hotel – a man named Bunce. His name fitted him. He was more than half-inclined to be fightable when I told him what I thought, but he explained that the man had stolen a ring and he was going to make him confess.

On asking for accommodation I was shown a miserable room, with the ceiling and walls dripping with rain water; I thought that I could do better – certainly no worse – at the *dak* bungalow, so I pushed off in the *gharry* to find, after a long drive, that there was nothing in the bungalow: visitors who used it brought their own staff and necessaries.

There was no help for it but to return to the hotel, and I was received by the landlord with jeers saying that, as I did not ask him about the bungalow, he thought I might as well find out for myself.

The daughter of the house was a hunchback who played a splendid game of billiards in spite of the fact that she was barely a head taller than the billiard table cushions. She used the rest all the time but had a small cane stool to stand on when necessary, and her cue was handled in such a manner when making her shots that her wrist was in line with her ear.

In the combined bar, billiard saloon and dining room was a notice that attracted my attention, and will possibly convey a better idea of what the place was like than any other details:

GENTLEMEN ARE REQUESTED
NOT TO FENCE WITH THE CUES.

There was a fight over cards the first evening between a Portuguese and a German captain, and any amount of bad blood in which Bunce joined. His daughter took no notice of it and went on scoring at billiards.

Coming downstairs in the morning I nearly broke my neck by

slipping on a large piece of yellow fat, which a pariah dog had apparently left on the second stair from the top.

Very annoyed and bruised I saw the hunchback girl smile broadly and when the servant told me there was no tea for *chota hazri*, only rum and milk was served, it did not improve matters. I sent for the landlord, who said he had heard of my accident and was sorry he had not seen it. His daughter, Lily, had. "Poor girl," he soliloquised, "It's not often she sees anything to amuse her in this dead and alive hole and I'm glad she was there. It's done her a lot of good," he assured me. When I spoke about the absence of tea he told me that the people who lived in his house could "drink like lions" and that he had no use for man who didn't know when he had had enough. [17]

Through the good offices of the local colonel of police Harry was able to obtain a more congenial billet in the bungalow of two married men. He stayed there for the rest of his week in Akyab and it became his regular abode in Akyab during his visits there over the next three years or so.

When I was living in a chummery at the back of Dykes & Co. in 1885, we had a supernatural visitor paying us nightly visits. A tall Sikh used to walk through the window whether it was open or shut and disappear down the stairs. At the bottom of the stairs there were two doors – one leading into British Indian Street and the other into Dykes & Co.'s workshops, both of which were locked after working hours.

Not only did every man in the chummery see this, but the dogs invariably barked and assumed every aspect of fear and aggression. I have on at least 20 different occasions rushed downstairs – not more than a dozen steps – with my sword bayonet or a big stick, determined to find out what it was and thrash it if it turned out to be a human being.

My dog, a plucky crossbred bull terrier would never come with me, but always barked until the man had quite disappeared.

One of the members of the chummery, a sickly nervous fellow, was so upset over it that when the other men were away at the Delhi Durbar in 1885 he did not sleep a wink, but paraded on the roof of the workshop with a loaded revolver for several consecutive nights.

We were all youngsters in the country: none of us could speak the language well; therefore we were unable to question the servants very closely about it – they merely said there was a *shaitan* about the building as it was a very old house.

I have followed downstairs immediately behind the mysterious Sikh and struck at him or in the corners where I thought he might be hiding in the dark – tried the doors and found them locked so that the man or whatever he was couldn't get out We never elucidated this mystery. [18]

In 1885 just before the outbreak of war [the Burmese war of 1885-86] I was travelling along the Arrakan coast from Rangoon, and at Kyouk Phyou was walking down the companion to get into a sampan, as I had to do some work ashore during the short time the steamer was there.

Seven or eight Pathans were on deck lurching about, insolent as a Labour leader with a gang of strikers and as I was getting into the boat one of these fellows spat on me. Without any hesitation I ran up the ladder and sailed straight into the Pathan getting two fine punches well home before he could gather what was up; these I followed up with a very lucky one under the jaw which knocked him out. He soon got round and I resumed my journey.

The Pathans seemed to think the fight no end of a good joke and every time I met them on the deck afterwards they were as good-humoured and sporting about the scrap as though I had been with them on some thieving excursion. Certainly they did not bear the slightest malice, and I have always felt cheerfully disposed towards them and their tribesmen ever since. [19]

Harry's action, while possibly working wonders as far as discipline and mutual respect go, could hardly be categorised as legitimate self-defence. Nor, I feel, could this next episode. He does not put a date on it but I am reasonably sure it must have occurred in his first few years in India. He would have been unlikely to have indulged in the Pathan lesson-teaching activity after it had happened. It is also one of the few occasions he makes mention of Harry Norton again – the young man whom he met on the voyage out. I find this slightly surprising as Harry Norton remained certainly an acquaintance all his life. Whether by coincidence or brought about by the one following the other's example I do not know, but the fact is that in course of time both made their English homes in Bournemouth. Harry Norton – by then Captain H. B. Norton, JP – was to live there and become a much-respected citizen, being made a Freeman of the Borough in 1938, after much work for charity and for the benefit of his home town. Both Harrys may have felt they had had a lesson of their own and a lucky escape – even if their motives were of the best.

Before Harry Norton built the fine edifice at the corner of Old Court House street, there were, in addition to his own residence, several native shops of a very poor class in the immediate vicinity, one or two drinking dens as well as some dealers of odds and ends – one being a bottle shop.

One Sunday morning I was talking to Norton at the corner when two sailors commenced to argue and then to fight. One, the bigger man, knocked the other down on to the bottles, and every time he tried to get up he was knocked back again – a most uncomfortable and worrying position for a Christian to be in during church time on Sunday.

Harry Norton called for fair play and to let the man get up, but the son of Neptune refused to listen until he was pulled away, when he let out a beautiful flow of language and offered to fight, telling us that he could tear iron.

Norton in those days weighed 14 stone of bone and developed muscle, and he wasted no time in fetching the iron-tearer a short arm jab that lifted him off his feet and on to his back.

Suddenly we noticed that the man's neck began to swell, veins became as thick as your thumb, his face grew distorted and black, and he showed every sign of a violent death. We both grew exceedingly alarmed and rushed to pick him up, to shake him or do something, when we saw a huge quid of tobacco very gradually work out of his gullet. The sudden punch had apparently caught the man by surprise just as he was changing sides with his quid and the drop on his back had jolted it down his neck.

There was no further talk of fighting after that, and the two men walked off together without giving any trouble or making any remark. Norton and I were quite well pleased that no disaster had happened, but we had such a shock that we resemble the man who was asked by a salvationist: "Are you saved?" and he replied: "I am, but I hardly like to talk about it." [20]

Writing in 1937, Harry recounts a sad story in which he admits to having been responsible for a man's death, although few would regard him as being culpable in the circumstances. The whole episode, together with that which immediately follows it, gives a good idea of the life he had to lead – tuning and repairing pianos in between these experiences. It is slightly complex as written, for the narrative contains a story within a story, but I omit very little. By the time of these events Harry had moved from the Crooked Lane chummery to that at the back of Dykes & Co., so it is not possible to know if the sick man was one of those 'decent chaps' whom Harry met on his first arrival or a friend from his later billet. Wherever they had met Harry wanted to help him if he could.

In 1886, after three tough months in Assam, I left Shillong for Darjeeling. The *tonga* journey to Gaubati, 65 miles, mostly downhill, was done in heavy rain. Cholera had killed or scattered the villagers which necessitated passengers helping with the ponies at each changing place, or effecting occasional repairs to the harness. Every halt meant a thorough drenching.

Having just recovered from a bad go of ague, I was not feeling up to much after having been soaked through eight or nine times during that day. Depressed as a half-drowned hen, I crawled on board the river steamer, meeting a genial planter, C. A. B. Anderson ("Cab" Anderson, a prominent character) who sent his bearer to give me a thorough rub down.

After a change and feeling more comfortable Anderson whispered in my ear that he had the finest remedy in the world, imported direct – a pocket flask of good scotch whisky. That turned out to be a full magnum champagne bottle. Wonderful to relate, we emptied it before going to bed. It killed my ague dead. Still more remarkable, although I had plenty of malaria I never had another touch of ague until I picked up jungle fever in the Ganjam Hills, thirty years later.

After Assam, Darjeeling seemed like heaven on earth, particularly from the back of a good pony, and Bob Sutton, once in our chummery, wrote to say that he had seen my arrival announced among the social events of the season (I had been fined ten rupees for furious riding) but would not permit trifles like that to affect our friendship provided I called to see him, as he had been in the sanatorium for weeks.

Poor fellow! Long continued malaria had atrophied his heart. He was skin and bone, but could talk of nothing else but Assam, where hospitality was simply showered on every stranger while the charm of tea garden life made him long to go there. We yarned and laughed, thoroughly happy, when the doctor walked in, Major Somebody, Indian Medical Service. He peremptorily demanded to know what I meant by disturbing a man who was so ill, particularly as he had given strict orders to keep visitors away.

Being young I profoundly respected doctors, believing that their object in life was to benefit mankind. I was also convinced that all non-Christians were heathens. I know a bit better now. But it was medical etiquette to deprive patients of every niggardly atom of enjoyment, covering ignorance by harsh methods substantiated with nasty medicine. Therefore when this Major Doctor ordered me off the premises I cleared, feeling needlessly guilty.

In spite of that, Sutton sent chits imploring me to come again as he was sick of everything. He did not want to stand again among a crowd of sweating Bengalis for nine hours a day. How would I like, he asked, to be in a room week after week counting the flies on the ceiling with not a soul to talk to? His letter concluded by stating that his servant had orders to sit outside my room until he brought me back.

Within ten minutes I was cheering him up but, as bad luck had it, the Major caught me again choking me off in a shocking way, rubbing it in about the patient's life hanging on a thread. In front of Sutton that did not seem quite the best way to keep a sick man cheerful, but like so many army doctors, he was more of a sergeant major than a surgeon major.

Two days before I was due to leave Darjeeling, Sutton wrote saying that he could hardly believe I would go away without wishing him goodbye. If I came between 12:30 and 1:00pm the doctor would certainly not be there.

With many reproaches for leaving him so long in loneliness, we soon got back on my trip through Assam. More than anywhere he wanted to do that trip. It had attractions.

At that time there was no railway. Steamers taking passengers to Dibrugarh might be weeks on the journey but with European captains, reckless planters, cheery civilians and good food at four rupees a day the trip was well worth taking. On tea gardens life was hard and solitary. Strangers were welcomed for they broke the monotony of months. Every planter you met, after he had finished bragging about the championship of his local brand of fever, always switched on to the boundless hospitality shown to strangers.

When I told Sutton that I had tried to sneak past a bungalow so as to be in the station before dark, and a planter had pointed his gun threatening to fill me full of lead if I didn't stop to have a peg (which meant as many as I could hold above six). Sutton made up his mind that Assam was a place worth visiting – not for the free drinks but for the welcome. That led on to talking about a sample of Assam hospitality served out to me...

Harry then continues with the story he told Sutton:

...Late one evening I fetched up at Koliabur Ghat intending to go to Nowgong, 52 miles away. Arrowsmith was the pontoon admiral (steamer agent) at Koliabur, an old hand hardened by many years in sail. He told me what to do, fixed up a dugout and, at dawn, saw me off with a small parcel of food done up in a piece of newspaper.

The route was along the Kullon, a sort of dead river with long stretches of sand but I knew nothing about that when I started. The river constantly shallowed which meant dragging the dugout for quite long distances. Leeches swarmed, but it is curious when leeches attack your calves how much they relieve the tired feeling. Mosquitoes swarmed in clouds keeping anyone from standing still.

The parcel of food turned out to be nothing but a piece of stale bread with half an inch of mildew on it, evidently a sample of Arrowsmith's humour to be related amidst roars of laughter when his pals came along. The boatmen, more hospitable, shared their coarse grain and as I had good teeth I munched with them, although, poor fellows, their idea of a feed differed from mine.

After a lot of hard work we came to a wide pool where some wild elephants were wallowing. One cannot argue with a herd of elephants so we came back.

I afterwards learnt that there is nothing to fear from a herd. The whiff of a cheroot will stampede them. The solitary bull is the elephant to be afraid of.

It was too late to reach Koliabur that night. The next morning about breakfast time I boarded Arrowsmith's flat.* My eyes were half closed with mosquito bites while my trousers looked as if I had passed the night in a slaughterhouse. The first thing he told me was that my steamer had gone aground and could not be in Koliabur before 4pm the next day.

This led me to ask Arrowsmith how I was to manage about food. I could hardly believe him when he said he had bought food for himself and did not intend going short for anybody. Moreover if he gave to me he would be expected to give it to everybody, a rather unanswerable piece of logic.

After thirty hours of hungry discomfort, thirty more ahead was a poor prospect for a growing lad. I offered to buy a tin of sardines if he would take a *dib* for it at which he went into a passion. Cursed with nautical fluency, finishing up by saying he'd have no more of my infernal impudence, and refused to take any further notice of me.

It was hot. There was nowhere to go. I searched the piles of cargo in hopes of finding some grain to eat. He must have said something to the lascars who pretended not to understand when I offered to pay a rupee for *chapatties*.

Neglected as a monkey's orphan, I furtively watched Arrowsmith through the *jhilmils* of this cabin with his back hunched up over his plate so that I couldn't see what he was eating while I was certain that the stony-hearted rascal needlessly rattled his knife and fork just to annoy me.

I asked Sutton to picture my time on that flat, each hour longer than a day at the dentists, without even a piece of mouldy bread to rub the cold sweat off my teeth, while the greedy old sinner, full as a bull pup, finished a quart of beer, picked his teeth and puffed away at a Trichy cheroot.

Fresh in memory, it must have been a graphic story for Sutton, after weeks of lonely misery, laughed and laughed. "If he'd been Arrowroot you might have eaten him," said Sutton. The tears rolled down his cheeks. How he laughed! With a sudden gasp he said

---

* The residential accommodation at the pontoon for the 'admiral.'

"Assam," then groaned, his jaw dropped with a half gurgle and he became strangely still. I went cold all over. Asked what was the matter. Implored him for God's sake to say something. There was not a move.

Absolutely appalled, I felt his heart but although there was nothing but skin and bone I could feel nothing of life. I gazed around horror-stricken. Had the doctor come in at that moment I believe I should have dropped dead on the spot, but I crept out on tiptoe, mounted my pony, rode across the bazaar to the boarding house too frightened to say a word to a soul or even to go to the funeral.

Had it not been for fear of meeting the doctor I might have said the Lord's Prayer, but I did nothing. I'll swear it was fifteen years before I comforted myself with the thought that if poor Sutton went on his last journey before enjoying Assam hospitality, at any rate he died happy. And Arrowsmith, who might have half killed me, killed Bob Sutton. [21]

It is curious that I should, so soon after this tragedy, have another experience of hardship aggravated by harshness.

After Sutton's death I took the early train to Sonada picking up a pony sent out on the previous day. July is a bad month in the Darjeeling hills and when I was about to mount a clap of thunder that almost cracked the mountain brought rain down with an absolute roar.

The *syce* said he knew the way to Murmah and, like drowned rats, we slid downhill until riding was impossible. Had I known more I should have turned back, but even when huge trees and rocks, as though shot out of a dredger, slid down in front of me it never crossed my mind that I could be killed. Often knee-deep in mud I pulled the pony across bad places while the rain poured incessantly. The pony trod on my feet, kicked me twice on the same place on my thigh; constantly slipping downhill with boots full of water wore my toes to the bone.

When I was hardly able to crawl, darkness was setting in and the *syce* said he didn't know where we were. It was impossible to smoke. I could have tied my Burma cheroots in a double bow.

About 10pm after 14 hours of struggle, a light glimmered

through the rain and I found myself near a bungalow. Shouting eventually caused a door to be unbarred and a carroty whiskered old man, evidently Scotch, demanded to know what I wanted. "Shelter," was my reply. "I don't keep a hotel," he said. "I know you don't but I claim shelter as an Englishman."

He looked angrily at the widening pool of water which streamed off me on to his verandah, then, in less hostile tone, asked if I would like a drink. He poured out a regular second mate's nip which I thought might stop the rattling of my teeth, so downed it in one to find it was nothing but neat lime juice. After watching the effect of his restorative he showed me to a room where there was a bed without pillows or sheets. Luckily it had a mattress, so peeling off my soaked clothes I took the *dhurry* off the floor, pulled it over me and in less than a minute was sound asleep. At 4:30 the next morning my worthy host turned me out, watched me put on my soaked clothes with the same interest as he saw me drink the lime juice, gave me a small cup of goats milk and, probably wishful to take advantage of the sweet uses of adversity, before telling his *jemandar* to show me off the garden, suggested that when in Calcutta I might buy tea from him.

To reach my destination was no end of a job; for the track led to the foot of a huge cliff round which a raging torrent scoured, making further riding impossible. The *syce* hobbled the pony with the reins while I cached the saddle under a pile of small rocks, then for two hours on hand and knees I climbed the hill and wore out the seat of my riding breeches going down the other side.

At a village – Namsu – incredibly tired, I sat on the plinth of a *modi*'s shop. The sun came out and in a cloud of steam from my sodden clothing with a thankful mind I filled myself up with coarse grain fried in rancid ghee. A *syce* came to ask if I was the sahib expected yesterday and said the pony was waiting. So I rode to Murmah bungalow where Reid, the manager, laughed over my experience until he cried, but gave me a change of clothing and some of the best tea in the world, with as much wedding cake as I could eat. Reid said that I had butted into the most notorious skinflint to the district, but it was wonderful that Hallifax had allowed me to stay the night in his house at all. [22]

Harry comments (in 1937) that old-time hospitality must be dying out as he rarely heard it mentioned by then. Perhaps the need for it in such atrocious conditions had lessened, if not gone altogether. I find it a little strange that nowhere in these accounts of difficult, even horrible journeys does he mention any problems with rescuing his belongings. If on the road for many weeks, or even months, he would have needed changes of clothing, shaving tackle and the like. Even more so, if visits to such establishments as the Murmah bungalow (where, clearly, his visit had been pre-arranged in some detail) were to tune and generally service one or more pianos, he would surely need a fairly sizeable box of tricks for the purpose which might be both bulky and heavy. What kept them dry and safe can now only be left to our imagination.

Harry makes little mention of the musical side of his life at this time, despite music being the reason for his coming to India in the first place. But it does get a mention when he deals with his visit to what many might regard as a particularly unlikely destination for a piano tuner.

Captain Hercules Burleigh was in command of the Asiatic steamer that took me to the Andamans on a business tour in 1886; he must have been a big baby to be so christened, and as he then weighed over 20 stone there must have been something in him when quite an infant to suggest such a Christian name.

As my cabin mate on the voyage I had Major Bromhead VC South Wales Borderers who, with Lieutenant Chard of the Sappers, greatly distinguished himself at the defence of Rorke's Drift in the Zulu War some seven years previously.

He was a stout, stolid man and of great interest to me, but I was unable to get a word out of him about anything. All he said was that he was surprised to know there were any pianos in India and that he wondered who played them.

When we reached Port Blair a boat with its crew of six murderers was placed at my disposal and I soon found out murdering was not their only accomplishment as they stole from me a meerschaum pipe during the first hour I was in their company. As however they did not wear a lot of clothes I managed to get it back without much difficulty, although I had no smokes out of it until I had given it more than one good bath.

M. V. Portman, with whom I put up, held one of the famous musical degrees issued by the Bogusville College of Music in Concord USA. The examination necessary for a candidate to pass was to make a resolution from G to F with one finger on the keyboard of a seven-octave trichord piano. Of course there was a substantial fee to pay, but the real test was that of musical knowledge, which luckily this gentleman amateur possessed.

He attracted quite a full congregation in the church and the ladies almost burst with envy and delight when he sailed down the aisle as a Mus. Doc. In the voluminous flowing robe of bright crimson of the Bogusville University of Music, and sat down to pump the wind out of the American organ.

Portman had half a dozen Andamanese boys – the real aborigines trained as table servants and very good they were too. Not much over four and a half feet high, they were as black as coal and had curly hair similar to that of Negroes, except that the curls were widely separated, each curl stood on its own ground and was so springy that if one was pulled out straight and released it sprang back with an audible click.

One afternoon Portman was busy listening to some weird native music, regretting that he could not write it down; and when I did it, marking certain notes as being a quarter tone sharp or flat, he suggested that I should work for him by writing native music. In those days native music was far less inviting to me (musically) than a dog fight, but he was so full of it that I did not flatly decline – with perhaps a trace of orientalism I thought about it after inwardly deciding against it.

That evening I found on my dressing table a dozen sheets of foolscap on which had been printed various questions on Indian music…

…I remember a few which show that he had given Indian music more than passing thought, although many of them were regular posers.

Describe accurately the varying rhythms such as 5-3, 7-3, 11-5 beats in the bar.

Give details of all stringed instruments, stating the number of strings, thicknesses of wire, intervals in tuning scale, whether fixed or moveable; and also state in tenths of an inch the distance between fingerboard nuts and bridges.

Write down the number of scales and intervals of quarter tones used in Bengal, Bombay, Madras, the Punjab and Burma.

If you have any knowledge of Chinese tunes state whether they are from north or south China.

Explain the difference between the Burmese eight interval scale and primitive Hungarian utilised in old time melodies.

Write down all the Hindustani operas you know.

By the time I had got through the first dozen of the questions I could see that any musician taking on the billet would possibly die of brain fag or musical indigestion in a few months, so I troubled very little about it beyond keeping the questions as curiosities.

When leaving Port Blair it occurred to me that I had met three VCs. They were Colonel Knox-Leet of the Somersets, Colonel Cadell, Commissioner of the Andaman Islands, and Major Bromhead, 24th foot, all of whom not only knew nothing about music but actually rather prided themselves on that fact. It was stated that Colonel Knox-Leet was the originator of the old story of stopping the band because the slide trombones did not work together, and when the bandsman vainly endeavoured deferentially to explain what the different parts meant for first, second and third trombones, the very gallant commanding officer retorted: "I don't care a damn! If my bandsmen have to shove a yard of brass down their necks on the line of march they shall all do it together!"

In later years though I met Captain J. F. Mackay, VC of the Argyll and Sutherlands who gained his decoration as NCO in the Gordons when fighting in Africa – and I take it that he had to be as brave as anyone to get it – well, he had enough music in him to suffice for himself and the three others, as many of the Calcutta Scottish will remember. Music was as necessary to him as food – he once said that music was his fourth requirement, and the order of his wants were food, shelter, clothing and music, which is interesting and to those who are really musical, fairly accurate. [23]

It might be expected that Harry's exposure to these many hazards in his travels, in addition to the burden of the Indian climate and conditions generally, might result in damage to his health. Mention has already been made of his attacks of ague and bouts of malaria (which are today commonly thought of as virtually synonymous terms, but which Harry plainly differentiated) but eventually there was a major breakdown in his health. Indeed it was for him a 'death experience'. Modern medicine, physical or mental, might have a different explanation: Harry always maintained that he did die and somehow came back to life.

In this connection he gives a rare glimpse of his beliefs. He was well acquainted with Church music and ritual, he laced his writings with quotations from and references to the Bible (often in a very caustic manner); and clergymen, particularly highly ranking ones, were often the object of his scornful writings. By the end of his life, however, I suspect he was more of a Christian than even he was aware of. These events occurred when he was very young, and the account is mainly taken from *It Was Like This!* written in 1918.

> Certainly, so far as my belief goes, I am convinced of a distinct individuality after death, and in full seriousness I give the following particulars of a most vivid and unfading experience of my own.
>
> Some people totally disbelieve in a future existence, others wish they could have it proved to them so as to remove the terror of eternal darkness, while many who are possibly much larger in numbers than could be casually conjectured have an unshakeable belief that they will preserve their individuality after death, for ever and ever.
>
> It may be that some may say that my experience proves nothing. All I can say is that I had to overcome many misgivings before I had the courage to write about it.
>
> On the Queen's birthday, 24th May 1888, I had to cross the Ganges somewhat lower down than Dinapore. In the middle of the river was a huge sandbank. It had been arranged that I would take a dinghy to the sandbank, walk across it and take a dinghy on the other side. When I got there no boat was visible and none came until sundown. I learnt later that 24th May was Calcutta's hottest day – 114 degrees – 45 tram horses died in one day.
>
> In Dinapore the following day I felt ill but thought it would pass

off. It didn't and eventually I was too done to go further, so got the train at Umballa, got as far down to Roorkee where I spent four days in the *dak* bungalow.

That was followed by 11 days in the Bareilly *dak* bungalow where I believe I had one cup of tea. Eventually I was put on a Calcutta-bound train and went straight to the Presidency General Hospital on 4 July where I spent several months. I learnt later that I had enteric, dysentery, sciatica, haemorrhage of the lungs and sunstroke. After having been ill for many months I had many bedsores in addition to all my other discomforts.

One day I died and went direct to heaven. It is said you go to that place only once and it is better to get there once than be ten times at the gate. Well, I have been there and walked along the side of a beautiful stream, with delightful green banks and shady trees, and the air as calm and genial as the finest summer's day in England.

I rested by the river feeling how beautiful it was to be there – knew that I had died and had no sorrow or regret – the freedom from all pain and discomfort seemed to be agreeable beyond words. So far as I could remember I saw no living form there, nor have I any recollection of anything but a place of peace.

After a time it occurred to me that I might go back to look at my mortal remains, and I remember going into the room, standing alongside my dead body and examining my features with much interest and sympathy. In those days I had a slight fair moustache and I remember most distinctly seeing the white skin between the hair on my face and head.

Addressing myself I remember saying: "Poor fellow! You've had a real bad time of it and you couldn't hold out any longer." Then I looked at my own spirit, just as you look down at yourself in the flesh, a shapeless, almost transparent bluey mass, as large as a full-grown man, and I again examined with curiosity and pity my wasted body.

Then I felt the rain on my face and I remember being aware that although I was dead the window of the room had not been closed and crows would be sure to come in and peck my face, which would be a pity as none of my friends had been to see me.

While feeling something akin to resentment I opened my eyes and gradually noticed that Colonel Crombie, the sister, *padri*, assistant surgeon and nurse were round the bed.

Then someone came in on tiptoe, but was signalled to go away by the nurse. I did not speak, just lay still with wonder and returning to life, thinking neither far nor very deep.

Very, very slowly I picked up strength, although for a period of over nine years I was a sufferer from fever, but the impression of that excursion away from the realms of this world has always been real and fresh in my memory.

Many long months afterwards I saw Colonel Crombie who told me that I ought to feel thankful that I was still alive as he had made sure I had gone west because it was such a long job bringing me round. [24]

Harry was never short of sympathy for those down on their luck, and I am sure that many such had good cause to be grateful to him for a helping hand of one sort or another. Writing in 1932 or 1933 Harry recalls a poignant chance encounter with a sad and anonymous stranger. I reproduce it for the picture it paints of what life so far from home can do to a man as for any more particular insight into Harry himself. On this occasion, certainly, there was little he could do. In a chapter headed *The Renegade*, he writes:

Life often lets us down with merciless suddenness and many who believe they are floating in deep water find themselves on the rocks before they can look around. As the old tag goes: There is nothing between a poor man and a rich man but a piece of an ill year.

Forty-five years ago I spent six hot weeks in the Punjab and towards the end of May the fierce dry heat half killed me. For several nights I had hardly slept and when I boarded a train the breeze, scorching though it was, sent me to sleep. When I awoke I was far beyond my destination, so to dodge paying for a journey I had no intention of taking, I hopped out, walked to the far end of the platform to avoid making myself conspicuous and to wait for the down train in the morning. Unrolling my bedding, I lit a cheroot and tried to forget that I had no chance of anything to eat until noon the next day. Outside the station compound were a number of transfrontiersmen, evidently on their way to a horse fair, who were attending some horses which were tethered nearby.

As it grew dark a man with baggy trousers, a big *pagri* with curly ends and fancy waistcoat, squatted with a sigh and wondered what I thought of the infernal heat. While looking him over, I hardly got past his Biluchi love-locks when he kicked off his loop-the-loop slippers and reassured me by saying it was all right – he merely wanted a *bukh*; wondered if my Burma cheroot was an orphan, helped himself to one and puffed away with evident enjoyment. When the stars came out he began to talk. Obviously familiar with the army, he mentioned various regiments wondering where they were; told stories about officers and men whom he referred to by their regimental nicknames, then drifted into talking about himself.

The son of a London stockbroker, he had passed out of Sandhurst into a British cavalry regiment, and was given an allowance which let him keep pace with the other officers. Often, when business was good, his father would send a draft for more than he expected. Occasionally, during dull times there might be a delay of a week or two in his remittances, but never long enough to cause him anxiety.

A run of bad luck at a race meeting brought settling day with insufficient to meet it. With a reputation for being well off he hated having to explain matters to the bookmakers, feeling sure that the incoming mail would bring all he expected. Unfortunately the squadron officer happened to be on short leave which made it easy to square his debts with the regimental money. Almost before he had grasped the gravity of what he had done he found himself standing with bowed head in front of the commanding officer who gave him a few hours to put things right.

Unspeakably dismayed he found his brother officers not only had nothing to spare, but they did not seem particularly keen on speaking to him. A frantic rush to the telegraph office gave him several hours of anxiety but no reply came – there was hardly time for that – and by night he found himself a prisoner in his own quarters, disgraced, heartbroken and, without real criminal intent, smashed. Hysterically dazed, he crept out of the bungalow and when he saw anyone approaching, hid in the *nullahs* alongside the road until they passed, and making his way to the station stowed himself in a third class carriage completely ruining what remained of this reputation by deserting.

Fearing arrest, he hid in cheap boarding houses in the bazaar of a large town until his few rupees went. To a white man India is little more than a vast prison, and applying for work among Europeans was risky, particularly as a deserter with a crime against him, and his training had entirely unfitted him for initiative in business. Further, he had been long enough in India to know that everybody knows everybody. At his wits' end, he met a travelling horse dealer who knew what had happened – and offered him a job as a sort of oddman and correspondent which meant burying himself among a gang of primitive cut-throats with whom he was about as popular as smallpox. Eventually to stifle the animosity of those around, he severed that last thread which bound him to his former existence by turning Mahommedan. Hating nobody, he had suddenly dropped into a life of verminous hardship as a deserter and a renegade.

"Had the guv'nor sent me half the money but sent it regularly this would never have happened," he said. "What was the good of writing home? As for poor mother, well, the Gazette would tell her all I could say, and while I was sorry for her, well, the less she knew the better and when you're down to the bottom fine feelings go."

Of course we all know that in such stories the real reason is never given. The sequel of being found out in any transgression is to throw the blame on somebody, or to invent a story which palliates the offence. The honour of a regiment would have been safeguarded by the regimental shroff had the delinquent been worth helping.

But that was his story and it was not for me to pass remarks. It went at that. Whether it was or was not true, there he was, an Englishman, evidently well brought up who, one felt, would never of his own free choice live the life of an outcast among such people. Whatever sins he may have committed, his atonement must have sponged them out with many scalding tears of regret.

Next morning almost before it was light we shook hands and parted with no suggestion of meeting again. He did not ask my name, nor do I know his, but a soldier friend some years later told me he had met him in Rawalpindi, still with the travelling horse dealer, a victim of circumstances, who without working it out had learnt from poignant experience that there is no substitute for punctuality. [25]

With so much time necessarily devoted to his employer's business, delayed journeys and at times ill health, it is a little surprising that Harry found much time for volunteer soldiering. It is evident that he did so, and with some distinction, although his progress can really only be guessed at from the writings of many years later. A landmark for him and for the Calcutta Volunteer Rifles seems to have been the appointment of a Colonel Frank Chatterton of the Indian Staff Corps to command the volunteers. He brought with him as adjutant Lieutenant A. A. Barrett (later to be Field Marshall Sir Arthur Barrett) and the sergeant-major of the Agra Volunteers. Of the latter Harry wrote:

> Many will remember Sergeant-Major A. Lees, and I am sure no finer sergeant-instructor ever served in the force. Full of humour, a fine shot, good boxer and excellent drill, he could issue a gas pipe to a recruit in such a manner that the lad would feel confident of winning the Viceroy's prize the first time he fired out of it. [26]

Of the two senior officers, commanding officer and his adjutant, Harry wrote:

> Both soldiers were keen and appreciative of whatever was done to help them. Their encouragement stimulated me. I raised the strength of F Company from about 30 to 113. On one occasion I had 100 men on parade. [27]

Taking the credit, as he does in that passage, for the strength of his Company it would have been interesting to have been told when he was promoted (perhaps elected) to non-commissioned rank. The highest rank he attained in the Volunteers was Colour Sergeant and he can hardly have reached that level in his first five years. He was undoubtedly a good shot and it was marksmanship which was one of his enthusiasms. He was one of those who took the view that excellence in drill movements was not enough for an army in wartime and he did all he could to improve the shooting skills of the soldiers. He would have been encouraged to do so by no less a person than the great Lord Roberts who, as Commander-in-Chief in India from 1885 to 1893, was trying to do just that:

> The effect of the Majuba disaster was beginning to be felt although military minds still held to the belief that a regiment that could march like a wall and wheel like a gate was efficient even were the

men, if placed in the middle of the parish they were born in, unable to hit it.

General Roberts was out to change that, not only did he encouraged the use of the rifle, but spent a lot of time on the rifle range. I fired twice alongside him on the Ballygunge range. He wasn't much of a shot but was just like any other man – free from side.

On one occasion Sergeant-Instructor Ben Vigrass, who had marched with the general from Kabul to Kandahar, was keeping the score. If a bull was signalled he would sing out loudly: "His Excellency the Commander-in-Chief Sir Frederick Roberts – a bulls-eye – FIVE!" Were a magpie signalled from the butts he would quietly mutter: "General Roberts – three." I saw the general's sides shaking with amusement. He was a great man.

When battalion commanders began to see that they would be in a bad way if their figures of merit were low on the range, they fell into line and offered all sorts of privileges to those who were efficient with their rifles. In one battalion leave was granted to those company commanders who showed the best returns on the targets, and one officer anxious to get away on a *shikar* promised the men four annas for every bulls-eye. To his disgust he was badly beaten by a far worse lot of marksmen and the other captain got the much desired leave. Over a half peg the loser complained to the winner: "I've never paid such price for bulls-eyes before. When I was a kid I got them at four a penny, but I'd like to know how you managed to beat my chaps." "Well you see," said the other, "you paid your four annas to your men but I paid mine to the markers." [28]

Such mild chicanery may not have been much frowned upon. I do not think that Harry could have been one of the participants – although I am sure at times he tells a story of his own actions, disguised as those of another – for he would never have been a battalion commander. He was certainly party to one piece of chicanery to help Colonel Chatterton win a wager. He tells rather a long story of the other man selecting names of those to shoot and he, Harry, realising that some were duds, stood them down and made three or so good shots take their places and their names. But "one man forgot his name so I informed the officer that the blushing blighter who almost let us down stammered; was nervous when questioned; so he passed all correct. Prestige was saved." [29]

One account of an incident, however, leaves me in little doubt that Harry is referring anonymously to himself and another. How else would he have known about it, for neither participant would have been likely to mention it to anyone else? If I am right in this, it also shows that Harry was a non-commissioned officer by the time it happened, and so before his first return home.

A rather curious tragedy happened in 1887 or 1888, when two non-commissioned officers in F Company, 1st CVR, were returning from the range. They noticed that the indicator on the breech block of the rifle pointed to the striker being cocked, so without hesitation the trigger was pulled. To the surprise of both men, the rifle went off. Luckily as they thought, the muzzle pointed skywards and they concerned themselves no more about it until they read in the *Indian Daily News* of an extraordinary occurrence in Chitpur Road, where a *durwan* was found to have been killed by a shot that struck him in the top of his head. They kept *chup* and, beyond the few in the know, the matter remained a mystery and was probably considered in the light of a visitation. [30]

Harry's first five-year term with Samuel Harraden would have expired in November 1888. He nowhere states the reason for his first home leave being postponed for six months. One possibility was his health. He had had his serious illness (and 'death') in the weeks or months following the end of May. But then one might have thought that a return to England would have been considered beneficial to his health. Another possible factor may have been his prowess as a shot. Through Lieutenant Whitehead he was selected for the Indian Team which was to compete for the Kohlapur Cup at Wimbledon in 1889. It was the last time the Wimbledon ranges were used, the venue being moved to Bisley thereafter. He said his team did badly – he being put off by the captain who gave instructions when his sights were on target, which put Harry off more than help him.

The only reference I can find to his first return to England after more than five years hard work is almost a passing thought in a short passage dealing with changes in his unit's uniforms.

In 1883 the Calcutta Volunteers had just discarded the rifle-green serge uniform and adopted khaki with dark green piping, which was very ugly. In 1887 or 1888 we were garbed in scarlet coats, blue trousers and white helmets...

Later on we wore khaki with white helmets, and I remember being very struck with the appearance of a bore on the Hooghly – the khaki water with white foam on top, which exactly resembled the Calcutta Volunteers in line on the march...

I was Left Guide of the Guard-of-Honour when the present Volunteer headquarters were declared open by the Viceroy, Lord Lansdowne *. We paraded in red serge on the morning of 1st April 1889 and it was fairly hot; it is so fresh in my memory because I was leaving for home by the P&O steamer *Thames* on the morning of 3rd April. [31]

* Viceroy 1888-94.

CHAPTER 3

IRISH INTERLUDE:
FROM DERRY FADDA FARM
TO MELBOURNE

I F DETAILS CONCERNING the early life of Harry are fragmentary and haphazard, those relating to Jennie are almost non-existent. Even her age was never known. It was known that her birthday was on 11th April and that she was two years or so older than Harry. When she died on 24th March, 1943, Dorothy – who was the informant to the Registrar of Deaths – gave her age as eighty-one. It was a guess: Jennie always refused to say how old she was. In 2003 I was fortunately able to see the entry of her marriage in the Church of St. Thomas in Calcutta. She had given her age on 5th February, 1894 as thirty-one. So she was born on 11th April, 1862, and was still not yet eighty-one when she died.

She was born Jane Agnes Larkin, the second daughter in a family of four girls and four boys. There were also two older half-siblings. The Larkin family were close friends of the McCormack family, and one of the McCormack family married Mary Larkin, Jennie's older sister. The McCormacks had two sons, Jack and Frank, and two daughters, Marie and Queen. Their home had been in Melbourne Australia from the last quarter of the nineteenth century. In due course Dorothy wrote to Queen to tell her of the death of Jennie, and Queen replied towards the end of 1943 (post taking a long time in those wartime years: the envelope was 'opened by censor') and giving some family background. This letter gives the most full and accurate written account of Jennie's early life that is now available to me. It is not very long, and was not written from personal experience. However, Queen McCormack (she never married) had the advantage of living with her Aunt Annie, Jennie's younger sister, often referred to as 'little auntie', from whom much of the information in her letter could have come.

Indeed she says in her letter that "aunt is writing you some details of your little mother's early life" but, if she did, that letter has not survived. Queen's letter does, however, throw a small shaft of light on what life may have been like in Ireland in the mid 19th century.

Grandfather Michael Larkin was a widower with two children, boy and girl, when he married Mary Clancy, our grandmother – at that time he was a gentleman farmer, well educated (a brother of his used to act as Irish interpreter for the judge in the courts) and lived at Derra Fodda,* according to Frank and Jack a beautiful house with mullioned windows – (mother) Mary, Matthew, John, Michael, Thomas and (your mother) Jane were born there.† They kept two maids and nurse Peggy (Margaret O'Connell) who was with them till she died at Larkin's Cross.

Grandfather did not own the farm – a wealthy man in London (Mr Taylor) owned it and an English agent in Limerick named Vandergast acted for him. He (Vandergast) wanted it for one of his friends but grandfather refused to leave and went to London several times to see the owner who refused to go against his agent. For seven years this went on. Grandfather was even going to law (there must have been a life tenancy attached to it – the owner would not even sell.) Then the day came and they had to go – mother used to tell us how Vandergast rode up on the fatal day on his beautiful grey horse and stood by while furniture and their beautiful cattle were taken out, and how grandmother had hidden grandfather's gun because he threatened to shoot the first man who moved anything. However all had to go and the family with Peggy the faithful nurse went with them to Larkin's Cross (hotel and farm) that grandfather owned. For some time after [grandfather] was Town Clerk – not called that – in Limerick. Aunt Annie and Aunt Maggie, who died years ago, were born there. Grandfather did not live very long after that but grandmother, who must have been a marvellous woman to bring up the family as she did, lived until 2 August 1895…

I must mention although our loved and devoted mother†† remembered every detail of their eviction from the farm she was never bitter towards England…

* Spelling varies – that in the chapter title I believe to be correct.
† I do not think this is in correct order of birth. At least one brother – John – was younger than Jennie, maybe two.
†† She had died some years before.

...The [half] brother and sister when young went to America to an uncle Larkin but did not live very long...

...Our mother was the first to come to Australia. She came to Melbourne to a cousin, Mrs Lyons from Echuca one of our country towns, but did not stay with her; she got a position in Melbourne. Uncle Michael (Mick) came next. Then your mother and Uncle John – Aunt Annie next – then Uncle Tom and his wife who were married in Ireland. Maggie staying with her mother and eldest brother Matt who became a postmaster. He married a niece of our father's and lived at Larkin's Cross till his death and now his son Joe is there with his wife and family...

Queen's reference to 'grandfather did not live very long after that' conceals another tragedy for the family. As well as his position in the City of Limerick, Michael Larkin also had some Customs and Excise appointment for which he had a tied house near the bank of the River Shannon. One night his duties called him out and he had to row across the river. While doing so he suffered some mishap and was drowned. When the family returned to the house after the funeral, they found all their belongings out in the street, and the successor in that post to Michael Larkin had been duly installed in the house.

All the Larkin passages to Australia were 'assisted immigration' paid for or sponsored by a Mr Tom Minahan, a friend and former neighbour in Ireland who had gone south several years before.

Queen gives a little more information about other branches of the extended family. The elder brother, Matthew, who remained in Larkin's Cross, had several children, many of whom emigrated to America where they married and had large families – as did those who made their lives in Australia. There must be many scores, if not hundreds of descendants of Michael and Mary Larkin in Ireland, England, Australia and America today.

As an afterthought Queen adds that Jennie was fifteen years old when she emigrated. In this she was mistaken. Dorothy's recollection – which she can only have got from her mother – was that Jennie was twelve when she made that journey "during the course of which she taught her little brothers the Catechism."

Whether she was twelve or fifteen the passage out must have been an ordeal requiring some courage on Jennie's part. Nothing is said as to who, if anyone, was accompanying her. Certainly no member of her immediate family (apart from her younger brother or brothers.) Perhaps kind adults on board, emigrating as she was, were glad to take the pair of them under their wing for the voyage. Conditions would not have been luxurious. The cramped, limited space available on deck and below, and the motion of the small vessel in which she would have sailed, would have been hardly conducive to teaching anyone anything, let alone their Catechism. The fact that she did so tells us a good deal about Jennie's commitment to the Church, which was lifelong. That may help to explain her sticking to the man who was to become her husband, despite all his faults. In her mind that, too, was a lifelong commitment.

But marriage was many years ahead – and I regret that I have no information at all about Jennie's life during the next fifteen or twenty years. I have to leave her as a twelve year old, disembarking with her little brother at Melbourne, probably to be greeted by an older sister who would introduce her to her new life in her new country.

CHAPTER 4

RETURN TO INDIA
AND BEYOND

ON 3rd APRIL 1889, Harry left India for his first visit home in
just on six years. There is no record as to how long he was
away; indeed there is hardly any information at all about that
period. I suspect it was something of an anti-climax. Instead of being
the centre of almost breathless admiration and pride as a great
traveller and achiever he seems to have been greeted with something
akin to indifference, even disbelief. The only reference I can find to
any aspect of his homecoming is a rather sad paragraph:

> I shall never forget my disappointment when after six years of
> adventure I went home for the first time. Eager to talk about where
> I had been and what I'd seen, I found that place names conveyed no
> meaning: Chhindwara, Chitpur, Chittagong, Chunar and
> Chowringhee were all alike; they aroused no interest; all fell equally
> flat. Then on top of this a friend of the family, after hearing a recital
> of the places I said I'd been to, bluntly said he didn't believe me. I
> was almost speechless with angry amazement, but it had its effect.
> For many years I shut the recollections down, and perhaps today
> feel regretful for I might have had some good stories to tell. [1]

Considering that, in the event, he was to write some half a score of
books, mostly crammed with stories – not all, it is true, purporting to
be of personal experience – his final lament may be taken with a pinch
of salt. But it points to his family not being very close knit, I hesitate
to say dysfunctional, which may explain why he makes so little
mention of them in any of his writings. Reference has already been
made to his assertion that on his return after his first leave he had only
eight pence. I would think that that was probably largely due to rather
heavy expenditures which might almost be categorised as reckless –
for he wrote:

During my first holiday home, in 1889, I went to Paris to see the
Great Exhibition and stayed a month at a very comfortable hotel in
the Rue de Rivoli. [2]

Harry does not identify the hostelry which he patronised on that
occasion, but I cannot believe that any 'very comfortable'
establishment located in that fashionable street in Paris could be
other than pricey. Perhaps his five and a half years in India had
enabled him to save a significant sum, and, with no dependants to
worry about, he felt "I earned it the hard way; now I'm going to enjoy
myself." And who could blame him for that? Especially if in part he
was also improving his mind.

There is nothing to tell us what else he may have done during that
first leave, nor the date upon which he returned to India. For return
he most certainly did, and to continue to work for the same employer.
He uses his reference to the French hotel as a starting point for an
anecdote in which he does not appear in at all a favourable light –
especially when one considers that he liked to stand up for the
underdog and disliked humbug of any kind:

One of the visitors; was a burly Britisher with two nice daughters
the right side of 30; and when the old gentleman found I came from
India he told me that he had been right through the mutiny in a rifle
battalion. He went further and mentioned that he had picked up a
fair amount of loot but could not get away with it all, so he had
buried 800 rupees and a lot of jewellery under the eighth milestone
from Cawnpore along the Bhitoor Road.

The daughters filled me with much enthusiasm as they were
firmly convinced that their dear old dad had buried a few dozen
diamonds from which the Koh-i-Noor might have been a chip, so
after hearing so much about this I went to my room and carefully
wrote down the details without appearing to take too much interest
in the story.

I happened to be in Cawnpore the next year and called on a
friend there to whom I confided my secret, and we arranged to start
out in a *ticca gharry* at four in the morning. He was to be dressed in
his volunteer uniform for the sake of effect, and we took a telescope,
a couple of brass stair carpet rods and a tape so that it might look

as though we were part of a scientific expedition and thereby create a good impression among the natives.

When we arrived at the milestone we lost no time in laying out the tape and stair rods, placing the telescope in a prominent position and getting to work. It was about the middle of October and not very hot until we began to dig. Luckily some of the local population came along, and by showing them some of the coins we had found (in our pockets) we managed to impress them for the digging, which went on until past ten o'clock.

My companion then began to enquire whether the old soldier had stated definitely that he had buried it himself or whether the battalion pioneers had been employed for a week or so on the job. I consoled him with the thought that this was perhaps the last day's work we might ever have to do, particularly if we came across the diamonds, and urged him to put his back into it...

I suggested to my companion that we had either dug past the treasure or if we went much deeper there was a danger of falling through the other side of the hole. We were not mean about it; we paid our Aryan helpers and left the government to fill in the pit as all their servants work for pensions, and besides what do we pay taxes for?...

That was my first and last experiment in hunting for treasure, and while I hardly expected to become suddenly rich I must own that the anticipation more than counterbalanced the disappointment.

It occurred to me that my old soldier friend might like to know about it so I wrote to him explaining that some dreadful thieves must have burgled his treasure as it was not there – that is, within 15 feet all round that milestone.

I expressed my regret at not being able to send his daughters a few diamonds as paperweights, and desired to know if he was quite sure that it was the eighth milestone, feeling that perhaps he might be able to give more accurate details.

Shortly before Christmas I received his reply which for a time rather upset me. The old warrior said he could tell from the keen look in my eye that I took in what he said and purposely gave the wrong milestone as he had no intention of giving away a treasure to a stranger, no matter how agreeable he may have been, and moreover he was coming out on a trip and meant to dig up the loot himself.

Just to encourage my Cawnpore friend I sent him the letter as a new year greeting, and he seemed to be quite cross about it - some people have no sense of humour but they will never own up to it...

I therefore wrote to say that if ever I heard of any more hidden treasure I would not tell him about it, neither would I permit him to help me find it, and that closed the whole romance. [3]

I cannot make up my mind which is the more surprising: that Harry should have embarked on the enterprise at all (whether on account of ordinary honesty or the rather obvious risk of having been taken in by the old soldier) or that, having done so, he should have written to the old soldier to tell him about it. And I wonder what he would have done if, improbably, he had discovered the treasure.

I am glad that Harry's attitude to the property of others was quite different when he came across another treasure by accident during the course of his normal work:

A strange experience occurred to [me] some years ago [probably the early 1890s] in Rangoon. While tuning a square piano, in the house of a wealthy Parsee merchant, a noise was heard which, on being searched for, was found to proceed from a diamond, as large in diameter as a four anna piece, which had dropped out of its setting into the instrument! Previously a servant had been accused of stealing this valuable stone; and on searching his effects, several small articles which he had stolen from his master were found. He was convicted and sentenced to a long term of imprisonment – a sentence in its severity probably more on account of the diamond he had never possessed than because of the almost valueless articles he had pilfered. On the stone being restored to him, the Parsee evinced no emotion, and received it without a word of thanks. It was only after incidentally referring, at the hotel that evening, to the discovery of the diamond that I learnt the story connected with it. [4]

Not only treasure did Harry find in the pianos he had to visit. Perhaps piano tuners everywhere from time to time come across the odd and the unexpected inside an instrument, but I suspect that the Indian selection is wider than most:

It is often surprising what is found inside pianos…I remember in a seaport town sitting down to tune a piano and was startled to hear two rapid reports with the thud of bullets plugging into the teak partition of the room. "It's all right," said the marksman, "I'm only seeing how close I can get without hitting you!" The wife of this gentleman was greatly distressed at the affair, as her husband was drinking, and she was quite unable to find out where he got the whisky or where he kept it. Later in the day I found a whisky bottle inside the bottom door of the piano, which showed that a knowledge of piano construction can be put to various uses! [4]

And again:

I once discovered the cast skin of a snake on the keys of a square, and it was apparently that of a large reptile too; needless to say I treated that piano with very great care for some minutes and felt uneasy all the time in case the snake might appear from the inner recesses at the treble end. [4]

And again:

It is of frequent occurrence that a horizontal piano is left open for some hours and then suddenly closed. If rats or mice wander inside the damage they do trying to gnaw their way out to the various chinks of light that show through the casework is simply surprising. Rats have been found inside pianos that have come on a ten-day journey, they are generally very lively in getting away as soon as they see the first chance of liberty. [5]

And yet again:

I have lively recollections of an experience in a bungalow near the Royal Lakes, Rangoon. Lying on my back to take off the pedal I was drawing the screws from the guide blocks when the whole lot fell, bringing down a nest of ants which had found a comfortable billet on the rocker. How many ants dropped down my neck I hardly like to estimate, but I remember going out into the compound with my body apparently on fire and undressing under the shelter of a very small bush. [6]

It was not only pianos to which Harry had to give his attention. The organ also called for his work from time to time. One such contained intruders which prevented any work.

> Some years ago I was in Oudh and at a certain station I was asked to put the church organ in order. After receiving the order, the padre casually remarked that he thought it was only right to inform me of a nest of hornets that was in the back of the instrument. Probably more out of curiosity then anything else, I asked him who would compensate me if I got stung and he indifferently informed me that that was my lookout. He quite appreciated my reply that, as I considered he must be more fitted for another world than myself, he might try to get them out himself first, and on his reporting "all clear" I would commence work. I did not tune that organ.
>
> Mice, snakes, lizards and insects of all descriptions abound in many organs and it is always best to approach a disused organ very cautiously before putting one's hands inside in a careless manner. If any cuts or bruises are received while at work it is advisable to take particular care afterwards to disinfect and thoroughly cleanse the wounds. [7]

Harry's work on his return to India was, at first, along much the same lines as had been the case in his first five years. But he was soon to find that piano playing was occupying more and more of his time, and he was particularly in demand as an accompanist. Not surprisingly there is not much reference to routine work of that kind, but Harry does give us his recollection of the occasional unusual or colourful event. One of those occurred during the visit to India in early 1891 of the future Czar Nicholas II and involved a 'little fellow called Professor Hayes' whose only claim to be called professor seems to have been that the ship in which he had come to India had been called *Professor*. He was, in truth, a shirt maker at the Great Eastern Hotel. Writing after the Bolshevik Revolution but before Ekaterinburg, Harry tells us:

> The Czarewitch – recently the Czar of Russia (and who will possibly fill that position again) – came to Calcutta with his staff, creating a tremendous sensation with the splendour of their uniforms. The young Prince was dressed as a Cossack Colonel with white

astrakhan coat and hat, while some of his staff had dazzlingly burnished eagles on the top of their helmets which glittered and glowed in the bright sunshine.

Some of this splendid array was accommodated by Harry's company commander in the Volunteer Rifles, and when they were all together in the building:

> On two or three occasions...any man in the Company who could sing went upstairs to entertain those great people with impromptu concerts...
>
> The Professor used to sing from music - that is, he read the words from the music sheet, and then not always correctly, and his magnum opus was *The Blew Alslaytian Mountains*, with the last few bars on tiptoe. Walking towards the piano, he leaned forward in a dramatic manner and remarked cheerily: "Drop it down a crotchet old dear! My copy's half a semi-breve too high." He then loudly cleared his throat, pumped his Adam's apple up and down a few times to see if it would easily clear his collar and was working freely, just as a taxi driver gives his engine a few turns, then started to sing.
>
> After giving his masterpiece, during which I had transposed the accompaniment twice, raising him a full tone each time, he sat down to talk to a Russian prince and would insist on calling him 'mister', reciting meanwhile his opinion of some of his customers and how trying they were. [8]

Harry's ability to transpose at sight led him at times to sail rather close to the musical wind. Once he found himself accompanying a tenor of whom he had formed a particularly poor opinion, regarding him as a pompous ass possessed of little ability and no musicianship. One of his items was a ballad of several verses towards the upper limit of his range. Harry transposed up a semi-tone between each verse with the result that the last two verses or so were rather far from euphonious. The tenor came up to Harry afterwards and said: "Mr Hobbs, I can't understand it. I could manage all the notes when I began that ballad, but I found it quite impossible to reach them at the end." Harry reckoned that his poor opinion had been vindicated.

Samuel Harraden, who had originally engaged him on behalf of his firm of Harold & Co, was not in Calcutta very often. One of his sons, Herbert Harraden, was in Calcutta for much of the time and was also a musician. Harry wrote of him:

> Herbert spent five years at Cambridge without being able to get a degree. Like his father he was a musician, but unlike him was without a trace of business capacity. The simplest problem in figures generally resulted in his saying, in helpless tones: "I really can't follow you." Even his compositions – and they were many – might have 17 bars in one part and 11 in another.
>
> As a pianist he was delightful company. He could not only play the piano; he could play with it. When trying over new music he could criticise, poke fun, change a couple of bars to hint that it had been stolen from a familiar melody, play a note as though stumbling over a half brick, or over emphasise a defect so that you laughed, all the while making a running commentary that filled those standing round full of enjoyment. In that Herbert Harraden was in a class by himself. [9]

It was Herbert, and particularly his arithmetical blind spot, which pitchforked Harry into the operatic limelight:

> One experience was conducting the opera *Rip Van Winkle*.* [Three named individuals] were responsible for the production; Herbert Harraden…was musical director. Although Harraden had been five years at Cambridge vainly striving for his degree he could not count beyond ten even if he took his boots off.
>
> The Lieutenant-Governor of Bengal signified his intention of being present and Harraden, finding the conducting meant counting beats and bars, suddenly caved in. He did not pretend to be able to count. The bandmaster of the British Regiment in the Fort was in hospital; hundreds of rupees had been spent, so as the very last resource I was asked to do it. Harraden was my boss and

---

* A French operetta by Robert Planquette produced at the Comedy Theatre in 1882 where it ran for over 300 nights.

the request was tinged with command, and fools butt in when wise men from the East End stay at home, but I took it on. How many in this world have been suddenly called upon to conduct an opera? One might more easily get over the dedication of a cathedral or take on the responsibility of launching a first class battleship but, before I could think, I found myself in the orchestra with a baton in my hand wagging away as if I had done it before. Well, faint heart never got into the divorce court and, like the man who fell out of a balloon, I was in it.

Time did not permit more than two rehearsals. During the first, the leader of the orchestra, a stocky Goanese and a good fiddler, resented being pulled up and hurt my feelings by saying: "I'm not a musician of five minutes standing." There was a certain amount of truth in that but it could not be tolerated. The subsequent exchange of pleasantries at which I made a better fist than I did at conducting, so upset him that he threw an epileptic fit in the orchestra and had to be carried out foaming at the mouth. The promoters of the show were nearly in the same condition but when the man recovered he came back quiet as a lamb. He must have felt that God had justly punished him for his bad behaviour.

There is no shame in admitting that I was never so nervous in all my life but in spite of that *Rip Van Winkle* ran for three nights to crowded houses. One performance was under the patronage of the Lieutenant-Governor of Bengal. It must be confessed, that the orchestra sometimes got home first, while at others I was the winner. But as nobody asked for their money back, and my portrait appeared in the illustrated papers, that must prove without doubt that my first and last essay into conducting what was very nearly an opera was a pronounced success.

As for the amateur actors! They had a good booze-up at a dinner afterwards. I didn't belong to their social circle, so I wasn't invited. The line had to be drawn somewhere. They had been generous enough with Anglo-Indian hospitality to permit me to pay for my own drinks at the theatre bar during the show, so missing the dinner didn't trouble me much. They had given me a first class opportunity of showing off which should be the greatest reward any amateur musician has a right to expect. [10]

Harry does not put a date on his conducting 'career'. I believe it must have been in the early 1890s.

He was not usually quite so much in the limelight. One suspects that the quality of musical performance in Calcutta was not up to the standard to which we are accustomed in this country today, but doubtless audiences were grateful for what they heard, and the performers often had more than merely the music in their minds.

The most successful amateur productions of the late 80s and early 90s were Gilbert and Sullivan's operas conducted by Herr (afterwards Chevalier) Mack. Most of the ladies were pupils of Loreto House. All were about the sweet 17 age and, as youth is the only beauty, highly attractive.

Mrs Mack, a large red-faced Englishwoman whose stays (they did not call them corsets then) creaked and groaned like a new hemp hawser taking the strain round a bollard, looked after them. She had the eye of a hawk, the strength and pugnacity of two butchers. Nothing ever happened to those girls while in her charge. The constant lover who got past her would have been a super Don Juan.

Herr Mack was an accomplished musician and a charming personality. He efficiently scored every bar in *Pinafore*, *Patience*, the *Mikado* and the *Gondoliers*. There may have been others but I have forgotten them. Amateur musicians, strengthened by bandsmen from the Fort, formed the orchestra. The theatre was always packed. In the *Mikado* and the *Gondoliers* I played bassoon and oboe parts on a large harmonium.

Good as they were it is doubtful if the ventures paid and it is still more doubtful if Mack paid anything for the performing rights…

Writing with a little experience, those who carry through schemes involving big financial risks, who can manage male jealousies and feminine feuds, must be blessed with an infinity of discretion for avoiding trouble, and be all tact in wriggling out of it. The ability to manage men, to say nothing about women, is a greater gift than being able to paint a picture. Those who have it and a stout heart as well are outstanding characters.

The Italian government recognised this by making Herr Mack a Chevalier, which is perhaps all he got out of his hard work. The young ladies did far better for, at the close of the season, it was customary to judge the success by the number of engagements. They were numerous enough to secure a full company the following year. [11]

Samuel Harraden died in the summer of 1897 and Harry records that Herbert had pre-deceased him. Furthermore Harry had established his own business, H. Hobbs & Co (later to be incorporated) in 1893. That is, assuming the accuracy of one of the business letterheads which I find in the documents available. As with many businesses H. Hobbs & Co had several different letterheads. Harry happened to use a sheet of business paper, probably many scores of years old, for a short personal letter, of no interest at all, in 1953. It proclaims:

H. Hobbs & Co Ltd – Est 1893

Pianoforte importers, repairers and tuners, player
pianos and extensive library of perforated music
Agents for Ky-Ko non-electric fans

How much of this wide-ranging business was set up at the time of its inauguration is not revealed. By the time of the publication of the second edition of his first book, *The Piano in India*, in 1914 Harry has more than half a dozen pages advertising his business. It sounds very substantial. 'Over 600 pianos stocked. Repairs are most thoroughly carried out and under expert supervision…Tuners sent on short notice to any part of India.'

Even assuming that it began as a rather more modest enterprise it seems that it must have been from the beginning in more or less direct competition with Harold & Co, Samuel Harraden's firm. It seems unlikely that he would continue as an employee of Harold & Co after establishing a business in competition with them. Indeed it is a situation which might well have caused a great deal of bitterness and even litigation, but I can find no reference to any such dispute. The business was always in the centre of Calcutta, first at Harry's apartment at 4 Esplanade East, then at 9 and later at 21, Old Court House Street. It became his main source of income. Harry gives us one small indication of the problems of setting it up.

Thirty-odd years ago [about 1900] I bought tickets for a soldier friend, A. E. Browne, now a retired major, which resulted in a win for him of Rs 30,000 [in] the sweep…promoted by the Howrah United Club…At the time I had just started business on my own account and Browne generously offered the use of the money for as long as I liked, without interest. The temptation was strong, as we were both poor men, so I consulted W. A. Langdon of the much lamented Alliance Bank of Simla, who promised to assist with Rs 10,000 whenever I required it. I was thus able to return the cheque and keep Browne's friendship. When it came to an overdraft, Langdon backed out but, knowing Browne, I told Langdon exactly what I thought, which resulted in threats from the bank's solicitors, demonstrating how difficult it is for an honest man to beat a bank. However I transferred my account and Percy Mould of the Mercantile Bank of India treated me well, so Browne actually did as good a turn as if he had leant the money. [12]

'Exactly what I thought' is probably a euphemism for a lengthy and loudly expressed diatribe of a highly defamatory nature, which I expect became recognised as a likely consequence of displeasing Harry. In later life he was once asked: "Didn't you ever get any writs for libel?" – "Certainly. Four in one day." – "And what did you do about them?" – "Took no notice." Plaintiffs would be likely to be put off pressing a claim once they realised he could 'justify' – that is, prove the truth of what he had said or written. Debunking humbug with the truth as he saw it was his stock-in-trade.

The founding of his own business would have meant a considerable change in Harry's lifestyle. While he may still have undertaken himself some of the tuning requirements of his customers, he probably was under much less pressure to be travelling in all conditions to all parts from the Punjab to Burma. He soon had London agents helping him to recruit staff, just as he had been recruited himself ten years or so earlier. His travelling was rather further afield. He had realised that there was a demand for pianos in India which would be better able to withstand the climatic conditions – the extreme heat and the extreme humidity – than the normally imported instrument, designed with Europe in mind. His skills as a tuner and repairer, his musicianship and his business acumen led him to approach piano manufacturers for them to manufacture pianos to include specifications of his own for dealing with the conditions in India.

He did not find this an easy task. Piano factories in England would say they were willing to comply with his requests – longer screws, pegging as well as gluing, for example, were two matters – but when the instruments arrived he found his specifications had been ignored.

This led him to search elsewhere; and Germany was the obvious country to which he would look for well-known makers of pianos. This entailed visits to Germany – and he evidently made many. At first he seems to have fared little better than he had in England. As well as looking for compliant piano builders he kept his observant eyes and ears open while there. What he saw and heard led him to have no doubt as to Germany's potential military strength. He believed that the make-up of the German army was rather different from the British. Writing in 1917, when the Great War was at its height, he recalled:

Twenty years ago when I first visited Germany I received an impression regarding the German army and the sort of discipline in force, which is worth recording.

I called on a manufacturer who could not speak English and as my German permitted me to do little more than count up to 20 we were not able to discuss intricate points of subjects such as the rise and fall of the Roman Empire.

However my host did the next best thing by planting a large tankard of Munich beer before me. Presently a big beefy soldier turn up, who told me – speaking in huge lumps of German – that he was the son and junior partner of the house. At that moment he was serving one year as a volunteer or officer recruit in the Guards, and the barracks were just round the corner.

After we discussed business – in which, by the way, I was done (but that's another story) – we adjourned to their swagger restaurant to cement my order with lunch. The place was full of non-coms of the Guards, splendid looking men, and I remarked: "What fine looking fellows these are!"

"They're *schweinhund*," was the reply. "You see that man over there?" (he pointed at a particularly magnificent specimen) "he's what you would call in England the sergeant. I had to pay him a shilling to leave barracks and now that he has seen me with an Englander I'll have to pay another shilling when I get back."

"I shouldn't pay him," I asserted.

"Neither would I if I could help it, but I shall go into the guard-room if I don't. If I go to war he's the first man I intend to shoot."

Further enquiries from the guardsman, and later on from various people in Germany as well as Germans in India, all tended to confirm the statement that the non-commissioned officers in the German army blackmailed their men. The conscript always cleared out of the army as quickly as he could, unless he happened to be very poor, when he remained and became an under-officer.

This means, therefore, that the non-coms are taken from the labourers, street-corner boys, and the social dregs of the nation. They like the army because it gives them a better home, food and prospects than what they might expect in civil life, therefore they remain in it.

With the number of socialists in Germany their men are all pretty well grounded in class hatred before they join up, and they have much satisfaction in taking it out of the well-off and better educated conscripts; therefore if they happen to be in a crack corps they do very well, which is interesting.

Possibly this state of things may partly account for the brutality shown by the German troops during various phases of the war. The British always claimed that their non-commissioned officers were the backbone of the army; the Germans freely admitted to me that theirs were more or less the riff-raff.

Socialists and others say that in Germany the human being commences with the subaltern – the German army doesn't claim humanity for their rank and file, but the superior grades make up for it. In the Opera House in Dresden and other public places I was interested to observe that officers who came in with ladies were always helped off first with their coats, the ladies standing until the men were made comfortable – a striking testimonial to the position of the soldier and the deference paid to his rank. [13]

Typically, but maddeningly, Harry tells us nothing of that 'other story' to explain how he was 'done'. I suspect they economised on his specifications, thereby occasioning him yet further trips to Germany.

Eventually, at a date unknown but which I expect was before the turn of the century, Harry met M. F. Rachals of Hamburg. Harry found in Rachals a piano manufacturer whom he could trust completely and whose workmanship he found second to none. There began a fruitful business relationship which lasted for some 30 years until, sadly, Rachals's business came to grief in the worldwide slump of 1929. Even in his first book, *The Piano in India*, Harry nowhere gives any account of how they came to meet, nor of their business relationship. It was quite close – Rachals and his wife certainly visited Harry's home in England more than once.

The nearest Harry comes to saying anything in print is in one of the advertisement pages in the second edition of *The Piano in India* where it is proclaimed: 'The famous Rachals horizontal and upright pianos are constructed on designs superior to any other. Their high reputation has been gained entirely by merit. For durability under all conditions and rich quality of tone, Rachals pianos stand alone. And H. Hobbs & Co are the sole agents.' But there is no hint that these superior designs were, in part at least, those of H. Hobbs himself.

No Rachals piano today can be less than 70 years old, but a few are still encountered by a modern tuner up and down the country. We are fortunate in having two in our family – one a grand, one an upright – both of which still give excellent service.

Harry's musical work in the 1890s included the writing of his first book *The Piano in India*. As he put it, it 'took a long time to write and saw the light in 1899. It nearly wore my brain to the bone but proved most useful.' [14] And in his preface to its second edition Harry expressed the "hope that it may further in a humble way the cause of the 'Esperanto of civilisation' in this country."

Despite his burgeoning musical business Harry still found time for his other love – volunteer soldiering. He became a very good shot and came to Bisley more than once. Even in this comradely activity he could get himself disliked – or worse. One suspects as much for the manner in which he expressed his views as for their content.

At a meeting at Bisley in 1897 I aroused hostility by expressing the opinion that the events were run on the wrong lines. Instead of starting competitions at short ranges and retreating to 1000 yards, it would be better to advance from 1,000 to 200. A trained soldier should be taught to advance. Those who made a business of rifle competitions were dead against improvement so nothing was done. I tried that idea in Calcutta and was unpopular...

...The Calcutta Light Horse with its Greek and German troopers was dubbed by us 'The Foreign Legion'. That was among ourselves, as many of them were our chaps' employers.

One morning I took a party of F to the Ballygunge Range to find the Foreign Legion at the firing point. As the range had been allotted to us, I pointed that out, but they refused to budge. Going back a couple of hundred yards I fired at a big wasps' nest close to where the Light Horse were firing. They were pretty light on their feet after that and my men were delighted.

In 1897 I backed myself in a level hundred dibs to win the Viceroy's prize of Rs 500 and a medal the following year. Not only did I win but was eight points above the next man.

With growing cares tempered with finding it too trying to sustain a reputation and poorer men resentful at leaving little to them, I gave up competing and lost many happy hours with good company in the fresh air.

I am still proud of what I did to help along proficiency with the rifle. Without really knowing it I was preparing for war and did better than I thought. [15]

But Harry's time in the Calcutta Volunteer Rifles was to come to an abrupt end. It would seem that this was, to some extent, brought about as a belated spin-off from his original caustic comment which had so upset the captain of his company. Writing 50 years after the event Harry's account discloses what must have been a typical Hobbsian episode, with the spoken passages (at least by him) being a good deal more purple than his recollection as a nonagenarian.

In 1899 the Hon'ble Mr W. E. Oldham CIE, ICS was appointed to the command of the Calcutta Volunteer Rifles. At the time I was colour sergeant, keen as mustard, but still hated by the captain of the company whom I had insulted 15 years previously. He made a false charge against me which brought a poisonous letter from Oldham, leading me to ask for an interview. Pointing out that in 15 years I had made my company the best in India, increased its strength from 30 to over 100, he cut me short: "It doesn't matter to me if your company is the best or the worst. I know nothing about drill or shooting. I don't pretend to. I am here solely on account of my social position and that is all that concerns me."

I told him that I could see no benefit either to India or to myself by serving under a man who was completely ignorant of what he was supposed to do, that snobbery blinded him to tolerate injustice and I would waste no more of my time under him, so forthwith resigned. He was blandly indifferent to what I had said. So far as I was concerned, he didn't consider me alive.

As might have been expected he was a sort of social emetic on the strength of the battalion so must have been asked to try for recruits. He advertised his willingness to take candidates for 'my regiment of pedestrian riflemen' leading me to ask: "If I join your regiment of pedestrian riflemen shall I be given a bicycle or a horse?" The pompous ass never replied.

While it must be admitted that all competition-wallahs were not so caddish as W. E. Oldham, he was by no means a solitary exception.

As Lieutenant Whitehead said, I saw things as they were; that must have made me independent. Then years of travelling about India, being able to sound my own reveille and comparatively a free man, gave me an independent outlook, unafraid of superiors, which so hampers government servants. Were a man rude to me he got it all back. Whatever complaints may have been made – well, I would be miles away before they reached me. What did it matter anyhow? [16]

I lost no time in joining the Calcutta Port Defence Corps to serve under a fine ex-Royal Navy officer, Captain Eaton W. Petley. What a change from the CVR! The Naval division consisted of pilots, river surveyors, harbour masters, dock masters, lightship men and men from shipping offices, while apprentices from ships were roped in and trained with smooth-bore nine-pounders and rifles. The Artillery Company was recruited from office men and the engineers had more professional attainments that could be found in any regular unit in the British army. And a happy family we all were.

There was no snobbery except that the engineers were dubbed the Brahmins – a designation which stuck to them.

Captain Petley was one of the bluff, hearty type, a sahib from the crown of his head to the soles of his feet, afraid of nobody where the welfare or the reputation of his command was concerned [17]...He commanded the Calcutta Naval Volunteers, later the Port Defence Corps, for over 21 years. For forethought, tact, discretion and that consideration for others which is the first essential of a gentleman he had few equals, and I have much pleasure in being able to pay my old commanding officer this tribute of respect. [18]

Harry thus began a period of very nearly 20 years in the Calcutta Port Defence Corps. As the last extracts from his writings would seem to suggest, he found it an improvement on the Volunteer Rifles. The change in command was doubtless a significant factor. Perhaps he found he had more in common with his new comrades, perhaps the work was more to his taste. Whatever the reasons, service in the Corps played a large part in his life, giving him his rank, providing him with certainly one trip to England and back and, indirectly, inspiring him, as we shall see, with the name Chingri Khal as the name of his home in England. In this last respect the inspiration was singularly long lasting in that, nine years after Harry's death, my wife Sheila and myself, having the need to choose a name for a new home, agreed to adopt the name of Harry's choice. And it so remains, considerably more than 100 years after he joined the Corps.

As the 19th century was drawing to its close and the world was looking forward to the dawn of the 20th with, in the English speaking world at least, considerable Victorian confidence, Harry probably had as good a cause as anyone to feel confident. He was in his late thirties, strong, fit and healthy. He had been in India for nearly 20 years. He was thoroughly acclimatised to his new country. He had founded his own business, which was showing every sign of flourishing and expanding. He was the author of a successful, if technical, book. He was more than able to look after himself in the competitive world in which he had arrived. He was a much-travelled man – not only between England

and India but also within India. Europe, especially Germany, had been visited – not to mention other parts of the Far East – China, Japan, and the Philippines. And – I feel it must be so, although there is not a word of it in his available writing – he went to Australia.

For by the turn of the century, in addition to all the characteristics I have summarised, he was also a married man. And not only a married man but a family man too.

Harry Hobbs
at about 16 (taken in England).

Harry at about 26
(taken in England, probably on his first return home).

*Jennie Larkin
in her early 20s
(taken in
Melbourne).*

*Derry Fadda
Farm in 1959.
Jennie's
birthplace.*

Jennie at about the time of her marriage (taken in Calcutta).

Larkin's Cross in 1959.

CHAPTER 5

FAMILY LIFE
MAINLY IN INDIA

HARRY AND JENNIE were married on the 5 of February, 1894, in the Catholic Church of St. Thomas, Middleton Row in Calcutta. Having stated that bald fact I have stated all that can be regarded as known, more or less for certain. I am acutely aware of the very unsatisfactory extent of the available information. We last saw Jennie as a young girl, probably as young as twelve, coming down the gangway in Melbourne Docks in about 1874. She re-emerges in our story some twenty years later as a bride in Calcutta.

How did this come about? I wish I knew. Family folklore, I suppose one could call it, has it that they met in Australia. That also seems the more likely alternative to a meeting in India. Harry was an inveterate traveller. Sometimes just to and fro from Calcutta. Sometimes using visits to England as the opportunity to explore new places *en route*. And by the early 1890s he was, if not in any sense rich, at least a man with fair prospects. It seems unlikely that Jennie, by contrast, had any cause for significant travel, still less the means to fund it. Her elder sister Marie had secured 'a position' in Melbourne, according to Queen's letter and this sounds like 'in service.' It is unlikely that Jennie found herself eventually in any much more lucrative employment. Where and with whom she had lived from her arrival in Australia is unknown, likewise where she was educated, the jobs she may have secured and the degree of independence she had achieved.

No stay of Harry's in Melbourne was likely to have been very prolonged. Apart from anything else from 1893 he had a business to look after in Calcutta, which would have required his personal attendance for much of the time, however efficient his manager may have been. It would be fascinating to know how long their courtship took. Was it on just one visit, or did it take two or more for Harry to win his bride? It would have taken quite a lot of courage on the part of Jennie to accept the offer of this young man from India, an Englishman and a Protestant, to leave her adopted country and so many of her immediate family and to make the second almost epic journey of her life, probably on her own, to a strange country, and there to throw in her lot with a man whom she cannot possibly have known for more than a few months, perhaps even only a few weeks.

So what was it that attracted these two rather unlikely people to each other? Early portrait photographs are interesting, and, perhaps, a little revealing. Jennie, in her late 'teens or early twenties has her hair swept back and tied at the back of her head. Very pretty one might say, without being a classic beauty, regular features, round, slightly plump face and kind understanding eyes. Getting on for ten years later, but I expect before marriage, her hair is cut fairly short and she wears an expression of some determination. In a photograph taken (I guess – most ageings are guesswork: few photographs are dated, but some reveal where taken) at or about the time of her marriage that determined expression is still to be seen, as well as the kindness. Capable of a lot of tender loving care, but hoping for, indeed expecting, as much in return. "I will be faithful to you," she seems to be saying, "now you be faithful to me." One can see how very attractive she must have appears to the young Harry.

As for Harry, photographs taken at roughly the same stages in life do not show much change apart from the gradual enlargement of his moustache. The earliest, dated 1880 when he was sixteen, shows him in some uniform – presumably that of a cadet or volunteer with the North Middlesex Rifles in which he served before he first went to India. Young, fresh-faced, shaven upper lip, he would be thought of as good looking but slightly arrogant. The next two studies of him show a very smartly dressed young fellow, with a distinctly military bearing, growing his moustache until it reached the size and shape which it retained, more or less unchanged, for the rest of his life. Handsome, many might say, but with a look about him which, to my mind at least, indicates a man whom it would be wise not to cross. Is that because of the rather severe central parting? Or does he have a very slight cast in one eye? His erect, confident and still slightly arrogant look is much more what one associates with a soldier than with a musician. Jennie might have been forgiven for feeling a little frightened of him, but I do not believe she ever was.

So what was the mutual attraction? Harry may have found there to be something of a shortage of attractive young women in India, apart from the wives of fellow ex-patriates. In Jennie he found someone who was certainly very far removed from the 'listless women with snaggle teeth and receding chins' he had come upon in Calcutta. She was pretty, vivacious, good company, and she dressed well and danced well and was good fun to have around. And she seemed to have fallen for him.

The 'chemistry' between them must have been absolutely right at the time. Jennie was by now past thirty. She may have been wondering if she was going to be left on the shelf. And here, from India, had come this dashing young man, who could be the life and soul of any gathering. To the end of his days Harry was a consummate raconteur, and even at twenty nine his experiences had given him a fund of stories to draw on. He could be as charming and fascinating to her as she could be to him.

His religion was undoubtedly a drawback for Jennie. The loyal Catholic in those days would certainly look for a spouse first of all among the Catholic community. To marry a spouse of a different religion – or none – would require a dispensation from the Bishop, the obtaining of which was by no means a formality. It usually required some evidence, or at least statement of belief by some responsible person, that the faith of the applicant would not be endangered by the proposed match. Jennie was by now over thirty, and at that age consideration would be given to the potential risk that she may not find a husband at all. It may well be that Jennie also had to face some degree of opposition to the marriage from within her not inconsiderable family in Melbourne for contemplating entering into a mixed marriage.

Despite all difficulties and problems their plans went ahead and Jennie set off for Calcutta to be married to her handsome young soldier-musician. I have no doubt that each was in love with the other at that time. Jennie, as I have already said, remained devoted to Harry until the day she died. Harry, on the other hand, with the passage of time grew out of love with Jennie. Reasons for this may suggest themselves as we proceed with the tale. Some time in the five years or so before she herself was married Dorothy once, exasperated by listening to Harry going on about her mother, was driven to asking him "Why ever did you marry her then?" She received the singularly unromantic reply "Because she looked healthy."

Healthy indeed she did look – but more than healthy, surely. Such letters as have survived from relatively early in their life together show love and, even more important, show the respect which Harry felt for her. Once he grovels low – uncharacteristically very low – in humble apology for some misdemeanour. Deeds speak louder than words very often and here again there are signs of his early love in some good, if not excessive, pieces of jewellery he gave her in their early years, and in the manner in which he provided for her in the home in England he bought and gave her. And despite many demands for economy and threats to reduce his allowance for running that home, he in fact never reneged on his obligation to provide for her.

Nowhere that I can find in any of his published books does Harry make any reference, even indirect, to his marriage, to his visit or visits to Australia or to anything connected with his marriage. And yet I believe it must have been quite an event in the social life of Calcutta.

With so little reference to it in permanent written form it is little short of astonishing that such an ephemeral memento of a wedding as the wedding present list should have survived. But survive it has. Mostly neatly written out by Harry, with some entries in Jennie's more sprawling writing, there are some fifty entries as well as the addendum 'And several more are expected – quite a dozen have not yet been received.'

Some entries may give the flavour of the occasion. A Mr T. M. Edwards (Best Man) gave 'an entire set of table cutlery. Two electro-plated breakfast cruets and a combination breakfast set and toast rack.'

The 'Young Ladies in Moore & Co.' (I wonder who they were) gave 'a set of desert knives and forks in case. Electro-plated and glass jam dish. Set of glass table vases (eau-de-nil and pink roses.)' While Madame Emilie gave 'a porcelain and brass table lamp.' I have to resist the temptation to conclude that these were the staff and madame of the local bordello: I am sure Harry would have had more consideration for his Bride's sense of proprieties.

By this time Harry Norton was plainly married: he and his wife gave an electro-plated ice jug (very many of the items are described as 'electro-plated', perhaps it was the 'in thing' at the time.)

There were presents from the Bandmaster to the Viceroy, from the Superintendent of the Detective Department of the Calcutta Police, from the Deputy Accountant General of Bengal; from the Garrison Sergeant Major and his wife; from Herbert Harraden (no ill feeling, it would seem, from the competition of H. Hobbs & Co. – he gave 'a Doulton ware and electro-plated salad bowl and server;) and from 'Miss Rogers – Bridal Bouquet.' Lady Elliott, the Lieutenant Governor's wife, gave the flowers for decorations.

Jennie's gifts to Harry were 'a pair of ebony hair brushes with silver monogram. Gold pencil. Dozen linen Handkerchiefs.' Harry's gifts to Jennie were 'An emerald & diamond ring. A curb chain gold bangle.'

I would think it was quite some party and can only regret that there is no record of it surviving. Who gave Jennie away? Were any of her relations present? No Australian names, so far as one can tell appear on the list. Perhaps there had been a farewell party in Australia before Jennie left, at which presents from her side had been given and subsequently acknowledged by Jennie on the long journey from Melbourne to Calcutta.

So they settle down to life in Calcutta. They had a flat, probably a rented one. Jennie soon became pregnant and her child, a son, arrived by the end of the year. Sadly he was stillborn.

Jennie must have become pregnant for the second time quite soon after the first distressing experience. A second son was born in 1895 who was healthy and survived. He was christened Harry Reginald Conway, or Harry Baba for short. One can imagine the Parents' delight at starting their family with a son to replace, as it were, the baby who had not survived.

As with most established ex-patriate families they had servants, including an ayah for the baby. One day when the little boy was around the two year old mark, he was in the care of his ayah and was being a little bit boisterous and noisy. His ayah decided to quieten him down. So she gave him some opium. She was all too successful. He died.

If the loss of their first son would have been distressing, the loss of their second must have been catastrophic. History does not relate any further details as to the circumstances. Not only would there have been their grief at their loss, but also, and potentially even worse, self or mutual recriminations at leaving Harry Baba alone with the ayah. If it had happened while the two were out together at some glittering social event there would have been even greater poignancy. If Harry had been routinely out at his business and Jennie was in the home, perhaps leaving unexpectedly for a short while, there may have been scope for the less kindly use of his tongue.

There is, however, only one reference to Harry Baba in all the surviving documents, and that is in letters passing between Jennie and Dorothy thirty years later. So I hope that the grieving parents were able to comfort each other and get their lives more or less back to normal after they had buried their son.

Certain it is that Jennie fell pregnant again quite soon. No doubt they were concerned that there would be no tragic accident this time and they wanted the coming infant to be born somewhere other than in India. So where should Jennie go? One might think that the obvious answer was Australia. Most of her close family were still living in Melbourne, a City which she must have known very well, and in which she would have had many friends in addition to her close family. Even Ireland could have had some attraction. An opportunity to see other close relations whom she had not met for over twenty years, and to see old haunts of which she had been fond. But no. The decision was made that it was to be London to which she would go for her confinement.

There were advantages in this choice to offset the undoubted disadvantages, stemming from the fact that England in general and London in particular were completely strange places for Jennie. Harry had Agents in London and business connections in London and Germany. He must have wanted to be with her as much as possible, even if he could not stay with her until the child was born. So they journeyed together to England in the second half of 1897. Whatever business Harry may have attended to, he must surely have had as his principal concern the well-being of his wife and the setting up of all necessary arrangements for her confinement. There is nothing to indicate what, if any, role in all this his own family played. Some of them would have left England by then, but equally there would have been several still in England and, indeed, in London. By early October he set off on his return to India, leaving Jennie behind.

On 12 November, 1897, Jennie gave birth to a daughter at 183, Hammersmith Road, Fulham. Dorothy always maintained that she was born within the sound of Bow Bells and so, technically, she was a cockney. Whether Bow Bells really can be heard in Hammersmith I must leave others to judge. They seem a long way apart to me. She was given the names Dorothy Effie Mary. Harry was informed by cable: 'Girl on November 12th. Both well,' which he received as he left the ship at Bombay. I am unable to say if he had helped in the choice of names before he left England. The name Dorothy would seem to have no family significance. Mary was the name of Jennie's oldest sister. Dorothy always understood the Effie was chosen to include three other aunts whose initials were E.F.E. I find this hard to follow. She had one aunt Emily Hobbs (Harry's oldest sister) but no other with the initial E and none at all with the initial F. Dorothy had believed that 'Effie' was a contraction of 'a fairy', which quite pleased her. It came as a rude shock when, well into her middle age, she read a little about John Ruskin whose wife, known as 'Effie' was, in fact 'Euphemia.' Dorothy had never felt in all her life the least like a 'Euphemia' but she was stuck with it.

Dorothy was baptised in the Catholic Church of the Holy Trinity, Brook Green on 19 December. Her birth was not registered until even later, on 23 December, the very last day of the sixth week, the informant being 'M. Bartlett – present at the birth' who lived at Shortlands just around the corner from the place of birth. The father was described as 'Pianoforte Maker (Master.)' Facts of no great interest in themselves, but which seem to me to indicate a lack of any close family around to help and support Jennie. Who was 'M. Bartlett' who had been present at the birth? And why was she, six weeks later, being the informant to the Registrar rather than Jennie?

There is very little information about the family life over the next seven years or so. Such as I have comes first from my recollection of Dorothy's recollection. There are the undoubted facts of the births of her brother and sister. There are some posed photographs which reveal the place where they were taken. And finally there is a letter written from India by Harry to Dorothy in October, 1912, for Dorothy's fifteenth birthday. In it he waxes very sentimental and emotional in reminiscing about her early life and his relationship with her.

Jennie returned to India with Dorothy as soon as she was fit to do so and could cope with the journey. It would be less trying in the winter months than in the heat of the summer if she were fortunate and missed a bad storm. Harry remembers 'How I used to waken you to see your eyes and how I used to be full of excitement when I thought you really knew me.' An unconventional way of bonding, perhaps, but it does seems to be referring to a very young child, still a baby in a cot or its equivalent.

Jennie took her baby daughter to Darjeeling in the hot weather of 1898. Separation was plainly going to be a frequent occurrence in the family. On their return Harry found Dorothy did not recognise him and he had to start again. Soon they were even closer. But Jennie by now wanted to see her family and to show off her child to friends and relations in Australia. The opportunity did not come until she was pregnant for the fourth time. At some time in 1900 she went to Melbourne, where her son Arthur (Arthur Noel Kevin) was born on 26 December, 1900.

In the meantime Dorothy always asserted that her earliest memory was of waving a flag at the celebrations in the street for the relief of Mafeking. Now Mafeking night in London was at the end of May, 1900, when Dorothy would have been no more than two and a half years old. Quite a feat to remember an event dating from that age, even an event so calculated to imprint itself upon the memory of an adult. Unfortunately I do not remember her specifying the City in which she was partaking of these jollifications. It can hardly have been London: why should she have been there then? Assuming that the relief of Mafeking was at least something of a cause for celebrations elsewhere in the Empire than London, she could have been in Calcutta or Melbourne.

Their time in Australia made the longest separation yet. Harry recalled it as 'nearly two long years' and that 'on your return you spoke with such a terrific Australian twang that I used to invite men up to hear you talk.' From then on the pattern was set for Jennie and her increasing family to live with Harry in the flat in Calcutta during the cooler months, while moving to Darjeeling to avoid the worst of the hot weather.

There were disadvantages at both places. Harry's home was a flat in Calcutta, without garden or other open space in which children could play. The Maidan and the Eden Gardens were not far away. But young children obviously would have to be supervised on visits to public areas like that.

Then there were many people nearby, some in the same building, who were friendly with Harry and his family. He may well have lived there a considerable time. Certainly by 1909, and quite likely by the turn of the century, he was in 4, Esplanade East, which remained his Calcutta home until the 1930s. Some of these friends, while good hearted and without malice, were almost oblivious to the needs of children. Dorothy rather liked visiting her father's chums. They would be relaxed and cheerful and wouldn't tell her off. Billy Bradshaw was one such. He was a fellow officer in the Port Defence Corps and shared a flat nearby with a like-minded bachelor ex-patriate. They were no strangers to the hard stuff and they would improve the flavour of their morning prunes (so useful to keep one regular in a difficult climate) by soaking them in whisky. It came as rather a shock to both Harry and Jennie when they noticed Dorothy was losing interest in her prunes. "Why are you not eating up your prunes, Dorothy?" she was asked. "Oh well, you see nowadays I only like them if they are soaked in whisky." "WHAAAT?" and, of course, explanations had to be forthcoming and certain places be put out of bounds.

On the other hand the separations involved in the family's move to Darjeeling must have been very trying for all concerned. For some time Dorothy was a boarder in the Loreto Convent there. Why boarding was necessary is far from clear. I have no address for them in Darjeeling. Dorothy could never have been more than seven and probably started at the school a good deal younger. They were in Darjeeling in 1902 and 1903. I believe Jennie must have been there too since there are photographs taken in Darjeeling of Dorothy with her brother, Arthur, and then with Arthur and her younger sister

Phyllis (Phyllis Margaret Norah) who was born in India on 30th November, 1902, soon after Dorothy's fifth birthday.

If Jennie was staying in Darjeeling with her two younger children one would have thought that Dorothy could have attended the Convent as a day girl. She had also been at a Loreto Convent in Calcutta, whether as a boarder or as a daygirl is not made clear in Harry's letter. It is not a long walk to the Convent (which adjoins St. Thomas's Church) from 4, Esplanade East. First days at school can be more traumatic for parent than for child sometimes, and Harry seems to have been affected worse than most. He remembered Dorothy's first day: 'You were in such a hurry to go to the other girls to play with that you could hardly wish me good-bye and I left the Convent with tears in my eyes and quite unable to sleep.'

He evidently went to Darjeeling to visit her there and to take her out for the day or two of his visit: '…I came up for you from the plains and called at the Convent with Mr Oliver giving a message that a gentleman wanted to see you, and you came in shyly on tiptoe looking enquiringly at Oliver while I was hiding round the corner; and both Oliver and I had tears in our eye when you made a rush for "my father" and we hugged and kissed like two big girls and were happy. Then I took you out of school and you were as happy as a grig when leaving school while every morning we would crawl slowly to school; you would be crying and I hardly able to speak because you were going back to school and the sadness of being the day without you.'

Nowhere is there any clue as to how Jennie fitted into this picture of desolate father and homesick daughter. She may have been in Calcutta with Arthur and Phyllis while Harry took the opportunity presented by a business visit to the north to call and see Dorothy. It is a little surprising that Harry's accounts of going to see Dorothy are of visits by him alone, not of both parents together, for they were a close family unit at that time.

That is not to say that they did not have their problems. Harry's temper, which led him to deal so effectively at times with politicians, soldiers, churchmen and others, would be unleashed all too often on Jennie. If Dorothy's earliest memory was a happy one, her earliest recollection of her parents was not. She remembered her father shouting at her mother. This was not an infrequent occurrence. Once

Harry worked himself up into such a paroxysm of rage that he ruptured a blood vessel in one eye and so became virtually blind in that eye ever afterwards. That is why in many a photograph of him he is to be seen with a monocle hanging round his neck and reposing on his increasingly substantial corporation. At times he wore conventional spectacles, especially in later life; but the sight of the affected eye never significantly improved. Even that experience, however, which some may regard as approaching the catastrophic, did not moderate his wrath when he felt aggrieved for some real or imagined reason. He would cool down and return to normal in time, which could be anything from a few minutes to a day or so, but it was a wearying experience and kept the household on tenterhooks as to what they might say or do next to set him off.

There is no doubt that he loved all his children deeply and tenderly. I have only letters between him and Dorothy, with very few exceptions, and so can only give details that may shed light on his relationship with his children insofar as Dorothy is concerned.

But even with his children he had at times a way of giving himself a laugh at their expense, which was unkind, even approaching the cruel. Certainly not to be approved in parenting classes in the twenty first century. Dorothy had a very clear picture of it in her mind and told me about it more than once:

"I remember so well sitting down to dinner with my mother and father. I would have been five or six. At the end of the meal we were having fresh sliced peaches. And daddy knew that I loved fresh sliced peaches. The bearer handed the dish to mother and she helped herself. Then he handed it to my father. I can see him now, helping himself to a few spoonfuls, hesitating, and looking sideways at me with a slight smile, and then helping himself to a few more. All the while I could feel my face getting longer and longer until, as he ladled the last slice on to his plate, I burst into tears while he threw back his head and laughed his loud and raucous laugh."

I hope Jennie quietly ticked him off after that – she was quite unafraid and capable of doing so, but history does not relate. Of course Dorothy did get her peaches in a few minutes, but what an unnecessary upset.

During this period of building his family, life went on for Harry much as before and his books contain many account of various happenings concerning his business and music, his volunteer soldiering and the extreme manifestations of the Indian climate. But he gives no information as to how they affected, or were related to, his family life.

In the case of climate, for instance, he had been in relatively small earthquakes in 1885, in 1886 and in 1888. But then:

> The most alarming earthquake of modern times affecting Calcutta took place on June 12th, 1897. It originated in the Garo Hills, but places as far apart as Manipur and Bombay felt the force of the shock.
>
> The weather was close and sultry and the temperature for some days previously had been very much above the average.
>
> Every building in Shillong was levelled, trains were overturned, fifteen feet of the Calcutta Cathedral spire fell on the roof of the Church. The building that stood on the site now occupied by No. 4, Esplanade East was wrecked, and remained in that condition for one or two years. The spire of the Free Church of Scotland in Wellesley Street fell into the compound but did no damage to passers-by.
>
> The Dalhousie Barracks in Fort William – always inclined to shake – quivered, then rocked, and the frantic charge downstairs of six hundred heavy-booted soldiers, who were at the time enjoying a banquet of tea and dry bread, did not help to steady that fine old building.
>
> One soldier's wife came down the lightning conductor in her nighties and lady-like fainted after performing the feat. A memsahib I knew was making a pudding for dinner when part of the building came down; it was hot and she was very scantily dressed, but she suddenly found herself in the street, still mixing the pudding and wondering how she came to be there. [1]

It seems to me to be considerably odds-on that the 'memsahib I knew' was in fact Jennie. She would have been some four months pregnant with Dorothy at that time, and one might have expected him to have had something to say about how this event affected her, even if she was not this particular memsahib, but especially if she had been.

One can make the same comment about the next climatic disaster when Jennie was some six months pregnant with Arthur:

> September 1900 was the wettest month in Calcutta that I can recollect: for ten days it rained day and night without stopping. *Dinghies* competed with *ticca gharries* for business in the streets of Calcutta and Hindus used the steps of the GPO as an impromptu bathing *ghat*, or took their dip in the seething maelstrom of the Dalhousie Square streets instead of the Hooghly.
>
> The tramways were blocked and big fish from the overflowed tanks got under the wheels of the car in Lal Diggie. Forty inches of rain fell in five days; streets were like rivers, and for an area of hundreds of square miles around the City there was hardly a dry spot.
>
> In Amherst Street the water was five feet deep while many other streets of the city were like rivers; no supplies came in for days; all the chickens were drowned; thousands of native huts collapsed; the young paddy rotted in the ground, while the condition of the poor was deplorable…
>
> Had the tides risen another foot and poured into the already flooded area it is certain that one of the greatest disasters of modern time would have befallen Calcutta, as it is problematical if any large building would have remained standing. [2]

Perhaps the most significant event outside his family which happened to Harry in the early part of the twentieth century was his good fortune in the Calcutta sweep.

> In 1901 with one ticket I drew 'Handicapper', second favourite of the Derby, winner of the 2,000 Guineas, in the Calcutta Sweep. 'Handicapper' was nowhere in the race, but as I had sold a quarter share and made a few bets I had a clear £1,000, which put me on my feet. That – the intoxication of sudden riches – being considered to be certain to send any man to the dogs (if it didn't friends would be disappointed), a few called to give advice, but most hoped to see if

they could get a bit for themselves, turning into life-long enemies, while all used a magnifying glass when talking about luck in the Sweep. [3]

His business had been going by then for seven or eight years and many may have thought of him as being already 'on his feet.' I am sure the unexpected cash helped him a great deal, whether on his feet or not, and would have been of considerable assistance in setting his family up in England in a few years time. His good fortune led to an adventure which could be called hair raising. The story is too long to be told here. For those interested it will be found in Appendix 2.

Harry's musical activities continued, albeit – at times at least – in rather more high-falutin' circumstances than in *dak* bungalows and cheap hotels:

[About 1902] an American singer, calling herself the Californian Nightingale starred India. She had a wonderful voice, dead in tune, and dead so far as sympathy went; her notes were as telling as a steam whistle. She was taken up by Mrs. Stevenson Moore who soon found she had welcomed the able better half of an Old Man of the Sea. You couldn't do too much for the Californian Nightingale. She expected it.

Worried to death Mrs. Stevenson Moore asked me to take over the business side of the Grand Orchestral Concert to be held at he Calcutta Town Hall under the patronage of Her Excellency Lady Curzon. I fancy Lady Curzon, hailing from the Bright and Breezy West, knew better than to refuse anything demanded by a 100 per cent American like the Nightingale from California. As soon as that vocalist found that she to deal with me she halted, struck an 'entranced' attitude, and, most obviously lost in admiration declared – "You have a most wonderful aura – I can see it covering you from head to foot like a perfectly marvellous crystal cloud."

When told it was second hand, and I preferred to lose the deposit rather than keep it, the aura dropped out or off and we got down to business.

I approached the Viceroy's Military Secretary for the loan of gilt sofas and chairs from Government House Drawing Room for the two front rows of the stalls. There was some trouble about that as there were no rules authorising the loan of Government property. When it was pointed out that sitting on hired sofas might mean taking away more than you bargained for he gave his consent.

I received Lady Curzon on the steps of the Town Hall and while showing her to her seats assured her that she would feel more at home in them than in anything I could hire. She was very charming and graceful, obviously easy to get on with.

The Californian Nightingale sang four songs. A lady played a piano concerto accompanied by the Viceroy's Band under the baton of Herr Buchner. I turned over the music for her. She missed 24 bars but Buchner had his men so well in hand that the hitch was hardly noticeable. The less important singers I accompanied on the piano.

After the concert was over I escorted Lady Curzon downstairs where she praised everything. Then I saw that the bandsmen had plenty to eat and drink; I checked the takings, counted the cash and went home to write column long critiques for *The Englishman* and the *Indian Daily News*. Most of the matter had been pinched from *The Daily Telegraph* and *Musical Opinion*, but it was better than anything I could think of myself, and went some way towards satisfying the insatiable appetite of our local musicians for that praise which is said to make the good bad and the bad worse.

The air of refinement, the gorgeous dresses, the uniforms of the staff and Buchner's thirty musicians staggered the Californian Nightingale. All she could say was, "Ain't it elegant? Great Lands! Did you ever see anything so elegant?" and she volunteered the statement that she "Didn't care if the concert was a loss it was so elegant but could she call tomorrow for the money?"

But, from my point of view, taking that as an evening's pastime after a day's work it was not a bad effort. [4]

Not a word, be it noted, to say that his wife was with him at the glittering reception wearing a 'gorgeous dress' and enjoying the social scene. I doubt if Jennie had any very great interest in music, but I feel sure she would have liked to have been at his side if she had been in Calcutta at the time. However, in a letter to Dorothy as long after the event as 20 October, 1937, and after the publication of his book in which the above account appears, Harry wrote, 'The day the

Californian Nightingale sang our barouche was run into and you were lost in the Eden Gardens. I didn't put that in because it might have looked overloaded, but there it is.'

Harry was just as much at home in the more light hearted side of music making, which probably was rather more common in Calcutta than the type of concert which the Vicereine attended. But again there is no suggestion that Jennie was there to join in the fun.

How, in these days of physical development, step-dancing has not been taken up is amazing. For suppleness, leg muscles, breathing, rhythm and concentration it is unsurpassed. No apparatus is needed. It can be practised in efforts lasting no more than a minute, it is attractive to watch and pleasant to hear.

John Torrens Hume, for many years Public Prosecutor in Calcutta, kept himself as fit as a gymnast instructor by step-dancing. Unfortunately, in a sense, those who had similar taste and ability lived in barrackrooms. They had long been schooled in the manner of the times, dancing to street organs on public house cellar flaps. If no organ was about they had competitions with other dancers demonstrating the variety and numbers of the steps

Cellar flaps made excellent soundboards and small crowds would collect to enjoy music, noise and rhythm and to encourage the performers. Owing to its association with public houses and street organs, public opinion classed the art as low and those able to step-dance as the associates of street corner loafers. Not that social exclusiveness troubled Hume. He went through life seemingly unconscious of it. Soldiers came to his house: with them he assiduously practised new steps and like others who enthusiastically take up a hobby, in his spare time he thought of little else.

Amateur acting had the great attractions for him and I often played his accompaniments in musical sketches, Box and Cox, the Blind Beggars and others. But it was in song and dance that he let himself go.

Dressed in clothes of many colours he would sing in a tuneless voice a happy-lover song, his eyes uneasily directed to the piano. The words might have expressed little more than –

I met a little charmer in the street (clickety clack)
She had such pretty bandy legs and feet (clickety clack)
My heart goes pit-a-pat
I'm sure I shan't grow fat
If I met that little charmer in the street. (clickety clack)

but once they were done with, his manner changed. Light footed and light hearted, he danced until he panted for breath.

So keen was he that he had to show you the latest step every time he saw you. One day on the landing of the police court he insisted on showing me a triple-tongued step to a tune he whistled, much to the interest of gaping Indian litigants who wondered what other phase of Sahib-logue eccentricity they would see.

Occasionally we started the provinces – Hastings, Dum Dum, Barrackpore, and took trips to Budge Budge when Hume, with half a dozen cockney privates of the East Surreys appeared as a noisy item:

Uncle Ben had six big children
Three were boys and three were girls.

The girls wore chignons and bustles while the boys wore magenta coats, blue silk breeches with pearly buttons, yellow waistcoats, green jackets and expensive tartan bows. For an encore Hume would give a turn at pedestal dancing when he was always sure of a vociferous reception.

Soldiers often put on a good show and were alright so long as they kept to the book of the words. When they strove for originality one saw that military gagging often contained humour of a quality which led more conventional folk further than they cared to go.

At a sort of command night at Dum Dum when the General and all the brass hats were present, Uncle Ben and His Six Big Children furnished one of the turns. It was a long item and the accurate clatter of seven pairs of clogs was a noisy marvel of accurate rhythm. The finale consisted of portly Uncle Ben falling down, the boys falling on him and the girls on top of the heap. An unmistakeable encore caused the curtain to be lifted, when soldiers' women, sergeants' wives and officers' ladies gave a start, a gasp and a shriek of laughter, for the skirt of the girl on top was found to be covering her head instead of the other end, while the display of anatomical details made it all too plain that she was not what her clothing led one to believe.

Hume, a most proper and simple-minded man, whose nature remained unspoiled even after thirty five years of the sordid surroundings of the police court, and who could never countenance anything improper, was quite unaware of the cause of the laughter. With pleased satisfaction at what the babu called 'the many loud applauses' he smiled and bowed time and time again. But somebody must have told him about it for he never appeared with Uncle Ben and His Six Big Children again. [5]

But public music making, whether it was of the frivolous or the more serious variety, came to an abrupt stop in 1903 or 1904.

After the time I had been twenty years in the country I found that although I was useful I was incapable of real improvement. One day it dawned on me that as a pianist I would never be worth more than two pounds a week. I could write the music to words for a man who couldn't sing, do almost anything with music but excel as a performer. My musical tastes were miles above my musical ability, so I dropped practice and gave up playing at concerts. I cut it all out and am glad I did. [6]

This decision did not stop his playing informally. Indeed as late as the Second World War, when he was in his late seventies and early eighties he frequently entertained Allied troops by playing in hotel bars and other places of resort, accompanying singsongs and playing popular tunes to cheer them up.

Harry's love of music had not diminished on account of giving up his efforts at professional music making. He remained in the piano business for decades thereafter and encouraged his family in music making and appreciation. Right at the end of his life he quotes an anonymous four line stanza, which does not seem to me to scan very well, but which may be said to sum up the feeling of all those who love music, from the ace performer to those – and there are many – who (as Sir Thomas Beecham said of the English) "know nothing about music, but simply love the noise it makes."

Captains and Conquerors leave a little dust,
And Kings a dubious legend of their reign
The swords of Caesars, they are less than rust,
But music doth remain. [7]

Harry's military interests continued unabated. He was soon promoted, or commissioned to the rank of Captain in the Calcutta Port Defence Corps. His evident enthusiasm for the Corps might have led one to expect a considerable fund of anecdotes about it in his books, but there are far fewer than those relating to the Volunteer Rifles. Much of the activity of the Corps seems to have centred upon Fort William. Harry gives quite a long description of the Fort, which was completed in 1781, in *It Was Like This!* [8] It is not to my purpose to repeat that here. Enough that the Fort, although by the end of the eighteenth century it did 'not come up to modern military requirements,' was still 'very useful; in many ways as an arsenal and headquarters for quite a large body of troops.'

Harry does not expressly say so, but the implication from his books does seem to be that such headquarters as the Port Defence Corps had was also in Fort William. But many of their exercises took them a good deal further afield.

In December, 1890, the Corps, then named 'Calcutta Naval Volunteers,' undertook a forced march from Calcutta to Diamond Harbour, a distance of over thirty miles. This was nearly ten years before Harry was a member and he did not take part. It was an event of some notoriety at the time of which Harry, again in *It Was Like This!*, gives a full account. [9] Elsewhere Harry makes a passing reference to the topography of this part of the Hooghly:

> There were, in 1798, a number of warehouses and a factory at Diamond Harbour, about 30 miles below Calcutta where ships find good anchorage. Close to it is 'Shrimp Channel' (Chingri Khal) frequently referred to in old books as the haunt of pirates. [10]

The translation Harry uses for the name of this small inlet is not that normally given. Prawn Creek is the English version which I have always understood to be the meaning of the Hindustani words. A meaning I once had confirmed quite by chance by a complete stranger. But this is a distinction with, perhaps, little difference.

In quite another context, and in a different book, Harry is describing what the Port Defence Corps contributed to the war effort in 1914-1918:

> …Another lot of Port Defenders went to France as a motorcycle unit and yet another was sent to Mesopotamia. There were several members who were medically unfit; with the few who were barred by age we did duty at Chingri Khal Fort down the river where every man soon had a snake skin waist belt; reptiles swarmed. We also furnished guards in Fort William and the Docks. General Strange gave us credit for our high standard of discipline and the manner in which we looked after our men. [11]

These are the only two references I have been able to find in Harry's published works to Chingri Khal or its Fort.

There are a few ancient sepia photographs which were taken in the Chingri Khal Fort. One of them shows a military-looking gentleman standing by the most ancient of weaponry while another squats behind it. A small gathering of men stand around, looking for all the world as if they had stepped out of an amateur chorus line in *HMS Pinafore*. It is inscribed on the back 'Captain & Adjutant J. Rowley, RA superintending the firing. Capt Hobbs firing the machine-gun, Chingri Khal Fort, Diamond Harbour, Feb. '06.'

Another is inscribed on the back: 'Firing old fashioned 9-pounders at Chingri Khal Fort.' Yet another has no inscription, but was taken inside Chingri Khal Fort. It shows a group of nine men, one of whom (the only one wearing his topee) is plainly Harry, posing in two rows on a grassy area. Beyond the grass is a bank topped by a fairly high wall in which several gun embrasures are to be seen. Sadly I feel there is no hope of identifying the rest of the group – many may be men whose names appear several times in Harry's books.

Despite the paucity of references to the Chingri Khal Fort, I have no doubt that it was a favourite place for the Port Defence Corps in general and for Harry in particular.

It must not be thought that the duties of the Corps were limited to the ceremonial, or to playing around with obsolete weapons. They had men of many different skills among their number who could be relied on in an emergency. Harry tells of one such occasion in the course of which he and several others were, for a short but significant period of time, exposed to very acute danger:

Fifty years ago * there were two Captain Pecks in Calcutta. One was in the BI, a quiet, harmless man who, because he had been paid four rupees on one occasion for singing a song, thought he ought to describe himself as a professional singer. The other, Peck of the *Deepdale*, was one of the hardest cases who ever set foot aboard a ship, and tremendously popular; that is, of course, round hotel bars.

One Sunday I was making what was then my usual trip down the river to Ooloobaria. Passing the *Deepdale* steaming along with a big deck cargo of coal, there was a loud noise. She had touched sand, shot all the cargo over the side and capsized. So far as I remember there were no casualties, but the wreck was in the fairway and had to be blown up.

The Engineer Company of the Port Defence Corps was given the job; some tons of gun cotton were said to be used. Naturally all officers were keen to be in on the game, so when the charges were placed we went in one of the river survey steamers and at dead low water got into a boat to place the fuses. The tide began to rise. In the Hooghli it jumps up a foot at a time, but everything being all correct the survey boat was signalled to that effect. Suddenly it was found that the nose of the jolly boat had got under a chain and we looked like being in trouble. There was a rush forward to depress the bow and we swung clear after using language which, though forcible, showed traces of religious teaching. Had the men in the launch pressed the button when we signalled, a boatload would have reported to the Great Pilot. Curiously there was not much of an explosion, nor much left of the *Deepdale*, and Captain Peck never seemed to bring another ship into Calcutta. [12]

Harry's interest in military matters was not narrowly confined, and if

* That is, in 1904.

he had what seemed to him to be a good idea he would put it forward at the highest level he could reach.

> While I was much interested in the Volunteers I took up anything likely to be of interest at the time. There is always something worth attention, much of it worthy of help. Difficulties in recruiting for the British Army led me to write to Lord Kitchener when Commander-in-Chief *, asking for an interview. I went to Treasury Gate to find him playing simple tunes on the piano. He rose, asked me to sit, spoke in rather a light tenor voice, was easy to talk to, different from what I had expected.
>
> My theme was the wasteful and cruel treatment of soldiers who served in India. Often lads of seventeen when they enlisted for twelve years – seven with the Army, five on the Reserve, with the further liability of another year if in India, meaning thirteen years in the service. The result was that men were over-excited about going home. As soon as the ship moored, to save money they were given a cheap suit of civvies, paid off and turned away to find themselves practically foreigners with no one to take interest in them. Far too often they became tramps. One never saw men who had enlisted in the Royal Marines on the roads. They were abroad for no more than three years, so never lost touch with the people they had been brought up with.
>
> My idea was that if the period of service was to continue to be twelve years, two years should be served at Home. Then no more than five years in India, finishing their Army service with one year with a Home regiment. That would give them time to look round, get acclimatised and find a sweetheart who would help them get a job. The danger of being dumped down almost immediately on arrival with nowhere to go would be avoided, the Army would not have such a bad name and in many ways there would be a saving of money.
>
> His Excellency asked me if I had thought what the cost would be were my suggestions adopted. I said it looked as if there would be a cost of 15 per cent on ship passages, but there would be advantages in other respects. Moreover the soldier was entitled to more regard for his welfare. He brought the interview to an end by saying the Government would not consider anything likely to lead to greater expense. [3]

* Lord Kitchener was C-in-C India 1902-1909.

A good idea, perhaps – and not the first to fall foul of the problems of Government expenditure.

As the year 1904 came and went some significant landmarks were passed. Early in the year Harry and Jennie celebrated their tenth wedding anniversary – that is, if they did celebrate it: I would have expected there to have been something at least to mark the occasion. Possibly even a piece of jewellery. By the end of the year Dorothy had attained the age of seven years, Arthur four and Phyllis two. Harry and Jennie were going to have to give serious thought to their children's future, particularly their future education. Was it satisfactory for that to be continued in India? And if not in India, where should they be educated? All the children were too young to be consulted, but the fact that Dorothy had had a bout of malaria could well have been something further for them to bear in mind in making their decision. Jennie may have hankered after Australia, or even Ireland. If she did, neither was chosen. I suspect that Harry, ever the patriotic Englishman, had no doubt that if his children were going away from him and away from where he could closely monitor their progress, they would go to England and nowhere else.

And so they had to accept that almost inevitable penalty of Empire building: long separations in the family. With some families that would mean children living with relations, or boarding at school, and only rarely seeing either parent. With others it involved husband and wife being apart from each other for most of their married life. The children have the benefit of one parent's care and attention almost continuously, but are deprived of the influence of the other to a very great extent. It must be a hard choice to make, neither solution being at all satisfactory. For Harry and Jennie, once England had been selected, it was no choice at all. There was no family in England with whom they could, or would wish to, leave the children. The younger two were too young in any event to be left with virtual strangers.

Perhaps with heavy hearts they accepted the almost inevitable, and began to make plans for a future which would keep the two of them apart for months, even years, at a time. And for Harry it would mean separation from his children for the same long periods. I am sure it was not easy, either in the choosing or in the execution. And I doubt if it was good for any of them in the long run.

Their problem was not in the least unique: probably thousands of couples every year had to contend with the same sort of agonising decision making. That does not lessen the individual pain of separation. It is well to bear in mind the sacrifices which had to be made by those who, whether in great positions of state, or in a very humble capacity, were playing their part in running the Empire.

Group at Chingri Khal Fort – Harry front row, extreme left.

At Chingri Khal Fort – 'Captain & Adjutant J. Rowley, RA superintending the firing. Captain Hobbs firing machine gun, Chingri Khal Fort, Diamond Harbour, Feb/06.'

4, Esplanade East. Harry's flat was on the top floor, 93 steps up.

The showroom of H. Hobbs & Co. at 9, Old Court House Street, Calcutta.

CHAPTER 6

FROM CALCUTTA TO BOURNEMOUTH

THE DECISION TO SETTLE HIS FAMILY in England was only the first of many which would have confronted Harry in early 1905. The next, and perhaps even more difficult one, was: whereabouts in England shall I find a home for them?

London must surely have been the first city he would have considered. He had been born there, he knew it and there would still have been members of his close family living in London. There would have been plenty of schools from which to choose, both for boys and for girls, not to mention museums, art galleries, theatres, music and all those things he would think were desirable to have within reach to improve the minds of his young family.

London evidently failed the test. Perhaps the very presence there of several of his siblings, not to mention his parents, told against it. Then again he may have felt it was not right for his family on the grounds of health.

Harry was a bit obsessed with health – his own particularly. He had his own fads and his own pet remedies, not all of which, I daresay would have found favour with medical opinion even in his day. His usual cure if feeling out of sorts was "take two grains of calomel", a rather violent purgative, believing as he did (and frequently asserted) that "a good set of bowels is worth any amount of brains." Had he somehow, I wonder, heard of that still small town on the South Coast, set among pine forests whose motto, adopted in 1890, was 'Pulchritudo et Salubritas' ('Beautiful and Healthy')?

Bournemouth at this time was still a very young town by English standards, not due to celebrate its first one hundred years until 1910. It was in no sense insignificant, having achieved County Borough status in 1900 with a population in the first decade of the century passing the 75,000 mark. Beautiful it certainly was in those days – wide roads, large gardens, both public and private, few dominating buildings and trees in abundance, and all set in the centre of the grand panorama from The Needles to Old Harry Rocks. It was (perhaps it still is) claimed to be healthy due to the perceived beneficial effects of 'the resinous odours of the pine trees.' On the basis of the proposition that if you believe something is doing you good, then it may well in fact be doing you good, the second limb of the motto was as justified as the first. But, even granting that, it seems unlikely that Bournemouth would have been a very obvious subject of discussion in the hotel bars in and around Chowringhee and the Esplanade.

There are two possible sources of information coming to Harry. He had a distant cousin, John (Jack) Breaks, who was a merchant navy captain, married to the daughter of the Senior Naval Constructor at the Royal Naval Dockyard at Portsmouth. They had a large family of three boys and two girls and they were settled in the Boscombe area of Bournemouth by the early part of the twentieth century. There is nothing in writing surviving to suggest that they recommended Bournemouth. They must have been in a position to do so. A further possibility is Harry Norton. In due course he was to retire to Bournemouth and, as has been mentioned, to be made a Freeman of the Borough. He could have had contacts with, or even a home in, Bournemouth by the time Harry was considering moving his family to England

The atlas would have told Harry that the town was reasonably accessible to London, and even more so to Southampton where many liners had their terminal port. There was a flourishing Convent School for girls (coincidentally almost opposite the cousins' home), which also had a junior department for boys. Jennie might have been glad to learn that the main Catholic Parishes were staffed and run by the Jesuit Fathers. One would like to think that the reputation of the Bournemouth Municipal Orchestra, the precursor of the Bournemouth Symphony Orchestra, which already had more than a dozen years of excellent service to British music under its belt, helped to persuade Harry in his choice of Bournemouth. He certainly patronised the Orchestra quite a lot when he was in England, but I expect in reality it was a happy bonus to confirm the choice when made.

Dorothy did not talk to me about the journey from Calcutta to England. She was well over seven years of age by that time and it must have been a great excitement and a memorable few weeks. Since the flat at 4, Esplanade East was being retained for Harry the upheaval may not have been too great; but that could presage extra problems on arrival, with a new home to be furnished and equipped from scratch. No house was fixed up in advance. The family stayed for some time in the Grand Hotel, which, as its name may suggest, was one of the first class hotels of the town. It was never the premier hotel of Bournemouth, as there was rather too long a walk to the beach for that distinction, but it probably had the largest garden of any of the hotels in the town, a garden largely made up of pine trees and rhododendron bushes. It was a splendid place in which young children could play and was a good foretaste for them of things to come. The Grand was probably too far from the sea to have retained the necessary clientele to make it viable in the period after the Second World War – but its future was inevitably blighted by the construction, shortly before that War, of a road through the garden, thereby depriving it of its best and most unique asset. It closed its doors and was demolished in the seventies.

Dorothy may have had some weeks to enjoy the garden. Even if estate agents had been instructed before they made the journey, and even if they had had sent to them in India details of some possible houses, the time needed to make their choice could hardly have been short, despite a fair degree of urgency. Harry's time in England was necessarily limited, and he may have had business commitments to attend to in addition to housing his family.

In the event they rented a house. I have no means of knowing why they rented rather than buying. It gave them the opportunity to take their time in finding somewhere they really liked for a permanent home. The house they chose as their first home was in Winton – 2, Bryanstone Road.

Winton at that time was a very small suburb, almost two miles due north from the town centre (The Square.) It had only become part of the Borough in 1901 and was still largely separated from it. A line of houses connected the large area of the Cemetery to Winton on the east side of Wimborne Road. On the west side of that road there was nothing beyond Meyrick Park Crescent until he first houses of Winton half a mile or more further north. Where there is today an extensive area of good quality housing there was nothing then but woodland. This woodland (Talbot Woods) extended to Talbot Village and Wallisdown. Beyond that was open country. The property they selected was the second house into Winton, on the corner of Wimborne Road and Bryanstone Road and backing on to Talbot Woods. It is still there, although looking rather different, being the Winton branch of Barclays Bank. But apart from the banking hall built on to extend the ground floor in the 1920s or 1930s the building is perfectly recognisable. It looks a reasonable sized, well built house with a garden at least large enough to permit a game of croquet to be played on its lawn.

Despite being readily identifiable by its number, and although only a rented house, Harry decided to name it. The name he chose was 'Chingri Khal.' "Why was it called Chingri Khal?" I asked Dorothy, probably many times over the years, especially when I was very young. "Oh the Old Man had enjoyed himself playing at soldiers in the Chingri Khal Fort and he liked being reminded of it," was the drift of her replies. I always found it a bit of a puzzle, made the more puzzling when, as I have pointed out, I found that the only two references to it in his books are as an eighteenth century pirates' den and a twentieth century exercise area, swarming with reptiles. On that evidence at first sight a very curious choice for the name of his home.

In February, 2003 I was fortunately able to satisfy my curiosity about his choice. In that month Sheila and I made a visit to India in order to find as many as possible of the places featuring so much in the various writings which have survived. Finding the Chingri Khal Fort was not easy. If it had ever formally born that name, it did not do so now. No one had heard of it. The researches of the local Manager of our Agents, Cox & Kings, had drawn a blank; there was nothing of that name.

However, our guide, Asif, whom the Agents had engaged to take us around Calcutta, had a hunch that he knew what and where it might have been, and so we set off to explore. It is a narrow, crowded and slow road to Diamond Harbour. After an hour and a half we were nearing the town, when we turned off the road into a cart track for a few hundred yards, then right again into a field and across the field close to the bank of the Hooghly where we stopped. Asif led us on a short walk and we found ourselves in a grassy area surrounded by the remains of fortified walls. Although most of the fortifications have long since fallen into the river, which has encroached into the interior, similarities with the old photographs could be detected. The original khal has silted up and been filled in, but its position was pointed out by a local resident, who also told us that the area was administered from Fort William, not by the local Council. I had no doubt that we were in the Chingri Khal Fort.

And thus I came to understand. It was not a mean, reptile-infested, forbidding dungeon at all. It was a place in which to relax; away from the road and from the town; a quiet and peaceful backwater, relatively clean and free from litter; its walls rose out of the river from which came a gentle breeze that helped to moderate the heat to a pleasant level. It was easy to imagine how, once their noisy soldiering exercises were over, the men of the Corps were able to relax and to enjoy their tiffin, a peg or two of their favourite brew and the pleasure of each other's company. I found it a moving experience to be at this spot – apart from Harry himself, the only member of his family ever to set foot there.

Once first given to 2, Bryanstone Road the name Chingri Khal has remained, first with Harry's family and then with mine. It can be said at least to have the merit of being, to all intents and purposes, unique, even if fiendish to spell and the subject of many an error. It has nothing whatever to do with 'Shangri La' with which it is often confused (sometimes, I suspect, deliberately.)

Having settled his family into Chingri Khal, Harry returned to Calcutta. Never again were he and Jennie to enjoy more than a few months together, sometimes at their home in England, occasionally in some other part of Europe and once in Calcutta. One cannot be precise as to how often Harry made the trip home. In the early years he came home quite frequently, every year, or every other year. There is little record surviving. What does survive tends to show a good, sound relationship between them, despite occasional pretty severe storms. They were only in their mid forties and the many prolonged absences and separations must have been the cause of much strain. The absence of their father meant that by far and away the lion's share of bringing up the children fell upon Jennie's shoulders. Harry often acknowledges her success in that task. The children themselves missed him a great deal, despite having something of a sinking feeling at the approach of any return home and wondering what will happen to set him off into one of his rages

He was back in Calcutta well before the end of 1905 and he and Jennie were in regular correspondence at once. All of his letters to Jennie from then on were among the hoard found on Jennie's death. Only one from that first year has survived, but an interesting one. It was begun on 1st January, 1906, and finished four days later. At that time the Prince of Wales – later King George V – was visiting Calcutta. It was not one of the major Durbars which took place in Delhi in 1902 and 1911, although it obviously caused a lot of interest and enthusiasm. I believe it is worth quoting extensively from this letter since it reveals a lot about Harry's attitude to India and to Indians as well as to his wife and to his children. It is all in typescript save for the very last handwritten word:

Calcutta. 1st January 1906

My dearest Jennie,

The one o'clock gun has just gone and I am off to Tollyganj with MacCabe to see the races. I was on parade this morning and got home at 10 to breakfast; there were thousands of people out and I should estimate about 6,000 troops on parade. I did not go to the parade ground but to the officers' enclosure where the march past could be well seen.

There has been a deal going on in Calcutta since the last mail left and I must send you all the papers so that you can see for yourself what has happened. On Friday morning [29th December, 1905] I went on parade and by 2 p.m. we were out again getting home tired out at 5.30. The sun was hot and shining in our faces all the time so you can imagine I was pretty red and not being used to standing still for hours felt the strain. After the parade we had to get ready for the Prince of Wales's Levee; the order was for officers of the Port Defence Corps to parade at 8.45 but we got there a little late and I do not recollect being in such a crush. The first to commence the shoving were the officers of the King's Own who all wanted to get in together and the squeezing and the scrambling was beyond description. Talk about one's early days at the theatre when there was some object in getting a good seat – it was nothing compared to this. One or two men fainted; Col. Carpendale was nearly mangled; a little Raja in front of me had his nose screwed on to an artillery officer's pouch and when we did get out of the crush the Raja remarked in his babu English – "Sir there is very much pressing" and I agreed with him. MacCabe went flying against the wall and I found myself turned round in the crowd holding on to the hilt of my sword and it afterwards turned out that I was holding another man's sword and pulling him along against his will. Over 4,000 men were at the Levee; I went through with the Cossipore Artillery and we were all home by 10 having a small bottle of simkin on the strength of it; my clothes were wet through and I felt tired having been on the run since six in the morning. The Prince looked well; quite an experience in its own way but of course so far as the Levee went it was just an ordinary affair.

On the Saturday morning I went to the Fort [Fort William] to see colours presented to the King's Own and heard the Prince speak; as I narrated it to MacCabe afterwards at the breakfast table it was as though I was myself speaking so pure was the English; There was no 'haw haw' about it but straight out speaking and he gave me a very favourable impression of his enunciation; wastes no time and is as rapid in his method of getting through anything as an up-to-date chairman of a limited liability company passing the annual accounts...

Later – I have returned from the races having come off a little to the bad but I am satisfied as I know that I cannot possibly do any good at any races as my luck does not run that way. It is good for me that it does not and that I can recognise it...

...I am dining alone and so will spend half an hour writing to you before going to bed. It has been a beautiful day and the crowds at Tollyganj and the Zoo were amazing; even at the Proclamation Parade there could not have been less than 100,000 people and at Tollyganj there were thousands of *gharries*; policemen of all sorts and from all parts of Bengal were there in thousands; the Prince was supposed to come but did not; Earl Minto* was there with his two

---

* Viceroy 1905-1910.

very fine daughters – they are exceedingly good looking and were most tastefully dressed – even I could notice this point about them and was struck with their appearance before I knew who they were. We had a deuce of a job to get home for some time, but MacCabe is such a skilful driver we lost but little time. On the road home we passed a *ticca gharry* in a tank where it had been carried by its horses. I do not think any serious damage was done though.

I did not receive much news by the mail beyond your letters. The great improvement in Dorothy's handwriting is remarkable and I was certainly surprised to see the strides she has made. I would dearly love to see them and have them all around me again as it appears to be such a long time since I was in that position although it is not much past three months. Time will soon pass now that Xmas is over and I shall be looking forwards to the next run home...

Thursday, 4th January 1906. I had a busy day yesterday one way and another although there was little business to do but it was the day of the illuminations and our building was as good as any standing out well outlined against the sky with the handsome military offices alongside and old Matthewson's place on the other. We had ours well done and all my verandah was decorate with coloured candle lamps giving the place a soft appearance restful to the eye. Opposite there were lights every yard hanging from the tramway wires and the roads were as bright as day.

Dalhousie Square was an absolute dream – never have I seen or imagined anything could be so effective and when I explain the fact that all the trees have been cut down so that one can see the Writers' Buildings on one side, the Post Office and the Telegraph Office, all of them smothered with little 'Chirag' lamps – some hundreds of thousands of them well I can only say that the Coronation in London * was but a penny peep show by comparison. The tank in Dalhousie square was half filled up and there were lines of chinese lanterns right around the tank while the water reflected all the lamps from the opposite sides of the Square.

Of the European shops Lawrence & Mayo were about the most effective and in fact all down Old Court House Street were blazes of lights and it was almost worth travelling all the way from home to see it. I do not know what H. H. thought of it but he must have been impressed.

---

* Of King Edward VII in 1902.

The streets were greatly crowded – more so than I have ever before seen them and one of the noticeable features was the manner in which many Europeans behaved, cutting the natives with canes and shoving them about as though they had no right on the street. To make matters worse there was a large crowd of very respectable natives standing around our premises and the road was far from crowded at the time when two soldiers of the King's Own charged into the crowd, hitting them across the face and cutting at their shins while one of them, a corporal, bashed them into the uprights of Matthewson's portico hurting them considerably. I called out to the corporal that he was to stop but he continued so I went up to a police inspector and told him to take the man's name. The corporal in an impudent manner demanded mine so I went down to him and told him he was a disgrace to his regiment and that I would not only report the matter to his commanding officer but would make a point of seeing him too. I have written a very temperate letter to the colonel and some good may result as there were many soldiers who were not on duty at all smashing into crowds of natives and hurting them severely simply out of sheer brutality. A well dressed native came up to me after I had sent the corporal away and said he had to thank me in the name of the people which was very kind of him as I did not like to be appearing to take sides with the natives against the Europeans although in this case it was more than I could stand. At any rate the private who was with the corporal saw that I would stand no nonsense so he began to move his pal away...

The crowning event was old Matthewson throwing out dozens of coronation medals to the crowd and there was a terrific scramble and almost a riot. It took two mounted police and others to clear the crowd away and Superintendent Swaine told Matthewson he would have him at the Police Court today which he well deserved as this took place at the time when *gharries* were permitted to travel along the street in rear of the processions and many were nearly run over while all the traffic had to be suspended. Of course it was great fun but might have resulted in a riot. I had a yarn with Matthewson after the show was over – 12.20 – and told him it was very dangerous, hoping he would not be very heavily fined; he said they could not send him to prison and he did not care about being fined although it will not be very gratifying to find oneself advertised in that manner.

This is practically the first day we are going to work after Xmas so it is time we made a start. Trade ought to begin to hum now as nothing has been done so far…

I find I am getting very fat and all my English clothes bought last year are too tight across the shoulders. This will not apparently last long but I cannot say that the hard work of this Xmas has upset me. I have not been out to dinner or done anything but work since I got back and that has allowed me to get lots of sleep at night so that I am fitter in the mornings. I do not think I shall ever adopt going out to dinner again…

Your very long letter of 11th Dec. came to hand late on Sunday and I sat up late reading it…It has suddenly struck me that this is fairly long as it is equal to two ordinary pages such as I before sent you but I feel that I could not write to a more appreciative audience and you will not complain at its length, prosiness or the errors which I know are numerous…

Poor little Arthur and his wish to come and see me for one day was a very nice way of expressing himself and I wish the lot of you could come here if only for a few hours just to let me hug you all and tell you how much I love you. Still the turn of the new year seems to make things appear different and time will not seem so long.

The behaviour at the tea party was very good and I can well understand how proud of them you were. All your nice training of them will now commence to bear fruit and I hope we may find our best desires in regard to them fulfilled. We live for the kiddies now and must do our very best for them in all respects…

Now I feel I must conclude and go down to work as I have given myself holiday this morning after seeing everything going on all right; I have sent you plenty to read and will be thinking of you on the Saturday you will receive it. A good half hour will be spent getting through this and I expect you will be amused at the many little errors my hurried writing had led me into but after all you have now plenty of news and that is after all is what is wanted in a letter. When someone wrote in a derisive manner to old Wilson who was once Editor of the Indian Daily News he replied that he only wrote for wise men and the opinion of fools who did not know what was meant did not concern him. Well I must say I do not like making mistakes or finding them out afterwards but in this case it is a big job compiling such a long letter and you must overlook all that appears ridiculous in style or composition.

With plenty of love to you and the kiddies hoping you are well
and enjoy good weather, kisses by hundreds to you and all, I remain
Your loving
Husband

In the meantime Dorothy had been enrolled as a pupil in the Convent
of the Cross in Parkwood Road, Boscombe, Bournemouth, starting in
January, 1906. She had just passed her eighth birthday and was to
remain at that school, sometimes as a daygirl, sometimes (less
frequently) as a boarder, for over ten years, until the summer of 1916.
Probably rather too long a time for a child to be in one school. But
Dorothy was very fortunate in that for the whole of her school career
the Headmistress was a Mother Kelly who was a quite outstanding
nun. Only twenty-six when she was appointed to the post, she
remained Headmistress for fourteen years and later, after a spell as
Superior (Reverend Mother) at another house of her Order, she
returned to Boscombe as Reverend Mother from 1925 to 1946.

Although Dorothy was very realistic about her time at the Convent
and not without unfavourable comment about some aspect of her
education there, I have no doubt that Mother Kelly had a most
profound influence on her, both in terms of day-to-day schooling as
well as her spiritual development. Dorothy remained devoted to her
throughout her life as she continued to live at the Boscombe Convent
after retiring from the position of Reverend Mother. After her death
in 1954 the community invited Dorothy to write a short life of
Mother Kelly, a task which Dorothy carried out with enthusiasm and
success once her initial reluctance had been overcome. It is a well-
written booklet, in which Dorothy acknowledges her debt to Mother
Kelly. It was, I am sure, in no small way thanks to her that Dorothy
became as staunch a Catholic as was her own mother, albeit, perhaps,
in a manner less Irish, less sentimental, less uncritical, less in awe of
'the cloth.'

But we are still in 1906, and there were other lessons to be learnt,
and only Jennie could deal with them. It was fairly early in their time
at the first Chingri Khal, but even so Dorothy was over eight years old
and really knew better. Jennie had once asked her, "When you grow

up, would you like to be beautiful or good?" Dorothy thought about it for a moment and replied, "Beautiful, because I can be good if I choose to be."

The family had a young nurserymaid. Her name doesn't matter, call her Mary Jane. She was quite young – in her mid-teens. The house was wonderfully situated for long woodland walks and Mary Jane regularly explored them with the children. One day, in the depths of the woods – or so it seemed to Dorothy – they came upon a clearing which was laid out in several well-maintained allotments. Mary Jane had a good look round and took it all in. The next time they had an outing she steered her young charges in the same direction. When they got to the clearing Mary Jane became quite business-like. She produced a bag or two from under her coat, and a knife or two from a pocket. "Now this is what we shall do; this will be good fun," she said. She posted Arthur and Phyllis to keep an eye on the paths leading to the allotments and she showed Dorothy how to help herself to a tasty selection of the fruit and vegetables. These they popped into the bags and then made their way home, enjoying much of their spoils on the way. This became quite a treat for the children. Many a visit they paid to the allotments. There was a bit of excitement, even of danger, a bit of secrecy, and quite a sense of achievement at the end. Inevitably they got bolder, and as they got bolder they took more than was wise, and thus it was that Jennie came upon some of the booty. "Where has this fruit come from?" "Oh, we collected it on our walks in the woods with Mary Jane. It's awfully good fun – very exciting."

Well, of course, that let the cat out of the bag. Mary Jane was sent packing and Dorothy in particular had to have a good talking to. "We took to it," she used to say, "like ducks to water. Mary Jane's encouragement was quite enough to overcome any scruples I might have had about stealing. It was a lesson to me in how easily someone properly brought up can be corrupted by another, older and more worldly wise."

Harry returned home to England in 1906 as foreshadowed in his letter. He refers in one of his books to having a bad passage in the P&O SS *Isis* that year when 'She corkscrewed into bad seas, devastating to the morale even of experienced sailors. For twelve hours I could not get out of my bunk, but with eyes shut tight held on to a stanchion like grim death." [1]

There seems to have been an effort made to keep in contact with the rest of Harry's family, but my basis for making that assertion is no more than one small photograph. Plainly taken in the garden of the first Chingri Khal it shows Harry, Jennie and their three children together with three men and one woman, and another small boy a little older than Arthur. They all have, to my eye at any rate, a very definite Hobbs family likeness. They all look very cheerful and one might have expected considerable family links to have been built up now that Harry's family was resident in England. But this did not materialise – at least I have no recollection of ever meeting any cousins or uncles or aunts on Harry's side of the family. I can offer no explanation. Harry's sister Annie, seven years younger than he, is to be seen in some family groups before the First War, and he mentions her in passing in occasional letters after that. At one time she managed a restaurant in London. She never married. One brother (Fred) went to South Africa and one (Jim) to Australia. The family seems to have fragmented.

In 1907 Harry was again back at home for much of the summer. He went with his family on not one but two holidays. Rather than stay in a hotel, in those days the family took a rented house for three or four weeks, and the entire establishment, including governess, servants, the lot, would upsticks and relocate in their holiday destination.

The first was in Bantham in south Devon where they took over Bantham House for their stay. A long way to drive for those days, but drive they plainly did in the 'old Vauxhall' - one of those cars which remind you of Sarajevo – with perhaps even Jennie taking a turn at the wheel. Certainly there is a holiday snap showing Jennie at the wheel, but it may simply have been posed. I would think she was not a good driver. She was certainly a menace on the road as a cyclist. She could not avoid riding at whatever she was looking at. Many's the time Arthur would shout at her "Don't look at the tram, Mother, look at me" and suffer the inevitable consequence of being run down by Jennie.

If one can judge from their holiday snaps they enjoyed good weather. They also enjoyed the company of Mr and Mrs Rachals and their family from Hamburg, with whom, by now, Harry had a very close and very thriving business relationship.

Bantham proved a great success and Dorothy often spoke of it with wistful nostalgia, despite it being the only holiday they had there. They were able to enjoy messing about in boats as well as playing on the very broad sweep of the beach – and without mishap, despite the tides which rush in and out in a quite alarming manner at that point on the coast.

In August the family went to Scarborough. Even further away. No holiday snap to show mode of transport. Those which are available seem to show a typical English family doing its best to enjoy itself at the seaside against all the odds. Whether paddling, or on a donkey's back, or simply posing with mother and father the children display that 'grin and bear it look' seen in its thousands on a long wet week by the seaside.

Perhaps during that fairly long time he had spent at home in England Harry had discussed with Jennie the shortcomings of the first Chingri Khal. Whether or not it was large enough, or convenient in its internal layout I do not know. Its situation left a certain amount to be desired. In the first place it was on the main road. Main roads were not what they are now, but it made it less than ideal. More important was the distance from the Convent. Winton and Boscombe are quite two miles apart and the tram journey was inconvenient. Possibly more important than either of these, the house was only rented and they really wanted to buy.

They were attracted to the newly developing area between Winton and Boscombe known as Queen's Park. This formed the northern part of the Malmesbury Park Ward (named after the third Earl of Malmesbury who was the ground landlord.) A large part of it (173 acres) had been made available to the Corporation for the making of a Municipal Golf Course which had been opened towards the end of 1905. The remainder of the land between Charminster Road in the west and Holdenhurst Road in the east was gradually developed over the years to come. The road made around the western and southern boundaries of the golf course was originally called Queen's Park Road. Later it was given two names, Queen's Park West Drive and Queen's Park South Drive. On the corner of what is now Queen's Park West

Drive and Queen's Park Gardens was a house that caught their eye. It looks from photographs to have been rather charming. It was built, perhaps, a little too close to the two roads on the corner of which it stands, but it had a large garden on the other two sides. Dorothy remembered it as being a somewhat cold house, especially in the large circular bays which are a feature of two of its four corners. It had the advantage of being on a much quieter road than the first Chingri Khal, and if it did not have Talbot Woods immediately behind it, there was the wide public open space of Queen's Park Golf Course just across the road in front. It was also a great deal closer to the Convent, close enough at a little over a mile for Dorothy to walk to school, which she often did. The one major disadvantage was that it was not for sale, but for renting only. Had it been otherwise I expect Harry might have bought it. In the event they took it on and it became the second Chingri Khal, although always accepted as another temporary home until they found something they liked which they could buy. It still stands, outwardly little different from its appearance in 1908, apart from the loss of a great part of its garden for building.

They moved in 1908. I feel sure Harry must have been home, both for the house hunting and the house moving. There is no documentary record of any such visit, and one could read Harry's next letter as indicating a longer absence than between six and nine months. If he had not been at home it must have been a big responsibility and a lot of work for Jennie.

Harry started a letter home on 24 March, 1909:

> My dearest Jennie,
>   I have just returned from the Trades Meeting where I have been elected a Municipal Commissioner representing the Trades Association and got in with the top number of votes; they say they want a man to speak his mind and they think they have got one in me. I shall attend the first meeting next Monday when the various committees are appointed.

There is then a break for more than a week before he resumes writing this letter. That gives an opportunity to mention Harry's own account of serving as a Commissioner. One might expect him to have been scathing about those concerned with the running of that large City, but quite the contrary is the case:

> I must confess that I started with the idea that the Municipality consisted of a lot of talkative, do-nothing cranks, but I grew out of that and found them to be a lot of very nice fellows with extraordinarily nimble minds among them. Of course one would occasionally hear squirts of verbosity about nothing in particular, but to hear them at something that was likely to affect their pockets one realised at once that they were mentally very agile and tenacious as bird-lime.
>
> …But after serving a trifle over two years I gave it up as I found that whenever I wished to say anything an Indian Commissioner had said it all and four thousand words besides. [2]

Having simply written of his joining the Calcutta Establishment Harry did not return to his letter to Jennie until 1st April. It contains many aspects of his day-to-day life in Calcutta from routine business to taking upon himself the task of medical orderly. All appears to be serene on the domestic front and, if his words are to be taken at their face value, he was much looking forward to his next trip home:

> April 1st
>
> I could not write any more then owing to there being a sudden rush on and since then I have been full up with volunteering; the books have had to be audited and even this has not yet been finished as Billy [Bradshaw] and I have to go down on board again tomorrow; there were meetings every day in regard to the bills and programme of the Distribution of Prizes which took place last Friday and what with seeing Captain Petley off yesterday which took several hours in the middle of the day, stocktaking and other little diversions I have been kept pretty busy all the week. Sorry to say we finished our financial year yesterday with what looks like a considerable drop and I only hope it may not last. Affleck* does not satisfy me in many ways; some asked how we were doing and he said he didn't care as he was sure of his 500/- a month and it therefore did not matter one way or the other. That is not the spirit one likes to see in a manager and I am thinking of making my stay at home a short one leaving

---

* Harry's manager from very early in the business until his death in 1936.

certainly before the last week in September as I must look after the business before anything. The clerk we have is a good man and I am satisfied with him; he appears to be too much for Affleck who will generally try to boss every man on the firm but this chap is a handful; he is quiet and thoughtful and capable of hard work and close application and will later find a bit of friction there I am sure. Still so long as the clerk has my interests at heart there will be a good break on everything and we may run along all right but in bad times I ought to be here.

Our Prize Distribution went off well last Friday night and I am pleased with the results. That Browne* is mad I am absolutely certain as he went so far as to issue orders that when I went up to receive my prize for the revolver match that not a man was to raise a hand and this was brought to me to my amusement; of course there was as usual the usual shout and I had more applause than ever, certainly more than any other man had taking a prize...

This morning we had the first rain since last October but it was insufficient to wet the ground; it certainly did not flush the drains and that is what is wanted to clear out the smallpox and other diseases. Bradshaw's man is getting on all right and my workmen who have smallpox are getting over it. Last Saturday I had a fine young Irishman turn up here en route for home and I was asked to take him for a run in the car; the car runs very badly but I took him round and before driving him home asked if he had been vaccinated; he said he would be done now so I drove him to Bathgates and asked to see the doctor who was out; the chemist's assistant refused to do it so I said I would, and did; I think I gave him a little more than was necessary but if he does not take it will be a wonder as he was properly done and no mistake...

McCabe is quite pleased at my election to the Corporation and great things are expected of me but I am determined not to be made use of until I well know the ground and those who think they are getting me cheap without my being aware of it will be mistaken. At the same time I will have my own views but I am going on as a student and not an agitator...

I am going to start packing up the various things but we have been so busy with packing up our own pianos for the rains as well as sending other people's pianos away also, that we have not been

---

* I presume the A. E. Browne who kindly helped him with starting his business – see page 68.

able to get through the work. We are busy in the way of small orders but the total is disappointing...

I was very pleased with Dorothy's letter that came this week and took it into Bradshaw for him to read; I then put it on the table to take out with me and never saw it again; where it went is a mystery but the fact remains I have lost it and I have searched high and low for it. The secret she has for me is, I expect some further success in music as that is what I read in between he lines but the disappointment to me is in not being able to reply to it and to read it over and over again which is what I generally do with my home letters...

I expect Phyllis will be shy when she sees me as her remembrances of her Dad are sure to be vague; as a matter of fact I expect we shall all feel a bit strange when we meet again as it seems years since I saw you and I have felt very homesick lately.

It is very amusing to read the ideas the children have about me and Arthur's notion that I am taller every time I come home is not a bad one; the fellows in the house were highly amused about his tact in avoiding a direct reply by saying I had not been measured lately shows an alertness about him that I would not have expected but he will be like most boys – up to a certain age he learns without knowing what he is learning and after that he begins to be sharp and intelligent.

Skating rinks are all very well but there is a crowd at the Pier not altogether of the best for the children to see and while it may be as well to let them have a turn at it when I come home and can take them it may be better not to permit it as a regular thing. I believe in children learning all those accomplishments but as you say they will be better in the open air than in a crowded place on the Pier. Still if I approve of it when I come home that can be one of the treats for all of them.

...I sleep on the verandah and it is very pretty to see the lights across the Maidan and the trams coming along the roads well lit up at night and I must say I enjoy the southerly breeze that comes across from the sea. It is simply beautiful to come upstairs after a hard and worrying day in the office to find the air fresh and clear up on the verandah and a breeze enough to blow you off your feet...

3.45 p.m. I felt the muggy heat so much that I fell off to sleep after tiffin; or rather after tiffin time; the tiffin was so poor that I did not eat it but this heavy weather makes me feel sleepy. This means that I have wasted half an hour of my time and must cut it from your letter which I am sorry for but there are others to be written and as you will soon be seeing me it is as well to get through the imperative ones.

To you and the children I send all my love and did I tell you how eagerly I look forward to seeing you all again you would perhaps hardly credit it but the fact remains I am very homesick and want to be with you and the kiddies again.

Hoping the weather is good and that everything goes well with you all, I am always, your loving   Husband.

The time scale envisaged by Harry might strike one as being a little surprising. He was expecting to leave for home 'in five weeks', that is, on about 6 May. He was thinking he would have to set off back to India by the last week in September after what he calls 'a short stay at home.' On that basis he could hardly have been back in Calcutta before November, which would have meant being away from his business for almost six months. Of course time actually at home with this family would be no more than four months, possibly a little less, depending on the sailings, but even so it seems a long time to be absent from the daily running of a business, especially one involving quite a lot of skilled technical work and with a manager 'who does not satisfy me in many ways.'

However that may be Harry presumably arrived at Chingri Khal sometime around the second week of June. Barely three weeks later something almost catastrophic had taken place – but what? All one can say for sure is that it looks as if it was without doubt entirely his own fault. His apology is as abject as it could be, without any attempt to shuffle any responsibility on to Jennie.

The letter is handwritten at Chingri Khal, as if he had settled down to compose it after Jennie had gone to bed, leaving it for her to read in the morning:

July 5 / 09

My dearest Wife,

For over fifteen years we have been married and I have found you to be a good wife and a Heaven sent Mother to our children. Above all there is one thing I cannot sufficiently express; my gratitude for the manner in which you have brought up the children to love and almost idolise me, and as you now know and have lately frequently told me, I have not been worthy of their love, neither have I been justly entitled to their respect.

Unfortunately I have been brought up in this world without love or religion, and know myself to be very much of a heathen. Some men, leading a rough life for many years might have turned out softer for their experiences: in my case the result has been that rough experiences have made me hard and difficult to keep in check, but I have loved you and the children and been as good as I could when my life is considered.

There is no occasion for you to tell people the reason I am leaving is because I am ashamed of myself and cannot feel the same in the house again.

Your anger and reproaches have all been deserved – I do not complain there but I do hope you will not smash altogether the idol you have built for the children – their father. I feel that you will not if you can help it and that you may try later on to think kindly of me – if only for the past and not for the present. Needless to say I will try to do all I can for your comfort while I live and hope you may later on feel some forgiveness in your heart for your sinful husband.

Although I daresay you do not believe me

I can still sign myself,

Your affection [*sic*] husband

H. Hobbs

P.S. I shall tell everybody that I have to return on a/c of bad news from Calcutta. HH

How could things have come to such a pass in so short a time? Merely indulging in verbal rowing would hardly seem to call for such a confession. Had he struck her? Perhaps, but that would have been uncharacteristic. Indeed the trouble seems to have been festering for some days, or why the reference to 'have lately frequently told me?' Why was he unworthy of the children's love and respect? Something which Jennie 'now knows.'

It is my tentative belief that the most likely explanation is in the revelation of Another Woman in India. Twelve years later there is no doubt at all that there was The Other Woman lurking in the background in Calcutta, albeit very discreetly; about whom more later. She could have been on the scene a decade or more earlier. Certainly by the 1920s she was not afraid to write to Harry when he was at home in terms which would leave the reader in no doubt as to their relationship. It could have been that one or more of such letters arrived at Chingri Khal soon after Harry's return and provoked more than one storm.

I regret that I am unable to say what the outcome proved to be. Harry plainly contemplated a more or less immediate return to India, but recognised that it could not happen instantaneously. Did Jennie dissuade him from the drastic course he was proposing? It would have been in character for her to do so. She was enough of a Christian to have a clear vision of right and wrong, and she had quite enough spirit to protest vigorously if Harry departed from the principles she expected him to follow. Equally she was enough of a Christian to be prepared to forgive when forgiveness was sincerely sought with such humble apology.

We find that their relationship apparently is back to normal in the next available correspondence, with no hint of harking back to this very considerable upset, so I expect he did not make a precipitate return but continued to enjoy his time over that summer with his children – and, I would hope, with Jennie as well.

Obviously Jennie kept his letter. She may have felt that it could even be needed as a type of insurance policy in the event of further problems arising. I do not recall Dorothy ever telling me about it. She would have had the opportunity to read it in 1943, along with all the rest of the correspondence, but, if she did, it never featured in any of her many chats with me about her early life.

One must give Harry and Jennie credit for doing what they could to get over this crisis. It could hardly have been easy. Eating humble pie was a pretty rare event for Harry and hardly came naturally to him; while Jennie would have had to have made a considerable effort to put behind her – if not entirely out of her mind – whatever it was that caused the ruction. There can be no doubt that both of them were devoted to their children who were still quite young (eleven, eight and six respectively) and who reciprocated the love of both parents. In the need to put their children first Harry and Jennie would certainly have had a principle in common.

Harry returned to India, either almost at once or, as I believe more likely, at his intended date in mid September. In March, 1910 he was presented with the Volunteer Officers' Decoration ('VD'). There is no reference to what has to be done to earn such a distinction, whether it is simply for long service, or requires some particular action or achievement nor, if the latter, what the achievement might have been. The presentation was made to Harry by the Commander-in-Chief, India, Sir O'Moore Creagh, VC (C-in-C 1909-1914) on 6th March, 1910. The Calcutta Port Defence Corps turned out in strength for a parade on the Maidan. I am sure a good time was had by all. It certainly made a good start to the year, foreshadowing, perhaps, the fortunate developments for his family which were to follow during his time at home that summer.

Jennie with her children, 1906.

The first Chingri Khal, 1906-1908.

Afloat at Bantham.
(Left to right) Frau Rachals, Dorothy, Arthur, Phyllis, Jennie, Rachals).

Jennie at the wheel of the old Vauxhall
outside Bantham House, summer 1907.

Harry, Jennie and family (with governess) on Scarborough beach, August, 1907.

In the garden of the first Chingri Khal.
(Right to left: Standing –? 2 Hobbs brothers, a brother-in-law. Sitting – Harry,
Jennie, Dorothy Phyllis,?Hobbs sister. On ground – Arthur and a ?cousin).

*The second
Chingri Khal,
1908-1911.*

*Harry, Jennie
and family in
the garden of the
second Chingri
Khal, probably
1911.*

CHAPTER 7

A PERMANENT HOME

O N 6th MAY 1910 King Edward VII died at Buckingham Palace. His successor, King George V, was crowned in Westminster Abbey on 22 June 1911. Harry's return to England in 1910 was probably entirely unaffected by either event. As will be seen the consequences of the latter event made his home visit a very short one, although a very important one, in 1911. But the train of events was started the year before.

As part of their scheme for the development of Queen's Park the Bournemouth Corporation had, by 1910, built a road linking the two radial roads already mentioned, namely Charminster Road in the west to Holdenhurst Road in the east. They called it Queen's Park Avenue. It runs along the bottom of a shallow valley which, at its eastern half, forms the northern boundary of the Queen's Park Golf Course. The western half of the new road was, by contrast, thickly wooded, mainly with pine trees, rhododendrons, bracken and other ground cover. No doubt it was hoped and expected to become an area of good quality housing, together with the other, smaller roads which were made to connect the new Avenue to the area to the south.

When Harry was at home he and Dorothy liked nothing better than to go out together for walks during which they explored the expanding area and kept their eyes open for a likely house to buy. One such walk took them to see the fairly new Queen's Park Avenue. Arriving at the bottom of the southern slope they could see the golf course to their right, open and countrified. No houses being built on either side of the road there. To the north lay the estate of a large Victorian house called Hadden Hall that was deep in its own pine forest. But what lay to the left?

Turning left, then, they walked through the trees of the Avenue. After nearly half a mile they came upon a group of four houses being built by the same builder, a Mr Rolls. They were immediately taken with the third of the four houses to which they came. All were quite different from each other. The one that took their fancy was probably slightly the largest of the four. Within minutes Dorothy was scampering all over it, choosing her bedroom, allocating the others to the various members of the family and generally laying down the proposition that this was the house for them, and didn't Harry agree and had he not better get on with contacting the builder and buying it before anyone else got in first. Her enthusiasm for the place was infectious and she carried Harry along with her.

The house was very far from completed when they first saw it. Indeed it was not completely finished before Harry's departure for India the following year. So Dorothy's choice of rooms must have been made in a building still requiring a good deal of imagination to appreciate what it was going to be like. Furthermore, at an early stage, before they moved in, Harry arranged for additions to the house to be built, including a large double garage at the rear with a full sized billiards room above.

So during the winter of 1910 to 1911 Harry would have been able to look forward to returning the following summer with the pleasant, even exciting task, of moving his family into the new house and supervising all the final details of the building, decorating and furnishing. In the event he did not have anything like the usual length of time in England, due to the arrangements made for the Coronation of King George V. As the trip was at the expense of the State it was obviously sensible to go along with it, even if time was made very short thereby.

A scheme was approved 'for the despatch of a contingent of Indian troops and Volunteers and Imperial Service Troops to England to attend the Coronation of His Majesty King George V, Emperor of India.' Detailed orders were issued from the Army Headquarters in Simla by the Adjutant General setting out in Appendices the names of all Regular (British and Indian) Officers and all Volunteer Officers. There were to be sixty-three Volunteer Officers, of whom Harry was one. Whether his name had been drawn from a hat, or whether he had been chosen by someone in the Port Defence Corps is not revealed, either in the Orders or in Harry's own account of the event.

It might be thought typical of Harry that in the passage dealing with the Coronation in *Scraps from My Diaries* he makes no mention of that ceremony itself, nor of the King, nor of any procession, nor of the part he or his contingent played in any of these, but concentrates on his own forthright behaviour, particularly what seems to have been at least a heated disputation, if not a bad tempered slanging match, between himself and the Commander of the Contingent.

In 1911 I represented the Calcutta Port Defence Corps at the coronation of King George V. The contingent left Bombay in the *R.I.M. Dufferin*. General Birdwood ('Birdie') was in command, a handsome, efficient soldier who told a good yarn and wasted few words...

He and I had several arguments particularly over the Volunteer Force, later the A.F.I. (Auxiliary Force India). One complaint was that they were not smart – not his idea what a soldier should be. I asked if he knew any units in the British Army that could compare with Corps like the London Rifle Brigade, Queen's Westminsters, London Scottish, the Artists and other London Volunteers. My own Corps...had an engineer section, some of the sappers being men in important jobs drawing as much as £100 per month. Royal Engineer Officers said there were more engineering attainments in that small unit than could be found in any body in the British or Colonial Army.

"We are able to earn our living, many filling posts your people would find it difficult to fill and in our spare time we do a bit of soldiering.. Some are slack, but there are always keen men who take up the hobby of soldiering, glad to have chances to pick up more knowledge in a soldier's duties. What's more without any real authority we manage large numbers of men and get all sorts of things done. I am a businessman and an amateur soldier. I am prepared to back myself in even money to beat any man in this ship with a rifle on the range, and to back myself 10 to 1 to beat any man with both rifle and revolver, right and left hand. Not that I can't be beaten but I know I have a damned good chance of winning. When it comes to the next war, we are the chaps you'll have to depend upon to fight for you."

He asked, "With those ideas do you salute?"

"Of course I do because that is part of the ritual. But I don't salute because I think you are better than me."

He was firmly of the opinion that "You are nothing but a bloody socialist," but even there he was wrong. I am a patriotic Englishman...

The Officer appointed as Adjutant of the Volunteer Contingent was a gentleman, too refined to deal with the rudeness shown by some of the Volunteer Officers home on leave, so that he hardly knew what to do. "Hand them over to me," said I, and was promptly installed as Acting Adjutant. When complaints about unanswered telegrams were shouted over the 'phone, I shouted back, "Why the hell didn't you prepay a wire, surely you don't think we are going to spend our own money on you?" A soft answer turneth away wrath, but a hard one has good stopping power, so everything went smoothly after that and the Lance Adjutant was grateful. I still hold two letters of his thanking me for what I did.

The Army & Navy Stores catered, charging ten shillings a day, which considering the excellent fare and attendance was most reasonable and greatly appreciated. Many visitors came to camp at Hampton Court and being most of my time on duty they had to be entertained. No end of notabilities had a drink at my expense, and I fancied myself when standing Earl Crowe, Secretary of State of India, a half peg. There is, in more ways than one, a democracy about the Army and I thoroughly enjoyed such exalted Company, regretting that it didn't last. [1]

Indeed time was very short. The contingent had sailed from Bombay on 19th May and had docked at Southampton on 10th June. The disembarkation orders, issued on board on 7th June, involved the entire contingent going to the camp at Hampton Court. They were in England for just over three weeks, sailing on Tuesday, 4th July. While provision was made for Volunteer Officers being on leave in England to report to the India Office in London, Harry travelled with the main body, his copy of the disembarkation orders, issued on board the *Dufferin*, is among his papers. He returned to India on the *Dufferin*, and some of the letters home which he wrote on board have survived.

Harry claims to have been on duty most of the time. Even if one takes that with a pinch or two of salt, it seems likely that he was glad to be around on the military scene. We get a glimpse from his last paragraph above of his evident liking for an opportunity to rub shoulders with highly placed members of The Establishment. I think it was something of a sensitive issue for Harry. His origins were rather humble, and his undoubted success in making his way in life had not resulted from him becoming a member of a learned profession, nor from becoming a Regular Officer. But on this occasion he was accepted among the Gentry. And not only was there the – presumably temporary – Officers' Mess at the Hampton Court Camp to enjoy. Two prestigious Clubs elected him an Honorary Member during his official visit. The Committee of the Naval and Military Club in Piccadilly 'have done themselves the pleasure to elect you'; while the Members of the United Services Club in Pall Mall 'hope that Captain H. Hobbs will favour them by becoming an Honorary Member.' Harry would surely have made a point of availing himself of the opportunity so presented to walk on hallowed ground – even if every other Officer (or, at least, every British Officer) in the contingent had been similarly honoured.

Then there was the Coronation Naval Review. That took place on Saturday, 24th June, two days after the Coronation itself. Harry – again one assumes with all or most of his contingent – was invited to join the S S *Mongolia* at Southampton, sailing at 10.30am for Spithead, a return railway ticket from Waterloo to Southampton being provided for his convenience on a special train at 8.30am 'Morning Dress will be worn.' Harry would not have missed that; it must have been quite a 'do', and, in any event, his invitation was not returned, which it would have had to have been if he had not been going. On the other hand his railway ticket was not used, and remains in its pristine condition as a nostalgic reminder of what railway tickets used to be like. I believe that this shows that he went to join the *Mongolia* from Bournemouth.

So in spite of Harry's assertion of being 'most of my time on Duty' it looks very much as if he took himself to Bournemouth very soon after the Coronation itself, probably on Friday, 23rd June; then got a train to Southampton for the next day's adventure at the Review of the Fleet, returning to Bournemouth at the end of the day. Obligatory attendances at the Camp at Hampton Court would surely have been few and far between, especially for Volunteer Officers such as he. And home would have been beckoning with much for him to do.

Although he does not mention it in his book, by far the most important family event of that summer was the completion of all formalities in relation to the purchase of the new house in Queen's Park Avenue, which thus became the third Chingri Khal. Harry had left in the *Dufferin* to return with his contingent to India before the family could move in, so a great deal of the responsibility would have fallen on Jennie. With a house that size and its extensive grounds the task would have been considerable, but it was probably a labour of love.

For they had undoubtedly picked a winner. From the outside Chingri Khal was an unexceptional house, perhaps; a fairly typical Edwardian building, almost symmetrical on its south front, with two large flanking gables. Plain red brick up to the first floor level, painted plasterwork above in a pale off-white, which lightened its appearance. It was quite a big house, but by no means enormous, with four reception rooms on the ground floor (the largest of which was 27 feet by 18 feet), six principal bedrooms on the first floor and three attic rooms on the second.

But the interior layout and its setting made it a very pleasant and comfortable home for the family. Mr Rolls had spacious ideas. The house itself was built on a plot with a 100 foot frontage to the road. On the east of Chingri Khal lay another 100 feet of garden, enough land for a rose garden and then a full sized tennis court. The largest reception room, known as the music room, looked east over this broad, almost level garden. The remaining reception rooms faced south over the front lawn, which was at a slightly lower level.

To the west, on which side lay the tradesmen's entrance there was a further 50 feet of land. Even if the western boundary of the property had been made there, it would have been a house in ample grounds. But Harry was able to buy the whole area between that potential boundary line and the boundary of the most westerly of Mr Rolls's four dwellings, thus giving a further frontage of 150 feet to Queen's Park Avenue. Whether Mr Rolls had had another dwelling in mind to erect on that site or not, he was willing to sell it to Harry and it became part of the grounds of Chingri Khal. It was quite untouched, covered with the ubiquitous pines, along with smaller trees, rhododendrons and bracken, and much else besides. Not surprisingly it was always known as 'the wood.' The house itself was well set back from the road, with a thick screen of evergreens before the front lawn. The land rose a little up to the house from the road and then behind the house it rose rather more steeply, the northern boundary being far enough from the back of the house for a fairly good sized kitchen garden to be developed. The house with its immediate garden was conveyed into Jennie's name; the wood into Harry's.

The third Chingri Khal was the first home the family felt they could really call their own. It remained Jennie's home until she died nearly thirty two years later. From the outset she adopted an open house policy: Friends and acquaintances came and went in profusion. As with most households in their income bracket there were servants for the family, inside and out. Cook, parlourmaid and chauffeur-gardener would have been the minimum. Often there would be more. Dorothy in particular made it her business to understand enough about horticulture to have a very clear idea of how the garden should be developed, and with the gardener of the day she did much work to lay it out and to plant it. As for the wood, she undertook enough work to tame it so as to make it accessible without spoiling in the least its wild, secluded and natural appearance. It was a wonderful area for children where they could play unseen and unsupervised and let their imaginations run riot. It also suited slightly more organised occasions, such as the occasional bonfire party, where bacon and eggs and other succulent delights could be cooked over a crackling wood fire. I feel sure that those who have experienced it will agree that the combined smell of wood smoke and of bacon sizzling in the pan is hard to beat. It will always evoke for me fond memories of the wood at Chingri Khal.

The lawn to the east of the house, perversely called the back lawn, was normally marked out as a tennis court, the necessary equipment having been acquired in the way of nets, posts and the rest of the paraphernalia. Tennis parties were popular both before and after the Great War, and many were held, formal and impromptu.

The kitchen garden, too, was made into a useful productive area, in which fruit trees, soft fruits and vegetables were grown. From an early stage Jennie invested in two or three hives of bees, and became a dab hand at donning all the necessary protective gear and dealing with the bees to the manor born. These creatures, however, sometimes gave rise to inconveniences when excited. One or more of them provided the occasion for a demonstration of the rather less sympathetic side of Harry's sense of humour.

One of the guests at a tennis party soon after the First War was a young man who appeared to most of the rest of the company as being rather more pompous, smug and self-satisfied than was either attractive or justified. For some reason a small, but significant number of bees found his copious head of hair a pleasing new resort. Having taken up temporary residence among the flowing locks, the bees became disturbed by the enquiring hand of the youth, and began to display their irritation by injecting their venom into his scalp. This produced quite an effect, the young man crying out and tearing violently at his well-prepared coiffure in a frantic effort to remove the offending insects.

Family and other guests, despite feeling that it might be regarded as a well-deserved put-you-down, were disposed to be sympathetic and to conceal as best they could the smiles which the performance was engendering. Not so Harry. Assuming an air of mock outrage he marched up to the hapless fellow, and barked at him in his most ferocious way: "How dare you come here and interfere with our pets." He thereupon burst into paroxysms of his raucous laughter, causing the rest of the company to lose such self control as they had so far been able to muster and to dissolve into giggles or worse. The youth had to fend for himself and do what he could to restore something of his dignity. I do not believe he ever went there again.

For more than three decades this large, welcoming house, with its pleasant, spacious grounds was the family home for two generations. Over the years inevitably it would have its sad moments as well as its joyful ones, but basically it was a relaxed, happy and hospitable home which was a source of delight not only for Harry and Jennie and their children, but, in due time, for their grandchildren as well. And it impressed itself as well in the minds of many a visitor, young and old, who would look back with affection and nostalgia to the time they spent at Chingri Khal. It had its own special warmth of welcome – and the credit for that must very largely go to Jennie who made it what it was from the outset.

The third Chingri Khal. 1911-1943.

CHAPTER 8

TO THE COMING OF WAR

ARRY'S SATISFACTION at the ultimate outcome of his short visit home in 1911 is very evident from the first letter he wrote during the voyage back to India.

R.I.M.S. *Dufferin* near Gibraltar
July 8th 1911

My dearest Jennie

We are due at Gib about 5 this evening and expect to have a good time there.

So far the voyage has been excellent – it would not be possible to have better weather and I hope we shall not have such a trying passage after all.

Colonel Binning * inquired very kindly after you: he tells me that his boy was at Hodder and Stonyhurst and says that they are splendid places for a boy to obtain a good start, so that is very satisfactory.

You will soon be leaving the Cottage, but I shall continue to send your mail there until I learn your new address. I hope you will be lucky in finding a suitable place in Swanage and that you will be very careful to ascertain any dangerous part or time for swimming so that the children can avoid dangers.

Since we turned round Cape St. Vincent there has been a deal of vibration in the *Dufferin* as we have had a strong head wind. I have been doing a lot of basking in the sun and am very brown but it is just right for sunning oneself and more perfect weather can hardly be imagined. My appetite is much better and I must confess that my trip has done me a deal of good. The purchase of the house too has taken some anxiety off my mind as well as pleasing me with my

---

* Of the Calcutta Volunteer Rifles.

141

purchase, and now that you have that you can take more pleasure in your home as it is your own…

The King sent us a nice message as we were leaving which pleased everybody and barring a few discontented ones who did not like coming away there has not been a growl from anyone.

I must say again how very pleased I am with the children who are growing up just as I would like them to be and I am pleased with their physical appearance as well as with their talent. We have three splendid children and are both very proud of them while we do all we can to make their lives happy. While we must make every effort now to have a house free from every encumbrance we must also start with being comfortable so far as our fittings, so please look after our friend Mr Rolls and ask him for anything that may be good and durable…

I must say again and again that the children do you credit and that I am more than proud of them…

Well, old girl – I'll drop you a few lines or a p.c. ashore and I now conclude with much love, many kisses and the hope that you are having few difficulties in the househunting

Your own loving

Harry

You could hardly hope for a letter more full of domestic bliss. It is the most affectionate letter from Harry to Jennie which has survived, and makes the later deterioration in their relationship so much the sadder – and, one might feel, so unnecessary and avoidable. Harry's satisfaction is very understandable. From departing for India when nineteen with only two borrowed pounds in his pocket, he was now at forty seven leaving behind a devoted wife, three children in whom he had the greatest confidence, and all of them comfortably settled in a large property, well provided for and with a future full of promise

Harry wrote separate letters to all four members of his family when near or at Aden. That to Jennie is, perhaps, a little less effusive, ending:

I wonder how you have got on about Swanage and whether you are comfortable.

Give my love to the children: be very careful about making enquiries regarding the unfavourable times for bathing and have Dorothy do as little reading as possible and then in the open air. She has a tendency to sit down all of a heap.

With much love to you, hoping you are well and everything going as you would wish

I remain,

Your loving Husband

To his two younger children his letters were quite short, but to Dorothy he gave more of a picture of life on board:

My own darling little Dorothy,

The heat was very great in the Red Sea, and last evening as we sat down to dinner we noticed a sudden lightness in the air and a freshness that was more like England. This was due to our having passed the gate of the Red Sea and out of the oven which is what it always feels to be. On deck it was quite cool and as I had been sleeping on deck for a fortnight I kept out although it was cool enough to sleep in the cabin. At 4.30 this morning the bugle sounded and we turned out. I have felt inclined to recommend that the bugler of ours plays in silence as it is a bit of a surprise to find a man standing at one's feet, blowing over your head:

However – we got used to it although one feels inclined to wish that someone would tread on the bugle.

As poor Herbert Harraden wrote once when he came through the Red Sea

> "Ah! Me! That awful Red Sea
> "No place in this World could more odious be.
> "If bad words are not right, it's excusable quite
> "To make use of a 'D', yes the biggest big 'D'
> "In the Red Sea. In the Red Sea."

And those aboard who felt that a few extra whiskies & soda would do them no harm as they were thirsty, felt the heat more than I, as I have hardly drank anything barring on my birthday, when I drank your healths in champagne and wondered whether you were thinking of me. I am afraid you were then in bed and fast asleep.

Tomorrow, the 26th July your holidays are to commence as far as I can remember, and I hope you have been successful in your exams although I think it might be better if you waited a year.

Now, darling little Dorothy, when you are holiday making, try to be as much in the fresh air as you can – do not hang about inside the house reading, but try to grow up strong and straight: there is plenty of time before you to read, but I want you to read 'The Newcomes' as that is a favourite novel of mine and a real standard work.

We do not leave here until tomorrow evening and I expect it will be a bit hot during the day. At 7.30 in the morning it is quite fresh.

Much love, many kisses and hoping you are well.
I remain
Your own loving
Father

The reference to schools for Arthur in the first letter to Jennie illustrates a curious feature of her relationship with Harry. They rowed about almost everything on occasions, the one exception being religion. Despite the manifest dislike, almost contempt, which Harry felt for most forms of organised religion he would only very rarely take up any difficult stance over religious observance. The education of his only son might well have provided fertile ground for problems; but no. He seems to have acquiesced in the choice of Stonyhurst, together with its nearby prep school, Hodder, without protest, or even demur. Living in a Jesuit parish it is, perhaps, not surprising that Jennie considered a Jesuit school for Arthur. It is a little surprising that she opted for Stonyhurst, purely on the basis of geography. Although a very fine school it had the disadvantage of being situated near Clitheroe, in Lancashire, some 250 miles north of Bournemouth, which must have made it difficult, if not impossible, for Harry or Jennie to visit Arthur during the term.

Particularly is this the case as Beaumont, at Old Windsor, another distinguished Jesuit school, was so much nearer and more readily accessible for the family. While attending at the Convent to collect Dorothy, Jennie had met another catholic mother, a Mrs Hickey. She had a son, John, between Dorothy and Arthur in age, who was due to go to Beaumont. John Hickey was to be a life-long friend of the family, and I would have thought that it would have been a very happy solution for the two young friends to have gone off to the same school. Jennie decided otherwise and Harry went along with her decision without any fuss or problem.

Harry's reference to 'the Cottage' could not have been a reference to either the second or third Chingri Khal, but to the first stage of the family's summer holiday which appears to have begun just as Harry left to return to India. Dorothy's school year had not finished: she must have been boarding for that term, or part of it. After 'The Cottage' – wherever that may have been – they did indeed, as Harry's letters foresee, go to Swanage for their main holiday.

It was when they were at Swanage that Jennie had one of those experiences which must have made her wish that she had more male support in her normal life than was the case in fact. As usual the family had moved, lock, stock and barrel, into a cottage, taking their kitchen and nursery staff with them. The immediate entourage consisted not only of Jennie and the three children, but also Rufus, a fully-grown St. Bernard, Jimmy-the-Dog (so called to distinguish him from Jimmy Breaks, their cousin), a mature cocker spaniel, and Cheng, a pekingese.

Their holiday home was half a mile or so from the beach, to which the children repaired each morning, together with at least one nurse or governess and probably Jennie on occasions. Of course, inevitably the whole menagerie came too. Picnics were not in vogue with them in those days, so the whole assembly returned home for lunch, repeating the process again in the afternoon.

It so happened that their route to the beach led them across a small green on which was tethered a goat. On the very first time they went past the goat, Rufus discovered that it was tethered, and by how much, and that there was a lot of canine fun to be made out of tormenting the goat. Day after day, and four times a day, Rufus would taunt the goat by barking furiously at it from just beyond the extremity of its tether, while the goat strained helplessly, tugging on the rope trying to get at Rufus, while the family laughed at the situation, calling Rufus after them when they had got beyond the green.

As luck would have it, after about a fortnight, Jennie had to go to London for the day, and she went off early by the train which at that time ran from Swanage itself to join the main line at Wareham. The family routine carried on unabated. All was well in the morning and on the way down to the beach in the afternoon; Rufus dancing around the goat, and the goat, beside itself with fury, trying to get at its tormentor. But on the way home in the afternoon there came about that misfortune which really should have been foreseen and guarded against. The goat broke its tether.

It was obvious to all from that instant that this was now a fight to the finish. Two weeks or more of goading and provoking had got the goat more wound up than it is wise to wind a goat. Rufus was a big and healthy dog, but a goat half wild with fury might be thought to be more than a match for any dog. The children were hustled away from the scene of mayhem, fur flying and considerable rampage. So Dorothy did not actually see quite how Rufus did it. But Rufus killed the goat, and trotted back to the holiday home, a bit puffed, and probably bruised, but otherwise very pleased with himself at having put paid to his enemy. In the meantime this had all so greatly over-excited Jimmy-the-Dog, who was the most docile, friendly and peaceful of creatures, that he ran off to the nearest farmyard and killed two chickens.

So Jennie arrived back from London, very soon after the scenes of carnage and slaughter, no doubt looking forward to relaxing in the peace of the summer evening, to find instead two very irate farmers on her doorstep. One held the carcase of a dead goat – a goat which, of course, was in the prime of life and at the peak of its value – while the other held the remains of two hens – both of which, of course, were in full lay and worth the very top market price. Jennie would have been less than human if she had not thought that life must have been much simpler on board the *Dufferin* than in the depths of darkest Dorset.

The next time Harry came home saw the introduction of what might be called another member of the family. "A piano for Dorothy," Harry announced when the large van made its unheralded arrival at Chingri Khal. And, sure enough, the men trundled in a Rachals six foot grand piano. One of those pianos designed by Harry for the Indian climate, and finished at his request in a satin oak case to go with the oak dado panelling and fireplace in the music room. There it was to remain until Chingri Khal was sold more than thirty years later. It then went into store for four or five years after the sale, when, after some restoration work, it was moved into Hereford House. There it stood for nearly forty years, only leaving when Dorothy herself left and came to live with Sheila and me in the fourth Chingri Khal.

The Rachals grand did not follow Dorothy to Winchester. Sheila by then had her own Steinway grand. Instead it was gratefully accepted by Dorothy's oldest granddaughter, Helen, herself a professional musician, who needed the piano and subsequently used it a great deal. It has had many vicissitudes in its long life. After Dorothy married it was considerably under-used, save as a handy flat space, and subject therefore to accidents such as the spilling of fluids into the body. At Hereford House it was also very under-used, although great care was taken of it and it was regularly tuned, if at rather long intervals.

But when it was moved to Helen's home it came into its own. Used regularly, mostly daily, and treated with love and respect, at the age of about seventy-five, this grand old instrument became a musician's piano. It had to be moved several times, once by crane into, and later out of, an upstairs window. On one disastrous occasion there was a burst pipe when Helen and her husband were away for many weeks. Their home was badly flooded and much water found its way into the Rachals. When Helen saw it on her return she feared that this was the end of the road. But not a bit of it. The piano was allowed to dry out slowly over several weeks. Much work had then to be done on it to renew the felts, replace the strings, and much else, but the frame, the soundboard and the case were all undamaged.

Its latest (in 2003) adventure has seen it shipped to Brazil, where Helen and her Brazilian husband and family have relocated in Rio de Janeiro. So now, at the ripe old age of nearly ninety, the Rachals, for the first time in the tropics for which is was designed, is giving forth more music than it had ever done in all its first three quarters of a century put together. It certainly proves Harry's point when he asserted that Rachals pianos would still be giving good service a century after they were built.

Although Dorothy was the most musically inclined of Harry's three children, and as a young woman she was quite useful on the piano, she never claimed to be a pianist. I can remember her playing a few well-known pieces (Schumann's Arabesque comes to mind) but opportunities to play the piano after she was married were not easy to find. "My hands are not the right shape for playing the piano," she used to say. Whether that was really the case, or something of an excuse, matters not; her first love on the performing side was singing. Even this did not survive her first pregnancy, and the loss of her singing voice was a considerable blow to her.

But her love of music in most of its many forms never left her. Doubtless she inherited much of that from Harry. He certainly did all he could to encourage her. When he was at home he would take her as often as he could to hear the Bournemouth Municipal Orchestra, playing under Mr Dan Godfrey (he was not Sir Dan in those days) in the old Winter Gardens, the conservatory, which looked rather like the Palm House of Kew in miniature. At that time the weekly symphony concerts were given on Thursday afternoons – a fact which probably speaks volumes as to the character of the audiences – but which may have made it easier for a teen-age girl to be taken, at any rate in the school holidays. There she was introduced into the world of the classics of the orchestral repertoire, as well as to much modern (as it was then) music, of which Dan Godfrey was such a whole-hearted exponent.

Not that the two of them, musical as they undoubtedly were, always appreciated that which they heard. "It was well before the first War that Daddy and I heard what I believe was the first performance in England of Debussy's Prélude à l'aprés-midi d'un Faune," Dorothy told me. "It was certainly the first time it had been heard in

Bournemouth or by either of us. Nowadays we enjoy it without turning a hair. But then I remember that we sat through it, and when it was over we turned to each other with expressions of incredulity on our faces and agreed that we had never heard such complete gibberish. You must never be too quick to write off the new simply because you do not understand it the first few times."

In October, 1913, for the first and only time since she came to England in 1905, Jennie accompanied Harry back to India after his visit home that summer. She found herself once again living in her old home at 4, Esplanade East for the six months or so that she was in Calcutta. In that time the children attained the ages of sixteen, thirteen and eleven respectively, and no doubt were old enough to be left in England.

But they were not left at Chingri Khal. Jennie had a friend, a Mrs Cole, who also had a son called Arthur, about the same age as Jennie's Arthur and who was willing to give the three children a home for the time Harry and Jennie were away. She lived not very far away in Richmond Park Avenue, where the thee children stayed at any rate during the school holidays, otherwise they were boarding at school, the girls at the Convent, and Arthur at Stonyhurst.

It was not a very happy time for them. Mrs Cole was one of those 'good Catholics' whose bigotry knows no bounds and who give the Church a bad name. The name of her house – 'La Roseraie' – whether or not a conscious play on words with 'Rosaire' – gives some indication of life there. Materially the house and small garden would have been a considerable come-down from Chingri Khal. But what was worse was the narrow minded approach to the children's activities. As an instance of this, someone had given Dorothy a copy of G. K. Chesterton's *The Innocence of Father Brown*. One would think today – probably most people would have thought then - of that being an entirely suitable and sensible choice for an intelligent sixteen your old to read. But not Mrs Cole. It must refer to a Catholic priest, and referring to his 'innocence' must reveal something improper. So Mrs Cole took it upon herself to confiscate the book and to burn it.

How Dorothy's faith managed to survive in that sort of atmosphere is hard to understand, but survive it did. All the children were very glad indeed when their parents returned together in he spring of 1914.

Whilst they were away something prompted Harry to write a brief note to Dorothy, probably enclosed in a letter from Jennie. Musical experiences often struck a chord in Harry's memory, and he recorded many in his published books. He does not say what jogged his memory of an event nearly twenty years before, but one can be glad that it has survived, perhaps against all the odds. It is written in pencil upon a scrappy piece of flimsy paper – little more than tissue paper. Despite the pencil, he has taken a good deal of care to write the manuscript music clearly. The little vignette of travel in India is mentioned in his books [1], but only here is the music revealed:

My darling old Dorothy.

In 1886 I was travelling for five days from Dhubri to Dibrugarh in Assam. No other European was on board the steamer. One night a flautist played this weird air outside my cabin. He played these eight bars – nothing else – all night – He knew them by heart – I haven't forgotten them since. You have heard me play them but perhaps you have forgotten them so here they are. Be careful to note that the last E is a natural – it ought not to be so marked but I have slipped in the ♮ in case. Grace notes very short. Make the most of the other.

20.1.14   Dad

Another musical experience, this time in the 1930s Harry recalled near the end of his life:

> During tiffin in a hotel in Kobe, a trio – piano, violin, and 'cello – played several items, among them something by Mendelssohn. The piano and the violin were in two sharps while the 'cellist interpreted his part in two flats. It was difficult to avoid applause – whether accidental or intentional it was funny – so I applauded vociferously. With Japanese grace the musicians bowed with smiling courtesy which rather discounted my irony.
>
> At dinner time the performance, and the mistake, were repeated. One could see then that the management recognized that travellers are supposed to want a band when they eat, so they provided one. Whether the performers knew anything about what they were playing was of minor importance – the band was there – "what have you to grumble about?" At the risk of feeling that it was a shame to ridicule, I again applauded, and the three performers were obviously delighted to find there was at least one musician in the Audience. [2]

Harry and Jennie arrived home in the spring of 1914, and all the family were thankful to be together again in Chingri Khal. Perhaps to celebrate, perhaps to compensate for the lengthy separation Harry arranged to take his family on what now would be called a cruise on a banana boat, calling at any rate at Lisbon, Grand Canary, Tenerife and Madeira. They were due to depart near the end of July by which time the storm clouds of war would have been billowing up even if they had not been obvious when the booking was made. For many years by this time he had conducted much business with Germany. Rachals in particular was an important customer for him – and vice versa – but there must have been many others. The year before he had made several visits to Germany and had, incidentally, seen the Kaiser three times. He had the lowest of opinions of the Kaiser, but equally he had no illusions about the potential military might of Germany. "If it comes to war with Germany," he used to say, "the Germans will show a fine set of teeth." He was never shy of expressing his opinions loud and clear, and this one caused him often to be accused of being pro-German and unpatriotic. He would reply that to state the truth can only be a benefit for his own Country. Certainly there was a significant proportion of the British public who adopted what he regarded as a most absurd view of the potential scale of the conflict if it came to war with Germany.

In two of his books he gives accounts of the outbreak of war as he experienced it; the first tells how that event may have cost him a fortune, but he would never know whether it did or not; the second illustrates the wishful and foolish thinking of many of his compatriots.

When war was declared in 1914 I was in Lisbon, in a banana boat with a crowd of excursionists bound for the Canary Islands and Teneriffe. How enthusiastic the Portuguese were! Even those lined up outside the banks hoping to find a soft corner in the moratorium forgot their troubles to cheer us. Unfortunately, most of the passengers, doctors, schoolmasters, and comparatively well-to-do folk had not been educated in pride of race; they did not realise what a splendid heritage it is to be born British, and they received the cheerful goodwill of our oldest allies in a foolishly contemptuous manner. I shall never forget the obvious sincerity of our welcome in Portugal, and when it is remembered how that admiration has since [by 1930] turned to hatred, what a pity it seems!...

As our stay was uncertain, we loafed about the streets of Lisbon, went to Cintra and other beautiful places, and, in a sort of way, settled down. A tobacconist persuaded me to buy tickets in a State lottery which was closing that evening and assured me that I should know the result before the steamer left. Suddenly orders came for us to steam at 3.00pm, so after taking our time over lunch in an old fashioned hotel, we decided to walk to the ship. In the main street was a huge crowd, and, amid great excitement, a fine band crashed out with a blare of brass; everybody seemed to desert the bank doors to push and laugh and shout. The guide explained that, when the lotteries were drawn, it was customary for the Governor to send his band to play outside the premises where the winning ticket was sold, and it did not take long to ascertain that my tobacconist was the lucky man. I pulled out my two pounds' worth of tickets; the guide looked and said something to the crowd who tried to make way, but the Portuguese are short and squat, and pack close, so that it was impossible to force a way through a dense mob of excited men and women. Meanwhile, my wife, sister, and three children, already imbued with the seriousness of war, were in a fever in case we missed the steamer, so with much reluctance I took a taxi to the docks and by the time we fetched up alongside, the vessel was casting off. After helping my party on to the gangway I settled with the guide and as a parting benefaction gave him my lottery tickets. With bare head, bent low, he thanked me profusely while I hastened up the ladder feeling more than a little relieved to set foot in the promenade deck. Looking over the side, I saw Fernandez, whose length was taken in his breadth, making record time for the dock gates, evidently keen on drawing my winnings. I often wonder if he still shows tourists the long deceased bodies of the Kings of Portugal in their glass coffin, looking, in spite of all their finery, like an over-ripe Stilton cheese sprinkled with crystalline sugar. Perhaps too I feel curious about how much he picked up over my misfortune and if, while scratching himself inside sacred edifices, he ever remembers the name of his benefactor. [3]

[When we reached Madeira] the war had then just started, and our steamer...was within ten miles of the fight between the *Highflyer* and the *Kaiser Wilhelm der Grosse* when the latter ship was sunk. To recall the attitude of the passengers on our vessel then, their insubordination in regard to lights at night, their utter incredulity about the war lasting more than three weeks, and the scorn with which they received any expressions about the ability of the Germans or their capacity to put up a good fight, filled my mind with wondering what they think about it today [in 1925.] When we left Lisbon the Captain addressed the passengers on two occasions explaining that he had been instructed to steam without lights, and asking all to assist in carrying out this necessary order. Two men, holding well-paid, responsible positions, flatly refused to comply. "We've paid our money, and why should we go about the decks barking our shins? Besides, whose afraid of the Germans?" To show their British independence they turned on their cabin light, pulled back their purdahs, and stood outside smoking and enjoying themselves. When the Captain and Chief Officer were brought by one of the crew, the two Government officials abused them; so the electric bulbs were removed without further argument. The next day they boasted of what they had done, and asked me to draw up a letter to the owners reporting the Captain for his officiousness. After hearing my opinion they decided to send in the complaint themselves, but for the rest of the voyage they cut me dead. One cocksure individual was full of gibes at the possibility of anything happening to anybody. The war was a subject for hilarious contempt, but when we reached Liverpool in August 24th, 1914, and he opened his letters to learn that the Government had taken away all the horses he employed in his cartage business, he burst into tears and went around the deck bleating: "The Government can't take my horses, can they?" "They've ruined me," etc., and there was no satisfaction in asking him if it was so very funny after all. [4]

The family evidently lost no time in making their way to Bournemouth. By 25th August they were sufficiently restored from the rigours (such as there may have been) of some three weeks at sea in wartime, to be able to attend at Dean Park County Cricket Ground where Hampshire County Cricket Club were playing in the County Championship. The last week in August has traditionally been 'Bournemouth week' for Hampshire County Cricket and the war was not being allowed to interfere with that. Two photographs survive of Harry and his three children. One of the photographs, helpfully, is a professionally taken post card inscribed on its face 'Bournemouth cricket week. Golf club tent. Tues. Aug. 25 1914.' The Company is well attired; the gentleman in suits with buttonholes and hats – boaters, panamas and (for Harry) homburgs – the ladies as for Ascot. Arthur is in school uniform with cap and Eton collar, the girls in party frocks with picture hats. They are enjoying the warm sunshine outside a flag-bedecked marquee, plates of sandwiches and cakes on small tables in front of them. Staff stand respectfully behind. A happy, relaxed and confident gathering, such as had regularly been the case since the reign of Queen Victoria.

Meanwhile, on the 23rd August the great fortress of Namur had fallen to the advancing German army and by the 25th the British Expeditionary Force had retreated back to the French frontier. The Channel Ports were under threat and plans were being considered for the defence of Le Havre. But life must go on, even in a crisis.

Jennie and her children, about 1913.
Clockwise from Jennie: Dorothy with Cheng, Rufus,
Phyllis with Jimmy-the-Dog, Arthur.

Bournemouth Cricket Week, 25th August, 1914.

A close-up of the family (Dorothy, Phyllis, Harry, Arthur).

156

CHAPTER 9

COPING WITH
ABSENT FATHER

B Y THE TIME OF THE outbreak of the Great War Dorothy was approaching her seventeenth birthday. Her relationship with Harry had been a normal, happy, father/daughter relationship apart from being witness to so many rows which took place. These mainly were between Harry and Jennie, sometimes with other members of the family, sometimes with outsiders.

It could be disconcerting to have a meal at a restaurant interrupted if Harry found his dish not quite to his liking. He would throw down his knife and fork and loudly call out "This steak is bad. Send me the Manager. I'm not going to be poisoned in any cheap-jack eating house." And so on until he ran out of breath. He seemed oblivious of the embarrassment to the rest of his party.

At home they could never be sure what might set him off on a violent tirade against some slight failure in the domestic arrangements, or make him take offence at an unguarded remark. Jennie became quite expert at acting as a buffer between the children and Harry. But all too often she was herself the target of his wrath.

Sometimes, it must be said, she knowingly pushed her luck. As in the case of the row over the drive. Chingri Khal had a gravel drive which went right round the house, and there were two entrances into Queen's Park Avenue. That to the east came up the incline just to the east of the house. But that to the west was aligned opposite the large bay window of the dining room. To most peoples' minds this was a mistake: you do not want those walking up to your house, whether guests making for the front door, or tradesmen making for the kitchen door (which was that side of the house) to be gazing into one of the main living rooms while they do so. But Harry liked it that way. He could sit at the head of the table and look straight down the drive into the road and make a mental note of all those who were passing to and fro, and very likely add some caustic comment for good measure. Jennie realised it would be hopeless to get him to agree to any alteration, so she made no mention of the possibility of any change.

She waited until he had gone back to India, his first or second such return after they had taken possession, before the garden had matured. She then had workmen in to move the drive a few yards further west. It was an obvious and considerable improvement to most eyes. The dining room looked out on to part of the front garden, and there was much greater privacy.

Jennie probably held her breath when Harry next returned. He did not notice the change on arrival. But as soon as he sat down for his first meal at the head of the table…well, there was hell to pay. Fury at the change – and without consultation at that. Jennie stuck quietly to her guns, uttered a few emollient phrases that were hardly true – "I didn't think you'd mind, dear," "I was sure you would think it such a good idea," – and did her best to pacify him. The storm eventually blew over and the drive remained there for good.

Such outbursts of temper were part of the family scene; they kept everyone on tenterhooks, but not otherwise involved. Dorothy enjoyed having her father around. He was a great storyteller, and he treated young children as if they were adults. No talking down. He found in Dorothy a very receptive listener and someone with whom he could have a stimulating exchange of views and information which he could respect and admire. She may have been the only one of his family who shared his love of music, at any rate to any significant extent. In short, they were close to each other, affectionately close, and intellectually close.

Harry had left to return to India by the end of August 1914. Although it is not altogether clear when, he certainly made the journey back to England at least once during the War. The most probable years were 1916 or 1917, but there is nothing in any document to tell us about anything which might have taken place. There must have been a great deal of correspondence at that time, and it is a pity that very little of it has survived. But that which is available to us today – just three wartime letters from Harry to Dorothy – gives much food for thought.

The first, dated 20th January, 1915, and addressed to "My own darling Dorothy" is quite short, on only two pages. Evidently in reply to her Christmas letter, he comments on her Christmas, and on a letter from Arthur. He gives her a glimpse of his work:

> …At the present time I am devoting as many hours as possible to the workshop as we have to rebuild so many pianos owing to the difficulty in getting them from home to say nothing about the expense. I have about fifteen pianos to rebuild and three of them are in hand so it is essential that I be there to push on the work.

She has lamented his absence:

> It is quite true…I have not had a Christmas in England since 1882 which is getting on for a time ago; how I should stand the cold and wet is a conundrum.

A later comment on is a bit more Hobbsian in tone:

> It is not nice to feel that your friends are growing away from you but not bad if they are merely growing up. Sometimes I cynically remark that the advantage of leaving home for years is that you have fewer people to borrow money from you but there is also the Divine command – "Honour thy father and thy mother that thy days may be long in the land that the Lord thy God gaveth thee!" and therefore if the stay in one's native land is a blessing then I have been deprived of many blessings for a number of years. However I have much to be thankful for and am never forgetful to offer up a silent prayer for the many benefits I have received.

And he ends more like a father at Christmas, perhaps, with:

> I have been sending you five shillings a week which is more, I believe, than I said I would but I will continue it through this year and on your eighteenth birthday will consider a dress allowance for you but you will have to remind me and give some information for me to go on so that you may not be altogether at sea when you have really to run a house for yourself or keep yourself. You can discuss this with me in a letter when you feel that you have time to do so.
> With many loving kisses. Hoping you are well. I am.
> Your loving Father

All of which might be thought to be a fairly normal letter for a seventeen year old to get from her father. But the next one is very different, and makes me wish all the more that I had been able to talk to Dorothy about it, what impact it had on her, did she show it to Jennie, were his allegations true, and to what extent? But I never saw or heard of it until after Dorothy had died, and I can only wonder how she managed to deal with the responsibilities he seems to be trying to put on her. Mature she may have been for her age, but she was still only a schoolgirl, with more than a year at school to run. It is six closely typed pages long, only the last word is handwritten, and he pulls no punches.

April 6th 1915

My old darling old sweetheart Dorothy,

Your long letter of March 2nd gave me much pleasure to read but also reminded me of my promise to ascertain the right sort of good books for you to read which up to now I have not done, much to my regret.

Stocktaking and getting ready generally to go away have taken up a lot of my time but I will make a real effort to go to Thacker Spinks today or before the mail closes to ask the advice of the best men there.

Your news is certainly not good and the health of your mother is an anxiety; She does not try to make the best of things and is worried over matters that I am afraid she ought not to be. When I was home I found one or two very suspicious looking men about whom I afterwards learnt were detectives and whom I also gathered were employed by your mother to watch me. There was no need in the wide world to do so but she has apparently got into the clutches of these people who have nothing to do but to blackmail their clients. Your mother borrowed £50 from Mr. Norton to pay detectives and now that they know she has squandered her money they keep her busy with all sorts of wicked fairy tales that merely take money out of her pocket and ruin her peace of mind. When I came away this last time I did not hear from your mother for over three months; later she sent word that I was driving about in a fine two-seater car and I first thought it was someone at home who told her these things. Now I have worked out the problem that my hard

160

earned money is being (or has been) wasted on scoundrels who merely spread silly reports destitute of truth and cause your mother much agony of mind.

Harry then sets out his detailed expenditure on his family, totalling, he says, £1,400 a year, and asserts the need to look after expenditure and not to grumble about small allowances. The Indian political situation and his age are against making money. Others are managing on far less. He then goes on:

I feel in this matter that your mother has prompted you to write to me on this subject and therefore I reply knowing that she will read it and be quite unable to agree with the figures or the statements but you have a wise head and will see how economies can be effected and how the money made to go further and to better advantage. It is possible too that the detectives are not taking money now – or it also may be that they are worrying your mother under threat of telling me and that is worrying her and making her ill. From my point of view I think that there must be something seriously wrong when your mother disregarded me for over three months – doesn't write a letter and then tells me that I am running an expensive car here while she has to walk. No one in Calcutta will deny that I am a very industrious man; I work hard and steadily and look after my business carefully and I do not find it is likely to benefit my temper or my health to have all sorts of unfounded charges made against me when I am working hard for the benefit of my wife and family...

It requires a business head to run a house; it also needs energy to realise that the servants will rob if they can and that they must be looked after and made to be careful; it is wasteful and wicked to owe money to small tradespeople as they have to rob you in return; they are unable to lend better off people their money which is what it amounts to and they have to rob to put the interest on the bills...

...Idleness breeds discontent and all the evils of Satan and no matter how old people are work is a necessity. I remember your mother telling me with much satisfaction that Mrs.Waring had her sister to help with the children and someone else to run the house and all Mrs Waring had to do was to look nice if anybody called. My remark to that was that she might as well have been a monkey in the house but the point is how much better are they off for that sort of thing now? The real point is to look after things – hustle about and keep busy and keep off grumbling. Work and hard work are good for people: when they find idleness brings on nothing but discontent and prosperity spells nothing but unhappiness then it is about time idleness and prosperity come to an end. Get busy; cut down your food when old and find plenty of inexpensive objects in life, are good maxims…Your mother is now better off than her wildest dreams ever anticipated and I believe she has less pleasure in life, less contentment and grumbles ten times more than she was working for a small wage. This therefore means that her prosperity has purchased nothing but misery where it ought to have bought happiness.

Now it is your duty to try to make life more cheerful by putting a different aspect on things in the house; you are in your eighteenth year with a wise head on your shoulders and I think you will grow up wiser and stronger minded if you know these things and look upon discontent and grumbling as a disease that ought to be cured. Try to find how other people manage on very much smaller incomes and then try to bring a mind desirous of bringing peace and goodwill into domestic life. Neither your mother nor I had much when we married and it is only luck and hard work that has put us in the position we are in. Personally I thank God every day for the blessings I have received; I thank God every time I go upstairs and realise the rotten stuffy rooms I used to live in and the comfort I now enjoy. And also I try to enjoy it…It pays to be cheerful; it pays to be well and it pays to go without food so that you may keep well. It pays to show people that you are contented as when you know you ought to be contented and are not – they despise you to your loss as well perhaps theirs…The cheapest thing in the whole world to buy is unhappiness – it is literally given away and fortunately it pays more visits to the rich than to the poor.

I find I have treated you to a sermon and while I shall think twice about sending it to you I think it will be better to do so than to let matters go on in the dangerous way they are trending. Ask your mother to write regularly to me and I will reply. Try to get her out of her despondency and bring her mind to bear – not on the wealth of the rich but to think back on what we were twenty years ago. If the recollections of those days do not do her any good then she is incurable.

Two days later Harry continues with the letter, says he has decided to send it, discusses books she might like to buy and concludes:

> Now do the best you can to see where the leakage is in the expenses and see that bills are paid promptly; there should be none to run on more than the month. The amount is liberal enough as I know quite well – if it cannot be made to carry through it's a sign that the spending of it is faulty. I do not want you to take sides or feel that I am dragging you in for trouble. Your mother makes unfounded statements that only serve to upset me and put me off work and after puzzling my brain for months to find who is telling her lies I have realised that she is paying away my money, running herself into debt to be bled by scoundrels who simply laugh at her. That she has employed detectives she has told me; Mrs Norton put her up to that and if anyone can find out anything against me then I shall be surprised.

> With much love and many kisses hoping you are well. I remain
> Your loving
> Father

Harry calls this letter 'a sermon.' He is right; indeed it is rather a good sermon some might think. But it is also a great deal more than a sermon. He does not want her to take sides, but it is hard to see how she could avoid being at least tempted to do so, and she could have reacted very sharply against one or other of her parents. That this did not happen – and I am confident that it did not happen – seems to confirm Harry's belief that Dorothy had 'a wise head on her shoulders.' But it still strikes me as a rather unfair burden to put on those shoulders.

Dorothy's 'long letter' must have contained some plea for more funds, lack of which was making her mother ill. Jennie's greatest fear always was that Harry might take it into his head to stop, or drastically to reduce, her allowance. What the truth was with regard to 'the detectives' I can only guess. I find it hard to think of a good reason for Jennie wanting to employ them. She had the letter of 1909, and maybe more evidence – she was certainly soon to get more evidence – as to misdemeanours of Harry. She never took, nor, I would think, did she ever contemplate taking, any proceedings in Court against Harry. If there were detectives keeping an eye on him they might well have been put there by someone else – he had made many enemies by then.

Dorothy was quite astute enough to know what was worrying her mother, and Harry's belief that she was writing in the way she did at Jennie's instigation may not have been in fact correct. It is not possible to know whether or not Dorothy and Jennie talked this letter over together. Whatever may or may not have been said between them there seems to have been no major eruption, and for that fact a good deal of credit should go to one or other or both of them.

Whatever their feelings may have been, family life at Chingri Khal carried on. Arthur by now was at Stonyhurst (the annual cost of that was put by Harry at £100, hard to believe today.) Phyllis had joined Dorothy at the Convent (that was put down at £90 for the two of them) and Dorothy continued there until the summer of 1916. No reference to the fact is made in any surviving letter, but it must have been a cause of much delight when she won a place at Girton College, Cambridge, where she read History, going up in October, 1916.

University life during the First World War was very different from that in pre-1914 peacetime, but Dorothy was nevertheless very happy during her three years at Girton. It cannot be said that she achieved great academic distinction, in that in 1918 she passed her History Tripos part I at no more than Class III. In 1919 she 'attained the standard of Ordinary Degree' (women not yet being admitted to Cambridge degrees.) Perhaps one can say that it was something of an achievement in itself to have been there at all.

The undergraduates in her year appear as a somewhat unsmiling even solemn group in their First Year Photograph, Dorothy looking as grim as any of them. That belies the reality of their eventual time together over the ensuing three years. Many long-lasting friendships were formed. 'The Year' began the habit after they came down of having an annual lunch, usually in London, which they all tried to attend. It is a measure of the bonds they made that the annual lunch continued for a good sixty years after they had left Cambridge, until reduced numbers and increasing frailty of those remaining caused it to come to an end.

But before Dorothy's time at Cambridge came to an end two events of importance almost coincided. By the autumn of 1918 her twenty-first birthday was fast approaching. Harry was well aware of this and happily his letter to her has survived. Happily, because it shows clearly that their relationship had not been damaged in any discernable way by 'the sermon' and its aftermath. And not only does it show his continuing affection for her, even leading to some rather exaggerated sentiments being expressed, but it contains the most remarkable tribute to her mother. It is not long, and is entirely handwritten:

September 10th 1918.

My own darling sweetheart Dorothy.

In the hope that this will reach you in time for your twenty-first birthday I am writing this well beforehand.

While I am writing, murder, rioting, arson and dacoits are happening less than a mile away: the mob is looting shops, wrecking motor cars, stoning the police and burning houses. All the troops are out and as the weather is hot and muggy to a degree, they are having a bad time.

Now this is to be a letter of congratulation on your attaining the full and mature age of twenty-one years, and I am afraid that it is almost too much to expect that the next twenty-one will be as full of happiness and comfort as those you have just enjoyed, but I certainly hope they will.

To be twenty-one and have a life full of interest before you with a real happy past is a very enjoyable prospect which makes me feel proud, particularly when I remember that your intellect has grown with your years and that you can now consider yourself as one of the most intellectual women in the British Empire today.

May I confess that this was a summit that I never dreamed you would attain?

The fact is that you owe the most of this to your mother – whose love and ambition to do her children well are boundless and yet one has restrained the other so that your career has been guided and guarded far more sensibly than I could ever contemplate. Had mine been the guiding hand I am afraid that I should never have looked so far ahead nor aimed so high. The fact that I have worked hard and with a certain amount of success is quite a secondary matter – the credit must go to your mother who saw clearly, kept right on and is, I am sure, as proud of you as any mother in this world.

When you were barely three you were disobedient to me and I ordered you to stand in the corner. You flatly refused and I was on the point of making you when your mother very tactfully arranged matters and I didn't therefore force my ideas of discipline on you. Often since then I have thought that that was the starting point of an affectionate confidence that will live as long as I do; there was not the too frequent break between love and discipline that often happens and we have grown up full of sympathy and love for each other. Had I started by making you obey first and placing love second neither your mother nor I would stand with you where we are today. The love your mother bears towards you is as wide as it is deep and I feel that you are as much aware of this as I am.

I shall send you a cable on Nov.11th and I hope to have your birthday present home in time too – if it should be late you will know that it is on the way.

Wishing you all the happiness that a 21st birthday can give you, I regret that I cannot be with you on Nov. 12th, but you will be in my mind and heart all that day and I shall be wondering how many other loving wishes for you to have Many Happy Returns of the Day will be sent to you in addition to the love and kisses of
        Your own loving
        Father.

The good wishes were completed with the arrival of the present (whether 'in time' or not), which was a very beautiful crossover ring of a diamond and two pearls. Domestic mismanagement, unpaid bills, detectives and the rest seem to have been forgotten.

And then – just thirteen hours before the dawn of her twenty-first birthday there came the eleventh hour of the eleventh day of the eleventh month. As she became an adult the guns fell silent and the world was at peace.

The family on the front lawn of the third Chingri Khal,
probably summer, 1916.
(Left to right) Harry, Phyllis, Annie Hobbs {a younger sister of Harry}
Jennie, Arthur, Dorothy.
(In front) Canute {so-called because he was a Great Dane}
and Jimmy-the-Dog.

Portrait of Harry, 1918,
by Philip Tennyson Cole.

CHAPTER 10

A BRIGHT YOUNG THING
AND A WEB OF DECEIT

WHAT IS IT THAT might possess a man to have his portrait painted? I am entirely inexperienced in such matters, but it seems to me fair to assume that the activity would be likely to be both time consuming and expensive. Promotion in his professional or business life may occasion the decision. A formal pose in the splendour of the robes of the higher judiciary or of those to be found in the groves of academe might be very understandable. Then again the boardroom of a successful company may need to have the founder of the firm gazing down on the work of his successors to inspire them to greater efforts. Or yet again the ducal palace may require a likeness of the most recent holder of the title of His Grace to feature alongside the many examples of his ancestors already on the walls.

Smug self-satisfaction might be enough of a motivation for some, perhaps. I daresay we could all think of a public figure whom we might believe (rightly or wrongly) to be capable of an action so redolent of Master Jack Horner. I do not think that Harry was such a man. He may have been self-satisfied, but I would suggest never smug. He was too much of a realist, too well aware of his own good fortune and of what he owed to others for his success in life. The undoubted fact is, however, that in 1918 he had his portrait painted by Philip Tennyson Cole who had a studio in Calcutta. Although Cole is not, I understand, thought of as being in the top rank of his profession, he was well enough regarded to be granted sittings by King Edward VII. He was probably able to command a substantial fee from Harry for the commission. The resulting portrait is a good likeness with a real sense of Harry's presense. The year – 1918 – is clearly to be seen under the artist's signature.

Harry was not in England during 1918. Indeed there is no record of his coming home before 1921, but I believe he would have made his first return trip after the war earlier than that – quite likely in both 1919 and 1920. Whenever it was that he came home, he brought the portrait with him. It used to hang in the music room at the third Chingri Khal, on the wall behind the grand piano, where it remained until the house was sold after Jennie's death. Dorothy chose it as one of the assets she wanted to keep, but it went at once into store, along with various other items, and was largely forgotten. It was not until after Dorothy's death, when we decided to try to do without any storage requirement, that the portrait emerged once again into the light of day. I am glad to say that proper wall space was able to be found for it in the fourth Chingri Khal, where it looks down, more or less benignly, upon the family as they go about their daily tasks – whether it inspires them to greater efforts I venture to doubt, but from time to time it might engender a respectful glance.

So the portrait never did hang in the boardroom of H. Hobbs & Co. (if there was one) nor in any part of the premises at 9, Old Court House Street – save for, perhaps, a very short time before being brought home to England. In the music room at Chingri Khal, Harry would have seen it, of course, when he was at home. But over the years he was away from home far more than he was at home, even on his longest stays at Chingri Khal. I believe that the portrait was not for him, or at least not primarily for him; it must have been a present to Jennie, something to make her feel she meant a great deal to him. Perhaps it was to try to make up for some of the things which he had written in the 'sermon' letter to Dorothy. It must remain a matter for doubt as to whether those feelings towards his wife were genuine or a sham. He had had to apologise profusely to her in 1909. In 1911 he complimented her quite effusively about the children. In 1915 he had written some pretty cutting remarks about her. In 1918 in his letter to Dorothy he had given her a glowing testimonial. The arrival of the portrait must surely have been intended to reinforce that testimonial. But was it real love and affection that lay behind his actions? Or a wish to be able to eat his cake and have it, on the basis of 'how happy could I be with either if one dear charmer were not here?' Or a rather devious device to lull Jennie into a false sense of marital harmony? He was soon to become very devious indeed.

170

In the meantime, Dorothy came down from Cambridge in the summer of 1919. As she herself was to acknowledge she did not have a very brilliant result in her academic work. In those days women were not admitted to Cambridge degrees. She attained the standard of Class III in Part I of her History Tripos, and only that of a pass degree for the rest of her time. That her success was only so modest can hardly be said to have been much of a misfortune: young middle-class ladies in the years between the wars were not expected to embark upon a remunerative career once their formal education was completed, and Dorothy was by no means alone in not doing so.

That generation of young women must not be dismissed as flighty or frivolous. The realms of higher education were still only partially accessible to women, while the professions were only grudgingly opening their doors to them. At any rate until they were claimed in marriage daughters busied themselves in assisting in the running of their family home, acting as co-hostess with their mother, being concerned in good works in their locality, and enjoying the social life that was available to them. The contrast with the war years must have been very great. Gone were the long and dreadful casualty lists which had had to be scrutinised so often. Gone were the shortages of food, services and amenities of every kind. And young men were around once more; not, perhaps, in the numbers really needed to match the demand, but enough to make it understandable that much hair would be let down with the release from war time tension. Add to that the changes in fashion and available facilities – clothing, dancing, music, transport, holidays and much more – which made a great contrast to the lifestyle of the pre-war years, it is not surprising that the young women of that time were often referred to as 'the bright young things.'

Rather to her surprise Dorothy found herself to be among the brightest of them. Surprise because she regarded herself as rather plain, being, as she thought, too big boned, too tall, too long a face and with long, lank dark hair with which she could do nothing. "Phyllis was the pretty one, not me," she would say to me, "with her very fair, very curly hair, finely chiselled features and great personal charm." But despite that rather stern self-assessment Dorothy found that she attracted young men in great numbers. Like the proverbial moths to a candle they were in fairly continual attendance upon her, and, as will be seen in her own detailed descriptions later on, some were lovelorn within a surprisingly short time of making their first acquaintance with her. In truth, of course, she was much better looking than she acknowledged, especially once she had learned how to make the best of herself. Her natural intelligence, sharpened by her good education, made her an interesting companion and a good conversationalist; her abilities on the piano, as a singer, and probably most of all as a dancer, coupled with her considerable sense of fun ensured she was good company to have around and not in the least bit stuffy; while her sound common sense stopped her letting things get out of hand. Aching hearts there probably were aplenty, even at times some broken ones; but disasters, never.

As Dorothy came home from Cambridge, so, shortly afterwards, did Arthur return from his final term at Stonyhurst. That October he went up to Oxford, to Christ Church. The choice is unexplained and approaches the inexplicable. For Dorothy to have been sent to Cambridge during the war years when Oxford was so much closer to Bournemouth (the journey from the South Coast to Cambridge is still a tiresome and difficult one), and then for Arthur to go to Oxford, where none of the family, at any rate at first, would have had many, or even any, friends or acquaintances, is somewhat bizarre.

The choice had this advantage for Dorothy, namely that Oxford was near enough to her home for the occasional trip to be made there to see Arthur and to join in some aspects of the social life of the University. The latter was something which she was able to enjoy to a fair extent in Arthur's three years as an undergraduate, although it has to be acknowledged that his time there was somewhat chequered.

In his first year a friend of his was sent down for good for some unspecified offence. This man decided to give himself a mock funeral, hiring hearse, horses, mourners, and being carried recumbent in the hearse, in black morning dress, top hat, weepers, the lot, together with a pint of beer in his hand, from his college to the railway station. Arthur took part in the cortege as a drummer. Inevitably the Proctors were on the scene, the procession along The High was stopped and Arthur, probably not alone, was asked, "Are you a member of this University, Sir?" Name and college follow, and he had to report to the Censor at the House after which he was rusticated. That is, sent down for the rest of the term.

Harry's reaction to that event is not recorded. He was immensely proud of Arthur and I expect he would have regarded it on a 'boys will be boys' basis. There is equally no record of any other events in the years 1919 or 1920. Jennie maintained her open house policy at Chingri Khal. Friends local and from afar came and went in profusion. John Hickey, the friend from Convent days long before the war, met his French wife Denise there. They were married in France and made their home in Paris where he practised as a lawyer, specialising in international law. Friends of Arthur from Oxford were often visiting. Many a young swain from the locality would appear in the hope of a game of tennis during the day or of bridge in the evening, with the added attraction of possibly advancing his cause. The whole family had learned to play bridge, particularly in its then modern form of contract bridge, Dorothy becoming a particularly keen and expert player. This was a fortunate feature of her life: bridge was to play a significant role in the years to come.

In contrast to the two previous years, 1921 does provide us with some facts, but it also throws up some mysteries. Harry undoubtedly came home, leaving Calcutta towards the end of March, and was certainly in Italy by the end of April. I doubt if he could have got to England and then out to Italy in that time scale, although I suppose it is just possible. He most probably went directly to Italy. His family, with the exception of Arthur whose university term would have begun, were with him and on that basis would have met him in Italy. He refers in one of his books [1] to spending 'some months in Italy and had the good fortune to hear Toscanini's orchestra three or four times.' In fact

I do not think it could have been more than 'some weeks'.

It was certainly long enough for the four of them – Harry, Jennie, Dorothy and Phyllis – to enjoy their own equivalent of The Grand Tour. It must have been at a time when Harry was doing particularly well in his business life. He was away from India for over six months in all. He took his family to several Italian cities (Ravenna, Venice, Milan and Rome certainly, maybe others), staying at all the best hotels, and with a guide permanently attached to them for the duration. For most of the time it was a great success, partly, perhaps, due to the guide and Harry getting on so well. "It proved the truth," Dorothy used to say, "of what Jack Point says in The Yeoman of the Guard: 'T'is ever so with simple folk; a celebrated wit has but to say, "Pass the mustard" and they roar their ribs out.' Daddy had only to say, 'Good morning, Signor So-So' when he came down to breakfast, for our Italian friend to burst into laughter and exclaim, 'Oh! Mr Hobbs, you are so amusing.' But he did get us all into a very jolly mood, and the Old Man rather enjoyed what he took as a compliment."

But even so they had their moments. Dorothy recalled many aspects, the beauty of the flooded church in Ravenna, the comforts of the Danieli in Venice, the amazing waiters at the Excelsior in Rome - "there was always a waiter standing behind every chair as we came to the table, each one more handsome than the last" – but the Excelsior was the scene of a major row.

Before she left home Jennie had arranged through her parish priest for herself and her two daughters to attend a Public Audience with the Pope (at that time Benedict XV) in the Vatican. Rather unwisely she had not told Harry about it, fearing that he might make some sort of trouble. It would probably have been much better to have told him well in advance so that he could get used to the idea and its implications.

Somehow they found a reason to encourage Harry to take a stroll up the Via Veneto, and perhaps into the Borghese Gardens, at the time they had to get themselves ready. In those days women had to wear a complete black outfit, long skirts, long sleeves, veils, the lot. They hurried into their regalia after they had seen him depart into the sunshine, and assembled in the parents' room, hoping to get a taxi to the Vatican before Harry got back.

But he beat them to it. Perhaps the sunshine was just a bit too hot. He opened his bedroom door to be confronted by these three ladies all in black, their white faces – particularly white at that moment, blood having drained instantly therefrom due to the shock of exposure and the fear of the consequences – showing through the carefully arranged veils. "Who's dead?" he demanded fiercely. As Jennie began haltingly to explain and he realised that he had been the subject of some gentle subterfuge, closely connected with popish goings on, there was a not inconsiderable eruption. "I'm not having anything like this – my family are not going to make an exhibition of themselves" and much, much more. He refused to allow them to go, they had to get out of their black, and they remained in the hotel for the rest of the day. Good humour was restored next day, but they had passed a rather unhappy twelve to eighteen hours.

Probably if he had been handled in a different way all would have been well. A few caustic comments would doubtless have been made, mainly directed at the Pope, and then he would have shrugged and let them go. But if indeed his anger was mainly engendered by the lack of candour he sensed from not having been told about it in advance, then one has to say he was a fine one to talk, and, from our comfortable chairs in the twenty first century, we might even feel like calling him something of a hypocrite.

It is impossible now to know when Harry first met Miss Florence Briscoe. Nor can I say with any certainty anything about her background, where she was born, how she met Harry, nor even her age. I do not believe she can have been less than twenty years younger than he, quite possibly as much as twenty five. From about the mid 30s until his death she was perfectly well known by the family in England as someone who was very much Harry's 'right-hand woman.' It became gradually accepted by everyone that she was more than a mere personal secretary – although that may well have been her designation in the early years of her association with him. But in the early 20s none of Harry's family had the slightest inkling of her existence. Whether the truth came to Jennie (or to anyone else, for that matter) at an early stage in the affair and she kept it quiet for the sake of the family as a whole is a question for interesting speculation, although I do not believe one can now achieve any firm conclusion from the available evidence.

That evidence consists of two letters, one written in 1921, the other in 1924. With the first of those (which includes a very small separate note) there are two envelopes. Now by the time I first came to see these letters there had been many opportunities for them to be taken out of the original envelopes and placed in others, and a Scenes of Crime Officer would regard them, therefore, as being suspicious, or tainted documents. The coincidences are such, however, that I am firmly of the view that the first letter and note and the two envelopes all belong together.

The letter is captioned 'Calcutta' and is dated 'April 7th '21', and 'Thursday'. The small note is headed 'Friday. 8/4/21' and plainly was inserted with the letter. The first envelope, into which the letter and note, folded as they are, fit neatly, is addressed in typescript to 'Miss Hobbs, 26 Hatherley Grove, Bayswater. London. W. England' and in the bottom left hand corner there is simply 'H'. It has Indian stamps on it and is post marked Calcutta. The date is a little obscure. One can decipher '8 APR 2.' And '2 20 .M' This envelope, with letter and note inside it, fits equally neatly into the second envelope. This is addressed in handwriting to 'Major Hobbs V.D. Hotel Excelsior Rome.' The very clear postmark is Padd[ington] 'W.2. 1.45 PM 29 APR 21 B'. The writing is not Harry's, it has more of a female look about it, but it has, particularly in the formation of the word 'Hobbs', an appearance very like that to be found in Harry's own signatures.

The contents of the letter, closely handwritten over six quarto sides, might have been expected to have caused a terrible rumpus had it ever come to the attention of Harry's family. From commencement to signature nothing much is left to the imagination as to the true relationship between the writer and the addressee. The writing is plainly that of Miss Briscoe – we had many examples of her handwriting in later years – and Harry is equally plainly the intended recipient:

My own precious Sweetheart,

Your letter posted from Aden reached me last Monday (4th) and with it came a letter from London. I am looking forward to her letters now and would be upset were she to miss a mail. I have written her a long letter this week and will also write regularly every week to her. It is d. good of her to say she will write to me every week as she must have plenty to do. You must also thank her from us both…

…I am feeling this separation more and more every day; and am anxious about myself as I cannot put my mind to anything – however you don't understand and never will…

…I was hoping you would have news of Arthur and I so sincerely hope that he is quite well again. Don't forget to let me know if you haven't already done so. I have thought of you every minute of the day my Beloved; and wonder what you are doing every time I look at the clock. Well, I suppose you are very very happy with all those whom you love so dearly with you…

…I'm only having a peg twice a week now. Just now (6.30 p.m.) I've opened a fresh bottle; the 1st new bottle since you left and there wasn't much left in the other. Having a peg now and I feel I want you very badly…

…I don't think I have any more to tell you my own beloved Sweetheart. Will write you a long letter next week when I hope I shall not be so depressed. Do write me nice letters my darling old Sweetheart and tell me all what you are doing – I am <u>very</u> <u>very</u> miserable without you – God knows but you will never know; and I feel now – today – that if you have to leave me for all this long time again I shall have to go away. I couldn't go through it again…

…only please come back to me soon. After all you don't realise what I feel, for you have a home and someone to love there and a home here with someone also who loves you here – but me, well, I'm beginning to wish that I was dead. I don't see what I've got in the future to live for. You'll continually be going away and the other six or five months is only an existence after all.

Altho' I am doing something from early morning till night my mind is going ten thousand to the dozen. I cannot help it. What will happen to me I do not know for I am terribly depressed.

Until I write again I send you a heart burning with love for you. You'll never know how much either, and you don't care much either or you would have taken me with you.

All I wish is that I don't have to go through any more years of this – because I couldn't – not even for all this great love for you. It's killing me.

Your miserable,

Florrie

The little note, basically telling him she is going out to post, begins 'My Harry' and ends 'Much love and many millions of kisses, Your own, 2½'

The 'she' referred to in the first paragraph must have been, it seems to me, the 'Miss Hobbs of 26, Hatherley Grove, Bayswater' and so one of Harry's sisters. It cannot have been one of his daughters as they were both with him in Rome. Harry had persuaded this sister (probably Ann, to whom he was closest, and who probably was the sister in the 1914 cruise) to act as a go-between when he was away from India on his way home so that Miss Briscoe could write to him in England, or wherever he may be, without exciting comment for receiving letters from India while with his family. He had only to say "a letter from Annie" if anyone should ask and there would be no suspicion. Miss Briscoe would write to her, the 'H' would indicate that it was in reality for Harry and Ann would put it in an envelope unopened and post it to wherever she knew Harry to be.

The contents of this letter so far as set out above – the rest is domestic tittle-tattle – show not only that Miss Briscoe loved Harry, and that he loved her (or she would not be going on in that vein) but that she was realistic enough to know and, indeed to accept, that he also loved, and was loved by, his lawful family in England.

It is not really a very edifying set-up; but before one adopts too censorious an attitude it is worth remembering the very artificial lifestyle with which Harry, along with many men separated by ten thousand miles from their wives, had to contend. Married bliss for the months at home: a chaste life in an unchaste world for the rest of the year. Small wonder many fell for domestic comfort in their overseas posting, wherever it may have been.

At this early stage (although one wonders if, in fact, the inception of the affair had been the occasion for the row in 1909) Miss Briscoe's own words show that Harry had not yet fallen out of love with Jennie, still less with his children. Jennie was, however, some two years older than Harry, and so by the time he was, say, approaching seventy in the early 1930s, she would have been seventy-two. Miss Briscoe would have only been about fifty: a considerable age gap. Harry may have been impatient with Jennie for her longevity (although it was a lot less than his, as things turned out) particularly with Miss Briscoe anxious to keep him with her, and maybe exhibiting that clinging, rather cloying, attitude she shows in her letters. This could have been the precipitating factor to cause him to express such hatred for Jennie, as we shall see he did.

It is a curious twist to the relationship between Harry and Miss Briscoe, that she was a rather devout Catholic – certainly during all the time her existence was known by Dorothy, when Dorothy and she from time to time corresponded, and much later on eventually met after Harry's death. Indeed by that time Dorothy had become very grateful to Miss Briscoe for all the care she had shown for Harry: she was thoroughly devoted to him and looked after him to the very end of his life. In those later years a priest was quite often in attendance socially in her apartment or Harry's (they never outwardly shared an abode), not to proselytise him, more for Miss Briscoe's peace of mind, and Harry seemed perfectly content with that..

To return to the letter of 1921, there is an even more curious matter to contemplate: how does it come about that I am able to read it and to quote from it? That it was with all the other old family letters I looked through after Dorothy died cannot be doubted. No more than I think one could doubt that Harry received the letter in 1921 at the Hotel Excelsior in Rome when having a high old time with his family. It must have been among all the large collection of old letters found by Dorothy in 1943, having been among Jennie's collection of her most intimate memorabilia.

I find it hard to escape the conclusion that somehow or other the letter came into Jennie's possession not so very long after its receipt by Harry. He may have believed he had mislaid it or thrown it away. It is not a letter he would have needed to have kept. It contains no instructions for any purpose which he would need to remember. Unless he was as sentimental about letters written to him as Jennie obviously was and kept them all for, maybe, years (and I have nothing to indicate that that was the case) there would have been no need for a detailed search in Rome. He may have felt some anxiety for a few hours or days as to whether his mislaid letter had fallen into the 'wrong' hands. But when there were no recriminations he assumed all was well, it had been thrown out somehow and that was that.

That there were no recriminations in Rome I am sure: if there had been a confrontation about the letter it would surely have led to the most almighty row, with very likely disastrous consequences for the whole family, and Dorothy would surely have remembered it and at some time or other would have told me about it. I feel, therefore, driven to the conclusion that Jennie somehow found the letter fairly soon after Harry received it, read it, and decided, however sadly and reluctantly, the best thing to do was to do nothing. She accepted the situation as one which at least meant that she kept her husband to herself when he came home, and kept him as the father for her children. Both features may have been in jeopardy if she had taxed him with it.

It must have been a bitter blow to learn of how she was being cuckolded, but she did not waver in her love, and she accepted what she probably recognised by then as the inevitable. The letter she wisely kept in case of need in the future. I do not think that any need to use it ever arose. If she ever subsequently quietly asked Harry about it when they were alone together at Chingri Khal there is nothing now to show for it. How many other such letters she intercepted in that way I have no means of knowing; all I can say is that there is just the one more, from three years later, which was in the papers I read in 1990. How many others there may have been in 1943 is likewise beyond telling. Probably none, for in the nature of things one can hardly expect Harry to have mislaid very many such potentially incriminating documents, and, if there had been one or two more, it would hardly have been necessary to get rid of them then simply for reasons of space.

The return of the family to Chingri Khal and the rest of that year do not feature in any book or letter. However, one short document and one short sentence in a letter seven years later leads me to believe that

Dorothy very nearly got married in 1921, and I do not know to whom. If this is unsatisfactory to the reader, it will be appreciated how exceedingly unsatisfactory it is to me.

The remark in the letter was to the effect that she had had her first 'love affair' at twenty-three, eighteen months after coming down from Cambridge. Her twenty-third birthday was in November, 1920, by which time she had been down from Cambridge for nearly eighteen months. So the summer of 1921 is about the right period for all this to come to a head.

Without more that phrase in the letter might simply mean that some young man had paid court to her in a really serious manner, leading them both to believe marriage might be possible. But I think the document shows that it went even further than that. The document in question is a Certificate of Dorothy's Baptism.

When a Catholic seeks to marry in a Catholic Church it is necessary for there to be produced a Certificate of Baptism which has to be obtained from the records of the Church in which the Baptism took place. The fact of the marriage, once it has taken place, is referred back to the Church of Baptism and is recorded in the original Register. Thus the officiating priest has it confirmed that the Catholic partner has received the first and most necessary of the Sacraments, and a significant safeguard against possible bigamy is obtained.

As we have seen, Dorothy was baptised in London and so to be married in her Parish Church in Bournemouth she would inevitably need a Baptismal Certificate. It is not surprising, therefore, to find such a certificate in her effects. What is surprising is the date given as the date upon which it was issued from the records of the Church in Brook Green: 21st July, 1921. I can think of no reason, apart from the imminence of marriage, which would make a young woman go to the trouble to procure such a document. And there would be little point in seeking to obtain one until the need for it was tolerably certain.

So who was the happy young man? I wish I knew. From later letters there are a few, a very few, tiny hints. I have dim recollections of Dorothy mentioning to me some of her friends of whom she had been particularly fond. One of them was her first cousin, Jack McCormack. He was the son of Jennie's eldest sister, Mary, and was about two years older than Dorothy. He visited England in the years soon after the first war and certainly they were both fond of each other. His home was always in Australia; he was much in evidence there when Dorothy and Harry stayed there in 1926.

Another possible young man who may have been engaged, or almost engaged to Dorothy was Mick L'Estrange. He was the eldest of three brothers, all of whom were in England during this period. His family also came from Australia, and had become known to Dorothy through meeting Arthur in Oxford. They certainly came to stay at Chingri Khal in this period, and again Dorothy became fond of them all, but particularly of Mick.

Over the years Dorothy mentioned both Jack and Mick to me as being young men for whom she had had a very soft spot in her heart, and perhaps had even been a little in love with them. She never told me that she had been engaged to either of them. But then she never told me that she had been engaged to anyone before my father. If I had asked I have no reason to doubt that I should have been given the full facts. I never had any reason to ask, at least not to ask probing questions. It is one thing to have a chat for half an hour or so about the past, quite another to seek out information for the compiling of a book. So it may have been neither of these young men who was so nearly married to her. I feel that one or other of them was the most likely, partly because of the Australian connection. Each would have been returning to Australia in a fairly short timescale. The degree of rush or hurry that that would have caused, coupled with the inevitably long, indeed virtually permanent, separation from her family may well have been features to make Dorothy pause and consider whether she was not taking a decision in too much haste and with too many uncertain consequences attached. Whatever the detailed proposals may have been it all came to nothing.

And so for Dorothy, by the end of the summer of 1921, it was back to the dizzy social whirl of Bournemouth life. Harry went back to India, no doubt to a rapturous welcome from 'his miserable Florrie.' And in the event it was Phyllis who was first, by many years, to be taken to the Altar. But that is to anticipate the following year.

BOOK TWO

TRIPE
AND TROTTERS

*Dorothy in a rickshaw outside the
Station Hotel, Kuala Lumpur.*

CHAPTER 11

MORE TRAVEL AND
A WEDDING

H ARRY'S JOURNEYS to and from India were often used by
him as an opportunity to explore some part of the world
with which he was not familiar, sometimes making a
considerable detour to take him through a country which he had not
previously visited. In the year 1922, however, for the first (and, I
believe, the only) time he was actually enabled to fulfil an official, or
semi-official, commission as part of his journey home. As he put it
in his Forward to his third book, *Digressions of a Ditcher*:

> In 1922 the military career of more than two thousand officers
> serving in India was about to expire under the painless influence of
> the Axe, and as Africa was opening her arms for immigrants,
> particularly those with money, while newspapers boomed the
> continent as the finest in the world, I was asked if I would go there
> to ascertain what were the prospects for these unfortunate Soldiers
> of the King.

Whether the book achieved its desired object is not to my purpose
here. A publicity leaflet within the pages of my copy quotes some
dozen highly complimentary reviews, from the *Times Literary
Supplement* down. The table of contents gives an idea of the territory
he covered: Mombasa; Nairobi; Nakuru; Coast Ports; Durban;
Johannesburg and Cape Town. Want of time prevented his including
Southern Rhodesia. In the first line of his text he tells us that he left
Calcutta in March; typically he nowhere says when he left from Cape
Town, nor when he arrived in Southampton.

Harry's brother, Fred, some 5 years younger than he, had been
living in Cape Town, or nearby, for many years and had a wife and
two daughters. Not unnaturally Harry's arrival in that City was the

occasion for a reunion. Harry writes remarkably little about it, and what he does write leads one to doubt if it was an encounter of any length or enthusiasm:

> An unusual experience befell me in meeting in Cape Town one of my brothers, after an interval of thirty-three years. Both of us waited until all the other passengers had left the platform, before either made up his mind to ask the other if he was the man looked for. Perhaps we were both disappointed.
>
> Drawn up outside the station was a string of hansom cabs, looking for all the world as though they had stepped out of the London of twenty years ago; the cabbies were just as weather-beaten, wore as many clothes, and perhaps waited longer for fares. It did not look as if there is much money in cab-driving in Cape Town. Two mounted policemen regulated the traffic at a crossing, but with ten vehicles a minute during the busy part of the day, the men had no real need to learn their job.
>
> In the Grand Hotel in Adderley Street, I was charged 18s. 6d. a day for an excellent corner room over-looking the station; a printed notice in the room detailed the rate – an honest way of running a hotel, even if unusual. [1]

No other direct reference is made anywhere to his brother. One indirect reference occurs when Harry is commenting on service in Cape Town:

> The hotel workers are mainly of Madrassi descent; they speak good English, wear a mongrel sort of Indian costume, and quite familiarly wish you "Good morning." An Indian army man rebuked one of them for not saying "Sir," so that particular khitmatgar cut him dead afterwards. However they are more civil and certainly more efficient than the white waitresses in one of the other hotels, who appeared to size you up after discussing you and your guests, and, if you do not meet with their approval, they let you know it. I took two young nieces out to lunch at a fashionable hotel a little out of town, and the sight of a man old enough to know better, laughing cheerfully with two good looking girls, was more than the Puritanical feelings of the waitresses could endure. Half way through the meal, I found two pungent cheeses on the table and requests for their removal ignored, but the narrow mindedness of the colonial girls consoled them for

any other drawbacks appertaining to discourtesy. Of course such a thing might happen in England, so perhaps it is possible that I was unlucky in striking an unusually bad patch. [2]

It follows that there must have been some socialising, but we are told no more about it than that – little more than an aside. While it must be accepted that his purpose in writing was not to give his readers family news, yet one might have thought that brother Fred could have been a source of useful information for his readers. Nothing about Fred's work, where he lived, how he had made his way in life, education for his children, and so many other matters relevant for consideration by an ex-officer contemplating moving to Africa. An insight into the family life of an English immigrant could have given an insiders viewpoint to put alongside Harry's own, which was necessarily that of an outsider. But he seems to have gone straight to a hotel and from all one can tell he never stayed with Fred and had little contact with him. Thirty-three years before takes one back to 1889, that is to say the year of Harry's first, and not very satisfactory, leave home from India. One would have thought they could have sat down and talked for a week without stopping. But there is nothing to show that they had anything much to say to each other.

At the end of his African tour Harry returned home from Cape Town on the *Windsor Castle* - 'a fine new ship of nearly 19,000 tons, which was on her first homeward voyage.' [3] In his final chapter – 'Homeward Bound' – of *Digressions of a Ditcher* Harry gives quite a detailed account of the voyage home, making an interesting comparison between the Cape route, to and from South Africa, and the P&O route to and from the Far East both as between the customs on board and as between the type of passenger travelling. There is far too much to reproduce in these pages. 'The most noticeable difference was the want of sociability' [4], the Union Castle ship being the unsociable one. But they did have a Royal on board, and she gets Harry's highest accolade:

Princess Arthur of Connaught was on board, and all through the voyage devoted herself to serving the passengers by attending every function in 1st, 2nd and 3rd saloons; concerts, sports, dances, presentation of prizes, when some hundreds of pounds worth were distributed; while, in addition, her Royal Highness sat through the daily auction sweeps. By a long way, the Princess was the hardest social worker I have ever seen on board a ship. [5]

One exchange with a fellow passenger which Harry records is worth repeating since it gives some insight into his own attitude towards Indians and to their relationship with the English (as Harry would usually call them: today one would have to say 'the British.')

> An elderly man in a sudden and belated turn of friendliness asked several questions about India and Gandhi in particular. I regretted that I had not been favoured with an opportunity of meeting that gentleman.
>
> "I knew him quite well," he said, "for I lived in the same town with him when I first went to the Colony. He was quite a nice chap in those days, but the colonials rubbed him up the wrong way, and he grew to hate them. When he found he could do little or nothing against us he went back to India. We made him, and now you people have to put up with him. I always laugh when I see the mess you're in. Damned funny, I call it!"
>
> Of course I had to say something, so after, "I suppose you think you are very clever?" I began to give my opinion.
>
> "I'll guarantee we can do more with Gandhi than you South Africans. Gandhi knows that the Sahib isn't a bad fellow, and you can take it from me that in spite of the lies told about us the Indian would always work for a Britisher in preference to his own countrymen, for the Englishman treats the Indian far better than the Indian does, and far better than the Englishman in England treats the Englishman."
>
> "May be!" was all I could get out of him. [6]

In ten to fifteen years time Harry was to have some very decided views on Gandhi. He may not have stuck to his belief that "we can do more with Gandhi," although I have not found any correction to this passage in his later works.

It took, he writes, thirteen days to reach Madeira and his description of his 1922 visit gives him the occasion to reminisce about his 1914 visit (see Chapter 8 page 153) in rather different circumstances. Whereas on that occasion his ultimate landfall was

Liverpool, on this it was to be Southampton, very much closer to Bournemouth, of course, but rather atypically he seems not to have been met at the quayside by any family members. Perhaps the early hour of arrival made for agreement for him to get the train.

He concludes his book with a rare personal insight into his homecoming and his feelings for his native land. If this does represent his genuine feelings at that time, it makes it all the more necessary to try to find a credible explanation for the fact that, in only a little over 10 years, he was virtually to turn his back on his homeland for good.

Southampton Water to a home coming Englishman is, on a bright summer's day, a delightful picture...

To arrive in Southampton Water at midnight, to see the lights all around and realise that you are home again was very comforting, for one does not love England the less for having passed years abroad. All of us look forward to a return Home as the golden prospect of life and a reward for labour, and Southampton adds to this feeling, for it is from the sea a beautiful sight. In the morning, the ease with which the baggage of hundreds of 1st, 2nd, 3rd and 4th class passengers was handled made you appreciate dear old England all the more, the 4th class passengers being kept to the last so that the wealthy ones could more easily get into the Pullman cars inside the dock gates.

However, after what one sees in various parts of the world, one must admit that working folk receive more consideration in England than they get anywhere, even in the more democratic colonies where poor people find they have to deal with autocrats in corduroys.

Driving to Southampton West Station [now Southampton Central] through the clean and peaceful streets, I was hailed by a Calcutta man in a small car who looked remarkably well in spite of having been eighteen months looking vainly for a billet. He said he had gone through two of life's greatest experiences – Love and War – and thought he might as well try the third – Destitution – so he drove up in his car and took his place in the queue of out-of-works who were seeking unemployment dole. "Would you believe it," he explained, "I've driven the dear little bus twenty eight thousand miles without an accident, and those blighters actually broke the windscreen. Why, they wouldn't even give me a chance to explain that I was perfectly willing to go on strike as soon as I got a job."

Of course we agreed it was perfectly shocking – 'red 'ot!' – and went on our way

While waiting for the train I met a Major of British Infantry with a number of men. "My word!" I said, "I heard you were killed in Gallipoli?" The last time we met was on the Calcutta Maidan, when his battalion had been, on account of their good conduct (that is what they told the men), specially selected for active service; and their exemplary character permitted them to form a unit of the immortal 29th Division. My friend was taking a party from the Holy Land for demobilisation and expected to be gazetted out himself. Comparing our watches, we decided there was time to celebrate our meeting. The young lady behind the bar said she could only offer us mineral waters.

"No, thank you! We're not thirsty! We merely wanted drinks," and that was the welcome home we two travellers received. There was the usual crowd of idle folks with vacant faces on the platform seats: barrow loads of strawberries wafted their fragrance around, porters were busy with milk cans, everything was delightfully solid and peaceful, and going home through the New Forest the recollections of those who were crazed about climate in Africa made one ponder. There was but one conclusion: – dear old England takes some beating after all. [7]

Harry's return home that year was particularly important. It was very necessary for him to be at Chingri Khal for the wedding of his younger daughter. It came as a surprise to no one when Phyllis had become engaged to her distant cousin Jimmy Breaks. He was the second son of that cousin of Harry's, Captain Jack Breaks, whose home had been in Bournemouth before the Hobbs family came to the town. Jack Breaks had been a Captain in the Merchant Navy. The two eldest of his three sons, Horton and James (Jimmy), both became professional seamen in the Royal Navy in which both had distinguished careers, each of them attaining Flag Rank in due time.

Living, as the two families did, only a couple of miles or so apart there was a good deal of coming and going, especially by the young, between the two homes. It had been obvious for many months, probably for some years that Jimmy and Phyllis were falling in love with each other. She was seven years younger than he, and inevitably during the four years of the war, at the outbreak of which she was only twelve years old, opportunities for them to meet were somewhat restricted. Jimmy had many seagoing appointments – he was serving on *HMS Warspite* at the Battle of Jutland – and Phyllis was at school. The school being the Convent of the Cross, just across the road from the Breaks family home, put Phyllis in a good position to visit when Jimmy was there on leave, but inevitably opportunities for them to meet were very limited until the war came to an end.

By 1919 Phyllis had turned sixteen and was fast growing up. The two families were on excellent terms with each other, good friends in every sense, but it was Phyllis and Jim who were to make the match; he by this time being Lieutenant James Breaks, RN. And so it was that on 18th August, 1922, they were married at the Church of the Sacred Heart on Richmond Hill in central Bournemouth. It was not the Catholic Church nearest to Chingri Khal: that was the Annunciation, only half a mile away, and a much more interesting (and some would say more beautiful) building than the Sacred Heart, having been designed by Sir Giles Gilbert Scott, the first Church he designed after Liverpool Cathedral. However the smaller Church of the Annunciation was only what is called a Chapel of Ease, served (by the Jesuits in those days) from the Sacred Heart and at that time was not licensed for marriages.

Probably the bigger Church would have been preferred in any event, for Harry was not one for doing things by halves, and the wedding of his younger daughter, the first wedding in the family, was not something to be passed over lightly. It was a big occasion, as the local paper's account makes clear. Headlining it as 'Fashionable Bournemouth Wedding' it says 'Great interest was evinced in a very pretty and fashionable wedding…' and continues to give detailed descriptions of the dresses and flowers worn and carried by the Bride, the Bridesmaid (Dorothy) and the Mother of the Bride; of the celebrants, the performers, the music and the rest. It continues 'A reception was afterwards given at the home of the bride's parents, when a large number of guests attended. The presents were numerous and costly, and came from all parts of the world, Major

Hobbs having travelled very extensively and having friends in all quarters of the globe.'

It was to prove a very happy marriage. Their first child, a daughter, was born the following year. Phyllis named her Dorothy Mary after the new baby's Aunt: a pretty compliment reflecting the close friendship as well as love that there was in those days between the two sisters. The two names were always together. 'Dorothy' on its own referred to Dorothy Hobbs. However, childish nicknames sometimes stick. Dorothy Mary's first stumbling attempts to pronounce her own name achieved, so it was thought, nothing closer than 'Toffee May.' This soon became contracted to 'Toff,' and 'Toff' she remained for the rest of her life, although to Dorothy, at least half the times she needed to use her name, still used the original Dorothy Mary. I think she was the only person to do so.

For the greater part of the next two decades the Breaks family were to make their home at Chingri Khal. Much depended, inevitably, on where Jimmy was stationed. When at Malta, which he was for two periods, the family lived there. When based in Portsmouth as happened from time to time, he took a house in that area. But for most of the 20s, 30s and early 40s they lived at Chingri Khal. It made obvious good sense. Arthur and Dorothy, in the natural order of things, were likely to be leaving Chingri Khal in a few years – as, indeed, proved to be the case. The house with its large garden would have been far more than Jennie would have needed, or even wanted, for herself on her own. At the same time it was an obvious family asset which it was highly desirable to keep intact. With the new young family in residence there so often and for such long periods it was able to become the same centre for social gatherings for the growing Breaks family that it had been for the growing Hobbs family a generation before. And so, in the course of a few years, when I was born and grew up in my home, only a couple of miles away in the centre of Bournemouth, Chingri Khal was still there, the family focal point with its ever open, hospitable door, and its large, enticing garden, warmed by Jennie's benevolent presence. It was indeed a wonderful place for children, and what good fortune for me to be able to share in it as long as it remained.

The third Chingri Khal in about 1926
looking across the "back" lawn to the music room –
the billiards room is to the right, beyond
and above the conservatory.

"Are you a member of this university, sir?"
Arthur (centre, in profile, with drum) having his name and
college taken by a Proctor (wearing mortar board)
Bullers (wearing bowlers) stand by.
The horse-drawn hearse waits behind.
About 1920.

CHAPTER 12

A BULLFIGHT AND A
POLITICAL FIGHT

WITH THE BIRTH of his first grandchild occurring early in the summer of 1923, it might have been expected that Harry would have been certain to have returned home that year. There is, however, nothing in any writings which are available to me today to indicate whether he did or did not do so. Perhaps any visit was relatively uneventful.

There are, however, three sources of information regarding the following year, 1924. The first came about in somewhat unusual circumstances. It will be recalled that Arthur went up to Oxford in the autumn of 1919. In the normal course of events he would have taken his Final Examinations in the Trinity Term (Summer Term) of 1922. This may have been put off for a year on account of his rustication after the part he played in the mock funeral. Whenever he did sit his examinations, unfortunately he ploughed them rather badly.

His parents did all they could to persuade the University to allow him to sit them a second time. However they were up against a difficulty. The House was not prepared to have him back. Whether on account of his lack of application to his studies and poor academic performance, or because of his behaviour generally in the previous three or four years is not now revealed. Without a College to welcome him back they were up against something of an impasse.

The solution which was reached, with the consent of the University Authorities, was for Arthur to be permitted to continue to attend lectures and to receive private tuition, provided he lived in the City of Oxford in a house in which there was adult supervision. Whether it was an express requirement that that should be parental supervision is not altogether clear, but that was certainly the effect. The consequence was that Jennie had to rent a house in Oxford for the duration of the

University terms, or just a little longer, to provide a base for Arthur.

So it came about that, when Harry invited the family to join him in Morocco and Spain on his way home in 1924 (or, just possibly, to go there with him after getting home), there was only one of them who could take him up on his offer. Arthur was in Oxford studying; Jennie was there, too, chaperoning him; Phyllis had a one-year-old to look after; and that left Dorothy free to be with her father in those exotic parts.

The overall consequence, therefore, of Arthur's academic problems was that the occasion was presented to Dorothy for writing to her mother describing her experiences in Africa and Europe. This she did with considerable clarity and effect, although now we only have three letters surviving, all addressed to Jennie at 22, Bardwell Road, Oxford. There must have been several more. I feel sure Jennie would have kept them all: the rest must have been destroyed in 1943.

The first is from Morocco:

> Hotel Transatlantique   [Fez]
> Tuesday 13th May, 1924
>
> My darling Mother,
>   So sorry I couldn't write yesterday. We had rather a trying journey from half past six in the morning till about two, without a stop except when the engine broke down owing to a choked feed. It was hot too – six people inside a limousine car and three in front including the chauffeur. Then when we arrived at the hotel we found hat they hadn't a room, but inwardly we were devoutly thankful as it was a filthy hole. We are very comfortable here, which is a first class hotel and there are lovely eats. Then I got rather a headache and...after we...had dinner...it was time to go to bed.
>   Daddy is very thrilled. There is some military mission going round – generals and colonels of every nation being shown Morocco I suppose – and the French General in charge entertains them at this hotel. I don't know how long they will be here, only a few days I suppose, but we were lucky to time our visit so well. We don't know any of them but they are so interesting to watch and beautiful to look upon.
>   Fez is by far the most interesting town we have visited so far. It is very hilly and the old Arab town is kept entirely separate from the

European part. This hotel is an exception, being adjoining the old walls. The Arab town is very old and very hilly and there is running water everywhere. The whole place is full of springs and in the patio of every native house there is a fountain, in the little narrow streets you can hear them all the time. There are many things of interest and beauty to be seen. However (and this applies to every part of Morocco that I have seen) the dirt and smells are bad enough; not as bad as I had expected, but often overpowering, but it is the disease which sickens me so. Most of the children run about bare headed and most of them have some kind of eczema. Then the next most common disease is of the eyes; then there is a good sprinkling of sores and deformities etc. out of which some hope to make a living.

It is very hot and one gets sticky just sitting still in the shade. Oh, one thing I have noticed is that ever so many of the Moors or Arabs are fair like Englishmen with ordinary blue eyes. One scarcely sees the girls. There are a few women in the streets closely veiled but I have never seen a blue eyed one. And even the children playing about are all boys – they tell me the little girls are put to work as soon as possible – and I suppose the better class ones are never let out.

…There is no fruit. Hitherto we have had oranges and bananas but now we've only oranges.

How is the baby? Jim? Arthur? My love to you all,

Dorothy

It would have been interesting to learn rather more about the military mission, not to mention any other places they visited in Morocco. There was also evidently at least one night spent at Gibraltar which could have provided more material for her views, and probably Harry's, on that ancient British possession. As it is we turn to Spain from where Dorothy, staying at the Hotel Casino Alhambra Palace, writes on 24th May:

The journey yesterday wasn't a bit uncomfortable, or rather worrying, because it was really too hot to be comfortable. We got up at 5.30 and crossed the bay on an ideal morning. We had no trouble at the customs and a carriage to ourselves until 3.25 when we had to change trains. Then we got on to a train with a Spaniard and a man and his wife got in after us – he was a Russian and she was a German American. They were very nice and rather interesting. The trains were slow especially the first one, but really extraordinarily clean,

197

with an absolutely clean towel and a bit of soap in the wash place! And the country was exquisite. We were travelling all day and I have never seen such a stretch of such continuously lovely country. If anything it seemed to grow more beautiful as we approached Granada, for we could see the snow covered Sierra Nevada in the background. Most of the arable land was under barley, olive trees or vines. There were one or two little woods and a fair number of hayfields just covered with all different coloured flowers. We passed through a mountain range with rivers and a few falls – some parts being very bleak with rugged granite peaks jutting out against the blue sky and others kinder and softer with wooded gorges and a river running between. The permanent way had few cuttings and considering the kind of country, few tunnels, so you can imagine what it was like. We went a most roundabout course following mostly the contours and our engine laboured up the hills and then with a whistle of delight ran down them again. The difference was quite perceptible.

In Gibraltar we had had our breakfast at about 6.15, and in the train we stopped for about a quarter of an hour to snatch a bit of lunch. In spite of it being such a little town we got a most excellent meal but had scarcely had time to do more than taste what was put in front of us. We arrived here and by the time we got our rooms etc. we sat down to dinner at 9.30. We had a lovely meal and at last I have come across a place where there is an abundance and variety of fruit. Apricots, cherries and strawberries (though the latter are supposed to be dangerous) and, of course, oranges. They are very fond, too, of dried fruit and have beautiful raisins and figs. The bread is peculiar but very good.

This hotel is really topping...I have a very nice clean room. Granada is at our feet. I could scarcely tear myself away from the window, looking at the lights all twinkling down below and feeling the cool, sweet breeze that comes from the mountains, and this mind you in spite of a very trying and long day.

At the last moment I was afraid of leaving a British Possession. I think the filth of Morocco must have made a greater impression than I had thought. Then I was afraid of the language (but now I see that I will overcome that fairly soon) and then I think the atmosphere of Gib is a little oppressive – one feels slack and lazy there. Now that I've arrived here and got away from everything I'm too pleased for words. I have such a lovely view from my room and I think that makes up for anything. This is a beautiful place although there are few people staying at present, and there is a happy, bracing atmosphere about everybody…

The following day Dorothy went to her first (and, I believe, her only) bullfight. It obviously made a great impression upon her. She wrote about it to her mother on 26th May:

The bullfight yesterday afternoon was most thrilling and I enjoyed parts of it immensely. There were six bulls, young ones of about 2½ years old, as this was not a big show, they're saving their best for Corpus Christi which is the great time in Granada. Well it was due to begin at 5.30 but was only nearly an hour late. However it was most interesting watching the crowd come in and the various vendors of drinks etc. wandering around among the people. The orange sellers were in the arena and the skill and grace with which they threw their fruit to their customers was amazing. The crowd itself too was most amusing, though Granada being half empty and the absence of horses kept the better class of people away. I saw no gorgeous mantillas or shawls but nearly all the poorer class women wear cheap large celluloid combs and 'mantillas' (like the square hat veils we buy in England) over them and the effect is awfully pretty.

Well, we had a sort of band there too that played at intervals and quite well at that, and then eventually four trumpets rang out and the orange sellers and the people who were tidying up left the arena post haste while two gents dressed in black velvet with short capes of the same material and black hat with multicoloured feathers in them came galloping in on two fine chestnut horses. They circled round and doffed heir hats to the President and generally did their parlour tricks and galloped off with the key of the bulls which had been thrown down to them.

Then the toreadors came in, in the usual fancy dress costume, but somehow it looks exactly right in the arena. Well, they go off to the side, the bugles blow, a door is opened and in rushes a bull and generally he rushes at one of the capes which the toreadors are holding. The bull almost always charges at the cape so that if it is held at one side the toreador remains unharmed. This part was really quite thrilling and not the slightest bit disgusting. I got excited like I do at the pictures. I was at the corner of a box, some Spanish people were on my left, and our young Russian friend on my right. I think my exclamations and excitement caused them more amusement than the show – at least at the beginning. Well, they play with the bull like this for some time and the bugles blow again.

This time it is for the banderillero to perform. He has two sticks covered with gaudy coloured papers and with a barb at the end. The object is to get the bull to rush at them quickly, to step to one side and to put these on his neck, if possible one each side of his spine. Yesterday the banderilleros weren't up to much, except one – but more of him later. There was another, however, a very brave man but with little skill (and you know how nerve racking it is to watch anyone like that) he fell near the partition and the bull was on him like a sheet of greased lightning. However the partition saved him from all but a wound in his arm and the others all dragged the bull off by his tail. Well, this part certainly is cruel. The barbs remain in, of course, and become covered with blood but somehow it doesn't look very real – beyond a few patches of red there is nothing horrible to see – and the skill and nerve and eye that are required are wonderful.

As you can imagine by this time the animal isn't in any too sweet a mood though one of them yesterday got fed up at this stage and trotted off to the door out of which he had come. Poor thing! Though with the shouting and the capes waving at him he soon got annoyed again.

The bugles again ring out and the matador goes towards the President's box and asks permission to kill. He takes a sword and a cape of bright red and plays with the bull. One man – I mentioned before – was wonderful. He scarcely moved and yet the bull was always on him. He was extraordinarily lithe and graceful as if he were made of steel springs, and I should imagine that one had to be so. The others were not exactly clumsy but they were not graceful. Neither were they any good. After having played with the bull for some minutes the matador decides to kill.

The bull, knowing perhaps of his certain doom, stands facing him motionless, while the crowd which hitherto has been noisy enough holds its breath like one man, while each pair of eyes watches critically both man and beast. The matador points the sword at the bull and then raises it slowly till the hilt is level with his own eye. For a second he takes careful aim, then lightly rushes and plunges it into the unfortunate animal just between the shoulder blades. If the aim is good the bull dies in about three minutes but he is generally fighting to the last.

Yesterday for my first bull the aim was a bit too good. I had been thrilled and terrified at first with the ordinary flag wagging, then horrified by the banderilleros and then when the sword had been plunged in up to its hilt and the bull coughed up pints of blood I thought I was going to be sick and faint. However I did neither and the bull died in about a minute, its heart having been pierced. With all the others there was much less blood. Then everyone claps or cheers if it has been a good show. Four sprightly mules gallop in and charge out dragging the dead 'toro', and in a few minutes it starts all over again with a fresh victim.

One bull yesterday was a demon and jumped the parapet three or four times to the great delight of the people, and one matador (the one I have spoken about) was splendid. He comes from Malaga and I shouldn't be surprised if he became famous some day. The people stood up and cheered him and when the show was over they carried him out shoulder high.

So that yesterday I saw four rare things (1) no horses at a bull fight (2) a banderillero injured (3) a bull jumping the parapet and (4) a matador carried out in triumphal procession.

...This morning we went over the Alhambra again and saw some more exquisite examples of Moorish architecture...and then our guide took us to his house. His wife and family apparently make lace and Daddy bought an exquisite mantilla at 300 pts, that's between £9 and £10. I'm so thrilled and surprised. It is an appliqué lace, black silk net with all different flowers embroidered over it in coloured silk. I have never seen anything like it except about here. It is rather loud, but it would look exquisite on a plain evening dress, and apparently that rather fine lace is the kind they make around here (Andalusia.)

All my love to you   from   Dorothy

It is pleasant to be able to record that the 'mantilla' which Harry gave to Dorothy on that occasion is still in the family. It is not what I, in my ignorance, would have thought of as a mantilla, being some fifty inches square with a twenty inch or so border of lace and tassel all round. I do not recall Dorothy wearing it: I expect she did in the years immediately after being given it. Today we keep it more as a memento and an antique.

Harry eschewed any suggestion that he was a politician. As he turned more and more to journalism, having given up public music making, he found many opportunities to put in his oar into political waters – political in the widest sense. In one chapter of his book *Talkeetalkeewallahs and Others*, an uneven collection of essays on a variety of topics published in 1938, he seeks to explain himself:

> In the ordinary acceptance of the term I am not a politician, differing, to this extent, that I see no reason to apologise to enemies of my country for being English. Current events, as well as British-Indian History, have always interested me, and often helped when I attacked those…pillars of finance, the 'Knights of the Golden Fleece', who plunder shareholders on the one hand and pillage them on the other – those philanthropists whose one aim in life is to put the silver lining of the other man's cloud into their own pockets. Making immense fortunes in many cases – more than their upbringing will ever permit them to spend – they have managed to obtain such a hold of their confederates in business that none dare open his mouth to protest when they know the Golden Fleecers were out to betray their political and commercial privileges. Unfortunately they have been more successful with the throats and pockets of their fellow countrymen than I have been in checking them. [1]

With this preliminary explanation he goes on to recount his early bag-throwing incident quoted in Chapter 1 (page 12). We have seen how, in 1922, he had expressed confidence that the English in India could, in effect, mould Gandhi to their satisfaction (Chapter 11, page 188), a 'guarantee' which, by the outbreak of the Second World War, I doubt if he felt had been honoured. By 1924 certainly (and ever thereafter) one of his *bêtes noires* was the activity of those of his own countrymen and women who denigrated – falsely as he would maintain – the work of the British Raj in India. If he was around when that was going on it could, and often did, provoke the mature equivalent of the bag of flour.

One such rumpus occurred in Oxford at what must have been fairly soon after his return to England from Spain. Trinity Term at the University may have been in its last week, or it may have just finished. The house in Oxford was available to him, and he kept his eyes open.

In 1924 the City of Oxford was plastered with placards advertising a meeting at the Town Hall where Mrs. Annie Besant and Srinivasa Sastri (an Indian 'Moderate' and, I believe, a bit of a Christian) were to speak. S.S. is a wonderful talker. Words simply squirt out of him; he talks so much and gets so far, that he can seldom find his way back to where he started. His best efforts begin with a flash and end in smoke. It is (rather unkindly) said that, wherever he goes, all the donkeys go lame – he's talked the hind legs off them.

To those unfamiliar with Indian politics, the difference between the 'Moderates' and the others is, they are all the same.

Some 800 people were seated when I walked in. Sastri, one time of the Y.M.C.A. (a connection few politicians brag about, mostly, I expect, they know too much about it), nodded approval while Mrs. Besant let herself go.

The gullibles present were told that disease in India was rampant. There were no hospitals. Millions were dying. The Indian Government was the vilest and most callous in the world. Famine-stricken wretches, women and children, clamouring for food were mercilessly clubbed and bayoneted by British soldiers. Quoting Gandhi and C.R. Das they warned the audience something to the effect that if this didn't stop British soldiers would be hurt, obviously alarming many of the people there.

Long residence in India, and intimate association with the people had taught Mrs. Besant (if she didn't know it before) that a half-and-half lie convinces nobody. But a real jump into the marvellous fixes somebody and a believer is always a broadcaster.

Up to then it had never occurred to me that anti-British propaganda could take such a shape or that people in England could believe such palpable silliness. When I queried some of the remarks, Englishwomen seated nearby expressed strong disapproval.

As Mrs Besant went on, out-doing the better half of Ananias, I could bear it no longer. Standing on a chair I shouted, "I have never heard such a pack of lies in my life. Do you believe that your sons, brothers and fellow countrymen, as soon as they set foot in India, turn into a lot of bloodthirsty brutes? As for that fellow Sastri!" Well, I won't say what I said about him. We had met previously…and as he doesn't belong to any warlike caste – rather the other way – he lost little time in pushing Mrs. Besant to the wings, and the pair made themselves scarce.

While I was denouncing that precious couple in unmeasured terms, the scores of Indians present made a rush. Ronald Raymond, an Australian, and a full back of the 'Varsity rugger team, shouted to me to go on. He and his friends kept the ring and I talked until the lights were turned out and the police cleared the hall.

After that I went to London. On my return a week later I found Oxford placarded with posters announcing that I was to speak at a meeting to be held in the Town Hall Assembly Room, to traverse the statements of the Rt. Hon Srinivasa Sastri and Mrs. Annie Besant, with Sir Patrick Agnew in the chair.

There was nothing for it but to carry on.

One Indian only turned up at my meeting. Raymond paid all expenses and I had difficulty in persuading him to let me pay for the hire of the hall...

After that I was advised by some members of the Indian Civil Service to ask Lord Olivier, the Labour Secretary of State for India, for an interview, and in a few days I received a letter from him making an appointment.

Most carefully preparing what I had to say I spent over half an hour with that nobleman who said I was the most interesting man he had talked to about India. According to India Office procedure he had refused to see any officials who really knew the country and the people so, as far as that went, he was probably right. But as he did not appear to know the difference between C.R. Das and Gandhi, I was unable to return the compliment. Neither was I able to attend the garden party to which he invited me.

...To hark back to the meeting at Oxford. After having spent forty years in India, proud of my country and happy in my associations with the people, it struck a queer note to find English men and women only too anxious to believe any foul statements made with the object of injuring England. But the belief in the ingrained brutality of their own people seems to be a feature of English suburbanism. They, judging by themselves, cannot believe that long service in the East brings, with experience, infinite toleration and sympathy. [2]

No doubt the family returned to Chingri Khal after these Oxford excitements. Unfortunately Arthur, who had sat his Finals again that term, still did not make the grade, but he did well enough to be permitted, under the same conditions, to sit a re-take in the December.

The problems relating to Arthur's education were not the only ones confronting Harry and Jennie after they had got back to Bournemouth. A letter came from Miss Briscoe. At this time she was alive and ill and just as miserable. This, the second of the two letters from her which survive from these early years, is dated June 20th 1924. It is written simply from 'Bombay', without giving any indication as to why she was there. Obviously it was not because she had been seeing Harry off: he would have left in early April to be in Morocco in mid May. Perhaps she went there for medical advice – she certainly got some while there.

The letter is written on quite different paper from the 1921 letter, and there is no accompanying envelope of any sort. Thus it is not possible to speculate on the manner in which it was despatched. It was certainly in among Jennie's letters when I first examined them, along with the first one. It poses the same questions that arose with that first one, in an almost more acute form. Omitting the domestic trivia and the full details (graphically provided) of her ill health one can see how no reader, intended or unintended, could have any doubt about her relationship with Harry.

> My own precious beloved sweetheart,
>   At a moment when I needed every ounce of affection and every word of comfort from you, your letters were given to me. The Dr. hadn't crossed the doorstep to go away – after telling me that he diagnoses gallstones…
>   Your letter of May 24 saved my life. My darling old sweetheart and I kiss you many many millions of times for it and send all my love.
>   I've been very unhappy and miserable since you've been away. Every day and all day my thoughts are of and for you – and I simply cannot get used to these dreadful separations. When I was younger I didn't mind it so much and found plenty of work to distract me – it's

different now and I can't. If only you knew how dearly I love you my Beloved you wouldn't give me any heartache. I know you love me very very dearly but I want your best love and the first – and I'm selfish about this and don't want to share your heart or your love with anybody. I only want you and only live for all the love can give me and to be able to look after you. I would do anything for you my Beloved old darling, oh surely you know how very dearly I love you...

...The time is half way through as I'm expecting you back by end of October – however if you are later I won't be angry my Beloved – only do take as much rest as you can. All this time I felt I didn't want to go home again as had you not been coming back alone I would have returned with a heart of lead – as I'd firmly made up m mind to sell off. The blow would have been too hard for me to bear – Now I am happy and will look forward every day to your return. I kiss you a million million of times for your very beautiful letter...

Now, there is little remaining for me to tell you my darling old Sweetheart. I've been writing this all the morning so will close now sending with this all my love – very many millions of kisses from Sweep [her, or their, dog] and hope that you are quite quite well.

Another heart full of love and a big kiss from
Your very own
2½

It seems to me inescapable that Jennie, who must have had this letter in her possession at the time of her death, got hold of it not so very long after it had been received by Harry. And for the same reasons as advanced in relation to the 1921 letter she did not confront Harry with it. How she was able to keep the knowledge of this persistent, and really rather outrageous infidelity to herself is hard to understand. It must have caused her a lot of anguish. Here was this much younger woman complaining bitterly that Harry was not putting her first, before his lawful wife and three children, and she resents his returning to his English home to be with them. Her reference to being better able to cope 'when I was younger' may indicate she was the cause of the row in 1909.

Harry did return to India on his own as she hoped he would do. However Miss Biscoe did have to share him at about the turn of the year with Phyllis who, together with Dorothy Mary (not yet called Toff,) was staying with her father. It is not possible to know the length of that visit. All one can say with certainty is that Phyllis had left by 27th January, 1925. Probably not long enough to be much of a problem for Miss Briscoe. But in due course arrangements were made for the end of that year which could hardly have been much to her liking.

CHAPTER 13

DOROTHY'S JOURNEY
(1)
FROM BOURNEMOUTH
TO CALCUTTA

THE EARLIEST SURVIVING letters written by Harry to his old friend Lt Colonel James Wyness, by this time living in retirement with his wife at Bletchley, date from 1925. There are four in that year, written in January, February, April and June. They are by no means solely concerned with family matters, but they are a source of some information about Harry's family that is not available from anywhere else.

We learn that Harry believes he has been badly treated by the newspaper which commissioned his African venture, leading him to '…be fed up with the whole thing. I gave up music because I considered myself to be a twenty-five bob a week musician; now I wonder if I am more than that as a journalist.'

Arthur 'has settled down, got his BA and commission in the Loyal Regiment with 2½ years seniority. On top of it he has knocked down an 8 year old boy, fractured his skull and broken his thigh, but I believe it wasn't Arthur's fault.' Indeed, no proceedings were ever taken against Arthur, even though the unfortunate child died. Jennie was in the car with Arthur, together with at least one other adult and a very young friend of the family, Joan King (now Mrs Joan Scott.) Despite being not quite five years old at the time she still recalls the tragedy. It seems the poor boy ran out in front of the car

Harry's letter to Col Wyness, dated 25th February, 1925 gives us a little – only a very little – information about a family visit and the start of his own brushes with the European Association:

My daughter and her beautiful baby went about on January 27 for Madras, Colombo and Tuticorin; I ought to have heard within the last four days but they haven't written. Arthur's appointment to the Loyal Regiment appeared in the London Gazette of January 30 so he is to get down to it. Having excellent references from Colonel Dawnay he has a good start; his Colonel is Walter P.H. Hill, late Royal Fusiliers. I hope he is a martinet to wheel Arthur into line...

I have interested myself in the European Association and the older I grow the more suspicious I become of the little bunch working it. In one of my comments I told them I felt like playing in a game where the cards were shuffled downstairs, and on top of it all they have been just about the greatest lot of chumps possible to invent or imagine. Needless to say I rubbed it in when the matter was brought to me and they felt mighty sick of themselves. It is too long to write but I am filing it for future reference.

Harry goes on to refer to 'learning more about the navy than ever' so it seems probable that Jimmy was out there as well, perhaps on a naval posting. There are no surviving letters home relating to this period.

In March Harry tells Colonel Wyness that he has decided not to return to England in 1925. His manager, Affleck, wanted to do so and he felt it unwise for both to be absent. He was not looking forward to the hot season out there, but he consoled himself with the fact that his health was good and he would be able to cope. No doubt much to her delight, Miss Briscoe was there to help him cope, although it is not clear whether she accompanied him to Darjeeling where he spent some time in The Club 'for a change.'

Even as late as the last letter of 15th June there is no mention of any proposal that Dorothy should come to India that winter. It was plainly Dorothy's turn to see once again the Country which she would have remembered from the time when she was nearly eight and younger. Phyllis had been there in 1924 to 1925, and Arthur was now subject to military discipline and so not in a position to take leave of the sort of length which would be needed.

Whether the whole project was at her request or at Harry's invitation I have no means of knowing. There are no surviving letters to Colonel Wyness between June, 1925 and September, 1926 – a pity, for there must have been some which would surely have enlightened us about all this. All that is certain is that it was decided that Dorothy would go out to Calcutta for Christmas with Harry in 1925, and come home with him in 1926.

During the summer and early autumn of 1925 the arrangements must have been made. One can imagine the state of excitement, even panic, that there was at Chingri Khal as the day of departure drew near. This was not for just a few weeks. Even on the original understanding it would be several months that she would be away – it proved to be longer in the event – and Dorothy may have felt many a passing doubt as to what she was letting herself in for.

Inevitably she would be in close contact with her father for most of the time and be separated from the rest of her family for all that time. Both quite new experiences, and ones which she may well not have relished unreservedly. The only exception to separation might have appeared to have been Arthur. His Regiment was due for a posting to India in the New Year and the three of them expected to meet out there. Dorothy would surely have been appalled if she had been told, after saying au revoir to Arthur a day or so before she left, that she would not see him again for almost exactly fifty years.

Inevitably all the buying of tickets and reserving of cabins, the massive packing operation, the round of good-byes to friends and neighbours, the last minute frantic bits and pieces which always seems to claim attention in the final hours before departure, all came to an end. There were the excited members of staff wishing Miss Dorothy safe journey, the last tender and emotional farewells to Jennie, to Phyllis, to Jim, to Dorothy Mary, a final wave at Chingri Khal and she was off. It was Saturday, 28th November, 1925.

The world is divided into those who are good sailors and those who are not. Dorothy belonged to the latter. The miseries which are inflicted on the seasick traveller by the motion of a ship can surely only really be understood by those who have had to endure them. Any sort of contact with the sea, especially the rough sea, could make Dorothy feel unwell. For her to be standing on the Undercliff at Bournemouth and to see one of the small paddle steamers, which gave so much pleasure to holidaymakers, leaning rather drunkenly against the side of the Pier when a swell was running, could trigger that awful feeling in the pit of her stomach and make her want to turn away.

With such a reaction likely to occur, her willingness to undertake her journey may be thought surprising. But, paradoxically, it was the longer sea voyages that were less daunting to her than the short ones. "I knew I would feel terribly sick for about the first ten days, but then I would get my sea legs and would thoroughly enjoy it all. On a short voyage I would only have time to be ill, and would spend half the time afraid that the ship would sink and the other half afraid that it would not."

The wily traveller to the East, who was not enamoured of the sea, would do his best to avoid the Bay of Biscay. This could be achieved by joining the vessel at Marseilles. A short channel crossing, and then overland by train, through Paris, to the South of France was the thing to do. That made even more sense if – as was likely – you were going by P&O, for in those days their English terminal port was usually Tilbury rather than Southampton. Joining the ship at Marseilles did not only avoid the Bay of Biscay, it also cut out the long haul down the full length of the English Channel. Bournemouth was also well situated to encourage the use of the added attraction of the ferry service from Southampton to Le Havre, which was an overnight crossing. You could get on board early, get to bed, and be asleep before there was any perceptible movement in the ship.

And for Dorothy on this occasion there was yet another advantage to be obtained by using this route: she was able to spend a few days in Paris with her friends John and Denise Hickey. They had, by this time, a baby daughter, Françoise (now Mrs. Françoise Parncutt) who was about the same age as Dorothy Mary. They lived at 34, Rue Parmentier, not far from the northern edge of the Bois de Boulogne, from where Dorothy wrote at least three letters home to her mother. We get a fascinating glimpse of middle class life in the Paris of the 1920s:

> 30th November. I had a very pleasant journey here yesterday & although I had slept all night in the ship I was tired enough to sleep most of the way in the train.
>
> John met me at the station and as there were so few passengers I got through very quickly and arrived here at about 12.30...

…After I arrived here we had a very nice lunch and then in the afternoon went off to a dance tea place called 'Hermitage'. It was very interesting to watch but impossible to dance. John and I tried, but it really was impossible. Then we arrived here about seven and had supper and so to bed.

1st December…Yesterday after I had finished writing your letter Denise and I went out to post it…rather late in the morning. It was bitterly cold here…with driving rain and half a gale blowing…We had lunch and after that John went back to work and Denise and I laid down. Denise's mother was here afterwards for a few moments just to see the baby and me and then we had tea…Denise and I sat and talked together…until it was time to dress for dinner. We had a very nice little meal and then went off to the theatre. John in a dinner jacket and Denise in her wedding dress renovated…We went to see a new French farce, or rather comedy, called 'Les Nouveaux Messieurs.' I understood most of it but didn't think it frightfully good. However it was nice to go out. We arrived here about midnight, when we went off to bed. The procedure in the morning is this. I am called and told my bath is ready at about 8.30 or 9.00 When I come back I find breakfast waiting for me, so I sit in solemn state in my room wearing my yellow nightdress, my black dressing gown and gold slippers and eating breakfast.

1st December. I am writing this tonight as I don't think I shall have time in the morning…I am to meet Mary at 10.00 a.m. at the Madeleine and arrange about my ticket to Marseilles.

I have had a lovely day. Denise and I, after a lazy afternoon with the baby, sallied forth to an 'At Home' in Paris where we arrived at about five. There were a lot of French women there – at least four of them were grandmothers and looked about forty, with little cloche hats on and skirts as short as mine, and do you know they really looked awfully nice. I talked a little to some of them and we had the most delicious tea. There were heaps of tiny cakes such as you love to see for afternoon tea – éclairs about two inches long and tiny tiny meringues covered with cream and chestnuts – and then at about six all the husbands came to fetch their wives. Out came all the cakes that were left over and everyone drank port. John came to fetch Denise and myself and we left at about 7.15. We then strolled along into the main streets and arrived at Poccardis for dinner – the same place where we went to last time. There I had the most terrific dinner and I am still feeling weighted down by it.

The scene appears to be set for a daily letter home – an ambitious project one might think. But, if there were further letters to Jennie written from Paris, surprisingly, they have not survived. By the time of the next letter now available, Dorothy is on board the steamer which will take her to Bombay.

It may be helpful at this point to introduce a family who feature from time to time in Dorothy's letters home. When Harry and Jennie were living together in Calcutta they met and became very friendly with a Mr and Mrs Pym. They were a Catholic couple and probably met Jennie first through the Church. Mr Pym was a jeweller. They had two daughters, both older than Dorothy by a few years, namely Zoë and Winnie. By the time of Dorothy's journey to India, Zoë and her husband, Tom Allan, were living in Assam where Tom was a tea planter. He was sometimes known as 'Barbara' after the popular song 'Barbara Allan.' They never had any children. Winnie married a Mr King, and they had two children, Joan (the young witness to the traffic accident) and Pamela. Sadly Mr King had left Winnie quite early in their marriage which, unlike that of Tom and Zoë, had never been happy, and Jennie had been a great help to Winnie and her children. Indeed, over many years both Harry and Jennie, the one in Calcutta and the other in Bournemouth, did a lot to help both families. One of the attractions to which Dorothy was much looking forward was a proposed visit to Tom and Zoë in Assam. As will be seen, she was not disappointed.

It also seems to me worth stating that I do not remember ever hearing anything fall from Dorothy that could remotely be called anti-semitic. From time to time in her letters home – the first time being right at the outset – she uses the word 'Jew' or 'Jewish' to indicate a particular appearance, mode of speech or behaviour, usually of a passing acquaintance, which she did not like. It would be quite wrong to read more into such phrases than that. This was, of course, many years before the holocaust was in anyone's contemplation. She was as horrified as most people when the maltreatment of Jewish people started to become apparent. She could well have picked up such a figure of speech from Harry, who no doubt was, at times, anti Jew – but then at times he was anti- almost everything – anti-Catholic, anti-Christian, anti-Pope, even anti-Jennie. Small wonder Dorothy sometimes picked up his phraseology. But she was never anti-Jew: she was never even anti-Harry, despite being a Catholic Christian, respectful of the Papacy and very fond of her mother.

So to Dorothy writing her first letter on board, in which she has adopted the practice of referring to Harry as 'Henry'. She writes from 'P&O SN Co. *SS Rawalpindi*,' a vessel which was to achieve great fame early in the Second World War by reason of her gallant, but tragically hopeless fight as an armed merchant cruiser against two German battleships, the *Scharnhorst* and the *Gneisenau*. But these were happier days. *Rawalpindi* had only been completed at the end of that summer: this must have been her second voyage to the East. Dorothy gets down at once to setting the scene and to introducing the personages she first encountered on the voyage:

Saturday, 5th December, 1925

My darling little Mother,

I have decided not to write a separate letter each day but to carry on with the same one, like a sort of diary, then I can go straight ahead with the news. But I'm afraid there will be very little at first because you know how long it takes to settle down, and especially if you are a seasick person like myself.

I haven't got a very good seat in the dining saloon but perhaps that is all to the good. I am in the corner and there are a couple of Jews, a man and his wife, opposite me. They behave all right, you know they eat nicely, but their talk is dreadful and so is their appearance. Being in the corner I have only one person next to me, but he is delightful - an old man who has been in India forty eight years. Unfortunately I don't know his name but I think he comes from Assam. He knows Zoë and 'Barbara' as he calls him, fairly well, and he remembers Winnie.

The lady in my room is rather a nice old thing, 'though I think she is a bit talkative, but she's most awfully kind. She is going out to her husband who I should think is either in the Forest or a Planter of sorts and I think she said she was going to Bangalore – but I might be muddling her up with rather a charming Scotch lady who is also going out to her husband.

The then 'cure' for seasickness was a pill called 'Mothersills'. Dorothy must have brought a liberal supply; she began taking them that first evening on board, but their success seems to have been only partial:

It is bitterly cold and has been quite rough. I felt rather ill at about midday today so I rushed to my cabin and took another dose of M. and lay down. I suppose I spent about 15 minutes over my lunch and then I went back to my cabin, got a hot water bottle and slept soundly till tea. I am all right now and it is much calmer…

Sunday. Dec. 6th. I have been lying down most of the day. There was dancing of sorts last night to a gramophone in the bit of deck outside the Purser's office. I had two dances (both with very indifferent people) and then went to bed as I felt sick. I have had to be very careful all day taking M. and lying down most of the time. It is too cold to go on deck, especially as I'm not feeling well. N.B. I can't make out who the old chap is who sits next to me, but he's a perfect dear. He asked me this morning if I was going to pray and I said "No, that I was of the Roman Catholic persuasion" He told me he was an R.C. too.

The rough weather, with its unpleasant physical consequences did not stop Dorothy making the first two of what she calls her 'clicks.' Men of all ages seemed only too anxious to be of service to her. One of the first two appears to have been badly smitten despite the ravages of seasickness which was affecting not only Dorothy, but also most of the passengers on board. It seems odd that, by comparison with her clicking speed, it takes quite a long time for her to introduce herself properly to fellow-passengers, and they to her.

December 8th. It has been very rough and I haven't been well enough to write – I haven't exactly been ill, but you know what it is like when the weather is bad…We are having a wretched passage, nearly everyone is ill so I cannot expect to be feeling my best, but we arrive in Port Said tomorrow and I'm hoping for the best from then on.

You will be pleased to hear that already I have had two clicks, the first being with a Jew of sorts called Manasseh. He has a wife and child and nurse on board but that doesn't deter him. I think he means well but doesn't even yet quite appreciate European ways. The other is a perfect darling – a boy going out for the first time to an engineering firm – not a bit good looking, but such a dear…

Wednesday December 9th…I am quite well now. I really did feel ill yesterday and scarcely knew which way to turn. This darned ship rolled and pitched like a cork and I began to feel that life was not worth living. This morning we put into Port Said and for the first time since we left Marseilles I saw the sun. It is still very cold though, and, now that we are steaming slowly down the Canal I cannot go on the windy side of the deck without a big coat on. So you can easily imagine that there is no question of summer dresses.

I went ashore with Mrs.Beckett, my cabin mate, who really is rather a dear. I think she is a colonel's wife but don't know. Anyhow we see little of each other during the day, which I think is a good thing, but get on very well during the times we are together in the cabin…She lives at Camberley. Oh and my charming old man is an Assam Tea Planter…but so far I haven't gathered his name. Well, to return to my trip into Port Said, I must say I don't think anything of the town. Mrs. Beckett and I went off to have some coffee and were so pestered and badgered by these awful people who were surrounding us that a policeman came and shushed them off. However they still came with their jade and amber necklaces and the policeman after them, so we had a lively time. We went to Simon Artz and I sent Arthur some turkish delight and some nougat…

I have met a pal of Henry's – an oldish man who has placed his deck chair at my disposal, and then there is my charming engineering boy named Bagnall who for the moment is my slave. How long it will last I don't know but it is a pity he cannot dance. However he has been waiting on me most of the afternoon and we are slowly steaming through the Canal so the stage is well set. I am going down now to dress for dinner…

In the next few days, perhaps on account of the calmer weather, shipboard life got rather more sociable. Names have been exchanged – but Dorothy was beginning to find that her clicks were showing signs of clicking a bit too fast for comfortable control:

Thursday 10th. I've met an old man named Leslie who knows Henry; he is very nice to me and has advised me to book by the Mail Train from Bombay, which I have done. I needn't pay until I get there so I shall be alright as Henry said if he did not meet me himself he would send someone with some Indian money to meet me. Well, this man Leslie, whom I should imagine had a tiny touch of tar, has leant me his chair and altogether put himself at my disposal. The chair I brought with me is useable – I have to get in and out very carefully and must move it with great care as two of the legs are broken, not to mention other minor injuries, but I shan't take it further than Bombay.

I had quite an exciting time last night with my devoted slave, who was on duty from about two o'clock till eleven – I couldn't get rid of him. However, he is only at the moony stage and is very young, so it isn't very interesting. The weather isn't up to much – white horses on a sea that other people say is calm. We are rolling about a good deal and, though I don't feel it, I'm not over thrilled with it.

Friday 11th. Only one week more. I shall post this at Aden if possible...Well, yesterday afternoon everyone lazed and than after dinner I danced. I don't think there are any great dancers on board but still that isn't their fault. I went on and could scarcely believe my ears when the band stopped and I found out that it was eleven o'clock. This morning it was very hot and I haven't been feeling up to much...

Lots of little things have happened. Everyone is more friendly...Well then, there is this other man who rather fastens on to me for the dancing – Manasseh – he's married but his wife doesn't dance "for the present" as he pointedly said. Well, tonight I am going to tell him I will have one dance with him and one only. It isn't that he's not nice but I don't like him and as he has found I am a good dancer he wants to cling on. I haven't got anyone to go and sit by so if I want to get rid of anyone I have to tell them to go point blank. Well, it is all a great world and I am learning a lot. They are getting up a concert and I hear that there is already an awful amount of friction about it. To begin with it is to be more of a cabaret show and they are proposing to form a Pindi Beauty Chorus of six (needless to say I haven't been asked). Well, imagine choosing six girls out of the ship. Most of the other hundred or so will be offended for life. Anyhow the woman who is running it isn't any Gladys and has a voice like a steam whistle – she drowns all the men. I must fly and dress for dinner now...

Saturday. This letter will be posted tonight and be taken off at

Aden tomorrow morning I am enjoying the voyage, but oh how I miss you… Last night I did an idiotic thing. I was asked to dance and looked around for someone who would look after my bag. There was nobody; so as everything was locked up in my cabin I took out my keys and gave them to my partner so that if my little bag was stolen or lost it wouldn't matter. Well of course I forgot about them and he – a Cambridge youth named Alistair Gibb – forgot too. It was hot and I decided to go to bed at about ten, when I couldn't find the man with my keys. Eventually I got him and all was well, but oh I felt such an idiot getting the deck steward etc. out to find this man, who all the time had been in the smoking room.

The Jews at our table are called Bettmann and Mr. Murray, the Assam Tea Planter who sits on my left, cannot stand them. He says they are Germans. She is a typical Frau with a coarse shape and both she and he wear mole coloured leather boots – flat heels – you never saw anything like them. Yesterday she was in a long yellow silk dress that Mr. Murray called a dressing gown and in reality it was a bit like it; anyhow with the boots she was a sight. Well, she is as broad as she is long, and her husband is a tiny little man, hideous, with cross eyes and glasses. Last night they started talking about Austria and Mr. Murray said the peasants "did" one. The old Frau began to get awfully waxy and I just saved the situation by talking about Paris or something.

This morning was very hot so I lolled about. I've met such a charming woman named Mrs. Smith who is going to Bangalore. Her husband I hear is head of the Government dairies…Mr. Manasseh met me last night and said, "I'm playing Bridge, but each time I'm dummy I am coming to dance with you." So I laughed and said, "No, one dance only." And sped off in the lift. He took the hint and I didn't see him for the rest of the evening.

John Bagnall has leant me his chair and I have given him my clock to mend, so we are quits. N.B. He thinks I am eighteen… I suppose this is really the nicest part of my holiday, and will soon be drawing to its close, but I have a sort of feeling that after all India will be quite nice and Henry really glad to have me.

The letter so far would have been Jennie's first news from Dorothy since she had left mainland Europe. Significantly, perhaps, it ends with two recurring themes during what she calls 'my holiday.' The first is her reluctance to acknowledge her age to her new found friends. Shortly before she left home she had celebrated her twenty eighth birthday. She always tried to keep quiet about her age throughout the journey. Whether this was to avoid putting off would-be suitors, or to enjoy the consequences of their error (which many seemed to make), or simply as a characteristic inherited from Jennie I do not know. She was never coy about her age as far as I can recall.

The second, and more important, theme, which often reappears in her letters home, is her anxiety about Harry's feelings towards her and to her visit. Without seeing any correspondence that there must have been in early preparations for her journey it is not possible to know much of the basis for her anxiety. He had never been an easy man, and his temper was short and could be violent. It is easily understandable that she might well have viewed the prospect of lengthy periods in Harry's company, and his company alone, with more than a little trepidation. As things turned out she had a fair mixture of loving generosity contrasted with unreasoning criticism and hostility. She carried on the next day, Sunday, 13th December, where she had left off to catch the post at Aden, starting with the passengers' attempts to entertain themselves and each other:

We had the concert last night, being Saturday, but it was an appalling show. No one could sing and the entire arrangements seemed dreadful. In the Second Class there is a Jazz Band going to India but it is a very second rate affair and the effect they get is more like a military band than a ragtime show. Well, they were by far the best part of the show. The worst was so bad that it was funny. (a) Two people got up to dance the tango about which they hadn't the faintest idea. For one thing they held each other about three feet apart and were never dancing in anything like time, and for another they kept on and on and on. (b) There was a man due to sing "When my sugar walks down the street" but he got too well primed up except to come on and mumble. Of course everyone thought he was doing it on purpose so they clapped him no end, so he wouldn't stop. There was the stage manager and some other man who was running the show trying to get him off but he would stand there with an inane grin on his face and murmur "Sweet sweet Tweet". Eventually they sent on two of the company who sang the chorus and marched him off – but he came on again in spite of everything. Then there was the beauty chorus. Well it was a complete failure as there were only three girls in it so they made up the other three with boys. Nobody knew what to do and they were got up in shawls with one shoulder bare. Two of the girls weren't used to this, hadn't their shawls on tight enough and so could scarcely move, they were so frightened of something slipping. However it ended all right and everyone said how much they had enjoyed it, etc., etc. I then tried to dance but the wind was so bad and I hadn't my hairnet so gave it up and had a little talk with my friend John instead. He was rapidly falling in love with me, but I think it was the Indian Ocean, or rather the Suez Canal.

There was to be more of both passenger self-entertainment and of romance. The former, it would seem, rather more successful than the first effort, and the latter – well, success or otherwise would depend on your point of view. Almost as an aside we learn of the presence on board of one of the most distinguished lawyer/politicians of the time, together with his wife, perhaps making preliminary researches for his work on the Indian Statutory Commission:

Monday December 14th. There is very little to relate – you know what a day Sunday is – everyone just sits around and is bored…I was chatting this afternoon with Sir Francis Couchman – at least that is how it sounds – and Mr. Leslie. He is the head of the Solicitors. Sir Francis is head of the railway, or some railway. They were both very nice, in fact I often chat with Leslie because our chairs are together. But now it has struck me that Henry had had violent quarrels with these men – has he? It will be distinctly funny if he has.

Tuesday 15th. I am afraid I have a confession to make. We had a Fancy Dress Ball last night and I didn't wear mine! The baggage room was terribly hot and, as the ship had started to pitch about a bit, I didn't feel like going down. Then I should have had to iron out my frock and, as everyone had been ironing and having hot baths all day in preparation for the evening, the whole of 'D' deck, where my cabin is, was like an oven. However it was very interesting watching the people. I should think there were more Spanish girls than any other kind. I suppose it was because everyone on board has a Spanish shawl – some of them rather wonderful ones, too. There was a Mrs.

Johnstone who had on a beautiful crinoline frock in gold, gold lace skirt in three flounces and a gold velvet bodice. She wore a Spanish comb and red roses in her hair and at her waist, and a shawl. The last item was a pity because although it went with her frock, it was a striped affair which I don't consider Spanish. The first prize went to a woman got up as a vivandière – a costume which I consider very ugly, but it seemed very popular.

There were no picturesque men's dresses, but some were really very funny. One…was a man in ordinary evening dress, a bit the worse for a night out, with his collar undone and the rouge marks of lips painted on it, paper streamers all over his opera hat and in his button hole, a woman's suspender hanging out of his trouser pocket and, to crown all, a bottle of Eno's Fruit Salts in his right hand. I would have given him the prize, but a man dressed as Cupid got it. He was perfectly hideous but very funny and he acted the part so well. He had on tights and a little pink tulle frilly skirt, a pair of very dilapidated wings attached to his braces and a miniature bow and arrow…

Dancing went on till nearly twelve, but I'm afraid I sat out the latter part with my devoted slave, who doesn't dance. There would have been no temptation to do so even had I met a single one who could dance even moderately well, I got so hot resting on fat men's tummies and being pulled about by thin ones. There was a buffet with claret cup, lemon squashes, ices, cakes, etc., and altogether the whole thing went with a swing. Even Sir John and Lady Simon came in fancy dress – nothing to rave about – but everyone seemed out to enjoy themselves and there was a nice atmosphere about it.

Mrs. Beckett says I must tell you that she thinks I am looking heaps better since I came on board – I am feeling better anyhow. My only fear now is that Henry will think I am too pale, or too thin. You know I cannot help dreading the meeting a bit, but hope for the best.

Wednesday 16th. Our one thought now is that we land the day after tomorrow – everyone is talking about it and the air of excitement about the ship is simply terrific, in fact a bit trying and I am beginning to look forward to getting it all over. That doesn't mean that I haven't enjoyed the voyage – I have and it's been topping.

Thursday 17th. I have a bit of news for you now only not a word outside the family – I've had a proposal from my devoted slave, and as I'm not in the least in love I told him that was the combined effects of the separation from his home and the Indian Ocean. However it's all been very interesting. Everyone here thinks I am about twenty and I haven't let on a word about being to Cambridge so I feel I can be as foolish as I like. I have had a good old laugh to myself at times – for instance I was told this morning that a girl of my age had no business to have read anything of Bernard Shaw and that apparently I hadn't been spanked enough…The pop came from John Bagnall, the man who is going to Assam to lay down plant for McPhail & Co. (or some such firm.) He…[is] fair and a bit shock headed, and very young. However he must be fairly good at his job or the firm wouldn't be sending him out P&O 1st class 'A' accommodation. He speaks with a north country accent and comes from Manchester. He has been on the research staff of Crossleys Oil Engines and he has a brother doing Classics at Queen's, Oxford.

I have done most of my packing – tomorrow I will write in the train.

Dorothy was as good as her word. The train journey was only for two nights – from Friday morning to early on Sunday morning. An Indian train rattling its way across the continent may not be thought to be the most likely of romantic hot-spots but it seems to have served to provide Dorothy with an opportunity for, well, perhaps not quite a conquest, and she does not call it a click, shall we say a considerable impact on an impressionable young man.

Friday December 18th. I am just writing you a few lines in the train… Last night the ship was very, very lively – unfortunately the packing had upset me just enough to prevent my sitting in the hot music saloon to hear Lady Simon present the prizes. From what I heard though it went off successfully. I sat on the deck a little with Jack – he's quite barmy about me now but you know what these ship board love affairs are. You needn't worry – it was in full view of everyone. Well champagne bottles were popping all night and some people didn't get to bed at all. I finished my packing and got to bed at about 1.30. It was very hot and I had been 'finishing' since 11 o'clock. They put on the clocks 45 minute during the night and I was up at six so you can guess I'm pretty tired now. Soon after I was up I got a letter from Cooks containing my ticket and saying that hey had some money for me. So after breakfast I went off with my devoted slave into Bombay, collected my money and came back to the train.

19th Dec. Saturday. I had a very pleasant night and altogether am finding the journey most comfortable if a bit dusty. Everyone has been so kind to me. Mr. Leslie has looked after me very well and bought me two brass trays at one of the stations coming through. He also bought me some chocolates and I had some from Jack before we left so that altogether I have done very well. I don't think I have had so much attention paid me in my life and I must say I have enjoyed it.

You remember my talking about Mr. Manasseh on the ship? Well, as he has been really quite nice and at the same time a bit persistent I thought I had better make friends with his wife who seems rather charming and I think likes me. I thought I would be on the safe side that way. Well, she has asked me to call; so unless Henry says "No" I will do so sometime later on.

The food has been quite nice on the train – I have had my meals with the lady who is in my compartment, a Mrs. Tarlton of Bird & Co., and her son, aged 24 or so, just to make it more interesting. Then I go in and have a chat with Mr. Leslie and then come back here and watch the continent of India unfold herself before my eyes, but so far I haven't noticed anything very interesting. They tell me we pass the best bits in the night. I am meeting Henry in the morning at about 6 a.m. I hope it will be all right…All the men say I must stay in India.

Tuesday…I've not written on Sunday or yesterday but honestly the only moment I have had to myself is now…

In the train I quite got off with Stewart Tarlton who drank my health and toasted me with "Here's to your eyes divine" which Phyllis can repeat to you. Then I had a chat with various pals in the train and to bed. At 2.30 Mrs. Tarlton got out and I was up at 4.30 a.m. the train got into Howrah at about 6 a.m.

By my reckoning that makes some four young men and three old men who were smitten by her, to a greater or lesser extent, on this first stage of her journey. It makes me feel rather proud of her that so many took her to be one of those 'very agreeable girls and none are over the age of twenty one.'

But now she had arrived at the buffers at Howrah Station, and we see her stepping down on to the platform and anxiously looking out for the formidable 'Henry.'

CHAPTER 14

DOROTHY'S JOURNEY (2) CHRISTMAS AND NEW YEAR IN CALCUTTA

A S THE TRAIN WOUND its way through the outer suburbs of Calcutta Dorothy's anxieties at the coming encounter with her father, whom she had not seen for over a year, grew in intensity so that she seems to have become almost paranoid about it. The train was a bit late, and she tried to console herself with the fact that his grumpiness, if not worse, which she fully expected him to show, would be due to no more than irritation at having to wait at the station, rather than her unwelcome (as she feared it might be) arrival.

She need not have worried: he welcomed her sincerely, and treated her at once with generosity. His fuller plans for their return journey to England the following year were made clear to her in outline soon after her arrival. But she did find herself leading a most curious life. They hardly ever had a meal 'at home', the only exception being early morning tea (*chota hazri*.) Nearly always they went to a hotel or restaurant, even for breakfast, despite Harry's apartment at 4, Esplanade East being on the top floor of that building. The Bristol and Spence's were the two Hotels most patronised at first and Peliti's and Firpo's the two Restaurants. Most of the places they were regularly visiting were in a fairly small area of the city around the northern end of the Maidan. Spence's was about a ten minute walk in one direction, The Bristol about the same in the opposite direction. Peliti's was even nearer, Firpo's rather further away. Even St. Thomas's Church, to which Dorothy usually went, was no more than a twenty-five minute walk for her.

The majority of the characters who are mentioned in her letters are explained and described as they appear. One, who appears in her pages many times, is not. C. L. Phillipps, or Old Phillipps, as she often calls him, is simply there. It is plain from the mention of his name in Jennie's letters in reply to Dorothy that he was a character already well known to Jennie. Most of the company surrounding Dorothy were male; at first probably because most of Harry's friends were male. Later – and not so very much later – the number of men around her was at least as much due to the attraction which men of nearly all ages seemed to feel for Dorothy. She gives a graphic account of it all, if at times a bit disjointed:

Tuesday. [23rd December]. I've not written on Sunday or yesterday, but honestly the only moment I have had to myself is now, and even now Henry has just come up and I have to write and talk at the same time...The train got into Howrah at about 6 a.m., Henry having waited some time for me there. He was tired and for a second my heart sank but then I realised that even if he were a bit grumpy the cold and the long wait were ample excuse. However, he was not and I may as well tell you that everyone tells me how he has been talking about my coming out and I think he is genuinely glad to have me.

We arrived here at about seven where I find that the back room has been most tastefully got up in royal blue and old gold for me, and I have my own bathroom. I believe the man who hired the room from Henry is in the furnishing trade. I had a bath, changed all my things and then Daddy gave me a topping little wristwatch surrounded with rubies or garnets and four diamonds. That is my Christmas Box – wasn't it sweet of him? Well then, we went to the Bristol for breakfast, beginning with mulligatawny soup. I can tell you that this place is queer living. For instance this morning I woke at 9. Henry had had his breakfast and I had my chota hazri of tea without milk or sugar and a biscuit. Then we went up to old Phillipps where I had a most extraordinary meal consisting of tea, toast butter and caviare, marrons glaces – at about 11 a.m. I shall have some tea now and then go on to dinner.

However I must tell you about Sunday. After that meal at the Bristol we went to the Eden Gardens to watch the cricket. Henry isn't a member so we sat on a bit of plank and I'm afraid I dozed off once or twice I was so tired. I suppose we got back to Esplanade East at about 2.30. I was done and I managed to throw off a few clothes and get on to my bed. I suppose I had been in bed asleep for about half an hour when I was awakened to see C. L. Phillipps Esq. and John Bagnall Esq. come to see me…Phillipps came to offer me a flat he has somewhere. I don't [know] whether he meant his Alipore house or not, but it was jolly decent of the old chap wasn't it?

John, of course, had just come to rest his eyes on me. I am afraid he is rather too much in love so I have had to write to him telling him how old I am – perhaps that will put him off. Anyhow I am glad he is here and that he hangs around because he is more of my kind than the others. He wanted me to come out to dinner with him. Instead Henry asked him to dinner at Spence's, where we all went later on, after Henry and I had been for a spin in the car and watched the cricket. We had hardly sat down to dinner when two other people joined us – both men and of not much class – however they were quite nice. I think that ends Sunday.

Oh, I've forgotten to say that Henry is looking very well and is happy and sweet and that I am going home with him via Australia, New Zealand and the Panama.

Now, on Monday what did I do? Drive and walk and a little unpacking in the morning. Lunch with Henry and four other men at the Bristol…We stayed talking till fairly late and then there was just time to change and go to a garden party to meet some Indian gent whom I didn't meet. However I met scores of people Henry knows and really, you know, I think I am doing him some good. For instance at this show I met a Mr. and Mrs. Griffin Chaive (name uncertain) and we all chatted together for some while. Then Henry introduced me to a Colonel I.M.S. who was with his wife, but he didn't introduce her to us. Then there were fireworks afterwards – most lovely fountains of silver rain and waterfalls, etc., etc. – better than anything that I have ever seen in my life.

Well, I was standing – I must tell you that of the five or six hundred people there, both black and white, I was one of about twenty women – well, the natives made a great fuss of Henry and of me so a chair was brought up and I sat down. Just behind me I saw Mrs. G. Chaive and Mrs. Colonel and after the show was over the Colonel came up and spoke to us and introduced his wife to us both, so you see it isn't going to be bad at all.

Had Dorothy been afraid that she would have found herself more or less ostracised in Calcutta? Harry had a reputation already for being something of a firebrand, and his business (still his main source of income) cast him as someone 'in trade' and so not quite in the best of society. By 'doing him good', Dorothy seems to mean showing to others that his family was reasonably civilised and so he may be civilised also, beneath a fairly rough exterior. The Clergy took it that way:

> I've met Barrie Brown who wants me to go dancing with him (he's only half my height), and a chap named Watson, who squints, and Goss, who's rather nice and oh! scores of men. Father van der Something was at the show and Henry introduced himself and me. He is Rector of St. [Francis] Xavier's and knows Fr. Nicholson and Fr. Bodkin being himself an S. J.* I think he was staggered to find that Harry Hobbs of the papers had a daughter who was a Papist.
>
> Then I have met all the firm and am to be allowed to call on Mrs. Affleck, which I must get done soon. I must say I think it is wonderful the amount of business that is done considering the state of the place. The office is most unprepossessing, and looks untidy and dirty, even if it is not. However it is none of my business and besides I haven't seen the other places yet.
>
> My old ayah turned up today and wanted to look after my babas. I told her I hadn't any. Thank God Henry asked me if I wanted her and I jumped at it, of course. I didn't say anything, but I felt a bit worried as here I was in this flat with nothing but men around me. You can imagine circumstances in which it might be very awkward. However I've got her now and she is not a bad old thing, though I should judge a bit slow.

Queen Alexandra, a Queen Mother very much loved by her family and by the public at large, had died on 17th November, only a week or so before Dorothy's departure. This sad event did not appear to make any difference to life on board the *Rawalpindi*, but it was still casting its shadow over Calcutta society at Christmas time. And Christmas this year for Dorothy was to prove a bit of an emotional trial for her. She was homesick for much of her time away, but particularly so over Christmas.

The Viceroy, etc., are in half-mourning so I am wearing my grey

---

* i.e. A Jesuit: as were the Clergy at Bournemouth.

coat and skirt and my mauve hat. The Cup is to be run on Saturday. We are lunching with C. L. Phillipps, then to the races...Isn't it fortunate that I had a grey dress?...Will you write to the Old Man and thank him for being kind to me?...

December 23rd 1925. I sent off the mail this morning. The ayah had called me and I was at the hairdressers at 9.15 where my hair was cut quite successfully. We had breakfast at the Bristol and then came home...

...I've been to the Polo and then I've been trying to get my dress done...Jack came round at about 10 tonight – Henry had gone to bed. I'm afraid he is going to get fed up with the boy coming here, but you know I haven't the heart to send him away – he has only just arrived, he doesn't know a soul and it's Christmas time; besides, I like him. Henry tells me he goes to bed every night at 9.30 so you can imagine what a lively time he has of it. Oh, I am seeing the queerest life you can possibly imagine. Well, Jack came and sat with me for about twenty minutes in the big room surrounded with papers, etc. etc., and a safe and the spirit stove and tomorrow's tea and some fruit and all Henry's day clothes on various chairs – even his shirt and vest, they are all carefully laid by the bearer, and Henry himself in the next room with doors wide open and two dreadful looking calico curtains as purdahs. It is really comic. To show you what a few friends he has to come up to see him, do you know he hasn't a drink in the place.

Christmas Day. Another day has gone without my writing, but I know you will forgive me. Yesterday I was so miserable that I just couldn't bear to write, even if I had had the time. I suddenly thought that it was Christmas Eve at home and I pictured you all at Chingri Khal and thought of how I longed to be with you. Daddy is perfectly sweet – it isn't that he doesn't mean to do me well or anything of that sort, but he just hasn't any idea of enjoying himself or anyone else; but I couldn't help thinking of how terrible it must have been for you at times – however it is best not thought about much less written of.

...There was Polo in the afternoon. Then I went out to do some shopping, met my friend, John, who gave me some coffee and then to Spence's to dinner – alone with Henry, of course. It was as quiet as a china service and I thought of you all at home, in the midst of bustle and excitement...We drank your health in liqueurs. Then I came home, got on to my work whilst Henry read to me out of his newer book. It is very interesting, much more so I should consider than the last one and much better written.* He stayed reading in my room until about midnight (I was up till one and still the frock isn't finished, this half mourning is a damned nuisance) and he chatted with me about the business [with] which he is fed up. However I think he quite enjoyed his little talk with me and is genuinely glad I have come. I try and be as nice as possible to all his friends because I think that may do him good. I'm sure most of them get startled by me – apparently they expect a strident harsh kind of woman, which you know I am not. I have already spoken of the lunch clique at the Bristol† – well, I feel rather extraordinary butting in, but I think they all like me, which is what I am out for.

This morning [Christmas Day] I was up at six and in Church at St. Thomas at seven. Then went to the New Market to buy a few flowers for Christmas and then came home and gave Henry your and my present. He said he was very pleased with the socks as he badly needed some, and I know he was glad we had remembered him. The flowers improve the place a bit, but it is still a sad muddle...

I've been to the Convent, just to wish them a Happy Christmas. Mother Xavier is in Assam but I saw Mother Christine who tried to be nice but somehow I couldn't stick her. Polo this afternoon and then dinner this evening with Barrie Brown, Campbell Forrester being the only other guest. It was quite an amusing show and infinitely better than going over to Spence's for the evening. They are both asking me out and I asked Henry if I might and he said "Of course", but I really don't think he wants even one evening off. We drank "absent friends" and you know I only thought of you all. Campbell Forrester is very amusing about his wife who he calls his "five foot ten and a half inches of American trouble." I am going to play tennis at his house on Sunday. Barrie Brown is a funny little man who scarcely comes up to my tummy but he is getting quite keen, is going to take me out dancing and already calls me "Dorothy." Races tomorrow so au revoir until tomorrow might.

Boxing Day...First of all I must tell you I have dismissed my

---

* *Digressions of a Ditcher* was published in 1925.
† In fact no more than the brief reference at page 226.

ayah. [Dorothy sets it all out in detail: breaking an earring, being very slow with her needlework; doing it all wrong: so much for her relief at having a woman around].

[The grey dress was not ready in time so] I wore all white instead…hat…frock…and even white stockings and I think that was as much mourning as was necessary. As a matter of fact all the really chic people in the Members' Enclosure were in black. The Vicereine looked a pukka Rachel. She was all in black and was being wheeled about in a bath chair, as she has just had an operation, I believe for cancer of the breast, poor thing! Well, the Countess of Lytton was also in black, she looked charming and must have been a very beautiful woman in her day. Lady Alexandra Metcalfe (Curzon that was) also present, and I think she looked the nicest. Her black was so light and airy. She had the thinnest of black silk stockings so that the colour of her skin came through, a thin frock of black georgette with lots of fine lace at the edge, all this with a black crinoline shawl and, just as an afterthought, a magnificent diamond brooch in it and a string of pearls about three feet long round her neck. She is most awfully pretty and looks so fascinating when she talks, but when she is in repose she is just a tiny bit too self-possessed. Isn't it a pity about the mourning! Of course after today it will only be half mourning but still it has spoiled much of the entertaining and in today's big race, one of the greatest events in the year for Calcutta.

Well, I had no breakfast this morning but a colossal and extraordinarily good meal (hazri) at Phillipps's at 11.30. This is what we had. Hors d'oeuvres – caviare, sandwiches, olives; soup – mulligatawny with rice and lemon; Grilled fish; lamb cutlets with tomatoes, peas and potatoes; pineapple water ice; then chicken curry, prawn curry and chicken pilau (I had to eat them all); then ham from Firpo's; local turnip [?]; plum pudding (the only item not first class); ices; dessert. I feel as if I never want to see food again, but it was delicious all the same. Oh, and we drank a German wine, and we had coffee.

We didn't go into the Members' Enclosure but we were in the reserved stand and paddock which was very select and, as all the Members were there too, and only went into their stand alongside us for the actual race, it was quite like being in the best place. The only fault was that I didn't get a very good view of the arrival of the Viceroy, but otherwise everything went swimmingly. There is no doubt that the racecourse is beautiful and everything is so well managed. Daddy met scores of people he knew and has introduced me to so many that I don't know where I am. Almost without exception men...I think everyone is a bit aghast, because of course it is not like Phyllis – I am with him alone such a lot and I am sure that those who don't see the likeness there is between us sometimes make a bad guess.

Old C. L. [Phillipps] gave me Rs.100 to bet with and I came out with Rs.104 having used his tips and gone wrong on my own guessing, so anyhow my day's racing has been successful, as I have kept it all, of course. Henry made Rs.100 (about) also, so the family ain't done so bad. C. L. didn't bet – he shared with Henry. It was a bit tiring – such a lot of standing about and so many, many people to meet just for five seconds conversation and then someone else. Also I felt a bit on show. It was afterwards we went back, drank to Arthur in Champagne [it was his birthday] and talked to the Old Man until seven. Then dinner at the Bristol and here I am writing to you.

I'm going straight into my little bed. My God it is hard, just an ordinary horsehair mattress on wood. At first I didn't think I could put up with it but I am beginning to like it now. And then the mail will be in tomorrow – oh joy.

Sunday. [27th December] Rather a dull day. High-ish Mass at St. Thomas's. It only rook thirty five minutes so would appeal to Arthur. Big hazri at the Bristol and then I stayed in, so sat on the sofa reading. Who should come in but friend John. He seems as much in love as ever – poor thing. I am dining with him on Monday night, so will give you all the news then. We didn't have tiffin but arrived at Mr. Campbell Forrester's [for tennis] at about 3.30. I couldn't hit a ball at first but improved rapidly and impressed them a bit. Henry was most awfully pleased. Poor old Henry, he means so well and yet hasn't the faintest idea how to enjoy himself. He is so proud of us all and so badly wants us to do well. It is quite pathetic to see him.

Well, *revenons aux moutons*, there were four men at the party who played tennis – our host and three others whose names I have forgotten, and a Miss Lloyd, Secretary of the European Association, whom I couldn't stick. One of the men's wives came for tea and seemed quite nice. The men themselves weren't bad and Forrester was charming, and still on about his American wife. He married her five years ago, mainly out of pique because his daughter and a woman he was keen on didn't turn up to meet him at Marseilles, and since then they have lived together about seven months. She comes for a fortnight and then goes off exploring or something of that sort. At present she is at the Riff Front but will be in Calcutta with her husband in February for a few days or so. He starts off by saying, "Yes, my wife – five foot ten and a half – big with it, fine woman, splendid woman – too much for me." It was a very enjoyable afternoon and I was especially glad to get the exercise

We had a quiet dinner and then went to a concert given in aid of local charities by the combined bands of the Viceroy and Governor, or rather orchestras. It really was most awfully good and almost up to European standards, but it started...late and went on until a quarter to twelve.

Tuesday [29th December]. I have started to get terribly stiff in my calves, and couldn't make it out how it was...Last night I discovered what I consider is the real cause and that is the ninety two steps about a dozen times a day. Otherwise, though I haven't noticed it and would scarcely have believed that there were so many.

On Monday nothing much happened, but in the evening I went out with Jack. We had a fairly good dinner at Peliti's. There were about two dozen people there and about five couples dancing – we were not one of them as my pal is going to learn dancing but won't try now. Isn't that annoying of him?...My dear Mr. Murray was at the next table. He also is one of McNeill's planters and with him were other men, both I think of the same firm...My young man is still very much in love but as he is going away on Sunday or Monday for some time I think he'll get over it...

I went to call on Mrs. Griffin Chaive this morning and on Mrs. A. K. [Mrs. A.K.Affleck.] The former was very charming and has asked me to play tennis on Tuesday next. The latter was most amusing. She pretended she knew nothing about my visit, whereas I had told A. K. the night before and he told me that she would be expecting me that morning. She has grown very much plumper and broader. I think she has now started and will become enormous...

...In the afternoon...Schoolie* Lever and the Doctor McDonnell came to call and to ask me to a dance on the *Effingham*

* i.e. Instructor-Lieutenant-Commander, R.N.

next Friday. I think Schoolie must have brought the other man so that they could have a combined verdict because just before he was going away he asked me if I would care to come to the races next Friday, so I have some pleasure ahead of me. They are both short but seem awfully nice. They stayed about an hour and after they went we had our walk. Then dinner at Spence's.

Wednesday 30th. Went to call on Mrs. Lees today. She kissed me both coming and going, which I thought a bit of cheek but otherwise was quite nice. And Henry came with me and dropped his card! – a thing I don't believe he's done for decades…

…You ask me to tell you about India and what I think of it. I am beginning to like it but of course began under difficulties as I knew so few people. However that is all right now and I don't feel so homesick. Christmas really was awful – I missed you all so much and everything out here seemed so strange. I am quite happy now and most awfully glad I came, as I think I have made Henry happier, apart from the fact that I am enjoying myself. The business is sound even if it has fallen on bad times, but everyone has suffered like that here this year. I don't think there is anyone to buy the business, which is a pity, but I often wonder now if it was sold whether Henry would have enough to do out here without it. I expect he would. In his way he is an important man. I have altered my opinion about the man Chapman because I see now he must have been an utter scoundrel. Henry though is like that, and though generally he won't put up with the slightest imperfection in people, yet occasionally he is imposed upon by someone whose insincerity and rottenness are apparent to everyone. What I wondered is that he put up with him for so long. On Sunday night, I don't think I told you, when we were walking home from the concert, Chapman came up to make it up – well it was hardly the thing to do was it when Henry was walking with me? Daddy didn't stop but said something about "I bear you no ill will, neither would I do anything to injure you, but I can never be friends." The next morning he got a letter from Chapman saying that Daddy had the good will of Horn (Chapman's brother-in-law) and that when Horn came down this week Chapman would show him Henry's letters and then Horn couldn't possibly have a good opinion of Henry, so that they had better make friends – did you ever hear anything so idiotic?

Thursday 31st December. Tomorrow is New Year's Day, and I shall be jolly glad when all the festivities are over. I can't help thinking of you all and how much I miss you, so I don't feel too cheerful. When everyone else stops celebrating and starts ordinary life again I shall feel less out of it.

Today we went to see old Phillipps who is taking us to the races again…soon after I got back John arrived to see me and take me out to lunch. He is a queer mixture, such a babe in some ways and so grown up in others. I've given up trying to put him off me. I've told him how old I am, that I am much too old for him, that I'm not in love with him, that I don't know anything about him and vice versa, and heaps of other things on the same line. All he does is to giggle and to say my line of reasoning is wonderful – until I've got exasperated. I think he is quite brainy in his own way but he isn't my kind in the slightest. I can't help liking him because his devotion is so dogged, but on the other hand his way of talking (he has some sort of an accent, but God only knows what – it isn't Lancashire or Cockney, but a cross between them both) and his manners, which are perfectly good, only he doesn't seem at his ease to my mind, would get on my nerves after a time. However he is safe to go about with and infinitely preferable to most of the men I meet.

I played tennis this afternoon at Campbell Forresters. Almost the same people there, and as I played badly I didn't enjoy it over much.

This evening I went to dinner at Spence's which was excellent. There was quite a merry throng there and we threw streamers etc. about…I am undressed and writing this letter at just after 10.30 so you can tell I haven't been very late… Tomorrow… I am getting up at 6.30 for the proclamation parade. Then straight on to Alipore for burra hazri, then racing all day, then dinner and dance. It sounds exciting, but how I wish I were back with you all…

Saturday. [2nd January, 1926] Yesterday went off as I have told you…but I was terribly tired. I had a very good time at the races – lost about 60 Rs., but as Henry had given me 100 Rs. I did not mind so much. Anyhow it is a mug's game…Well this time old Phillipps had his secretary with him, a half caste woman, who I think is quite respectable, but of course no one else does, on account of the old man's awful reputation. That is one of the reasons why I don't like being out with Phillipps. Everyone I expect thinks the worst. At the races Campbell Forrester, who is a dear old soul, came up and asked me who the lady was. When I said "Secretary" he said "No, niece. They always call them niece here."

I saw some people I knew – mostly men – including the doctor of the ship who gave me a good tip for the last race. We went back to Alipore where we drank champagne and ate cake. And then I came back and changed, dined at Spence's and then on to the ship for the dance.

It was a very good show and I thoroughly enjoyed myself. I danced most of the time with Schoolie and with the Doctor. The time seemed to go like a shot. My programme was filled up right from the beginning... I got home at 1.30.

Well today [Saturday] needless to say I got very tired especially as I had wakened at 7.30 this morning so I told Henry I was going to lie down – this was at about 12. When he came up at about 1.15 to call me I couldn't be roused, and, when I did wake up at 2.15, I had no idea that anyone had been in the room, much less spoken to me or touched me.

Then I was just starting the climb up here after lunch as Henry was going off to see the cricket at Eden Gardens, when I heard a voice behind me "Miss Hobbs will you come out to tea with me?" and it was the little Doctor of the *Effingham*...Well I said yes, but of course it was too early to leave then so we came up to the flat – not a soul in it of course – and all my manicure set was laid out as I was intending to polish my nails. I sat down and began, but he insisted on doing it for me. Remembering what Jimmy had told me about N.O.s, I let him, but I was intensely amused, and needless to say that is the first time I've ever had a man manicurist.

I then changed into my white frock...and off we went to Firpo's. It really was funny. I was sitting there whilst he was putting away his hat etc (in reality he was safety-pinning his shirt which had lost a button just under his tie) and I saw two familiar faces, but I wouldn't pretend to notice them. Of course you can guess who they were. Violet and Beatrice Briggs. Violet couldn't resist the temptation to come up and speak to me. She said, after a few preliminaries, "How you've improved! I saw quite a pretty girl come in but I said to Beatrice, 'surely that can't be Dorothy Hobbs.'" Rather a back handed compliment, but still she meant well. She looked very old, but not nearly as loud as she used to be…

Tonight Henry, Jack and I went to dinner at Spence's but Henry was a bit argumentative and bored. We had asked the boy for his last night and as he was staying at Spence's we didn't pay for his dinner, neither did he have anything to drink, so it was a cheap show for us Afterwards I asked him round here where I found that one of Henry's native brokers has sent some flowers, so of course I immediately started to put them in water. Jack wanted to help so poor old Henry got fed up and went to bed and switched off his light. Well I felt a bit uncomfortable but decided to take Jack along to my room and have a talk. After all it is a bed sitting room and incidentally the nicest in the flat. I told him it wasn't a bit of use his thinking about me as that while I liked him tremendously etc. I wasn't a bit in love with him and that I was much too old for him. He said I was as far away from him as the stars and that he knew he'd need 10,000 Rs. a month before he dared ask me again but that he was going to work for it. Oh, I also said that we hadn't anything much in common and he said he thought we had enough. Well, it has ended there and he goes off to Assam tomorrow.

Sunday. [3rd January] Went to the 8.30 Mass at Durrantollah (or however it is spelt.) then Henry and I went for a stroll around the New Market and breakfasted at the Bristol. I came home and rested a bit and then went out to Ballygunge…to tennis…It was a pleasant afternoon. I was the only girl…Schoolie Lever came to call for me and took me out to Firpo's for dinner – being Sunday there is no dancing so we went on to the pictures afterwards where we saw an amusing, though really terrible, film called 'The Wages of Sin.' You can imagine what it was like from the title. However we talked most of the time and the dinner was lovely…I like Schoolie most awfully, and only wish the ship were staying longer. By the way, he is a very clever little man and seems to have leanings towards our Church.

Monday [4th January]…We had the two sailors – Schoolie and the little Irish Doctor – round to dinner. We talked at Spence's till 10.30 then came on here and talked and I sang until 1.30 so you can imagine what a go we have had. Daddy admires Schoolie tremendously and Schoolie stood up to him wonderfully in an argument. He says our house must be marvellous, with a heretic such as Henry and all the white sheep. It has been a funny evening. They loved my singing and of course Daddy loved to hear me too, and was so proud. I can see him now, sitting there looking as pleased as punch. He accompanied me to some of my songs, and Schoolie to others. We talked of you all at home and sat round and the men had drinks and I had tiparis, which I adore, and then after every few songs we'd have a rest and start on religion again. The Doctor is a little fat man and a bit of a lame duck as far as Henry's opinion goes, but he is a dear all the same.

That's what makes it so difficult with Henry. He shows his intolerance so obviously, and if he thinks a man is not as quick witted as himself he's bored straight off. He can't bear people talking to me. Schoolie and I were talking religion once or twice this evening at the table and he would butt in so I told him straight out to let us finish our bit and then he could have his say. Schoolie can argue with him, the Doctor doesn't bother. Then of course Henry gets gushing to the one and takes no notice of the other, so I have to put my spoke in again and be extra nice to the one who might be feeling slighted. It makes things a bit awkward, though, and I have to be on the *qui vive* all the time. Poor old Henry, he is unaccustomed to late nights and 1.30 a.m. is a bit thick for him. I wonder whether he will have a thick head tomorrow. He fancies he isn't over well so has had no dinner tonight, but has had about four whiskies instead, which I think is rather an idiotic procedure.

It is now nearly 2.30 so I must fly...

Tuesday morning. [5th January]...Zoë Pymm is coming down next week for a day or so...I am quite excited at the thought of seeing her.

I am really enjoying myself and having a much better time than I had anticipated. It is really quite settled about the trip round the world – isn't it exciting? Only I wish I had more clothes. I suppose I've really enough, but I'm thinking I ought to have had some riding kit and some more tennis dresses...Will try and write this evening.

Wednesday morning. [6th January] No time to write yesterday. Went to the Rotary Club with Henry and Schoolie Lever. Quite interesting. I was introduced to Lord Meston, the speaker of the day, and lots of other people nearly all of whose faces and names I have forgotten. After that I went out to tennis with Mrs. Chaive, but played so badly I don't like thinking about it. Flew home, changed into my grey frock and red hat...and went off with Henry to the At

Home on the *Effingham*. Henry met heaps of people he knew and thoroughly enjoyed himself, whilst I, in my own quiet way, thoroughly enjoyed myself too. I was seized by a Paymaster Snotty right at the beginning, which made the dear little Irish Doctor very annoyed. Well, we all had tea together and then the Doctor and I danced and had a long talk interrupted though by the Snotty* who came up to ask for a dance. The Snotty gave me a long lecture on getting married – how it was by far the best thing to do, and at the same time to arrange it so that there would be plenty of cash, which he considers extremely important. Of course I was intensely amused by all this. Well, I danced with several other people and was really sorry to say good-bye to the ship…It poured with rain all the afternoon.

Henry read to me when we came home and then Schoolie called for me and we went to Firpo's to dinner and dance. I enjoyed it immensely, but it ended at 12 and my pal wanted a drink so we went to the Grand and found the bar closed there, so I suggested a drink here. So in we came at 12.30. I suppose he stayed an hour, just talking, as Henry, like a mean hound, had told him I was at Girton. Now that spoils everything generally, so I have made Henry promise, this morning, not to tell anyone else. Unfortunately I now hear that we rather disturbed Henry in the next room and that he didn't get to sleep till 3.30 after that. I'm so sorry, but he wasn't a bit annoyed with me. I thought I had better tell you in case he wrote about it to you.

Wednesday evening. [6th January]. Vaughan Jones came round this morning to ask me out to tea to the Saturday Club. Sir Willoughby Carey and his two daughters were there and about five or six other men, including Blunt who is really rather a dear, though I think he does probably drink too much as Henry says. I think it is an awful pity to see these youngsters have five or six chota pegs between 7 and 8 in the evening and then start on martinis, gins and other cocktails. I was asked if I had just left school – wasn't it sweet? Schoolie and the young Doc both thought I was very young but now that Henry has split on my being at Girton it only wants an addition sum and they know how old I am. More or less of course.

I wish I could describe a bit better the extraordinary life I live out

---

* i.e. Midshipman.

here. Schoolie told me that the night they came to our place for dinner they were shown into the room – remember we only have one. (Schoolie was telling me this tale later when I had suddenly noticed a heap of gents' underclothing in the corner.) "Well," he said, "when we came in we scarcely knew where to sit as every chair seemed to have its quota." So you can picture the main room in our flat after dinner. Then there are the extraordinary people we meet. (By the way I ought to have told you about Lord Meston as Henry was pleased to have introduced me, but as I didn't chat to him for more than about half a minute and couldn't hear his speech very well, I'm afraid I've nothing more to add, but remember the name, and remember that I did tell you about him.)

Well, darling, no more now. I won't tell you how much I miss you, but oh if you knew how I long to see you once again! I am always thinking of you and wondering how you are – doesn't it seem ages since we were together?

The Bristol Hotel, Chowringhee, where The Heretics Club met for lunch.

CALCUTTA ADDRESSES IN THE 1920s.

Peliti's premises in Government Place East, the scene of many celebrations.

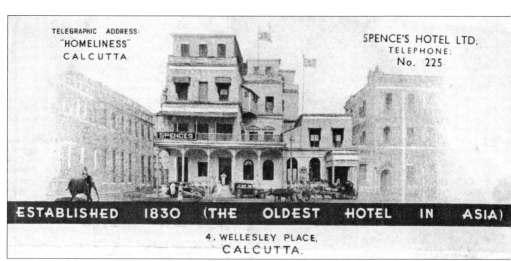

Spence's Hotel, 4, Wellesley Place, later managed by Harry.

240

CHAPTER 15

DOROTHY'S JOURNEY
(3)
A MONTH IN CALCUTTA

OROTHY'S ACCOUNT OF the holiday period was contained in just three letters. The last Chapter sets out the greater part of them.. Letters from both Dorothy and Jennie are couched in often very emotional terms of affection. Jennie frequently refers to Dorothy as "my beautiful Gloire de Dijon" – a reference to a climbing rose (even then rather an old rose) with double golden-buff flowers. Some thirty years on Dorothy was to give me just such a rose to plant against the north wall of our then home: I have often wondered if at the time she had had in mind her own mother's pet name for her. For her part in her letters Dorothy often refers to Dorothy Mary as 'my Wild Rose.'

Letters between Bournemouth and Calcutta would take just under three weeks, in quite a regular and reliable pattern. Inevitably Jennie's comments and (sometimes) advice would reach Dorothy long after any potential problem had come and gone. Fortunately there was little disagreement between them. First reaction to the love sick 'slave' is quite terse and to the point, but not in the least censorious, and comes in a letter from Jennie dated 12th January, which Dorothy could not have received much before the end of that month.

> The proposal was very thrilling but I do hope you will not marry anyone younger than yourself: as a rule it does not lead to happiness.

She did not add – as well she might – that that had been her own experience. Two letters later (dated 27th January) Jennie describes how she shut up tea time gossips about Dorothy's possible emotional entanglements with a canny mixture of bluff and prevarication:

On Friday I went to Mrs. Russell Cotes to tea and bridge. Mrs. Clayton and Mrs. Cross sat next to me at tea; both made kind enquiries about you and said you would be getting married. I said I did not think so, in fact, I said you might become a nun. Oh they said did you want to, did I want you to? I said no I did not and you did not, but you never know. I thought that would stop them – and it did. I said you were having a good time, liked India and were very interested in all you saw. Both sang your praises and I suppose I did too. I said you were sweet and good and that was the best gift one could possess.

She had confidence in Dorothy's good sense but is none the less concerned that she might be overtaxing her strength and so become incautious in those she might meet or in what she might say to them or do with them.

[To] answer your letter. The only discordant note in it is Mr. P[hillipps] taking a dark woman to the races with you. She may be quite respectable as you say, but no one else will think so. However I don't think it has done much harm and perhaps you did not go again. He has no sense in some ways, in others he is clever.

...Please do not write my letters at night. I would rather have shorter ones than you should give up your sleep. And you know how your Daddy likes you to be energetic in the day time I hope he is quite agreeable to your dancing but you will understand him better than I can tell you by now...I can quite understand your Daddy getting bored for no reason but you must not take any notice...I quite understand the life at the flat. At least I want no imagination for that. Of course when I was there it was clean and tidy. It had to be then. But you can now understand your Daddy never wanting anything to be removed. He is not houseproud, although in some things he is particular, but not in the house...I want you to enjoy yourself and do not make yourself too cheap: be particular who you go out with.

Jennie, along with the rest of the family, was plainly very pleased for Dorothy that the long way home had been decided upon by Harry. They were not alone in that. Dorothy had evidently sent a Christmas card and a letter to Mrs Ada C. Beckett with whom she had shared a cabin on the *Rawalpindi* and who was now in Orissa. Having observed, no doubt, Dorothy's effect on the men around her, Mrs Becket replied with considerable encouragement:

…You are very lucky to be going round the world on your homeward journey. Nothing like travelling and seeing other countries and peoples for giving one a broad and sympathetic outlook on life in general. My one and only bridesmaid did just what you are doing and married just two days before the first anniversary of my wedding day. She is now the Countess of Portarlington. We came out to India on the same ship – her first visit to India – and she went on round. I hope you will have a real good time and don't break too many hearts on your meteoric flight round the world!

When Dorothy began a letter home on 7th January that 'meteoric flight' was due to begin just two months ahead. The holiday season was over, many had left Calcutta and she was finding life a bit quiet. She had been to see Mrs Manasseh, the wife of one of her first two 'clicks' on board the *Rawalpindi*, a course of which Jennie expressed her approval in one of her later letters. Dorothy did not think much of the home she shared with her husband's family – 'how I should hate to live the comfortless life of the average Anglo-Indian.' A couple of invitations, one to tennis and one to a dinner dance, brightened the horizon, but

…Lunch was a bit quiet at the Bristol but all the same quite interesting. Watson and Newman of *The Statesman* were the only two there but from what I gathered they are both very much amused by the way in which Henry orders me about, so I laughingly said that Henry was the troop sergeant and I was the troop. Later a lecture on the League of Nations, which was intensely dull and then another lecture at the Asiatic Society on life in an East Indiaman at the end of the seventeenth century which really was quite interesting.

Friday January 8th…Mr Tapissier came round to our table at Spence's to night and talked for a while. He and Henry are both very keen on rubber, so I was learning all about it. Henry has bought today 500 Ayer Plason Rubber Shares, and is going to invest as much more as he can. Two pianos were sold today so he is quite pleased with himself, but still business is bad. That does not mean that this place is being run at a loss. I think Henry told me he drew about £3,000 out of it last year, if not a little more – I think he said about Rs. 50,000, with the rupee at 13 to the £, but I'm not sure – but this is still poor in comparison with what it has been and what it might be…

Saturday January 9th…Henry and Affleck had a slight brush this morning but it was purely over some technical part of the business. I don't like A's attitude in the shop, but there you are!…

I am afraid all my good intentions as to work remain unfulfilled. You see, if I am not going out I chat with Henry, and then our meals take up such ages. For instance, today I have done absolutely nothing, yet here is my timetable. Ayah calls me with tea at 8 a.m. I am downstairs at 9.15. Henry is at Tompsons talking to Wiggett. I go to fetch him, then off to the Bristol to Breakfast at about 9.45. A Stockbroker chats with Henry. Office at 10.30. I rush upstairs, see my room is done, downstairs again, a little wait for Henry, then out to see an I.C.S. Judge in a nursing home who's just had his appendix removed; then St. Paul's Cathedral, Henry knows the Verger so more talking.

Home again by 12.30, hardly are my things off when there is a knock at the door. Henry wants me. So down I go to have a look at another peculiar man, and then someone else comes in so that by the time Henry has "just answered this letter" and finished talking it is 1.30, so off we go to lunch which isn't over till 3 p.m. Then we come home, have tea and then it is after 4 and we have to go to the hospital. I was sitting in the car outside the Hospital for nearly an hour this evening from about 5.30 to about 6.15. Not that I mind. I was perfectly comfortable.

After that, as to day was Saturday, we went to the Grand for a cocktail. Stayed there an hour, came home, rushed my bath and dressing and by the time we had walked to Spence's it was 8.45. Dinner, and now I am writing to you. You see we walk to all our meals, we never have the car for them – and we generally meet someone or something that delays us so that the time we waste on that a day must be over 2½ hours…Now please don't think I'm grumbling…because I'm enjoying it very much. I've only told you because I thought you would like to know how my programme was worked.

Whilst we were waiting outside Peliti's, Edouardo [Peliti] came up and spoke to us. He is such a nice man and has the most interesting face. I think he must have liked you tremendously for he asked after you most anxiously – this, by the way, while Henry was inside getting the ice – and asked me to send you his love. "Love" my dear, so you see what he thinks of you…

[Tuesday 12th January]. In the evening we went to dine at Mr. [Edouardo] Peliti's flat. He is a dear. Poor man I think he is terribly cut up about this affair of his.* We had a lovely dinner and then talk, talk, talk, between the two men. P. was going for Henry in a gentle kind of way, told him it didn't pay to make so many enemies etc., etc. but H. wouldn't have it. However P. scored once or twice and Daddy admitted, "Perhaps you're right." Part of it was interesting, but most of it was very dull. The man who marries me will have a Silent Wife. I have done the training.

Whilst one might understand Dorothy's last, almost exasperated, prognostication, it was never the case in fact. She had inherited too much of her father's ability to talk. It is not clear from whom she inherited her skill and enthusiasm for tennis. I found this a most surprising revelation when I first read these letters. For all the time that I remember Dorothy she never played any active ball game of any description. I was told that she had sprained her knee when a teenager in a fall off her bicycle and so was unable to run properly. But these letters reveal a young woman keen on tennis and, at times, quite good at it. One man invited her to play golf (likewise an activity in which I never recall her partaking) although maybe as much for her company as for her game.

Wednesday 13th January. Just as we were leaving for lunch Oliver telephoned and took me out in his car to the Jodpore Golf Club for tea. He seems quite nice, though I should say a bit of a flirt. He is going to lend me some clubs and I am going to play golf with him on Tuesday morning. I've got to the stage now where I don't mind what I do and I might as well try to play golf as try to do anything else. I had a very nice tea and we wandered around the links beforehand, and I was just too delighted with it for words. The whole

* There is nothing in any letter to explain the nature of this 'affair.'

place is most beautifully kept. Little woods here, a string of palms there, and about forty little lakes, some with water plants, some with rushes, and then up towards the clubhouse, about a dozen tennis courts. There is a magnificent lawn in front of the house and then a large and long veranda and both are bordered in flowers in quantities that I have never seen before. Yes, it is an awfully pretty place.

Well then this evening, dinner with Wile and he brought along a pal and then he took us to the theatre to see Ruth St. Denis and Ted Shawn, with chorus, in their dance show. Unfortunately Henry was just the tiniest, tiniest bit depressed and kept silence. I am afraid I am the unwitting cause of it. You know how men chatter when girls are about – mostly leg-pull and frivolous stuff – and how out here especially, where girls are comparatively scarce, all their attention is on her. Well it was tonight, that's all. I don't think Henry really minds, he is a dear to me I know, but he just can't get used to it – he's absolutely at sea. Anyhow I enjoyed it, and the dancing was lovely. It is now nearly 2. a.m. so I will close down.

In a very short additional letter, hurriedly written the following morning (Thursday, 14th) and posted at once with the main one, Dorothy sends Jennie a present:

I haven't forgotten that this letter ought to reach you in time for the anniversary of your wedding*. You know how I shall be thinking of you and wishing you well on that day. I am sending you £10 which I hope you will spend on something for yourself. Henry will give me any small money I may need so you might as well have this. It might help.

Even on the figures she had quoted in her main letter Harry could hardly have been regarded as anything other than comfortably off. In fact she was to learn from him (if his figures were right) in only a few days' time that he was a great deal better off than the drawings from his business as stated to her on this occasion might indicate. And yet

---

* On 5th February.

here was Dorothy sending her mother a very generous present – surely worth £200 or more in today's money – not just out of love and affection but on the basis that 'it might help.'

Help it surely would. Over the holiday period Arthur had been equipping himself with uniform and other necessaries for the posting of his regiment to India later in 1926. Harry had sent him £20 for the purpose, of which he had spent £18. He was going to draw two months pay in advance before going out, when he heard that he was not going in the first draft. So with no pay in advance, little normal pay left, and only £2 from his father's allowance it was small wonder he asked to borrow £5 from Jennie. She did lend that to him, keeping back a cheque for a similar amount that Dorothy had sent Arthur for his birthday (Boxing Day) so as not to be a burden on her. Then Jennie wanted the fiver back, as she wrote to Dorothy on 17th January:

> …I am writing to Arthur to return me the £5 I lent him. He said he would return it last week. I really cannot let him have it: I need it badly myself. I know you won't mind if I send him your birthday present. I expect that was what he wanted but would not ask for it. Poor boy he has no idea of managing. I hope he will learn now.

These seem to be such small sums to be causing financial problems. Jennie had a big house to run, with the inevitable overheads, and several servants to pay. Harry was the sole provider, and did remit the money, but not always as promptly as he might, and often with much complaint as to how short money was and how expensive was the Bournemouth establishment. In most of Jennie's letters there is some reference to problems with bill paying and anxiety over the arrival of funds from India. By no means all were concerned with Arthur's preparations for travel abroad. It all seems to be rather an unnecessary burden on Jennie which could have been avoided. Harry was in no sense hard up – but that did not prevent him writing to Jennie that money was scarce. One would think it would not have been difficult for him to have removed altogether from her shoulders the day-to-day anxieties about meeting the normal household expenditure. Even in those days arrangements could surely have been set up with the Banks for the smooth running of Chingri Khal, but these were problems with which Jennie was to be faced for the rest of her life.

In the meantime in Calcutta Dorothy was settling down to a routine of meals out ('the food is so frightfully dull – there never seems to be the slightest alteration in the menus of the Bristol in particular'), tennis parties and the occasional dinner dance. Friends of Harry's would often turn up for one of their many meals in the nearby hotels, and some she got to know quite well. One such was Herbert Dudley, the Governor's Bandmaster, for whom Harry had a great respect as a man and a musician – feelings which were reciprocated. Although he ended his life in South Africa, Dudley always remained in contact with the family. He made occasional visits to England on one of which in the mid 1950s he generously took me to a Promenade Concert in London when his still accurate ear and musical knowledge made him a most interesting companion.

In mid January Zoë and Tom Allan were in Calcutta for a friend's wedding. Dorothy had several meetings with them during which arrangements were made for her to make her eagerly awaited visit to their tea garden in Assam, leaving on 6th February. That still left her with plenty of time for a surprising number of odd and awkward encounters.

> Saturday, 16th January. [Last night] I went to Firpo's to dinner. You know, Campbell Forrester's affair. Well the dinner was excellent but I've never been among so many scotch people in my life. Some of them I couldn't understand at all. I suppose we were a party of about sixteen, but all the men were married except a Jute man of about forty, named Peter Mudie, but he didn't dance. However the others weren't bad. Mr. Barrie Brown was on my left. He's a funny little man but I've come to the conclusion that I don't like him. You should see me dancing with him. It's a scream – I watched us in the glass at Firpo's. He was in tails and has the funniest little figure you ever saw, whilst I towered above him like a Spanish Galleon in full sail.
>
> After that we went on to Campbell Forrester's house where we only stayed for about twenty minutes as it was getting late and the men started on chota pegs. There was a woman doctor in the party, named Headwards, who in a way attached herself to me – a terrible looking female but not bad hearted – and we determined to get away before everyone fell asleep, or got too tight to speak. We had great

difficulty in refusing the offers to take us home – everyone had a seven seater and a wonderful driver etc. etc., but we went home together in our host's limousine. Every man squeezed my hand as we said good-bye, including Peter Mudie, but I think they were all a little amorous with drink and I was the only available girl on the scene.

[Today] Joiner gave me a lift to the Saturday Club where I was dancing with rather a charming boy named Becker. He is one of the 'heretics' who come occasionally to the Bristol to lunch. After a while the party grew and I got hold of the best dancer I have met so far in the person of Golledge who is quite charming as well.

Sunday. [17th January] I was just coming home from Spence's with Henry…it was about 10.15 [p.m.]… who should be standing at the top of the stairs but John Bagnall. He couldn't carry on without sight of me apparently and had come in after having some sort of scratch meal somewhere straight from a fifty-four hour journey from Assam. He says he is consulting engineer for McNeil's and can go about pretty much as he likes. So he decided he was needed in Calcutta. Poor boy!…

I am not going to Durruntollah any more as this morning I felt quite ill in church. What it must be like in the hot weather, God only knows. I am going to have the car in future and will drive to the Fort, where I understand the church isn't quite so smelly.

I came home after a chota hazri at the Bristol and…put on tennis gear and went off with Henry to 33, Alipore where we had been invited by old C. L. [Phillipps]. By the way, I've found out why Henry didn't take Phyll and the baby out there last year. He told me himself that he was awfully sorry as he was sure the old man would have made them some glorious presents, but that that German woman was there until the spring and it was well known that they were not getting on, so he never went himself. Old P. doesn't even know that Phyll was out here, but he was telling us himself one day a little bit of news about the Fraulein or his wife – she is his wife, you know, and he's pensioned her off. He says she was a little mad and from what I gathered was impossible with his friends. At the same time the old man himself is a bad hat in many ways and still (at about seventy or more) retains the morals of a tom cat. However he has many good points and I expect the good predominate.

Well, to return to our show today. When we arrived we found a charming little Parisienne doing hostess – Madame Firpo, wife of the restaurateur – and that about twenty-six people were expected for lunch. They arrived in due course – the most extraordinary bunch you ever saw. Mostly Armenians, and you know they are no beauties.

However there was Mrs. Clark, a Eurasian who murdered her husband (her first husband.) At least so Henry says. I expect you will remember the story. Her husband was a pilot and coming home earlier than he was expected he found his wife and a girl they had staying with them and a man named Pugh, I think. You know Pugh killed the husband with a dumb-bell and then shot himself. Henry says Mrs. held him down whilst the man did the actual killing. Anyhow he was playing bridge with her all this afternoon but I don't suppose they talked of it.

…I mustn't forget to say we had had lunch on his [Phillipps's] long table – there were the usual luscious things to eat and today for a wonder the place looked clean and the furniture had shed its shirts and the staff were in fresh clothes. I can't let the old man down always, can I?

Tuesday, [19th January] I have had a nice but tiring day. Was out at 8 with Oliver, and played golf at Jodpore – don't you think that was brave of me? He lent me his clubs and after a few trial swings I started off, and really I don't think I have ever played so well in my life. Of course that isn't saying much but still it was very encouraging for me. Unfortunately I went into one of the tanks twice and the chochras had to paddle about a bit and find the wretched ball. Then we had breakfast under a tree on the lawn and then home…

Afterwards I went out to lunch with Mrs. Manasseh. She is rather charming and I did so enjoy home food after so many meals in hotels. It was a hen party and there were seven of us. Three were Australian…ladies (who were no Gladys Coopers and were enormous women.) They said that they came across no humour in India – nobody ever seemed either amused or amusing – but they made two exceptions. One was 'Kim,' which is the *nom de plume* of Mr. Newman who writes his column in *The Statesman* under that name, and the other 'Mr. Hobbs.' Of course I had to tell Henry when I got home and he was fearfully bucked.

Wednesday [20th January]…Last night…Henry had been invited out to a Masonic Dinner so I had asked John Bagnall to take me out and then on to the pictures. We dined at Spence's. I chose it as I don't want to spend too much of his money. [We] went to see Douglas Fairbanks in 'Don Q. the son of Zorro' but it wasn't up to much. John is getting too love sick for words and I'm beginning to feel I can't cope with him. He won't talk, but simply sits and gazes at me. He doesn't dance, or drink (much), or smoke, or play cards. This sounds rather saint-like, but that is the last thing he is. I should imagine he had come from a poorish north country family and had worked so hard that he had never had time to do these things. Well the result is that he has only one social side left – talking – and he can do a little of that at times but lately he seems to have dried up completely – anyhow when I'm with him.

It so happens that one letter from Harry to Jennie survives from this period – written on 19th January. It is perfectly friendly, detailing his proposals for taking out life insurance for Arthur and giving her some news about the deaths of two old friends whom she would have known. He also sends her the itinerary for the journey home. Of Dorothy he writes she 'is well and as she is writing long letters to you it looks as though my details will be unnecessary; at any rate she is enjoying herself and has much to be thankful for.' She may well have agreed broadly with him about his final observation, but I have some doubt as to whether she would have wholeheartedly included the attentions of those of the opposite sex. Her letter continues:

Friday January 22nd…In the evening [yesterday] I went out with Oliver. He called for me at about eight and we went off to have dinner at his club – the U.S. Club – at least they have a special sort of bungalow attached where ladies can be fed. After we went to the Palais de Dance which is just on a par with the Westover [in Bournemouth] in appearance, though the crowd I should say was slightly better. I, however, didn't have much opportunity of judging, as there were at most eight couples dancing. Of course there were a few odd men knocking around. Oliver doesn't dance badly, but not well. I had a most amusing evening.

He started on about marriage during dinner, and all the various friends he had had and the little sidelights on their marriages. At the dance he started talking about Romance, how it didn't always go with marriage, which was a great pity. He then said he was romantic, then that no one should ever let the great opportunity of making a romantic marriage slip by, and then that I was romantic and that no one could say that I was not "with those kissable lips of yours." On the journey home he tried to put his arm round my waist but I told him he'd kill us both (i.e., he was driving.)

Now what do you think of your pal Oliver? He is old enough to be my father and yet makes love so shamelessly. However, I don't mind – not in small doses – and I think I see through it all. I don't think he is the slightest bit in love with me but (1) he may want to flirt around a bit or (2) he may really consider me thoroughly 'eligible.'

I shall soon be getting a thoroughly rapid brain, as none of the older men seem to be talking anything else but "love."

It was dancing ability that gave the young, and the not-so-young man the possibility of getting close to Dorothy – geographically as well as socially. A good dancer could find himself whirling her around the floor even if she found him unattractive in other ways. Weeks before, on the *Rawalpindi,* she had found herself enjoying dancing with the married Mr Manasseh, despite not otherwise very much caring for him personally. Now his brother came upon the scene, with even greater ability for the light fantastic but perhaps even fewer other attributes giving rise to personal attraction.

Saturday [23rd January]...I danced at Firpo's with Manasseh's elder brother who is a bachelor. He's an awful looking Jew but quite attractive, I suppose because he dances fairly well. I had only met him once before at the races, and had heard he was most keen on dancing, and I am quite glad I went. He is one of those energetic dancers and has the idea of the three steps all right but is inclined to pull his partner about a bit. We tango-ed and it was an exhibition dance on our part for about five minutes. However I enjoyed that and think the exercise has done me good.

Jack Bagnall came round to dinner and took me to Chota Wembley after. It was quite amusing. We went to what they called a Rodeo which wasn't at all bad. Well they had a steer riding item and we were in the front row just behind the wire fencing of the ring. Well this beast made a charge and came straight for me. Everyone got up round us and John put his arms round me – what he intended to do if the thing had broken through I don't know, as it was pulled up in time. But I have wondered since whether the steel wire fence would have given way. Needless to say I was too terrified to move.

Sunday night. [24th January] Just after I had finished writing this to you yesterday my devoted slave Jack came in. He looked rather ill and shaky – I felt so sorry for him. You know I am far too tender hearted where men are concerned and always imagine they are worse off than they really are. However, to return to my pal. He said he had been up most of the night and had come round thinking he must see me once more before he went away. He is in terror of being sent back to Calcutta whilst I am in Jalpaiguri, and thence on to the wilds of Assam when I come back again, and so missing me as we leave on March 7th. I have told him that if I come back to India I'll probably be married to someone else, but I think he still thinks he's going to be the lucky one.

Dorothy seems to have felt that Jennie might find this parade of admirers, described in so much detail in her letters, a source of anxiety as to whether the next thing she would hear is of wedding bells being rung. So she sought to reassure her mother in this letter, a passage which carried on naturally into describing how one of the (ineligible, and, to be fair, never a suitor) male acquaintances lived.

Your letters came today. Of course you know, darling, that I wouldn't even fall in love with anyone without you could make a very certain guess beforehand, and I hope that so far you have made a pretty certain guess that I am not in love with anyone, because I am not. Nor do I think there is the faintest likelihood of it. I'm beginning to think I am growing more like a man every day. I scarcely ever speak to a woman at meal times and the conversations we do have are extraordinary. For instance, today we spent the day out at Watson's place. Watson is one of the Bristol lunchers and his place is about fifteen miles up the river on the Howrah side. There were two other men there. We talked Sir Oliver Lodge and Arthur Waves* during lunch and religion at dinner, at which we were sitting until a quarter to ten. So you see everyone was interested.

Watson is a manufacturing chemist, married, but wife and three children are at home. He and the other partner have this lovely house up the river with a garden that slopes down to the water's edge. The place is very nicely kept, beautifully clean and dustless inside and quite nicely furnished for this country, while the view from the verandas over the river is the most beautiful sight I have yet seen in India. The Hooghly isn't a crowded thoroughfare here, but there is a

---

* There is no clue as to what she means by the reference to these two men.

fairly continuous stream of traffic in the way of small craft, generally very picturesque, passing up and down. On the opposite bank there were luxuriant palms and greenery, etc. and some rather fine temples just tucked away here and there. The tennis lawn, where we played, overlooked all this, too, and now I come to think of it I don't wonder I didn't keep my eye on the ball.

Of course Henry arrived too early. He's so mad about punctuality that he loses all his common sense, so for lunch and tennis (they asked us afterwards to dinner) we arrived at 11.30 a.m., which I think is too early. We had two things for lunch that will interest you. One was curry. It was the best I have ever tasted, and even Henry, who is so mad about old Phillipps's curry, admitted that; and the other was a 'game pie.' At least they called it that only it was really done in a large dish in aspic, with mushrooms and hard eggs and not turned out and no pastry. This I think is quite an idea and I mean to try it when I get home. I think the game used was black cock or perhaps wild duck. Only breasts were used.

Dorothy's letters home contained many instructions to her mother, all meant with Jennie's well-being in mind. How she was to have her hair done, where to get a new dress or hat, how to take care of herself, and not to over tax her strength. At times she seems almost bossy, but Jennie was always glad to have Dorothy's views. Dorothy was also adept at what might be called gardening by remote control. By now she had a good working knowledge of horticulture and gardening generally, having been very much the driving force behind the creation and development of the garden at Chingri Khal, doing a lot of the physical work in it as well as giving the gardener orders. It may be thought that a little bossiness appears in the next passage in this letter:

I want you to tell the gardener this AT ONCE. He is to save all the droppings from the fowls* and dump them in a part of the garden where there is no likelihood of contamination by the pine trees. By the end of March, if he starts off right away, he ought to have some good manure. Towards the end of March would you send for Arthur Radmore† to come and prune the roses. He promised me he would

* There was a large chicken run as well as kennels by the entrance to the wood.
† The proprietor of a rose nursery at the eastern end of Queen's Park Avenue.

do so and I don't think he will charge you so much, and he may not charge anything, as after all they are his roses. Well, when this has been done the gardener must fork in the fowl manure well into the roots of the roses. He must get it into the beds and not just lay it on top. Later, in about May he must get and use an artificial manure that Radmore recommends…He will give you the name as I have forgotten it. Do get this done, darling, as I want the garden to look nice, and especially for Phyllis as she'll just about be getting up when the roses come out. I often have wondered how the bulbs have done but as no one has said anything at all about them I am afraid they must have been a failure.

The reference to Phyllis getting up is the first mention in the correspondence that Phyllis was pregnant with her second child, a pregnancy which must have been known to the family from before the time when Dorothy left for India. It was to become quite a topic for discussion in their letters during later months. It was strange that Dorothy used the impersonal phrase 'the gardener' rather than his name. Arthur Hall had been their chauffeur gardener for some time already by the date Dorothy left home and was to remain in Jennie's employment until after the outbreak of the Second War. So he was quite one of the family. As for news of the garden, Dorothy was not allowing enough time for the post containing it to get to her. Jennie, together with Hall, obviously had her return very much in mind. Most of Jennie's letters have some reference to the garden; two will give some idea of the enterprise:

12th January. The gardener has put up the trelliswork in the rose garden and very nice it looks. You will be pleased to hear that the camellia, which was near the peach tree, has been taken up and put in the conservatory and is actually blooming for the first time. I mean the buds are just forming. The cyclamen are also are also bursting forth and are looking so healthy. The one you gave me is still in full bloom in the drawing room and the azalea in the drawing room has still got numerous buds on. The Australian plant is bursting into bloom and that pretty one I got at Jean's is going to bloom. The freesias look very healthy…and today Hall and I discovered the first bloom. I think there are about fifty geraniums in the conservatory; also some marguerites and all ought to be in full bloom by Easter. The bulbs are above ground all looking very healthy. I am getting the names from Hall, so I will be able to tell you next week which are the most forward.

17th January. First of all I am sending you a list of seeds for the flower garden [it contains the names of three bulbs and thirty three seeds]. Hall informed me that you were partial to blue. I told him your Daddy liked cornflowers. He said Miss Dorothy is also fond of blue flowers. So I got forget-me-nots for you and the cornflowers for Daddy. Hall has been asking me about them. He said you wanted them for the garden. So I said yes…The garden ought to look lovely when you come home…P.S. I think the garden will be a blaze of colour by your return…Hall tells me the snow will do the bulbs an immense amount of good. The ones in the conservatory are looking so healthy; in fact everything in there is doing well.

Dorothy evidently need not have worried: the garden was in good hands. The promise of a colourful garden on her return may have made her the more homesick. She was showing signs of having had enough of Calcutta.

[26th January] I think Calcutta is a very *cutcha* place and I can understand now why Henry thinks our house at home is so wonderful. Even the hotels and the restaurants are fifth rate with the exception, perhaps, of Firpo's which is third rate. My room is about the most artistic thing I have seen yet but that is *cutcha*, too. I have left out one thing: the racing; and that is first class – I must give it its due.

I had a letter…from Zoë asking me to stay up with her until 24th, as she wants to give a dinner party on the 23rd. I sounded Henry and he said "Of course," but in such a way that I felt bound to refuse. So I wrote to that effect to Zoë saying I could only stay my bare fortnight. What is more amusing is that Henry thinks I'll be bored up there – among people I like and with a camp week going on; he never dreams that I might get a bit bored here – so he said today that all I need do was to write to him from Jalpaiguri and he'd send me a wire to come back. I think he's a bit jealous of me.

This afternoon I played golf with Oliver and did one hole in 5, which is a record for me, as it was a fairly long hole. All the same I think golf a rotten game (so sorry for the word you hate so.) We had tea out there and then he had dinner with us at Spence's. He was almost as affectionate as he was last week only somehow now I feel more capable of coping with it. I think I have made him feel that he must proceed more gingerly with me. Only I wish to goodness he wouldn't say ENGland instead of INGland – the way we and other civilised people pronounce it.

By this time there was only a little over a week before Dorothy was due to go to Assam. Much of her next letter describes similar happenings; more tennis, dinner dances, and some talks to learned societies. In addition, however, the attentions of some of her amorously inclined men were getting almost too much for her. She was thankful that she would be going away quite soon. Furthermore she became a little involved in Harry's business affairs as an observer, as well as giving vent to some fairly critical comments about him and his friends.

Friday January 29th. I went out to dinner with Oliver last night and the Palais afterwards. I now feel I can cope with him. He tried to kiss me but I laughed him off each time last night, but I have come to the conclusion I don't like him so frightfully.

…You know I wouldn't say this to anyone in the world but to you all at home, but as a general rule if Henry knows a man who is in a decent position socially, that man is no good. Always excepting the heretics' table for lunch. All the army people are rankers and drop their 'aitches.' Mr. Dudley nearly drives me mad at times, though he's quite a decent sort otherwise, and the amount of fifth rate people I have met would send you to your grave. However it is very interesting and I only hope I am doing good by coming out here.

Later. The more I see of Henry the sorrier I am for him. He has absolutely no manners, poor chap, and is very often positively rude to people. I do hope my being out here isn't worrying him too much.

I had a letter from John Bagnall today…he told me about meeting [Zoë] at the Club in Jalpaiguri on his way up to Binaguti where he is staying with K. D. Murray, the darling old chap who sat next to me in the ship. Isn't it strange that they should all meet?

I am glad that her attitude to Herbert Dudley mellowed over the years. By the time I remember meeting him she had quite a soft spot for him. He was certainly a thoroughly upright and decent man, as well as a fine musician. The softening process was evident in this same letter:

> Saturday. [30th January] Dudley came in at dinner and had his with us. He is a nice little chap and very boyish in his enthusiasms, which is all the more surprising when one considers he is very nearly fifty.
>
> Sunday 31st January...Mr. Joiner had very kindly asked Henry and me and so we went to the Fogt's house in Cossipore. It is a beautiful place with two courts, one green, and the other one a hard red court, but both were beautifully kept. In fact the whole place was beautifully kept and most artistically furnished – something really first class about it. And though the house is spoilt in a way by a bad approach, for one has to go through the Jute country – native villages and Jute go-downs inextricably mixed up - yet when you get there everything is shut away and there is the house and a garden full of flowers, the tennis court, beautiful lawns and the river. It surprises me to find anything so beautiful in Calcutta, which may be the city of palaces but they are only [beautiful] when viewed from the distance. Close to they look very *cutcha*. This Sunday and last have been very happy days and have been spent in very happy surroundings.

Dorothy evidently felt that the main event of the following day required a rather less public forum than her main letter home which, she no doubt rightly assumed would be read by all and sundry. So she wrote a separate small letter to Jennie.

> [Monday] February 1st...This is a private note, not that here is anything in it of a very private nature but I thought that what I had to say had better not go in the general letter that I had sent and also I thought I would leave it to your discretion to tell the rest of the family. It's purely business anyhow.
>
> The first is about Henry's income. He told me the other day when we were talking about shares that his income must be about nine thousand pounds (£9,000) a year, which I thought might interest you. I suppose therefore that he is worth about a hundred thousand, always assuming that the business could be sold for what it is worth, which I am afraid is not the case. Anyhow you will be relieved to hear he is by no means a poor man.

The second is that tonight we gave a dinner for Leas, Taylor and Jones. Henry is making them directors for the time he is away. This means that they will be on equal terms with A.K.A. whilst Henry is away; will have an equal voice, each one of them, in running the business and also will be able to get an insight into affairs which has not been so easy so far. All this ought to bring out any good qualities that they may have; but beyond their Directors' Fees of Rs.32 a month they will not get any money out of it. Henry then went on to urge them to improve themselves both from a business point of view and from an intellectual standpoint. He had offered to pay for them to have correspondence and bookkeeping lessons, and generally gave them good advice. He then explained that A.K.A. had only two and a half years to stay on in the firm and that while he (i.e., Henry) was making no promises he wanted to be able to rely on them when A.K.A.'s time was up. He was glad that I was there, as I had heard all that he had to say, and if anything happened to him [I] would keep his word.

They all seemed tremendously pleased about it but remember this is confidential – don't tell anyone, except one of the family if you think fit. I have at least in this been able to help Henry, as he has repeatedly said how glad he was I was there to hear what he had said and what arrangements he had made. He says my presence made his words so much stronger because so much more binding. So I'm very glad I came.

In her main letter Dorothy reported on the Rotary Club lunch on that Tuesday – excellent speaker, bad meal – after which Harry spoke "rather uselessly;" he could not "keep to the point." The following evening there was yet more dancing.

[Wednesday 3rd February]…To night I went to Firpo's – or rather this evening. I went with the elder and single Manasseh who is the brother of the one who travelled out with me. There were heaps of people I knew at Firpo's this evening and so it was most interesting. My partner and I got up to do the Tango. About half way through we were joined by another couple and in spite of being so much in the limelight, as one might say, we were given three encores. Mrs. Griffin Chaive told me she had heard some people say we were very good dancers and then someone chimed in with "I should think they were professionals." So when I see him again I am going to tell him. As a matter of fact he asked me to go to the Kalimpong Dance at the Saturday Club, but, as I didn't know him frightfully well, I refused – said I had another engagement…he has asked me to keep tomorrow night open for him and I have agreed – Firpo's being the destinations – although Oliver has already written for tomorrow too. But, as Oliver has got to the 'trying-to-kiss-me' stage, I think I'd prefer the Jew. What a choice!! However, neither of them is bad. Oliver is the better looking and a terrible dancer. Manasseh is quite frankly ugly and not a bad dancer but I expect he would be more difficult to handle were he roused. He told me today he was forty and my grey hairs were most fascinating.

The day after the completion of the last letter saw the arrival of some long awaited good news by cable from England. It had been confirmed that Jimmy Breaks was to be appointed to the Royal Yacht, *HMS Victoria and Albert*. It had been expected for several weeks, but the delay had been causing the family to get close to giving up hope. It was, of course, a considerable feather in his cap, and would mark the start of a period in his career when both he and Phyllis would have great opportunity for an interesting as well as a social time. Dorothy was obviously delighted with the news, writing to them both to congratulate, as well as expressing her delight in her letter to Jennie.

The day's events, however, were going to provoke another 'private' letter to Jennie arising out of the evening's activities which had been foreshadowed at the end of the last letter. Man trouble! And only three days to go to Assam!

[Thursday] 4th February. I went out to Firpo's with Manasseh…Saw lots of people I knew at Firpo's – that is, one or two including Zoë and Mrs. Paull and her two daughters. Zoë came over to speak to me and I introduced her to Manasseh – Adrian, isn't it an awful name? She had come with a message from Mrs. Paull asking me to go to their flat tomorrow night to a fancy dress dance, or ordinary clothes if I liked. I told Zoë I couldn't manage it as I was going to the Torchlight Tattoo with Henry. Later I went to thank Mrs.Paull and she insists on my coming after the Tattoo. Says the dance is going on till four a.m., and a young man in their party, before I was introduced or anything, simply implored me to come or, he said, he wouldn't sleep tonight if I refused. Whilst I was dancing with Manasseh this other chap followed me around the room with his partner and made eyes in the most unblushing and amusing manner. Manasseh and I did the Tango, almost an exhibition, and got on quite well. He has the making of quite a decent dancer, but he's a bit old – 40. He thinks I am about 22. How would you like what Harry calls a Baghdadi Jew for a son-in-law! But there isn't any hope in that line. What a life!! What a day!

The final exclamations were no doubt induced by the complete events of the day which Dorothy chronicled in the short separate letter of the same date.

I have come in after rather an exciting evening and feel I must tell you all about it. I have marked this letter 'Private' because I don't want you to leave it lying about, but of course let any of the family read it as you think fit.

You know that Mr. Oliver had asked me out to dinner to night. Well, as he had tried to kiss me all the time he was driving me home last time and was prevented not so much by me as by the fact that he had to drive his car, I wasn't keen on going. I didn't want to explain to Henry and I had another invite so accepted that. But I'm afraid it was out of the frying pan into the fire.

I was asked out to 2/1 Russell Street to dinner and naturally thought Mrs. Manasseh would be there. No. The brother has his own flat, and quite apart from hers, and I had dinner with him solo. However that went off all right, and I suppose these things are done so often now and girls are so free that nobody minds. Only I would have insisted on a dinner at a restaurant had I known that it was not at Mrs. Manasseh's flat. However it cannot be helped now. He is quite an interesting man but looks simply terrible – you have no idea how ugly he is, but I'll explain when I see you.

Then we went on to Firpo's – about that I'll tell you in the general letter – and then he drove me home. He started by putting his arm round me but I stopped him. Then I talked hard, but I knew what was coming and couldn't keep up the conversation long enough. He started on about asking if R.C.s said it was wrong to kiss, and I said "No, of course not." Taking the bait like an idiot. He then begged and implored me to kiss him and I wouldn't and didn't, but he kissed me about twice and kissed my hands. I got him cool in the end, but I think he thinks I'm a bit in love with him. Thank God I am going away. It was quite exciting though, but I wouldn't like this life long. No home comforts and a lot of trouble looking after oneself.

Enough problems, one might have thought, before her departure on Saturday evening, but, having dealt with the younger, if not very young, men, Dorothy found herself having to grapple with Father Trouble.

Friday 5th February. Today is the anniversary of your wedding, darling, and needless to say you have been in my mind even more than usual. Zoë Pymm and I got a wreath each from Chattergee in the New Market. They were beautiful ones and looked so sweet and fresh and we went off to the cemetery where she laid hers on her father's grave and I laid mine on the two little brothers. I did not know what day to choose and then thought that as you would know nothing about it on that day, the anniversary of your wedding, so it would not upset you, and that afterwards, when you heard about it, you would be glad to know that I had chosen 5th February. The grave was quite decently kept and looked so pretty with the flowers. I thought of you and of them and said a little prayer. Zoë and I then went on to her father's grave where we again stopped and then home.

In the afternoon I went to Firpo's…Whilst I was there Zoë came in with an extra special message from Mrs.Paull saying I must go to her dance tonight. When I got home Mr.Watson was there as he came with us to dinner and to the tattoo. I had already spoken of the dance at Mrs. Paull's, but Henry had taken no notice. He has developed a habit of not paying any attention to what one says. So I said I was going.

He waited till Watson had gone in for his bath and then started. He wasn't a scrap angry with me, but he went on about the Paull's in the most shocking manner. Don't tell anybody, and of course I cannot tell Zoë. He said the most awful things about Mrs. Paull's mother and about Jews in general, though he admitted he knew nothing against these people themselves. Anyhow I wasn't allowed to go, and as I didn't think it worthwhile having a row over this, I left it. But I was more annoyed than I can say because I knew he was jealous of my going out, and annoyed because Mrs. Paull hadn't told me when I first met her (it was only half an hour) how she knew Daddy and thought what a fine man he was etc., and especially because when we came home, instead of letting me go to bed, they sat down and talked rainfall for a solid three quarters of a hour. So now it is just as late as if I had gone on to the dance.

Well, the dinner went off badly. Henry had been annoyed and it apparently makes him a worse host than ever, although the guest was his friend and he had invited him. At the Tattoo it was all right. The Tattoo itself was quite interesting although a bit drawn out. Some items were very fine. There was a night attack on a trench, with a tank and armoured cars thrown in. That was done exceedingly well and one or two of the soldiers who were 'shot' did their parts extraordinarily well, just rolling over and giving one or two convulsive kicks before they 'died' and so on. I got a bit frightened at the guns myself, as I am a creature that dislikes noise. Then there was some wonderful trick riding by the Senide Horse. I think perhaps that was the most interesting of all the items, but I must say it was all good. Oh, but I mustn't miss out the Massed Bands which were excellent.

I really enjoyed it and appreciated all the work and forethought entailed. The setting was rather beautiful – they must have had an artist on that – and so was the music. The only thing against it was that the intervals were too long and many of the items could be shortened by one half. Also if I had been allowed to go on to the dance afterwards I should have enjoyed myself ever so much more.

It was a somewhat sad note on which to end her account of her first stint in Calcutta. The cause of it was plainly still rankling with her even after the journey north. But the next two weeks were to be the highlight for her of the whole journey, which would very soon have made up for the disappointments of the last few days in Calcutta. They were to be the only significant time from December to August in which she was not virtually constantly in her father's company. I would hesitate to suggest that this is necessarily cause and effect: but it is certainly true that he was not an easy travelling companion.

CHAPTER 16

DOROTHY'S JOURNEY (4)
HOSPITALITY NEARLY IN ASSAM

NEARLY – BUT NOT QUITE. The Dangua Jhar Tea Estate at which Dorothy was to be the guest of Tom and Zoë Allan is in North Bengal and not in Assam. The tea gardens in the Himalayan foothills go in an amazing sweep practically from the Burmese border – Cachar and Sylhet, then Assam and then into Bengal to the Duars and finally the Tarai District and Darjeeling. Jalpaiguri itself is under one hundred miles from the border with Assam, just about half way there from Darjeeling. Not an insignificant distance, perhaps, but in terms of the distances involved on the Indian Sub-Continent not enormous. I like to think that poor Bob Sutton (he who laughed himself to death at Harry's misfortunes in the Assam that he, Bob, so longed to visit) would have regarded the hospitality Dorothy was to enjoy there as a fair example of the subject of his dreams.

But before that was to happen, Dorothy's last few hours in Calcutta were not the most carefree of her time out there. Why Harry should have wanted to be so cantankerous just before she left is a bit of a mystery. It could only have served to have made Dorothy all the more delighted to be away from him for a couple of weeks. She had an overnight journey and continued her letter on the evening of the day she arrived, harking back to the day of departure.

[Saturday 6th February]. Went...to say good-bye to old Phillipps. Now how can Henry complain about my going with the Paulls who are really decent people – he is a pilot – and yet I am seen in public with a wicked old man like old Phillipps whom everyone knows hasn't even the morals of a Tom Cat? I sometimes wonder what sort of a reputation I should have in Calcutta if I were here long enough...

I am afraid I was getting on Henry's nerves yesterday. He insisted on playing one of my accompaniments…after lunch. He didn't know it and made a hash of it. Naturally I hadn't said anything because I only sing to please him. I must tell you that Mr. Dudley was there. We then started to play patience and he started on about my singing. How that I didn't concentrate on it and so sang sloppily. He then went on about my not sending him books he liked, so I could see he was in one of those nasty moods of his when he is thoroughly happy in making other people miserable. However I was in too much of a hurry to feel miserable as I had to see that my packing was done.

We had dinner at the Bristol – a miserable affair. Henry was then thoroughly upset that I was going away from him. Quaint, ain't he? We got to the station and I found I had a very comfortable berth waiting for me, and my ayah there and the bed made up. Then Zoë was late and only caught the train with about three minutes to spare. I got such a fright and poor old Henry and Dudley were just going to make an effort and heave me and my baggage out of the compartment when up she turned. We had a very pleasant journey and I slept most of the way.

They arrived at Jalpaiguri the following morning and were driven by Tom to their bungalow in the Dangua Jhar Tea Company's premises on the Rungamalli Tea Estate. Dorothy was entranced by it, and especially by the garden.

There is a great bush of bougainvillea out in full bloom…and lots of roses and sweet peas, the best I have yet seen in India and quite as good as any we have at home. It makes me rather homesick to see the familiar flowers and to realise how long before I see them at Chingri Khal…The place is so home like, and such a change from Calcutta on that account. We had breakfast, and just fancy! it was the first breakfast I have had in India that didn't mean ninety-three steps up and down, plus thirty up and down.

The social life she was about to enjoy so much was in no small measure due to the period of her stay coinciding with 'camp week', or, more correctly, two 'camp weeks' in succession. These were occasions, it seems, when the local military returned to a nearby base, let their hair down, and enjoyed to the full the comforts of mess life, club life and of such female company as may be around. Because of the numbers involved, on this occasion at any rate, not all the military personnel could be accommodated, and so one half came for one week, the other half for the next. Not only did that result in a great amount of tennis, dancing, dining and partyfying generally, but Dorothy was doing so in company of young, and some not quite so young, men whom she found rather more congenial than those, in the main, whom she had met in Calcutta. So congenial, indeed, that Zoë, who was in much the position of an older married sister to Dorothy at this time, there being nearly seven years between them, took upon herself the mantle, almost, of matchmaker, certainly match-suggester.

But, in advance of the general jollifications beginning, Dorothy found herself having to be off with the old love before surveying a somewhat bewildering array of potential new ones. I have to confess to being a little surprised at the abrupt way in which her devoted slave makes his final appearance in her letters home.

> [Sunday. 7th February]. I must tell you that poor old John Bagnall tried to come in to see me today, but couldn't. So is coming tomorrow. He is going down to Calcutta and then on to Cachar in Assam.
>
> [Tuesday. 9th February]. Went to the club yesterday. I saw John Bagnall for about half an hour. Poor boy! I suppose that is the last of him.

And so, it would seem, it was.

The fun and games began that day, although not at full steam because the band was not due until the Wednesday evening. But that did not prevent the fun beginning. A Mr. Tony Gurdon, the local manager of the Imperial Bank of India and a bachelor, who lived much closer to the Club and to the Officers' Mess than the Allan's bungalow, put a room in his house at the disposal of Dorothy and Zoë. They could use this as a changing room between tennis and lunch and bridge and dinner and dancing. There was plenty of all of it. Men far outnumbered women and Dorothy, along with most women, I daresay, was booked for every dance. She was very pleased to be taken for seventeen and a half and also to find that the standard of the dancing was a good deal higher than it had been in Calcutta. And she was much in demand: by the end of Tuesday her dance card was fully booked for the week.

That day the entertainment was at the Officers' Mess where, at dinner, Dorothy found herself sitting between the Adjutant and a man

> …who is a Darjeeling Solicitor. He says he knows Henry etc. etc. and so of course I was at once suspicious and now find out I was right, as Henry's friends are nearly always shady and Zoë says this man is a bad hat.

Dancing followed, to a gramophone, without apparently anything particular to report.

Dorothy starts her next letter (next one to Jennie, that is: she states – almost complains – that she "wrote nine letters last week", including more than one to her father) with a brief description of the ambience at the bungalow – very different from that in Calcutta, before continuing with the saga of the dizzy social whirl.

> You cannot imagine how much I am enjoying it out here. It is so beautifully clean and quiet, and the garden is so peaceful. There are pigeons cooing away just now and the bungalow is bathed in nice warm sunshine. It is like being at home once again and I am very happy.
>
> [Wednesday 10th February]…We had [dinner] in Major Gow's bungalow in Jalpaiguri. He is an I.M.S. [Indian Medical Service] doctor and a bachelor but is rather run to death by a Mrs. Nelson who is wife of the local I.C.S. [Indian Civil Service] man. Hence great scandal, though I am sure there is nothing in it…He is one of those cheerful little Scotsmen… He gave us a glorious dinner – Zoë, myself, Mrs. Nelson, Tom and Tony Gurdon… It was a very cheerful party that left for the dance later on. Well then, I had a great time. I have got off with a policeman from Howrah who is going to take me to Firpo's when we get back, and I had a glorious 'flirt' quite in the public [eye] with Major Gow, so I expect my name is mud with Mrs. Nelson…

[Thursday 11th February]. We went in to see the point to point which was quite good only, of course, I did not back the winner. However my horse didn't lose his rider – a pal of mine – and didn't quite come in last, so I've that much to be thankful for. Then tea and we danced a bit before dinner and then dancing again. I have had a great time and don't think I have enjoyed myself so much in my life...We had dinner again in Mess but it wasn't up to very much last night as I was in rather a draught and had the leg of the table and of the chicken to contend with. However it really was an enjoyable show...

...Zoë says I am a success. In any case I am having a heavenly time...I have three flames in particular – Hutchinson, Le Brocq and Tony Gurdon...Everyone raved over [my frock]...and over my frock the night before...When the doctor (Major Gow) came into the drawing room he made me get up and turn round and then he hugged me because I looked so nice. We had a lovely dinner and then on to the dance, where, as usual, I have a stream of partners. I'm afraid I am getting dreadfully spoilt, but oh mother darling it is a pleasant process.

Hutchinson is tall and fair with a snub nose and very blue eyes. He is very amusing and one of the most charming boys I have met. But he drinks like nothing on earth and I think is half seas over all the time. He is the last person who ought to be out here because he must have company and plenty to do. He is quite brainy, but it makes me feel very sad to see him running to seed like this.

Le Brocq is another adorer. He's a policeman, though only a baby one, and is tall and dark and is stationed in Howrah. He is going to take me out as soon as I get back to Calcutta.

[Saturday 13th February] was a great night. First of all in the afternoon we went to watch the games – no sports...Everyone was there in their finery...Well, it was very pleasant sitting there surrounded by young men, but nothing reportable happened, it was just amusing. Then we had dinner in Mess, and I was taken in by a young South Lancs. Sub, who was very tall and fair and quite a good dancer. The dinner was a tremendous success. Prizes were given for the sports, there was a perfect din at the end, each squadron toasting "the ladies" etc and then all joining in to "the Colonel" etc. etc., and from there we went into dancing. I have found about four quite good dancers, and the others are chosen because they are so nice. I enjoyed it tremendously, but at the same time I felt a little sad. You know I am far too tender hearted and all these 'troopers' have been so nice to me, that I got quite sorry to say "good-bye." You see the second week of camp means another lot in because generally the gardens cannot send their full contingent together. Some, though, will be staying on. They have made me promise to try and come out next year…

After the dance we went to a supper party given by Major Gow. I sat next to Hutch, who is quite barmy about me, calls me "the fell lady" and "the princess" etc. As a matter of fact that doesn't look amusing, but if you had met him it would have been different. He is so nice…but it is such a pity to see him – he's never drunk but he does drink too much and is as thin as a rake. I think that is one of the things that has struck me most out here – the pathos of the men who see very few women. They then come into camp where there are one or two girls like myself about, and in a way they look at you with the eyes of half starved people, and in another they are frightened of you as an ordinary woman would be of taming a tiger…

…The supper had champagne complete and I had one or two tender farewells afterwards. Tom drove us home and we were in bed at about 2 a.m.

[Sunday 14th February] In the morning we had one or two callers. First of all Colonel and Mrs. Drysdale called. Then the Adjutant and Mrs. Grimes. Then Hutch was brought out by two of his pals, and Major George Webb, who is an old man and a perfect dear. He has made love to me quite shamelessly and to Zoë too, so we are quite safe. Hutch was very upset at leaving me and I was rather sorry too, as first of all it is nice to have someone buzzing round, and secondly he is such a good dancer and probably would be first class at home. Zoë herself will tell you about all the kissing that has been going on – first her and then me all in the open sunlight or in the blazing porch the night before. However he's gone now, and I'm sorry.

George Webb stayed to lunch and then Zoë and I went to the station to see him off. Le Brocq was there and I had another tender farewell with him. I think he has it just as badly as Hutchinson only he isn't such a good dancer and I shall be seeing him in Calcutta so it wasn't quite so tender…

Monday [15th February]…I am told I may expect a proposal from Tony Gurdon, if not up here, later, as he is going home this year, but personally I don't think there is anything in it…My programme is already nearly full for the week, and I had one or two introductions last night and we chatted a bit and then went on to

Tony Gurdon's for dinner. He is just beginning to make love a bit – I must see if I can get him really going...

I must not forget to tell you that Zoë has a wonderful way of cooking peas, which I should advise you to try. They are put into an earthenware jar with salt, pepper and butter (1 oz. or more.) The jar is covered and then placed in a saucepan of boiling water. No water is added to the peas and after about an hour or more they are more delicious than it is possible for me to describe. With English peas the result ought to be wonderful.

Wednesday [17th February]...The Colonel has called me his A.D.C. so I am feeling quite bucked about it. I have met one or two charming men but not so appealing as last week's lot. How[ever] as they have only been here two days so far one shouldn't really judge them...I have clicked with a young electrical engineer named Bearpark – isn't it an awful name? I thought it was Barepart when I was introduced to him and was too shy to write it down in my programme...His mother runs a hotel or boarding house in Darjeeling where he has invited me any time I care to go up there. He plays tennis rather well and I am supposed to be playing with him this afternoon – it's a great world.

Then there are one or two quite charming people in the S. Lancs, but I have come to the conclusion that the Navy do you better every time than the Army.

In this first letter from the Dangua Jhar Tea Estate Dorothy more or less managed to keep to her normal routine of writing her account of a day's activities on the evening of that day, or on the next day at the latest. But the pace of the many entertainments got so fast and furious in the second week that she was defeated and had to resort to relying on her memory, which she regretted because (so she wrote) "I have already forgotten much of it." But, in truth, she could hardly have written more.

[Monday] 22nd February...I have had an exhausting day every day for the last week, and a late night for a fortnight. The house has been full...Zoë had wanted me to stay on here 'till Wednesday. I asked Henry and he said "Of course, but you will miss the Garden Party at

Government House," and sent me the invitation. I immediately wrote back and said I would leave tonight and go to the Garden Party tomorrow. He answered: "Will meet you at Sealda* Tuesday. Garden Party will be a dud show." What are you to do with a man like that? However I was still determined to go when I was invited by Mrs. Nelson, wife of the Deputy Commissioner and Colonel Evans of the South Lancs. to a dinner and dance on Wednesday next, so I telegraphed off to Henry and wrote as well asking if I might stay on. I think that it is just as well. I don't like missing the Garden Party, simply for Henry's sake. I wish you had been here to give me your advice. Anyhow I have tried to do the right thing, and if I have chosen wrongly, well it's just bad luck, that's all.

Mother darling, I have had the time of my life up here. I don't think I have ever enjoyed myself so much in my life. I must try and tell you all about it. Roughly my days have been... Tennis in the morning, tennis or races or polo or sports in the afternoon. We come home from tennis in the morning – at least I did, as no one else in the house played – and had a bath and lunched. After lunch change and pack all our gear for the evening. My fitted suitcase has been a positive boon – the time we would have wasted without it and the inconvenience we would have had to put up with would have been unthinkable. We used to leave all this at the Bank. Tony Gurdon lives on top and for a bachelor has a beautifully appointed place – in fact it would do any woman credit. He also has a marvellous servant named Surami, who does everything, cooking when a special dinner is needed, speaks English, and unpacks our suitcases. Zoë and I share mine on one room and the Paull girls (who incidentally are perfectly charming) have another room and their own case. At first Surami fought shy a bit, then he opened the case, then he took out the dresses and hung them up and finally we arrived and found the room strewn with my pink undies etc., etc. Zoë and I were fearfully tickled. When we had changed we dined either with Tony or else at the Mess with some young man or other, then danced, then supped, danced a bit more and so to bed. It was very late at times I can tell you.

Tony Gurdon is very keen. He is thirty-four, I believe. Of course that is one of the delights of my existence up here. Everyone thinks I am about twenty-two; and so it appears that Tony thinks himself too

---

* i.e. Sealdah – the railway station in Calcutta serving the North East.

old for me. However he is terribly shy and I am afraid I laughed at him a bit. He and Tom are very friendly and it is a perfect scream at meal times when we are all together. You see, Zoë and Tom are all out for me to marry Tony, but Tom knows that the poor old chap hasn't got the guts to make love himself, so he gives him a good example, makes eyes at me and holds my hand under the table etc., while Tony looks a bit sheepish. He holds my hand too, or rather I sort of let him, but it is rather a farce. You know, darling, I am not much use at encouraging men – especially in public. Now don't say too much about this – I'd rather it didn't go beyond the family and Mrs. Pymm and Winnie [Zoë's mother and sister], because he is coming home this year and will probably be in Bournemouth. Anyhow, let me know what you think of him.

My darling, I never knew it was possible to have so many love affairs in a fortnight. However I must leave them now and go on to the tennis.

Dorothy then goes on to describe in considerable detail, if not quite as a 'ball-by-ball commentary', how, on Thursday, she came to win the women's doubles of the tournament after which, together with her partner, she was due to be presented with a small cup by the Colonel's wife. But the presentation was not until Saturday.

On the Friday evening there was a more-or-less impromptu concert in the Mess which Zoë was helping to run, both administratively and on the piano. It had got about that Dorothy was something of a singer and so she was roped in to take part, along with many others including the Adjutant, who sang duets with Zoë; one of the 'Paull girls,' who also sang; and "a perfectly killing young policeman" called Springfield, who did two comic turns. There had been little or no rehearsal, but, from the blow-by-blow account which Dorothy includes in her letter home, a lot of talent was found and put to good use. Dorothy received many compliments on her singing, but it was as much for Zoë's sake that she was glad it was so successful.

Zoë is most awfully pleased about it. Her party has done so well. But I expect it will cause a good deal of jealousy among the other station ladies who did not perform at the concert or win anything at tennis.

The climax of the week for those back for the 'camp week' came on the Saturday. Inevitably, perhaps, Dorothy's account is peppered with he descriptions of the young men who danced attendance upon her.

I think I mentioned a lad in my last letter named Bearpark...Well, he plays tennis rather well...He was just a little bit in love with me and asked me to dine with him...So I had dinner with him, privately so to speak, in Mess on Friday before the concert. He is an engineer and awfully well liked by everyone – you'd love him. He and Hutch were the two who were most in love, I think, and were the two who never attempted to hold my hand. I just let the others hold my hand as it pleased them and didn't affect me in the slightest. But I drew the line at kissing. I told them all that they were "too young" and when they said they were willing to learn, or had old ideas, or something like that then I said I was too young and got out of it that way. It has been funny.

Oh yes, there was another I didn't hold hands with although we sat out in a car – my dear the car was quite in the light and so much more comfortable than the hard benches on the veranda – [who] was Mr. Salthouse, good old Salty, or the faithful Salt, only he took a sort of a fatherly interest in me. Pulled my leg fearfully about always vamping "Long fellows." They say I always pick out the tallest men and then make eyes at them. And when we were not talking about the girl he was engaged to in England, he was making love to me for poor Ralph Hutchinson who left last week. So I don't count Salty, though I think everyone thought we were a bit keen on each other because we were such friends...

Bearpark's people run a boarding house in Darjeeling and he has asked me to run up and stay with them. I've had another invitation from old pa Hutch to go and stay with them, so you see I have done quite well over the camp.

I have had a letter from Manasseh. He is going away on the 25th so thank God I'll miss him. As a matter of fact he has my English address, but perhaps he'll drop me if I never write again.

I've had a letter from Godbold – one of my long fellows and so good looking. I think I'll send it along to you as it will probably amuse you as it did Zoë and me and then make you a little sad as it did me. These poor boys on these terrible tea gardens are absolutely starved for the sight of an English woman, and especially single ones.

And I've had three letters from Ralph Hutchinson. I met the old father on Friday. The son had written to him about me. He came up and spoke to me and said he had heard all about me from his son. I believe the old man is a bit of a devil. He is a retired policeman and knows Henry, and has asked us both to go and stay with them in Darjeeling, so I suppose I have passed the old man all right. To his astonishment, but not to mine, on Saturday I saw his son strolling up to me on the polo ground. Of course he is quite barmy and he certainly drinks too much, but is not so tight as he seems. For instance he and his pal were here on Sunday morning from 9.15 until 1.15 and all they had besides the tea for their hazri was one gin and ginger. Yet people said "You sent young Hutch away from your bungalow rather lit up this morning." Which was impossible.

Well, to return to Saturday afternoon, we just chatted instead of watching the polo. His friend Dolman came along too. Dolman is rather good looking and dark...We went back to the Club and danced from 5.30 to about 7. Then changed and then into Mess for dinner. It was a very rowdy affair, or, rather, cheerful. I sat at the Police Table with a man named Webster, and Springfield [he who had done the comic turns in the concert party] was on the other side, so I devoted most of my attention to him. He is perfectly killing and has large black eyes which he rolls about in the most amazing manner. There were speeches and toasting and then the awards of cups for the sports. Mrs. Cooper [her tennis partner] and I got a good cheer when we went up for ours – the only ladies' event – and then off to the dance. I'm afraid the dance was a bit of a scramble because there were so many people about and everyone was a bit merry. At 12.30 off we went to supper. Old pa Hutch insisted on giving me champagne. After supper we danced again and then Zoë and the two [Paull] girls went off at 3 a.m. while I waited for Tom to finish a rubber. We sat on the veranda of the Club with Hutch, Dolman, the Prince (i.e., Cooke) who is rather a darling. He is another policeman. And De La Longerede, who is a planter, a dear little chap. After it was over, he and the Prince carried me to Tom's car and held a hand each. Till we were well away from the porch. It was a great night!

A great night indeed. But the cold feel of anti-climax is readily discerned in her account of the following day.

On Sunday Hutch and Dolman arrived here at 9.15 for breakfast. I was the only one up and I was in my bath. Later, two other men turned up. They all went away soon after one and then in the afternoon the girls left. Then dinner with Tony, after having played bridge at the Club and lost. And so to bed. And now I have spent the entire morning and most of the afternoon writing to you. I haven't told you half what has happened but I cannot remember much of it now beyond what I have put down...

She had put down a great deal – twenty closely written pages could hardly have given cause for any complaint of lack of news as to what she was doing. She had originally been due to leave on the Monday; the various changes of plan gave her that day for writing. On the Tuesday, after they attended the 'soldiers' show' at the local cinema in the late afternoon, Zoë's birthday was celebrated with a small dinner party at Tony Gurdon's house, the Adjutant and his wife being the only other guests. All very quiet, although "I had another letter from Ralph last night in which he sent me rather a delightful poem about myself." The verses, I fear, have not survived. The very long letter was concluded by a short separate letter headed "Private":

[Wednesday] 24th February...Well, what I really wanted to say was about this man Tony [Gurdon] who is going home this year and so you may see him in Bournemouth. Zoë and Tom are all out for me to marry him. Needless to say he hasn't asked me yet and I don't know whether he is so frightfully keen or not, but things have come to the pitch that Zoë has said "Don't turn him down right away, Dorothy, if you cannot say 'Yes' right away." So if you see him be awfully nice to him because he is really rather a dear, but don't think I am in love with him or anything of that sort. He is too much of an old woman. Why I'd far sooner marry Hutch, who certainly drinks, but gives me a bit of a thrill. However he isn't in the running either. I've told Phyllis he proposed in a sort of way. I told him I wasn't going to marry anyone.

On the following day Dorothy began her journey back to Calcutta and her account of the last few events in Jalpaiguri (which included the dinner that, in the end, caused her to delay her return to Calcutta) was written on the train.

[Thursday. 25th February] Last night's show was a ripping affair. The dinner was at Mrs. Nelson's house. A lovely champagne dinner, everything beautifully cooked and served. I wore my mauve floret frock and sat between two long fellows (i.e., over six feet two inches) named Newton...and Palmer. They both admired my frock and I think I got off again. Palmer says he is coming to see me in Bournemouth as he gets leave this year. But he is nothing of a dancer...in fact he's not very interesting in any way except that he pays me attention, and, as you know, that, if it doesn't appal one, is always interesting. We danced on until about one and then we went into the billiard room which was deserted and drank black beer. There were just we five, Zoë and Tom, Tony and myself and Zoë's click, a little Captain Clark. I held Tony's hand and he was thrilled. Altogether it was a most amusing show and a nice wind up to my stay in Jalpaiguri.

It has been very sad saying good-bye to Jalpaiguri where I have spent some of the happiest days of my life. Zoë and Tom came to see me off at the station. All the young men had gone, but still two remaining flames did not desert me at the last; and so Tony Gurdon and a sub from the PWV, who is staying on at Jalpaiguri were there too. I have told Tony I expect to see him in Bournemouth. Zoë is dying to come to Calcutta and to see me before I leave, which will be in ten days time now. She and Tom looked the picture of health and so fresh looking. That was my last sight of them as the train steamed out.

Jennie might have been forgiven for wondering just how long the queue of would-be suitors was going to be, stretching out from the drawing room at Chingri Khal and down the drive. And how was she to remember whether this one was to be encouraged, choked off, or simply treated with indifference? And she would have been well aware that there were many thousands of miles to go, many countries to visit, and doubtless many young men lining the route. I believe she would have taken it all in her stride.

CHAPTER 17

DOROTHY'S JOURNEY
(5)
LAST DAYS IN CALCUTTA

THE TRAIN JOURNEY from Jalpaiguri to Calcutta passed off without incident and Dorothy found Harry glad to see her and "looking very well." The heat was oppressive – a storm was thought to be brewing – but that did not prevent her social life continuing as before, with its occasional unusual features and hazards.

Friday [26th February]. Had lunch at the Bristol where the heretics seemed very pleased to see me, and then later I went to Firpo's with Springfield, whom I met in camp. He is rather a dear and will come and see us in Bournemouth. I have asked him to stay as he is a sahib and I feel sure you would like him. I went to the pictures with him after he had dined with us at Spence's…

Saturday [27th February]. Young Le Brocq phoned me up in the morning and asked me to lunch. We went to Firpo's where I had a lovely meal and then came back about 3. I then went out to tennis with the Paull girls. There was a largish party there. All the men seemed decent sorts and sahibs. Mr. Paull is a pilot and seems absolutely devoted to his wife and children and they to him, and I could swear that no one there was the slightest bit fast in any way. You just ask Zoë about them. Well, I think Henry is annoyed about my going there…The tennis wasn't up to much but the whole party were so nice and cheerful. These are the only girls I know in Calcutta. We danced until seven to a gramophone on their veranda and they gave me such a cordial invitation to come and see them at any time. I went away feeling happy and having enjoyed myself just as I might have done at Chingri Khal.

In the evening the heretics table gave Henry and me a dinner at

Peliti's…I danced up to 1.30 a.m. and quite clicked with Vaughan
Jones and Becker, who are both decent sorts. It was a peculiar dinner
in a way but went off very well and I, being used to these quaint
gatherings of Henry's friends, enjoyed myself immensely.

Sunday [28th February]. I was terribly tired but I had to go to a
Rotary Club picnic up the river. You don't know how sticky these
shows can be, with a lot of second class people, uncomfortable chairs
and too many folk for the size of the launch. We landed at
Government House, Barrackpore, and played games. Or rather I
watched the others running races, egg and spoon etc., etc., but I
considered that with my previous late night it would be silly to go
capering about in the sun at midday. I had had no breakfast and we
were due back on the launch at 1 p.m. But she had got stuck on the
mud somewhere and couldn't take us on board till nearly two.
Everyone was waiting there, it was fearfully hot and we all thought of
our lunch with more and more concentration. However it ended up
more pleasantly than it had begun, as there was a thunderstorm
about 4.30 which cooled the air a bit, and then a cup of tea made me
feel lots better. We landed home about 6.00 p.m.

That evening Harry and Dorothy were joined for dinner at Spence's
by Henry Le Brocq, a meeting which had been arranged on the
Saturday with the full agreement of Harry, who seemed to get on
perfectly well with Le Brocq. After dinner Harry came home while
the two young people went to the pictures at about 10.00 p.m.
Nothing unusual or remarkable about any of that. Dorothy was
therefore entirely unprepared for the next morning's effort by her
father.

Monday [1st March]…[Henry] came into my room before I was
properly awake and said, "What time were you in last night?" He
often asks me this and I tell him. So I said, "About twelve thirty."
"Um, I didn't go off till twelve and I didn't hear you." Still it seemed
normal to me and I wasn't prepared for the shock that followed. He
turned around and raised his voice. "You are doing too much
gadding about and going out too much. You have got yourself talked
about. However it's too late now." And with that his lordship strode
out of the room. You cannot imagine how ill I felt, then I felt furious
and then again sick. However all the time I realised it was an attack
of spleen. He had got your letters, including Phyllis's about the car.

Personally, I don't think that had worried him, but he has heard from Arthur and not given me the letter to read which he does generally. Then I went to the Paull's on Saturday and apparently he didn't realise it until I started talking about them on Sunday night. And then he heard people teasing me about the camp, and I suppose he is a bit jealous.

Fortunately I didn't make any reply or there would have been a row. I was too shocked to speak. After I had got up and dressed I felt better and we just carried on in the usual way. You know, darling, I really haven't done anything wrong. People will talk about me in any case because I am my father's daughter; but, even if I wasn't, having been seen at the races with old Phillipps and that rotten crew must have been enough to damn anyone. As a matter of fact I don't think anything has been said, and I don't care. What I am sorry about is Henry saying things like that puts another rivet in the barrier that there is between us.

He came in this morning at about eleven. He knows he has hurt me and looks very sheepish. Well, I was having my lie down and he sat on a chair and sighed and then said he was very worried. I couldn't ask him what it was about, or help him in any way. I was frightened he might rave there and then about me or one of the family so I just said nothing. I suppose now he will go on at you about my gadding about, and you know…that up to leaving for Zoë's I had a pretty rotten time – well, no, not that, but quiet. However I'm not letting it worry me in the least.

Dorothy was plainly right not to let herself be worried by Harry's unreasonable outburst. She had experienced that sort of thing often before, and was to have to put up with much more before the end of her travels. By the evening of that day she and he were playing bridge after dinner with friends – "just the four of us, and, as I took nearly Rs 6 off Henry, I felt I had done a good day's work." By the next day all seemed fine and they were both able to enjoy – if that is really the right word: it is the word she used – rather unusual goings on, even for Calcutta.

[Tuesday 2nd March]. This evening I went out for a ride in the car with Henry. He is in a very pleasant frame of mind, so I feel everything has blown over. I came back, washed my hair, dressed and we went to the Rotary Club dinner dance at the Grand Hotel. We arrived at eight, chatted 'till nine and dined 'till eleven. I danced one dance and then came away. An old lady named Mrs.Warren…offered to give me a lift and I was only too glad to accept. Henry stayed on and arrived back here at just on 1.00 a.m. I didn't know anyone who danced and as it was then 11.10 I thought it was quite sensible coming away. The dinner was most excellent…but the toasts and speeches were far too long.

However I enjoyed it all immensely because I was watching Mrs. Wentworth Lewis, wife of the Editor of *The Englishman* and the President of the Club. She was the only woman at the 'High' Table, seated between Sir Somebody or Other and the R.C. Archbishop of Calcutta, and she was as tight as a lord. I nearly had hysterics watching her. She started to sing "For he's a jolly good fellow" when they toasted the King. She shouted and laughed terribly at perfectly serious parts in the speeches, she shouted out to Henry to "Shut up" when he had said "Hear hear", and when he introduced his guests she went into a loud burst of laughter, for which within a minute she came over and apologised. The last I saw of her was after the meal she was fingering the Archbishop's chain and then she leaned across him and kissed the cross on his chest. Daddy says another drink and she'd have kissed His Grace as well. Nice little lady, don't you think, and aged about twenty-four.

Wednesday [3rd March]. I shopped this morning, played tennis with Le Brocq this afternoon, which went off quite well, and then went on to the Saturday Club…I didn't get home until about eight so I had to do a very quick change for dinner. Le Brocq took me to Firpo's where we danced and now I am writing to you. I saw Oliver at Firpo's and have come to the conclusion that I don't like him. However it has been a pleasant day. Henry was in a very good mood and I think he quite likes the young policeman, but we shall see in the morning; he seemed very cordial tonight…I have had another letter from Hutch today saying, "Why don't we get married?" Poor boy! He's such a dear and I have given him such lectures! Le Brocq is another flutterer, but so far I think I must be callous or something.

Thursday [4th March]. I have never had so much to do in such a short time. We are leaving on Sunday morning and I haven't started my packing yet, and almost every second of the last week has been occupied. This morning I went to Howrah Botanical Gardens with Le Brocq. He is madly in love but hasn't proposed and won't, I don't think. He's a nice lad and I quite enjoy going out with him.

I think India is a very unsettling place for a woman to live in if she is married. The amount of admiration that floats around her is so great that she must always be wanting it, and so is never really contented with her husband. At least that's what I feel.

I rested a bit this afternoon and then went out to the Saturday Club with Vaughan Jones. There was another girl there and three other men, all nice. I danced until about 7.30 when I had to fly back here and change, for it was our dinner tonight. Although Vaughan Jones is engaged to an American, as I believe, I think he would be the latest click – what a pity I'm going away so soon.

Oh, I must tell you this. Whilst I was having my bath this morning, Henry came into my bedroom and shouted out that by mistake he had opened a letter to me. As I was curious I got the ayah to hand in the letter. It was from John Bagnall and it began "My darling little girl." I've been chuckling all day when I picture Henry reading that.

The time was so short before they were leaving Calcutta that Dorothy was only able to write a very scrappy conclusion to the letter she had started on the Thursday of her final week, leaving it until she was on board ship before settling down to write what she called "a good solid letter" to tell her mother all about the last few days. There was quite a lot to tell.

On Thursday night [4th March] we gave our own dinner [at Peliti's.] We had seventeen guests in all, and of them only four were women, but it went with a tremendous swing. The dinner was excellent and we danced in between the courses. There was a good deal of speech making. Henry made one and even I had to get up and say something. I blush now sometimes to think of the nice things that were said about me that night in public. Everyone tried to persuade Henry to bring me out again next year, and one lady…has offered to bring me home next year at the end of February, so if anything is to persuade him that will. I don't know that I particularly want to come out but I am beginning to feel I ought to, even if only for a short time. However that is all on the knees of the gods.

To return to this dinner, we had all kinds of wine and champagne. I think it cost Henry about Rs 400. We went on dancing 'till one a.m. I think I got to know nearly everyone that night, and the women were so nice to me. Now in my opinion all this is doing Henry good, and ever so many of the men have said, "You don't know how much good you have done your father – he is looking ten times younger and ten times more genial since you have been here." At the same time it was very sad saying good-bye to so many people who had been so charming to me. I wonder if I shall ever see Calcutta again!

On Friday morning [5th March] I…played tennis at the Devonian Club with…eight women in all…We didn't have anything very great in the way of tennis. It was blowing up for a storm and the side that played against the wind invariably won, but we had a lovely tea and quite interesting conversation, of a scandalous nature. In other words the subject turned on Mrs. Wentworth Lewis and her disgraceful behaviour on Tuesday night. Everyone had heard about it if they had not been there and I didn't realise till that afternoon that the Rotary Club is quite an important show in Calcutta, not only as a club but also socially among the wives of the members. They are all very proud of entertaining the Governor Designate of Bengal and the Archbishop of Calcutta and everyone was and is simply furious that the new President and his wife should have let them down so badly. For he was a bit tight himself and she was hopeless when she arrived so he ought never to have brought her. I also heard that she kept asking the Archbishop for his ring and that she chucked Sir Hugh Stevenson under the chin.

Henry went to the Calcutta Scottish dinner [that] night while I went out with the Paull girls. I have not told Henry that I went out to their house because he cannot stand them, although he has never seen them. I haven't lied to him. I just have said nothing.

Well, before I left I received such a nice present from Le Brocq in the shape of a large bottle of lavender water, and a little fancy box containing two bottles of Honbigants scent and a box of powder. You know how I love getting presents. Henry Le Brocq is rather a dear.

Zoë arrived to stay with the Paull's early on Saturday morning so I went round to have breakfast with them at about eleven. I took Mrs. Paull some rather nice flowers and thanked her for her exceedingly nice hospitality to me. There was no reason for it as she probably loathes Daddy as I hear that she loathes old Phillipps and knows all about him too. Zoë was looking very well and oh I was glad to see her. Why she'll be seeing you just after you get this letter, or it will seem like that. I gave her all kinds of messages for you and the family.

Then the last heretics' lunch on Saturday morning…How sad it all was saying good-bye! They have all been so sweet to me…and you know it has not always been an easy situation. Almost every day I have been in Calcutta I have had lunch and been the only woman among five, six, seven or eight men. Never have I been made to feel the slightest bit of an intruder.

As far as I can remember the rest of the time I spent with Henry Le Brocq, going to the pictures, then to Firpos and then his dining with us at Spence's. He had wanted me to go out with him afterwards, but I thought it best to stay with Henry (Hobbs) his last night.

I haven't offered to help him with anything. He gets muddled and then bad tempered. He got properly *gubbrowed* over the names of the people for our dinner. As we had five Watsons it was a bit confusing so I found out the initials myself and did it off my own bat. But with packing or anything of that sort he's terrible. He doesn't tell you what he wants done 'till the last second and than he shouts out something that he doesn't mean, such as, "Put it in the suitcase," when he means, "the Gladstone bag at the other side of the room." So I left it entirely to him and his bearer so that if anything does go wrong like it did this morning I shan't be to blame.

That morning's adventures, for which she was not to blame, properly belong to the next Chapter. Most families would expect some degree of panic on departing after such a long time and for such a long journey and one can imagine the final hustle as the two of them, each with luggage for several months being carried behind them, made their way down the ninety three steps to a waiting gharry.

Dorothy's feelings were very mixed. She was on the start of her passage home which would culminate in joyous reunion with her mother, her sister, her niece and the rest of her family, as well as re-entering through the hospitable doors of Chingri Khal. On the other hand, she had had a lot of fun in India and felt she had been a help to her father. Would she ever see Calcutta again, as she had asked in her letter, and doubtless had asked herself very many times in that week? All those breakfasts and lunches at the Bristol and Spence's, all those dinners and dances at Firpo's and Peliti's; all the tennis, the golf, the races and the socialising; together forming such a large part of her life day by day – and a good deal of Harry's life as well – were they all for ever in the past?

Had she been told the answer to her ruminations she might have been even more sad and felt even more nostalgic. Yes, she was to return to Calcutta, but not for thirty years. The circumstances then to be so changed as to be almost unrecognisable. India no longer 'British'; her father no longer alive; she a mature married woman accompanied by my father; not dances, parties or innocent flirtations, but conferences with lawyers, accountants, bankers and the like. And, to cap it all, she, effectively, the guest of…Miss Briscoe.

"Miss Who?" she would have said. For that is surely the most remarkable aspect of her voluminous letters to her mother. Nowhere, anywhere, neither in the 'public' letters, nor in those marked 'private' is there the smallest, slightest, most tentative hint of even the existence of Florence Briscoe, let alone any clandestine relationship she may have had with Harry. How had he kept it dark? How had he kept her quiet? Both questions call for an answer, and I fear no answer can be proffered with any feeling of confidence.

Unless the letters from 1921 and 1924 are a lot of fantasising rubbish – which seems unlikely, apart from anything else, when one considers the elaborate scheme set up to get mail from her to him – it is almost beyond belief that no one in Calcutta had come to realise what was going on between them. And in the Calcutta of those days, where most people seemed to have plenty of time – and appetite – for gossip, once one person had a suspicion the whole City would know. And, even if the majority would possibly try to spare Dorothy an unwelcome revelation, one would expect there to be at least one person, at any rate, probably claiming to be a 'good friend,' who would be only too glad to drop a gentle hint which would let the cat out of the bag. Harry and Miss Briscoe must have been amazingly discreet over many years.

The silence of the mutual correspondence on this aspect of Harry's life also tends to confirm that Jennie, if she had read those two letters, had not revealed them to Dorothy. Were it otherwise there would surely have been some mention of it, Jennie urging Dorothy to try to find out what might be afoot, and Dorothy reporting on such enquiry.

As for Miss Briscoe, how ever did she manage to cope? From the time of Dorothy's arrival towards the end of December, 1925, until Harry's ultimate return to India in the autumn of 1926, he was virtually continuously chaperoned by the unwitting Dorothy. The only exception being her two weeks or so in Jalpaiguri. One pictures 'his 2½' becoming quite frantic. From December to March he was there, yet unapproachable. From March for six months or more he was to be away altogether. The miserable Florrie might be expected to have been very miserable indeed. But she seems to have kept her peace, and she did not kick up any rumpus. All credit to her, one might say, for that.

So at least Dorothy was not burdened by any anxieties as to the possibility of her mother having a rival in Calcutta. She set off in blissful ignorance of any such threat. Just as well – she had to contend with enough of her own difficulties. With Harry around they were never very far away.

SS Rawalpindi – *from Marseilles to Bombay.*

SS Arankola – *from Calcutta to Rangoon.*

SS Houtman – *from Soerabaia to Melbourne.*

The manager's bungalow at Danguar Jhar tea garden, after storm damage in 1931.

SS Marama – *from Sydney to Auckland.*

SS Ruahine – *from Wellington to Southampton.*

CHAPTER 18

DOROTHY'S JOURNEY
(6)
FROM CALCUTTA TO PENANG

DOROTHY REALISED, quite correctly, that the next six months or so were going to be spent very largely in close proximity to Harry, with little in way of a break. Some of the forebodings she had felt on the train from Bombay re-surfaced as she said good-bye to Calcutta and the many friends she had made there since she arrived. His moods were very unpredictable; he could be hurtful in his remarks; he was prone to take offence unreasonably. It was almost a relief when something went wrong for which she could not possibly be blamed: it reminded him, or should have done, that he was no more immune from error than anyone else. Their departure was certainly rather more adventurous than had been intended, the effect of which seems to have caused Dorothy to be rather disjointed in her account of it.

B.I.S.N. S.S.Arankola

[Sunday] 7th March. My dear, wasn't it a scream! We nearly lost the boat! Henry couldn't find the tickets and the gangways were taken away! We had to scramble in through a hole in the side and our luggage would have been left ashore if I had not directed proceedings from the deck and got them to put our things in. Our wretched coolies brought our baggage on to the ghat, but not on to the ship. Henry was rampaging round giving orders. Then he couldn't find the tickets (incidentally, he had them in his pocket all the time.) When we arrived we found all our luggage on the ghat and the gangways up. We only had about three minutes to go. I had to scramble into the ship through and over other peoples' stuff in this hole in the side.

However, we've arrived and so has our baggage, so I suppose we have much to be thankful for. I have a cabin to myself and am quite comfortable, though I cannot help dreading all this long travelling together and wish I were going home. The sea is almost dead calm but I feel the motion a little – it gives me a headache, and I feel I want to remain quiet. I haven't taken any mothersills yet and will try to do without it. I have slept this morning and then began to write to you as we came down the last part of the river. We are now at sea and there is a beautiful sunset. Good-bye India and all my charming friends. This last month I have been happy and I am sorry to be leaving.

Monday [8th March]. Father van der Swergen is on board, a wonderful man. Henry and I played bridge with him this afternoon. I lost again. My luck of late has been too terrible for words, but I console myself by thinking how lucky I ought to be in love. Then I have got hold of the Italian Consul for Bombay who has come and chatted with me. However as we are getting off tomorrow there is little opportunity for making friends – not that there is anyone really thrilling to make friends.

Tuesday morning [9th March]. We arrive at Rangoon at about two o'clock today – this letter has to be off in a few minutes. Nothing much happened yesterday. I chatted religion with the Italian Consul who has given me his card and promises to show me over Rome when I go there. There were two American women with us. I am afraid they were missionaries, but anyway we had an interesting evening.

The *Arankola* duly arrived in Rangoon on the Tuesday afternoon, but they retained their cabins on her for one more night, before transferring to another British India Steam Navigation ship, the *SS Egra*. By what I can only assume is pure chance, there happens to be in the collection of letters a letter from Dorothy to Phyllis written on this second vessel, which covers much the same ground as the letter to Jennie. One short passage in the letter to her sister, reflects her interest in the social future for Phyllis, and her possible need for formal evening wear, once she had had her baby and was free to enjoy Jimmy's appointment to the Royal Yacht. It shows you never know whom you may meet on board ship.

...I met a girl on board...whose brother, with her too, runs a dressmaking establishment in London. She was quite nice and told me her brother was at Magdalene, Cambridge. He designs the frocks and has had some good successes. She interviews, etc., etc. She says the price of a Court gown is from £40, and told me to call in myself, or that he would be very pleased to see you. Ask for her brother or her. The name is Norman Hartnell, 10, Burton Street (Berkeley Square or Bond Street.) Of course it isn't much use for you now but you never can tell when you may be wanting something that will have to be just right, so I remembered the address.

I am confident that Dorothy, at any rate, never had a Hartnell dress.

In her letter to Jennie, Dorothy gives an account of her impressions of Rangoon. They had only that afternoon and much of the following day to see it, and certainly tried to make the most of the opportunity. It ended with what sounds to have been an embarkation on to the second ship of her voyage considerably more traumatic for Dorothy than even that on to the first. And Harry, who really ought to have been full of abject apologies, seems to have persuaded himself to take offence at the consequences of his own fault in failing to take adequate care of Dorothy in the first place.

[Tuesday 9th March]. After we had strolled into the local shipping office we went to the Strand Hotel for a look around. Henry met some friends of his and then we had tea, and whilst we were having it we saw the Bombay Italian Consul, so asked him to come over and chat to us. His name is Scarpa and is quite nice. Interesting, you know, but, well, a foreigner.

This had taken us up to about five o'clock and Henry wanted to see the town so the three of us went for a motor ride. I don't think you have ever been to Rangoon. Henry was here thirty six years ago and of course he thinks it has deteriorated. I, on the other hand, was very much impressed. Of course it is a small town and nothing much of a shopping centre, but already they are putting up some fine buildings. The residential part is perfectly delightful. Some of the old wooden houses are left and some of them are quite pretty, but the new ones which are being put up all over the place are charming and, while I think they are consistent with the Burmese style of building, they remind me a bit of England – our kind of house. The gardens were well cared for and a mass of blossom. Most of them seem to be near the lakes.

There is this wonderful Pagoda all covered with gold leaf. We saw that, but did not go inside. It stands on a mound at the edge of the lakes, dominating the whole of Rangoon. There is a drive round the lakes and all these beautiful residences around.

Then we went to the bazaar, which I must say is dirty, although the stalls in themselves were nice and clean. I think the Burmese are a most picturesque looking lot. In the bazaar all the best stalls were presided over by a woman, keen and intelligent looking and spotlessly clean. She was generally smoking a big cigar. In the streets I kept on confusing the men with the women. Both wear these long gaily coloured skirts and keep their hair long. As a people, from what I saw of them in the streets etc., I think they are much more intelligent than the Bengalis. Now Henry thinks the world of the Bengalis and fancies they can do no wrong and I think he was awfully fed up when I said they were idiots compared with the Burmese.

We had dinner on board the *Arankola* that night in port, and afterwards played bridge with another lady who was also staying on board and one of the ship's officers. He and I won against Henry and his partner, and you know how that pleased me. I am afraid I love beating Henry at anything.

[Wednesday 10th March] We left the *Arankola* at about 10.30 a.m. and meandered up to the office of *The Rangoon Times*. Henry knows the editor who is rather a charming man. We had a chat and saw all over the works and it was quite interesting, although I didn't understand much of it. It was terribly hot at the time and, as I am much fatter than when I left England, I felt the standing about even more. We were then given a ride round the town and to the famous lakes and were shown the new club which is in the process of being built. It is going to be rather a wonderful place and will make Rangoon even more attractive than it is now.

We came back and had lunch at the Strand Hotel, which is, it appears, the only really decent place in the town and certainly it was good. Lunch, as you know, lasts a long time and when we got up it was three o'clock. Henry, who was much bothered about our luggage, tore off with the editor and left me at the Strand. He knew we had both been asked to tea by Scarpa and that I had accepted, so that I was quite safe, etc., but he never made any arrangements about my getting back again, and, as I had never been on this ship, and didn't know where she was exactly, it was a bit rough on me.

However, to return, the Italian is most interesting. Unfortunately I had not known him longer or I would have found out a great deal more about him. I have an idea he was attached to some Embassy in a commercial way. From the political point of view he was most interesting, and had known Mussolini and many of these big bugs and had signed one or two treaties for Italy. Of course he may have been pulling my leg or trying to appear great, but somehow I don't think so. Well, then something must have happened, what I don't know. He got fed up with life and chose to come out to India on account of its religion. Now, he is a good Catholic and yet he gets his comfort from Buddhism. If only I had known him longer I'd have found out what really was worrying him. As it is we had some delightful conversations…[He] had been at Peliti's on the Thursday night when we were giving our dinner and had seen us. He said I had looked so "imposing." I was rather amused and felt I must tell you…

A Burmese guide came along later when we went out for a drive, and we talked religion. I had wanted to go inside the Pagoda, but, as I couldn't without taking off my shoes and stockings, I admired the view. That I think is a filthy habit. Scarpa had had a cake made for me especially and had bought me two papeetas.

I got to the Hotel – no message from Henry. So I had to find out where the *Egra* hung out, which was mid stream; and how to get to her, which was by sampan. My dear they are the most terrible little eggshells, and I was absolutely terrified. I had to have two shots at getting on one, as it was quite dark although only just seven and I found they were expecting me to wade through some yards of mud. I insisted upon another place and had to jump from a barge eventually. I thought once or twice I was in for a ducking but fortunately it only took three minutes or less to get to the ship and then I was safe. My Italian deposited me quite safely and I arrived in for dinner.

I got a distinctly cold reception from Henry, who went to bed directly afterwards, had no breakfast this morning, and never spoke through lunch. However he's all right now and I haven't said a word to him. I felt very annoyed at being treated like a child in front of the ship's officers, but still more annoyed when I found out that sampan travelling is dangerous, and particularly so by night as they don't carry lights and no one will take any notice much if you get upset.

He had never told me a word about embarking.

However all's well that ends well. I am not in the least bit worried or upset and I have found out that, where possible, one should take no notice of him, and really I shouldn't have told you anything about this, and the time in Calcutta when he said I was talked about, but I thought that as he might say something when he gets home it might be quite as well to have heard about it before, and also once I have told you, darling, it is off my mind.

[Thursday 11th March]. I wasn't out of my room this morning when I was given a note from my Italian who wanted to come and say good-bye. He turned up about eleven and I think saw Henry. He must have stayed about an hour and though it was quite interesting I was glad to get rid of him. He was a bit womanish in his way. I do seem to attract the most extraordinary job lot in the men line. I've now got in with a Swede.

It was terribly hot this afternoon…as we slowly steamed out of Rangoon. I just lay in a long chair and panted. Just to cheer us up the doctor had told Henry that on the *Arankola* they found a case of small pox among the second class or steerage, I forget which; but how lucky we were that we were not kept in quarantine!

I have such a nice cabin in this ship – one to myself. I mean a single berth, shower and beautifully comfortable, and the Munro's just opposite. They are an oldish married couple whom Henry knew in Calcutta and she has taken quite a fancy to me. We have chatted together a good deal today, and then in the evening I've played bridge with Henry, Fr. van der Swergen and the Swede, whose name I don't know. I think the trip is going to be very interesting and the time will soon pass. I shall be home in no time and then, I suppose, longing to be on the move again.

Friday [12th March]. This is really a most pleasant voyage. There is nothing to do but laze and talk and play bridge. I played again and lost this afternoon, but I lost through bad play. Since dinner I have been talking with the Swede. He comes from Stockholm where he is a professor of geology at the University. He is giving me his card and says if I ever go to Sweden he will do all he can to help us. He recommends it especially for winter sports. So I am going to note that down in my address book. He is about forty and is quite charming, but I believe he is already married, so don't get romantic…

I left Henry up in the smoking room playing cards with the father and two other men, all hard at it. Strange how Henry is always in with the church… For the first time I have noticed the Southern Cross!! I am loving this journey! Good night! P.S. She is rolling about quite a good deal at the moment and yet I can only tell it by watching my dressing gown swing upon the door, so you can see how I've improved.

Next day life on board continued in much the same way, the extreme heat making her very sleepy after quite small exertions at deck tennis and letter writing. In her cabin "the iron plates were too hot to touch" in the afternoon, when her side of the ship was in the sun. Her cure for feeling a bit sun-sick, rather than seasick, was "a little angostura soon put me right." Her delight at the next port of call was somewhat blunted by what is, I suppose, every traveller's nightmare in every era.

Sunday [14th March]. We arrived in [Penang] at about four or five [in the morning] and got off the ship at about ten. We are staying at the Easter and Oriental Hotel, which is a perfectly splendid place…All we have done so far is to drive through the town to this hotel. The town itself is spotless and I have the most glorious view from my room. I am on the ground floor and look out on to a terraced lawn with flowers dotted here and there and a palm tree just outside. [The lawn] is about thirty feet broad and then comes a stone paved path and then a drop of three or four feet and then the sea. All kinds of picturesque craft are floating on the sunny waves and then on each side majestic looking mountains covered with tropical vegetation. I am awfully thrilled with the place. The food seems excellent and the attendance also. Chinese servants, of course.

The worst has happened. Henry, who deserted me at Rangoon and then got huffy because I was a few minutes late for dinner, whose sole job from tiffin on was to see that the luggage was trans-shipped, has left my big cabin trunk behind and his own cane chair. At least I am almost dead certain it was left behind at Rangoon and not at Calcutta. I'm a bit worried because it contains my ermine, my Spanish shawls, my black silk coat, all my silk nighties, my grey coat and skirt, my jumper suit from Jane Craft and my tennis racquet, books, etc., etc., so I hope it is found soon. On the other hand I hope it will be a lesson to Henry not to be so cocky in future.

A lesson it undoubtedly was, but I have to say that I do not think it was one which was particularly well learnt by the pupil. The excellence of the hotel, which the letterhead reveals to be under the same management or ownership as the Raffles in Singapore and the Strand in Rangoon, was sadly not matched on their return visit only some two weeks later.

We went for our drive...and I am absolutely enchanted with the island. The only fly in the ointment is it is so hot. From two until five it is soaking all the time and I feel so terribly tired. What strikes me is that the place is so beautifully clean, after Calcutta.

Well then, we came back and eight of us from the ship had dinner together, at Mrs. Munro's suggestion. Munro is returning from Duncan Bros and they all say he is very wealthy. Mrs. is a dear. We had champagne for dinner and altogether had a very cheerful meal. I was so sorry our time to part had come, as I had been very happy on that ship. Most of them went [in the] morning, including my darling Swede and the Munros.

[Monday 15th March] This morning we went to see about my trunk. They are going to wire. I hope it turns up all right. Then we went on to the Bank where we chatted with the manager...

I am going to try and get some silk here but I am afraid Henry is unwilling. However for this hot weather I must get myself some new clothes. A dress is almost through for one morning, and you know how neat one has to look in a hotel.

Mr. Henshillwood, a married man who is down here on business, has his meals with us. He is quite nice, and brightens things up a bit for Henry. You know I am afraid Henry misses the nicest people. If we have time enough I get to know some who are fairly decent, but in the beginning I find him with the worst of the lot, invariably.

Then in the afternoon Henshillwood, Henry and I took the funicular and went up the hill about two thousand feet. We got beautifully cool up there and the air was very invigorating and there was the most glorious view. Penang at our feet, all the ships in the harbour, the straits and then over to the Malayan mainland. This is a most beautiful spot, but everyone tells me that Ceylon is even lovelier.

It was too hot for more than one drive the following day. Even Dorothy did not feel up to joining in the dance in the evening, despite band and floor being "quite good." But she ended the day a bit more optimistic about getting silk out of Harry: he "actually came into a silk shop with me." An optimism which was proved next day to be justified, but not without a display of petulance on the part of the lesson-learner – still too cocky, perhaps, certainly too impatient.

[Wednesday 17th March] …in the afternoon we went to see the snake temple, which was very disappointing from one point of view, but horrible from another. It was just a smallish room with a recess in which was an image of Buddha. There were all kinds of books and candlesticks, chairs and shelves and on these were snakes coiled round, varying from a few inches to six or seven feet [in length.] None of them moved, but I loathed it and it made me feel quite ill for the rest of the drive home.

Then I bought some silk – sort of pink corded… We had been on this drive with Henshillwood, who, as I have said before, is rather a delightful Scot, and coming home. I said I wanted to get this stuff, so we stopped the car outside the silk shop and went in, he and I. Henry remaining outside. I suppose I was about five minutes getting my stuff; but then Henshillwood thought he'd make his wife a present, so started looking at all kinds of lovely stuff and we both forgot the time. Suddenly Henry tears in and shouts out to me about "Do you know this car costs five dollars an hour?" So I flew and got into it. Henshillwood didn't hurry and was at least another seven minutes before he turned up. As he was paying his share I suppose it didn't matter, but I was very amused to watch Henry, who couldn't go for me as I was being kept waiting too.

Ever the efficient needlewoman and dressmaker (activities which she called "my zimbalverk", that is "my thimble work", a phrase taken from the German nun who had taught her needlework at the Convent) Dorothy cut out the silk herself in the Hotel. An hour's job before breakfast. She had found a dressmaker in Penang who had already made up one length of silk from Calcutta for her "quite nicely", and she got him to undertake the same task with this local purchase. She does not reveal whether the job was done that day, or collected on her brief return at the end of the month.

S.S. Van Hogandorp

[Thursday 18th March]. I was sorry to leave Penang today, for though we shall see it again coming through it will only be for a day or less…what I liked about it was its extreme beauty. I felt that I need do nothing but eat, sleep and laze in that Hotel beside the sea. It was just lovely.

We embarked at about 2.30 this afternoon. There are only six first class passengers, all Dutch bar ourselves, but they all speak English and speak it well. We had the most extraordinary dinner: Vegetable soup; small solid meat croquettes; then fish baked in a cheese custard and boiled potatoes and a sauceboat of melted butter. The others waded into this as if it was gravy; then some excellent steak with spinach, and then there were oranges and bananas. Fruit in the tropics has been a disappointment. Nothing coming up to the quality or variety we get at Chingri Khal.

I have spoken to some of the Dutch men and to the only other lady, who is rather nice, but as we get off so early tomorrow there is no need to start making friends. I have felt very sick once or twice, but when I am not feeling very sick I'm feeling perfectly well, so that is already an improvement on the old days when I felt wretched all the time.

This is only a 600 ton boat and we are right in the stern for meals and all. There is only one bathroom and lav for us all, so I hope it won't be awkward tomorrow morning. This is a part of the world where baths are more than necessary.

Plainly this short overnight stage in their journey was not the most luxurious of their travels. I am glad to say we are spared any details of problems, if any, over their toilettes the following morning. Such mundane matters must have been driven from her mind by the excitement of the new discoveries.

CHAPTER 19

DOROTHY'S JOURNEY (7) SUMATRA MAYLAYA AND SINGAPORE

THE NEXT FEW DAYS were to involve a great deal of travel ashore visiting local beauty spots, interspersed with fairly short stays in hotels or on board ship or train. Not many opportunities for dances or for making new friends, but that did not prevent Dorothy from chatting up, as we should probably call it today, any likely fellow traveller. On the other hand she had plenty of scope for reporting to her mother about the many new places to which she was taken, as well as some of the mishaps along the way. Obviously often very delighted with her explorations, one can nevertheless sense her basic longing to be home: she frequently says so and she quite often compares what she is experiencing with England.

The passage across the Straits of Malacca to Belawan, the port for Medan, and then on to Medan itself in Sumatra took well under twenty-four hours, and they were soon travelling again.

[Friday] 19th March. We arrived at Medan this morning. I had a lie down and then [we] motored out about fifty miles to this place, Brastagi, which is nearly five thousand feet above sea level. It is quite cold, thank God, and I am feeling twice my usual self. Everyone speaks English well and the place, so far as we have seen in the two hotels, the two towns and the little villages we have passed through, seems well run and extraordinarily clean. The scenery coming up was magnificent and reminded me once or twice of England. I get so homesick at times. I think on the whole tropical vegetation is grossly overrated. The flowers are nothing to the English flowers and the fruit is most disappointing. For instance, I had strawberries today, but they only tasted wet.

Oh I did quite a nice bit of work yesterday. I chummed in with a man in the ship – I'm afraid I'm becoming quite shameless about these things now – and we chatted away for some time after dinner. Today he came up to us in the hotel at Medan and is giving us an introduction to the director of the largest newspaper in Java, a man he has known for over twenty years. If it hadn't been for me we shouldn't have had it; so I'm beginning to feel useful as well as ornamental.

This is such a lovely spot…and you would enjoy it so. There is a golf course round the hotel itself and the view down over it and the lawns and gardens of the place is simply lovely. I have a lovely room with bathroom and a little sitting room and Henry has the same. He seems to be paying out like a lamb. At times I don't know him, he's so mild. On the other hand his clothes are too terrible for words. All his collars are frayed and he wears them long after they are dirty "because then they will be thrown away." We may have to move out of here for the night to another hotel because of some expected rush…

Saturday 20th [March]. We are staying on in the hotel, or at least I am as Henry has had to sleep in the Bungalow a little way off, but I also have had to change rooms. However I am still here which is a great blessing.

I find this place absolutely enchanting. The scenery is too magnificent for words. My room hasn't a bathroom or other conveniences, but it is almost over the entrance to the hotel in front and the view is glorious, straight over a valley of green meadows and occasional copses of lush tropical vegetation, surrounded by hills, some of them ten thousand feet in height. Henry says those across the valley must, some of them, be fifty or sixty miles away. The light is always changing, sun and shadow chasing one another, and sometimes the hills are veiled in mist and some blue in the haze. At the back there is an extinct volcano with a steaming sulphur lake in the centre – I believe we are going to see it.

Dorothy was able to enjoy some dancing after dinner on the Saturday. They had a quiet day on the Sunday before their main excursion on the Monday.

[Monday 22nd March]...Henry and I took a car and left the hotel at ten to eight. . Well, I think the journey was close on a hundred miles. We went right across this plateau, which stretches from the hotel right to the borders of an immense inland lake. To give you some idea of its size I might say that there is an island in the centre, which by no means fills it up; and that it alone supports 80,000 inhabitants. Well, we drove over rolling country with the mountains all round, but in the distance, and then we began to see a rift which made us realise that though we were driving on more or less flat country we were very very high up. The sides of the lake are 2,000 [feet high] and sometimes almost sheer. We dropped down to one of the villages and I should think it was within a quarter of a mile, although of course with the zigzagging we did, the actual road was much longer. We needed coats and jerseys on the top but when we got down it was like an oven. There we saw the bazaar – filthy – and we think we saw rashers of dog. At any rate I saw them selling dogs alive and I am sure they were destined for the kitchen. We were also entertained to a dance by a very very old man and a boy of about 12, who was exceedingly clever.

Dorothy was writing this account the following day, Tuesday, and must have run out of time before that evening's activities. There is an obvious change in the writing. I feel sure there must have been more to tell about the lake with the island (which she does not name, but I believe was Danau Toba) and their journey back to the hotel. By the time she was able to get down to continuing her letter, it was Thursday, nearly another two days had passed, and she was too full of the intervening adventures to carry on the narrative from where she had left off. Her account is, once again, rather disjointed, and is best set out as written.

Thursday [25th March]. Since I last wrote we have been experiencing some of the delights of travelling, but first of all I must tell you about the party on Tuesday. It was terrific. Everyone sat down and had drinks until well after nine so that I was positively famished when we began eating, but oh what a meal we had! Hors d'oeuvres that beat anything I have ever had. They put a large block of ice on a plate and the ice was hollowed out underneath so that it could hold a light. We had smoked salmon, lobster, caviare and pate de foie gras. The rest of the dinner you will see from the accompanying menu (which I expect I'll forget)* but you can imagine that it was equally good. The wines were champagne and a sparkling burgundy, which were drunk more or less together, and some had sherry with their soup. After dinner it was a bit sticky. We didn't finish until eleven and had to dance to the gramophone until one. There were twelve in our party, equal numbers, but none of the six men could dance, so I rather bought it, being in demand.

Oh I was tired the next morning. We motored down to Medan. There we had lunch and lost the luggage. Henry had sent on his suitcase (a trunk really) and two little things of mine by the hotel bus from Brastagi, which always puts everything off at the Medan station. Henry saw it at the station, which is about as far away from the Hotel de Boer as Plummers is from Bobbys† and told them to send it along. Now Medan is about fifteen miles from its port, and our ship sailed at four. The station people put our things on their delivery van and forgot to say ours must be dropped first. So there we were in a taxi, with Henry nearly mad with rage. I was rather amused, but he contained himself and really it was annoying. Then we had the most hair-raising journey to Belawan, averaging over forty miles an hour through villages and all, but we arrived and had about three minutes in hand to catch the boat, which we did.

Henry had no cabin, so slept in the saloon, but he thinks he was more comfortable because they put down a lovely bed for him on the settee – I gave him the two pillows I didn't use and he got all the breeze, whereas the cabins were stifling. Well then, there was some fuss about paying, in which I hope we will win. Next, it was fearfully hot yesterday, it made me feel quite ill, and the ship was a bit smelly and very crowded so it wasn't over pleasant. We arrived here (Penang) at about nine this morning and found that there is no room at this hotel. I suppose they will give us lunch and then we will have to beat it for Kuala Lumpur.

You don't know how much I enjoyed Brastagi – it was such a change and everyone was so nice and friendly. The views and the walks were so beautiful and I loved the fruit – terongs and passion fruit – but I am longing to get on. I haven't heard from you for over three weeks…so that, although I am fed up with not being able to stop two nights here, as all this continually changing forms of

* It was lost rather than forgotten.
† A reference to The Square in Bournemouth: about 300 yards.

journeying is rather trying, yet the sooner I get to Singapore the sooner I'll get some mail...

Later. I think the mail goes out today but I felt I must just let you know that most of our troubles have cleared away. They have found us rooms here, so we are staying two nights. My trunk was found at Rangoon and is now on its way to Singapore, so that's all right, thank God. Henry can't find the menu.

This hotel [the Eastern and Oriental] is packed, hardly room to breathe, and the service during lunch was terrible. A P&O liner is in and I think all the inhabitants, I mean passengers, are lunching here.

Somehow I am awfully homesick today. I suppose it is seeing all these people going back. I am longing to be on the boat from New Zealand.

A very short addition was added by Dorothy to explain that Harry was not writing that week, she did not think he was feeling well and had developed inflammation and a sty in his good eye. In her next main letter she complained

> Henry is going deaf as well, or else he won't pay attention. I have to shout at him all the time now – very tiring. Mostly we sit in solemn silence.

Splendid as Dorothy had found the Eastern and Oriental Hotel the first time they were there, she was glad not to be staying more than the two nights in this occasion. She only had a "tiny little room with a punkha gone bust", the replacement fan not efficient, and all in annexe ten minutes walk from the main hotel. She used the one day as a washing and mending occasion. She lamented to Jennie that she had not been able to buy her any silk because "I haven't any money...and I don't think he'll bear much more, and I hate asking." She could not resist a little dig at Harry over her luggage.

> My trunk is being sent on to Singapore and ought to arrive on the 31st. We sail for Java on the 2nd, so ought to get it even if the ship is a few hours late. So far I haven't heard why or how it happened, but I do know it fetched up at Rangoon and was not left behind in Calcutta. So it was Henry's fault.

The next two stages were to be by train. Their itinerary included Kuala Lumpur, but, with a stop intended to be of no more than twenty four hours, impressions could hardly be more than skin deep. They were fortunate in having a friend there, a man named Spring, who must have been known to Jennie, as he is mentioned by Dorothy without any introduction or explanation. Then on to Singapore, where they had from Tuesday to Saturday. Time, one might think, for a good look round, but Dorothy does not have much to say about it.

Saturday [27th March]. I do write to you in some funny places. I am now in the train going to Kuala Lumpur, and I'm sitting up in my sleeping berth – the carriages are arranged like the French ones...Henry has been in a great mood all day, and has been positively nice. I don't mean to infer that he has been nasty, but he certainly has been quiet and gloomy of appearance if nothing else.

It is terribly dusty and filthy in this train – I mean smutty – although it is so beautifully kept. They haven't got good coal.

Today has been a terrible day. I am beginning to feel the heat so – or perhaps it is that rotten room. Thank God I'm out of it!

Sunday [28th March]. Station Hotel, Kuala Lumpur. We arrived here at about 6.30 this morning. Spring came round at about 10 and took us out in his car. We went to see some planter friends of his...who have a lovely bungalow, and than came back and lunched here. We all separated then until about five o'clock when we again went out driving until seven or after and then went to dinner with Spring in his hotel. Now we are back...

I cannot tell you how good Spring has been in taking us around, nor how charming. We have had the most lovely time and I know Henry has enjoyed himself. The country around is absolutely exquisite, with the most wonderful drives. The roads – well, I have never seen anywhere to touch them – they are all like billiard tables and I am told they are like it all over the country. Of course a great wave of prosperity is coming over the country and it is quite evident already. I wish I had the money to buy rubber shares!

To return, everything is well laid out and well cared for. I thought Penang was clean, but it is very grubby in comparison with Kuala Lumpur, even the Chinese and Malay quarters are respectable and clean, while the European parts are a series of beautiful bungalows dotted in a Garden of Eden. Generally each one is on a crest of a little hill – the place is surrounded by small hills and tiny grassy valleys with wooded sides – and their gardens are lawns with all kinds of flowering bushes and trees scattered along their slopes. The buildings in the town itself are really rather marvellous, the old Moorish style has been adopted and most successfully. I was reminded very much of Casablanca but I think the buildings here are even better. Altogether I am rather in love with the place...

Henry is very impressed with Spring. We had a long talk after dinner about shares and the future in general- at least I listened – and from what I heard them saying the F[ederated] M[alay] S[tate] is the country of the next ten years. Rubber is going to boom and the possibilities in almost everything round here are immense.

We leave tomorrow at about 6.30 a.m. for Singapore...The mail comes tomorrow – I'm so excited.

Dorothy's reference to the arrival of the mail was to its arrival in Singapore. They were half a day late getting there – more muddle, but this time not the fault of either of them – and the mail contained little from home. They had changed their itinerary slightly, and letters from Bournemouth had gone to Sumatra. Whether it was much compensation I doubt, but the fact is that that some of Dorothy's admirers from India managed to get letters to her. One obviously still quite smitten.

Monday 29th [March]. In the train. As you see, she is rocking a good bit. Well, we missed our show this morning. Last night Henry enquired the time the train left, and they said 8.30 a.m. I was ready just about 7.00 when the porters came rushing in. She left at 7.05, but I realised it was impossible to get on to her so didn't even leave my room. Henry ordered his baggage to be left too, but he went down to the platform and was just in time to see her steam out. In reality I was very glad as now we are travelling by night and it is comparatively cool, whereas had we been in time this morning we would have had to have faced the heat of the day, and it was terribly hot today – thunderstorms about.

Singapore. Hotel Europe...This seems a most interesting town with all kinds of lovely things. We went for a stroll around this evening and there are crowds of Chinese shops at the back and most interesting they appear to be too...

[I] had a delightful note from Lordon, two from Le Brocq and another from Hutch to whom I think I have lost a bit of my heart.

However nothing serious he winds up "If ever you change your mind and want me just cable 'Come.'"

Tuesday [30th March]. I went out this morning with a Mrs.Cooper who we had met on the *Egra* with her husband. They are staying here and last night at the dance I had a go with him. Lots of the *Hawkins* men were here and Prince George was in the lot, so they say. If I saw him I didn't recognise him. Mr. Cooper, who has something to do with tin, says that the Admiral here is just off to the Royal Yacht. Well, this morning she and I trailed off. I wanted some silks, but couldn't afford their prices…Whilst meandering round in our Jinrickshaws we came across the Swedes again. I had thought they were in China, but they were to leave today, having been to Java. It was so nice seeing them both, particularly my dear Professor Quincil, who blew me a kiss at parting. Stevens, Henry's ex-partner came to lunch and after tea took us for a spin in his car. It was very dull.

Thursday [1st April]. My box has been cleared and is now lodged in the hotel, although the less said about it the better. No; I don't mean that; what I mean is that I haven't opened it, but it looks all right, and I haven't said anything much to Henry.

I shall be so glad to get home. We have had nothing but muddles about our rooms at hotels. We are now leaving tomorrow, Good Friday, for Batavia and only this morning I discover that we have no rooms reserved. We have cabled but God only knows what luck we will have.

Their departure on Good Friday marked their final farewell to the Asian mainland and to travel by train. Bad sailor as she was, Dorothy was positively glad to back on board a ship. And particularly a Dutch ship: she always maintained afterwards that they gave the best service, food and accommodation of all those vessels in which she sailed on this prolonged journey. Her first experience of one was quite short, only from Good Friday to Easter Sunday to get to Batavia (Jakarta) from Singapore, but enough to whet her appetite for the two weeks or so which they would be spending on a similar vessel en route from Java to Australia. Before that happened, however, they were able to enjoy fully a very worthwhile visit to Java.

DOROTHY'S JOURNEY (8)
JAVA AND THE GREAT BARRIER REEF

I T IS NOT AT ALL CLEAR how the itinerary followed by Harry and Dorothy was chosen. It seems certain that Dorothy played no part in it at all – in outline it may have been decided before she even got to India in the first place. There were subsequent alterations, and again she was apparently not consulted about them. It must have been Harry who made the ultimate decisions, whether with or without advice from Travel Agents or others with experience of South-East Asia. Dorothy's reaction to the various places they visited, and hotels at which they stayed, reveals a very mixed degree of enthusiasm.

Was it worthwhile spending such a little time in so many different places? One can understand the brief stop at Rangoon: Harry wanted to see again a City to which he had been many years before. But in the three weeks from 12th March to 2nd April they experienced Penang, Sumatra, Kuala Lumpur and Singapore, not to mention the various forms of travel between them. While there was much in which to take delight, the effort was considerable and the discomforts at times irksome. One suspects that they might have done better to have visited fewer towns and stayed in the good hotels a little longer.

The next two stages of their journey were rather different – and different from each other. Harry must somehow have learnt that Java was worth exploring in some detail, and they took over three weeks to do so. True, this involved a lot of travel, but at least they were always in the same country, and it does seem that the effort and discomfort – both of which were again, at times, considerable – were regarded by both of them as having been well spent. Travel was mainly by car, and when not by car was mostly by horse or pony. Riding was another talent of Dorothy's, whether previously learned or acquired simply on these necessary rides, that I had no idea she possessed. I never saw her on a horse, nor had I any knowledge of her ever having ridden one.

The Javanese tour did not give a lot of time for socialising. This was to come again, perhaps not surprisingly, on the voyage from Java to Australia. Moths were then around once more in some number, while Dorothy found that her sea legs were more secure. She rather relished the foretaste of those two weeks in the relatively short passage between Singapore and Batavia.

K.P.M. S.S. Plancius

[Saturday 3rd April]. We left Singapore yesterday. As soon as I boarded this ship I was delighted. It is about six thousand tons, while the Egra, in which we came from Rangoon, was about four, but otherwise what a difference!! I have the most topping cabin to my self. The dining room and the smoke room- drawing room are most comfortable, while the feeding and service are excellent. This line beats the B.I. into a cocked hat.

I am sorry to say I have a little fever. I think I have had it for some days, which perhaps accounts for my feeling so irritable for the last few days. However it isn't anything serious…But all the same I love the ship, and am looking forward especially to the fortnight on board one of these ships going down along the Great Barrier Reef to Australia. Unfortunately we arrive in Batavia tomorrow, because I'm so comfortable I don't want to get off. I wonder if we will find any accommodation.

You have no idea how beautiful it is. We are steaming through a warm sea studded with tropical islands. I can see their shining beaches from here, and would love to get off and spend a few hours on one. This is a fairyland…Isn't it funny that I, who am so seasick, should so love the boat? I wonder now if I have any sea legs or if I'd be upset were it a bit rough.

Easter Sunday [4th April]. It has been a tiring day. Henry called me at five o'clock. The Passport Officer was to be on at six so we got our luggage ready too but that wasn't necessary as we didn't get off the ship till about eight and it took ages to get all the baggage ashore and then through the customs.

The first person we saw in this hotel [which Dorothy does not identify] was Henshillwood, who had breakfast and lunch with us. Unfortunately he left for Soerabaya this afternoon by our boat so we won't have him to chat to. I have a very nice room – this appears to be the hotel in the place – with my own veranda and bathroom. No hot water is put on anywhere, but there are lovely cold showers. It is very hot and there are no punkahs at all in the rooms – only in the dining room and lounge and there they are few and far between. The Dutch doctors say that they are bad for you, so we just sweat on and try and sit in a draught.

The breakfast is most excellent...and for lunch I had the national dish which is called something in Dutch which means Rice Table. It consists of rice with about twelve or fourteen different things such as chicken, fried bananas, shrimp salad, meat croquettes, nuts, chapattis, chutneys and in fact anything you like to think of...When they have it in a private house they have anything from twenty dishes up and people go on eating the whole afternoon...We went for a drive around the town but it is very uninteresting and cutcha. Much worse than India...

Monday 5th April...We have...arranged for a motor to take us round the Island. It will take us a fortnight or longer, and I am getting quite excited at the thought of it.

Tuesday 6th April. Even Henry, who always says he expresses no displeasure – and, incidentally, no pleasure – says he'll be glad to leave tomorrow. The climate is very trying – not so much the heat, for I don't think it is as hot as in Calcutta when we left it – but it is oppressive and dull. Everyone says there is nothing doing here.

The amount of half-castes in the place is amazing. I think them awful. And the women – I don't think I have ever seen such a set of colossal women. The Dutch men are big and gross and are accompanied by crowds of these enormous women who waddle about the place and dress excruciatingly, but I must say they look fairly cheerful; for all the fat and their terrible clothes...

Daddy is a most peculiar person. I know nothing about him and vice versa. I sometime wonder what he is thinking about when we are sitting or walking together in silence. I'm afraid I must be a terrible disappointment to him. You see he was so upset at my coming out to him that he never said he was glad to have me, nor did he make a fuss of me in any way. I cannot always be making advances so we remain silent for the most part. He thinks differently from what I do. At other times I feel desperately sorry for him with his blind eye and his weakening ears, but he is so calm that one cannot be sorry for long. Of course, he gets angry and flustered, but never pleased – if only he'd be human occasionally, but there you are! One person he adores is Arthur, to whom he has written at every opportunity and who, I suspect, doesn't care a rap.

The imminent departure of the mail to England caused Dorothy to break off her letter at this point – without even a signature – and so her reverie about Harry was interrupted. Comparing what she did manage to write then with her first letter home after her arrival in Calcutta one is left feeling that she was being rather unfair to Harry this time. Her room had been redecorated, he had gone early to the station to meet her, he had given her "a topping little wristwatch" and she did think then that he was "genuinely glad to have me."

On the other hand she had had a number of less agreeable experiences with him since then, which may have to some extent caused her to alter her opinion. Nothing would have pleased her more than to have had a really close rapport with her father, but he seems to have been a man who did not easily get on to very close terms with anyone, not even his willing daughter, and, perhaps, still less with his wife. She – Jennie – knew him as well as anyone could, obviously, and her comments on this passage, cut short as it is, would have been interesting. However her letters in reply, while making a point of acknowledging those she had had from Dorothy, do not refer to this one. It must have arrived at some stage, but it may have been very delayed by the post and so arrived too late for Jennie to answer what, by then, would have been a letter three or more months old.

I feel sure she would have given Dorothy some advice or comfort. The only place in her letters where she comments significantly about Harry is in that which was begun on 27th February. She had plainly received Dorothy's letter telling about the last week before she went to stay with Zoë.

After deploring the ploy of Manasseh in securing a dinner *tête-à-tête* with Dorothy as being "not what I think a gentleman ought to do" and then warning Dorothy to "beware of old men, darling, I think they are more amorous than young ones," she wrote

> I felt so sorry Daddy did not let you go to that dance; but my darling he is peculiar and of course does not understand women and he must be very trying at times. But, poor man, he has a lot to worry him as all businessmen have and you, I am sure, with your tact must give him a lot of pleasure and pride. He misses you and he is upset, I expect, with Arthur.

Because of the change in their itinerary Dorothy did not receive this letter until the end of April when they got to Soerabaya. But, even without it, there were so many adventures in Java which they both enjoyed that she seems to have cheered up considerably by the time they embarked on the last stage before Australia.

Grand Hotel Selabatoe
Soekabatoe

> [Wednesday] 7th April. I sent off your letter this morning in such a hurry that I never finished it and now I don't remember where I left off...
>
> Well, we have started our long trek through Java. We have a very comfortable car, a seven seater Fiat, and, if today is to be any criterion, we ought to enjoy ourselves immensely. We left all our heavy stuff at the hotel. It will be shipped and we will pick up the boat in a fortnight's time in Soerabaya. We left Batavia this morning at about nine and motored straight towards the hills, arriving at a place called Buitenzorg at about eleven. The drive was delightful and we were so glad to get out of the mugginess of Batavia, even though up here it isn't very much better. Well, at Buitenzorg they have the most beautiful Botanic Gardens in the world and I spent an hour wandering round. I could have spent days and days. There was a clump of water lilies 'Victoria Regina' almost as large as our tennis lawn, and I was particularly struck with a fernery of tree ferns, which had the most fairy-like appearance. I was awfully sorry I couldn't stay longer.

We had lunch at an hotel, Belle Vue I think, where we met a man from the ship *Plancius* which had brought us from Singapore. He was a perfectly charming man named Goodfellow, a Natural Scientist...He had lunch with us and afterwards we chatted about his various expeditions in different parts of the world. He was so nice, and when I next go to the Zoo in London I am going to ask for him.

Then we drove from Buitenzorg to this place where we arrived at about 5.30 and are staying the night. The hotel isn't up to much but still quite clean. We are now more up in the hills being over two thousand feet above the sea but it is still warm. The drive here was rather marvellous and we went through the usual Javanese thunderstorm. They say it rains here nearly every afternoon. In reality there is no variation in the climate and no wind but this rain comes nearly every afternoon and so everything is always beautifully green.

Daddy seems in a very nice mood and I think he is enjoying it too, which is a great relief to me.

Grand Hotel Preanger
Bandoeng

[Thursday 8th April]. We had the most lovely drive today. We were up at about 6.30 and left the hotel at 8.30. By the way there is no hot water so I wash in cold. We arrived here in time for lunch. This is a most comfortable hotel and the food seems excellent. They have a Ryst Tafel (Rice Table) here today but unfortunately we didn't know until it was done. However there seemed to be ever so many more dishes than in Batavia. Everything is beautifully clean. I have a room, a bathroom and a veranda like a sitting room where I am writing this.

I cannot attempt to describe the drive, all through tropical vegetation with the mountains always on one side of us and sometimes on both. Here we are in a town that is on the slope of a hill that borders a plateau. The latter is extraordinarily fertile and the green terraces of the paddy look awfully fresh and green. We are surrounded by mountains and several of them – all the biggest – are smouldering volcanoes. Try and imagine how beautiful it must be.

This afternoon Captain Ohthardt came out with us (Henry had got pally on board the Egra) and took us out up the hill to see the sunset. We could see for hundreds of miles – but there, I cannot

311

paint the picture myself in writing, so I must tell you later on. Well, this Dutchman, a Flying Corps Officer, came on to dinner. He is quite nice and he and Henry talked about the Eurasian question most of the time. Henry is very interested in it, and so am I for that matter, because there are such quantities of them, and they are received everywhere with open arms.

Friday 9th [April]. Another lovely day. Captain Ohthardt has practically spent the day with us, showing us round and having his meals with us. He took us up this morning to the Observatory at Lemblang or some such place, from where we had the most wonderful view of this town and the surrounding mountains. Then we went to the aerodrome where we saw a good many planes. Two took off while we were there. We saw the repairing plant and went into the mess for coffee. Then we went to his special office – the photography department – where he is head, and there I saw all the latest appliances and also some marvellous photos especially those made into maps…

We came home via the bazaar, which is beautifully clean. They have tanks to keep the fish alive and gold fish seem very popular in the local kitchens. Harry bought a quantity of mangosteens which he says are the finest fruit in the world. There is no doubt about it that they are delicious. I feel I ought to be ill as I have eaten so many today, about thirty five I should say, not to speak of papaya for chota hazri, hazri and lunch, and chickos for dinner. However I think Almighty God must have given me an inside that can cope with almost any quantity of fruit I like. Whereas half an egg, or an orange will almost lay me out. We had rice table but I only had one or two dishes of it. You should have seen Captain Ohthardt tucking in! I don't know how these Dutch people cope with it!!!

This afternoon…off we went again with our friend. This time we saw a sort of nursery where they grow all the flowers for the government gardens and produce new varieties. The only flower that was doing much now, for it is really in between seasons, was the dahlia. I was given an enormous bunch on leaving. I had never been very keen on them but now I see their beauty and have made up my mind to grow some at home. Only here they are so beautiful, with long stiff stems and each one not only a different colour, but a different size and a different shape. Some of them on the desk now are nearly thirty inches long. We came back, dismissed the car and walked through the town looking at the shops. The shops here are shut from about one till about 4.30, when they are open again till seven or half past. They are all brilliantly lighted and things are not dear as there are no taxes on clothes, etc. The town is beautifully clean and the natives also and they dress quite nicely, seem very well behaved, and look awfully happy. We were taken to the Club and sat on its terrace in the main street watching everything and I was extraordinarily impressed. The buildings, while unpretentious, are very pretty and in keeping with the rest of it. This is a most beautiful spot. I just cannot describe it. I am so sorry we are leaving tomorrow.

Grand Hotel

Ngamplang

Saturday 10th April. We had a most glorious day, but a bit strenuous. Up at six and out just after seven. We seemed to be going for miles and miles right through the mountains and through tea estates most of the time. The Dutch have all the latest improvements and hope to capture the Assam trade. Their estates are gloriously laid out and appear very well managed. We must have mounted well over four thousand feet, and it was heavenly. The air was like champagne and the scent of the tea bushes never seemed to leave us. When we came back we meandered through the town and bought some more mangosteens, but a native (of India I mean) who saw our great basket of them told me that I mustn't eat too many or I'd get "belly ache." After lunch we motored here – about fifty miles from Bandoeng…The journey was a bit hair-raising. We were given another car and another driver at Bandoeng and he is a bit of a goer, although I must say a splendid driver. Well, we came unexpectedly to a bend in the road and had to get into first to take the hill with safety. It was like going over a precipice – quite the steepest thing I have ever seen. We had about six 'steps' like this and I got the wind up properly. Thank God we arrived all right.

This is a most delightful hotel. My room looks out onto a terraced garden with all kinds of plants in flower and then beyond that right over the valley to the mountains in the distance. It is so beautiful. Java has completely exhausted my stock of adjectives, but really…it is lovely and if you could see it too you would realise that it is impossible to overrate it…

Sunday 11th April…Well, every day I want to say we have had a wonderful day but today I think the adjective is really well earned.

We set out by car from here at about 6.10 and arrived at [Grand Hotel, Tjisoeroepan,] in an hour's time. Here we got on ponies and went up to the Papandajan Volcano then back again and then home. It took us from 7.30 to 12.30 to go up and down, and with the exception of the last climb and the time for having something to eat – I should say about an hour in all – we were on horseback.

Just imagine me in my tussore get-up, astride on a pony and climbing up and going down the most dreadful paths imaginable for four solid hours. At first I was a bit nervous but in the end, on the little flat bits, I trotted and even cantered. Needless to say I am feeling fairly stiff now, but I have fairly made up my mind to learn astride when I get home. Daddy and I laughed a good deal about my mounting and dismounting as I was awfully shaky at first, and as we were going up to the crater he had insisted on my getting off the horse, or rather pony each time we came to a steep bit going downhill. When we were coming home however it was practically all downhill, and fearfully steep, but I was too tired to get off and walk it. So you see I have had some riding in spite of everything.

Now I must tell you about the ride itself which was lovely, all among little forest paths up the mountain, with waterfalls and little pools here and there and rather a profusion for these parts of the world of wild flowers. We went through one or two bamboo thickets which I always think are so delightful – they are always so cool – and then gradually as we neared the crater the vegetation grew more and more stumpy and then disappeared.

We dismounted and walked up the last bit and were nearly choked by the sulphur fumes. The wretched hill was sizzling away and clouds of steam were rising…However, apart from the interest of the thing, I think the ride up was the best part, as the crater has been enormous. Then one side was blown out, and it was through this break that we went. Now there are about five or six smaller spots, all close together, in the rifts of what was once the large crater. It was rather impressive to hear the rumblings and to know that at any moment we might be blown up. Papandajan is known to be dangerous, and has been much more active this last year. Its temperature is always being taken, and as a mater of fact we met one of their scientists who had been up to inspect her as we were going up.

Their activities for the following day had to be curtailed because Harry was a little unwell. A reaction to the riding of the previous day in all probability. It did not keep him *hors de combat* for more than a couple of hours or so, but enough to shorten their outing, and to cause them to decline a suggestion of an expedition involving ten or more miles on horseback. They gave themselves two short local outings before an early night before what was to be an early start the following morning. All of which Dorothy was able to cram into a short letter and post it just before they departed, leaving her main letter until the next place on their tour..

Hotel Bellevue,

Tjilatjap

[Tuesday] 13th April. We have had such an exhausting day but it has been all so lovely that I have enjoyed every minute of it…We were out at six and arrived here at about quarter to six in the evening, having been out all the time. We had nothing to eat but mangosteens and a few sandwiches – no breakfast, lunch or tea – but it was worth it. My, how I am longing for my dinner.

It was rather amusing when we arrived here, which is the only hotel – and not bad really – in a very one eyed town, to find the Madame of the place sitting on the lawn with her infant and two pyjama-clad men. That is to be seen at any time in Java but I had never been so close to it before. Well, we asked for tea, which came, but as usual here there was nothing to eat, so I asked for a few biscuits, explaining how hungry we were, so she sent us round not biscuits but toast, butter and pancakes!! It is very hot and the mosquitoes are making a meal off me so I shall be glad to leave tomorrow.

Now for the drive, well it was glorious. We seemed to be driving along the lesser roads all the time. From Gareot we went entirely by the little lanes to a mountain lake called Pendjaloe…Then we went on through the mountainous and then hilly country coming south-east all the time. It is just like a park or a botanical garden, and has almost every kind of scenery except snow.

We landed up at a little place called Kalipoetjang where the car went on board a river steamer and Henry and I went upstairs to the first class place which in any ordinary ship would have been the bridge. We were thirsty so, as we had to wait some time, Henry walked up to the village and bought two coconuts, green, for us to drink the milk. Incidentally I don't like it. Then, as we still had to wait, he amused himself by chopping up the nut inside and throwing it to the chickens on shore, which of course collected round the ship at once, never having had such a feed in their lives. One fell into the water but managed to get out again, poor thing, it was so eager for the unaccustomed fare, and Henry just loved it. We sailed at two, going down the river for some miles and then along a soft lagoon with fishing villages all round and then up the straits here. So we had the entire time from about one o'clock on the water. It was such a change for me and so beautiful. I just loved it. The only thing was the pangs of hunger became rather insistent at times. You see neither of us knew we were out for so long a trip.

Grand Hotel de Djokja

Thursday 15th April. We left Tjilatjap yesterday morning. It was hot and I was glad to be away. We motored about twelve miles and then had to cross a river in a sort of raft made by two boats being joined together with a cross piece large enough to take the car. I was afraid there might be an accident as the whole arrangement looked so frail, but it went off splendidly…

Then we went up to the hills to a place called Wonosobo…It is rather an inferior hill station but very crowded on account of the Javanese New Year Festival which is on now. We got terrible rooms in the Annexe and the service was appalling and unfortunately we weren't able to see anything of the place because it simply poured all afternoon until about eight. You would have been amused to have seen us – Henry and myself playing patience, and an Australian Pole watching us and trying to talk to us. He only knew a few words of English, so there we were trying to talk German!

By the way something rather funny has happened. When we were coming back from Papandajan, the Volcano where we both accomplished such feats in riding, we were both in hysterics at the thought of how stiff we were going to be the next day, but Henry in particular was almost beside himself commiserating with me and saying "well, I suppose for the next few days you will have to have your breakfast off the mantelpiece" and then going into peals of laughter. But what a different man now! It doesn't strike him as

316

being humorous in the least that his behind should be sore and not mine! I have to lend him my lanoline and talcum powder while he moans a bit in the car.

I was very glad to shake the dust of Wonosobo from my feet, as we were very uncomfortable. Today is the Javanese New Year so for the last few days and nights and especially last night they have been letting off crackers to frighten off the devils. Last night they had a thin time and I'm sure won't come back for another year. Result though for us was that we had very little sleep...

...The road was most interesting. Mountainous at first, we passed four large volcanoes, which looked very magnificent in the clear morning air, and then on to one of these fertile plains growing rice and sugar. Then a little later on we got to the hillier country and branching off we paid a visit to the famous Borrobuddha temple. It's really just a monument – a mass of carved stone covering the entire peak of a small hill – and has no 'inside.' It is very old and was made in the time when Java was Buddhist (it became Mohammedan about four or five hundred years ago) and all the carvings are supposed to represent the different incidents in the various lives of Buddha. It is startling and interesting rather than beautiful, at least from my point of view, because I don't like oriental things as a general rule. The whole place was crowded out with natives who were making merry; and I was quite intrigued with their booths for selling things and their entertainments – it was a sort of fair – but we did not stay long as it was very hot.

So hot indeed that they left a day earlier than planned, despite the hotel being "first class." They spent one night in Madioen ("a one-eyed place, hotel pretty appalling, filthy pillow case, and the squalor of the whole thing and greenfly and mosquitoes and ants just to cheer one up a bit") and one night in Malang ("hotel clean and of good class") before arriving in Tosari.

Whether because of the heat, the travel, the changes of hotels or simply their close proximity to each other for so long, Dorothy found her father particularly difficult and again wondered, rather sadly, about her relationship with him. They had had "a bit of a row at Djokja" which seems to have been nothing more than he shouting at her when she was, as he thought, late for a meal.

He's such a funny man. He doesn't pay any attention to what one talks about, so I don't say much, and he won't make any definite arrangements about the time for meals, so I'll just have to be ready. At Djokja he had just committed himself to letting me buy some leatherwork for you and Phyllis and I think the thought of that irritated him. Anyhow you won't get it now as we left before I could get any money out of him. Also he needed a dose of medicine.

He is rather funny about that too. He will buy the various purgative waters he sees in the chemist shops and, as they are of different strengths, and as neither of us can read Dutch, he doesn't know where he is. At Bandoeng he bought a bottle of stuff – about a pint size - and told me it only lasted three doses; while at Djokja he bought another pint bottle of something different and had to drink the whole lot before it acted. He'll kill himself one day. Poor chap!!

…We are perfectly friendly, so don't worry. I often wonder though what his real opinion is and what especial crimes I have been guilty of in his estimation. However I have done my best – all that I could think of and I only hope that I haven't done any harm to the rest of the family; or that you or Phyllis will be able to think if not say "What a pity she didn't do so and so" etc. It is only now that I realise how brave it was of me to come at all.

And again, writing briefly from Tosari, one can sense the curious lack of rapport there seems to have been between father and daughter.

Henry had a hot bath in the spring last evening. He stayed in an hour and I began to get anxious but he came out looking quite fit so I suppose no harm was done. I play patience now with him quite a good deal but I often think of all the needlework I have to get done and wish I wasn't wasting so much time He has spoken to some other English people here so he is happy now with someone else to talk to. I feel so sorry for him at times. He is so lonely.

Tosari was intended to be the starting place for their ascent of the Bromo, the huge volcano in eastern Java. Their only full day in Tosari was the Monday when it rained so much in the early morning they decided to put the expedition off to the next day, although it would mean carrying on afterwards to Soerabaia before they could really rest.

So they had Monday in Tosari. English friends whom they had met in Batavia introduced them to "A Jew, a Dutchman, quite kind hearted but awful looking. I don't know what is the matter with me, because I seem to have a fatal attraction for these kind of people." He certainly appeared rather taken with her, and she did not find it easy to shake him off. "But I must tell you, the little Jew told me he thought at first that Henry was a Jew. I of course immediately told Henry, but I don't think he finds it as amusing as I do." If he had had romantic ideas he had an odd manner of showing them that day: he presented Dorothy "with two pairs of men's arm bands (which they wear for badly made shirts when the arms are too long) which he said I might like to use as garters."

Tuesday had to be the day for the Bromo if they were to do it at all. Despite the fact that the rain first thing was as heavy as that on the day before, they made the effort, and felt it was worth it, but tiring. Evidently writing early the following morning just after getting up, Dorothy gives a full account.

> Oranje Hotel,
> Soerabaia

[Wednesday] 21st [April] 6. a.m. …We were up yesterday morning at half past three but as it was wet the coolies refused till it cleared. Henry went in a sedan chair and so did the Jew and one went for me too, but at first I rode. I had a beautiful little pony, intelligent and sure-footed and I found her very easy to manage. The way was terribly steep in parts and frightfully slippery. How my pony managed I don't know, but you should have seen me packed on his back there and going up sides of a cliff like those of Bournemouth, only all of mud. However I didn't come off and I only lost my stirrup once which I think was a bit of an achievement.

We were on the road just at six when it was fine, but about another thousand feet up we ran into a sort of Scotch mist, which made everything still quieter and more mysterious. There were ever so many casuarina trees – a kind of pine tree, very slender, with very fine long needles – and they looked perfectly beautiful covered with all this dew in little beads, suddenly coming before one out of the mist. Before we got into it I forgot to say that we had the most wonderful view of the plains and of the sea and of Soerabaia, seventy miles away! The path wound through a casuarina wood, and then to the top of a ridge where there was a path about six feet wide and almost a precipice of four or five hundred feet on each side.

We then got on to another hill and had to descend a bit – we were right in the mountains going from one to another. Then we started to climb again and went up and up on these terrible mud paths when suddenly without any warning we found ourselves on the edge of an extinct crater with walls a thousand feet down and almost sheer. There at our feet was the 'Sand Sea', which must stretch for five miles at some parts, and these terrific serrated walls of stone of a thousand feet on all sides. In the middle of this rises the Bromo and another crater, but extinct. As a matter of fact I cannot describe it to you. It was unbelievable to my eyes looking almost artificial and so enormous.

Then we had to get down this thousand feet. We all walked and the road was terrible – track I ought to call it. Then I got on my pony and cantered and trotted across the sand sea occasionally coming back to see how Henry and the Jew were getting on in their sedan chairs and eventually we came to the Bromo which was roaring away like a furnace. It was windy and very cold. We clambered up a few hundred feet then got on shank's ponies and the last bit to the rim of the crater – two hundred and fifty steps. When we came to the top there she was just as one would imagine a deep inverted cone with serrated sides and clouds of steam and sulphur smoke coming out of her throat and a roar that made even shouting almost useless…

I rode back and did some more cantering across the sand sea and climbed up this thousand feet on the pony's back which I think was a bit of an achievement. Then we started to descend. Oh! It was a great day. Unfortunately soon after we had started from the top of the cliff, as I wasn't dressed for the part, I got in the sedan chair and was carried home.

"Home" in this context meant the hotel at Tosari. Dorothy does not describe the journey to Soerabaia, nor that town itself. The heat and discomfort of the place made her feel ill. The great joy was the receipt of mail from Jennie and from Phyllis and from Jim – the first for about two months. A Dutch rubber broker whom they had met in

Malang took them for a drive and then to his home. "The next morning a topping book on Java arrived for me from him but I haven't seen him since. Wasn't it nice of him?" The day before Dorothy had been sent "a beautiful bunch of roses" from the Jew who had been their companion going up the Bromo – "However I managed to avoid him for the rest of my stay." Not even these pleasant gestures reconciled Dorothy to Soerabaia. "I shall thank God to be out of this awful heat, with no fans to make it bearable."

On the weekend of the 24th to 25th April – Dorothy does not give the precise day in her letters – they embarked on another vessel of the Dutch line KPM, the *SS Houtman*, for their long voyage to Australia. Dorothy was not well at embarkation: she had had a fever since the ascent of the Bromo, which the great heat in Soerabaia did nothing to relieve. They had one port of call at Makassar, after a day or two on board. There they took an excursion to see some waterfalls in extreme heat, followed on the return leg by a soaking in a tropical rainstorm – all of which did nothing to improve matters.

However the sea air coupled with the excellence of the ship got her to rights in a day or so. She had little memory of Australia from her time there more than twenty years before, and for some reason, had prepared herself to find Australians not to her liking. People must have said things to her in the past which had prejudiced her outlook. She was soon disabused – and was glad to be. She started in a cabin which she had to share with an Australian girl ("awfully nice") and transferred after Makassar to a single cabin, mainly because of the quantity of luggage she needed with her. The change involved going down one deck, which similar prejudices (similarly ill-founded) made her, at first, reluctant to do.

Tuesday 27th April…The real reason against my going on to another deck was that we had heard that the officers of the ship were a bad lot and thought nothing of trying to look in the cabins etc., etc., but so far I haven't noticed anything untoward.

The ship is very comfortable and the food good. The people seem quite pleasant and so far I haven't met any of the poisonous Australians we hear so much about – however that has to come, I suppose.

I have started playing games as I am not in the least bit sea sick, and anyway it is gloriously calm…Today I have recovered and am full of beans

I am enjoying the voyage and I think that now that it has started to get cooler it will do me good. I am sitting at the table next to the chief officer and opposite me is a man, aged about fifty, who has a terrible face but isn't a bad sort. He's an Englishman named Woodward and has promised to take me out in London to his Club. But you know what men are – they're full of promises which they've no intention of keeping. The Purser is a Dutchman who pays me a little attention, but is very nice and does all he can to make me comfortable in the ship so I am quite glad to keep in with him. Henry is chairman of the Sports, but somehow I think he is thoroughly miserable.

Continuing her letter the following day, Dorothy took up again the theme of Harry's less than contented frame of mind. News from home, or the lack of it, had played a part. Arthur had had an injury, not a very serious one, playing rugger which had kept him a little while in hospital and had caused him to miss the contingent's posting to India. There had also been some concern about mess funds, for which, although a sergeant had been arrested, Arthur was not said to be culpably responsible, but evidently a small sum – under £50 – was needed to help to rule a line under the incident. Then Phyllis was thought to be developing come complications in the later stage of her pregnancy. In due time this was found to be a false alarm. But it was real enough then to those so many miles away. Finally, as the newspapers would have told them, England was coming to the boil in the dispute which culminated in the General Strike. All of which would have affected them both. Dorothy was always a little inclined to make a drama out of a crisis, even a relatively modest one. I expect she inherited that from Harry, who even enjoyed making a fuss over relatively little, as being a good way of attracting a modicum of sympathy and attention to himself.

Wednesday 28th April…I don't think Daddy is very happy; he feels so out of it when men like Woodward and Col. Toll pay a little attention to me just in the course of ordinary politeness. Now Daddy – of course I know he doesn't mean it – will ask a whole lot of men to have drinks before he asks me, and, if I happen to come along when they are already ordered, I have to ask for one for myself. Also I think he is worried about Arthur. He adores Arthur. In Calcutta he wouldn't open any letters from home until perhaps Thursday when he had to answer them, except Arthur's. And when writing, Arthur is the one who always comes first. At the dinner we gave, he got up and said in his speech that he was grateful for all the hospitality shown to me and promised to Arthur (we did not know then that Arthur was remaining in England) and that "when my son comes out you will see the best of the family." – a pretty poor compliment to me, especially as I was there – and to Phyllis and you. However they shouted him down over that, but he made no graceful aside to cover it up. Just went straight on. Well, now that Arthur hasn't even written to acknowledge the money, he suspects something and I can see he is very worried.

Thursday 29th April. I have clicked with Mr. Woodward. It appears that his brother once commanded Arthur's Regiment. I suppose he is about fifty-five and is awfully ugly – he has a sort of prizefighter's face without the slightest glimpse of good humour. However it is quite interesting. Last night he seized me after dinner and talked till 11.30, quite a good deal about himself. Henry likes him, so everything in the garden is rosy. The Purser, a Dutchman of about thirty-five is another moth, so I always have the two to play off against one another. Then there is Colonel Toll, so I am fairly well off for men. There are two rather nice girls on board, Miss Anderson, of whom I have spoken before [it was with her that Dorothy had shared a cabin for two nights or so] and Miss Collins, who is quite young and very pretty. She is a New Zealander. I don't think the Aussies are a bad crowd, although they do make one feel a bit of a foreigner.

Inevitable shipboard life included the Sports and a Concert. The competition of the former engendered, Dorothy reckoned, a lot of jealousy. She was "trying to be as careful as I can." The latter, despite regarding herself as having done the lion's share, she considered "an awful fiasco, but I think it was moderately enjoyed." She was able to see the funny side – even if one may feel that it could become tedious very quickly:

It is rather amusing that the Captain, who has really a terrible voice, will sing the most awful sickly songs like 'Little Grey home in the West' in English with a Dutch accent, and he will go on. If one goes

323

to the piano after dinner up he comes and starts his singing, and really it is awful.

Despite this, perhaps irritating, feature of life on board, as time went by Dorothy was obviously enjoying the days at sea more and more. And her principal admirer was getting ever more pressing in his attentions.

Friday 30th April. I am knocked out of most of the games, but am getting much better at them all, and I just love them…You will be glad to hear I am very comfortable on this ship and so far have met with nothing but kindness from everyone in the ship.

…This man Woodward seems rather keen and gave me a box of sweets yesterday evening – he has just come up and asked me whether I write about things in general and give you a vague outline or whether I tell you exactly what people say and do. I evaded the question by telling him I told you all about my meals and what clothes I am making. It is a funny world. He really is quite nice – I couldn't stand him touching me, but still I feel quite sorry for him. If only he weren't so ugly.

Saturday 1st May. I have never believed that any voyage could be so beautiful as this one is. We are more or less hugging the coast all the time. The sea is like oil and we thread our way through tiny little islands all the time. The mainland itself is rather wonderful – sometimes with sandy beaches, sometimes with trees growing down to the water's edge, and sometimes with rocky cliffs; while behind tower the hills in ever varying shapes, and the cloud effects and sky scenes all go to make everything of absorbing interest. I feel I could sit and watch all day long. I just love life on board ship.

It now turns out that this man Woodward is a retired Colonel. He really is getting quite keen and, because he is he, I'm beginning to think it must be obvious to others too. Whether you can understand that bit of reasoning I don't know – I mean he is oldish and gruff and used to ordering people about and so it must seem strange to see him nice and charming to me. However I don't think it is serious and he'd never touch my heart so don't worry. But you know how I love telling you about my affairs. Strange to relate, he has the cabin next to me and sometimes when I am dressing he shouts to me to sing. His latest is to call on me before dinner and give me a drink.

Sunday 2nd May. I have had a great day today, and am fairly tired.

I played in the finals of the deck tennis and lost, which I think rather annoyed Henry. However, my partner and I won the ladies doubles against the winner of the singles and her partner, and I won the mixed doubles deck quoits with the Captain. So I didn't do so badly...

We have been passing through the most enchanting seas imaginable. By all kinds of little islands, and then at four o'clock through the Whitsunday Straits, with Whitsunday Island and its lighthouses on our left. Thank God for the six weeks going home, which we must have now, as I just love this life. It is so healthy and I am getting in such a lot of games. Altogether I am simply loving the voyage and don't want to get off the ship in the slightest.

I am getting quite friendly with the women on board and I think they have taken me to their hearts – at least the younger ones have for certain, but I am waiting to see the Australian at home before I pass any criticism about them. I have been doing a lot of needlework...and I think that that strikes them as wonderful that an English girl should be able to sew and to play games etc. One girl told me "But then you sew and are a good sport and play the piano and that's exceptional for an English girl." I think they start off by despising us, but, once they find out we can be natural, they are rather nice. Now this, of course, only applies to those I have met on the boat who I suppose are the better class.

Monday 3rd May...I have had a glorious day again. It is getting much cooler and as a result I feel much better. Also I must tell you that I have had a sort of proposal from Woodward. At least it isn't one really, but he told me he didn't know me well enough to have the courage to tell me something and he was going to ask me something in London. Anyhow we will count it as one, only don't mention names except to the family as any of these people might be known. It seems so funny to have a man of his age so barmy about me – though only temporarily, I expect – and I suppose most people in the ship have noticed it, although no one has mentioned anything to me. However, I am afraid he hasn't a chance. I told him he could say what he liked to me but he mustn't touch me ever – I couldn't stand it. So he said – but I won't tell you all that as you must know what men say. Anyhow I enjoyed it.

I have also the Purser and the Chief Officer in tow, not that I go about with them in particular but the former is the most important man in the ship from a passenger's point of view – for instance he finds lost property, is on the Sports Committee, gets me apples when they are not on the menu (and the Australian apples and pears are glorious) and looks after the barber's shop. I don't think I said that the barber went ashore at Makassar and missed the ship. So one has to deal with him (the Purser.) And the Chief officer I sit next to. Oh well, it's a great world.

Great indeed the World may be, but sea voyages do not last for ever, and the magic spell which a voyage of many days so often casts upon the susceptible traveller all too often gets broken by a landfall. The ardent but ugly Colonel seems to have experienced just such a dose of reality, and exits our story in a manner reminiscent of that of the devoted slave two months earlier. Australia, to which we must now turn our attention, was to have other interests and other problems.

The view from the top.

THE ASCENT OF PAPANDAJAN, 11th April, 1926.

Dorothy inside the crater.

*Dorothy and Harry on horseback
after descending – Papandajan
smoking in the background.*

*Dorothy at the
Borrobuddha temple,
15th April, 1926.*

*The car boarding
the raft crossing
a river from
Tjilatjap to Wonosobo,
14th April, 1926.*

The main crater of the Bromo across the Sand Sea.

Dorothy at the Sand Sea inside the Bromo, 20th April, 1926.

CHAPTER 21

DOROTHY'S JOURNEY
(9)
AUSTRALIA

THE PLANS DRAWN UP by Harry – it must have been his work: Dorothy nowhere mentions being consulted – were for visiting Brisbane, Sydney, Canberra and Melbourne, and allowing for well over eight weeks in Australia. One might have thought that, coming by sea as they did from the northern tip of Queensland, they would have gone to those cities in that order. However, for reasons which are completely obscure, they almost reversed the order, thereby giving themselves much extra and – it would seem – unnecessary travelling. It did, however, have the advantage for them of remaining on board the *Houtman* as far as Melbourne.

Brisbane was to be their first port of call, the vessel being due to dock in the evening. That gave nearly a full day for the Colonel to make his final attempt to press his cause.

[Tuesday 4th May]. During the day, Woodward made quite a set at me. He is making all kinds of plans to take me out in London, etc., etc. I wonder if I shall go if he asks me. I think he is one of those people who have had more experience than I can cope with. We have talked a good deal and argued about things and then, just as we were getting into Brisbane, I got exasperated with him and left him. He came to say good-bye but, as I was with Mrs. L'Estrange and Mrs. Lord, I only shook hands – we didn't make it up so to speak. However I don't care, as it doesn't affect me in the slightest. He's promised me all kinds of presents and the last two days made love most violently – and it all meant absolutely nothing to me.

Colonel Woodward is not mentioned again. I expect he had put Dorothy out of his mind before he was far from the dock gates at Brisbane. It was probably just as well that Dorothy was busily occupied. The meeting with the two ladies whom she mentions was entirely unexpected. Mrs L'Estrange and her sister-in-law, Mrs Lord, were waiting on the quay, much to Dorothy's surprise. Potentially awkward farewells with Colonel Woodward were thereby avoided.

Mrs L'Estrange was the mother of Mick L'Estrange about whom I was speculating in Chapter 10 as a possible fiancé, or nearly a fiancé, for Dorothy in 1921. Her husband was a doctor, but a sea-going doctor, and so he was away from home for very long periods. They had three sons. Mick, the eldest, probably several years older than the second, Harry (who was 21 in December, 1925), while the third, Jack was close to Harry in age. The whole family had spent some six years in England including the early 1920s and it is quite obvious that all of them had the most happy and sentimental regard for the Hobbs family and Chingri Khal. To everyone's regret, of all that family Dorothy would only be able to see Mrs L'Estrange. The Doctor was away at sea, on a long voyage to England and back; Mick was on a sheep station at Longreach, some six hundred miles north-west of Brisbane; while Harry and Jack were together on another station at Ashley, a little closer, but at nearly three hundred miles south-west of Brisbane, still too far away to make the journey in those days.

By now Dorothy was quickly coming to terms with Australian people, finding that she enjoyed their company, and also she discovered that they enjoyed hers. But Harry seems to have arrived on Australian soil determined to be abrasive. As Dorothy recounted, writing on the short passage to Sydney:

[Tuesday 4th May]. I was so ashamed and fed up with Daddy…Of course, he doesn't mean what he says; at least he says things that sound far worse than he means them, but other people are not going to make allowances for that. Well, there we were [in the] evening with Mrs. L'Estrange and her sister-in-law, who seems a very nice woman, but apart from that was going to invite us on to her husband's station etc. I pointed out the Purser and Mrs. L'Estrange said "Quite a nice looking man!" when Henry came out with "Yes! These men are engaged in order to be nice to the Australian women."

Well, I don't know how it reads nor whether I have remembered it exactly but it sounded dreadful. So rude and so unnecessary. If he'd only left out the "Australian." Mrs. L'Estrange came to the rescue after an awful pause, and carried off the situation quite well, but whether Mrs. Lord will now ask us out to her station remains to be seen. So far I quite like the Australians and get on with them very well, but Henry is going to have a perfectly miserable time unless he can be decent to them.

A real upset was to develop out of that remark of Harry's. But in the meantime they had the two day journey to Sydney. Although the *Houtman* was continuing (with them) to Melbourne the farewell dinner was held on the approach to Sydney:

> [Friday] 7th May. Last night there was a nice dinner. Little souvenirs were given round (I got a brooch and Henry got a pair of sleeve links all with enamelled K.P.M. flag) and the Captain stood champagne all round, and slowly we steamed into Sydney harbour. This morning we must have been up at five to pass the doctor. We were in a little cove right at the entrance of the place, which is the quarantine anchorage for all ships and then we slowly came up to the town. The morning was cold and slightly hazy – just like England on a spring morning – and I felt terribly homesick. The views were exquisite and I for one was thoroughly glad to be out of the Tropics. We are now going ashore and will be back soon after lunch as I think she sails at four.

The opportunity was taken to sign off this letter and to post it on their short foray into Sydney. Dorothy was certainly impressed by the beauties of Sydney Harbour. Even before the building of the Bridge (not completed for another six years) let alone the Opera House it was a magnificent sight. However, she had little time to write about it in that letter and by the time of the next she had been thoroughly put out of sorts by more serious father-trouble, and Sydney was well in the past.

Menzies Hotel
Melbourne

[Tuesday] 11th May. Sorry I didn't write for the last few days, but Henry was a bit annoyed and when I get upset I just cannot write. In addition I've had a very bad cold and the sea was a bit rough so your instalment got the go-by.

It was like this. You remember in my last letter my telling you about his remark to Mrs. L'Estrange about the Purser and Australian women? Well, we were walking quite happily in Sydney when he started on against the Australian women again, so, thinking my opportunity had come, I wanted to point out how unwise of him it was to make these remarks to Australians. He was furious, said he would not be talked to by me, that I showed a perpetually hostile spirit, and that his remark about the Purser was a deliberate hit at me because of my disagreeable behaviour with the man "knowing his reputation."

Quite barmy, my dear, and quite untrue in every way, but you know how these things upset one at the time. I cried a bit and then felt sick so couldn't eat any lunch so, as a result of both I suppose, I caught this cold. However, he didn't mean it I know, and he's been better since. I sometimes look at him and feel he hates me. I used to think you were overstrung once, when you used to say the same thing, but I've come to the conclusion he just can't stand women. I keep wondering why he brought me with him, I think his idea is to sicken me so that I'll never want to go to India again, but I'm convinced I ought to go, although I don't suppose I will. Well, I didn't think much of Sydney after that. I felt awfully ill on the Saturday and Sunday and we arrived here yesterday morning, berthing at about eight thirty.

The nature of Dorothy's letters rather changes in Melbourne. Although they stayed at the same Hotel throughout their fortnight or so in the City, they were almost all the time in the company of relations, and moreover they were relations of Jennie. Thus there was a great deal for Dorothy to tell her about how they were, how they looked, dressed, and behaved, and all the many details which would be fascinating to Jennie at the time, but are of less interest generally now.

It is very pleasing to read that all their encounters with relations in

Melbourne were a very considerable success. All of them were as welcoming and as friendly towards the pair of travellers as anyone could hope for. And they met a considerable number. First and foremost one must put Jack McCormack. He was the son of Jennie's eldest sister Mary. She, together with her husband, had been dead for many years. Indeed the four McCormack children – Queen, Jack, Frank and Marie – had largely been brought up by Annie Larkin ('Little Aunty') who was the only Larkin sister left in Australia by the time Mary had died. Jack was still a bachelor at this time. He was some two years older than Dorothy, being, of course, her first cousin. He had served in the First World War, and for some time had been in England.

It was Jack who rose to the occasion of this visit by his cousin and his uncle by marriage to look after the latter in an almost royal manner. He took Harry in hand and showed him round and introduced him to a lot of notable men in Melbourne, took him to his Clubs and generally made a fuss of him. Harry simply loved all of that and as a result thought very highly of Jack. Meanwhile Dorothy spent a lot of time with Queen and with Little Aunty, and also with Marie, the youngest of the McCormack four, now Marie Farrell. She and her husband Ted, together with their little daughter Pat (at that time referred to as Bubbles), also lived in Melbourne. All got on well with Dorothy and all had a great deal to tell her about the family, past and present. As much as Dorothy could remember was relayed back to Bournemouth in her letters.

In addition, there was at least one occasion when Dorothy and Harry were present at an even more extensive gathering of the clan. Jennie's three brothers, John, Mike and Tom turning up together with their two wives and three children, not to mention a McCormack Aunt (Anne Doherty), all with their memories of Jennie, and all anxious to meet Jennie's husband and daughter.

The hot and cold aspect of life with Harry is demonstrated, however, even in Dorothy's first letter from Melbourne, despite the fact that

> I think Henry is quite impressed with them and he has been really charming, just as he knows how; so, so far, everything has been running smoothly.

Dorothy's longing for home was getting no less, and she was a little anxious that he had not yet finalised the booking of their return passage, although – months in advance – "he has booked again, P&O for Bombay on October 18th." And if he was pleased with the reception given them by Jennie's side of the family, he was not an easy companion for Dorothy.

> Henry is in the devil of a temper – if only he'd book us home I wouldn't mind; only I hope it won't reflect on you all. I don't quite know why he is huffy – says I've been persistently rude or something. However, I'm getting used to these things now and don't worry. I've been thinking I wish Jim were here. The next best thing to Jim himself is to copy his method, not to get upset. I think Henry is one of those people who get worse when you get upset.

Perhaps Dorothy was too forthright in her opinions and attitudes for Harry's liking. Having plenty to say for yourself, despite it being controversial, was fine in a man, even a young one – part of manly growing up – but in a woman… Notwithstanding the family doing their best to fête them, there was another bust up in a day or two.

> [Thursday] 13th May. I posted the mail yesterday. I had had a row with Harry- over such a little thing, but it had worried me overmuch because I could see he was really hurt. However we made it up in the evening and he has been perfectly sweet since, and now I am beginning to think it has done a lot of good and cleared the air. I know you will be glad to hear this, so I am sitting up after twelve to write it to you.

Dorothy gives no further details in her letter. She once told me of an incident, which could well have been this one – it does not otherwise appear at all in the letters – in reply to a remark of mine to the effect that it (that is, the whole Journey) must have been a marvellous experience. "It would have been if Daddy had not had such an uncertain temper," she said. As an example of how his demeanour tended to spoil things, she told me how she and he had gone into a

Bank. Dorothy was undertaking some transaction and the assistant asked for a detail which she did not want to give him as she thought it irrelevant. Harry intervened to point out what the man wanted. She turned to him and said "No: its none of his business." Meaning of the assistant's. He misheard, or misunderstood her remark to have been "No. It's none of your business." Meaning Harry's. He would not speak to her for the rest of the day. A pretty poor basis for a row, one might have thought, at most a minor misunderstanding which should have been instantly put right.

As for Melbourne itself, it would have been well known to Jennie from twenty-five years or so before this time, and Dorothy only gives one brief account of her impression of the place.

> [Friday 14th May]. By the way I must say I am impressed with Melbourne and its fine streets. Some of the suburbs are beautiful and there is an air of well-being and solidity about the place that is undeniable. The shops are beautiful and the things are ever so much cheaper than India, although dearer than England. The women in the streets are not smart but they are quite tastefully dressed – quietly and sensibly – whereas in Sydney they were awful – got up in sky-blue jap silk and worsted imitation silk stockings and terribly made up or else without a vestige of powder. Sydney women seemed to have very hard faces.
>
> Everyone has been extraordinarily polite so far and we haven't come across that impertinence that is supposed to mark the Australian spirit of democracy. Taxi men, servants etc., etc. all "Sir" Henry and really are very polite and obliging.

The large get-together of so many of the Larkin family took place at the home of Little Aunty, Queen and Jack. Those three still lived together. Dorothy stayed for dinner in the evening. Jack took Harry to a recruits' show where he, Jack, spoke; typical of the sort of event he had lined up for Harry's interest and entertainment, which Harry greatly enjoyed. After taking Harry home, Jack came back to take Dorothy home. In a short passage she gives about the only clue as to whether Jack could possibly have been the hidden fiancé of five years before.

[Monday 17th May]. Jack called for me and took me home. We had a long talk. He made out he was still a bit in love with me and is most humble about never having written. He says he was ill at the time "but," he said, "that isn't it. I can't write letters. If I had written I'd have said too much, so I didn't write." – whatever that may mean.

And whatever we might be expected to infer from those few cryptic sentences. Jennie, of course, would have known all there was to know and so would not have needed explanations. It is pretty clear that at some time in the past Jack had been "in love" with Dorothy, but when, and to what extent? And about what might he have been expected to write and be apologising for not having done so? Answers to those and to other questions can only be guesswork without further evidence.

Dorothy then allows herself to speculate about Queen, in terms which tell us as much about herself as about her cousin. And she also makes it clear that by the day after the family gathering she and Harry were on even better terms.

[Tuesday 18 May]...I feel awfully sorry for Queen. She's so nice but she is growing into an old maid and is beginning to look like it. You know, a cheerful-but-blighted-at-the-same-time look. As soon as I begin to look like that, and some of you will be the only ones who will tell me, I shall marry the first man who comes along. Queen ought to have been married ages ago. She's so nice and would make such a nice wife...

...Henry has been such a dear – partly I expect because he hasn't seen too much of me – anyhow, he has been so nice that I bought him a bunch of cornflowers and put them in his room. He was quite touched and has been wearing one.

She ends this letter with another example of remote controlled gardening.

...Don't worry about the rhododendrons as they won't make any new wood until May or early June and then, when they have flowered, I think the tops ought to be pruned to within three feet or so of the ground. That will strengthen the new shoots. Of course only top the ones that have already been cut too much and don't let him clip them like a hedge, but more or less unevenly. I explained both to Hall and to Jim before I left.

Their time in Melbourne continued with daily comings and goings between members of the various related families, all of which Dorothy records for Jennie's benefit in much detail. She was full of praise for the way "your relations," as she referred to them generically, had looked after the pair of them, entertaining them and driving them round by car or taxi. When the time came for departure on 25th May – I assume by train – they were given the royal treatment:

> The cousins sent us off splendidly with flowers and chocolates and a book for me, a lovely bag for you from Aunty and a spoon for Dorothy Mary from Bubbles. Henry has been fearfully impressed. Jack introduced him to all kinds of nice men, and through him he has got an almost official invitation to Canberra.

A comfortable overnight journey got them to Sydney, where they booked into The Australia Hotel. Mrs L'Estrange was waiting for them at their hotel and was to be much in evidence for most of the rest of their time in New South Wales and Queensland. By this time Dorothy had had letters from all three of the L'Estrange boys, each one showing in his own way considerable affection for Dorothy and her family. For that reason, and because Mick is the other candidate for the role of fiancé, it is worth setting out some quotations. In their own right they are interesting, describing the life on a sheep station, but that is rather remote from Dorothy's journey.

From Harry on 29th April:

> Dearest Dorothy,
> ...Doesn't it seem terrible that we all won't be there to meet you after we had planned such wonderful things to do? Remember when Jack and I stayed at Chingri Khal and we had such a wonderful time and we swore that when you came to Australia we would try and pay some of it back. Moonlight surfing parties, dances, passionfruit cake

and all the real and imaginary fruits that we used to tell you about. I swear we will have it some day; but if only you had come three months earlier we would have all been in our house together instead of as we are now, scattered to the four winds and the house let…

…Jack and I often get jobs together and sometimes as we ride along we go over all the happenings of the six years in England and when we think of the glorious times we had at Bournemouth we get sort of wistful and say "Wouldn't it be wonderful if we could meet Dorothy now and have a good old talk again just like we used to at Chingri Khal." I wonder when we will meet again…I haven't forgotten all the dancing you taught me and only wish we could have a few evenings together as we used to…I…was dancing with…the best dancer in Australia and she said that Jack and I were the two best dancers she had come across so far in Queensland, I laid it all at your door…

My love always   Harry

Alone of the three brothers, Harry wrote a short second letter to Dorothy three weeks later. Could his commencement of this letter be of significance?

Dearest Big Sister,

Wish you really were. I often think how nice it would be to have a sister…Jack and I were just saying today that we would give a month's pay (a vast sum when you have earned it) to be with you and Mother in Sydney. Just think of it. But you must come again. We won't take "No" or "Perhaps" for an answer…Goodbye and all my love. Jack and I are always thinking and talking of you.   Harry

Jack, for his part, wrote between Harry's two letters on 9th May, and provides his own tiny, but characteristic, vignette of life at Bournemouth.

Dearest Dorothy,

Welcome to Australia. I cannot tell you how disappointed I am at not being able to get down to see you…we will have to go on waiting for your return visit…I hope you had time to go out and see Strathmore, our home, it really is a lovely place, and when you come out again you are to have the Louis Quinze Suite…Sometimes I go

339

out by myself the whole day, and then I think over all the happy times in England. As I have told you before I did not enjoy anything so much as our stay at Chingri Khal, and often we talk over it together. Those nights at the King's Hall* were wonderful, and the evenings that we used to play bridge and Mrs.Hobbs used to bid up like anything. I only hope that some day they will come again.. The people here are very good to me, but somehow I never feel at home...Well good-bye, Dorothy, for the present, and do come out again to see us, we will always be waiting with much love,

from Jack.

Mick's letter was the last – he had written two or three times earlier in the year, but these had not managed to get to Dorothy. It is worth mentioning here that, in a letter to Jennie in January from Calcutta, Dorothy refers to getting "most charming letters from Australia – no, not from Mick; he is a broken reed so I've turned him down – but from Harry and the Doctor." Another enigma. Why a "broken reed?" What had she "turned down?" Whatever the answers, she had plainly written to Mick when in Australia. He, in his reply, is much more intense than his younger brothers: there is clearly something mutually recognised but not openly admitted.

Dorothy Dear,
   You don't know how happy I was to get your letter last Sunday, but it is damnable to think that you are so close and yet I am unable to see you.
   I am glad you like Australia so much, but England holds my heart just as securely each year. Unhappily I cannot forget. "Life is made sweet by memory but possible by forgetfulness." Did I ever tell you that the thing which fascinated me most in all mythology was the river Lettie? You can guess that I have spent many, many hours musing on the mutability of human affairs…
   …What you say about Oxford I shall treasure with the other things you have said to me. I have a copy of the Shropshire Lad and often read it; I find something new each time.
   …Do you remember the morning of the Merton Ball when we went to the [Blyth's] house in Holywell for breakfast, Arthur in his pyjamas with "scooter leg"? Douglas Blyth had the odd spot and

* The ballroom at the Royal Bath Hotel.

wanted to kiss everyone and Mrs. W. was terrified he would try to kiss you and you would be annoyed...I wish we could have danced again, but perhaps it is just as well that we cannot. I shudder to think how out of date my dancing must be...

Very much love, dear,   Mick

It is a little sad to have to put on record that, despite all that evident affection and good will, not to say love, shown by the L'Estrange family, Dorothy never again did visit Australia, nor, so far as I know, did she ever again meet any one of the L'Estrange boys.

But for their six days in Sydney they had the company of Mrs L'Estrange who helped to show them round and introduced them to charming and helpful people – sending Australians still higher in Dorothy's good books.

Thursday saw them "doing the famous harbours, but, as the sun got too much in my eyes, I have a terrible headache" – what a shame not to be able to enjoy one of Sydney's greatest assets. Friday saw the arrival of the mail and, as a result,

Henry is in great form. He has been interviewed by the press, twice I think, and he has had a topping letter from Arthur which has made him proud as punch...Next...he got a letter from Bramley* who wants to join him in the business. Daddy is delighted and I only hope it will come true as Henry has got tired of the business and would, I think, be happier in some other job He is as excited as a kid and has had no dinner tonight on account of writing off letters...He is as sweet as honey now he has had news from Arthur...

Saturday [29th May]...This evening we all went to hear the Don Cossack Choir, and I think Henry enjoyed it although he went to sleep once or twice. He says if Bramley takes over the show entirely, which he would like, he would try and get on to a Financial Paper like *Commerce*. Mother, pray hard that everything goes well. Daddy, I know, feels hampered by the business and I'm sure would be happier if he were rid of it.

For whatever reason, the proposed deal with the man Bramley never came off. The business, such as it was by then, remained Harry's until

* Not otherwise identified.

the end of his life. Meanwhile in Sydney Dorothy indulges in a little liturgical criticism, and shows herself no ecclesiastical sycophant.

> Sunday [30th May]…I went to St.Mary's this morning where the Archbishop of Sydney preached. He isn't up to much and was dead against mixed marriages, which he dragged into his sermon, which was supposed to be on Our Lady. The singing was absolutely excruciating so in the end my nerves were so on edge that I could have cried. The church, though, is a beautiful building, and the crowd seems quite decent – much better than in Melbourne.

The mail arrived from England on the next day, Monday, and with it the welcome news of the safe birth to Phyllis of a second daughter, Phyllida Jane, both doing well. The medical scares had proved groundless.

That day also saw a meeting with Harry's "brother Jim, who is simply too awful for words. I saw him for a few moments when I came back. He dresses like a working man and looks like a pig." And later the two of them were taken to a Palais de Danse, in the party being "a man…who's gone barmy on me, but I'm a bit mistrustful of him. Lockyer is his name, an Englishman and he wants me to go out 'fishing' of all things on Sunday. I shall refuse, I think."

They spent all Tuesday in the train to Canberra – Harry got fed up with the journey and "wasn't in too sweet a mood this morning, but has completely recovered by now, thank goodness." Writing from the Hotel Canberra, Dorothy gives her impressions of the new Capital to Jennie.

> [Wednesday 2nd June]. Well, this is an extraordinary place. Absolutely raw, the Hotel is nice. Quite simply laid out but with good things, and is very comfortable. It has beautiful courtyards, with lawns and bricked paths round the flowerbeds, and will be ever so much prettier when some of the trees grow a bit more. Opposite is the new Federal Parliament which we went over this morning. This was quite nice, but nothing to rave over in my opinion. I expected something more luxurious, both in size and in fittings. The building is squat and all the rooms are low. Knowing the beautiful Australian woods that there are, I expected ever so much more panelling than I found. However, it is all very unfinished and so unfair to judge. Well,

then it all appears waste land, although you can see some of the roads indicated and in the distance a few groups of houses – the coming of the township. The weather has been dreadful today – just like a wet day at home – and so the outlook was depressing. I am glad I have seen Canberra.

After two nights in Canberra they took a car to a sheep station, Foxlow, to which they had been invited by people whom they had met a short time before. They had the misfortune to be involved in a motor accident as they left Canberra, but they were unhurt, and, it seems, their journey not impeded. It was "a most beautiful station, very small. Fifteen thousand acres, eight thousand sheep at present, but generally twelve, and about six hundred cattle. They have just imported a Red Poll bull from the King's Stud in England. The Homestead is simply beautiful, panelled hall with English oak, dining room and lounge, good bedrooms, nicely furnished...in fact one might be in a lovely country home in England."

Friday was spent in the train returning from Canberra to Sydney, where they spent that week-end. Dorothy tried another Church, but seemingly not with a great deal of success.

Sunday 6th June. I went to St. Patrick's this morning, but it was very disappointing. The building was hideous and I have never seen so many cheap statues in my life; there must have been over fifty of them, all crowded together and higgledy-piggledy, so the place reminded me more of a cheap china shop than of anything else. And the singing! And the organ! Our little church at its worst was up to Queen's Hall standard by comparison. However the sermon was good and I felt very devotional in spite of it all. The amusing part was that Henry, who had come to call for me, arrived early, and was dragged in by some enthusiastic Holy Roman to hear the singing, "the finest in Australia." I met him outside and, not knowing that he had heard it all, I started off by saying how terrible it was. It was lucky in a way that I did as I had the first whack, and he couldn't say much more.

Dorothy continued with a bit of a summing up of her time in Australia, although they had nearly another month there ahead of them.

You know I like Australia. We have met such charming people for one thing and it is so nice to be among loyal Britishers for another. But all the same I wouldn't like to live here. It is not only out of the way, but far away…Of course we've been very lucky. Your relations did us absolutely splendidly in Melbourne and Jack was simply marvellous in showing Henry round. Got heaps of men to meet him etc., etc. and Henry simply loved it. Here we haven't met so many men, but we have met some topping people who have been most kind…Well then, Henry's own relations are very much of a come down, and I'm sure he will never have the face to say anything to you about yours now. His brother Jim is Kentell* in his best clothes. I expect they were Jim's best clothes, too, and a nephew (I suppose Jim's son) is friendly with one of the waiters here and sent Henry a note through him. It is a good thing Daddy doesn't live here, as they'd be on him like a plague of leaches. Well, I'm not going to own them, so that's that. Daddy looked so refined and gentlemanly beside his brother. He said he was so glad Jim had seen me. I suppose Jim was impressed. I don't think he realises how glad I was to see Jim – for your sake, darling, that's all.

They had just the week-end in Sydney on their return from Canberra before they were off again into the Blue Mountains, to Jenolan, principally in order to see the caves there. They made the journey "in what they call a parlour car, which is a sort of char-a-banc, only more glorified than I had ever thought could be possible. The seats were most comfortable and the travelling was a cross between a Pullman car on the railway and a limousine motor." They had bad weather going there, leaving Dorothy disappointed in the scenery, but sunshine coming back gave her plenty of opportunity to enjoy all there was to see. Caves and scenery made quite an impression.

Tuesday 8th June. This morning we did the Lucas Cave and this afternoon the Orient Cave with part of the river cave thrown in. In the latter they said there were 1,400 steps, which I think may be a bit exaggerated, but I know that having tramped up and down the Lucas steps in the morning and then those of the Orient, we were fairly well exercised when we sat down here to tea…The caves'…colouring is magnificent and the settings most weird. They are all lit with electric

* A predecessor to Hall as gardener at Chingri Khal.

light. Some are very small so that you have to bend almost double to get into them; others are enormous, and one certainly had a most beautiful domed roof. Last night one of the caves had like a beautiful spray of green weeping willows against its walls. This morning we went to a part called The Cathedral, which it was not unlike, but the most notable feature (after its height which was over a hundred feet) was a formation which was like a window in a church. That was really rather lovely. This afternoon the Orient Caves are just like jewel boxes, flower groves and silk all mixed up – mostly pink, gold, white and all shades of terra cotta to brown…Fairyland; too beautiful to be true.

We had the most glorious trip down in the sunshine and saw the Blue Mountains at their best. They really are rather wonderful – they seem to be covered with a blue gauze, which I think is caused by the gum trees: as soon as any hill in the distance is covered with gums it looks blue, just like the mountains

They had three fairly hectic days in Sydney. At least Dorothy did: Harry got a chill on his return from Jenolan and stayed in a couple of days. He eventually absented himself on Saturday to spend the evening with his brother, "such an idiotic thing to do" was her comment, but he was more or less back to rights on Sunday.

Just as well, for they had to take the Brisbane train from Sydney at 3.30 p.m. on the Sunday. This involved passing over the site of a major train disaster, which had taken place only on the Thursday before, when the Brisbane Express had fallen off a bridge and down an embankment. As they went over the bridge they could see the overturned rolling stock and the flares of the men working to deal with it. It seems they must have been lucky that the line was reopened so soon. They had to change trains at the border with Queensland, because of the narrower gauge in that State, and it was 7pm. on the Monday before they thankfully were able to relax in their Hotel – the Lennon's.

They had ten days awaiting them in Brisbane, rather longer, one might have thought, than they really needed or wanted. It provided Dorothy with the opportunity for much socialising with various families in the City, mainly at the introduction of Mrs L'Estrange. "Brisbane," she wrote, "is a cross between Bournemouth and the

Riviera, without any smartness, of course. I like it better, I think, than the other towns in Australia," although much of the unfinished state of the streets and buildings, while understandable, she found unattractive. She was much taken with the home of the L'Estranges, as the boys thought she would be, despite it being let to tenants. But she was critical of the people she saw in the streets.

> I cannot get over the crowds of men lolling about the streets, nor the quantity of drunks there are about…It strikes me as being very sad to see the number of street loafers there are. Not beggars or down-and-outs, but quite decently dressed people, men, who seem to do nothing but hang about at the corner of the streets and fairly stink of beer. They are young-ish and not wretchedly dressed and are supposed to make their living by racing. The Queensland girls, such as I have seen, are neither pretty nor smart…

But not so critical of church and churchgoers.

> Sunday [20th June]…I went to Mass at the Cathedral this morning and enjoyed it very much. The crowd was ever so much better than in Sydney or Melbourne and so was the singing, although that isn't saying much. The building itself isn't bad, although I understand it is not the real Cathedral which has yet to be built. However they have three windows over the High Altar which are the most beautiful things I have seen in Australia.

A letter from Harry to Jennie happens to have survived from this time in Brisbane. Only noteworthy in its apparent normality and pleasantness ("My dearest Jennie…Much love. I hope you are well, growing reconciled to Arthur's departure and, like us, looking forward to our homecoming. Your affectionate Husband."). He gives her his opinion that "Dorothy…is improving under the experience of travel and, I think, will be found benefited by her experience. At any rate she needed such a schooling and the money will not be entirely wasted." I somehow doubt if Dorothy saw that at the time: I think her reaction might have been a little volatile – orally, or in writing, or even both.

Their social outings that week included an all day outing to Bribie Island in Moreton Bay; three hours each way by boat for two and a half hours on the island, where friends had "a tiny little place." Most of the time there seems to have been spent preparing, eating and clearing up after an alfresco meal, starting with oysters (Harry being deputed to open them, in the course of which he slashed his thumb "which bled like billyoh") and ending with tinned pears. Much effort for very little, although Dorothy, perhaps unexpectedly, enjoyed the boat trips to and fro.

At 8am on Friday, 25th June they got on the train for Sydney ("with great relief") and, after the necessary change at the border, arrived n Sydney at 12.30pm the following day. They still had nearly a week before they were due to sail, and it seems to have been a question of how to kill the time before they left. Harry took Dorothy to a show. It was

> ...very poor...when he had paid 8/8d each for the seats I was sorry it was so indifferent. I feel so sorry for him as he gets such a little pleasure out of his life. Lately, though, he is becoming just a shade more broad-minded. I only hope it goes on, although I am afraid you won't notice it in his ordinary life as it only affects his political opinions so far. But I have hopes!!

Sunday afternoon was enlivened by a visit they paid to

> ...The Domain – a park – and listened to the tub-thumpers. Most of the cranks of Sydney were there I suppose. Members of Parliament, Loyalists, Religious, Communists, I.W.W., and eating and drinking fanatics and, oh the most terrible people. There was one man with long silky hair and a beard talking on sex and another man dressed in shorts and a running vest and literally nothing else, who spouted about vegetarianism and sex and everything. We ran into him tonight as in the deserted streets more meetings were being held after dark. I never knew there were so many gasbags in the world, nor so many people qualifying for the lunatic asylums. The religious people, too, are terrible and their singing was the cruellest thing you could imagine.

They had some friends to dine with them at their hotel on the Monday. Dorothy organised it and felt she had done so badly, explaining to Jennie in much detail where she felt she had been less than clever. She then allows herself the luxury (if that is the right word) of a fairly prolonged reflection on her father and his complex character. By now she had had the opportunity of observing him closely for over six months, and so, this being the last significant comment that is available, it is worth setting out her conclusions. Her lead in comes with the end of their little party and being alone together with Harry.

He said when he came up here he was glad it was all over. Now really I had enjoyed it, but I think he feels the strain of being on his best behaviour. I don't think he has ever dressed so much nor been among so many decent people as since I've been with him, and I don't think I'm conceited or that I'm flattering myself when I say that I am an asset to him as I know more or less how to behave and can be nice to people without gushing over them. He also feels out here that his position is anomalous – forgetting that this is a very democratic country.

One result is that it makes him more inclined to sell out of the business and go on a newspaper permanently. I know he feels the strain of being on his best behaviour with me and the decent people and clothes (although I must say he does wear filthy collars) but I think he'll miss it when he gets away from it all. Poor Daddy! He is only now getting a taste for the things he has affected to despise. If he sells out of the business is he going to improve in the way he can? Because as a newspaper man he could hold a good position and, through my being in Calcutta, I have helped him towards knowing a few decent people, so he may become a bit more civilised and less brutal than he has been so far. But with the business still on his hands he cannot.

It isn't what other people think, because when I was there I saw that many people knew him and would be nice to him...There are...for instance...all the friends I made. It is he himself. He cannot face people with that place he now admits he loathes. You must pray that Bramley will buy. India is a place of short memories for all practical purposes and in addition Henry would be a much happier man. I think perhaps the slights and snubs he received when a young man have helped to sour his nature. I feel so sorry for him at times and hope and pray that I will please him for the rest of the journey.

You know, darling, we are not a scrap alike – he and I – and we would not pull along together at all were it not for our mutual advantage. It would be much better for me to have a pa on a newspaper and much better for all of us if I can get him to know a few decent people, so I am continually 'at' him. On the other hand, although he and I have scarcely a taste in common, he wants me on these journeys because I'm a stand by. Of course, I am very fond of him and he more or less likes me, but I am under no delusions about his reasons for travelling about with me.

I am longing to get home, but I feel sometimes I ought to go out to India again with him. Mind you he doesn't want me, I know that and I would rather be at home with you. Of course I could visit various people out there but the bulk of my time would be spent in Calcutta and I have to go so gingerly with Henry, whereas at home with you I'd just love it. Still, as anything may happen in this changeable world even Henry might change his opinions; should I accept if he offers to take me out again? As a matter of fact I have an idea that you and I will go out this time, and if not this year, next.

But in truth Jennie never went to India again and Dorothy did not do so in Harry's lifetime. Nor, indeed, so far as I am aware, did either of them see again any of those Australian relations whom Dorothy had so much enjoyed meeting. And as for the business, it was never sold, whatever the reason may have been, and was still going strong, or possibly not so very strong, thirty years later. Their last few days were unremarkable and they set sail at 3 o'clock on the afternoon of Friday, 2nd July for New Zealand, their last country to visit before the long voyage to England.

CHAPTER 22

DOROTHY'S JOURNEY (10) NEW ZEALAND AND HOME

OROTHY HAD ARRIVED in Australia in a state of some apprehension as to how she was going to like the country and its people. She departed in a very positive frame of mind, with all doubts and hesitations dispelled, even if she found the place expensive. Writing after they had settled into their first hotel in New Zealand, the Grand at Auckland, she wrote

> [Tuesday] 6th July…We've left Australia, with many regrets and with great pleasure – regrets because we would have liked to have seen more of the country and of the people, especially the people because we were very lucky and met some perfectly delightful Australians; and pleasure because we are now on our way home…On Friday [the day they sailed] I had to fly off after lunch to the bank when I sent home the remainder of my money, £50 to wit. I have one pound left, which means that in less than two months in Australia I spent twenty-nine pounds – isn't it awful? I have bought nothing; the money has gone in theatres, pictures, teas and taxis, which are very expensive… in Australia.

She was to find New Zealand even more to her taste. But before that she had to get there, and the crossing was more than a little trying.

> I taxied to the ship, quite a short journey, and got on board to find I had a cabin to myself and so had Henry, so we were both happy. We set off, I mean sailed, at three and I had tea. But no sooner were we out beyond the Heads when she put her nose into it and that was the end of poor little Dorothy Mary. I am still feeling the effects. I got up for breakfast the next morning but went to bed immediately after,

and stayed in bed all day Sunday too. Monday was a bit better and I got up for lunch, but felt very sorry for myself. I sat in the smoke room and watched Henry play bridge and this morning I just crawled up for lunch. I think I felt worse this morning than at any other time as I developed a terrible headache, although it was beautifully calm. Also my old trouble of wind came back to me and I felt I couldn't digest anything but the smallest and driest of food, so I have lived almost entirely on water biscuits...Even the Captain told me he felt ill and Henry frankly admitted being upset by the motion. We arrived at 3. p.m. instead of 7. a.m., so you can see that we didn't have any too easy a time. However it is all over now and yesterday evening I quite enjoyed. I have come to the conclusion I like shipboard life even if it is rough and the people are dullish.

Despite her mainly restricted diet, Dorothy was able to assert a most favourable account of the cuisine on board. At the time there was no adverse criticism from her of the food on the *Rawalpindi*, but these four days to New Zealand brought forth quite a stinging rebuke to her Line.

The last five hours or so on the boat were very enjoyable as we were coming down the coast and passing various islands, and altogether New Zealand looked rather enchanting in the sunlight. The attention on board the *Marama* was excellent and the food even better than that of the *Houtman*. When I think of the P. and O. feeding in comparison I almost blush to think that a great British line should show up so poorly against a potty little Dutch line and a potty little Colonial line. However, there it is, and Henry is full of praise for the Union Steam Ship Company and the *Marama*.

No doubt she would have been encouraged by the excellence of the *Marama* to look forward to the long voyage home even more than she already was. Little did she know...

First impressions of New Zealand were excellent – apart from the music.

By the time we got our luggage away and arrived here it was nearly six. We had dinner at 6.15, which is the time here apparently. Just as the clock struck the quarter the band in the lounge struck up 'God

351

Save the King' and I remembered that we were truly in the most patriotic country in the world. Otherwise I might add the band is too awful for words – excruciating, and worse. The food here is excellent and the hotel very comfortable. We are waited on by girls who are the most spotlessly dressed in white and seem very efficient. So far I have heard no accent. The people seem an even finer looking lot than the Australians, though the Victorians in Melbourne must run them pretty close.

They had no more than eleven days in New Zealand, and confined to the North Island, but in all they managed to visit six different places, with quite a lot of sight seeing in all of them, save probably the last, Wellington, from where they made their final embarkation. Dorothy's one letter, which she reckoned would only get home some four days before they did, gives a full description of the many fascinating places in their tour.

They had one full day in Auckland, which they toured 'in a char-a-banc.' Despite 'it being very cold here and I am half perished with it' she thought 'it seems a pleasant place and the people very fine looking. I was especially struck by the children who seem positive young giants.' Then they were on the move.

Waitomo Hostel

Thursday [8th July] We had a very pleasant journey here arriving about 4.30…We went over the caves. They are nothing to the Jenolan Caves in N.S.W. in beauty or comfort as they are very wet and muddy. Before we went inside we had to put on gigantic hob nailed boots which they hire out for the purpose. You should have seen me with my short skirts, a vast expanse of fat leg in a woollen stocking and these terrible boots. As a matter of fact they were quite comfortable and most useful as otherwise we'd have been sliding about all over the place. Daddy and the men looked even more comic than us, because he had tucked his trousers into his socks and so converted them into very long plus-fours. The caves were interesting – vast and very white, but as I said before nothing to the Jenolan. However, there was one spot where we embarked on a little boat and went along an underground river in the dark and the top of the cave was covered with glow-worms – just millions of them. They were reflected again in the water and the whole effect was fairylike in the extreme. I am very glad I saw it…it was worthwhile coming.

This hostel isn't up to much – the cats sleep on the beds, as several people found out when they entered their rooms, the rats are making the most terrible row imaginable, and, as this is a wooden house, their efforts are meeting with considerable success. The food isn't bad. Henry is arguing with the Americans and God only know what they will think of him.

Grand Hotel,

Rotorua

[Friday] 9th July. We have just arrived at the Grand Hotel. Last night was awful – in a way. I told you the hostel is built of wood. Well, the water cooling in the pipes made the most astonishing noises and the rats were absolutely unbelievable. I have never heard such an inferno in my life. Then, in addition, the partitions between the bedrooms being very thin, you could hear each movement and sound in the rooms on each side. The man on my right couldn't sleep and I could hear his bed creaking as he tossed and turned, while the American couple were on my left and he snored so loudly all night that neither he nor his wife heard the rats. Eventually I slept and when I was called at 7 a.m. this morning the rats were quiet but the snorer was still at it… So far this seems the nicest hotel we have been in, but as I haven't had a meal yet I mustn't talk – more tonight.

[Saturday] 10th July. Well, there wasn't any more last night as Henry seized me and we played bridge solidly till after twelve. I take back what I said about the nicest hotel, although it is very good. The food, though, is nothing as good as at Auckland which was really more comfortable in other ways too.

We have been out on an all day trip round various lakes and geysers and active and quiet volcanoes. It was very interesting. We went over two lakes in launches. One of the lakes was boiling in places…We saw some of their famous trout in a stream by the road – the water was almost black with them, and now is the spawning season. They say they will be much finer and more numerous later on.

Then tonight we went to a Maori concert and saw the famous Haka done by the men. The women are quite nice looking but all the older ones are tattooed over their lips and chin so they look as if they are wearing a beard and moustache, which I think completely spoils them. They sang one or two items jolly well when they were sticking to their simple native tunes, but they murdered 'Annie Laurie.' They also had a ball on a string in each hand and swung these awfully cleverly to time as they sang. Altogether I enjoyed it…

Sunday 11th July…This morning…it poured…When I was called this morning I thought we were having an earthquake, though I'm almost certain it was nothing but the wind in these wooden houses. The room was literally shaking with it…It is bitterly cold and I am absolutely frozen with it. I think I am very difficult to please as regards weather…

We went off to a place called Waka – the native settlement of Rotorua. It is really an old crater and is filled with all kinds of steaming pools and geysers. Unfortunately it was still wet and it had rather a depressing effect. I couldn't help feeling how it might go up at any minute. Every little crevice and crack in the ground was steaming. The village itself was quite uninteresting, being made of matchwood, although they had a show place to demonstrate their old ways of living. The geysers were not playing very well, but it was quite interesting…

After that we went to the Baths…We had what is known as a radium bath. My dear, it is simply glorious. No bathing costumes, a lovely green pool about four feet deep. If you had told me last year that I would have got into a bathing pool with six or eight other women all with nothing on, I'd have died at the thought. Yet there I was and I enjoyed it immensely. The bath was quite hot and bubbly and after I went and had a hot shower. I came back home all aglow and went to sleep and had the best night you could imagine.

Geyser House Hotel,
Wairakei

[Monday 12th July] We left at about nine in the cold and rain but it got much better as we came along, and as we were driving in an open car we were duly thankful. The drive was very pretty and much like Scotland. This isn't a bad Hostel and I gave Henry the room with the radiator, as he seemed to be feeling the cold…

After lunch we went to see the famous Geyser Valley, which is marvellous beyond description. There are all kinds of geysers playing – generally about every fifteen minutes, but what adds to the whole business is that the valley itself is so pretty, with all kinds of bubbly springs, some of a most lovely blue and others green. One, which was very small, was entirely surrounded with red thermalite so it had a pinkish look, and others, which became geysers, looked absolutely lovely when playing. I shouldn't like to live here though as I'd be too frightened of the whole place blowing up.

Then I had a bath here…'The Avenue Bath,' so called because you walk down a long avenue of pine trees for about half a mile and then, on turning to the right, we came to a little shed on the edge of a lovely green pool. There was a little waterfall at one end and an overflow at the other. It was very hot. I just loved it. We were there out in the open air, in a beautiful steaming hot pool, with trees and fern all round and the darkening evening sky. I don't think I have ever enjoyed myself so much.

In the evening…we went out at about eight and saw a famous blowhole – a place that they call the safety valve for New Zealand. Steam is always being forced out at a tremendous pressure, I believe a hundred and eighty pounds a square inch. When we came home we went for a bath in the swimming pool, which is just next to the hotel. No costumes and a lovely warm blue pool about thirty or forty feet long. I swam around and realised that I had never lived until then.

[Tuesday 13th July]…I was up at seven for another bathe in the swimming pool, and then after breakfast we went to the famous Wairoa Valley, where we saw the origin of our baths. The Avenue Bath, the swimming pool and the Fairy Pool are all pools of the same stream – I suppose about two miles or under being the distance between the first and the last…The first is the hottest, only just bearable, the other two being quite comfortable.

Well, the stream that feeds them comes from some of the various pools in the Wairoa Valley which, like the Geyser Valley is another large volcanic crater, which contains all kinds of hot pools. Some of them were too lovely for words, and there are three of them which are quite famous, a cloudy blue, a clear green, which they say is over a hundred feet deep and very, very lovely (called The Emerald Pool) and a cloudy red pool, a colour we would call crushed strawberry. This latter is surrounded with ferns right down to the water's edge, although the temperature of the water is just on boiling point. But its colour, which is due to iron and this red stuff the Maoris used to make paint out of, called 'hematite', is quite unique, and the 'Claret Cup' is the only one of its kind in the world. We then wandered down the valley, passed all kinds of little pools – all nearly boiling - and along a stream whose bed was first green with copper and then pink with iron. The vegetation all around was very thick and mossy, with scrubby trees and ferns. Oh, it was lovely.

In the afternoon we went over the Geyser Valley again, which I think I enjoyed more than the first time. Also we saw the geyser called The Eagle's Nest play. It is so called because it is surrounded with gigantic stakes which have been washed there at some time or another, and they have all been more or less petrified. It looks exactly like the nest of an enormous prehistoric bird or monster.

There is another geyser there too, which is a quiet pool for about four minutes, and then you see a rock which is submerged at one side, move slowly up and down. Then the water shoots up for about three minutes. Well, this time I sat on a rock some distance off, but where I could see into the pool with safety, more or less, all the time the geyser was playing, and I could feel the shock of the rock bumping against the bottom of the pool. It was rather a terrifying experience and I was quite glad to get away. At the same time the Geyser Valley is lovely and I think Wairakei beats Rotorua every time the bell strikes.

Before dinner I went down to the Fairy Pool. This is a little pool about fifty or a hundred yards away from our bedrooms. It was dark when we went, but all this place was lit up with electric light. The pool is round – about fifteen feet across and has a waterfall coming into it about four feet wide and at a height of about six feet. As you may imagine the force in this little fall is pretty big. We bathed as usual with nothing on and I got an immense pummelling from the water, far better than any massage in a Turkish bath.

Oh dear! I did enjoy myself in those baths. I think the Fairy Bath was perhaps the best, but all of them were lovely. It was glorious being out in such beautiful surroundings, in the clear frosty air, with the open sky above and ferns and moss around and these hot pools. I bathed in the swimming pool after dinner and felt so sorry I was having my last go. I was in with another girl, and, although we had shut the gate, a man wandered in and I shouted him off. He was as scared as a rabbit, and the other girl and I were tickled to death, as we were really all right, up to our necks, and the water was cloudy, so nobody could see even our shoulders. We thanked heaven, though, that we had had our last five minutes chat and hadn't been caught coming out.

I am left wondering how the male of the species managed to get a look-in at these various delectable hot pools. Mixed bathing in the altogether was not an activity encouraged, or even permitted at all, in those days. Perhaps they had certain times set aside for their use. Dorothy does not tell us if Harry had a swim at any of them, nor, if he did, what he thought of the experience. Their time in New Zealand was fast drawing to its end.

Masonic Hotel

Napier

[Wednesday] 14th July. Last night it was very cold and I woke up with my nose frozen. It has been a lovely day though, clear, sunshiney and frosty. We have been motoring all day. We left Wairakei at 8.30 and saw Lake Taupo, which is a gigantic lake right in the centre of the North Island, with snow covered mountains around and a smoking snow clad volcano right bang in the middle of the picture. The road here wasn't too bad, from the point of view of surface, but we took all this time because it was so steep. We crossed a range of very steep hills and most of it was awfully hair-raising. The views were exquisite although the country for the most part was very barren. The last thirty miles or more, though, were through the most beautiful, fat, pastoral country, just like England at its best; and it made me excited to think how near I was to seeing you all again.

This town is on the seashore and my room looks over the beach. I shall be rocked to sleep tonight by the breakers, although I am sleepy enough…

Midland Hotel,

Wellington

[Thursday] 15th July. By the bye, whilst I think of it, Henry is really seriously thinking of bringing me out here in the winter of 1927-8, as he was talking about it the other day. Why this pleases me is that it shows that he has not been so terribly disappointed with me this time,. Though I shall need a very great inducement to come away again –anyhow for a long time yet…

We were up at seven this morning and away in the train at eight. The train was slow but very comfortable…We arrived here at about five…This is a very pleasant hotel, but I wouldn't care if it was a pigsty, as we are only to be here one night. We embark tomorrow evening before eight, and sail at daybreak on the following morning, Saturday. I have a cabin to myself and so has Henry…

357

I like Wellington. So far it seems a nice clean town and, above all, its harbour contains the *Ruahine* which is to take me home. This evening the labels arrived; and when I saw 'Southampton' in real letters I nearly went mad with excitement.

Well, darling, be good till I come and give them all my love. I'm just longing to see you.

All my love,

Dorothy

And there the letter comes to an end and the correspondence stops. This is quite understandable: no later mail could possibly have got to her family before she did, even if Dorothy had tried to send a letter from Colon at the far end of the transit of the Panama Canal, their only stop in the entire five weeks. Understandable it might be, but it is also a great pity. Dorothy mentions having the idea of writing a daily record of their journey home. If she did so, it has not survived.

I suspect she did not. Her excitement is almost palpable at the prospect of her voyage home, mounting as it does when embarkation is imminent, so as to make her 'mad' on seeing the labels. She had learned to cope with her seasickness, and knew she would get over it after a few days at sea. Every sea journey so far she had been able to enjoy. Even the *Rawalpindi*, rather surprisingly deprecated in her letter from New Zealand, had given her a memorable time. The trip on the *Houtman* had been a real highlight of their travels since leaving Calcutta. She must have been dreaming of an idyllic five weeks of good food, good company, mild flirtations perhaps, certainly comfort and relaxation. All of which would be very rewarding to write up for future reference – if it had been like that.

But it was not like that. If she had ever started a diary of those five weeks, she may well have given up in despair. The voyage was not a success. There were several reasons for this. The ship herself was partly the cause of their disappointment. The *Ruahine* had been built in 1909. Although only a little over 10,000 tons she carried no fewer than 520 passengers, 56 of them in first class. After this voyage in 1926 she was refitted and the passenger accommodation reduced to 220 in one class. At the time with which we are concerned she was probably both cramped and somewhat worn out in appearance.

So it was that the first problem for their five weeks on board became apparent more or less at once. Their two single cabins were very small and dingy. Their hearts sank as soon as they saw them. Harry's protests were to no avail. The refit must already have been planned – the Company was probably well used to criticism of the accommodation – but nothing could be done about it then. Loud mouthed and ill-tempered complaining – which was something of a Hobbsian speciality – does not usually endear even an always-right-customer to the service provider. It was not a happy beginning.

The second great disappointment became evident very nearly as quickly. During her several journeys by sea in the previous eight months Dorothy had enjoyed cuisine which was always reasonable and seemed to get better and better, culminating in that on the *Houtman* and then, with her most enthusiastic endorsement, on the *Marama*. They were hoping for the best on the long voyage home.

But the food on the *Ruahine* was very bad. The Purser's department invoked the General Strike as an excuse. That may indeed have made for difficulties when they were victualling in England at the end of May or early June. Reasonable foresight could surely have coped with the problem, even in England, let alone in New Zealand before the return leg. But no. They had indifferent to downright bad fare all the time they were on board. By way of example, one evening for dinner the only hot dish available on the menu was tripe; on another the only hot dish was pigs' trotters. Harry was appalled. He was, in any event, fussy about what he ate, and the quality of it. More or less every meal presented him with the excuse (indeed, it must be acknowledged, the reason) for a loud and vociferous tirade directed to the steward and anyone else in authority who was nearby, and to the Line in general. It made for a wearisome as well as a distressing time for Dorothy, fearing some sort of rumpus on most occasions when they went down for a meal.

Adversity which is shared sometimes brings people closer to each other. Not so on this voyage. Harry would always maintain that no one was a greater snob than the returning colonial. As has been seen from her descriptions of earlier sea voyages Dorothy had enjoyed meeting fellow passengers, and had often attracted quite a lot of attention. It was not like that on the *Ruahine*.

I doubt if the phrase had been invented by then; today we would say that the first class passengers soon sussed Harry out. He may have been called 'Major' but he was not a professional soldier. He had never been one, not in the British nor in the Indian Army. Only an Officer in a Volunteer Corps. He no longer even thought of himself as a professional musician. He was something of a journalist, but that did not amount to much and really hardly counted. No: he ran a piano shop in Calcutta – he was 'in trade.' As such he had really no business to be in the first class at all, not being a professional man nor belonging to any gentlemen's club. And they were made to feel it.

The atmosphere was exemplified by the events following the concert given by the Don Cossack Choir. This fairly prestigious ensemble (which, coincidentally, Dorothy and Harry had heard in Sydney) was travelling in the second class. Whether the first class asked them to perform for the first class, or whether they offered and were accepted, is not clear. The concert took place in the first class, but the Choir insisted that the second class should be invited to attend as well, so as to make a worthwhile audience, and to include their own travelling companions. That was duly done and the second class did attend the concert in large numbers. It passed off without any problem, and was much enjoyed by all.

In order to show their appreciation and gratitude for having been asked to the concert, the second class passengers invited the first class passengers to a dance they were having fairly soon after the musical event. Both Harry and Dorothy went down to the second class accommodation for the evening's entertainment. They were the only people from the first class to do so. Many sad and disappointed passengers came to Dorothy and said, "Are no other first class passengers coming to join us, Miss Hobbs?" "Where are the rest of your fellow passengers from the first class, Miss Hobbs?" "Why are no more coming from the first class, Miss Hobbs?" All very pertinent enquiries, to which Dorothy had no answer except platitudes, proffered with the maximum of embarrassment on her part.

Some idea of the lifestyle on board may be gleaned from a short passage in a letter which Harry wrote to his old friend Colonel Wyness on 24th August, only two days after arriving at Chingri Khal:

New Zealand is wonderful so far as hotels and volcanoes go – they were splendid. But the *Ruahine*, a Tripe and Trotters Liner, was about the worst sample of travel I have experienced for a long time. My cabin, a single berth, less than half the size of an ordinary cabin and charged £10 extra for, was a tricky swindle. And for the first time in my life I created scenes at table and abused the Chief Steward like a pickpocket. I have also sent in a demand on T. Cook for £50 for putting me on such a packet. However I'm home again and feel pretty cheap today after living on bacon for breakfast, bread and cheese for tiffin, a piece of meat once in a way for dinner. The vegetables ('owing to the strike') were not fresh; I imagine it was the great strike of 1921. Pastry from last voyage; second-hand tea, apples cured of seasickness five voyages ago, rotten mangoes and resurrected breakfast rolls, tapioca pudding without sugar, eggs or milk – just tapioca neat - and I cursed the Chief Steward in my best manner. He never had anything like it. "Take this to the Chief Steward with my compliments and tell him, if he'll eat it, I'll never see the blighter again in this world and, with good fortune, not in the next either" generally attracted attention. "What's the scotch for rotten?" "This cutting from a draught buffalo must have been found a month after he died fifteen years ago" and so on – they began to look round and as the saloon was small and my remarks were fired just when there was quiet, sort of hit the bull's-eye every time.

There is no record as to whether there were any social occasions in which everyone joined with mutual enjoyment, evenings of bridge, tournaments of deck games, or congenial dancing partners. Scenes like those which Harry was so proudly setting out in his letter to his old friend could only help to sour the atmosphere still further. Poor food, general discomfort and the rather icy relationships with fellow passengers made Dorothy all the more impatient to be at the end of this long voyage.

So when, on 22nd August, a day later than scheduled, the *Ruahine* sailed into the Solent, with the Isle of Wight to port and the Hampshire coastline to starboard, she felt that only the reunion lay ahead. Packing was all done, the last meal had been eaten, only innocuous brief encounters with fellow travellers would occur in the last hour, all was at peace. Nothing could happen now to upset her father and the disappointments of the voyage could be put behind her. Alas for vain hopes.

On past Calshot Spit into Southampton Water. Any vessel of some size makes a splendid sight as she makes her slow and stately way along that historic entry to England, whether from ship or shore. The New Forest and Fawley to the west, the mouth of the Hamble, Netley Hospital, with its curious oriental appearance, and Netley Abbey all to the east, and, again to the west, the long thin line of Hythe Pier all came and went. Sights familiar to some, and surely making the 'delightful picture,' as Harry called it, for all the eager passengers on that bright Sunday morning.

The *Ruahine* had nearly seven thousand carcases of New Zealand lamb to discharge before leaving for London that afternoon so she kept in the western channel, the River Test. She made for berth 38/39, just short of the International Cold Storage Company's refrigerated building at berth 40 to which she would move once her passengers had been disembarked. On board the passengers all gathered, as passengers do, along the ship's rail to watch the docking and to see if they could spot friends and relations on the quayside. For there was a crowd there as well, and some hand waving and fluttering of handkerchiefs was starting on both sides of the narrowing watery divide. And then, entirely unexpectedly, began the final, for Dorothy devastating, dénouement of the voyage of the *Ruahine*.

The eyes of the Hobbs Reception Committee were as sharp as any on the quayside. They quickly spotted Harry and Dorothy standing side by side among the crowds of fellow passengers. Jennie, Phyllis and Jimmy were in a state of high excitement at the approaching reunion, and Jimmy, characteristically, couldn't wait to make the first contact. He was quite accustomed to making himself heard from one cruiser to another in mid-Atlantic in a gale, and, cupping his hands about his mouth, and giving Harry the uplift in rank which the family often did, he roared across to the *Ruahine*:

"WELOME HOME COLONEL –
HAVE A GOOD TRIP?"

Well! What an opportunity! Five weeks of pent up fury and frustration had only partly been relieved by the almost daily eruptions in the dining saloon. Here he had the perfect amphitheatre.

362

His tormentors were a captive audience, officers supervising the docking, at least some of the crew on deck carrying out their tasks, and unsuspecting passengers all around him. Never one to let a chance like this slip from his grasp, in a rasping bellow, audible all over the dock basin as the vessel came ever closer to land, and to Dorothy's mounting horror, with a ferocity worthy of Vesuvius at its least benign, Harry Hobbs blew his top:

"BLOODY AWFUL.
I CALL THIS THE TRIPE AND TROTTERS LINE.
OUR CABINS WERE A COUPLE OF PIGSTYS.

THE FOOD HAS BEEN DISGUSTING ALL THE TIME.
ROTTEN OR STALE. NO CHOICE. BADLY COOKED.
BADLY SERVED. A DISGRACE TO ANY OWNER.
A REAL STARVATION SHIP.

THE OFFICERS AND CREW ARE A HOPELESSLY
INCOMPETENT LOT. THEY DID NOTHING
WHATEVER TO HELP.

THE PASSENGERS HAVE BEEN A COLLECTION OF THE
MOST POISONOUS SNOBS I HAVE EVER HAD THE
MISFORTUNE TO SAIL WITH."

And so he went on until the tirade was silenced by a prolonged blast on the ship's whistle, and the general clatter of the gangways coming aboard. Harry, pleased as punch with himself at having put the record straight, as he would have regarded it, then turned on his heel and stalked off to disembark.

Dorothy, in a state akin to shellshock, just about managed to trail along in his wake, not knowing how to avoid the outraged stares of her former travelling companions. As he marched down the gangway she somehow stumbled after him, fell into the arms of her joyful mother, and wept.

Despite the final minutes of her travels being rather more fraught than she had bargained for, Dorothy had soon got over the experience and was revelling in life back in Chingri Khal. So much to see in the house and garden, so many people to visit, so much to tell them all, she had plenty to keep herself occupied. The routine of that life never seemed to tire her.

Harry duly returned to India in October on the passage he had booked when in Australia. Life would have been a good deal more peaceful after his departure. Letters from him to his family after the return have not survived. There are, however, those he wrote to Colonel Wyness, which give just a little idea of what went on.

Plainly he had come close to promising Dorothy, towards the end of their New Zealand tour, that he would bring her out to India again on his return to the East the following year. That never materialised for the very good reason that he did not come home at all in the summer of 1927. It is not clear why he stayed out there. In February he wrote 'Have not yet made up my mind where to go this summer – maybe China, Canada and Home!!' The next mention of his movements is in August: 'After all I changed my mind about going home and spent nine dull weeks in the Club in Darjeeling returning three weeks too soon as the weather was poisonous owing to a monsoon without rain.'

There is no hint as to what may have caused him to have that change of heart. I expect Miss Briscoe put her foot down. She had not had him to herself for nearly a full year from December of 1925, and had not seen him at all for about nine months of that time. Perhaps she said "stay here with me this year, and give me a holiday in the Hills or else." The 'else' might have been going her own way, telling Jennie, or any other of the steps open to a woman scorned. Who can tell?

At Chingri Khal the household was a little smaller than hitherto. Arthur was stationed in India. Phyllis and Jim with their two little girls had a house in Cosham and so were only intermittently in Bournemouth. Dorothy did not seem to be getting any closer to finding herself a husband. Despite passing her thirtieth birthday in November, 1927, she was neither showing nor feeling any concern at being still the maiden aunt to her much loved nieces. "I never had any doubt that I would marry at some time," she once told me. That may have had a degree of hindsight in it, if one remembers what she had written about becoming an old maid when discussing her cousin Queen in a letter from Australia, although I do not doubt her general confidence.

She had every reason to be confident. There was no shortage of admirers and she was content to bide her time. She thrived on the attention they gave her. She recalled a summer's day a year or so after her return when, because it was pleasantly warm and sunny, and she had plenty of time, she decided to walk home to Chingri Khal from the centre of Bournemouth instead of taking the tram. It was about two miles. Once you are at the top of Richmond Hill, leading North from The Square it is flat and fairly straight along Wimborne Road and Charminster Road until the final hill down towards Queen's Park Avenue. In those days the open top trams had quite a struggle to get up that first hill, but along Wimborne Road they soon got up to their top speed of about twenty miles an hour.

As she was walking alone along Wimborne Road she heard the clattering of a tram approaching her from behind and getting up to top speed. As it passed her she heard a shout "Dorothy! Dorothy!" She looked up and saw one of her young men leaping to his feet on the top deck. He ran to the back, tore down the spiral staircase, and leaped off the fast moving tram. He ran straight up to her, took her by the arm and said "let me walk you home." "Oh!" she said to me, "after that as we walked along I felt on top of the world!"

By the end of March, 1928, Harry was planning his route home for the summer. This time there was nothing to prevent him. If she had been his stumbling block the year before, Miss Briscoe probably resigned herself to the inevitable. The route he chose was via China, Japan and Canada, writing to Colonel Wyness en route from on board the Canadian Pacific Ship *Empress of Canada* 'on the edge of the North Pole steering for Vancouver.' He eventually got home to Chingri Khal on the 19th July, where Jennie, Dorothy, Phyllis and his two grand daughters were there to welcome him. Jimmy was still on the Royal Yacht – 'he is a good fellow and much thought of,' he wrote to Colonel Wyness. Arthur was on his way to Canada, having resigned his commission in the Loyal Regiment some six to nine months before.

Despite his homecoming Dorothy still had invitations to social gatherings that were for herself on her own. Hardly surprising in the case of a lively young woman in her thirties. Along with the rest of her family she was a keen and good bridge player and was much in demand to make up a four.

Leo and Kathleen Sharkey were not particularly close friends of hers. Dorothy had got to know them first as fellow Catholics, and had been to their house on a few occasions. Their invitation to a bridge party not very long after Harry's return was therefore no great surprise, and gave promise of a pleasant enough evening, if not a particularly exciting one. Neither Harry nor Jennie had any reason to want her at home on that occasion – so she accepted.

And thus it came about that one evening in the summer of 1928, she found herself, not for the first time, in the Sharkey's house, 'Asenby', West Overcliff Drive.

BOOK THREE

FROM ONE
CHINGRI KHAL
TO ANOTHER

Pat at the time he met Dorothy.

CHAPTER 23

WEST COUNTRY INTERLUDE:
FROM EXETER
TO BOURNEMOUTH

IF THE SET OF HIS JAW LINE, as seen in an early photograph, is anything to go by, Constable Samuel Tucker would have been a formidable match for any would-be crook or troublemaker on his beat. He was the elder of two brothers. There are probably more Tuckers in the County of Devon than in any other part of England. Their family had come from the Braunton area, between Barnstaple and Ilfracombe, where they were farmers. They were of tough, Devon yeoman stock; good, upright Bible reading Protestants, and intensely loyal to County, Country and Queen. Most Devonshire men will swear by their County: it is no accident that the motto of the City of Exeter, the County Town of which they are so proud, is 'Semper Fidelis.'

The younger brother, Ephraim, remained close to his roots. He founded a successful retail shoe shop in Barnstaple which, until well after the end of the Second World War, still carried on business under the rather resounding title, emblazoned in very large letters along its frontage, 'Tucker's Boot Emporium.'

Samuel, by contrast, became a career Policeman. He had the physique for the part; tall – well over six feet – big build in proportion, very straight and piercing blue eyes. He married Mary Parker, a very pretty woman with clear complexion, full figure, straight nose and a look of determination quite reminiscent of her husband's. The two of them certainly made a very handsome pair. She was rather well connected, being descended from Admiral Sir Hyde Parker, he to whose signal to 'disengage the enemy' Lord Nelson chose to turn his blind eye during the Battle of Copenhagen. Sir Hyde was himself a great–great-grandson of a seventeenth century Bishop of Salisbury, so

369

one might assert that Mary Parker had in her blood something of a tradition of service to both Crown and Church. They had just one child, a son, who was born on 16th April, 1866. They called him Albert John, no doubt, in part at least, in memory of the late Prince Consort, so recently lost to the Country.

By the time of which I have records Samuel was an Inspector in the Devon Constabulary and was stationed at Kingsbridge in South Devon. Both he and his son, in their respective spheres, were winning golden opinions from others. Bert – for that is the name by which the son was known – was a pupil at Kingsbridge Grammar School. Most of his school reports survive. The earliest, for Michaelmas Term, 1878, shows him coming fourth in a class of eleven, aged under thirteen and more than eighteen months younger than the average. He was first in Scripture and Religious Knowledge, having studied 'Chronicles II, Daniel, Ezra, Nehemiah, St. Matthew's Gospel Chapters 1-20, Maclean's O. T. History pp 92-124.' Quite a tall order to go alongside much English (language and literature), History, Geography, Mathematics, French, Latin, Drawing and Writing.

In 1881 Bert was awarded an Exhibition, worth £20 a year, to go to Devon County School – West Buckland School – to start there from January 1883 when he was four months short of his seventeenth birthday, and where he would be a boarder. The award was timely for the family was soon to move from Kingsbridge upon Samuel being promoted and transferred to Exeter. His imminent move brought forth a letter from the Head Master of the Grammar School on behalf of himself and his wife:

Nov. 7. 1882

…We wish to express the regret we feel at hearing you are leaving the Town. During the three years we have been here we have had many opportunities of observing your uniform courtesy and anxiety to give all assistance in your power to the residents in the Town and we have conceived very high esteem for yourself personally.

If at any time I can do anything to further your views, or those of you son, will you kindly let me know, and I shall be only too pleased to use any influence I may possess.

Believe me,

Yours very sincerely,

D. F. Ranking M.A. S.C.L. F.R.A.A.T.

Although reports from West Buckland have not survived, three letters over the years from the Head Master show Bert was regarded as highly there as he had been at Kingsbridge. Consideration was being given to his taking the Civil Service Examination as early as September, 1883. In a letter of 20th January, 1885, the Head Master wrote offering to keep Bert on for another term and to extend his exhibition for that purpose as

> It would give him a little more time to arrange as to his future and he would be very welcome here.
>
> I should be glad if he were to be successful in the forthcoming Civil Service Examination. I need hardly say that it will afford me great pleasure at any time to bear testimony to his excellent conduct.

It is not clear what was the outcome of his sitting of that examination, nor what, if any, post he took up in consequence of that outcome. What is certain is that in 1887, the year he attained the age of twenty-one years, he entered the employment as a clerk to Mr H. W. Michelmore, a well known and highly respected Solicitor in Exeter.

He speedily made his mark in his new career, for at the relatively early age of twenty-four he felt sufficiently secure and prosperous to get married. His bride was Blanche Martin, the older of two sisters, with a solid Devonshire background. Bert had inherited much in the way of good looks from both his parents, although to my eyes those heavy Victorian walrus moustaches, which Samuel grew in later life and Bert when in his twenties, add nothing to a man's appearance. Blanche, by contrast, and inevitably only judging from photographs, appears to have been somewhat plain. Perfectly pleasant, no doubt, efficient, and quite capable of running a home, but not a woman to cause heads to turn as she passed by.

They were married on 7th August, 1890, and made their home at 50, Culverland Road, Exeter, very close to Samuel and Mary who lived at number 12. A daughter soon followed, Winifred Blanche, ('Winnie') born on 28th April, 1891. Their second child was not born until 3rd May, 1895. This time it was a son. They named him partly after his father and partly after goodness knows whom, giving him the names Percival Albert, names he always detested, and which,

*Samuel Tucker
(G-pa) –
a determined-looking
policeman.*

*Mary Tucker
(G-ma).*

*Albert Tucker
and
Blanche Tucker
at about
the time
of their
marriage.*

inevitably perhaps, were shortened to Percy. Their family was thereby completed.

Percy's schooling followed along predictable lines. For a little while he was in what was then called a 'Dame's School', which we would now call 'Nursery School.' The two ladies who ran it, Miss Gitsham and Miss Ada remembered him well enough to send a card when, nearly thirty years later, he was married "Wishing you long life, every happiness and prosperity. May you always keep a smiling face as you did when you were <u>little Percy.</u>" Which may give as good an indication as one could hope for of what he was like as a very small boy.

He next attended Mount Radford School in St. Leonard's Road, Exeter, a highly regarded day school, run by Mr Theodore Vine and his wife. No reports or other documents survive to tell us about his time there. The only exception is a rather splendid photograph of what is evidently the start of a school outing, soon after the turn of the century. The large four wheeled vehicle is drawn by four horses. The coachman wears a white top coat with buttonhole and a white top hat. Mr and Mrs Vine ride at the rear. Young Percy – probably about six or seven – is one of those turning round to look at the camera. If the entire school is on board – and there is a considerable age range – it cannot then have been a very large establishment.

It was at about this time that Percy witnessed – or, perhaps more accurately, almost witnessed, for he was hustled away as the incident developed – a dramatic rescue by his father from the beach at Woolacombe. This small town on the north Devon coast was a favourite holiday place for the Tucker family. A day's outing from Exeter might be no further than, say, Exmouth or Ladram Bay. They went further afield if spending a few days away, and Woolacombe was their usual haunt.

Bert had been a good athlete at school, but it was as a swimmer that he excelled and he was a leading light in swimming circles in Exeter, coaching and encouraging young swimmers. Woolacombe has a fine sandy beach, but is known to be a place where particular care at times has to be taken owing to a strong undertow at certain states of the tide. On Thursday, 23rd July, 1901, the family were on the beach. Bert was changing in a bathing machine preparatory to going in for a swim. Two men were bathing together and got into difficulties, another man went to their help and himself got into the same current. One of the original two, a Mr Howell, managed to get to the shore, but the other, a Mr Wood, and his would-be rescuer, a Mr Spiers, were being drawn out to sea. The bathing machine proprietor, knowing Bert and his skill, called him from the machine. The North Devon Journal for 25th July takes up the story:

> ...Mr. Tucker (who is a well-known swimmer...) performed a very gallant act. He waded to and swam through the breakers, and managed to reach the two men who were struggling in the water. Tucker grasped Spiers as he was sinking, and swam with him towards the shore, from whence Mr. Hadingham (a medical man) a visitor, Tom Price [bathing machine owner] and his wife (who worked bravely and indefatigably) were pushing out a long pole attached to which was a rope. After Tucker had placed Spiers on the pole, the latter was washed away by a breaker, the brave Exonian again going to his aid, and eventually succeeding in getting him into shallow water. There was not sufficient time to render aid to Mr. Wood, as he had meanwhile sunk and was drowned. The wife and child of the deceased were upon the sands, but were unaware of what was transpiring, the sad news being broken to them by Mr. Howell and his wife. When brought to the shore, Spiers was in a most exhausted condition, and a considerable time elapsed before the efforts at artificial respiration were attended with success. Mr. Tucker was warmly complimented on the great gallantry which he displayed in saving the life of Mr. Spiers. The affair caused a profound sensation at Woolacombe. Under all the circumstances is seems marvellous that not more lives were lost...

Once his father was back safe and sound, Percy was told the whole story and was able to see the aftermath. He was only a little over six years of age and the whole incident made him immensely proud of his father, and increased the influence, already considerable, which his father had over him. And all the more so when, in November, Bert was awarded the Royal Humane Society's Bronze Medal for saving life.

In due course, not surprisingly, Percy followed in his father's footsteps to Devon County School. All his school reports are available and show he began there in the Summer Term of 1909. He would have been fourteen at the start of that term, a little older than one might have expected. The reports show good and steady progress, without outstanding brilliance academically, and considerable satisfaction with his general conduct. In addition he was, rather like his father, a very good all-round athlete. In his case he was particularly good at football, running, hurdling and the high jump.

The Head Master's comments tell us quite a lot. In April, 1911, 'a good, quiet influence in the school which is very valuable;' in July 'will make an excellent prefect and football captain;' and in December 'a good prefect and Captain. I am sorry he must go – he has the good wishes of us all.' He was, by then, just sixteen and a half years old.

Why did he have to go? The answer lies in the family tragedy of that year. Bert's mother, Mary Tucker, had died after a long illness in April 1910. She was sixty-seven, not a great age, but a fairly respectable one for those days. Samuel continued to live at 12 Culverland Road, with a housekeeper to help look after him.

In the summer of 1911 Blanche was taken ill. Cancer of the uterus was diagnosed – incurable, inoperable and fatal. She died on 4th September when she was only forty-seven years old. Bert was completely devastated by her death. So overcome with grief was he that at her funeral he could not walk unaided up the aisle of the church. He had to lean heavily on the arm of his daughter, Winnie. She was twenty by then, and able to be something of a tower of strength for her father – and she was to need a lot of patience and understanding in a very short time as well.

Percy, as the son only a little over the age of sixteen, must have felt the loss of his mother deeply. But in later years he spoke very little about her, and she is, therefore, something of a shadowy figure in the past. School term began on 26th September and there is nothing to show in his report that he was late in getting back to School after the summer holidays.

Bert, however, was inconsolable. So distraught was he that it was considered wise for him to take a short holiday with Winnie to try to start the healing process and to come to terms with his loss. So the two of them went for a week or so to the Runnacleave Hotel at Ilfracombe, probably after getting young Percy off to West Buckland.

They were far more successful than Winnie had ever bargained for. Staying at the same Hotel was a Mr Hooper with his three daughters. They had not been there more than a few days when Winnie was horrified to realise that Bert, with Blanche barely yet cold in her grave, was starting to make eyes at the oldest of the three, Edith.

If she protested at all it was to no avail. She may not have felt able to protest. For all his sterling qualities, both public and professional, Bert was not an easy man in the domestic field. He knew what he wanted and he expected to get his own way. And he wanted a wife to run his home and to be his mate. He returned from the recuperative holiday in Ilfracombe with his grief assuaged and a new wife at least something of a distinct possibility in the not too distant future.

Meanwhile Percy, distressed though he no doubt was, had returned to West Buckland where he had a successful term. It is not easy to understand the connection between his – or, for that matter, Bert's – personal bereavement and the inability to continue his education. He was doing very well at school and would be expected in the ordinary course of events at least to have finished that academic year, and possibly stay on for one more year until he was over eighteen. The family's finances could hardly have been affected much, if at all, by the death of Blanche. Bert was coming up towards completing twenty-five years with Mr Michelmore, having been his Managing Clerk, a highly responsible and important position in the firm, for some time. His future would have appeared – and, indeed, it was – completely secure. He could hardly have needed Percy at home to give him comfort and solace in his loss: that was being provided elsewhere. So it remains something of a mystery. Perhaps it was simply a spur of the moment idea coming into Bert's head which, once there, was not to be dislodged. That would be very characteristic of Bert.

His last term at West Buckland ended on 19th December, 1911. By January, 1912, Percy was registered with Guy's Hospital as a future Dental Student. Why dentistry? Because Bert had so decided. His only explanation to the young Percy was "It's a fine Profession, my boy." Well, no doubt at all it is indeed a fine profession, just as any career involving the relief of pain and personal care for the human individual would be regarded as a fine profession. But it was a strange thing to make that decision for his son without any consultation or discussion.

The choice was all the more curious in the light of a most generous offer made by Mr Michelmore. He obviously knew Bert, his Managing Clerk, very well indeed, and knew his family. Doubtless he was much affected by Bert's sad bereavement and did what he could to help. He also knew Percy, and had formed a very favourable view of him. It probably came to his attention that Percy was to leave school rather earlier than might have been expected. He reckoned that this quiet, rather shy young man, who nevertheless was personable and got on well with those he knew, had the makings of a good solicitor. So he offered to take him as an Articled Clerk without fee.

Articles, which would have set Percy firmly on the way to becoming a Solicitor, could be an expensive item in a parent's outlay for a son. To have them free was, in effect, a considerable gift, as well as an informed expression of confidence in Percy's future abilities. Percy himself had, as yet, no very fixed ambition for his future career, but he was glad of the offer and would have been very happy to have taken it up.

Furthermore, even as early as 1912, Bert might already have had at the back of his mind the possibility of his taking Articles himself with a view to qualification. 'What a firm Tucker & Son could be' – one might have expected some such thought to have crossed his mind. The obvious good sense of encouraging Percy to take up a legal career is such that it is hard to understand why Bert did not accept his employer's offer with enthusiasm. But no: dentistry was the career for Percy. Bert had so decided and that was that. Whatever may have been the feelings of Percy, whether or not he was heavy of heart at a missed opportunity, Mr Michelmore's offer was declined. Percy had no option but to go along with what father had laid down.

Percy was too young to embark upon his dental studies. It was not until April, 1914, when he was close to nineteen years old, that he entered Guy's Dental School. I do not know how he spent the intervening two years. Neither he nor his father would have tolerated simply idling around. He certainly passed some examinations in scientific subjects early the following year, 1913. So perhaps he was

378

in some local college. He may have worked for some of the time on a farm. The family had been farmers two generations before, and maybe cousins and others were known to them with whom Percy could do a useful job of work. It was long before the days of a 'gap year' being commonplace, let alone a gap two years. I am sure his time was well filled.

Meanwhile Bert's courtship of Edith Hooper, who was ten years younger than he, proceeded satisfactorily for both of them. Her home was in Purley, in Surrey, now part of the Borough of Croydon, which even today is something of a long hike from Exeter. At that time the opportunities for them to meet must have been very limited indeed. Perhaps their relationship developed as much by correspondence as through personal contact. There is nothing in any remaining document to indicate when they came to regard themselves as engaged.

On the 14th September, 1912, they were married in St. Mark's Parish Church, Woodcote, Purley. That was the second Saturday after the first anniversary of the death of Blanche. Not even Bert, one likes to think, would have thought it right to remarry before that day had passed, and perhaps the first Saturday (which would have been the 7th September) was thought just a little too obviously the end of a 'can't wait' period. Again I have nothing to indicate the extent to which Bert's family came to Purley to support him, save that Percy was certainly one of the two witnesses signing the Register. And if he was there, at only a little over seventeen, Winnie would surely have been there as well, whatever inner feelings she may have had over the whole affair.

To assume the role of Stepmother is no easy task, and the prevailing circumstances could have made Edith's position a very uncomfortable one. Fortunately her personality was such that she succeeded in making a success of that delicate relationship, where many others might have failed. She was no great beauty, but she was tall, straight, with an excellent dress sense, nice looking in a motherly sort of way – although she never had any children of her own. Without in any way being an intellectual, she was an instinctive good manager and housewife, and she knew how to play the part of supporting spouse to a prominent local professional man.

She loved all her new stepfamily. It has to be said that Winnie never became entirely reconciled to the principle of widowed men marrying a second time. She often said she did not think it ought to be allowed. This feeling undoubtedly stemmed from those experiences in Ilfracombe, which resulted in her having few good words to say about her father thereafter. But Edith, obviously, could not be blamed for Bert's sudden recovery from overwhelming grief, and she and Winnie had as good a personal relationship as one could wish.

As far as Percy was concerned there were no reservations at all. She was a very loveable person, who loved and was loved by all those who knew her. From his point of view his father could not have made a better move or a better choice.

Bert's difficult nature was made evident to Edith all too soon after his marriage to her. It was while they were on their honeymoon in Devon that he had a letter from his father. Samuel had written to tell Bert that he had married his housekeeper, Bessie Conibear. There had been no prior indication to any of his family that this was on the cards, Samuel was seventy-two, Bessie was thirty-eight. And what is more they had married on the very next 'working day' after Bert's wedding, that is Monday, 16th September.

One might think there was a lot of good sense in such a union, provided the two of them were genuinely fond of each other. But Bert was furious. Was it the thought of having a stepmother eight years younger than himself, and only two years older than her 'daughter-in-law'? Whatever the reason, so angry was he that for the rest of that day he refused to speak to Edith at all. As if it were her fault. Of all men, one would have thought he was the least well placed to complain. But there it was, Edith had to cope with his mood: she often had to, and she coped extremely well.

Whether real significance is to be attached to it or not, there are subtle differences in the information supplied to the two Registrars by – it must be – the respective bridegrooms. Bert describes himself as 'Accountant', as, indeed, he had on Blanche's death certificate, rather than 'Solicitor's Clerk' or 'Managing Clerk.' He describes his father's 'Rank or Profession' as 'Gentleman.' Samuel has no compunction in calling himself 'Police Pensioner,' nor his father as

'Farmer.' His witnesses included 'W. C. Tucker' whose identity is a mystery. Obviously not his brother – 'Ephraim' – nor his brother's son – 'Lionel' – nor his grandaughter (unlikely in any event) who was Winifred Blanche – perhaps a more distant relation, male or female. Had Samuel been at St. Mark's, Purley, two days before? His plans to marry must have all be laid by then, and yet not a word to anyone of those who would at least be interested, some even delighted for him. Perhaps he was a little afraid of the reaction of those for whom delight would be far from their response.

In addition to all these matrimonial excitements, that year, 1912, also saw Bert complete twenty-five years in the employment of Mr Michelmore. He was presented with a handsome and inscribed silver salver 'as a token of esteem and regard for his services.' But his time with Mr Michelmore was coming to an end. Whether his employer knew of his intentions at the time of the presentation is not known. What is known is that on 10th January, 1913, Bert became articled to Mr R. W. Cocks of Exeter, for a period of three years. Mr Cocks had only been admitted as a solicitor himself ten years before. With a family still to support, Bert must have had some special financial arrangements securely in place. There were no economic problems arising from this move.

In April 1914, Percy set off for London and began his studies at the Guy's Hospital Dental School. That would have cost Bert a great deal more than if his son had been articled to Mr Michelmore, although he did not provide Percy with an over-generous allowance. "I used to have to decide if I would buy an evening paper for a halfpenny and walk half the way home to my digs, or get a bus all the way," perhaps paints as clear a picture as one can get of life for the young student. He made a good start, finishing his probationary work by July, 1914. A spirit of competition arose between him and his father: which of them would be qualified first?

Meanwhile two events were brewing. For quite some time Winnie had been courted by Charles Hibbs, a young teacher of almost her own age and who had been a close family friend for many years. He was a particularly good friend of Percy as well, although there was a four year age difference. The two young men had often had outings together, camping on Dartmoor, rowing or sailing in the estuary of the River Exe, and similar adventures. It came, therefore, as no surprise and a source of all round delight when Winnie and Charles announced their engagement. They were duly married in Exeter in fine style on 1st August, 1914.

It was an anxious time to be taking such a step. Only three more days and the World was at War. Charles had very soon departed on military service. It is not clear precisely when it was that Percy likewise joined the Army. He was still very much a student at Guy's, passing the two parts of his first Professional Examination in September, 1914, and January, 1915. That more or less marked the half way stage towards qualification, and he decided that was the time to give his service to his Country. Perhaps a little surprisingly Percy did not return to Devon to join a Devonshire regiment. In February he volunteered in London and joined the 2nd City of London Regiment (Royal Fusiliers.) He was commissioned a Second Lieutenant on 6th May, 1915.

He had made three decisions at about the time of his going into the army. The first was almost trivial: he grew a moustache. In that he was following family tradition, albeit to a less luxuriant extent than his father and grandfather. Once grown, he retained it for the rest of his life.

The second decision was to do something about his name. The passage of time had done nothing to reconcile him to 'Percival Albert' nor to 'Percy.' The problem of what to do about it was readily solved by the happy accident of a short, presentable acronym from his initials: P.A.T. He decided to call himself Pat, and asked all who knew him to call him Pat. The family found it difficult, not surprisingly, and he continued for some time to sign himself 'Percy' to them. But in time most of them co-operated, including Edith, and made the change, although Winnie and Charles tended to revert to, for them, the old and familiar 'Percy.' But Pat he became, for all except the most formal of purposes, and we shall refer to him as Pat from now on.

More fundamental was his abandonment of all forms of religious belief. He had been brought up in the Church of England, and educated at a Church of England School where he seems to have done as well in 'Divinity' – as religious instruction is referred to in his reports – as in any other subject. He remembered, and could quote, extensive passages from the Old Testament. He always retained a huge admiration, even love, for Exeter Cathedral as a building; a fascination which in later life was to lead to an enthusiasm for visiting the old churches of English towns and villages. But from about the time of attaining his majority he had no belief in any Deity, after life, or any other Christian doctrine. He became, and remained, unconvinced, uncommitted and unconcerned.

Such a conversion is rarely a matter of a moment: it occurs gradually over a period of time. There is no knowing when it began in Pat's case. It would seem to have been complete by the time he joined one unit in the army and realised, on studying whatever records were available, that there were not enough Baptists to make up an Officer's Party for Church Parade on Sunday. So he put himself down as a Baptist. And thus could enjoy Sunday in a manner more congenial to himself.

Pat was assigned to the 3rd battalion of the 2nd Londons which began to form at Tattenham Corner, Epsom, moving in May, 1915, to Tadworth under canvas, then at the end of that month to Bury St. Edmunds and finally at the end of June to billets in Ipswich, where they remained for close on a year. As *The 2nd City of London Regiment (Royal Fusiliers) in the Great War (1914-19)* puts it 'the life was very pleasant and the residents very kind.' But after so many moves it 'had an adverse effect on the efficiency of the troops.' [1]

It was while he was living in Ipswich that he found himself billeted in the home of a family named Prentice. They had a daughter called Olive, about the same age as Pat. It so happened that his twenty-first birthday came while he was living with them. How long in all he enjoyed their hospitality is not clear, but long enough for him to retain nostalgic memories of that period and of the family who were kind to him at a time when most young men would have preferred to have been able to celebrate at their own home. For Olive he may well have had some romantic attachment. There is no indication of any other young woman being the subject of attention from Pat, either in Exeter, in London or during military service. That is not to say there were none: but I doubt if there were many for whom he had had any very strong feelings. Despite his ability to get on with others, and the friendships he made among his fellow officers, he was a bit of a loner.

Bert in the meantime had successfully taken his final examinations in November and was duly admitted a Solicitor, obtaining his first Practising Certificate in February, 1916. He went into partnership with Mr Cocks to whom he had been articled and they practised together in Exeter as Cocks & Tucker. Bert and Edith moved from Culverland Road, where the family had lived since Bert's first marriage, to 24, St. Leonard's Road, a larger house on the opposite side of Exeter City Centre, by coincidence not far from Mount Radford School. Also in 1916 came the arrival of the first grandchild. (Blanche) Mary Hibbs was born on 29th June, much to everyone's delight. Winnie and her new baby continued to live in their family home in Paignton while Charles was still away on war service.

The period of waiting for the 3/2nd Londons started to draw to a close in the summer of 1916. They had adopted the title of 2/2nd Londons on the disbanding of the earlier 2/2nd Londons after their service in France and Gallipoli. As 2/2nd Londons they were part of the newly formed 58th (London) Division. They moved first to a camp outside Ipswich, then to a hutted camp at Sutton Veny, near Warminster, where serious training for action began in earnest. On 21st January, 1917, the new-style 2/2nd Londons, Pat – by this time a full Lieutenant – being among them, embarked at Southampton for France. The History of the Regiment makes a rare reference to the daily life in its account:

> The Battalion was doomed to a rough passage; and everyone was glad when the ship finally reached the shelter of Havre at the chill hour of 1.30 in the morning. After spending the best part of a day and a night in this port the Battalion took train to Frévent, the concentration area of the Division, arriving there after fifty bitterly cold hours in the usual French troop train. Thence a tired unit tramped to billets at Bonnières, which Lt Col Richardson described as 'poor.'
>
> It was at Bonnières, and before its departure to fresh billets at Ivergny on 29th January, that the Battalion taught itself the art of what the men called 'winning' or 'knocking off.' The Padre, quite unashamed, admitted the attempted annexation of firewood from the orchard of the good lady who found herself his temporary hostess. The attempt, however, was a failure; the lady was suspicious,

and the Doctor, conspirator with the Padre, was caught in the act. As the Padre tersely sums up, all they could say at the time was 'No compris,' to which the good lady replied, in effect, with 'No fire.' [2]

For, in truth, the Battalion had marched into the one of the worst winters in living memory. The cold was more intense than had ever been experienced by most, if not all of them, and would have made it a miserably uncomfortable, even unbearable, experience even in the relatively benign conditions of peacetime. But in the context of war, particularly in the trenches of war, it defied description. Almost Pat's sole comment was "even the whisky froze solid in the bottle." The imagination can readily picture the sheer misery of the life.

There were a few weeks mainly devoted to training, although for a short period they were at the front and came under fire, before their first real experience of the front line. A little south of Arras the Germans were believed, correctly, to be planning a strategic withdrawal to a strengthened Hindenberg Line to the east.

Information as to [the enemy's] actions and, if possible, his intentions was eagerly desired; and the five days, or rather nights, from 2nd March that the 2/2nd Londons spent on this sector were busily occupied in active patrolling. The German defensive position hereabouts hinged on two very important points, the Blockhouse, a strongly defended salient in his line, and the Talus, a machine-gun post established in an embankment some 200 yards in front of his line; and although this system was carefully probed, no sign of weakness could be discovered.

The 2/2nd Londons held their trenches with three companies in the front line and one in support, and, during the period, were subjected to heavy shelling by high explosive and shrapnel. They were relieved on the night of the 7th March by the 2/11th Londons, and move back to billets in Bailleulval. In this village they stayed, amid intermittent high explosive and gas shelling by the enemy, until 16th March, when they moved into fresh quarters at Bienvillers. The object of the move was to enable them to be in a position to take over next day part of the front line north-east of Monchy. [3]

But the German withdrawal had begun and the men of the 2/2nd Londons were among those advancing over the former German lines, not under fire, but in conditions far from easy or pleasant. The Colonel reported:

> The difficulty of moving in the dark and rain across a maze of heavily wired trenches, carrying everything on the person, had exhausted everyone, and it speaks for the keenness of the men that we were able to repair the roads sufficiently to enable the cookers and ammunition carts to be brought up by 6.00 a.m. [4]

The 2/2nd Londons took up their position in the line in the early hours of 21st March.

> The night was foul, the darkness pitch, the rain pitiless and hard, the ground strange to everyone, pitted with shell-holes and mine-craters, and liberally bespattered with mud. It is small wonder that finding one's position became a matter of real difficulty. [5]

The first actual contact with the Germans took place on 23rd March when they captured an advanced post resulting in casualties to the 2/2nd Londons before the rest of the garrison was withdrawn.

> The Battalion remained in the line for three days in most uncomfortable circumstances. Snow had fallen, and was followed by a biting wind. Little cover was available for the troops; and as a result of the severe weather the men suffered from the exposure. On the 24th the Battalion was relieved...and returned to Boisleux au Mont, but not before it had suffered five casualties (two dead and three wounded) by shellfire while the relief was being carried out. [6]

The Battalion had a month at Achet le Grand refitting and retraining during which the Brigade of which it was a part it came under the command of Brigadier General B. C. Freyburg, VC, DSO (later Lieutenant General Lord Freyburg) until the late autumn of that year. Pat was always intensely proud to have served under such a distinguished Officer.

The 2/2nd Londons next saw action at the first Battle of Bullecourt. This small village was within a small salient in the Hindenberg Line and its capture was regarded as an important objective. It was very highly fortified and its capture was a prolonged and costly process. British and Australian infantry were involved for the first half of May, the 2/2nd Londons being part of the relieving force in mid May. Communications were difficult and they were ordered to dig a second trench, two companies undertaking that task.

> The enemy's shellfire which had been heavy all day, now increased to an intense bombardment and caused the 2/2nd Londons many casualties…Despite the heavy shelling and the extreme difficulties of communication with the battalions in front, the 2/2nd Londons succeeded in supplying them with water and in evacuating many of their casualties during the night.
>
> The morning of the 14th May passed uneventfully; but at 2 p.m. the enemy subjected the British position to another intense bombardment. This lasted, in all, for close upon fourteen hours, and culminated at 3.30 a.m. on the 15th in the delivery of a fierce attack. At the junction of the 2/3rd Londons with the 14th Australian Infantry Brigade on the right the enemy forced an entry into the trench; but the 2/3rd Londons, to whose support 'A' Company of the 2/2nd was hurriedly sent forward, quickly drove him out and restored the situation. The fact that this was the thirteenth attack in ten days and that the troops employed were of the 3rd Prussian Guard is proof that the enemy was in deadly earnest in his attempts to regain this part of the line…
>
> On the night of the 16th/17th May, the 2/2nd Londons relieved the 2/3rd Londons in the right sector of the Brigade front… signs of still further attacks by the enemy were not wanting, and great vigilance was required on the part of our men. Vigorous patrolling, night work to clear the dead, continued strengthening of positions, and improvements in communications, were necessary and made so many demands on the men that fresh labour had to be sought from the transport personnel of the Battalion. Of these days in the line, 2nd Lieut. Harper's diary records the gruesome fact that 'the sun on the dead lying about made the line almost untenable.'[7]

At last, after further heavy shelling on 18th and 19th May during which one officer was killed and another injured, the 2/2nd Londons were relieved by the 2/11th Londons on 21st May and marched to camp on the outskirts of Bihucourt.

It must have been at about this time that the earliest surviving letter home from Pat was written. Written simply from 'France' on 23rd May, 1917, it is a strange mixture of the tragic and the banal.

Dear Dad & Edith,

At last another opportunity occurs for letter writing, I hope you received the post card I sent a few days ago.

In my last letter I told you that we would shortly be going into the line, well, we did with a vengeance. They pushed us straight into "the fiercest fighting on the Western Front" and for about a week had about the hottest time in the way of artillery bombardment that any troops have experienced in this war. Men who went through Gallipoli & the Somme say that they never struck anything like it. Of course I cannot give any details as regards casualties but in the rest camp where we are now, many less bivouacs are required than were before we went up. Am thankful to say that I am here without damage.

Your letter dated the 5th was sent up whilst we were in the line & seeing that you had been to Woolacombe made me think about the lighthouse near there where we used to picnic.

Have you sent any letters since then, as I believe some were lost on the way up to the line through the carrying parties being knocked out?

By he way I saw Major Michelmore whilst up there & spoke to him for a while, he seemed quite fit & is on the Divisional Staff.

Did you get the British warm I sent back in a sandbag?

Leave started last week & 2 officers are going per week, don't know when my turn will come. Capt. Ellis went from the line & he promised to write to you when in Blighty, He left me in charge of the Coy. which was then in the front line. The responsibility was a bit of a strain but things went all right & it was a relief to get out of that inferno back to the country which is now at perfection. Since then I have had the rotten job of writing to the people of some of my boys who were killed. The men were splendid & the Brigade has gained the thanks of the C in C & quite a name. I believe my name was sent forward but don't know if anything will come of it.

Yes, I should be glad of some thin underclothes, I believe I mentioned it before. These Aertex short drawers are the best; also will you send a pair of puttees.

Well, there isn't much more, please let people know that I am still going strong as am still in charge of the Company & there is a lot to

do in the way of reorganisation & refitting. Will write again soon.
With love,   Percy

On 28th May it was back to the front line for the 2/2nd Londons,
Captain Ellis evidently having returned from leave to take over
command of 'C' company from Pat. Some success had been achieved
in capturing part of the Hindenberg Line to the east and south of the
village of Bullecourt, but that to the west and north was still in
German hands. Plans were laid for the capture of this section the
2/2nd being positioned some half a mile or more north-west of
Bullecourt. 'Most careful' preparations were made, with detailed
training and practising of the particular tasks each unit was to
undertake. 'The actual attack [was] rehearsed three or four times
each night until every man knew exactly what he had to do.'[8]

Even with such careful practice the party detailed to put down
forward tapes and ducking board bridges over communication
trenches lost its way – and all but two of its personnel. The
Hindenberg Line had two lines, in fact, the front line and the support
line. It was intended that the front line should be taken on the first day
of the attack, the support line on the second. Meanwhile, during the
attack on the front line the artillery was to keep up a heavy
bombardment of the support line to prevent reinforcements being
brought up.

After three postponements the attack went ahead on 15th June.
The History of the Regiment takes up the story:

> All was now ready. At 2.50 a.m. the British barrage opened; and 'C'
> Company (Capt. Ellis) on the left and the two platoons of 'A'
> Company (Lieut. Roberts) on the right advanced to the attack, in
> company with 'A' Company of the 2/4th Londons. As the ground on
> the left was much broken by trenches and sunken roads, 'C'
> Company, with the more difficult task before it, was allotted a
> frontage of about 180 yards and was disposed in four lines...
> ... [Later] 'C' Company, on the left had reached the Hindenberg
> Line front line, and its two leading platoons (Lieut. Tucker and 2nd
> Lieut. Heading,) in company with personnel of the 2/4th Londons
> on their left, failing to recognise their objective, went far beyond it.
> Eventually they reached the enemy's support line, where they

captured 17 prisoners, but suffered heavy casualties themselves from the British standing barrage, now concentrated on this spot to prevent the reinforcement of the German front line. Among the casualties were the two platoon commanders, both Lieut. Tucker and 2nd Lieut. Heading being wounded. Ultimately the remnant of this party managed to extricate itself and, with its prisoners, rejoin the remainder of its company. With regard to this incident, Lieut.-Col Richardson's personal diary records the fact that 'the men were keen and went too far.' [9]

Pat's own account does not give a great deal more detail, understandably, perhaps. It comes in his next letter after the one already set out, but written in pencil in a very shaky hand, in places almost illegible. He writes from 102 Red Cross Hospital, A.P.O.2, BEF on 'Wed 20th' – that is of June, 1917:

Dear Dad,

Just a line to let you know that things are going quite well. This is an effort by the left hand, hope you can read it.

Did you get the letter the padre wrote for me?

Expect you read that we captured a bit more of the Hindenberg Line last Friday. Well, the 2/2 were in it & I was hit whilst going over the top. The first bit went through my right foot & has probably broken one of the small bones. I managed to get along for some way till a shrapnel bullet hit my right arm close up to the shoulder & broke the bone. After that I had to go back & it took some time. Still I eventually reached our line with about 6 Bosche I picked up on the way – the usual Kamarad type.

They took the bullet out of my arm at the C.C.S. & next day came down here at Rouen by train, an awful journey, about 10 hours. Ellis & 2 other officers of our Coy came by the same train. C Coy went in with 5 officers, 1 was killed and 4 wounded. The Battn [?] did very well but were let down by people on flanks & mauled.

They are awfully good to us here and the grub is A 1, chicken every day, glad to say I eat well but it is rather trying being in one position always.

Well, there isn't much more & it has taken an awful time to write this bit.

Don't worry about me for I'm getting on quite well, please let everybody know the address for I cannot write to all.

Hope things are all well at home.
With love   Percy

There is a lot of understatement in that letter. In fact all Pat's injuries were caused by what we would nowadays call 'friendly fire.' They did indeed overrun their objective, whether due to their own fault or inadequate prior instruction is now a useless speculation, and at the support line were victims of our own all-too-accurate artillery bombardment. At least two bursts of shrapnel hit Pat. The first hit his feet. Both feet. He may at first have thought just a broken bone. He carried on, despite great pain. The second burst, which broke his right arm, put him effectively out of action. A right-handed man, with a broken right arm can hardly be a useful soldier for long. How he managed to bring in prisoners along with himself, as well as to carry, or help to carry, a wounded man back to our lines is not easy to imagine: but he did.

Whether he knew it when he wrote his first letter home, and was trying to avoid unnecessary (as he might think it) anxiety for his family, or whether he was still unaware of the extent of his wounds, the fact is that his injuries were far worse than he portrayed. The broken arm was not, in the result, of very great moment. Once it had had time to heal he was left with little more than a rather dramatic scar on his right upper arm. He regained full use of that limb.

The feet were another matter. Massive quantities of shrapnel had been blown into both of them. It was never possible to remove it all: much of it remained there for the rest of his life. Whatever damage had been done by the initial entry of the metal – and that would have been considerable – was greatly compounded by the stresses and strains to which he put his feet, first in continuing to advance, and then in the long haul to return to his own lines, involving much activity over difficult terrain. One wonders how long the "some time" was in fact. If the pain had been just about bearable at first, so as not to put paid immediately to his ability to remain mobile, it was excruciating by the time he eventually got back.

To conclude matters military, the Battles of Bullecourt were not completely successful. The first day's fighting did secure the front line, but the second day's 'had nowhere been attended by success.' The History of the Regiment sums it up thus:

Bullecourt represents one of the finest achievements of the 2/2nd Londons, not so much from the results gained as from the endurance and self-sacrifice displayed by all ranks; throughout the battle the men behaved with splendid courage and cheerfulness in very trying circumstances. As the result of the heavy casualties sustained, the personnel of the Battalion underwent an extensive change; and although the Battalion served with distinction throughout the rest of the campaign, Bullecourt was, so far as its original personnel was concerned, its first and last great engagement. For this reason it is especially satisfactory that the battle-honour 'Bullecourt' was selected as one of the ten to be born on the Regiment's Colours. [10]

And as for Pat's actions there remains a bit of a mystery. If his name did go forward, as he wrote in his earlier letter that he thought it had, he received no formal decoration apart from the normal Campaign Medals. He did receive, however, a citation – if that is the right word for it – from Major General Fanshawe, commanding the 58th (London) Division. It is a small printed card (I presume it is card: it has been in a frame for over eighty years) saying: 'Your gallant conduct on...has been brought to my notice, and I take this opportunity of congratulating you on the good service you have rendered to your country,' and it is signed by the General.

In neat handwriting appears first his name, but as '2nd Lieut.' It is true that the Official History at times credits him with being a full Lieutenant and at times does not. But, according to his letter, he was temporarily in command of his Company: would that not require him to be at least a full Lieutenant? His Certificate of being Disabled and Discharged, dated 24th July, 1919, certainly refers to him as 'Lieutenant.' Was it a slip in compiling the card? He would hardly have been promoted after disablement.

And then the citation is filled out '...conduct on 15th May, 1917, near Bullecourt.' I have always believed – and I am sure I was always told – that this document relates to the day upon which he was wounded. It was not until, for the first time, I read in detail the relevant passages in the History of the Regiment, and looked at the detail of Pat's letters that I realised that, on its face, it does not relate to that day. He was wounded on 15th June. There can be no doubt about that. But his Battalion was in the vicinity of Bullecourt on both dates, seeing action on both dates. Did the clerk preparing the card for the General's signature make a careless slip? Or was there something else that he did the month before, something that caused his 'name to be sent forward?' And, if there was, what was it? I do not believe I shall ever know. I doubt if Dorothy knew. Pat would not talk even to her about his time in the trenches. As she put it to me, "It had been so awful that he did all he could to put it out of his mind completely."

Pat began upon a particularly bleak and miserable period in his life. There are no medical reports surviving, and one is left to speculate upon what the state of a foot will be like after the trauma of first shrapnel followed by considerable and energetic use. He was many months in hospital in Rouen and had operation after operation. Whether he had the best medical skill available in those days or not, the surgeons were unable to get his feet right. He was in great constant pain. He remembered a visit paid by Queen Mary to the hospital, during the course of which she came to his bedside. He was heavily sedated after the latest attempt to operate which had left him in agony, but he had the impression that she spoke with a strong German accent and asked "Vos it der shrapnel?" He may have been mistaken: he was in no condition to be an accurate reporter.

Obviously, in due course he was returned to England where he remained in hospital for a considerable time. It was not until October, 1918, nearly eighteen months after he had been hit, that he was able to return to Guy's Dental School to continue his studies. They gave him three months' credit for fees. After a gap of well over three years it cannot have been easy. But what made it worse was his health. After all that had been done for him he was left with two feet, still with metal in them, neither of which had any natural arch. He always had to have shoes specially made for him to give support for an arch that did not exist. His feet had set in such a way that each was splayed outwards to about 45° from straight ahead. So that together they were almost at a right angle to each other, and his walk in consequence was rather unusual, even clumsy. Running was out of the question.

He struggled on and passed Part I of his Final Examination in May, 1919. But by then he was quite done in and was unable to continue. Whether on account of his feet on their own, or, as I suspect, his general health as well, he had to have a prolonged period away from work. I believe more operations, more time in hospitals, and more pain and disability. This was surely the moment for him to have considered his position and re-thought his future career. The injuries he had sustained were about the very worst that could befall a young would-be dentist.

Or, to put it another way, few young men with badly disabled feet would consider dentistry as a first choice among professions to take up. Especially in those days, when the dental surgeon did not sit beside a patient lying prone on a reclining chair, but stood behind a nearly upright chair. Of all professionals the dentist then was on his feet virtually all the time he was working. I do not know whether Pat already had reservations as to how much he actually wanted to spend his life in dentistry. I do know that, once qualified and practising, he did not enjoy his work and soon came to hate it. If Mr Michelmore, eight years or so after his offer to Pat of his Articles free, had been unable or unwilling to renew it, there would have been many Solicitors in Exeter who would have been only too glad to do so. A wounded soldier from the Western Front, son of one of their own number, would surely have been welcomed with open arms. But no. Whether because of Bert's insistence, or a reluctance to make a decisive change in his plans, Pat carried on ultimately as he had begun.

After the medical attention he needed, he spent several months working on a poultry farm in the Home Counties trying to regain his strength with fresh country air and not too much hard physical labour. He rather enjoyed his time with the chickens, and would later talk about such things as the respective merits of the Light Sussex as compared to the Rhode Island Red. I wonder what his feeling were as he retraced his steps to Guy's Dental School. He did not do so until June, 1922, after a gap of just over three years, and more than eight years from the time when he had embarked upon his studies.

Although he wanted to take his Part II of the Finals in the November he was advised not to do so until February, 1923, because of the long breaks in his studies. He was successful on that occasion and was duly registered as a dentist (LDS, RCS Eng.) on 24th April, 1923. He was a fortnight short of his twenty-eighth birthday.

For a year he got experience doing various locum jobs, while registered at his home in Exeter. He then became an employed dentist in a practice in Great Malvern. All I know of his time there is that on one occasion he was a little alarmed when the patient walking into his surgery proved to be none other than Mr George Bernard Shaw. "I hope you do not mind the attentions of a dentist," said Pat by way of opening gambit. "My dear boy," replied the celebrated playwright, "what greater pleasure can there be than sitting in a comfortable chair watching another man work?" I daresay that put both at their ease, and they got on well for the rest of that (their only) session together.

After some three years at Great Malvern Pat was keen to get his own practice. He was now well over thirty and felt it was high time to have the benefit of professional independence. So he kept his eye open for any opportunities to join as a partner or to acquire a practice of his own. He eventually came to learn of the dental practice for sale of a Mr Godfrey Deane Webb, which at that time was situated in fairly newly built surgeries at Hereford House, Hinton Road in Bournemouth

He was a little taken aback the first time he went to see it. A fortuneteller, a few years before at some funfair or other such establishment, had gazed into her crystal ball and told him she saw black and white, there would be connections with black and white in his work. He walked up the short path from the road to find that the front door, along with its substantial glass and wooden surround, was painted black and that the area in front of it under a portico was paved in white, with large black and white checks on it. It did not influence him greatly: but it did strike him as more than a little odd.

He was attracted to this pleasant, seaside town and to the practice which was very close to the town centre. Although the surgeries and offices above had been quite recently built, they were annexed to an early Victorian building, the waiting room at the front and the dental workshop at the rear being actually within that Victorian house. They together made pleasant, spacious professional accommodation. Pat decided to go ahead.

Mount Radford School treat, about 1901. Percy is 5th boy from the left.

*TWO
VICTORIAN
OUTINGS*

*Winnie, Blanche
and Percy
in the woods,
about 1906.*

Percy, the dental student.

Pat, the young subaltern.

Pat recuperating on a poultry farm, about 1922. The strain is showing.

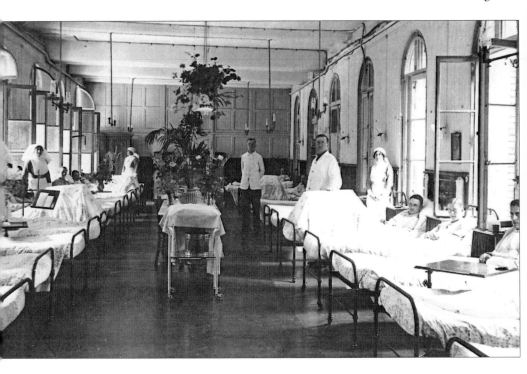

Hospital ward, Rouen, 1917, awaiting Queen Mary.
Pat is 2nd patient visible from the left.

With the assistance of an advance from his father of £925 he bought the practice from Mr Deane Webb for £1,250, furniture and stock at valuation. Unfortunately – although it is not clear that Pat realised it was unfortunate, or how unfortunate, at the time – the consideration for the purchase price was the goodwill only. Hereford House itself was not included. He had to rent it from Mr Deane Webb. And the rent was high.

Formal completion was on Christmas Day, 1926; Pat moved to Bournemouth and carried on the practice from early 1927. He decided not to take a lease of the residential accommodation which existed in the remaining part of the Victorian house. It might even have been occupied by someone else and so not available at that time. It is not insignificant that neither the garden at the front, nor that at the back, both really very small, were included in the lease. Mr Deane Webb kept as much as he could under his control.

As a single man Pat had a number of options for living accommodation. He could have gone into digs, and been looked after by a landlady. If he had wanted to be a bit more extravagant he could have bought or rented a flat or a house and installed a housekeeper, and possibly more staff. Instead he chose to avail himself of the facilities offered by the small private hotels with which Bournemouth was liberally supplied. Without wishing to be unkind to those establishments, which often provided long-term and perfectly satisfactory homes for many, it was probably rather a depressing lifestyle. One such hotel he patronised, I think probably the first, was in fact the very next-door building to his surgery. Ellerslie Mansions Hotel was a late Victorian building, replacing an earlier one of a similar type to Hereford House, quite large, a bit gaunt, but perfectly adequate. From there he moved to the Osborne Hotel, a short walk away on the far side of the Central Gardens. For a change as much as for anything else. He always remained on very good terms with the Plummer family who ran Ellerslie Mansions – they were, after all, his next-door neighbours.

But whatever their merits there was one undoubted disadvantage: apart from a few personal possessions he might have in his room, absolutely nothing was really his own. Furthermore the fellow guests tended to be on the elderly side. He was not a very gregarious man and he had few close friends. His sister and brother-in-law had by now moved to Winchester as Charles had been appointed to a teaching post at Danemark School in that City. Their second daughter, Betty (now Mrs Donald Judd) had been born in May, 1926. Pat had learned to ride a motorcycle in the Army, and now had one of his own. Winchester is about forty miles from Bournemouth, a manageable distance for a day trip, and he would occasionally make the journey to see the four of them, when his visits were eagerly awaited by both his nieces, especially by Mary, who was now coming up to eleven years old. He was a very popular uncle.

He kept in touch to some extent with the Prentice family who had befriended him all those years ago in Ipswich. In the box containing family photographs there is one of Olive Prentice in the countryside, dated 1927 with simply the word 'me' on the back. They must have been in touch with each other, but nothing at all enduring in the way of a romantic attachment was in the air.

However, Pat did have two things he enjoyed. One was a game of golf, despite his injured feet, and he was an early member of the Hazards Golfing Society which met for golf on various courses in the Bournemouth area. He was also a keen, and a very able bridge player. A young single man who can be relied on, not merely to make up a four, but also to play a good hand, was a considerable asset for a hostess who was trying to arrange a bridge party. And an evening of bridge would make a very pleasant change for him from dinner at his hotel followed by early bed, even if it did mean meeting new people and being sociable with those he hardly knew.

Dentists often get plenty of opportunity to talk to their patients and invitations to bridge could easily come from one who learned of his interest in and enjoyment of the game. Whether they were his patients and had talked about bridge, or whether they had discovered his prowess at the game through meeting him at a bridge party, I do not know. The fact is that Mr and Mrs Sharkey invited him to such a party at their home, and so he found himself, one evening in the summer of 1928, knocking on the door of 'Asenby', West Overcliff Drive.

CHAPTER 24

A BIT OF A WHIRLWIND

"A S SOON AS I MET HIM I knew this was the man I was going to marry." So Dorothy asserted to me on one occasion. I don't doubt that at that time she believed it to be the case, but I suspect that the benefit of the hindsight of, by then, fifty to sixty years had to some extent coloured her recollection. The evidence of the letters she wrote to Pat in the short period of their courtship does point to some hesitation on her part before taking the plunge. But it is certainly true to say that they were interested in each other very quickly.

There is a difficulty confronting the historian in dealing with these letters from Dorothy. Unlike those comprising her long journal to her mother, she has not dated any of those she wrote from Chingri Khal (often in pencil) save by giving the day of the week. They are on small writing paper and in very small envelopes which have not been through the post. At least they are neither stamped nor franked. Some have Pat's full address, some only one line of it. Some go to Hereford House, where he worked, some to the Osborne Hotel, where he was living. How they got to either destination is far from clear. Perhaps she had some faithful courier (Hall, the chauffeur-gardener, is a possibility perhaps – but that does seem a little unlikely, apart from a little detail from the events of the following year) or she may have put them in another envelope which Pat did not keep. I am glad he did keep the letters and that they have, rather amazingly, survived. I wish Dorothy had kept his too, but, if she did, they are not available to us now. His letters certainly came by post. But with hers it is not possible to be entirely confident that I have got them even in the correct order. Apart from a few clues within the letters (Bournemouth Cricket Week, for instance, as we have seen in another context, is at the end of August) it is largely a matter of guesswork. What I believe to be the first letter does read as if they are being a little cautious with each other. On the other hand there had plainly been some serious talk involving at least some mention of the possibility of marriage, or 'religious conditions' could hardly have arisen. The date may well have been Thursday, 23rd August.

> Thursday Night.
> My dear – thank you so much for your letter. Please write whenever you feel inclined – I just love getting your letters.
> It didn't arrive till the 6 o'clock post this evening, and in a way I knew it could scarcely come any sooner, even if you did write last night, which you did. The point, though, is this, just to show you what a Doubting Thomas I am. I began to wonder whether our little discussion about religion & religious conditions had made any difference.
> This is to say that you must forgive me coming on Saturday, but tomorrow – and that is today when you read this – I shall come and see you. I shall be at the cricket, steal away just after 5.30 & meet you at 6. But where!! In the Arcade. What a place, but the only one I can think of. I'm afraid this time I cannot stay long but – another time. However could you come round after we meet tomorrow and have some dinner with us – don't change - & then Bridge after.
> What do I think of you as? Well I tell you some day.
> Forgive the pencil! I am writing upstairs in my room in secret.
> My love to you
> Dorothy

It would be characteristic of Dorothy to have made some reference, sooner rather than later, to the Catholic Church's rules and regulations relating to mixed marriages. They were a good deal more stringent then than they are today, and many a man could be put off, or insist on ignoring them. She would have regarded the former as disastrous and the latter as unthinkable. Pat, as we have seen, had by this time been without any religious convictions for some years. He never raised any problems or objections to religious practices as far as Dorothy was concerned. She told me that he said, early on in their engagement, "I suppose you want me to become a Catholic?" To which she replied, "Only if you want to." And there the matter was left.

By the end of August arrangements had been made for Dorothy to take Harry on a motoring tour to Scotland. Curiously the intended trip did not include Jennie. There is no hint as to why that was so. Harry had written to Colonel Wyness on Saturday, 1st September, telling him of the plan and seeking to make an arrangement for the two of them to stay on their way back in a hotel in Bletchley, where Colonel and Mrs Wyness lived, so that they could all meet.

A Hobbsian eruption very nearly put paid to the whole enterprise. It is by no means clear what precisely caused this outburst, which seems to have been pretty violent while it lasted. Dorothy only puts part of it down on paper.

Monday [3rd September?]

My dear – Strange, isn't it, that I should be the first to write after what I said last night.

It was the high jump for me this morning. Scotland is off, thank goodness. Unfortunately many other things are off too, including dancing, late nights, the use of the car etc., etc.

I can't come tomorrow night. I can't face seeing you tonight as I shall have to relate to you the story of my woes & will probably cry - & a woman looks awful with red eyes. Don't ring me up – I scarcely knew how to speak this morning. I will some round and see you one evening later on in the week.

Mother has been a perfect brick but please don't think it is anything to do with you (there's a badly constructed sentence – but you get the meaning I hope) Henry just violently disapproves of my way of life, that's all – and I'm so ridiculously sensitive.

Don't worry. I shall be seeing you soon.

Love   from   Dorothy

It looks as if Harry was treating Dorothy as if she were a tearaway teenager rather than a mature woman of over thirty. I expect it was a case of Jennie to the rescue, not for the first time, and she succeeded in mollifying the irascible Harry. It seems to have taken her nearly a fortnight to do so, for it is not until Friday, 14th September that Harry writes again to Colonel Wyness:

Owing to uncertainty I have not been able to tell you of my proposed movements; then the weather has been so good that I've enjoyed the rest. Dorothy and I leave here on Monday for Worcester, thence to a friend near Chester and then en route for the Lakes and Glasgow returning via Bletchley.

Evidently Dorothy had not much been looking forward to driving her father to Scotland and back. Probably not so much on account of the labour involved in the driving as to being in his sole company for a fortnight. But in the event she enjoyed the trip well enough, especially as their relationship seems to have been restored to an even keel. The rumpus seems to have been forgotten in small romantic subterfuges.

> Sunday [16th September?]
> My dear. You are just walking up and down the lawn with Jim and I have stolen away to write. However I shan't be here long – someone is sure to disturb me – perhaps even you.
>
> One day I will write you a proper letter. But this I will post so that you get it sometime tomorrow – to console you or comfort you, or perhaps merely to tell you that I am sorry to be going away.
>
> I have enjoyed having you with me this afternoon though I am afraid our plans of bathing went awry – did you mind so very much? Of course if I'd known about the bathing I'd not have suggested tea with the Reid's, but I am glad you have met Florrie. She's as straight as a die & I'm really awfully fond of her.
>
> Each night you know what I shall be thinking. And yet in a way I am glad to be going away – publicity looms up & I want to avoid it – at present.
>
> You are just in the next room now – do you blame me for ending?
> I send you all my love, Pat darling, & remain
> Dorothy

The following day Dorothy and Harry set off on what, even today, would be regarded as a fairly significant drive. I doubt if Harry was at the wheel for any part of the journey: Dorothy did it all. I expect he had driven a car in Calcutta, but in England he seems to have been content to leave all the driving to Dorothy. She was a very experienced driver by then, and had no qualms about that task, although both cars and roads were very different from those of the twenty-first century. Less traffic, obviously, but probably plenty of it in the town centres, and they would have had to go through many town centres on their way north. At least she did not have to cope with the old Vauxhall – the pre-war open car – but with the new Vauxhall, which looked more like a shoebox with a wheel at each corner. High, square, with very large windows and plenty of space inside, but no boot; it was the sort of car she always liked. "A car in which a man could sit wearing a top hat with ease."

Unlike her daily bulletin to Jennie during her Far East Journey she only managed three letters to Pat in the fortnight or so that she was away. They are curiously different from each other in style and content. The first was written from the Grosvenor Hotel in Chester.

> Tuesday [18th September]
> My dear – we went to Stratford-on-Avon yesterday & then here today. We have had lovely runs and I am enjoying myself immensely. We hope to be in Glasgow on Friday night & will probably stay until Sunday. Write to the North British Hotel – I will leave an address with them in case of forwarding.
>
> I keep wondering whether you remember me. I have a host of questions to ask and things to tell you – most of them unimportant but still!! However I must thank you for your dear letter which came on Monday & which I read in my bath.
>
> We have to be off now to see some pals of Henry's, so this is merely a note to tell you I am well and looking forward to my return.
>
> Darling I send you my love.   Dorothy

After that short, fairly subdued, almost prim letter with Dorothy wondering if Pat remembered her, the next one, written from the North British Station Hotel in Glasgow, goes right to the other extreme.

> [Friday] Sept. 21st
> My dear love – your letter was waiting for me and I have already found time to read it through twice. Daddy is now going to have his hair cut so I am stealing away to write to you.
>
> So strange that you should tell me of your ideal girl – I was going to ask you to tell me so that I could point out how far I fell short, but then you said in your letter that I was a most blessed of Eves & I am content, Adam darling. Anyhow I will wait till I can talk to you a bit

more definitely before I start showing you my feet of clay.

One thing, though, has been rather on my conscience. You remember saying "But then you are different and you know you are" and I said "Yes"? Well I don't really think that I am different from any other woman, though we are all variations of the imaginary normal. However I admit that my peculiar education might have made some superfluous difference & that was really what I was thinking of when I agreed with you. Perhaps I had better tell you about it although it isn't very interesting.

I won't talk about my home life for that will be evident to you as time goes on (if you haven't grasped it already.) I was then sent to a Convent where I was scandalously overworked – through kindness, of course. But you can imagine what a quiet convent life is like. Then I should have gone abroad, but the War came so I was sent to Cambridge instead. Can you imagine the change! Well I didn't do frightfully well there either, as I only got honours in the first half of my Tripos, & as I expect you know, to get an ordinary B.A. isn't anything. However, I didn't mind much & I am sure that Cambridge did me heaps of good. Especially on top of the Convent. I think it was 18 months after I came down that I had my first love affair – at 23 – and that did me more good than anything. However, you see now what I meant when I agreed I was different

Now for some news. I clicked good and solid at Chester, but he's married, so don't worry. Then we took your tip and stayed as the Old England at Bowness, and my dear it was lovely. Now I wonder if you will be shocked! They gave me a room with a double bed – I stretched my hand but I was still terribly lonely. I have been thinking of you in each place – wondering how much better it would be if we were seeing it together. I have promised to show you so much, Oxford, Cambridge, the beauty spots around Bournemouth, & you have lightly hinted something about Devon. I wonder! So many things I wonder. How many of my dreams are you going to bring true? Dear, how much depends on you & how little can I tell you to help you because I don't know myself. I am sure your idol was – is – not indecisive – but I am.

But News! News! We 'did' the Lakes – rather heavy driving – and for the first time I was tired on arriving at our destination. However it (Carlisle) is a lovely old place & I thoroughly enjoyed seeing over the gloomy old Castle with its grim dungeons & tales of horror that almost made me sick. We saw the Cathedral, too, rather a 'beaut' as

Dorothy Mary would say, and then on here this morning.

(1) I don't suppose we will be home for at least another week.

(2) I don't smoke till after lunch

(3) I am getting fat, for Henry insists on three square (very square) meals a day. My interior economy isn't as it should be, my skin ditto ditto and my figure ditto ditto, only more so – do you mind? A great big fat ugly old squaw will be arriving back at Chingri Khal with Henry.

Oh my dear, my very dear one, I am so longing to see you again. You know I think of you just as I have told you. I want to help you and comfort you & give you my arms & my mouth and — and — and 'your own' and, and. But you must add on yourself. Only remember I have told you & that I am thinking of it all

I send you all my thoughts to nestle in your heart with me, and my love

Dorothy

By contrast her third and final letter on this tour, written from The Cairn Hydro, Harrogate, on Monday 24th September, is brief to the point of being terse, even curt.

My dear. – I shall be home fairly soon – probably on Saturday. Thank you so much for your letter which arrived this morning, I was so glad to get it.

This isn't a proper letter – just to tell you that I am well & looking forward to seeing you.

All my love to you from   Dorothy

P.S. Write to The Felix Hotel, Felixstowe. Will be there Wed. or Thurs.

Assuming, as seems safe to do, that Dorothy and Harry had arrived back at Chingri Khal by the end of September, or very early October at the latest, there is a gap of nearly three weeks before we have another letter kept by Pat which shows the course of their romance. Perhaps the telephone sufficed for communication in the interim, apart from meetings out of surgery hours. Whatever the cause it is safe to date the next available missive as having been written on 22nd October. It reveals something of a turmoil.

Monday morning

My dear – this is going to be so difficult to write & yet I must.

Since Saturday things seem to be different. Doubting Thomas has returned – first for us both, though your letter on Sunday morning made me feel a little better about you but I have been thinking & thinking & I know that I still doubt myself. Things are different. I feel I am caught in a net or a wild bird in a cage, and one that I have made myself. Please don't think that I harbour any unkind thoughts about you or that I blame you in any way, my dear. If I blame anyone it would be myself but I don't think I even do that.

It is only fair to us both that I should try to tell you exactly what I feel.

Passion has been awakened in me – I don't know how to deal with it, my doubts are whether it is on account of that alone that I have said I loved you.

Our present stage cannot go on. I want you to help me understand myself. I feel that everything is wrong, and yet I cannot put my finger on the spot and say, "This is it." So I ask you to help me. If you love me as you say you do your great love must be able to help me.

The present situation is impossible. I am not a bit unhappy – perhaps a little sad, but I am harassed.

I am writing because when I see you I seem to want just to be happy & not to think. Perhaps this will break the ice & I can talk.

If I can I will meet you at the Bath at 6.10 tonight & unless you want to put me off, don't 'phone.

Dorothy

P.S. This is all so bald. Please try & help me to explain tonight.

Whatever the reason may have been, their next meeting was not until the Tuesday. It did take place 'at the Bath' – a reference to the Royal Bath Hotel, which is opposite the eastern end of Hinton Road and Westover Road, five minutes walk from Hereford House, and always a favourite family haunt. At dinner there that evening, however precisely it may have been spoken, they came to regard themselves as engaged. Pat had obviously hoped, even expected, that that would have been the case, and had given Dorothy an orchid by way of corsage to be worn during the meal. Somehow by the end of that week the, by now probably fading, bloom came back into his possession. From then until today that symbol of the culmination of their courtship has been pressed within a folded piece of card and kept in the envelope containing Dorothy's next letter to him. The florist's foil wrap has all its brightness, the asparagus fern retains just a trace of its original green, and, although of the orchid itself there is little more than a shrivelled brown remnant, the whole is quite recognisable and remains a touching relic of the happiest of occasions.

The letter itself gives some idea how happy the occasion was – and how different from the many encounters we have heard about from Marseilles to New Zealand. It is written 'Outside Bmth Central.' Dorothy must have taken someone – very likely her father – to catch an early train, probably to London for the day, and then could not wait to write. Pat had been busy already, with the help of the Post Office of those days: you could hardly do so much now. A full day had elapsed. Family activities at Chingri Khal must have been considerable, otherwise Dorothy would surely have put pen, or pencil, to paper the very next day. In the event she wrote a happy mixture of the ecstatic and the practical.

Thursday [25th October]

My dear – after all you are really my dear now – 'my dear love, my true love, who has my heart forever.'

I was so glad to get your two letters – you are a dear to me and I am pleased to know you are happy. I feel still too dazed to know what I am doing. I don't feel deliriously happy or thrilled, but I feel something far more wonderful – just as if I am sunk in a sea of happiness & contentment & everything else is a little misty & far away & doesn't really matter very much Otherwise yesterday would have been very trying. Old Father Sidgreaves is eighty-nine I think & stone deaf. We played Bridge (?) I leave the rest to your imagination.

I shall drive terrible carefully to Portsmouth today. I am going to tell Mother on the journey. I suppose I ought to have told her on Tuesday night but – well I have liked gloating over my happiness by myself.

Do you think you ought to write to, or see your father? He will probably be rather hurt if he thinks you have not asked his advice –

besides he might not approve of me and then the fat would be in the fire.

I am terribly afraid that I shan't be able to manage this evening – still, I'll see. Our plans are these, aren't they? You will go to the Osborne when finished. I will ring up there first & if you aren't there, then Hereford House.

I must fly now to my breakfast.

All my love darling   from   Dorothy

I do love you darling so much

Dorothy's family knew of the engagement by the week-end. She could hardly fail to have been anxious as to what Harry's reaction would be, but it seems all was well. In a letter to Colonel Wyness on the Monday Harry refers to two family landmarks.

On Friday Dorothy became engaged to a Dental Surgeon down here – a very pleasant, sound fellow whom I like. They are to be married next May when I return to England. Phyllis gave birth to a 10 lb daughter on Saturday and when I saw them on Sunday both looked very well. I have much to do as you can imagine.

So general sighs of relief all round. The birth of a third daughter, Elizabeth Ann (now Mrs Gerald van den Brul,) to Phyllis may well indicate some of the reason for there to have been a rather hectic household at Chingri Khal. The journey to Portsmouth on the Thursday was no doubt for Jennie and Dorothy to see Phyllis, even for Jennie to stay for the approaching confinement.

In the midst of her joy, Dorothy was wise enough to suggest to Pat that he got in touch with his father. She had not yet met any of his family. Time had been too short. Without knowing the date of the Sharkey's party it is impossible to be precise. It would not have been very long before the first letter, and so only eight to ten weeks from first meeting to becoming engaged. And two of those weeks were when Dorothy was away with Harry. Not, perhaps, the shortest courtship on record, but quick enough for all that – and why not? They were not inexperienced teenagers and were quite capable of making a rational decision without consulting distant parents, but even so it is sensible to keep them in your confidence, and thereby on your side, as much as possible.

It was not until after they were engaged that Pat took Dorothy to Exeter to meet Bert and Edith. On the way, referring to Edith, Pat said to Dorothy, "She's not my mother, you know, but she's a jolly decent sort." Which summed her up very well. The visit was a success, although in one respect a trial for Dorothy. She had a broad taste in food, but one thing she could not abide was offal, and kidneys in particular revolted her. For dinner the evening they stayed for the first time, the meal began with very thick kidney soup. Delicious for some maybe, but for Dorothy almost impossible to get it down, let alone keep it down. But she did it, and they didn't notice any problem. Pat knew what a struggle she must be having – and admired her all the more for the effort.

The last letter of this series which he kept – it might even have been the last altogether until she went abroad, for they would be seeing each other often enough one would think – is short, to the point, and wholly unnecessary. But then lovers are not always logical. When it was written is obscure and irrelevant.

Tuesday

Darling.   I feel I must write & just tell you I am thinking of you & longing for tomorrow night.

have just read Florence Nightingale in the Express and thought that although we both agree that I'm not a Modern Woman, yet unblushingly I am not a Victorian, am I? And aren't we both glad about it?

I must fly to my lunch now – I do so want to go on writing – to tell you I love you darling. It's a filthy day, & I've been out in it this morning so I know, but I'm feeling so happy after writing this little 'talk.'

You'll go on thinking of me won't you? & we'll see each other tomorrow.

Till then – I still love you   Dorothy

On the reverse of the letter Par, for some reason, has written in pencil: 'Charm is an atmosphere of graciousness surrounding a personality which appeals to our aesthetic sense as beauty of conduct.' Where he got that mouthful from I have no idea. I doubt if he tried it out on his fiancée. If he had she would have probably laughed till she choked. I expect he, too, was 'in a sea of happiness and contentment' and everything else was 'a little misty.' It is easy to lose one's way a little in a fog.

But the fog soon cleared and there was much for everyone to attend to in the next few months.

Hereford House in 1926 – no pavement yet outside the gate.

Godfrey Deane Webb in his horse and trap outside
10, Bath Road, probably soon after the turn of the century.

*Harry
at the hustings,
Calcutta,
25th January,
1929.*

*Dorothy at the wheel of the new Vauxhall
outside the front door of the third Chingri Khal.*

CHAPTER 25

POLITICS IN CALCUTTA –
MATRIMONY
IN BOURNEMOUTH

ARRY LEFT ENGLAND on the last day of October, 1928.
After what he described to Colonel Wyness as 'a record run'
he was in Bombay by the early hours of 15th November
and, presumably, back in Calcutta on the following day. He did not
waste much time. Within well under a week of getting home after
some eight months absence he was causing a typical rumpus.

This concerned the working of a body called 'The European
Association,' the precise nature of which is now more than a little
obscure. Membership seems to have been open to European
businessmen with an agenda very similar to a Chamber of
Commerce, with which Harry from time to time in his writings
compares it, even confuses it. He was a member for many years,
including, for some of that time, being on its Council. Despite that
involvement, he had a very low opinion of the Association, of its
activities, and of those who ran it. Writing to Colonel Wyness on 21st
November, 1928 he gives some idea of what sort of a cat Harry could
be when let loose among political pigeons.

> I had a scrap at the European Association meeting last night, and
> while I completely knocked out the clique who run it, so that they
> could not reply to a single charge nor parry my expressed contempt,
> but not a soul of the 32 members present supported me. Just fancy a
> body with 2,000 local members turning out 32 strong at the Annual
> Meeting. As I told then, that didn't spell apathy – it spelt contempt,
> and as far as I could see they deserved all of it. Eventually being called
> to order I socked it to them by refusing to accept the ruling of the
> Chair and went on speaking. They had most of what I wanted to say

and the meeting closed like wet blotting paper on boiled rice. The *banchutes*!

Harry makes no mention of it in this letter – perhaps the idea had not yet come to him – but by the 25th January, 1929, he was contesting a seat in the Bengal Legislative Council at a by-election, his first, and only, attempted entry into active politics. Writing nearly ten years later in *Talkeetalkeewallahs and Others* he refers to this election and uses it as an opportunity for venting his wrath on the European Association.

I will admit that I once stood for election to the Bengal Legislative Council. But those in control of the European Association, a so-called political body, who are distrusted and despised by their fellow countrymen and are like the Radical charlady whose contempt for patriotic men was expressed in few words: "They are my pet abortion." To defeat me thousands of rupees were spent and our political leaders lied like truth. Then, with usual capitalistic unselfishness, they sent all the bills to the man they had implored to stand against me. He was said to have ruefully confessed that the victory was more expensive to him than it was worth…

A curious sidelight on Bengal politicians was flashed by some Indian members of the Legislative Council, some of them Gandhiwallahs, who expressed regret over my failure.

"What a pity you didn't get in! There are many things we could have told you to say which we couldn't. You don't care for anybody."

After that election the European Association, fearful of exposure and keen to prevent too many hearing my jibes, jeers and insults, were careful to hold no meetings. When the obligatory Annual General Meeting came off, they had waited for a moonless night, and fixed upon the cricket pavilion in the middle of the Eden Gardens to present their report. Boasting as they do of a membership of 1,800, about the usual number turned up – something under twenty-five, I happened to be sick at the time the meeting was held or there might have been two dozen present.

The most autocratic organisation in India is not the Government, nor the Congress, it is the Chamber of Commerce in each of the Presidency cities. Animated by the slogan – Peace at any Price – their policy has been to kowtow to the enemies of their country so that the leaders in the Chamber could get away with their pile. Any man on their staff who dared to express an opinion contrary to the Chamber would not only get the sack, but he wouldn't get another job in India…And what is more nauseating, they have worked below ground to bring democracy into a land where there are no democrats, but where hereditary and traditional despotism has been accepted and absorbed by the soul of the unfortunate people. Those who know much about India (and few of them do) understand how few men are produced in the tropical world who have any capacity for progressive and just administration. The fact is that Chamber of Commerce politics are a matter for profound contempt and distrust, and a striking example of British cowardice…

If I have not accomplished anything during my years in India I have enjoyed the luxury of telling them at various meetings exactly what I think. As I have put it more than once – there are far too many third class heads sticking out of first class windows, and I have occasionally derived amusement from giving them a crack as the train goes by. Jeers, ridicule and insults have never drawn a retort. So at the Annual General Meeting following that already mentioned I referred to the Cricket Pavilion incident. "So fearful are these people of criticism that they are afraid to hold meetings. When one must be held they select the most out-of-the-way hole they can find. The Members of this Association can, therefore, confidently look forward to finding the Annual General Meeting held in the morgue of the small-pox hospital."…

That is the sort of stuff I have given them during more years than most of the British now living in India can remember, and while I must admit I have never been supported but once, I have never been contradicted. Of course, if looks could kill I should have been dead many times…

After several years on the European Association Council I eventually decided that trying to checkmate disloyalty was too profitless so, fed to the teeth, I declined to serve any longer, as "I never attend the Council meetings without feeling as if I had a rat in my pyjamas." That compliment was rubbed in on many subsequent occasions with a few others that came to mind, and never once drew a retort of any kind. My charges were admitted and my insults accepted with philosophy by those who knew they were unanswerable.

Not so many years ago, several of our political partial patriots, demi-semi-officially entertained Mr. Gandhi to dinner, and, further to express their profound admiration for the man who was out to "bend the British Lion" they arranged that he should address a Meeting. The Chairman, later several times President of the European Association, full of delight at such an opportunity coming his way, obsequiously dusted Mr. Gandhi's chair with his pocket handkerchief. Merely because I stood to ask – "Are you going to sleep with that handkerchief under your pillow tonight?" he looked as if he would like to scratch my eyes out and in. It was rather a shame to so needlessly ruin one of the proudest moments in his patriotic life, but that is what happened. [1]

Small wonder Harry was heartily disliked by a considerable slice of the body politic in Calcutta. It may be surprising that he did as well as he did in the Election. He was pleased enough with his performance when he wrote to Colonel Wyness on 4th February about the Poll the week before.

Dengue fever left my liver out of order; I took calomel. After 7 weeks of sloppiness, fever, aches and pains, and walked like a two year old once more. Have been fit ever since and thoroughly enjoyed the contest for the Bengal Legislative Council, where I polled 708 to my opponent's 829. The European Association Council did all his work for him; they had organisation and I had none; you cannot improvise organisation, even in politics. I am quite well satisfied to be defeated for I wanted to go Home and certainly did not wish to have to return in July as that is a pretty bad time for an old stager. I hate to lose a fight but having lost it I can take it in good part and already there seems to be a feeling of freedom for a week or so absent from my mentality.

Harry returns to the election in his next letter, of 18th March.

I had a good scrap with the European Association over the election but am leaving on the 14th April for Dorothy's wedding, so I'm glad not be a member. May have another try at it next time as there will be an election towards the end of this year. The European Association are now afraid to call a meeting for they know I'll strafe them, and, as it happens I'm by a long way the most forceful attacker

417

they have, they funk chancing a meeting.

But, despite his strafing propensities, and the neat vitriol he liked to scatter around, many admired him a great deal. Writing to Colonel Wyness after he had got back to Chingri Khal he recalled a dinner he attended shortly before his departure. He does not make it clear whether it was one in his honour or not – his friend probably knew already – but it seems he was honoured at it, and is understandably pleased.

> At the Calcutta Dinner I had a wonderful reception. Just fancy being told by prominent men with whom I was never on friendly terms that I was one of the greatest men Calcutta has ever produced! Men repeated remarks of mine made years ago: my writings were recalled and altogether I was even more surprised than gratified for it never occurred to me that people had such good memories. Well, it is something to be able to scrap after all – it is far better to be abusive than to reply to critics – people enjoy a scrap and never see a real need for explanations. Slosh him is a good motto, even when it may be diluted with unfailing and unblushing modesty.

Which may be an excellent philosophy for dealing with political type wrangles, but can be uncomfortable to live with in the saloon of the *Ruahine* or across the dining table at Chingri Khal.

He was to leave for Rangoon on 14th April, where he would join *SS Gloucestershire,* which would bring him to Plymouth on 16th May.

Meanwhile, in Bournemouth, the course of true love was running as smoothly as it ever does. There is no record of the first two to three months of their engagement: Pat and Dorothy would have seen a great deal of each other, and I would expect Christmas for the two of them to have been largely at Chingri Khal. From the start of 1929 Pat's pocket diary is available (for a very tiny pocket: it barely covers a matchbox) and at least confirms the considerable extent to which he was there.

But there was an interruption, and probably not a very welcome one as far as either of them was concerned. A large skiing party had been arranged some months before and there was no getting out of it for Dorothy. Two of her closest friends, who were to be her two adult Bridesmaids, Hilda Cartwright and Florrie Reid, were among the group as well as Jennie and Mrs Reid from the older generation. Before leaving Dorothy wrote a farewell letter in similar terms to those she had used three months earlier.

January 29th 1929

My darling Pat

I hate writing this to you – it is perfectly awful going away. I would like to be able to tell you of my happiness in being with you all these past months & darling I do so want to thank you for all your love & sweetness to me. You know you will always be in my mind whilst I am away & at night I shall lie & imagine I am in your arms. Think of me too – I feel your love for me is always round me, wrapping me from the world & everyone else but you like a thick mist. I get comfort & strength from you & you make my dreams come true, so remember I am relying on your love all the time & that I am pouring into your life all the love that I am capable of giving.

I'm coming back soon darling   from   Dorothy

The party left that evening for Southampton; from there they took the ferry to Le Havre (telegram to Pat: arrived safely); then train to Paris, Nord; met John and Denise Hickey; then across Paris to Gare de Lyons (long letter to Pat, so far so good, still well, still in love and still in one piece); then train to Villars, changed at Lausanne and again at Bex on to a funicular (telegram to Pat: arrived safely); and then a long letter to Pat written once rooms were settled, on the day of arrival, 31st January. By today's standards – even by yesterday's – that sounds as if Cupid was making rather a lot of hard work. A labour of love, perhaps. I expect they both enjoyed it.

They were just the fortnight at Villars, returning in the same way, arriving at Southampton early on Saturday morning. Pat had spent the night at the South Western Hotel to be able to meet them. In addition to the two letters and two telegrams mentioned above he had received a further eleven letters and two telegrams to prove that absence makes the heart grow even fonder. He had responded to much the same extent, so the mutual consolation was complete.

The skiing had not been good: it had rained soon after their arrival and then frozen, and even the experts were falling and breaking bones. But they did a little on the nursery slopes – another activity I had had no idea Dorothy had ever tried her hand at until I read the letters. She describes all their activities, meals, clothes, ailments and outings in considerable detail, looking forward to her return even more than when she was going round the World.

Interestingly, the party had celebrated Jennie's thirty fifth wedding anniversary on 5th February 'by having a bottle of the native wine – such rashness,' which leaves one feeling they were normally rather abstemious.

The following day, the Feast of St. Dorothy, as she points out more than once, Dorothy raised (coincidentally?) the question of her wedding ring.

> Do you mind much if I change my mind about the wedding ring? We were talking about them yesterday, and of course everyone is against me, but I do like those rings all set round about with stones. I think they are called eternity rings. I'd like one in diamonds. Of course, darling, I don't want to land you in for more than we can afford, but you did say I could have one, didn't you? I think it was at the Bath on a certain Tuesday evening.

'All my worldly goods' may have loomed rather large at this change of mind. However it happened, she changed her mind to the opposite extreme before the event to the unusual, but to her extremely satisfactory solution of a very plain platinum ring

In the same letter, and in her next but one, Dorothy touches on something even more practical: their future home.

> I wish you'd settle with Mr. Deane Webb about the flat. I am frightened that if we don't make some definite arrangement the opportunity will be lost. Seeing it without that dreary furniture I am sure we could manage a baby there too, supposing we have one. So carry on...
>
> ...It was rather interesting to read about the flat, especially as I

had just written that I thought you had better settle with D. W. Our letters must have crossed. I believe that the tenants should do the redecoration, but am not sure, so that if he does it that will be a help. I suppose he would let us put in a geyser ourselves. We must have some way of getting a bath in the summer & cannot keep the range going in the hot weather, but I don't think that would be a very expensive matter for us. It is rather thrilling to think that you might be taking possession so soon. But I do hope you will be comfortable. Your charlady must do for you in the mornings and I must see what I can 'lend' you.

Dorothy's reference to 'the flat' is to the living accommodation which was contained within Hereford House, and which was not included in Pat's lease of his professional premises. It had become available with the departure of tenants toward the end of 1928, and, being 'over the shop', had obvious advantages as a first home for the newly engaged young couple. "You won't mind if we live in the flat to start with?" Pat had asked in all innocence one day. "Of course not," was the reply of his devoted fiancée. There were disadvantages as well, obvious or not according to the eye of the beholder, but you have to start somewhere, and one can see the sense in taking the opportunity of renting it along with the professional part of the building.

It may be just as well that she could not see into the future when she agreed so readily to his suggestion to live there "to start with." Hereford House was to be her home for fifty-seven years.

People had kindly rallied to give Pat some social life while Dorothy was away. His diary is quite full of bridge, golf and other engagements, not to mention one week-end when he went to Portsmouth to stay for a night with Phyllis and Jim. After Dorothy's return the frequent appearance of the two letters 'CK' in the diary show how often he had occasion to be there.

Towards the end of April, Pat moved into his new home. It was by no means ready for them, more furniture and equipment was needed, but he had signed the lease and was paying rent, so it made sense not to pay hotel bills as well. A bit of camping out was a small price to pay in the circumstances.

Harry had written, just after their engagement, that the marriage was to be in May. In fact the date ultimately chosen was Friday, 21st

June. It gave them more time for preparations and, perhaps more important to all concerned, it gave Harry more time to get home and settled down in Chingri Khal, where he duly arrived on 16th May.

Bert and Edith had come to Bournemouth to stay, both in early March and over Easter. On Low Sunday Dorothy got Pat to come to High Mass at the Church of the Sacred Heart where their marriage was due to take place. There were very few occasions when that happened after they were married. On 24th May Bert and Edith came to Bournemouth for the day. Partly, I daresay, to meet Harry, whom they had not yet seen, but also with sad news. It had been hoped that Samuel, Bert's father, would be well enough to attend the wedding. But he was eighty-eight years old, and had started a sharp decline in his health and strength. It was thought unlikely that he would even live to see the wedding.

Dorothy had never met G-pa, as he was always called, and so the following week-end Pat took Dorothy to Exeter to see him. She remembered a huge prone figure in his bed, conscious and alert, but little more, yet who was able to give them both his blessing. He died the following Wednesday, and they made the journey to Exeter again that Saturday, 8th June, for his funeral. They may have been forgiven for thinking that it was just as well that his death had not come any later.

There was less than a fortnight to go. Harry put it, rather obscurely, to Colonel Wyness in a letter of 7th June:

> So glad to know you are coming to the wedding and of course we shall be most pleased to welcome you…There is excitement here, but I manage to hold up scattering the (skimmed) milk of human kindness in seedlets and cuttings as usual.

Pat had difficulty with his Best Man. Having the wedding on a Friday, rather than the more conventional Saturday, caused problems. It is a bit of a mystery to me why they did decide on a Friday. Pat's first choice was his brother-in-law, Charles Hibbs. This was hardly a surprise – they had been friends since Pat was in his teens. But Charles was a schoolmaster, and it was in the middle of the summer term. It was quite impossible for him to absent himself from his duties for the day. As it was he had unpleasant criticism after the event for allowing Mary, his older daughter, to be a Bridesmaid and so not sending her to school. Once it became clear that Charles would not be able to come, Pat invited a great friend from his Army days, Geoffrey Mitchell, a bachelor like himself, as his second choice, and this was arranged. However, quite close to the last minute, something arose in Geoffrey's domestic or business life which made it impossible for him to be there. and Pat turned to his future brother-in-law, Jimmy Breaks, who was only too happy to help out.

For her part Dorothy had no fewer than six bridesmaids. Three pairs. Hilda Cartwright and Florrie Reid, who had been on the skiing holiday, as the two adult bridesmaids; Mary Hibbs and Joan King (Zoë Allan's niece) as two older children; and Dorothy Mary (Toff as she was now called by nearly everyone) and her sister Phyllida being the two youngest.

Dorothy made one decision which startled, almost shocked, her mother. They inevitably had to discuss the transport requirements for a considerable number of people for the two mile journey from Chingri Khal to the Church. Dorothy refused to have a special limousine for herself. "I shall go to my wedding in our own Vauxhall, and Hall will drive me there and back," she declared. Jennie's protests that this was not the done thing were to no avail. It was a big spacious car; she knew it and she was fond of it. Hall had been with them several years already and they had done much to the garden together. She had her way. Possibly it was a small 'thank you' to Hall for being a courier the year before. So a long length of broad white ribbon was bought and he spent many hours in the last week or so tuning the engine and washing and polishing and cleaning every visible surface so that the Vauxhall shone like a showroom car.

Hall had plenty to do, for the reception was to be in the garden. That, too, had to look its best, and Dorothy did not have much spare time for gardening in the last couple of weeks. But he was in his element. The lawns had their final mow before the marquee went up on the 'back' lawn, edges were trimmed, flowerbeds weeded and all was got ready.

The day was fine and sunny. The caterers arrived and began to set out the buffet. Bridesmaids still remember the huge quantities of strawberries and cream that seemed to abound. It was that time of year, so well they might. With just a quarter of an hour to go, and, of the family, only Dorothy, in all her finery, and her father, in top hat and tails, left in the house, Harry took out his watch, looked at it and barked, "You can't go yet: You will be early. No Bride is ever early for her wedding." And with that he marched up and down the hallway at Chingri Khal, watch in hand, for what seemed like ages to Dorothy clutching her bouquet, but which was probably no more than five minutes. Then it was out to the gleaming Vauxhall by the front door, Hall, in his best suit and peak cap holding open the door, his chest bursting with pride at being about to drive Miss Dorothy to her wedding, and they were off.

Dorothy had experienced many occasions in the past which had been marred, even spoilt by events, sometimes outside anyone's control, sometimes due to her father. It is really pleasant to be able to record that this whole day passed off without any hitch or cloud of any kind.

The local Paper rather went to town. 'Brilliant local Wedding;' 'Mayor of Bournemouth's Good Wishes;' it proclaimed. There followed detailed descriptions of dresses, flowers and the rest. Harry welcomed everyone (trust him not to miss an opportunity for holding forth) the Mayor, Mr Charles Cartwright (later Sir Charles) proposed the main toast. A few platitudes, perhaps, but who can avoid them on these occasions? "Life's greatest adventure…pleasure of knowing the bride since she was a girl…sweet disposition and shrewdness…highway of marriage not totally one of roses…ups and downs…sure…they will find sincere happiness." All of which was 'cordially received with cheers for the happy couple.'

Pat replied appropriately; Bert thanked Harry and Jennie, "Hospitality and Major and Mrs Hobbs are synonymous," he declared; and the record states they were 'accorded musical honours' without specifying them. The family GP, Dr Leslie-Spinks, proposed the health of the many bridesmaids, and Harry's old friend Colonel Wyness replied on their behalf 'in a witty speech.' The guests can certainly be said to have had their moneys worth.

The press did not report the entertainment provided generally by Jimmy Breaks. Once he had got the bridegroom to the Altar and back to the reception he had no more onerous duties left than the reading of the telegrams. So he took it on himself to enliven the proceedings by walking round the guests proclaiming, "What a day to be married! 21st June. Longest day – shortest night. What a day! What a day to be married!!" The hilarity generally was raised several levels, thus showing that, despite the occasion being somewhat formal, with Victorian overtones, it was in no sense straight-laced.

'Mr and Mrs Tucker then left…among a perfect flurry of good wishes…The honeymoon is to be spent on a motoring tour through England.' Well, that is what the Paper said. In fact, rather predictably, the tour was to be in Devon. Predictable because Pat thought that Devon, his County, had no equal in England, or anywhere else in this world. He was never happier than when he had that good red soil beneath his feet and before his eyes. He wanted to show it to, and share it with his new wife. Not that Dorothy was in any sense a stranger to Devon, but she certainly saw it from then on in quite a different light.

Brides are often nervous at what they have let themselves in for. Bridegrooms, too, for that matter. Dorothy had another cause for being nervous. When he drove the Vauxhall away on the first leg of their journey (it had been leant to them by Jennie) it was the first time Pat had ever driven a car. He was an experienced motor cycle driver, which must have help him with the general principles of driving, but he had never previously been at the wheel of a car. He insisted on driving the whole time, and rarely exceeded thirty miles per hour in his concern for Dorothy's comfort and safety.

They went first for just the one night to the Haven Hotel at Sandbanks. Only five or six miles for a first effort, and probably enough for both of them. It gave time for a leisurely dinner – of consommé, sole bonne femme, roast duckling new potatoes and peas, asparagus, strawberries and cream, petits fours and dessert. That is known because Pat kept their signed menu. The following morning, not very early, but before they were ready to leave, there was a knock at their bedroom door. Pat opened it and outside there was a member of the hotel staff with a drop-side cot. It was never known if this was simply an error by the housekeeper, or the work of some friendly wag. Whichever it was, they had a good laugh and took it as a good omen.

Dorothy and her Bridesmaids
(Left to right, back row)
Florrie Reid (Evans), Dorothy, Hilda Cartwright (Waring)
(Left to right, front row)
Mary Hibbs, Toff, Phyllida, Joan King (Scott).

Pat and Dorothy –
an informal moment between formal poses
in the garden of the third Chingri Khal,
21st June, 1929.

It was not only the menu which Pat retained. He kept all the receipts from their honeymoon hotels. Their one night at the Haven seems to have been rather expensive (£5. 17s. 3d.). Then to the Victoria Hotel at Sidmouth (the drive took from Noon to 5pm and it can hardly be more than about 70 miles, perhaps less: slow and careful driving indeed) where they stayed five nights. That cost Pat £15. 14s. 0d. – much better value, even if they did charge extra for fruit (6d. a day) and strawberries and cream (1/10 on two days and 1/11 on a third.) Visits were paid to old haunts of his at Ladram Bay and Exeter. Their next port of call was the Palace Hotel, Torquay (four nights: £12. 9s. 6d.) Visits again to old haunts, of hers this time, at Bantham and Thurlstone. Then two nights at Two Bridges Hotel on Dartmoor (£3. 16s. 11d.) followed by one night at The Royal Hotel, Bideford (£1. 18s. 8d.) and finally five nights at the Runnacleave Hotel, Ilfracombe (£13. 16s. 5d.) Many well-known North Devon beauty spots were within reach, including Clovelly, Appledore, Westward Ho! Lynton, and, perhaps the most haunted of all, Woolacombe. On 9th July they returned to Bournemouth. They had been away for eighteen nights in six different establishments at a total cost of £53. 12s. 9d., or just under £3. 0s. 0d. a night for the two of them. And the car was unscathed.

But being back at Bournemouth did not mean being in their own home. The flat was not yet ready, so they were staying at Chingri Khal. The very next day they went to Maples in London to select some more furniture. Other domestic equipment had to be obtained, servants to be sought, interviewed and engaged and much else to be done. It was not until four weeks to the day after their return from Devonshire that Pat and Dorothy started their move from Chingri Khal into Hereford House, that is it took place on Tuesday, 6th and Wednesday 7th August, 1929.

This was, in truth, the moment at which the honeymoon ended and reality had to be faced.

CHAPTER 26

THE MARRIAGE STAKES

I
N MOST, IF NOT ALL, marriages that are successful there has had to be a good deal of adaptation on the part of both husband and wife. And usually it will have been the wife who has had to undertake the greater amount of that adapting. Particularly where, as so often was the case before the Second War, the husband is the only breadwinner. He has to carry on as before in factory, office – or surgery – and the changes in his life are mainly confined to his off duty hours.

This was certainly true in the case of Dorothy and Pat. For him the changes in his lifestyle were wholly beneficial. His own home 'over the shop,' run by his devoted bride, was almost beyond comparison with a small room in a private hotel or guest house which had hitherto been his lot. Inevitably it was a bit more expensive to run such an establishment, as compared to the charges of a modest hotel, especially as at that time they had at least one, maybe two servants, but that extra expense was not beyond his means. It was certainly well worth the outlay.

Inevitably he had far more female chatter in his private life than before, but most of that would be with Dorothy. He was very much in love with her, they were very good friends and had much in common. If it was a price at all, it was a small price to pay for the new comfortable life at Hereford House. Furthermore Dorothy did all she could to cosset him. She was always acutely aware of the nature and extent of his wartime injuries, and that he became very physically tired on account of them. So, for instance, in an era when professional families usually dressed for dinner (black tie) she said they would not do so. She was an excellent carver, having acquired that ability as the eldest daughter, and the one most often at home. It involved standing at the carving table or sideboard, so she continued

429

to carve in order that Pat could be seated as much as possible. There was only one telephone number for Hereford House, a switching arrangement causing it first to ring in the professional part during professional hours. When the telephone rang in the domestic part, whether during or out of surgery hours, Dorothy always answered it. In theory this was 'because it might be a patient,' but saving Pat the effort also played a part. Even if he were in the same room as the instrument when it rang, and she in another, he would never pick it up, daytime, night time, week-end or whatever, she would come post haste to answer.

An objective observer would conclude that Pat did very well out of the changes resulting from his marriage.

From Dorothy's point of view the position was rather different. To understand why it is necessary to describe in a little detail the home into which she moved. 'The Flat' was the most unflat flat it would be possible to imagine. The oldest part of Hereford House comprised the western half of an early Victorian building, which had originally been one dwelling. The original staircase was in the eastern half of the house. When the building was converted into two more or less equal parts a staircase to the western half had to be built. This was achieved by gutting most of the rear half of the building, creating a void, almost square in cross-section, and running the full three stories high.

The staircase was built around this void: seven steps up, turn right, six steps up, right again, seven steps up and you were on the first floor landing. Here were the drawing room and dining room. Repeat the same process to get to the top landing, off which were three bedrooms. To make up for some of the space lost in building this space-wasting staircase, a small extension to the rear had been built, comprising kitchen and scullery on the first floor, bathroom and lavatory on the second. Access to these 'offices' was from the main staircase. After the second flight of steps, six in number, one could turn left instead of right, and up five steps to the kitchen. Ceilings in the rear extension being lower than in the main house, when that process was repeated on the next level up the additional steps to the bathroom were only two. Thus from dining room to kitchen it was seven steps down and five up, from bedroom to bathroom it was seven steps down and two up. The whole domestic part being confined to the first and second floors.

Not very long before Pat bought the practice, Deane Webb had moved it from premises in The Square to Hinton Road. To house it, he built a substantial extension to the west of the Victorian building in what must have been its garden. With typical perversity he did not ensure that the new first floor level corresponded with the old. Main access both to the new professional part as well as to The Flat were through the same front door, which was in the westernmost bay of the old building. Double doors further in opened to the bottom of the stair well. The rest of the ground floor of the old building was a waiting room in the front and dental workshops at the back, and part of a large hallway – more wasted space.

On the outside at the front there was a very small garden area, a little grass, a few flowerbeds and much privet and euonymus hedging. Deane Webb thought that patients did not like to be seen going to the dentist, so he did his best to screen the front door from the road. At the back the arrangements were unusual and curious. Upper Hinton Road runs steeply up from Hinton Road, being about at second floor level at the back of Hereford House. Steps ran all the way down to give access to the back of the surgeries. At first floor level a bridge spanned the back yard and gave access to the domestic kitchen. The garden itself was not far from vertical. The first third was quite vertical, being a brick wall supporting a pathway, the second third was a very steep grassy bank, also with a pathway on top, the third third was a sloping area, in the main thickly covered with evergreen bushes. Technically, none of these grounds were included in Pat's lease. Deane Webb sent a man around now and then to mow the grass and clip the hedges. In practice Pat and Dorothy did a little to the garden in the early years, being careful not to make their work too obvious: Deane Webb could have objected to anything he did not like. At both sides they were completely overlooked, and the areas were far too small and inconvenient for any sort of sitting out to enjoy any sunshine.

When first built Hereford House would have had quite a fine situation. Hinton Road runs behind and a little above Westover Road, in which had been built a rather prestigious row of early

Victorian villas, each with a significant garden front and rear. Hereford House would have overlooked the back gardens of those villas, over their roofs and on to the central gardens, the sea and to the Purbeck Hills and Old Harry Rocks. By the 1920s all of those villas had been demolished to make way for a high-class commercial street of shops and various places of entertainment. While some attempt was made to make the appearance of this development reasonably agreeable from the central gardens, no thought at all was given to how it looked from the other side. From Hinton Road the buildings could only be described as very, very ugly, made no more pleasant by the long, relatively low shed-like structure that was the 'Old' Westover Cinema. From the top floor of The Flat it was still possible, just, to see over the tops of these hideous buildings to the sea. That came to an end in 1935 with the building of the 'New' Westover Cinema which put a huge, boldly pointed brick wall almost directly in front of Hereford House, and truncating the shed-like structure, the remnant of which is still there and in commercial use.

It must be acknowledged, of course, that many a first time home for a newly married couple has less going for it than the flat. Nevertheless it was a considerable come-down from the space, both inside and out, at Chingri Khal. Dorothy once told me that she had "felt almost imprisoned in the place" at times in the first years, but "we were very happy together, so it didn't really matter." That feeling must have been brought about in no small measure by being so close to Pat's workplace.

For her life style, unlike that of Pat, was not made any easier by 'living over the shop.' For him it brought domestic comforts instantly within reach. For her it meant treating her home for what it was, a professional household which must be kept quiet for those professional purposes. Chingri Khal had not only been an open house, with friends dropping in more or less as and when they wished, it was also a rather noisy one. Not in an unpleasant way, but an impromptu game of tennis, or coffee break might be followed by gramophone records being put on, or the piano being played, or Dorothy might sing a few songs. Nothing of that sort could take place while there were patients in the house. It had to be silent, silent as the morgue, if possible, while they were around. And when they had gone, Pat was tired. Although in later years he grew to like music a bit, he was not at all a music lover when first married (perhaps because as a small boy he had been made to try to learn the violin for a short time with complete lack of success.) The last thing he wanted then, when off duty as it were, was to have to listen to the piano, a record, or any singing in the only room in which he could relax. And so piano playing and singing became almost activities of the past. They had been quite an important part of her life, and accomplishments which had meant a lot to her, and their curtailment was a considerable wrench for Dorothy.

In addition to her new husband, whom she adored, marriage brought into Dorothy's life two other men who were not quite such good news. The first was her father-in-law. Bert was not an easy man. He did not have a placid and relaxed temperament. He was a clever man, a fine mathematician and an able Solicitor, and had made his place in the world through his own effort and ability. In Edith he had found an ideal wife. In no way presenting any sort of intellectual challenge to him, she ran his home smoothly and efficiently. She put up with his ill-tempered complaints about various aspects of her housekeeping, many of them entirely unjustified and probably due to some error on his own part. She was submissive and did not answer back. That suited him. He could cope with a woman like that.

But he found in his daughter-in-law a rather different woman: an intellectual as well as an intelligent woman. Such a woman he really did not trust. Probably she made him feel vulnerable, sensing as he did that she was as clever as he. Their relationship was difficult. And bridge made it more so. Bert and Edith both played the game, Edith on a rather hit-and-miss basis, Bert more astutely.

They lived far enough away from the newly-weds for visits to be rather well spaced out through the year. But they did take place as Pat's only break from his work. Not much of a break at that, really: their 'week-end' tended to be from after lunch on Saturday (there were patients in the morning) to Sunday evening. And there were also visits the other way. A rubber of bridge was frequently played, but it was always awkward, and became more so. Bert was a very bad loser, and his temper would get much on edge when he lost. And in particular he did not like losing to a woman. Dorothy's play, like that of Pat, was careful and skilful, and Bert knew enough about the game to realise that Dorothy was into the finer points of play to a much greater extent that he was, even with his mathematical ability.

These occasional evenings of bridge got more and more uncomfortable until, on one occasion when he was outplayed by Dorothy who had played her hand to considerable effect, there was a bit of an outburst. He got very angry and accused her of "only playing in order to win." The gathering broke up in a degree of disarray and some distress. And Pat, who greatly admired his father and, as we have seen, was inclined to do his father's will to the letter, found himself having to say that he would not allow Bert to play bridge with them again.

But at least Bert was eighty miles away in Exeter. And moreover Edith was always a great friend and much loved by both Dorothy and Pat. By contrast the other new man in Dorothy's life was much more on the spot. He could hardly have been more closely on the spot. He was their landlord, Deane Webb.

Godfrey Deane Webb was first registered as a dentist in October, 1878. He had no qualifications then, but was enabled to register because he was 'in practice on 22nd July, 1878.' In 1881 he obtained the Irish qualification of LDS, RCS (Ireland). Why Ireland? I have no means of knowing. There was nothing Irish about him at all. He was, outwardly at any rate, a very typical English Victorian gentleman. Of medium height, spare of build, by his seventies he was still brisk in his walk, grey haired but only very slightly bent, always formally dressed and with a rather forced mirthless laugh. He was a bachelor and of considerable affluence. He had arrived in Bournemouth in time to be able to make shrewd investments in properties in this new, and rapidly expanding seaside resort. Not on the scale of the really big landowners, such as the Meyrick or Cooper-Dean estates, but significant all the same. That shrewdness, coupled with a tight-fisted nature, secured for him ample resources for moving in the best of Bournemouth society.

That he did move in such society there can be no doubt. In 1910

Bournemouth celebrated its first centenary. A book, *Bournemouth 1810-1910*, was written by the Borough Librarian and a Magistrate to commemorate the event. Deane Webb's copy of the book has inscribed on the flyleaf: 'To G. Deane Webb Esquire with affectionate regards from Merton & Annie Russell Cotes. 3rd February, 1912.' Sir Merton and Lady Russell Cotes, as two of the only four Honorary Freemen of the Borough, were probably at the pinnacle of the Bournemouth social scene. They were the donors to the town of the Russell Cotes Art Gallery and Museum, the owners of the Royal Bath Hotel, and he sometime Mayor of the Town. And Deane Webb was the recipient of their affectionate regards. He could hardly have climbed higher up the social ladder, with the economic resources to be seen when and where he should be seen, and the prestige which went with an opulently run dental practice.

His home was at 10, Bath Road, in what must have been one of the earliest surviving house in Bournemouth. It was a two storied, stucco finished, early nineteenth century house, set in its own reasonably sized garden, about a hundred yards from the sea at the pierhead. My recollections of it are of a gloomy, depressing establishment, but I now realise that it would have had great potential to be made into a bright, cheerful and attractive home. Modern improvements have swept it away to make space for a car park. In Deane Webb's time it was largely hidden from view behind its thick screen of euonymus and other dark green shrubs and trees which pleased – and suited – his saturnine temperament. Among the many other properties he owned was the next-door house, 12, Bath Road, a taller, rather more gaunt building, from a slightly later period, rather in the style of Hereford House.

To run his home for him he had a housekeeper, Miss Carter. Louis Carter had been his chief receptionist and assistant in that branch of his dental practice, which he had once carried on in Welbeck Street in London. In his Bournemouth practice the same functions had been performed by Ellen Noble, a formidable old lady – at least she was old by the time I knew her, and was certainly older than Miss Carter – known simply as Ellen. Ellen was installed in the basement flat at number 12, Bath Road, together with Beatrice Thorne, her niece. Although she spent almost all the year in Bournemouth,

Beatrice's home, that is where 'Mum' (Ellen's sister) lived with the rest of her family, was in Worcester.

It was generally believed by Pat and Dorothy that both Miss Carter and Ellen had provided services, in London and Bournemouth respectively, which were outside the normally recognised extent of assistance in the running of a dental practice. There was, as a result, a good deal of tension between these two ladies, one being within the master's fold, the other consigned to the basement next door.

The move of the dental practice from The Square to Hereford House seems more or less to have coincided with Deane Webb's retirement from practice. He was by then close to seventy years old. His registered dental address was changed from The Square to 10, Bath Road in 1927 when Pat bought the practice from him. He never saw a patient at his home, but he did continue to see a patient occasionally at Hereford House, although he never retained any direct financial interest in the practice and any fees due to him simply went into the practice account. For that purpose, if for no other, he retained the key to the premises.

This enabled him to come and go as he pleased. In fact he retained an office in the new wing. The two rooms above the two ground floor surgeries were offices. One was Pat's, the other was used by Deane Webb, whether retained formally in the lease or not I am unable now to say. His coming into the professional part of the house was not a matter of much concern: many people were inevitably doing so all the working day. But he would also come into the private part of the house. Particularly when Pat and Dorothy were away. They would realise from something he said, or others said, that he had gone in there for a prowl round, seeing, as landlord, that nothing was happening of which might disapprove. There was, for instance, quite a to-do, a few years after they were married, when Pat and Dorothy were upbraided by an indignant Deane Webb because when redecorating they had painted a frieze blue, rather than leaving it white. White paint was what he liked, and was going to have, and they had to sign an undertaking to restore it to white if they ever left the house. As tenants with responsibility for interior decorations they were quite within their rights, and he had no right in law to make this demand.

In consequence Dorothy felt for many years that her home was not entirely her own. There was always this dictatorial figure in the background with the authority, real or assumed, to say what may and may not take place there. And for those who came regularly into the professional part there was nothing to stop any one of them from having a look around the domestic quarters if they so wished. Why Pat did not put a sensible lock on the communicating door between the professional and private halves of the house is almost beyond understanding. I expect the reason was part of the principle upon which he seems to have run the practice – "We must not upset Deane Webb."

For in truth the practice he had bought had been run on almost absurdly extravagant lines. The four principal rooms added by the 1926 extension were each quite spacious enough to be a surgery. If more thoughtful use had been made of the space given over to a large hall, there might even have been adequate accommodation for four dentists. Two would have had plenty of room to spread themselves. A sole practitioner had far more space than he could possibly need.

The staff was greater in number than really needed. There were two 'dental nurses', who were not really dental nurses at all. The were dressed in a smart uniform of dark blue dress, starched white apron and cap, with stiff-starched collar, cuffs and belt. Quite a performance it must have been to put it on. One of them was Beatrice, the niece of the formidable Ellen (who had retired by the time Pat took over,) the second was a woman called Gladys, and between them they opened the front door, answered the telephone and boiled the kettle to take hot water into the surgery. Yes, Deane Webb had built his extension for a dental practice without laying on hot water – only cold went to the basins in the surgeries. Neither of these assistants could undertake much work of the sort one is used to finding a dentist having at his elbow today from his dental nurse. Nor were they capable of secretarial work. A secretary was also employed. There were two dental mechanics in the workshop and usually an apprentice as well, and a cleaning lady came daily, completing the staff of seven on the payroll.

It made for a good show of five star facilities. But the combined outlay, especially when the top market rent was added, was hardly a sensible collection of overheads for Pat to shoulder, particularly once he was a married man, soon to be a family man, and unendowed with the fruits of successful speculation. So despite the outward show of some style, even opulence, and despite his popularity with his patients and skill at his work (which I believe he had), the reality was that money in his pocket was always in rather short supply.

In this somewhat unpromising set-up the young married couple began their life together. Changes in life style, awkward and in many ways unattractive accommodation, lack of privacy, a difficult landlord, and a need to be very careful with resources, all had to be faced and dealt with. But both Pat and Dorothy had one priceless asset to help them: each other, and the love each had for the other. That was to sustain them through all their years ahead.

CHAPTER 27

THE FIRST DECADE
(1)
FAMILY GAINS AND LOSSES

A QUESTION AROSE ABOUT the Rachals grand piano, given to Dorothy nearly twenty years before. Before they moved into Hereford House, Harry had said. "You will take your piano with you." But Pat and Dorothy demurred. They had only the one living room in the flat, and they thought it would be too small to allow a grand piano to take up so much space. In this they were wrong: some fifteen years later the grand piano was moved into the lounge at Hereford House without in any way overcrowding the room. Probably Pat's lack of enthusiasm for music played a part. But at this early stage they decided to leave it where it was.

"All right; I shall get Rachals to make you an upright," declared Harry. He was as good as his word. Sample veneers were sent from Hamburg for them to choose the style of the case. No doubt Harry sent a specification: it was not to be a piano for the tropics. He took himself to Germany to see Rachals and found a critical situation there. Writing to Colonel Wyness from Chingri Khal on 15th September that year he reported:

> [I] have returned from Germany where I found my friend Rachals in a very bad financial state and hardly likely to survive the change of fashion which rules his goods more or less out of the world. The other people seem to be carrying on but there is a long story of bankruptcies in that land of shattered ideals. Fashion makes and breaks even more than does religion – make a thing unfashionable [and] it is the same as preaching a blood-and-fire crusade.

The new piano duly arrived and was installed in the lounge in the flat. Sadly, it was the last piano made by Rachals. The slump caught up with him and he went out of business, never to restart it. It must have been something of a loss for Harry for whom Rachals had been a principal supplier, but his business continued for nearly thirty years. The new upright was not much used in its early years, but it came into its own after Sheila and I got married when it was loaned to her on a more or less permanent basis. It has never had a major overhaul and is rather worn out, but it still remains in the family; a good instrument of its type, with a fine, rich tone, and is yet another tribute to the workmanship in Rachals factory.

Meanwhile the newly-weds were getting down to the serious business of having their own home in which to entertain friends and relations. Two days after completing the move into the flat they had Harry and Jennie to dinner. A week later it was Phyllis and Jim. Three days after that it was the turn of Deane Webb, with whom they invited his half sister, Stella, and her husband, Mr Trevanion, a well-known solicitor in Poole, and for many years Clerk of the Peace for that Borough. And at the end of that week Bert and Edith came to stay for a night or two. The newly engaged servants must have wondered what had hit them, but I daresay the pace slowed down somewhat after the first flush of enthusiasm. There is usually plenty to enthuse over in the first few months after setting up home together, excitement for Dorothy and Pat being increased by the knowledge, which came to them around the time of their moving into Hereford House, that Dorothy had become pregnant on their honeymoon.

Such outward manifestations of that excitement as there may have been will have to be left to the imagination. There is no further record of what they did during that period. Dorothy was certainly determined that she would make the new baby a christening robe. Catholic tradition recommended baptism as soon as reasonably possible after birth, (it took place, in fact, on 21st April – before Dorothy was considered sufficiently recovered from the birth to attend) which would not leave enough time for making the garment from the start after its sex was known, so the job had to be begun before the birth. No question of guessing whether to do it in blue or pink, it had to be in white. One lesson she had learned very well indeed at the Convent was how to use needle and thread, a skill which lasted her until the last few months of her life. The result, just completed during her lying-in period, was an intricate and beautifully made robe which has been used for three generations.

Jennie was convinced she would never get it finished in time. So convinced that ultimately she took herself into one of the large stores in central Bournemouth and bought a pink satin ready-made robe. It has been handed down along with its hand-made rival. She need not have troubled: it has never been worn. Probably, however, it reflects the general assumption on both sides of the family, that the new baby would be a girl. Dorothy was sure of it. Not that she wanted a girl particularly, but there were her sister with three daughters, and her sister-in-law with two daughters, it seemed almost inevitable that she would have a daughter too.

It therefore came as a considerable surprise when, on 8th April, 1930, she gave birth to a boy. To have produced the first grandson on both sides of the family was no small achievement for the two of them, and they were thus able to bask in the general chorus of congratulations which ensued. In order to show due respect, or deference, to both grandfathers they called me Henry, after Harry, and John, after Albert John, and Martin, because they liked that name. It was a name with some associations with the family. Pat's mother's maiden name had been Martin. Dorothy was born at Martinmas. (A rarely used equivalent to Michaelmas, November 11th, in the old sanctoral cycle, being the feast of St. Martin of Tours, while November 12th was the feast of Pope St. Martin I. These two holy men are of some antiquity, having died in the years AD 397 and 655 respectively, the former especially being remembered in France.) Pat nearly put the kibosh on it, however, by saying to Dorothy "There have been a lot of famous Martins haven't there? Martin Luther, for instance." "What a thing to say to a good Catholic mother," came the retort – but they had a laugh and did not change their minds. Martin, the name to be used, was placed last, as I have subsequently been told, in order that I could hyphenate the surname with it if I had so wanted. I never have so wanted. Dorothy had in mind her bank account once being confused with that of another person of the same name. Quite a lot of foresight, perhaps, but resulting in formal documents, such as my Passport making me appear as 'Henry.' And I have never felt in the least like a 'Henry' – not even the Henry who features so much in these pages, although I daresay others might spot some connection. At least I have always been grateful to them for choosing 'John' rather than 'Albert' as the means by which to pay due respect to Bert – otherwise I should have been stuck with the acronym 'HAM' which I feel could have cultivated an image that I would not have welcomed.

It is a shame that there is nothing remaining in the family archives to indicate Harry's reaction to the news of the arrival of his first grandson (he was to have four more in all in due course.) Probably some pungent or witty comment was included with his genuine delight.

He had, of course, long been back in Calcutta when the event occurred. He had left to return to India on 9th October of the previous year by the P&O SS *Razmak*, joining her at Marseilles. There must have been a good deal of correspondence between him and his family in Bournemouth, but none of it has survived. There are available most of the letters he wrote to Colonel Wyness. The first of these, written on 12th November, 1929, after he got back gives us some idea of Harry's feelings about changes in India:

> …I can see the finish of the Europeans in India. That is, those of my class who work all their lives, have a permanent stake in the country, play the game and treat people properly. The day of the adventurer will return and the country may progress more under them than through the honest, if stodgy, efforts of salaried Europeans who hate to see innovations if they bring more work or risk pensions. Whatever any single man can do is so little that it isn't worth while wasting time with a bunch of bare-legged blatherers whose only outfit is brass and wind.

But the changes he perceived seemed to have improved his enjoyment of the journey out, and show that his views on the infamous *Ruahine* were in no sense merely prejudice against shipboard life:

The run out was pleasant. Fewer snobs than ever now: the political change had robbed most of the Purgatives from Purgatory of their self-esteem. There was little to find fault with regarding the bearing of officials who are just like ordinary folk now. A good job too. In this age of ball bearings over-bearing is out of place. Still the crowd on board were quiet, friendly, well-behaved, and, so far as the ladies went, without reproach. Of course the system of lighting the decks stays ardour, for it is only the class in lodgings who canoodle on the tops of buses. Full marks for the passengers on the *Razmak*.

Harry had lost none of his contempt for the European Association whose Annual General Meeting took place on 10th February. Writing next day to Colonel Wyness he included, for reasons which are somewhat obscure, a barbed lance in the direction of both the previous Governor of Bengal and the current Viceroy, in a typical diatribe:

> The Annual General Meeting of the European Association took place last evening. I knocked off work at tiffin time and sat down to drafting my speech when I attacked Lord Lytton and Lord Irwin, jibed at them for their failure to accomplish anything but scorn from the people they sought to placate. As Colonel Crawford told me deliberate lies last year over my election, I warned him he was 'for it' and he got it too. He looked as miserable as a glandered goat and, of course, couldn't reply. Those detailed to attack me couldn't. When remarks were made reflecting on anything I said, I shouted out and refused to accept them. The result was – a splendid effort. I think it was the finest speech I ever made, but there was a fat planter in one of the seats who was my greatest asset. I don't know his name, but he laughed until he rolled on the floor and of course enabled me to put in one or two hits which, not reported, hit just as hard.
>
> All the way through I have insisted that Gandhi is a blighter but I made no reference to him beyond accusing the European Association of making a business of being frightened by every bare-legged blatherer who can squirt out a few words in babu English. At any rate I had a wonderful reception and came away triumphant. Whenever I take on the downing of another seditious body, they will think twice before going for me.

He was writing again to Colonel Wyness on 29th April in which letter he tells him of a new venture in his life. Not, I may say, a word in it about the arrival of his grandson, although by then the news must have reached him by cable, but his new undertaking might have thrust it out of his mind.

> Did I tell you that I've taken on the management of Spence's Hotel as a Special Director? I sacked two men one after the other. The first was bowled out clean; the second nearly went to jail but he hopped it pretty quick when I told him to disappear. There being nobody else, I took it up and find it the finest sort of job in the world. Were I just 10 years younger what a hit I'd make in the job!

He made enough of a hit as it was. He was just coming up to his sixty-sixth birthday, an age at which many men – perhaps most men – are seriously thinking of retirement, if they have not already retired. This was a completely new venture for him. He did not give up the business of H. Hobbs & Co. and he retained his private address as well as having living-in accommodation, but he remained very much in charge of Spence's Hotel – the oldest Inn, he would say, in Asia – for three years at first, and then, after his visit home, until well after the Second World War, turning it round into a successful establishment. He ruled it with something like a rod of iron, ably assisted by Miss Briscoe. He would inspect the kitchens four times a day while she, in true spirit of Harry Hobbs, would take out her false teeth to harangue the servants in their own tongue. As Joan Scott now recalls, Spence's 'was [Harry's] pride and joy, and very pleasant to stay in. He used to go down to the markets and bazaars himself quite often to, pick out the best fruits, for instance, especially pomelos which <u>had</u> to come from a certain area.'

In addition to keeping the staff up to the mark, Harry had no use for dishonest guests, or those who, for whatever reason, would not, or did not pay their way. Writing to Colonel Wyness on 5th August he seems to be relishing his new work.

> Considering all things I am glad I never left off work. The ruin overshadowing England; the crushing taxation; the depression which grows would make me a miserable being. Now I can chuck my weight about, barge into any number of tin gods, watch my money

disappearing certainly, but less quickly than others'. Nevertheless my course of instruction in Spence's Hotel is staggering. It had never occurred to me that Europeans could live all their lives without the faintest knowledge of what honesty was. Talk about a gang of dacoits. They are like children brought up in brothels and who have no idea of morality. I've sacked seven thieving Europeans and given none of them a character. Some of the residents couldn't make out what dealing with a man like me was. They thought they were merely to stand on tiptoe and I should cower. The last to try that on was Stanley Oakes. That spotted specimen of a mixture of two inferior races 'terroarised' the staff. He had his food specially cooked; two special puddings for tiffin and dinner; a tin of fruit; asparagus four times weekly, and, to my surprise, he was paying 250 a month. Well, he sent in an 'ultimatum' and was staggered to find that the reply came, "Then you are taking the manager with you." So I sacked the manager and saw Oakes off. He will have to buy his food now. Curiously, I've known Oakes 37 years and never had a row with him. He knew it was no good trying to boss me, and when staff were instructed to say, "Please tell that to Mr. H." he was right up against the bulkhead. I wish he had given me an opportunity to choke him off, for he would have got it right in the neck.

There can be no doubt that it was not a good idea to get into Harry's bad books. Anyone who did was likely to have at least an uncomfortable time, quite likely a very difficult time with him, depending on the extent to which he or she may have been in thrall to Harry. No one would have been more acutely conscious of this than Dorothy. Her eight or nine months journeying with him could have left her in no doubt how thin the ice may suddenly become if he felt crossed.

No correspondence between Harry and anyone in Bournemouth during the early thirties has survived, and his occasional letters to Colonel Wyness only rarely, and briefly, mention his family. Pat and Dorothy were still relishing life together, and life with the added bonus of parenthood. Pat could get quite sentimental, particularly at special times for the family. For the recipient things written on such occasions are almost always much treasured, although subsequently, in the cold light of another day, they may appear slushy, or even insincere, to another reader. I do not believe there was the slightest insincerity in the message Pat wrote to Dorothy on their first Wedding Anniversary. Dated 21st June, 1930, it was obviously written to accompany a bouquet he had arranged for a florist to send to Chingri Khal where they were staying, probably for the week-end. It shows the strength of his feelings, which I do not doubt were fully reciprocated.

> A few flowers, Darling, wishing you many happy returns of the day and to tell you again how much I love you and realise how much I owe to you for all this last wonderful year.
> You have been such a wonderful wife and now are a wonderful mother, so we two boys will try so hard to make your life happier and happier.
> My love darling always   your own   Pattie

That year there was no Harry to complicate matters. Indeed he did not come home in 1930, nor in 1931, nor in 1932. Quite why that was so is nowhere stated in any existing document. Letters to Colonel Wyness show that he took himself to Darjeeling for two to three weeks in the worst of the very hot weather – he would usually say not for long enough – and one is left guessing why he did not make the trip home more often. My own guess is twofold. First he had the new responsibility of running Spence's Hotel and may have felt unable to take quite so much time away from his duties as would be entailed by coming to England. And then there was Miss Briscoe. Not only was she probably rather possessive where he was concerned, as demonstrated in her letters from the 1920s, but to him she probably appeared a much more youthful and attractive companion. He had been sixty-five soon after Pat and Dorothy were married. By then Jennie would have been close to seventy, and looking an old lady, although still perfectly vigorous and, in the main, healthy. Miss Briscoe was probably still under fifty. Domestic life may well have been more congenial to him in Calcutta than in Bournemouth.

446

However, by the summer of 1933 Harry's first commitment to Spence's Hotel came to an end. He resigned his seat on the Board, but remained a resident as he had a considerable disagreement with the landlord of his private apartment. In his diary for 15th May and later he wrote:

'Yesterday, Sunday, I decided to move from [4] Esplanade [East] to the premises formerly occupied by Thomas Cook & Son, 9, Old Court House Street...If there are regrets about breaking with associations extending to thirty two years, there are compensations. The landlord of No. 4 is a wall-eyed Bengali, classified even by his compatriots as a "very bad man," hates the English, but loves their money. His agent called on me and admitted that Mitra (the landlord) was "very much agitated" at the idea of an empty house, so I shall refrain from shaking him up too suddenly by keeping the unpleasant news from his ears until his eyes have seen the flitting of my crowd...Had the landlord been decent I would have remained, but he is one of the new type of Bengali who looks upon rudeness as a sign of fitness for self-government. At the end of this month he won't consider it quite so profitable.'

It was more often his fellow Europeans with whom he fell out. His relationships with Indians tended to be very good indeed, especially those who, in one way or another, looked to him for employment or support. This is clearly demonstrated in Harry's graphic account of his departure from Spence's in his diary entry written 'About 150 miles north-west of Port Said' on 29th May, 1933:

Then there were the goodbyes. Men came from all sides. Newspapermen wanted to write me up, and by threat of libel actions I dodged being done to death in that manner. Then the Babus wanted chits. Now it happens that I put a touch of originality into a testimonial and two of the Babus – Majumdar and Probodh, who have treated me well, had their eyes come out of their heads like organ stops when they read the nice things I wrote about them. My fame spread. Everybody wanted chits. Eighteen were through when I shut down. The head cook – Kanai – ...blushed like a girl when I handed him a splendid testimonial, shook hands and thanked him for all he had done. It went round that my chits read better than the

Bible or the Koran and much disappointment was evident when I could write no more.

...It was hot and trying and by the time I reached the station – 5 p.m. – I was just about cooked. The office staff of Spence's Hotel presented me with a gold mounted Swan pen with a letter of appreciation. Then all the cooks, *durwans* and *khitmagars*, bearers and sweepers stood outside to wish me a sad farewell. It will be long before they have a man who treats them like human beings. The barman who met with a bus accident and broke his wrist walked two miles to the Station to pay his salaams. I thanked him, gave him a rupee to pay his taxi fare back, but his eyes were full of tears when he departed. Then a *khit*, whose twelve years old daughter had fallen off a verandah and no hospital would take her until I paid 25/- for the ambulance to take her there – he came to pay his respects. I hung about until the train started while my boots filled with sweat and then took off my clothes (having a coupe to myself) got into pyjamas and singlet and did not change until we reached Bombay.

The staff need not have worried; he was back in the saddle soon after his return. By the end of 1937 he was congratulating himself on seven years as 'Managing Director' of the hotel.

Harry's passage home in 1933 was on the P&O *SS Ranchi*, a sister ship to the *Rawalpindi* upon which Dorothy had made her journey to India in 1925. She and Pat had not had any holiday since their honeymoon four years earlier, so they decided it was an opportunity to give themselves one by going to meet Harry at Marseilles and returning with him in the *Ranchi* to Tilbury. By then they had a full time Nanny, in whose care I was doubtless left, whether at Hereford House or Chingri Khal memory no longer tells me. They crossed from Southampton to Le Havre and thence train to Paris. A night, perhaps two, with the Hickeys was followed by train to Marseilles. They joined the ship on 3rd June, she sailed early the next morning and they were in Tilbury by 9th June. Six nights on board, some excellent food, and a few hours ashore in Gibraltar gave them a worthwhile break.

Harry was in England for four months, for nearly all that time at

Chingri Khal. And probably during most of his stay he was relaxing and enjoying family life. Writing to Colonel Wyness on 28th July he paints rather a happy and relaxed picture:

> …Am well. Went to London for 2 days and have rested, loafed, read, made notes, watched the grandchildren play, smoked Burmas (only 4 a day against 16 when I was a man) played billiards, called to see nobody, had 'flu and fever and recovered. A real holiday in weather too beautiful for words…and the whole run on that selfishness which cultivated to the nth degree spells comfort.

Not a whisper in any of his letters from that period (there are not, in truth, many of them) to suggest any domestic discontent. Nor do I recall any sort of row or rumpus at Chingri Khal during his time there at all. Only one, perhaps – and do I remember it, or have I just been reminded by being subsequently told? – caused unwittingly by myself. Harry and Pat were playing billiards, the billiards room being on the first floor at the end of a longish corridor, and then a couple of steps down to a polished floor. I ran excitedly along the corridor to see their game, took the two steps down at a leap, landed on a loose rug which shot across the floor, my feet went up in the air and my head crashed backwards on to the step I had so unwisely descended. Much bawling and many tears, comfort from Daddy and fury from Grandpa at idiots who left loose rugs on polished floors. But he might have paused to consider how many times he had walked over that rug without thinking of removing it.

No sign, therefore, of lack of domestic harmony. It is true that we – that is, the grandchildren – always called the two principal bedrooms, at opposite ends of the first floor, "Grandpa's bedroom" and "Granny's bedroom." We accepted that without question. It may have had little significance in itself. More married couples then had separate bedrooms as a matter of course than perhaps is so today. It may have had little significance.

At this time Jimmy was first at Greenwich and then at Dartmouth, and so Phyllis and my three cousins were permanently living at Chingri Khal. I was frequently taken there, and consequently Harry saw a great deal of all his grandchildren, and we of him. I wish I had a fuller recollection of that time. I had only turned three years old a

449

Dorothy holding Martin, 1932.
Pat's favourite photograph:
he kept a copy in his wallet.

*Dorothy and Pat
on board* SS Ranchi,
early June, 1933.

couple of months before his arrival. Although I can dimly recall my third birthday, my memories of Harry from that time are hardly worthy of that title. A cheerful, rather loud, and a somewhat awe-inspiring old man sitting at the head of the dining room table, rather larger than life, who told us stories that made us (and him) laugh and who made up doggerel nonsense songs for each of us, is about all I can honestly say I remember.

Other incidents have been mentioned to me over the years, which help to make me believe that I remember more than in reality I do. He was certainly the provider of the wherewithal to buy ice creams. The Walls Ice Cream man, with his tricycle and its blue and white cold box in front with 'Stop Me and Buy One' boldly displayed, would regularly be stationed at Five Ways, the junction of Queen's Park Avenue with the main Charminster Road, some two to three hundred yards away. If we heard the cheerful jangle of his bell (not the monstrous electronic things of today) Elizabeth and I would go and stand in front of Harry, wriggle and look hopeful. He would get the message, emit a guffaw of laughter, fish in his pocket and produce two one-penny pieces. Instant transports of delight, and we would run off to buy our favourite snow fruits, a sort of water ice in a triangular cardboard tube, about six inches long, and just a penny each.

But perhaps the single most reliable indication of his summer at home is to be found in the photograph which was taken by Pat on Harry's sixty-ninth birthday party, 21st July. He is sitting in the garden of Chingri Khal, cheroot between his fingers, with all four grandchildren around him. You could not hope for a more relaxed and contented group.

When, in mid October, the time came for Harry to return to Calcutta he did not find departure any less sad and difficult than had so often been the case in the past. In his diary for 7th November, after arriving back, he wrote:

> It was hard lines leaving. Little Elizabeth Ann made a dramatic show, the more effective because it was unconscious. She walked in, jumped on my lap, hugged me for a couple of minutes and silently walked away with her head down. I went in half an hour later to kiss her while she was asleep. Then patted poor Binkie [a springer spaniel

belonging to Phyllis] who didn't know he was losing a good pal, and that if a thousand sahibs walked up the drive, this one won't be he.

I find it hard to believe that his final sentence was anything more than a recognition that it would be a long time – certainly in a dog's life – before he was again 'a sahib walking up the drive.' One could, however, look upon it as prophetic. For Harry never again even so much as saw Chingri Khal.

After such a happy stay – for that is what it would appear to have been – it may seem a little strange that he never paid another visit before the coming of war greatly altered everybody's lives. He was approaching seventy, he had resigned from the Board of Spence's Hotel, he could keep his business going, or sell it, and all his Indian assets for that matter, and live in some comfort in Bournemouth. The climate may have played a part. He had not experienced an English winter since he first went to India in 1883. It seems he was lucky in the summer of 1933 in finding much warm sunshine to enjoy, but he would have been under no illusions as to what it could be like at other times of the year. And there is just no telling how much influence Miss Briscoe may have had in causing him, in effect, to stay in India rather than to retire to England. Other events in the coming years may suggest themselves as further reasons for his continuing to live in India.

That autumn and winter history was repeating itself for Pat and Dorothy. Just as she had become pregnant on her honeymoon so, it would seem, she had become pregnant on their short holiday on the *Ranchi*. If not then, it was certainly very soon after. Her second child was expected, not long before my fourth birthday, at about Easter time, which was early that year, Easter Sunday being 1st April. No christening robe causing any panic this time. She had already embroidered my initials upon it, and the new baby's could be similarly added at her convenience once names were decided after birth.

So they waited in confident expectation, but also wondering quite where this new arrival would take them. The flat at Hereford House was just about big enough for the three of us, but a fourth would surely make it too small. They had one bedroom, the one or two servants, together with Nanny, had another, and the smallest of the three bedrooms was mine, and really only big enough for one – at any rate for any length of time. Change would certainly be needed. But there was no hurry. Time enough to make any real plans after the event.

The same team was booked to look after Dorothy in her home confinement as had been in attendance in 1930. The family doctor, Dr Leslie Spinks, would be there, and also Nurse Hughes, the midwife who had helped in the delivery of myself and of two of my cousins. An experienced team in whom they all had confidence. Nurse Hughes would be living in, and so my room would be needed for her and the new arrival. When things started to warm up I would be taken to Chingri Khal until there was once again room for me at home. Pat would make do with a camp bed in the dining room.

And this was the plan of action which came into effect in the middle of Holy Week. On Wednesday, 28th March – Spy Wednesday it is sometimes called, as being the day of the betrayal by Judas – Dorothy went into labour, and by evening time the second stage had been very quick and easy and there, placed in her arms was – a baby boy. Another son! Great delight all round. Pat, doubtless, was quickly by her side. "Both fine," he was told.

Next day, Maundy Thursday, I was taken to see my mother and my new baby brother. In the unenlightened customs of those days he was in a cot in the next door room – my room. I had a look at him: just a little baby. Probably the first I had ever properly seen. Then some time with Dorothy in her room before it was time to go back to Chingri Khal for lunch. "I'll just have another look at the baby," I said, and went next door. The baby looked exactly the same as before. Not terribly exciting for a four-year-old, that would probably come later, but another glimpse – 'till the next time.

On Good Friday morning Dorothy was handed the baby to try a feed, perhaps, or just for a cuddle. As she held him she thought something was not as it should be. She was quite experienced with young babies, having been close to her sister when her nieces were very young, as well as having had one of her own. What had she seen?

Head held awkwardly? Movements of arms or legs not natural? Bad colour? Laboured breathing? It gave her a cold knot of fear in the pit of her stomach as she said to the midwife, "Nurse Hughes, there's something wrong with this baby."

There would have been no surgery for Pat that day so he was on hand to telephone to summon the doctor. But the doctor gave no comfort. There was, indeed, something very wrong, and nothing could be done to put it right. As the awful realisation dawned on her she thought of only one thing. "Pat, if he's not going to live, he must be baptised at once."

Baptism was probably the last thing on Pat's mind at that moment of emotional turmoil, but he was enough at one with Dorothy to realise how much it meant to her. Good Friday is a busy day in most Churches, and would have been particularly so in the principal Catholic Church in Bournemouth. But at least the Jesuits had several priests in residence there. Pat, despite his now closer acquaintance with the Church, was not one of its greatest admirers, but even he was impressed by the speed at which the response to his call came. It seemed he had hardly put down the receiver when there was a ring at the doorbell and a priest was there.

The feelings of Dorothy and Pat can only be imagined, not described, as the little heartrending ceremony took place in their bedroom in which the Sacrament of Baptism was administered to the dying baby and he came into the Christian family. They chose the names Justin Richard. I have no idea why. Perhaps they hardly knew why themselves. Nurse Hughes, presumably present, most probably was wondering whether she could have acted in any different way during the confinement. And the doctor; was he there? Did he go back to the Wednesday in his mind and ask himself if all this could have been avoided?

Justin lived just one more night. On Holy Saturday his breathing failed and his short life came to an end.

Inter cranial haemorrhage, it was called, and haemorrhage into the fourth ventricle owing to rapid second stage. In other words, a perfectly healthy little boy fatally injured in the last few moment before and during his birth. I do not believe there were recriminations against the team, although Dorothy always believed it was her doctor's fault. He retired soon afterwards and a replacement was needed and found. Pat had to go to Chingri Khal to tell Jennie, and doubtless to tell me as well. I do not recall any great display of grief. I do not doubt that both Pat and Dorothy grieved deeply, particularly as they may have thought it was the last chance – as, indeed, it proved to be – for Dorothy to have a second child.

Unlike (as I suspect) both Dorothy and Pat, I had not bonded in any sense with my brother, (in an almost uncanny experience I find I have bonded with him much more in thinking about him for the purposes of this book,) and took his death as a rather flat, factual event. The Catholic Church has a simple funeral service for very young children and that must have taken place some time in Easter week. I was not present, which is something I now regret. Today children are not insulated from family events, happy or sad, but it was then evidently thought I should not be involved with something which might 'upset' me. Little Justin was buried in a tiny plot in the Catholic corner of the Central Cemetery in Bournemouth. Once or twice over the ensuing years Dorothy took me to visit his grave. She would always refer to him as "your baby brother" and never as "Justin." I never asked her why.

But life had to go on. My fourth birthday was the following Sunday, Low Sunday as it was – very low for my poor parents. Again, I do not recall any blighted occasion. They were unselfish in seeking to preserve an outward show of normality, which may have made it all the harder for the two of them. Phyllis would have sympathised, Jennie, with her history, would have understood only too well, but it was to each other that they looked for mutual comfort and support, and they did not look in vain.

One consequence of this disaster was that it removed any need for moving out of Hereford House. If they had had any thoughts, let alone plans, for a change, they were put aside. We fitted into the flat, just about; there were some real benefits from continuing 'over the shop' and Chingri Khal remained nearby.

It was not that Hereford House was anything other than a very happy home, but it would be unrealistic not to recognise that there were inevitably some things it lacked: space inside, garden outside and company for me. I grew up enjoying the benefits of being an only child, such as undivided attention from parents, while the disadvantages were much ameliorated by being so frequently at Chingri Khal in the company of my cousins. They were close to being three older sisters, and at Chingri Khal I played endlessly with them, sometimes on my own. Indoors and out, in the nursery, in the music room, in the billiards room, on the lawns, in the wood. Oh! especially in the wood where we had trees and thickets, open spaces and hiding places, paths uphill and paths down, hammocks, and ropes, and – well just about everything imaginative children need to keep themselves absorbed for hours on end. Visitors came and went in considerable numbers. We had the occasional bacon and egg party round a bonfire in the wood (that wonderful smell!) One birthday there was a garden party with a Punch and Judy show. The whole place wove a magic spell for me which has never gone away.

On the way from the back door up some steps into the wood there stood a large wooden building, which served as dogs' kennels, and next to it was a chicken house and chicken run. The kennels were put to good use when Phyllis acquired a mate, Rosie, for her springer spaniel, Binkie, and bred a litter of pups. Six there were in all, three dogs and three bitches. One of the dog puppies was given to me for my fifth birthday. Jip soon endeared himself to us all, but perhaps especially to Dorothy. She was the one who gave him most of his needs – his meals, his walks and his groomings – and so got the greatest response from him of us all.

It was at about this time that the Local Authority decided to change the numbering in Queen's Park Avenue. Chingri Khal had been number 15 from the first; now it became number 23. Not a big change, it may appear, but a sign of the times. We should now say that the density of houses in Queens Park Avenue was to increase. It was a hint of the much more drastic changes which would come in due time.

From 1930 Bert had been a sole practitioner, with offices at 5, Cathedral Close, Exeter, which, although not large, were fairly prestigious premises almost next door to Mol's Coffee House. He attained the age of 65 years in 1931 and a couple of years or so after that took in a partner. Robert Hilton had only been admitted in 1932 and no doubt thought he had done quite well for himself on getting a partnership with so senior a colleague.

By 1935 Bert evidently thought he could take time off to give himself and Edith a good long holiday. With that in mind he booked for the two of them to go on a Mediterranean cruise. Cruising was not so widespread then as now. Few ships were built for that purpose. Rather it was the use to which the more elderly vessels were put when they had ceased to be viable competitors on the North Atlantic Run. The *SS Homeric* was just such a ship. At 750 feet in length she was large but not one of the largest of them. Built as the German *Columbus* she had been ceded to Britain and thence to the White Star Line soon after the end of the Great War, but had proved uneconomic on the ferry service to New York. From 1932 she was used solely for cruising, and by 1935 she was due to be scrapped. The three week cruise to the Eastern Mediterranean and Istanbul was to be her final voyage before she was laid up.

For reasons which are obscure, the departure of Bert and Edith on this doubtless pleasant, but hardly momentous holiday was treated as an occasion for a great family send-off. And so on 14th June we were all on board. Pat and Dorothy and myself on the one hand, Charles and Winnie and Betty on the other. Only Mary was unable to attend – probably at College. All dressed in our Sunday best, buttonhole for Bert, flowers for Edith, we assembled on the boat deck for a family group to be taken by Pat. One might have thought they were going away for three years rather than three weeks. But it was fun seeing all the big ships, I greatly enjoyed it all, and we waved until the *Homeric* was out of sight.

By 1st July she was on her way back, not long out of Catania, when Pat received a telegram: 'Dad very ill – Edith.' He assumed it meant his father was dead. He was right, as a second cable, received not long after the first, made clear. Apparently Bert had played a few games of quoits or deck tennis and then gone up to Edith, sitting on a deck chair nearby, lit his pipe and dropped dead in front of her. All very unexpected as well as shocking for the family and, indeed, for all those on board *Homeric*. Pat would have been prepared for Bert to have been buried at sea, but he was not consulted and his father's body was brought back to Southampton in a coffin – presumably she was a big enough a ship to carry one or two on board on a 'just in case' basis. The crew provided a twenty-four hour a day companion to look after Edith, who, understandably enough, was completely distraught.

So it was a sad second visit to Southampton which was made by Pat on the return of the *Homeric*, sailing up Southampton Water with her flag at half mast and unloading the coffin first of all, followed by Edith's disembarkation. The funeral took place soon afterwards at Exeter, both Pat and Dorothy obviously attending. I was not taken with them. Again, I would think, a mistake. I had been told of his death almost as soon as it was known, but was still considered too young to attend a funeral.

Despite the difficulties which had arisen between Bert and Dorothy, Pat was fond of his father and admired him greatly, so his sudden death, at the not very great age of sixty-nine, came as a considerable blow. The blow was made all the greater quite soon after the funeral when it became clear that Bert had carried forward his advance of £925 for the purchase of the dental practice as a debt owed by Pat to his estate. It had been understood by Pat that it had been an outright gift. The matter could not have been properly reduced to writing at the time, for there need surely have been no cause for misunderstanding. It was probably more fair to Winnie, the other ultimate residuary beneficiary, that regard should be paid to such a substantial advance on division of an estate which was not very big. It was the feeling that his father had not been frank and open with him which caused Pat to be sadly disillusioned.

But there was work to do; Edith had to be helped, the estate wound up, and the house in St. Leonard's Road sold. Edith took a lease of a flat on the top floor of Retreat House, a large Georgian house on the bank of the River Exe between Topsham and Exeter. It enjoyed magnificent views; south downriver to Exmouth, and west across the river and Exeter Ship Canal to the distant hills and tors of Dartmoor.

Over the years it proved to be a popular place for us to visit for the occasional short stay.

An additional benefit of having my cousins living so close at hand was that I was able to share their Governess with them. Miss Harries had been engaged by Phyllis to start off the education of Phyllida and Elizabeth and in due course I joined in. It involved a few hours on weekday mornings. She was a middle-aged lady, kind but firm, who gave us a good grounding in the three Rs. It put off for Pat and Dorothy any decisions about my education. One of the earliest surviving letters from Harry to our family – to Pat, rather unusually, he mostly wrote to Dorothy – mentions education.

> Don't be in too much of a hurry to send Martin to school. He will develop all the quicker if allowed to lie fallow for a year or so. I rather think there is too much schooling. Nothing can take the place of a good home.

I can only assume that this was written in response to hearing that I had been put in the care of Miss Harries instead of a more conventional school. Pat and Dorothy always felt a little uneasy as to how any decisions they took would be viewed by 'the Old Man' in Calcutta. His support and, even more, his praise was greeted as a welcome relief, his disapproval, or worse, could be very upsetting. So much depended on his good will in relation to Chingri Khal in particular. He frequently complained about the cost of keeping up the large house, and how it must be cut down. And then both Dorothy and Phyllis had allowances from him – Dorothy about half that of Phyllis, in view of the latter's much larger family – and these never appeared to be entirely secure.

Later, in a letter to Dorothy commenting on one aspect of Bert's death, he adds, 'I am writing a special letter to Martin by this mail so that he will grow to remember one of his grandfathers.' The letter, written from Spence's Hotel on 19th September, 1935 is the earliest surviving letter from him to me.

My dear little grandson Martin,

From all I hear, and from what I have seen from your photographs, you are growing up big and strong, obedient to father and mother, always doing what they tell you. Go to bed at the proper time, clean your teeth, and wash behind your ears – always wash behind your ears.

They tell me that you have grown so tall I should hardly know you if I met you in the street alone – but I hardly think that, do you?

Of course you would hardly know me, as you were so small when you last saw me, but I am sure we should be the very best of friends in one minute, aren't you?

Do you remember the song I used to sing about you? It was something like this –

"Pat dear! Pat dear, would you guess the truth?
Pat dear! Martin dear! Bless the little youth!
O do get up and light the fire,
Turn the gas a little higher,
Run and tell my Aunt Maria
Martin's got a tooth."

You always liked and laughed at that song when it was sung by
Your loving old
Grandpa

I must have taken his words seriously, for he comments in a letter to Dorothy early the following year 'Funny about Martin washing behind his ears. I have chortled over that many times.' I have passed the injunction on to children and grandchildren, but doubt if they took it in as I did. At least they will have to say of me "the backs of his ears were clean."

It was at about this time that the relationship between Dorothy and Phyllis became strained. It is not to my purpose in these pages to deal with how or why – and, in any event, neither the how nor the why are altogether clear. The two sisters had been such good friends up to and beyond Dorothy's wedding that it became a great sorrow to

Dorothy, adding to her other anxieties about the extent to which they could rely on Harry to keep funds available for Jennie to be able to run Chingri Khal, not to mention their own allowances. He was always writing in his letters how bad trade was, how much money his business was losing and the need to reduce the English outlay.

After the end of the summer term, 1935, at Dartmouth, Jimmy was sent to join *HMS Kent*, which was on the China Station. His journey by sea took him across the Indian Ocean in September from Colombo to Penang. Harry joined him at Colombo to have the length of that part of the voyage with him, doubtless catching up with some, at least of family news. The birth of a son to Phyllis in March, 1936, completed the Breaks family who, as Jimmy was in the Far East, remained at Chingri Khal. And also it gave Harry his second grandson (his third if you count little Justin.) He was named James after his father and Henry after his grandfather. With five grandchildren able to enjoy Chingri Khal it must have been to some extent a spur to keep the place going. But it was a near run thing.

A tennis party, August, 1913. (Left to right: Harry, Jennie, [Capt Griffiths] Dorothy, [Mr Griffin] [Mrs Griffiths] Phyllis, Arthur, Annie Hobbs.

A wild corner of the wood.

21st July, 1933, Harry with his grandchildren on his 69th birthday party.
(Left to right: Toff, Martin, Harry, Phyllida, Elizabeth).

June, 1936. Garden party with tea on the front lawn and...

Summer, 1938.
Bacon and egg
party in the wood.
"Another rasher
please Dorothy."

...Punch and Judy show on the back lawn.

465

Family group on SS Homeric, 14th June, 1935.
(Left to right) Charles, Bert, Winnie, Dorothy, Edith; in front: Martin, Betty.

The Homeric sails on her (and Bert's) last voyage.

CHAPTER 28

THE FIRST DECADE
(2)
THE UNPREDICTABLE FATHER

IF THE PROSPECT OF ANOTHER grandchild to see, making five in all now, made for a temptation to Harry to pay another home visit in the summer of 1936, it was set at naught by the death in early May of Affleck, the manager of the business of H. Hobbs & Co. It was as sudden and as unexpected as had been that of Bert the previous year. Affleck had been Harry's right hand man at least since 1918 and his unexpected death must have put a great deal more work on Harry's shoulders, both in the short term, dealing with his funeral and helping his widow (who lived with him in India) to cope with the immediate aftermath, and in the longer term in keeping the business going and finding a replacement. And all to be fitted in with his work in running Spence's Hotel. Their relationship had been very close, although it had somewhat soured in recent years by Harry discovering what he thought was dishonourable, if not dishonest conduct on the part of Affleck. Diary entries and letters from Harry tell us something of his state of mind. As so often with Harry that was not entirely straightforward. In his diary for 4th May, 1936, after describing Affleck's death, he goes on:

> None will deplore his departure as sincerely as I do. He ran the business of H. Hobbs & Co. I used to spend 3 hours there in the mornings, but he did the work. Conscientious, capable, efficient and blessed with a good memory with infinite patience, he succeeded where all others would have failed. And now at 72 I find myself with 2 businesses, other enterprises to carry out and the man on whom I could most depend, with all his knowledge, gone for ever.

While in a letter to Colonel Wyness of 7th May, 1936, he adds, in his only reference to Harry Baba that I have spotted, 'I haven't felt so dismayed and distressed since my first little son passed away forty and more years ago.' He is rather less adulatory three weeks later:

> As you can understand, there has been a lot to do for me to pick up the reins of my business. Affleck must have known that he was in a bad way so he neglected things. After the row over Spence's Hotel where he betrayed me and had the full length of my tongue as well as a drop of 400 a month, feelings were strained. I forgave him sufficiently for us to work together without exchange of confidences but the feeling of a father to a son departed. The story and its implications, unfolded since his death, surprise me.

In his next letter to Colonel Wyness, on 8th June, Harry (rather unusually) comments on the domestic set-up at Chingri Khal. The Colonel and his wife had visited Bournemouth recently and seen all the family – both families – and had written to Harry to tell him all about it.

> …The house cannot be kept on for the Memsahib. It is far too big and the expense of running it takes not only all I make, but I am constantly selling shares to pay for it. I reckon the piano business had lost 3 lakhs of my money during the last 12 years and there is no possible chance of picking any of it up. Could I sell out I should be a great loser. I can now make a bit for my subsistence which I might not get if I wasn't here. Unfortunately, nobody at Chingri Khal seems to believe that times are trying. They know they are with other people but when I write about it I am convinced that they feel I begrudge sending the money – that I have plenty. The Mem considers that she ought to stay there until she dies. Then the grandchildren come in. While they are able to enjoy living there I consider the outlay worthwhile for they might as well have a happy childhood while it can be given them. But when they go it is foolish and wasteful to keep so big a place going for one person. The taxes – income and municipal – amount to some hundreds a year and I am spending my savings as my business has lost, and is losing, so much.

While ten days later he wrote to Mrs Wyness, commenting again on her account to him of that visit to Bournemouth, and raising another curious reason for not staying in or retiring to England:

> My daughters are certainly lacking in the blunt vernacular of their father – more of that polish acquired in circles different from those of his youth. Well, that cost quite a bit to put on and I sometime wonder if it was worth it.
>
> The grandchildren are delightful, and I left home mostly because I was too fond of them. Treating children always as if they are grown men and women, never caressing or kissing them, respecting their dignity as much as I might that of a 17 year old girl, attracts them tremendously. There is a little boy of 6 nearby who always leaves his parents when he sees me. He is treated like a man and grows proud of himself. I too am proud to find children taking so quickly to an old man. The izzat of people is strongest in childhood but few of us recognise it. No baby talk about me. "How are you, old man?" never fails to charm and attract.

So, while Harry remained in India for yet another summer, Pat and Dorothy, taking me with them, went on holiday to a hotel at Perranporth in Cornwall. It was their first 'proper' holiday since their marriage and I have no doubt they badly needed their fortnight's break. Harry wrote that he thought they 'ought to have had a month there.' But two weeks was the most Pat felt he could be away from the practice.

It was to be the first of several very successful holidays taken with another family, that of Max and Vi Stothert, with their daughter Susan, (now Mrs Tony Hall) nearly six years younger than myself, who also lived in Bournemouth. Max, a Chartered Accountant practising in Bournemouth, was, like Pat, an early member of the Hazards Golfing Society. All four had quite a lot in common. They were frequent guests in each other's homes for an evening of bridge. Max was always full of good ideas, and could carry Pat along with his enthusiasms. It has to be acknowledged that Pat could be slow to accept a new proposal, and it was good for him – and good for

Dorothy too – that he had this spur to some decisions about his leisure time.

For her part Dorothy continued to get much social pleasure from bridge. For some years she had been a member of an informal group of ladies – they called themselves the Bridge Circle – who met weekly, or fortnightly, through the winter months in each other's homes for an afternoon of bridge. Usually three or four tables, with a rather sumptuous tea in the middle, laid on by that week's hostess. I rather liked to be around at home on the occasion of the Circle meeting at Hereford House when the tea was being cleared out of the drawing room. There were usually some delicious tit-bits left over: small sandwiches with the crusts cut off; bridge rolls with tasty fillings; cakes and éclairs, even, if I was lucky – oh joy! – a meringue. They did themselves well – and so did I.

The end of that year saw the Abdication Crisis, and that produced a typical outburst from Harry in his Diary for 15th December. He had been a considerable admirer of King George V, and had written movingly about him at the time of the Silver Jubilee, and at his death. Indeed, he had given a broadcast address on Indian radio for the Jubilee, of which he had been extremely proud. But he pulled no punches about his successor:

> So King Edward VIII has gone! Of all the silly, childish, contemptible actions – well, commend me to the ex-King Edward VIII. And to broadcast piffle about the "woman I love." As if a man of 42 could ever be smitten for more than an hour or two over a woman of 40! Said he couldn't carry on without her. And how long will he be able to carry on with her? If it says anything it plainly demonstrated that he was unfit to carry on as a King. I don't wonder that he has to be strongly guarded. A mean-hearted, cowardly fellow and a prize ass in the bargain.

The reaction in Bournemouth to such a tirade was likely to be 'thank goodness he can fulminate about something like that; it distracts him from finding fault with us.' For his growing impatience with his family in England gave all of them a considerable degree of unease as to what he might do next. Jennie became increasingly the target of barbs and insults, while he would take umbrage at any criticism. Dorothy was in pretty regular correspondence with him, and Pat would write occasionally. Only Harry's replies – probably not all, but a fair selection – are available.

The end of the year 1936 found Harry writing to Pat in a rather jaundiced way, complaining of being greatly overworked 'with three unsuccessful businesses on my hands.' The three in question were his own piano business, then Spence's Hotel and finally he was acting as Liquidator for another firm. He asserts he is working from 7am to 10.30pm or later. As for another home visit,

> As far as can be seen there is no chance of another run home. Actually I have washed that out and decided to work until I die or until I can go no longer – that is when completely fed up. But that doesn't matter very much so far as I can see.

Dorothy may have ventured to chide him for something like causing Jennie financial concerns and then felt obliged to apologise. For on 4th February, 1937 he wrote:

> I am glad you are sorry for whatever you said. Knowing what I do for my dependants I resent ungracious complaints made out of ill humour. For a short time I have to live there is little satisfaction gained by unkindness. With so much to do it is easy to drop writing altogether.

On 30th June he again takes exception to something she had written, ending with an early barb in Jennie's direction:

> Generally, when writing a letter which is not friendly, the effect of it should be judged before posting it. I am working here pretty hard and find my efforts the cause of discontent more than appreciation. It may be that I have too high an opinion of my liberality, but I also occasionally wonder what would be my position were I dependent upon my dependants.
>
> What strikes a queer note is the fact that at 73 I should be looked upon as the wage earner – a mean one at that. Years ago when I was

making a mighty struggle to earn a living, any expressed anxiety about meeting bills that were falling due never failed to bring a reminder that "And I want some money too." The callous selfishness and disregard of my worries used to make me wonder what sort of a soul the woman possessed – just about as much as there is in a deal plank.

Despite this antipathy to Jennie, which grew in his mind over the next few years, he was considering an alternative to coming home which would result in them meeting again. To Colonel Wyness he makes occasional reference to Jimmy's naval postings. In December, 1936 he told the Colonel that Jimmy was returning from the Far East having been appointed as Commander (E) to *HMS Warspite* 'the most mechanically up-to-date ship in the Navy – the flagship of the Mediterranean Fleet and is due for 2½ years there.' And on 4th May, 1937 he wrote:

Jim Breaks goes off next month to the Mediterranean and wants me to go to Malta to stay with them. If possible I will have a bang at it. Getting on for four years since I got out of the heat. Darjeeling no longer suits me. Either the dirt about or the altitude affects my inside – not my heart but I may have a run up to Darjeeling next month to try.

But such a meeting had to be put on the back burner. The *Warspite* developed some problems with her engines and was not ready for her Mediterranean tour of duty for several months. The *Warspite* was in Portsmouth and took part in the Coronation Review of the Fleet. Jimmy was able to have the use of one of her boats in which a large number of friends as well as relations were taken up and down the lines of ships at anchor in Spithead. We had to start very early in the day, so as to be off the *Warspite* in time for the Review itself. Many cars set out together from Bournemouth to Portsmouth, quite a long and difficult drive in those days. But how worthwhile it was! The mile after mile of huge grey vessels looked magnificent in the summer sunshine. Foreign as well as British and Imperial ships were there – representatives of nearly every Navy in the world. The crews mostly gave a cheer to any passing boat. We thought the biggest cheers came from the German and the Japanese vessels. There is probably a moral to be drawn from that, but I do not know what it is.

The reign of Miss Harries had to come to an end, which for me meant that the reality of school began with the summer term of 1937. By chance the previous year the Jesuits, who already had a substantial foothold in Bournemouth, running both the central Parish of the Sacred Heart, and also the Boscombe Parish of Corpus Christi, strengthened their presence by opening a new school. They bought the substantial premises and grounds of Grassendale, a former girls' school in Southbourne, and founded a hybrid, part prep school (because it took boarders) and part grammar school (because it took boys up to School Certificate) which they called St. Peter's School. It made a fairly sudden appearance on the Bournemouth scene. Dorothy had already more or less promised the nuns at her old school, the Convent of the Cross, that I should make a start there in their boys' department. She was not sorry to give the new establishment a little time to get over any teething troubles, and so it was to the Convent that I made my first foray into formal education in April, 1937.

Some six weeks before, I had distinguished myself by getting whooping cough, and made many loud, dramatic and alarming whoops for several days. Having got to school I further distinguished myself by somehow or other acquiring a black eye. The reader, I realise, will not believe me when I say that I have no recollection of the latter at all, although the former is very clear in my mind. Harry comments upon both of these events to me, seemingly more put out by the first than by the second. On 2nd March;

My dear Martin,

What's this I hear - that you have whooping cough? Now how did you manage that, and what are you going to do about it? I am very sorry to know that you are so worried and hope when the next letter comes you can report – ever so much better, thank you!

I have sent you a magazine with fine pictures which I am almost sure you will like. When you write you can tell me.

I send you ever so much love, and hope I shall see you one of these days, even if you have to come to India.

And now, buck up old man!

Your loving old   Grandpa

While on 8th July:

…Now I learn too that you go to school although [it] didn't read too good to know that you butted into a free fight and got a free black eye into the bargain. Well, well, and dear me! You know the story of the boy, 7 years of age, who rushed into a house where a row was going on and asked, "Please what's the matter? Father wants to know, if there's going to be a fight, can he join in?" I hope your Daddy didn't take a hand in the free fight as he did quite enough in fighting the Germans…

You didn't tell me what you did with the money I gave for your birthday. I hope that didn't finish up in a free fight also.

Well, you wrote quite a good letter – much better than I ever thought of getting – so I give you full marks and will look out for the next one.

With my love to you, and to your father and mother.

I am   Your loving old   Grandpa   H. Hobbs

Harry's letters to me – and, I expect, to his other grandchildren – were always in this style, cheerful, encouraging and often with a bit of worldly wisdom thrown in. Letters to Dorothy, as well as his diary pages which he often enclosed, frequently contained matter which was either disturbing in its implications for the future, or insulting to other members of the family, especially Jennie, and to The Establishment, political and particularly religious. We shall see the vituperation towards Jennie working up almost to fury as the years went by.

The summer of 1937 brought news of Arthur's marriage. Pauline, his wife, had come to England on her own beforehand to meet everyone at Bournemouth. She and Dorothy liked each other at once. Arthur did not come with her, either then or later, but Dorothy was very glad for his sake that he had found a wife whom she so liked and would help him in his life in Canada.

474

Harry's new role as a hotelier proved to give him a lot of satisfaction, and in a letter to Dorothy of 27th October, 1937, he sets out at some length his achievements, as he saw them, and how he went about it:

I am pleased about Spence's Hotel which shows something after 7 years hard work. The place was in the doldrums. Rascally British staff – 11 cases of picking pockets and robbery from the rooms in 14 days. When I sacked the men I suspected, no more robberies. The European of a low class is miles worse than Indians because he splits on his pals. But the insults, threats, abuse to which I had to retort, took a lot of tackling. Whichever way I turned I was defeated – but only once. When I found out what was wrong I waded in, not only to the staff, but to the frequenters of the bar, and also several of the residents. I must have had 30 people blackguarding me at the same time. The surprising thing being, they were believed.

Now all staff are engaged on terms which first insist on immediate dismissal. No notice nor any pay in lieu thereof. Then no man is allowed to take a drink from customers. That stops sponging. As I drink very little I set the example. Tell men who ask me to have a drink – "I am the cheapest man in the world to know. I don't take drinks and I don't smoke cigarettes." And it is surprising how much it is appreciated. I can approach everybody for a gossip, and men offer a drink, knowing I won't accept, but to show good feeling.

But I am a firm believer that without dignity there is no stature. I respect the dignity of all the staff, European or Indian. The result is that I am most certainly not robbed for spite. And the man who does rob (I have found none for a long time) would be badly got at by others on the staff. The place is small but even then it numbers about 110, most of whom are partially or wholly fed.

Were I starting in life again I think hotel management would offer most advantages. Of course it is one thing working for a Company when you have a controlling influence in the number of shares, and losing your own money. But I have taken it properly. The filthiest place in India has been turned into the cleanest, and by the same staff.

If the letter contains rather a lot of self-satisfaction, it is probably true to say that he had quite a lot to be satisfied about so far as Spence's Hotel was concerned. It is such a pity that, with so many talents at his disposal, building family relationships featured so little.

It was during the course of the year 1937, the *Warspite* being still in Portsmouth, that Jimmy rented a house in Cosham, and the Breaks family moved out of Chingri Khal. That left Chingri Khal feeling rather empty to me, but it was not, at that stage, going to be for a very long time, and I enjoyed a few days visit to stay with my cousins and seeing round many Royal Naval vessels in Portsmouth Dockyard.

When commenting in November on Chingri Khal being the home only for Jennie, Harry wrote that necessary roof repairs should be done 'in an economical way.' In a passage which foreshadowed worse to come, he went on:

> Actually I do not own the house and am not going to trouble about it. A small bill I may meet when it suits me, but the best thing your mother can do now is to live in an hotel where she can have company and not be entirely alone to be preyed upon (perhaps worse) by servants. It is a good job you are in Bournemouth as you and your mother get on so well and she can fall back on you. It means, of course, some extra worry for you but that cannot be helped.

It was just as well that Dorothy also got on reasonably well with her father. He pulled no punches as time went by over the need for economies. At least she was able somehow to keep the lines of communication open with him on a more or less amicable basis. But it must have been the case that much of the 'extra worry' to which Harry referred was brought about by the feeling of insecurity he engendered, and as to which he seems to have been oblivious.

In January, 1938, he wrote that the allowance to Jennie was to come down – 'And if matters do not improve the allowance comes down too pretty heavily, so just make that as pleasant as possible. I have done my best and earned a lot of ingratitude to say nothing about never having been shown the slightest consideration for what I did.'

By early 1938 the *Warspite's* refit had been completed and she had sailed to Malta. Jimmy took a house in Malta. His family had been there for several months in the early 30s and again went out to join him. They had returned to Chingri Khal before leaving for the Mediterranean, and it was a very sad and tearful occasion for me when I had to say "Good-bye" for what I knew was likely to be, for an eight year old, a very long time indeed. And it was not only the Breaks family which went to Malta. Jennie was also persuaded to go with them, or to go out to join them. In a letter to Colonel Wyness on 21st April Harry wrote:

> Jim's family and the Mem have gone to Malta, so Chingri Khal is empty. I was going but it looks as if no opportunity offers. Might as well die here seems to be my attitude now.

Jennie's imminent departure may well have provoked the request, or order, or statement of opinion from Harry in his letter to Dorothy of 7th April:

> It is scandalous that enough is paid in taxes to keep a single woman in luxury and there is now no need for it. Moreover, I cannot live very long and it will eventually happen whatever is done to prevent it. Your mother could live in a hotel on the amount paid in taxes and it would give me a chance of taking things easier, not that that ever bothered her. All she thought of was dress and dancing, with a bottle of whisky tucked away nearby.
>
> Chingri Khal has to be sold. I have said this often enough but if it isn't – then the money will not be sent home for taxes and that will ensure a sale right enough. I work here at an age when I ought to be able to take it easy. Any day I may crack up through the heat, or something suddenly go wrong. It will upset the mode of life in Chingri Khal whichever way you look at it, so why not get ready now?

However, he ends with 'Herewith draft for the taxes.' His next letter to her, only four days later, does not mention the house and ends 'Herewith a draft for forty pounds.' Dorothy must have sent this last letter to Jennie in Malta for there are three postscripts in her handwriting, one telling Jennie of the 'Chingri Khal must be sold' directive, the other two relating to how bills are to be paid. And in his next, dated the same day as that to Colonel Wyness, when asking for some sketches of Calcutta to be sent to him he says 'No good sending them to Malta as it looks as if I cannot get there,' giving as his reason the ineptitude of his replacement for Affleck, a man called Lees.

In his next letter, dated 28th April, Harry returns to the sale, or lack of it, of Chingri Khal – although how he could have expected anything to have been done in the short time in question, let alone with Jennie out of the country, is hard to understand. But then much of his attitude is hard to understand.

> Your mother will have to spend some of her own money for a month or two. Only the other day someone mentioned – "Mrs. Hobbs dresses so beautifully." Well – she can cut that down a bit and keep herself for the time being. The Budget is out. As anticipated, the income tax is up. Now that means more money wasted and as there seems to be no intention to sell the house, well, perhaps the Government will sell it when the taxes are not paid.
>
> The least that can be done is to sell one, or two, of the plots on the west side. The few hundred pounds they will realise will carry over these appalling bad times of which you, in England, do not appear able to imagine. If you imagine you do not believe. However, that is my ultimatum. I am not going to send money. I cannot afford to go away, particularly as one of my few Europeans is leaving and poor Lees is utterly incapable of thought…I have now reconciled myself to remaining here until I die and my obituary notice may be – 'He worked for others until he could work no more.' That's about all. I shall, before long, stop writing.
>
> Your affectionate father   H. Hobbs

He was, indeed, quite affectionate to Dorothy, but he never seemed to be able to understand that she was close to, and very fond of, her mother. He never spared Dorothy's feelings when he wanted to rant about Jennie. That is what he did in his letter of 27th June.

> I am sorry about the house and for your mother but she squandered money like a drunken sailor. Some years she got through £4,000 and,

of course, denied having a quarter of it and envied the wealth of people on £250, who probably made a better show of it with the money. She has lived all these years in undeserved luxury. Never on any occasion has she shown the least interest in my work – not even from the day she married. I consider she ruined Arthur, but had she possessed a spark of sense she would have saved something, instead of squandering it all on drink and dress.

But what will continue to rankle is the cold-bloodied manner in which my explanations of hard times were received. Nothing will lead me to forgive that. All my generosity was forgotten – I was just a mean old swine trying to keep them out of money and for all the interest displayed I might as well have been a shoeblack in the street corner of Newcastle. Many a time I felt it would be good were I completely ruined so that she could have a much-needed lesson, but, so far as I could, I kept my obligations – which she never did. All she thought about was dress and dancing. She could drink enough for six men without turning a hair. One little action I cherish. While receiving from me £4,000 in a year, she stopped taking The Times when I got home as she could not afford 2d a day. Like Irish people, generous with other people's money – mean and selfish with her own. But if she could point out to any regard for me I shall be surprised. She married to gad about. She had no other creed except childish idolatry but for all the good she was to me I'd have been better without her. Luckily, having a bad wife threw me on to my own resources; for that I am grateful. But I'm not sympathetic. After all, if you sow, and live long enough to reap – well, you have the crop – it's yours.

Your affectionate father   H. Hobbs

Receipt of a diatribe like that would hardly be calculated to give Dorothy a cheerful start to her day. With such an attitude towards his wife of over forty years it is all the more surprising that eventually he did bestir himself to visit the Breaks family in Malta for with them there was also Jennie. His visit there is confirmed by a letter of a very different character which he wrote to me on 29th August, 1938. His letter was evidently prompted by an early effort on my part to use the typewriter which Pat had for use in the practice. There had also been a small typewriter in a little room (we called it 'the little room' – I suppose it was a dressing room) at Chingri Khal on which I had experimented a bit. But its ribbon was worn to shreds, and no one thought to replace it. So my effort to Harry was most probably carried out at Hereford House. It caused a bit of a hit – and brought me a welcome reward.

> My dear young Martin,
>   I thought it was very clever of you to type a letter to me. Really the way you young chaps grow up is startling. Only the other day you were very small, but you used to sit next to me at table ad I'd give you water, tell stories, make you laugh, and all that. And now you type me a letter. WONDERFUL!! I hope you will keep it up.
>   I am leaving Calcutta on Thursday for Bombay and stopping for a short time at Malta where I hope to recover my health. I have been very ill and am not well yet but able to do something provided I lie down every now and then.
>   Heaps of love. I send a prize of ten shillings for that letter you wrote on August 10 and for which I thank you very much.
>   Your loving old   Grandpa

No mention to me about any problems regarding Chingri Khal, for which, no doubt my parents were very grateful. They never mentioned any such problems to me at the time. As far as I was concerned life just went on.

But not quite as before. For one thing I changed schools. Having been in the hands of the nuns at her old school for a year, Dorothy decided that the time had come for me to go to the new Jesuit School, St. Peter's at Southbourne, starting in the summer term, 1938. I was not to be a boarder. The distance was not great, about five miles. A trolley bus route (the old Bournemouth trams having been withdrawn in 1936; I saw the last one leave the Square, decorated all over) could take me from very near home to quite close to the School if transport by car was not possible at any time. In later years I was able to bicycle to school. I do not believe there was any problem about this choice of school: although there were a number of good boys' schools in Bournemouth where I could have been a day boy. Pat would certainly have learnt from Dorothy and from friends how first class was the teaching in a Jesuit School. He was content to go along with her decision.

And then at some stage during that year we moved into Chingri Khal. I have no means of knowing how Dorothy managed to arrange it, either with her father and mother or, for that matter, with Pat. We were, in effect, almost a family of 'house sitters.' The staff there – cook, parlourmaid and Hall the gardener at any rate – remained after Jennie's departure. I had not had a Nanny for two or three years, and so there was no need for anyone to come from Hereford House, nor was it necessary to keep any servant at Hereford House on the domestic side.

It cannot have been an arrangement without involving both some inconvenience and some extra expense for Pat, even if only in his need for daily travel to Hinton Road. I do not know what, if anything, Harry paid Dorothy towards the outgoings at Chingri Khal. It is a very frustrating fact that, by what I can only assume is pure coincidence, the bundle of letters from Harry to Dorothy (and to Pat and to myself) has a gap in it from that letter to me in August, 1938, until a letter to Dorothy in October, 1939. By a further coincidence the letters and diaries sent to Colonel Wyness also have a gap from the end of June, 1938 until September, 1939, after which there is very little remaining from that source.

However it was financed, it was a period of great delight for Dorothy. She was back in her old home, which had not yet begun to decay, either outside or inside, and where she was, even if only temporarily, in charge of both house and garden. Hall was still around tending the garden, although there was no car for him to look after. The Vauxhall, which had taken Dorothy to her wedding, had often been loaned to them until it finally wore out in the early 30s. From which time Pat had had his own car.

For me, too, it was a very happy time. Not that I was unhappy at Hereford House, but the whole ambience of Chingri Khal made for a very relaxed and contented household, especially for the young. It was sad not to have my cousins around, but school friends came from time to time, and I found I could enjoy myself in both house and garden without any difficulty even when on my own.

It was only Pat who did not like it. It was not just the two miles to work. He wanted nothing but the best for Dorothy, and he was prepared to go to any lengths commensurate with his means and ability to provide her with that best. But he wanted it to come from what he could give her, and was uneasy if it came from elsewhere. It was almost as if he were jealous of anyone or anything who could provide, independently of him, something for her with which she would be happy. I do not believe that this difference of feeling about the changed life-style caused anything in the way of a serious disagreement between them. I was certainly never aware of any such disagreement, let alone a row, between them. Pat was quite sensitive enough to know how much I liked being there, and he would have known that it was not a permanent arrangement. Even if he expressed his preference for Hereford House to Dorothy – as, I expect, at times he did – it did not come to my knowledge then, nor for many years.

There was a Mimosa tree in the front garden, to the right, the west, of the front lawn, between the lawn and the west drive. *Acacia Leguminosae dealbata* does not normally grow very big in this country, although it sometimes does so in southern counties. This one was in a sheltered spot, with acid soil and it must have found something it liked in its position. It was quite a big tree, of a 'Y'-shape formation, one limb extending significantly over the lawn. On a sunny afternoon Jennie liked nothing better than to have her tea sitting up at a table under the Mimosa tree, where the sunlight was pleasantly dappled upon the white tablecloth as it found its way through the fine fern-like leaves. In the spring and early summer there might also be the tiny yellow puff-like flowers hanging above your head, and some falling on to the table. Since afternoon tea for Granny usually included fresh white toast, cut into small triangles without the crust, together with marble-sized pats of butter to spread on it oneself, as well as, perhaps, a tasty sandwich or two and a cake with jam and cream in it – with such a spread it is no wonder that her grandson liked to join her. Under the Mimosa tree was where Granny had her tea, it was always so, practically hallowed ground.

We were there all the winter of 1938 to 1939, and celebrated Christmas there – for the first and only time away from Hereford House. Children tend to regard that which is familiar as having always been so, and which will always be so in the future. All about Chingri Khal seemed to me to be a fixed star in the firmament. Nothing seemed ever to have changed about the place in my conscious memory. True my cousins were away, as well as Jennie, but they would soon be back, and then everything would carry on exactly as before.

There were severe frosts that winter. The garden, and especially the wood, looked even more magical when all was still and frozen. Snow fell also, and I made a big snowman on the back lawn. Then one morning I woke up and looked out. It was a sad sight. One of the two limbs of the Mimosa tree was lying right across that half of the front lawn. If the tea table had been there in its proper place it would have been crushed flat. "What's happened, Mummy, can we put it right?" But, of course, we couldn't put it right. The frost had got into the 'Y' fork and torn one limb completely away from the other. All that could be done was to have the wreckage cleared away, and then, as if to seal matters, the advice was that the remaining part of the tree was now unsafe and so it had to be completely felled and removed.

I found it very sad to see the remains carted away. The impermanence of all things was brought home to me. No more tea with Granny under the Mimosa. Perhaps it was from then on that I realised more change was inevitably going to take place as time went by.

But further immediate change was only for the better. The coming of spring saw the return of Jennie, followed soon afterwards by the return of my cousins. In consequence we, Pat, Dorothy and myself, went back to Hereford House. Pat was relieved and pleased, Dorothy happy if he was happy, and, if I did not have Chingri Khal around me all the time, it was only a short drive or bus ride away.

And so life was pretty well back to normal, even if the teatime menu had to be taken under a different tree. And in any case teatime when there was a houseful of children was usually rather a different affair; taken in the room called the nursery, with much high spirits, quiz games as to who had which bird, or flower on their plate, and a huge chocolate cake which Cookie had baked. It always looked a mountain of a cake – and never did any cake taste better.

Then there was a holiday in the offing: I could look forward to that. Our friend Max Stothert had a client who farmed and owned a hotel on the tiny Channel Island of Sark. He suggested the two families again combined for a fortnight or so, and Pat and Dorothy agreed. It was three years since their last proper holiday in Cornwall and they no doubt felt they needed another one, even if it did take Pat away from the practice.

It proved a great success. The weather was kind, the food excellent, the hotel friendly and comfortable and the experience of Sark uniquely restful. So, with unbounded confidence for the future, before leaving they booked their rooms for the following year, 1940. Reality was dawning on them on the return crossing. Our outward passage had been at night from Southampton to St. Peter Port. For some reason on our return we had a daytime crossing to Weymouth. There was thick fog all the way, the ship's whistle sounding regularly and frequently its mournful note. I was not told until long after we were back at home, but Dorothy was scared all that voyage that we would be torpedoed. The day was Monday, August 28th and the World was holding its breath.

CHAPTER 29

THE SECOND DECADE
(1)
THE IMPACT OF WAR

THE FOLLOWING SUNDAY MORNING, 3rd September, the three of us went to Chingri Khal. I wandered out into the garden – alone because the Breaks family were away that day. I knew there was anxiety in the air, one could not get away from it. Even in Sark a fellow guest, who had arrived not long before our departure, had come up to Pat and asked him, "Are you going home because of this war they say we're going to have?" "No," Pat had replied, "our time is up."

So it came as no very great surprise when Pat walked into the wood to find me a little while after 11 o'clock. I was on the roof of the chicken house. Why that was a bit of a favourite place to sit in the sun now completely escapes me, but there I was. "The Prime Minister has been speaking to us on the wireless," he told me, "and we are now at war with Germany." Half expected it may have been, but that made the news no more welcome to me. If I look back twenty-one years from today, and realise what a short time ago that appears to be, I understand with what dismay the prospect of war with Germany again must have been received, less than twenty-one years after The Armistice. The horrors of the Great War were still very vivid recent memories. Pat and Dorothy would surely have shared such feelings with many millions of other people. Pat, especially, with his experiences of the trenches in the worst winter of the Great War, would have had cause to be distressed, even though he was certainly unfit for any military service. That did not stop him joining the Auxiliary Fire Service, although he proved not to be up to their standard of fitness, and he was not with them for more than a few months.

However my parents showed no distress to me. Regret, perhaps, coupled with a quiet determination to face up to whatever lay ahead. And to face up to it with confidence. "You must never say 'If we win the war,'" was Dorothy's injunction to me that day, "you must always say 'When we win the war.'" I think I obeyed that directive implicitly, and never doubted the sentiments that lay behind it.

The events of that day were somewhat different in Calcutta. Harry sets some of them out in his Diary for 4th September:

> Plenty of excitement for some of us. War was declared at about 10 yesterday (our time) and I was walking on the river bank trying to get a breath of fresh air when a man told me, so I drove back to the hotel finding everything quiet. Half an hour later news came to my room of the arrival of the police, special constables and some Bengal Armed Police, for our Germans. We had seven in the hotel and one woman. The woman's husband was to be taken away. Poor soul. She wept and moaned and, being unable to talk English, her loneliness must be acute. The men were gradually assembled; one man was absent but he came in half an hour later, then all were allowed fifteen minutes to pack. They had to take bedding as accommodation was said to be primitive. I saw that the police party all had drinks and something to eat. The seven prisoners were, at my request, allowed to have their dinner and the police very kindly waited until they had finished their icecream, when all shook hands, the whole party thanked me, and they were off in motorbuses to Lall Bazaar (our Scotland Yard.) Two Germans only were at the Grand Hotel. A hostile mob of 1,000 people waited for them and, but for the police, would have killed the pair. The difference in Spence's Hotel and the Grand was most marked. The Grand gives the police a lot of trouble. I see that they are helped.
>
> At Firpo's the other night when it came to singing the National Anthem two Germans sat and hammered the table with their beer bottles. They were thrown downstairs and both are still in danger. An appeal to the German Consul resulted (so I'm told) in telling them that had Englishmen acted similarly in Germany they would have been shot. They might. We shall see.
>
> At the Casanova two Jap ship officers were seated at a table near to the stage. Some men from the *Isipinge* (a South African ship) told them to get up. They pointed out that they were already seated and doing no harm, but they got a hammering and were stripped naked

before being thrown into the street. Giving them a bit of Tientsin, so the crowd said.

There was little outward change in those first months of the phoney war. The blackout was the main exception. That was quite a performance at Hereford House, which had some awkwardly large windows, particularly the window which ran almost the entire height of the staircase well. Less immediately obvious, but in the long term of much more concern, was the exodus of people from Bournemouth. It was not very great in those first months, but it was certainly there. The audited accounts of Pat's practice have long since been disposed of, but his ledger remains. A small, lockable volume, it lists a summary of his takings, expenses, gross and net profit throughout all his years in practice. In 1939 gross profit was down by a fifth on the 1938 total, and in 1940 it was down to little more than two thirds of that total. And this despite reducing overheads. Some staff had gone, one of the so-called dental nurses, Gladys, had left before the outbreak of war and not been replaced. One of the dental mechanics had also been called up.

That caused another anxiety for a time. Our principal mechanic, Harry Padwick (another Harry!) was of military age. If he had been called up as well, it would have been virtually impossible for Pat to carry on. He had lengthy and difficult negotiations with those concerned with organising the call-up. They ended successfully, but it was a stressful time.

And it was some time fairly early in the war that Pat, very likely Pat and Dorothy together, had to undertake a considerable task of what would now be called counselling. Beatrice, the one remaining dental nurse/receptionist, came back from one of her periodic visits to Worcester where she had stayed with 'Mum,' and any others of her family, for a holiday. She was in floods of tears and great distress because she had somehow learnt while she was there – whether by chance or deliberately told I do not know – that 'Mum' was not her mother at all. Her real mother, she was told, was Mum's sister, that is, Ellen, with whom she had lived for very many years as though they were aunt and niece. And so contemporaries she regarded as brother or sister were no more than cousins. To make matters worse 'Mum' had been unable (or unwilling) to tell her who her father was – plainly not the husband of 'Mum'. So in her distress Beatrice had asked Ellen, who, when confronted, had admitted maternity. "Well, who is my father, then?" demanded Beatrice, and received the quite impossible reply, "Mind your own business." Ellen maintained that wholly unreasonable stance up to her death towards the end of the war, so that the mystery was never completely cleared up. But it always seemed to me that as she grew older – she remained in my family's employment for very many years – Beatrice grew more and more like Deane Webb. It seems significant that in Deane Webb's will he refers to her as 'Beatrice Noble' (that is, the surname of Ellen, her mother) when leaving her a legacy of £100, but in the Codicil (in which he reduced that small legacy to £50) he calls her 'Beatrice Thorne' (the name by which she was always known.) He obviously knew Ellen was her mother, and most probably because he was her father. Perhaps a typical example of Victorian 'respectability.' She continued to live in that basement flat, with Ellen and, after the latter's death, for as long as it was available, that is, until Deane Webb's estate came to be wound up.

In the early months of the war Harry's letters were rather more restrained in relation to Chingri Khal and Jennie. He sent food parcels and some money when he could to both families in Bournemouth. He was sympathetic to the wartime plight of everyone, but had lost none of his tendency to underline how ill he was, or had been, and how hard he had to work. In October 1939, he wrote to Dorothy:

> ...Don't grumble about the difficulties, they haven't started yet...I feel very tired now and work of one sort or other falls to me whichever way I look. If it is better to wear out than to rust out, the man who wears well is your affectionate father   H. Hobbs

While in January, 1940 he sums up his own opinion of himself, in a passage which is characterised by a complete absence of any false modesty:

That Martin may not be able to have recollections of his grandfather is to be deplored, but you can bring him up to know that, if the old man was not famous, he was an important man in India, suppressed by the press and more or less banned by the upper class of Europeans for his fearless exposure of their ways, and unceasing attacks on them whenever opportunity offered. My warnings on political matters show how correct my judgment had been. Of course I've paid for it by being boycotted in business, but am openly feared.

From Dorothy's point of view the first year or so of hostilities was particularly noteworthy in bringing to an end the era of the domestic servant. The live-in 'cook general' who, as the term implied, cooked what she was told to cook, prepared and cleared up all meals and kept the house clean, disappeared from most professional households. The younger women were working in some form of war work – factory, farm or services – the older women did not want live-in jobs, nor full time ones. Certainly, at least, that was Dorothy's experience. Part time cleaning and general helping could still be available, but, for the majority of people, that was the most one could find. So in 1940 she had to learn to cook.

Being Dorothy, she learned to become a good cook very quickly, and a very good cook indeed after a remarkably short period of gaining experience. She always maintained that we lived much better after servants had gone. "I am naturally far too greedy," she would admit, "and so I made sure, as best I could, that everything came to the table as I liked to enjoy it." The whole experience was a challenge to her – as it must have been to countless other housewives across the land – and was one she took up with a degree of relish and a considerable measure of success. But it was hard work having to start when well into her forties.

As for something more specifically war work, that came to be provided, indirectly, by the use to which Bournemouth was put by the authorities. This fairly large, pleasant, seaside town, which had little to attract massive aerial bombardment, was selected as a place to which servicemen from all over the Empire would be sent on their first arrival in Great Britain. From memory, it was mainly those from Australia, New Zealand and Canada who came for their first experience of the Mother Country. And they were in Bournemouth in very large numbers.

It so happened that Dorothy was elected to be President of the Bournemouth branch of the Catholic Women's League in the first winter of the war. In early 1940 she and several others of her branch realised that there was a considerable need for some form of civilian care for the welfare of these young men. Many had left home for the first time, many were very homesick, some were unhappy, all were a long way from home.

The crypt of the Church of the Sacred Heart is a sizeable area. It includes quite a large hall, with a stage at one end. There are several more manageable rooms, including a library, a tea and coffee room and a kitchen. It is possible to enter and leave, not only through the church buildings, but also by means of direct access to Richmond Hill, through a door with the title (which I have always thought rather forbidding) above it of 'Catholic Institute.' Dorothy approached the (not very approachable) Rector, as the Parish Priest of Bournemouth was designated, to ask permission for the C.W.L. to be allowed to use the Institute as a club for servicemen. Permission was granted, and these intrepid ladies lost no time in putting their ideas into action.

The result was a considerable success. For virtually the entire war the club was open for long hours every day. It was open to men and women of all the services, of any denomination or none. The clientele was constantly changing. It would be Catholics who would get to hear of it first, so there tended to be more Catholics than others around, but none were turned away. Activities ranged from full-blown functions, such as a dance, or a Christmas party, to no more than a cup of tea and perhaps a sympathetic chat. But the place offered somewhere that was different from the barrackroom, where they could be quiet, and read their letters from home, and write their letters back in peace and quiet. There was no doubt in anyone's mind that it was performing a very valuable service which was greatly appreciated.

It inevitably involved a lot of work by the women of the League.

There always had to be at least one of them on duty throughout the hours of opening, and Dorothy did all, and more than, her fair share of that. To such an extent that Pat occasionally was moved to suggest that she needed to spend more time at home with her family. A view which I supported from time to time.

But Dorothy stuck to her guns, the success of the whole venture being its own reward. Harry was pleased to hear of it, writing at the end of May, 1940:

> Very gratifying to know you have so important a post and I am proud to know you are doing something for the benefit of our men. For years I have taken books and papers to the men in the Fort who are appreciative as they have so little to read…What you say about the garden and getting poorer interests. We shall all be as poor as a churched mouse, as some babu put it.

My attitude must have become apparent in due time and been reported to him for, more than a year later, he comments and pays Dorothy a rare compliment:

> Young Martin's request for you to keep to your own pure family was decidedly good. He must have known more than you think. Well, it is much for a boy to be proud of his family and testifies to the way you brought him up.

The second half of May saw the terrifying collapse of France and the start of the Dunkirk evacuation. By mid June the world looked very different from the cliffs at Bournemouth. Instead of Germany being safely tucked away round the corner in the North Sea, it was just over the horizon right in front of us. And, as if to confirm the awful happenings on the other side of the Channel, Bournemouth was filled with the evidence of them, in the form of thousands of French soldiers lining all the streets of the centre of the town. Hinton Road was no exception. Straight out of our front door and there were hundreds of them. A beaten army if ever there was one. Clad in their steel helmets and heavy greatcoats, despite the heat of the blazing

June days, they looked dejected, defeated and demoralised. Well they might, for their future was uncertain and the plight of their families unknown. 'If this can happen to the great French army, surely the finest in the world, what is going to happen to us?' Many thought along those lines.

And not only in Britain. Arthur cabled from Canada offering to provide a home for me and my cousins for 'the duration', as we called the uncertain period of the length of the war. There was a sense of urgency in the air, and I was acutely conscious of it. All my clothes were marked with nametapes in preparation for a sudden departure. "Whatever happens," said Dorothy to me, "we have to make sure you do not fall into the hands of the Nazis."

Her reply to Arthur is full of heartfelt gratitude, but also expresses the rather agonised doubt about the whole prospect of such an upheaval;

> ...I cannot begin to tell you how moved I was to read [your cable] and to think that you were willing to do so much for us and had not forgotten us – never since the war began have I been so near to tears – and, my dear, as for thanking you, I simply cannot – it is quite beyond me...there are no words to express all we feel.
>
> On...Wednesday night we had our first air raid warning. The sirens went off at 12.30 a.m. and the All Clear at 3.10. We all came down and huddled under our staircase in our dressing gowns with our eiderdowns around us. We had chairs and dozed off after a bit – there were two rather big explosions earlier on, but they sounded rather far away – as, in fact, we found out after that they were. I looked at Martin sleeping there in his chair and thought how awful it was that he should have to go through this.
>
> As for sending him out to you, we cannot make up our minds yet what to do. At first, directly I got your cable, I made enquiries, and found that it would be almost impossible to send him out privately – there are so many regulations. However the Government are now taking a hand and the schools too so we are waiting to see what plans materialise...
>
> I feel at times that I simply cannot bear the thought of letting Martin go. After all he has never seen you and scarcely remembers Pauline, and it might be years before I saw him again. If he were really homesick or ill it would be quite impossible for me to get to

him, and if/when you leave Canada, how is Pauline going to manage? I do realise, though, that compared with his safety, such thoughts count for little, but it is a terrible position to be in…

So there was hesitation. Yet again we all held our breath. The German army did not seem to find it as quick and easy to get across the Channel as it had to cross the Rhine. Instead of fleeing an invading army we watched dogfights in the sky. Tiny aircraft weaving to and fro, pretty white vapour trails behind them, high above our heads against the clear blue sky of those glorious summer days. Our new Prime Minister, Mr Winston Churchill, called it the Battle of Britain. And it seemed we were winning. He told us it was our Finest Hour. Was this the time for departing?

The Government itself was ambivalent about it. There was indeed a scheme for evacuation and many took advantage of it. We probably did not know at the time, but Mr Churchill, while not forbidding evacuation to Canada, had expressed his view to the Home Secretary that he 'entirely deprecated any stampede from this country at the present time.' Pat and Dorothy had probably made up their minds not to send me to Canada before the scheme was abandoned after the sinking of the *City of Benares* on 17th September by a U-boat. That disaster, involving as it did the loss of many hundreds of children, probably only served for them to confirm a decision already made.

I expect they were glad to have been able to decide to keep me at home. I know I was glad to stay.

Sometimes it is the small, and relatively unimportant things which cause the most emotional reaction. As if to emphasise the likelihood of it pouring when rain falls, in the midst of all the turmoil of military disasters and national peril, Jip, our springer spaniel, was taken ill. He was a young dog, only a little over five years of age but he managed to develop some form of internal ulcer. He was obviously in pain; the vet, Major Stothert (formerly a military vet: the father of our friend Max) could do nothing to relieve, it and for some days he lay about, not eating and growing weaker.

I realised he was unwell, but not how ill he had become. It was before the end of the summer term, and I was at school when the Major called again. He told Dorothy and Pat that nothing could be done for Jip and he advised having him put down. They had no choice but to agree. "I cried more over that dog than I ever did when mother died," Dorothy told me long after the event, "I knew I should never see him again, whereas I was confident that I would see her. Poor Jippy ran happily out after Major Stothert, and jumped into the back of his car. When I last saw him through the rear window being driven away, looking perfectly normal and content, I completely broke down."

Probably it was a last straw after all the traumatic events of the previous couple of months. She had recovered by the time I was back that day, and I was, strangely, only told that the vet had taken Jip away to look after him. Even more strangely (as I now think it was) Pat chose to tell me that Jip was dead one morning, maybe the very next morning, as he was driving me to school. Perhaps it was to give me very little time in which to grieve. I could not arrive in tears, and so I had to gulp, and pull myself together very quickly. If I had not managed to do so I might have had an uncomfortable day at school.

I evidently told Harry all about it in my next letter to him. In his reply of 24th September he wrote:

> To lose a dog is always a sad experience. In my time I've had many, all different in character but all full of devotion. The man who doesn't know the devotion that a dog can give, has missed quite a lot in life.

All hopes of taking up their bookings for another holiday in Sark had obviously been abandoned weeks, if not months before. They nevertheless managed a long week-end at a hotel near Shaftesbury in Dorset despite scares of invasion and air raids. I think the two of them were desperate for a short break.

And then it was back to the task of running the house, the many aspects of which fell increasingly on Dorothy's shoulders alone – although she did train me to be quite useful on the domestic scene, from which I have benefited ever since. Running the house included using all the cunning and guile which she could muster in dealing with the shopkeepers. I presume all housewives had their own technique for getting the best out of their family's rations. I daresay many verged on the unscrupulous in pursuit of the well-being of their family, a charge which Dorothy would probably have cheerfully admitted.

She had always tried to be friendly towards those with whom she had to deal, so it was natural for her to adopt the principle of being as pleasant to the shopkeepers as possible, and to spread her bounty – such as it was – to as many grocers and others as she could. You had to register with the shop which was to supply you with certain items. Bacon, butter and cheese are examples. She registered for each with a difference grocer. If, within her relatively modest budget, she spent well at a small grocer near Chingri Khal – where her order would count for more than in a town centre establishment, although she did patronise one of them – she might expect to be told of unrationed, rare items coming into the shop.

However she managed it, the results were eminently successful from our point of view. They may not have been universally popular. "I do not like shopping at Macfisheries," one patient declared to Pat. "Oh, indeed?" Pat replied, pricking up his ears, for he knew very well that Macfisheries was where Dorothy regularly bought excellent fish. "No," continued the rather disgruntled patient, "whenever I go in there, there seems to be a woman walking up the side of the shop calling out 'Archie, what have you got for me today?' and it seems like favouritism to me." "I understand," said Pat non-committally. And well he might be non-committal: he knew very well he was hearing a first hand account of Dorothy's activities. She had known Archie a long time. He knew she liked a Dover sole, and, if he had a few in, he tended to keep a couple back in case she came that morning. And that account was of her turning up in hope. During lunch that day Pat and Dorothy had a good laugh at his tale, and shared it with many friends in the ensuing weeks.

Sometime there was a *quid pro quo* to pay for the care and attention they received from their suppliers. One Christmas Day morning there was a ring on the telephone which I answered. It was not Archie but the manager of Macfisheries; could he speak to Mrs Tucker? So Dorothy came to the 'phone. "Oh, Mrs Tucker, do you think you could possibly speak to your husband for me. I've woken up with the most raging tooth-ache and do not know how I can get through the day – could he possibly see me?" Dorothy went to Pat and told him. "You'll have to see him: these are the people who are keeping us alive." So come he did, and went away a happier man.

Things seemed to happen on Christmas Day. In 1939 we drove to Chingri Khal for Christmas Day lunch, all in our very best best. That involved passing the door of Mr Green, our Butcher, of whom Jennie was also a customer. He was a very cheerful, outgoing man. "Tender?" he would loudly proclaim of his beef, "Tender? Tender as a woman's heart! Angels' food!" He knew his job through and through. That morning he was open. "We must stop and wish him a happy Christmas," said Dorothy, so Pat pulled across the road and stopped outside. Mr Green spotted the car, and, before any of us could get out, he hurried up, wiping his hands on his apron as he did. "A very Happy Christmas to you Mrs Tucker," he said leaning across the driver's seat and shaking her firmly by the hand. She smiled and responded appropriately. A few more words of greeting and we were on our way. Dorothy then ruefully counted the cost of their momentary stop and greeting: her brand new white gloves were bloodstained, and ruined. All in a good cause, she had to say to herself.

On Christmas Day, 1940, they had an interesting experience starting with the usual telephone call. This time it was the Royal Bath Hotel. Pat was much the closest dentist to the Bath, and among his patients were the Proprietors, the Head Waiter and the Head Porter. So they tended to give his name to a guest requiring dental attention. On this occasion, they said, it was a Norwegian gentleman who had arrived the night before. We were not away, nor having a big meal, so he came soon after 2pm. It transpired that he had flown into Poole by flying boat the previous evening. "I have recently been able to get myself out of Norway," he told Pat, "and I have come to England to bring Christmas Greetings from the Norwegian people to our King Haakon who is living in exile in London." It was getting on for 3pm, and Pat was finishing the necessary work, so he invited his patient to come upstairs to listen to our King George VI giving his Christmas message to the Empire. He was very glad to accept, and was introduced to Dorothy and to me. He was a most impressive man, and I am sure they had a very interesting conversation with him. All above my head, I expect, and I recall none of it.

Then the wireless was switched on. I would think we were as patriotic a trio as you could hope to find, but we would have stayed on our seats. Not so our guest. At the first sound of the drum roll he sprang up and stood rigidly to attention until the last notes of the National Anthem had faded away. We struggled rather sheepishly to our feet, looking and feeling more than a little awkward and embarrassed. We did all sit down when the music stopped, and remain so until the end of the King's speech. After a few more pleasantries our Norwegian friend left. I have often wondered who he was: we never saw or heard from him again.

Another happy spin-off from the Christmas season owed its origin to an idea that came to Pat as that day drew near. Great numbers of servicemen were billeted in two large requisitioned blocks of flats, Bath Hill Court, situated behind Hereford House and to the east. Their messing facilities were provided at the Winter Gardens. Not the old glasshouse. That had been pulled down with the completion of the Pavilion. In its place the Corporation erected an indoor bowling green, covering a very large area and with a completely flat main floor. It was to become after the War a very pleasant Concert Hall, but it was now also requisitioned and turned into a massive dining hall. In consequence there was a fairly constant stream of young servicemen walking to and from the Winter Gardens; and the most direct way to and from Bath Hill Court was along Upper Hinton Road and so passed our back door.

After consulting with Dorothy, who enthusiastically agreed with his plan, Pat chose an opportune moment to hang about near our back entrance and then to choose a likely looking couple of lads, stop them, and invite them to Christmas Dinner. Dorothy always got hold of the largest turkey she could find. We had got into the wartime habit of sharing Christmas Dinners with two or three friends who, like us, had only a small number of children. It meant several

Christmas Dinners and only one to prepare ourselves – rather a good bargain and it made the food go further. For us it meant using the large hall by the surgeries as a dining room, plenty of space, therefore, for guests, even extra ones.

The two young men were delighted and accepted. When the time came a few days later it was only one of the original two, the other was a replacement for some reason: it did not matter, both were charming. Particularly the first one – to whom Pat had originally spoken. All were Australians. This one was a Sergeant Pilot, from a family of sheep farmers near Brisbane, Phil Devine. He quickly became a friend of the family and while in England made as many visits as he could to Bournemouth. On one of those he took me for a treat to see the latest Walt Disney epic, *Bambi*, which was just on general release. He was a quiet, sincere and charming young man, obviously very glad to have some contact with family life in England. More than one Christmas dinner he shared with us, both at Hereford House and at Chingri Khal. It was a happy chance that Pat went up to him in the first place.

In the winter of 1940 to 1941 Jennie's health started to fail. She had had a tendency to laryngitis for some years. Now, as she entered into her eighties, it was turning to pneumonia and she had the first of a series of small stokes. For two years it was a case of two steps back and one forward, as she declined into a bed-ridden invalid by early 1943.

The Last Sacraments were administered to her several times as a crisis came and then went. Dorothy was present on most, if not all, of those occasions. Sad as they would have been, she did have to laugh on one of them, not the very last. Jennie alternated between being very devout, being unconscious and being only semi-conscious. Always having enjoyed a little flutter, and having tried to follow form a bit for that purpose, the sport of kings must have been on her mind, despite the ministrations of the priest. As she started coming out of a period of unconsciousness she opened her eyes, pulled herself together, and gasped out, "Don't forget. Five bob each way on Irish Duke." Apart from giving way to fits of giggles, no one around her bedside took any notice of what she said.

This was a pity. The horse won.

At first Harry's reaction to her declining health was really quite civilised. On 28th March, 1941, he wrote: "I am glad to know you mother is better and expect she will live longer than me," before going into some detail as to how ill he was. But only a week later a note of bitterness is creeping in.

> Sorry to learn of your mother's attack of pneumonia. I thought she was bedridden and therefore kept warm but I suppose the usual insanity – open doors and windows always; then complaints about the house being cold. How many times I've been ill and, at others, uncomfortable because doors and windows were kept open in spite of remonstrances. What did it matter about me? I had to get used to it at Home and had my food forgotten all about. Then I think of the devotion of my bearer on 25 rupees a month – and think. Of course to those in rude health open doors and windows may be all right but to ignore requests from the breadwinner, home from a hot country, struck many unpleasant notes. They added to the load of unforgiveness. It may be unfortunate that I remember these things, having so few to record on the opposite page.

The next month his letter was more about the progress of the war, and he probably meant some of his more vituperative passages quite literally as written:

> I was glad to see it stated that the reason the *Hood* was imperfectly armoured was through the fools and traitors who would not sanction an increase in the Navy. To put a few of those gasbags up against a wall in front of a firing squad would do quite a lot of good.

While religion gets its turn (it came round very frequently in his outpourings) in June – a relatively mild imprecation.

> That's about all. Plenty of worry about but – plenty of food, so I never sit down to a meal without sympathising with people at home. I never pray to God for anything. My religion is one of thankfulness. No mumbo-jumbo to keep lazy professional Christians, whose

principal occupation is idleness, free from anxiety. There are sufficient mugs in the world to believe the priesthood is pally with God. I decline to believe a word of that. Hope founded on humbug is a fine trade. Luckily it isn't that of   Your   affectionate father   H. Hobbs

But as 1941 passed into 1942 and Jennie was still alive, albeit in a very weakened condition, Harry's impatience with her turned to dislike and then, if he is to be taken at his word, to positive hatred. On 20th May, 1942 he wrote:

> ...I have no more use for...[your] drunken old mother... and to think that horrible old fraud believes she is pious because she performs a bit of judu now and again...And to think what a fool I've been to show that horrible old woman any consideration at all, when it never entered her head to consider me any more than she considered the policeman in the next city, makes me angry. If she goes to Heaven I hope I'll be lucky and never meet her. If matters move as I believe they will I shall not lie awake a moment worrying about that old woman who has such good treatment and is so utterly worthless...I've lived long enough and had a fine life with the exception of a marriage failure...Moreover misfortunes teach – often the only course of instruction. The pity is that that horrible old scarecrow is getting hers too late, but I hope she has some before she finds out what a bad bargain she made in paying priests to save her selfish soul. Luckily the only time my hatred rises is when I read your letters about her. I have no more sympathy for her than I have for a piratical Jap or Hun. If, therefore, you can refrain from mentioning her to me I should be grateful.

He seems to get almost hysterical about Jennie the following year. In ending a letter dated 10th February, 1943 – in which he comments that he has not heard from Dorothy for some time, acknowledging that that may be due to the war time postal problems (for she was a very frequent and quite regular correspondent with him) and so nothing from her can have prompted this outburst - his language is quite horrible.

> ...It is that dancing old scarecrow which has set so bad an example.

Booze and going round on her deformed feet while doing mumbo-jumbo in Church after having been tight every night of the week. A horrible old fraud with as much gratitude in her rotten heart as any pariah dog. It wouldn't hurt my feelings a bit if I knew she had a few testimonials like this the day before she finished this disease called her life. However she has worked out her own damnation. Unhappily she had done her damnedest to ruin her children comforting her rotten soul with a chunk of idolatry to make her feel good.

Your affectionate father   H. Hobbs

The effect that receipt of such a letter would have had on Dorothy's composure can readily be understood. And all the more poignant because that letter probably arrived very close to the time of Jennie's death on 24th March, 1943. As luck would have it, I had had some weeks off school earlier that term with rather a bad attack of chicken pox. In the irritating way that children sometimes behave, I had succeeded in passing that on to Pat in the form of shingles. This unpleasant illness had put him to bed for several days and made it very difficult for him to be the help to Dorothy with funeral arrangements and the like as he would have wished. In fact he was not well enough to attend her funeral: a rather splendid Solemn Requiem High Mass at the Sacred Heart followed by interment in the Cemetery, not far from her little grandson, buried there just nine years before.

Whether this letter was the final straw I do not know, but it was at about this time that Dorothy asked Pat to become a buffer between her father and herself. The frequent appearance of letters containing this sort of abusive material, mainly directed at her mother, was becoming increasingly a source of distress to her, and the arrival of a letter from India would all too often be followed by floods of tears. So Pat agreed that he would open every letter from Harry and read it. He would tell Dorothy whether or not it contained hurtful things about Jennie, or, indeed about anyone or anything else. Only if he told her it did not would she read it. If she did not read it, she answered it as best she could with Pat's assistance.

It is hard to understand why Harry persisted in writing in this vein. The occasional barb continued almost to the end of his life. When one bears in mind some of the earlier letters he wrote, his

501

glowing tributes and his abject apologies, his lack of fidelity and her perseverance despite it, the home she kept for him and his preference for India, it all seems so inconsistent with a man who proclaimed himself as someone keen to see fair play. Plainly he did not like it when a hint of criticism could be detected in any letter from Dorothy to him: he seemed quite oblivious to the effect his letters might have on her. Not to mention Jennie, for he continued to write to her. None of his letters to Jennie since the very few remaining from Dorothy's Journey of 1925 to 1926 have survived. I am sure all were carefully preserved and found by Dorothy in the weeks after Jennie died. It is useless to try to recall any now: I certainly had a few read to me, but probably none which Dorothy might have found really painful to read out. All have been destroyed. Perhaps it is better that way.

Jennie's death made one thing very certain. The sands of time were running out for Chingri Khal. Harry's letters, both for some years before, and immediately after her death, had contained many a directive as to what should happen to the house. Although he frequently acknowledged that 'it is a beautiful place' and would quite have liked it to have been kept in the family if possible, he appeared to resent Jennie enjoying it and kept issuing directives. Sell it, sell the plots of land (that is, the wood), take it over yourself, were some of his demands.

As it was not in his name but hers he could do nothing directly, only apply pressure as we have seen. But now that Jennie was no longer alive, it was inevitable that the place would be sold up. Jimmy and Phyllis did not want to buy it, with their family growing up and likely soon to be leaving home. Even more so, it would have been far too big for the three of us, even if Pat would have contemplated such a move for an instant. No, Dorothy had to face up to the fact that the end of the road for her old home was now in sight. And it was a prospect which filled her with sadness.

Bournemouth got off relatively lightly during the war. It was not important enough to be the target of a full scale Blitz like Southampton, or Coventry or so many others; it was not historic enough to be selected for a 'Baedeker raid' in the manner of Exeter and Bath. When the German target was one of the Midlands' towns the Alert would go between 8 and 9pm, and the All Clear between 5 and 6am. Through virtually all the period of the alert, German aircraft could be heard overhead, their unsynchronised engines giving forth a menacing, throbbing drone, and we could only hope they would not drop a stick of bombs to cheer us up en route, or to dispose of any left over on their way back. For night after night we slept as best we could in the large hall downstairs, later sometimes in the 'Morrison' steel tabletop shelter (named after the Home Secretary in whose time they became available) at the bottom of the large stair well.

Both Pat and Dorothy were heavy smokers. Dorothy realised that these disturbances were causing her to smoke half the night as well as all day. She was also well aware of my dislike of her having the typical smoker's nicotine stain on her fingers. She determined to give it up, and she managed to do so. Although occasionally reverting, briefly, to having a very occasional cigarette, the Blitz was the main cause for her stopping. Alas Pat did not take the same course; he may have paid dearly for that. Most of his adult life, certainly for so long as Dorothy had known him, he had had the most awful smoker's cough, which he did nothing to counter. I did not like either of them smoking, and I did tell them that, when I grew up, I was not going to smoke, but I was going to drink. That, at least, is a promise I have kept: never a single puff and – well, just a drop now and again is positively good for you.

Occasionally the town got some German attention all to itself. A noisy night in early 1941 saw the destruction by fire of Woolworth's in The Square, and of the Canford Cliffs Hotel three or four miles away. And sometimes there was a bomb or two, or a few land mines – once, it was asserted, a sea mine, which fell just over the cliff on to the Undercliff Drive, fortunately not on top of the cliff or there would have been much devastation. But from our perspective the greatest damage was caused in the 'hit-and-run' daylight raids by a single aircraft, or a small group of them. One Saturday afternoon a single bomb was dropped behind and above us, killing two elderly ladies sitting in their garden having tea. We happened to be having tea five miles away at the time, but we still felt the severe tremor. It was just as well that we were away from home. Most of the windows in the back of the house were blown in; there would have been a lot of flying glass.

But the worst incident was the daylight raid at lunchtime on Sunday, 23rd May, 1943, when a small flight of German aeroplanes dropped several bombs and machine-gunned the crowds sunning themselves in the gardens. Two big stores were badly damaged, Beales, only two hundred yards from us, subsequently burning down in spectacular fashion. Two hotels were destroyed, with considerable loss of life. Pat packed a Gladstone bag with first aid kit and went out to render what assistance he could. He was gone for some hours. There was much help needed. In due course Dorothy found herself providing refreshments for the fire fighting crew positioned just opposite our front door. They were Canadians. They enjoyed her jam tarts: she had finished them only seconds before the raiders came over. "All of this is on the Canadian Government, Madam," said the chief officer, and, sure enough, a few weeks later a food parcel came labelled 'With Compliments of the Canadian Government' written all over it.

The streets were a sea of glass, and we had several windows, in the front of the house this time, blown in. Our apprentice mechanic brought himself in, very kindly, to see if could be of use, and he helped with running repairs. In the midst of all the death and destruction Deane Webb, who had walked the short distance from his home to see if we had been affected, was fussing around the house as temporary window covers were put over the many broken panes, 'Mind my white paint' he was heard to say more than once, trying everyone's patience not a little.

By now Deane Webb was well into his eighties but was still almost as much of a shadow over the practice and how it was run as he ever had been. However, he was capable of acts of generosity, on both the small and the larger scale. Once, early in the war, Dorothy and I were going out for a walk and we paused at the window of a rather superior – and expensive – gentlemen's outfitters in Westover Road where the ties were displayed, and we were arguing about which one we liked the best. "Choosing your wardrobe?" we heard Deane Webb ask as he came up behind us, and we explained. "I like <u>that</u> one best," I asserted, pointing to a dark green tie with multi-coloured medallions on it. It was pure silk, very expensive, all of 8s. 6d. (42½ new pence.) We all laughed and went on our way. When Dorothy and I got home, the green tie with the coloured medallions was there waiting for me, and it remained in my wardrobe well into the nineties.

It was a similar impulsive thought which came to him at the end of one of our dreary visits to his house. He got to his feet and remarked to Dorothy "I know you are fond of beautiful things." He reached up to a fairly high shelf and took down an *objet d'art* which he handed her. "I would like you to have this," he said. It was a metal urn, some four to six inches tall, in very bright ormolu, and mounted on a small pillar of heavy pink and white marble. I have no idea of its value. It was certainly very ugly indeed. Dorothy, of course, expressed delight and much gratitude. I was most impressed: it looked like gold to me. I was disabused when we got home. It was a bit of an embarrassment: we had to keep it on view in case he turned up, but it was not a thing of beauty. However it is the thought that counts, as they say, and that thought made at least some impression on Pat.

Of much more substance, when the time came for my starting at boarding school in 1943, he gave Pat the fees for either my first term, or my first year. I was not told for many years, and memory now fails as to what I was told. But whether for a term, or for a year, it was a significant gift, even allowing for the relatively low level of fees in those days. Pat was far from well off, and the help was most gratefully received. And it gave him, he thought, good cause for much hope for the future.

CHAPTER 30

THE SECOND DECADE
(2)
SEPARATIONS

FROM SOON AFTER the drama and tension of 1940, there was another, quite different problem, that had been growing in importance. What was to be done about my further education? Miss Harries had been an obvious convenience; a year at the Convent had been too short, and I had been too young, for it to have been any sort of bone of contention; while the appearance of St. Peter's was almost manna from Heaven. Dorothy had been determined that I should be at home for as long as possible, rather than going to a boarding school at seven or eight. Her brother had had to go away at about that age, and she did not want to repeat the experience in the next generation. I believe Pat had no problem at all with my going to St. Peter's. He had met many Jesuits through being married to Dorothy; he had got used to them, and recognised that the teaching, discipline and general set-up there was second to none.

But St. Peter's had no Sixth Form, and would not prepare for University entrance. Besides they both hoped that I should go on to a Public School. But where? Arthur had been at Stonyhurst, the great Jesuit school, in effect their flagship. But that was hundreds of miles away in Lancashire, and was not a journey they would countenance in wartime conditions. Beaumont, situated in Old Windsor, was much nearer. It also was a fine Jesuit school, John Hickey had been there, and his son was there by the early 40s. But still Dorothy hesitated. She was not altogether sure that a further five years with the Jesuits was what she wanted for me.

It was rather a lonely position in which Dorothy found herself. As there was really no question of my following Pat and his father to West Buckland School, he came close to opting out of all decision making about my schooling. Even if he had hankered after my following in his footsteps, and I have no particular reason so suppose that he did, he did not try to press its cause. He just left it all to Dorothy.

Inevitably Harry put in his oar, although the fragmentary nature of the surviving correspondence does not always make the context clear. Writing in February, 1942, he was quite encouraging:

> Don't trouble Martin too much about getting on at school. 'Clever boys – dull men,' is often true. And you may remember that fine old priest, Father van der Mergel, who went with us as far as Penang.* He was head of St. Xavier's College. His opinion was that boys don't start to think until fourteen; education today may pre-date that by a year but boys should not be forced. However expect you know more about it than I do.

While in June, 1943, by which time, of course, the die had been cast, he was changing his mind from something he had proposed (probably emphatically) some time before.

> Perhaps I wasn't quite right about the Public School for Martin; he is clever, but it is a great misfortune to a boy to be an only child. Too much care of him is taken; too much fuss is made of him; all that sort of thing ruins a boy. He should get away from his mother or she will find that, after spending 21 years of her life in safeguarding him, another woman will come along and turn him round the other way in 21 minutes. Sell the house and use the money. Get him away from home so that he can have his head punched and punch other heads.

I am glad I did not come to read this last extract until quite recently: I have to state that I do not recall being either the recipient or the donor of any head punches.

Working it out for herself, Dorothy remembered something which Jimmy had told her when he had been at Dartmouth. As Second-in-Command one of his duties had been to accompany the College teams when they visited other schools in the West Country. One of those schools had been the Catholic school of Downside, some twelve miles south of Bath, and he had told Dorothy what a fine

---

* See Chapter 18: the spelling varies thus.

school it had seemed to him to be, and how much he had enjoyed the company of its headmaster, a Father Trafford.

She was familiar enough with the educational opportunities available to know that Downside was a Benedictine school. She thought a friend of hers had sent a son there. A search of a road map showed that it was even nearer to Bournemouth than Beaumont was. So, in the summer of 1941, she decided to write to Father Trafford, reminding him of Jimmy and making preliminary enquiries. If she did not know that he was by then Abbot, she soon found out when he replied, putting her in touch with the Head Master. The latter also replied, sending a prospectus and other information, and encouraging them to pay a visit to the School with me.

The visit did not materialise until the Easter holidays the following year. All three of us went to stay for a long week-end. Pat's car had been laid up six to nine months before, because the petrol allowance was so small he did not think it worth keeping it on the road. So it was the first of many journeys by train on the old 'Somerset & Dorset Joint Stock Railway,' usually known, with a mixture of affection and exasperation, as 'the Slow & Dirty.' It tended to be both.

I was given merely a matter-of-fact explanation that we were going to see a possible school for me, probably for the following year, and I went along with that quite happily. I was not aware of there being any problem between Pat and Dorothy about it, and, indeed, there may not have been any outward problem. However, It would not have been at all surprising if each had approached the encounter with the Head Master with more than slight anxiety.

Pat would certainly have had some questions before even fixing a visit. "Who runs this school?" "It is run by the Benedictines." "Who are the Benedictines?" "They are probably the oldest order in the Church, much much older than the Jesuits." "They are priests, then?" "Probably most of them are, but not necessarily. They are an order of Monks."

Monks!! What would have been Pat's first reaction to hearing that? The sound Protestant education he had been given probably said little about monks, and what it did say was likely to have been highly uncomplimentary. Christmas cards depicting fat, carousing men, sinister tales of underground passages and fraudulent exploitations of the gullible and pious may all have featured in his imaginatiion. Did not Bluff King Hal get rid of all of them? And did not Good Queen Bess complete his work when her half-sister, the grim-faced Bloody Mary, had tried to put the clock back? Could he allow his only son to be educated by such as these?

I doubt if he said any of these things to Dorothy, but he would have been less than human if doubts about the whole prospect did not come into his mind. And she for her part must have known that he may need some convincing. She needed a bit of convincing herself, for, apart from Jimmy's chance remark some years before, she knew nothing about Downside and not a lot more about the Benedictines. Inevitably, Pat had signed the promises then required of the non-Catholic party to a mixed marriage, which included bringing up any children as Catholics, and to him a promise was a promise and had to be kept. But there are always limits, and a wholly inappropriate establishment might well stir up some very disagreeable disputes, and she did not relish the thought of any such thing on top of her father's attitude to Jennie.

So one Friday soon after Easter, 1942, we set off by train to Shepton Mallet for three nights at the Guest House for Downside, at that time in the building now used as the infirmary. It was then run by the senior classics master and his wife, Mr and Mrs Neville Watts. They made us very welcome that evening and it made a good start. Our appointment was for mid morning on the Saturday. That gave us time after breakfast next day, therefore, just to have a quick look at the Abbey Church. We had caught a glimpse of it from the taxi the day before. Pat had already started to develop his interest in churches, as buildings, and this one looked as if it might be promising.

It was only a short walk up Abbey Lane, next to the Guest House, before we were in the shadow of the huge building. Much larger than any church in Bournemouth, perhaps larger than any church I'd ever seen up to then, except for Exeter Cathedral. But mere size is only a small indication of what, if any, aesthetic delights there may be inside and Dorothy lingered in the tiny porch, set in the temporary west wall, looking at books, pamphlets and the like on display in racks. Pat, with little interest in them, and more impatient, opened the door into the north aisle.

"Dothie, Dothie, look at this," he exclaimed with a bit of a gasp. We followed him in. The serene simplicity of the north aisle, followed by the grandeur of the nave, the choir and the great east window almost took our breath away, and we stood open mouthed at the end of the Church which was still and silent, with that almost palpable feeling of quiet you only experience in a very large building completely enclosed. Then a man – a layman – appeared from somewhere in the Church and offered to show us round. He had, apparently, shown many round in peacetime: there were few customers in the war. But we had to thank him and decline; the time of our appointment was getting near.

So it was back down the Lane with another favourable impression in our minds, and along the main road to the School entrance, up the winding drive to the door we were advised to try. Our ring was answered by a maid, who seemed to be expecting us. She led us along what seemed to me to be miles of corridors, some narrow, some wide, some dark, some bright, until she asked us to wait at the foot of a long, broad staircase. A few moments later I saw a tall, lean figure coming down the stairs, his black habit, only a couple of inches from the ground, swaying gently from side to side with each step down. He greeted us.

"I'm Rudesind Brookes," he said, "the Head Master asks me to give you his apologies for not being here himself. The news came through this morning that the father of one of our boys has been killed in the Far East. The Head Master felt he had to go and break the news to the boy himself, and, as the boy is in Cornwall at the moment, he will not be back until late tonight. He knows you are staying for the week-end, so he hopes you will be able to meet him tomorrow after High Mass. In the meantime he has asked me to show you round and answer any questions I can."

With that he took us to the Head Master's room where he and Pat and Dorothy were on the same wavelength in a trice. The reason for the Head Master's absence was impressive, rather than anything else, and Dom Rudesind could deal with most academic questions. Then he took us on a tour of the School, of the Abbey Church (where he showed us much more than any normal tourist would have seen, including vestments, communion plate and other treasures) before returning with him to his room in the School where he was Housemaster of Roberts. By the time we came to take our leave we were not merely well informed about the school and its environment, its history and tradition. During the course of our talking with him it had emerged how he had been a late vocation, that he had served in the Irish Guards during and after the Great War, becoming, as Lieutenant, ADC to the Governor and Commander-in-Chief of Malta before deciding in his late 20s to become a monk. "I would like to be able to go back into the Army as a Chaplain," he said, "but the Abbot wants me here at the moment. I am hoping he may change his mind one day."

Both Pat and Dorothy were completely captivated by his easy charm and impressed by his personality and achievements. For Pat in particular it opened his eyes to the reality of the Benedictine tradition. Doubts and fears and hostile stereotypes went out of the window in an instant and were replaced by enthusiasm. By the time they were alone together in their room at the Guest House he said to Dorothy, "If my son can be educated by a man like that I have no objection of any sort to his coming to Downside."

From then on it was all plain sailing. The meeting with the Head Master the next day was completely satisfactory. Dom Christopher Butler was a very different character from Dom Rudesind. Very much an intellectual, a classics scholar (he spoke fluent Latin) and a theologian, he nevertheless had a great ability to get on with all whom he met. Even as a gauche schoolboy, going to see him in his room in the Monastery after he became Abbot some years later, I found that it was always easy to talk with him, whether about serious problems, or daily trivia. My parents liked him at once and the upshot was that I was entered for Downside, for either that September, or September, 1943, depending on how I fared in the scholarship examination, and to go into Roberts, the house presided over by Dom Rudesind.

Of all the many decisions which Pat and Dorothy must have made for me in the first score or so of years of my life, I have no doubt that the most important and the best was the decision to send me to Downside. By the time we left after that week-end (the old Slow and Dirty did not operate on a Sunday at all) I was very happy at the prospect and told them it felt a bit like leaving home.

In fact by the time I got there Dom Rudesind had indeed achieved his wish and gone back to the Army. The Abbot had relented by the end of the summer term following our first visit. He did become a Chaplain to the Irish Guards, served with great distinction and was awarded the Military Cross. He never came back to work in the School, being assigned by Abbot Butler, as Dom Christopher had become by the time he left the Army, to various other Downside-run establishments. But I never forgot that first visit, and the huge part he had played in smoothing what might otherwise have been a very difficult path for Dorothy. Entirely unwittingly, I expect, from his point of view. Just another couple of prospective parents with their son to be shown round. Almost routine. And yet crucial for us, especially for me. So it gave me enormous pleasure to meet him again for the second, and last, time more than forty years later, at the Easter Reunion at Downside in 1984. It was in the Abbey Church. He was very old and frail, and was being assisted by a much younger Monk (who had been in the School with me.) I told him about that bright April day, forty-two years before. Of course he did not remember it: how could he? I told him I owed all of this – gesturing rather expansively around the church – to him. I don't think he altogether believed me – "My dear boy" was his delighted, if sceptical, response - but he was tickled pink to be told it. It was the truth. I was glad to have told him. By the end of that year he was dead.

I duly sat the Downside scholarship exam in the summer term of 1942. The papers were sent to St. Peter's, so no travel was involved. To no one's surprise, I imagine, I was unsuccessful. Just as well as things turned out. And not merely because I would really have been too young to start there at twelve. On a Saturday the following May – as it happens the week-end before the bad hit-and-run air raid at Bournemouth – a tragic accident occurred at Downside when a naval aircraft crashed near the cricket pavilion, killing nine boys, and injuring many others. They were nearly all younger members of the school, and it is more than likely that I would have been in that

Downside Abbey Church in the 1940s – before the re-ordering of the Sanctuary.

Jennie in about 1930.

Harry in August, 1947.

Edith in 1939.

*Dorothy with Matthew Larkin
at Larkin's Cross, June, 1959.*

vicinity had I gone there a year earlier. The disaster was reported in the national press, only very briefly, but enough for Pat and Dorothy to know about it, and to be glad I was still at home.

Later that summer term I again sat the exam. Some financial easing of the school fees was essential for Pat to feel he could afford to send me there, as well as to indicate that the outlay might be a sensible investment. We were all pleased that this time there was enough of a success to secure both: I was awarded an exhibition which both produced enough reduction in the fees to make the outlay of the next five years just about affordable, and made Pat and Dorothy think that it was worth affording it.

To have to prepare for my leaving home for boarding school at the same time as helping to prepare her old home for sale made that summer a sad one for Dorothy. I had outgrown my 1940 clothes by then and so there was another rush of marking with nametapes. My measurements had to be taken and sent to the school tailor who did a brisk trade in fitting out-grown Regulation Suits for new boys. This was important with clothes rationing and clothing coupons being scarce. Another, shorter, visit to Downside to see the Head Master was fitted in during the second half of the summer term. It was just as successful as previously – but I was conscious of an uncomfortable sinking feeling in the pit of my stomach; leaving home was soon to be a reality, not just a talking point.

The previous two years had seen September holidays in Devon with our friends the Stotherts, but we took ours on our own earlier in 1943 to be ready for both these substantial changes in family life. Dorothy and Phyllis selected what items they wanted from the furniture at Chingri Khal. Once the Breaks family had moved out to their new home in Ferndown, a few miles north of Bournemouth, these items were taken out, together with Dorothy's grand piano. The auctioneers brought in other articles sent to them for sale. The garden was hardly tended – just enough to stop it becoming a wilderness and putting off a purchaser. My visits to all my old haunts became fewer and fewer. I have no recollection of a farewell occasion. Maybe fortunate if I did not have one: I had quite enough sad dreams afterwards about the place as things were.

Dorothy had a last look round. I am glad I was not with her. There was so much for her to recall: the first discovery with her father, thirty-two years before; peaceful days and family gatherings; parties in the house and parties in the garden; laughter and tears; weddings and receptions; departures and returns. Too many memories, too big a wrench. But there was a future ahead which needed her attention. She shut the front door firmly, and walked down the drive for the last time.

Thursday, 16th September, 1943, was a difficult day for us all and a bad day for Dorothy in particular. It was the day for new boys to arrive at Downside, a day earlier than the rest of the School. Pat had decided he would take me there this first term, and that meant the same train journey, and an overnight stay in the village, returning on the Friday. It happened also to be the second day of the sale of Chingri Khal and its contents. The house and the wood (the latter a separate Lot: it was in Harry's name, not part of Jennie's estate) were auctioned on the Wednesday afternoon, the contents over the next two days. The house itself fetched the almost ridiculously low price, as we should think today, of £3,000. Half of that was site value (five plots) – the wood (three plots) went for £1,000. Dorothy could not bring herself to go to the sale: Hall was there and reported to her by telephone.

To cap it all a letter arrived that very morning. I think it was the Christmas Holidays before they told me: they did not know I happened to be by the bathroom door when Pat opened the letter – he usually brought up the post to read before he shaved. I heard his horrified gasp, "It's Phil," and then Dorothy's heartbroken wail "Oh no." The letter was from the Air Ministry. Apparently on 24th June Phil Devine, by now commissioned as a Pilot Officer, had had an accident on taking off. His aircraft had crashed and he had been killed. He was only twenty-two. Our name and address had been spotted among Phil's effects and, sensibly, they decided to let Pat know. We had all been very fond of him, he had become virtually one of the family, and Pat and Dorothy had begun to feel almost *in loco parentis* towards him. It was curious, perhaps, that they did not tell me, nor I comment to them more or less instantly. I expect they did not want to add to my emotional turmoil; and I did not want to comment if they did not mention it.

So it was rather a tearful Dorothy who said good-bye to me after an early lunch, when I set off with Pat in the taxi to Bournemouth West Station. She nevertheless managed to write a short but welcome letter to me that evening. By the time Pat returned on the Friday she was "feeling much better" as Pat reported in his first letter to me on the Sunday, redolent with good, fatherly advice. Thankfully, they seem to have had a very normal time once he had returned.

Correspondence on that pattern, two letters a week each way, continued regularly throughout my time at School. They were also punctilious about coming once a term to stay in the village, take me out, and meet some of the masters, certainly Head Master and Housemaster. There was little in the way of Half Term in those days. If they had not come to Downside it would have been the full twelve to thirteen weeks of the term before we saw each other. I think they enjoyed doing it, rather than finding it a tiresome chore: certainly I was always glad to have their visit.

The rest of the war years continued along much the same pattern. The practice had rather picked up after the severe dip in 1939 and 1940 and was bringing in much the same as in the mid thirties. Pat and Dorothy felt some need to economise to counterbalance the school fee obligation, making do with a short break at a hotel in Brockenhurst in the New Forest in both 1944 and 1945. The New Forest may not have been Devon, but it was a short train journey to Brockenhurst where they liked to go for a day out, usually for a long walk through the Forest. In the early summer of 1944 they were nearly arrested, having blundered into the normally empty woodland to find themselves surrounded by soldiers, tanks, guns and military artefacts of every description. They had stumbled upon the preparations for imminent invasion. Some quick talking, absence of a camera, the return railway tickets and, I daresay, an honesty of appearance, and they were allowed to retrace their steps without further hindrance. How any sort of secrecy was maintained is a mystery. No one could, or did, try to stop them strolling to the cliff top at Bournemouth, half a mile from their front door. From there the bay seemed to be full of shipping as far as the eye could see, from The Needles to Durlston Head. D-Day was soon after that. I saw none of it: it was all during the summer term, and we were not distracted at school very much by these momentous events, although, of course, we read about them in the newspapers.

It was the same the following year when VE Day was celebrated. We enjoyed the consequent whole holiday, or perhaps it was two whole holidays, which the Government decreed must be given to schoolchildren. I think the Head Master thought it a bit over the top, but we got all that was laid down. There being no television, and as any newsreel which came to our weekly film show was always weeks, even months out of date, I never saw the images of the excited crowds in London, nor do I recall even hearing Churchill telling them that "it is your Victory."

Likewise the General Election was entirely conducted during the Term, including the short period of the 'Caretaker Government' between Polling Day and the counting of the votes after the Service Vote had been brought to this country. My parents were, however, able to take me to a political meeting in the summer holidays occasioned by the by-election at Bournemouth when the sitting member (Sir Leonard Lyle) was elevated to the House of Lords to make way for a Conservative middle-weight (Brendan Bracken) who had lost his seat. It was an interesting experience for me; they wanted to get me as well informed as they could.

By contrast to the celebrations for the end of the War in Europe, VJ Day, was in the middle of the summer holidays. By August 14th, 1945, we had returned from our stay in Brockenhurst. On the nine o'clock news we were told that the Prime Minister would be speaking at midnight. "You'd better stay up to listen to this," said Dorothy. It was long after the normal bedtime for a fifteen year old then, but I jumped at the chance. We all suspected that it was the end of the War, and this was something not to be missed. So we were all listening in when Mr Attlee told us, shortly and simply, that, indeed, Japan had surrendered and that the War was over. "What a pity it wasn't

Churchill," was Pat's comment, and we all agreed. The National Anthem was played on the radio and Pat turned up the volume, and opened the windows for the benefit of any non-existent pedestrians in Hinton Road.

I was soon in bed, too excited to get quickly to sleep. Besides, what was that noise? It sounded like voices. Could it be cheering voices? Dorothy came into my room. "There's some excitement going on in the town," she said, "get up and get dressed and we'll go out and see what it is." I was ready in double quick time and we went out for the most exciting hour imaginable. The Square was packed with people, thousands and thousands of them thronging the pavements, the roads and the gardens. The occasional car could hardly move. On the roof of the traffic shelter in the middle there was a band from some American unit, playing with great gusto, their drum major twirling his baton to look like a dish of silver. Everyone was in the happiest of good humour. It made a memorable end to the six years of War. We could put all that time of sadness and danger behind us and really look forward to the future with confidence.

The war years had brought welcome news of the birth of a son to Arthur and Pauline in 1943, whom they called Harry, and so the name Harry Hobbs continues to this day. A second son, Walter, born about two years later, sadly developed an illness in infancy, never satisfactorily diagnosed, which retarded his mental, but not his physical development, and he has had to spend his whole life in an institution, lacking any real rapport with anyone.

In January, 1945, came the surprising, but welcome, announcement in the New Year's Honours List that Harry had been awarded the MBE. The precise occasion for this honour was, and remains, a little obscure. He eventually told Dorothy, when she was able to ask him, that he had helped someone, who held some official position in the Indian Establishment, and who was down on his luck. But whether it was a personal or a professional problem, or the help was practical or financial, was never made clear to any of Harry's family. There was a double cause for rejoicing at that time as Dorothy Mary – Toff, as she was always known by everyone by this time – was married on 6th January, at the Church of the Sacred Heart like her mother and her aunt. Her husband, Ian Collie, and she had known each other for many years, as Ian's home had also been in Queen's Park Avenue. It was cause of much regret that Harry could not be home for the event.

It was around this time that the existence of Miss Briscoe became openly acknowledged, although the earliest surviving letter mentioning her is dated as late as 1951. There is nothing now available to tell me when it was, certainly after the end of the war, that news came from Harry that he and Miss Briscoe intended to get married. I believe it was the first I had heard of Miss Briscoe, but the situation did not seem to cause Dorothy much surprise. Indeed, she was quite glad to think that someone would be out there, willing to look after her old father, who was by now over eighty. Both families sent good wishes and congratulations by telegram, but in the event nothing happened. They never did get married. By this time they each had a flat in Park Mansions, he was number 11 and she was number 6. Harry continued as Managing Director of Spence's Hotel, and Miss Briscoe continued to assist.

Writing in 1954, Harry recalled an incident from this period. The passage tells us a good deal about how he viewed himself, and India, and Partition, and Independence, and a whole lot more:

> Often accused of insulting people, which was partly true, I can claim to have attacked dishonesty, cowardice and disloyalty for fifty years and never once been contradicted nor accused of exaggeration.
>
> There are none so cheerful as the successful scoundrels, but not when I'm about. Dishonesty has made British merchants cowardly, and cowardice breeds disloyalty. Never once have they said a word about the partition of India, nor even muttered a protest against the base desertion of India. Times without number have I jeered at British merchants over this and been secretly hated, boycotted and ostracised, while every thing I say – and I talk sense – is suppressed. Even the papers were ordered not to take down anything I said at meetings.
>
> Shortly after the war ended I went to see a sick man who started to introduce me to a lady visitor. She said, "I know you Major Hobbs;

I used to work for the European Association. They were always afraid you would come to their meetings. How they hated you!" I think I ought to have "How they hated you!" on my tombstone. [1]

I think it is rather a pity that no one told him – at least I do not believe anyone could have told him: he would surely have reacted if anyone had – that the motto of the Emperor Caligula was *Oderint dum metuant.* ('Let them hate provided that they fear.') It would have suited him very well, and he could have incorporated it into his letterhead. It would have looked very jolly emblazoned over the main entrances to his business and to Spence's Hotel.

As the war progressed Deane Webb became rather less active, although my no means unable to get about. He attended Jennie's funeral, for instance, looking much as I had always remembered him. But the occasions for him snooping around the house seemed to get fewer. Thus encouraged, Dorothy began taking risks with the garden, such as it was, at Hereford House. She had gradually been able to prune properly the rhododendron hedge at the front wall. "If I do a little at a time," she would say, "the chances are that the Deane Webb will not notice." She was right; he did not notice. Nor did he notice other improvements, a bit of planting here, a flowerbed made there. We were greatly daring when we found, in a derelict former garden on the level above Upper Hinton Road, known as Parsonage Road, a considerable quantity of crazy paving slabs. No one was ever going to miss them, so we took to going up at dusk and coming down with a couple of slabs or so each, and tossing them over our back fence to start with. All quite fun. Shades, I suppose, of Mary Jane and those expeditions into the Talbot Woods. Whether it was lawful or not, we did it, and thus we were able to improve a few paths at the back. Nothing could conceal the unsatisfactory features of the garden, particularly its outlook, and how it was overlooked, but Dorothy gradually got it producing more flowers than one would have ever thought likely. Deane Webb never complained, but by the end of the war his health was evidently in decline.

I had had no idea of it at the time, and did not come to any sort of realisation of the situation for many years, but it was the case that Pat thought he had good grounds for believing that he had expectations from Deane Webb. For merely a straightforward business relationship there would have been no need to be so considerate towards Deane Webb. The manner in which the practice was run virtually did not change at all. "So as not to upset Mr Webb." No locks were put on the private part of the house to keep it private – that is to keep the landlord out. "So as not to upset Mr Webb." Rent reviews upwards were accepted without demur; so were more stringent clauses in the lease on renewal if the landlord so required it – which occasionally he did – all in the same cause. At least once each holiday, before and after going to boarding school, I was taken with them when we all went to see Mr Webb. I expect they went occasionally without me during the term. We would sit in his dining room. About as dark a room as one could hope to find. Thick, dark curtains, very dark wall coverings, dark furniture and lit only by one table light, and the light over the large picture above the fireplace. I would gaze at this painting for what seemed like hours, until the grown-ups made a move, wondering what on earth it was. Almost entirely black, it was hard to discern any detail beyond a dull orange sun, rather low down in the frame. Was it rising or setting? There was no means of telling. That sole spot of colour only seemed to emphasise the great gloom otherwise surrounding Deane Webb.

Nevertheless Pat felt there were grounds for optimism. Especially once Deane Webb had very generously paid my first term's (or first year's) school fees. But it went back long before that. For all his hardness as a landlord, Pat had always got on personally quite well with Deane Webb, who tended to call him "My boy." And when he said from time to time, as he did, "You'll be all right, my boy," together with a slap on the back, it did seem to be a fairly significant token of good will. After all, he was a bachelor. His only relative was his half-sister, Stella, who had no children, and she died some years before he did.

Having lived a long life, he might well have many friends as well as old retainers to whom he would want to give legacies. But there was no obvious person to inherit the bulk of his estate and so what about

Hereford House? Pat knew he had paid a high rent for many years. Had Deane Webb got it in mind to leave the place to him? He was believed to be worth a significant amount – not huge wealth, but enough to make the value of Hereford House only a fairly small proportion of the whole. Pat became convinced that the considerable burden of rent for home and practice was nearing its end. That seemed the most likely manner in which he would "be all right."

Thus when Deane Webb died just before Christmas, 1945 – on 19th December – Pat felt that the Season of Good Will might have something rather significant to offer him. It therefore came as a considerable blow when he found what Deane Webb had actually done. He left many pecuniary legacies, personal and charitable, about fifty of them, ranging from £10 to £2,000. Pat received £500. So far so good. To Louis Carter and to Ellen, in addition to pecuniary legacies, he gave each an annuity for life. Then came, for Pat, the crunch.

Deane Webb 'recommended' that the rents from Hereford House should be used towards satisfying these annuities – which totalled £850 a year – and only when no longer required for that purpose should the property be offered to Pat to buy if he wished, and then only if he were personally still in practice there. The price at which the place was then to be offered to Pat would be a sum Deane Webb would disclose secretly to one of his Trustees.

Pat was advised that this clause in the Will was invalid and unenforceable because it purported to be no more than a recommendation, not an out-and-out direction. Just as well, probably, that this was so. For what Deane Webb wanted to do was to tie up Hereford House, and to keep Pat paying an exorbitant rent in order to provide for the future of Deane Webb's two former mistresses. As it happens Ellen had died before Deane Webb, but Louis Carter was a much younger woman, probably still in her sixties. The house may have been required for her annuity for a score of years. After all that Deane Webb had said to him, this seemed to Pat not just a let-down but a slap in the face.

The situation was complicated by further bad drafting of the will and its codicil. The residue of his estate was originally divided among five charities, two of which were hospitals. As a result of the outcome of the General Election, Deane Webb (rightly) assumed that the hospitals were soon to be nationalised. So he cut them out, the codicil simply saying the hospitals 'shall not receive any share' of his residue. As the will did not state expressly that the share each hospital might have had was to be split between the other three charities, the Revenue claimed the hospitals' shares as an intestacy. Litigation ensued, and Pat was helplessly caught up in these wrangles.

Pat felt it was essential for him to retain Hereford House both for the practice and as his home. The possibility of moving both elsewhere seems not to have been considered. The solution eventually arrived at was for him to make an offer to the charities in the hope that they could be persuaded to sell to him at a price which was not out of his reach. I was aware of some of these problems. Dorothy rather bitterly once said to me that there was no organisation so uncharitable as a 'charity' and they were being even more tight-fisted than Deane Webb. However, eventually they accepted an offer of £7,250. This was a good deal more than the pre-war value of the place, which had been the secret price given (unenforceably) by Deane Webb to his Trustees, but I am not possessed of detailed figures. He had to obtain a mortgage – privately, through a Client of his father's old firm – of £5,000. The whole saga was not completed until September, 1948, after close on three years of considerable anxiety. The litigation continued, but, I believe, was ultimately compromised; I never learnt to what effect. The new arrangements would have resulted in a considerable reduction in the outgoings from his rent, but was still a millstone around his neck which he was not able finally to pay off until three months before he retired.

Despite these difficulties Pat and Dorothy maintained a cheerful exterior. A curious facet of Pat's character revealed itself in 1946. One of his patients let slip the fact that a relative of hers was running a small hotel in Woolacombe. This small Devon town, it will be remembered, had been the scene of many Tucker family holidays over the turn of the century and beyond, as well as of Bert's gallant rescue. The opportunity to go there again with his family was too good to miss. So a fortnight or so was duly booked up, and Pat was much looking forward to showing Dorothy and me around his old haunts, and for us to enjoy them all with him, just as he had done with his family.

When the time came it proved, alas, an almost complete disaster. The summer of 1946 was mainly very poor. We drove to Woolacombe through deluging rain, and could see the corn rotting in the fields around us. It was cold, wet and miserable for virtually all our time there. But what made it really almost unbearable was the hotel. A small affair, made out of two suburban houses, next to each other, but not physically linked, it was cold, bare, and uncomfortable and the food, even considering the rationing difficulties (worse in peacetime than they had ever been during the war,) was execrable.

On the one morning when there was a glimmer of sunshine for a few minutes, which she saw as she woke up, Dorothy said facetiously "What a lovely day for a swim." Pat took her at her word, and came into my room and said "Dothie says it's a lovely day for a swim, let's go and have a dip before breakfast." The beach was just the other side of the road, it could have been tempting. But of course there was no sunshine by the time we were down there. The sea was unbelievably cold, and neither of us stayed in more than a very few minutes. After which it was "Run up and down the beach to keep warm while we dry ourselves." Not even mad dogs would join Englishmen 'enjoying' such an early morning swim, and we never attempted another, not at any time of the day. I promptly got the most frightful cold and sinusitis. Altogether typical of a thoroughly unsatisfactory holiday.

But Pat seemed hardly aware of how unpleasant it had all been. After I had gone back to school they met the Hibbs for lunch. Dorothy was walking with Winnie, and telling her about all this. "It sounds rather a waste of money," was Winnie's comment. "Oh yes," said Dorothy, "a complete waste of money." Pat overheard this exchange, and was very deeply hurt and offended. He took Dorothy to task when they were on their own. He seemed oblivious of the failings of every aspect of that time away. He wanted the best he could get for her; he had provided this holiday to his former haunt, and so, in his mind, it must be regarded as the best, despite reality.

She felt she had to stick to her guns, and make him see and understand the reality of the position, and that she was not in any way blaming him. No use pretending all was fine when it was not. I think she succeeded in explaining her opinion to him. But he always retained that tendency to want to regard something as excellent if he had set his heart on it being excellent, regardless of its real worth. Unlike his father-in-law, he did not relish complaining about any sort of service – and he very rarely did so.

By contrast the following year we had a memorable fortnight or more in Scotland at a hotel in the Trossachs, which was being managed by the former head waiter of the Royal Bath Hotel. It was a marvellous summer, the sun shone every day all day, and the hotel and the food and the scenery were all first class. A day in Edinburgh, going to two events at the first International Festival, was a splendid bonus. It all more than made up for the disagreeable experience of 1946.

There was no holiday for me the next year, 1948. My last term at Downside ended on 24th July. On the 19th August I had to join up to start my National Service. It was something of a culture shock for me. It was an upsetting time for both Pat and Dorothy, and her tear-stained face as the train drew out of Bournemouth Central did nothing to make me more cheerful on my journey to London. It was to be for a period of about fifteen to eighteen months, later extended to twenty months. After that it looked like being Oxford. Why Oxford? Probably because as a small boy I preferred dark blue to light blue, and had always wanted Oxford to win the Boat Race. Dorothy, obviously, took the side of Cambridge. I had the mortification of Oxford's long series of defeats in the 1930s, but that did not put me off. And then Arthur had been at Oxford. So Oxford I chose. I had got the necessary examinations under my belt. I had not got a University Scholarship, but Christ Church, my chosen College, largely because it had been Arthur's, had offered me a place. The Local Authority had indicated they would give me a grant. Pat was prepared to underwrite the rest.

In fact Pat was coming up to what he later was to call his 'good year.' The National Health Service started to operate on 5th July, 1948. In the planning stage there was much opposition from the medical and dental professions. If I knew, let alone understood, the arguments both ways at the time (which I doubt) I recall little of them now. "It will put a premium on bad work," was one of Pat's comments. Dentists were offered high fees for each procedure carried out, regardless of time spent, or conditions at their premises. Dentists were sceptical as to how long that level of pay would last. It was going to mean the end of Pat's voluntary work at the Hospital Dental Department. Every Tuesday morning since he had begun in Bournemouth in 1927 he had given his services at the Hospital. Other dentists in the town filled in other times. Thus those who could not afford to pay for treatment would be seen free of charge. At least that change would give him an extra half day a week.

The dentists in Bournemouth voted against going into the scheme, but soon had to alter their attitude. Regular patients were waiting for them to change their minds. Institutions like schools were making enquiries. So in a very short time all were in the fold. And the initial benefit can be seen from Pat's accounts. His takings were good in 1948, second best to date after 1946, but 1949 saw a rise of more than a third in fees received. The Minister for Health, Mr Aneurin Bevan, then decreed that Dentists' fees would be cut by 20%, and that was swiftly followed by a further 10% cut. By 1952 Pat's takings were back to the level of the early 1930s, or only a little above. But he had had his 'good year' and that helped him to cope with my prospective University career.

By chance, St. Peter's School all those years ago had had a small laboratory and a very well qualified scientist in the Community to teach science. Greek was not taught. So I got into Downside on a science ticket. It was natural that I kept to the sciences. Physics and Chemistry were my main sixth form subjects. I got my place at Christ Church after a scientific set of exams, mainly Chemistry. But I had very little idea what I wanted to do with any scientific learning.

During my time in the army I came to he conclusion that I did not relish the prospect of reading Chemistry. But what else could I take up at the great age of twenty, which I would have attained by the time I was discharged? The answer seemed to be Law. For good or ill, I decided to ask to change my subject from Chemistry to Law. Largely on the basis that, if I had to start from scratch, I had better choose a subject where everyone will be starting from scratch. So I wrote to the Senior Censor at The House and told him what I wanted to do. He simply replied that he 'noted' that I wanted to read Law. As simple as that. No questions asked, no complaint, no comment.

I told Pat and Dorothy – whether in a letter or when home on leave I do not recall – and they did not demur. Indeed, neither of them attempted to influence me in any particular direction in my career then, or at any other time. I suspect that Pat had had so much direction as to career in his early life that he felt that the less he interfered the better. I also suspect that Dorothy would have been only too glad to put in her oar if I had asked for advice. It may have been foolish of me, but I never did ask them for their advice on career moves in any respect at all that I now recollect, and they seemed content to let me do what I decided to do.

Part of the reason for my being a little independent minded at that time was undoubtedly due to my being away from home for quite long periods at a stretch. Although I was never posted abroad during my military service, for most of the time I was far enough away from home to require at least a 48 hour pass to make the journey to Bournemouth seem worthwhile, and such passes only came up infrequently.

It is not surprising, therefore, that I was not at home on the day in late August 1949, when a telephone call came from Jimmy. Typically, he used a naval metaphor. "Panic parties out," he announced excitedly, "the Old Man is coming home."

CHAPTER 31

THE THIRD DECADE
(1)
THE SPOTLIGHT ON HARRY

THE NEWS CAME without any warning and thus made the maximum impact on both families. It transpired that this was in no sense a return of the wanderer to end his days in his native land, nor even an extended holiday. Rather prosaically, it was 'for purely medicinal purposes.' Apparently Harry had been experiencing some medical problem which was not being helped by his normal primary cure of three or five grains of calomel. The medical people in Calcutta thought he probably needed an operation. If I was ever told the precise nature of his condition, which I doubt, I have long forgotten what it was. The doctors advised more up-to-date techniques than available in Calcutta and suggested he came to London. He had become a Mason in the early part of the century, and, although he had not been a very regular attender at their functions, he had kept up his membership. Thus enquiry of the Royal Masonic Hospital procured the promise of accommodation and treatment for him should he come back to England.

Whatever the immediate occasion for his homecoming, it was obviously going to be a major event for both families. Dorothy looked forward to it with a mixture of emotions. First, there was great delight that her father, dearly loved for all his troublesome characteristics, would once again be around, even if only for a short time. For all her life, up to the fourth year after her marriage, his long absences from her home had been regularly interspersed with prolonged periods with her, abroad or at Chingri Khal. But for sixteen years now he had been away. Difficult years. Years of war, years of death and change, years of maturation. She had missed him and, in many ways, been regretful that he had not been able to make his regular visits home.

But then, on the other hand, she was fearful. What would he be like when back here living with one or other of his now independent families? Would he still be subject to those furious outbursts of temper? Would he vilify her mother again? Would he be a domestic tyrant and dictator? Would he get on with Pat – or even with her?

Whatever reservations she had at the back of her mind, and there were plenty of them, sheer joy at the prospect of meeting him again was certainly uppermost in her approach to the day, which was not far ahead. He was not going to use the P&O Line this time. It was before the era of the jet airliner, but well into the era of air travel. Slower than the jet was to make it, air travel was nevertheless vastly quicker than the sea voyage. Two days or so from leaving Dum Dum, the Calcutta airport, and he would be in London. Mid September was the intention, and so they had to make arrangements quickly.

One decision was quickly made. He had announced his intention of staying, when not in hospital, either at a hotel or at a club in London of which he had kept up his membership. Both families agreed, and persuaded him to agree, that when not necessarily in London, whether in hospital or elsewhere, he would stay with one or other of the families in their home.

My National Service kept me away from all preparations. I was not very far away, but far enough not to be able to get home easily. The camp at Lydd, in the middle of the Romney March on the South Kent coast, was some eighteen miles west of Folkestone. From there, it was a good train service to London. A 36-hour Pass, letting one off duties at noon on Saturday, would only give time to get to Bournemouth late that evening, and require one back by 2359 on the Sunday, so having to start back by mid-afternoon. A game not worth the fairly considerable candle of cost and effort. But a visit to London was another matter, and so I was able to be in on the Great Reunion.

Harry's flight was due to land in the late evening of Saturday, 17th September, close on midnight. He would stay the first night or two at his Club, situated in Whitehall Court, not far from Trafalgar Square. Pat and Dorothy had been able to get a room there as well, and one for me for the Saturday night only. I had 'civvies' at camp for off-duty outings, but only relatively scruffy ones. Dorothy brought with her my best suit and other necessary accessories so I would not look out of place in such surroundings. I arrived that afternoon, but it was thought better that I should get a normal night's sleep rather than join the reception party which was going to the airport. So it was Dorothy and Pat, and Phyllis and Jimmy who went to greet him on his first arrival in England after so long.

Dorothy was a little concerned as to how he would be. How frail had he got? Would his illness have made him weak and debilitated? Would his first experience of air travel have exhausted him? She need not have worried. When he first appeared through customs he was as fresh as if he had just got out of a taxi from a couple of blocks away. Upright, vigorous, full of talk in his loud, even strident voice. But when he saw Dorothy it was "Who is this?" Probably no one had told him that she had gone (prematurely) very grey, even white, and he did not recognise her. That was soon put right, and she embraced him delightedly. And so the high-spirited talking went on, in the cab to Whitehall, and into the Club. So much to talk about, so many anecdotes, stories galore and a lot of laughter. It was now well into the small hours of Sunday morning, but his voice did not moderate. Up to the area of their rooms, where, inevitably, there were other rooms, but the high spirits continued.

Then another door opened and an irate, elderly, protesting figure emerged, clad in pyjamas and dressing gown. "Don't you people realise the time?" he complained, "some of us want...er...er...can that really be old Harry Hobbs?...Good Heavens yes it is...Harry, Harry how wonderful to see you after all these years..." and they were off with more uproarious chat. It was three in the morning or later before any of the welcoming party got to bed that night.

I managed to sleep through all these high jinks. My turn came at breakfast next morning for which I had got down in good time, before anyone else of our party. I confess to being somewhat nervous. I had last seen him as a larger than life character, telling stories to make me laugh, but very much the head of the family, presiding at the top of the table. And I had been only three years old, little more than a baby. Since then I had learned something of his reputation. Now I was a soldier of sorts. Not much of a sort, I felt he would think. The call-up authorities must have seen my Higher Certificate in science and decided to put me into REME (The Royal

Electrical and Mechanical Engineers.) Few were getting Commissions by then. I doubt if I would have been given one even if they had been going in profusion. I was not, and I knew I was not, the military type. Not at all the sort of young man, it seemed to me, to appeal to Harry. Before demobilisation I had risen to the dizzy heights of Paid/Acting/Corporal. By this historic moment I doubt if I had even one stripe. I remembered that Dorothy had said to me, many months before, "If you had got a Commission in the Guards, the Old Man would probably have given you an allowance." Some hope. I felt very apprehensive.

And then I saw him marching into the dining room. I got to my feet, a firm grip of my hand and shoulder, a kindly smile and a blue eyed twinkle and his loud voice, "Hello Martin, how are you enjoying the army?" I had expected some such question and had prepared some such answer as "Oh, not too bad, thank you Grandpa, I'm coping with it all right." "Well, I suppose that that is as much as one could hope for," was the realistic comment as he sat down. And so the ice was broken, and it became fun.

I have often felt it was a great pity from my point of view that he did not make this trip six or eight months later, by which time I was out of the Army and waiting at home to start at Oxford. As it was I saw very little of him. That first Sunday flew by. Lunch en famille, tea probably and then I had to leave soon afterwards to catch the train back to Folkestone. And during the rest of his time I was able to get myself only one 48-hour Pass. That let me depart from after duties on Friday afternoon, again to 2359 on Sunday. Two nights at home – worth the travel and expense. But it was a very little time in which to get to know him at all well. Had I been aware then of all the details of his past life that I know now, and realised that this was my last opportunity to talk to him, I may have tried harder to persuade some understanding officer to allow me a little more time to be at home while he was there.

For he was at Hereford House quite a lot. He went there after that first week-end for a day or two before going into the Royal Masonic

Hospital. That proved to be much less traumatic than many had feared. Whatever his complaint had been, the doctors managed to treat it. He did not have to have any operation. The time he spent in the Hospital was quite short and he was able to enjoy his families in England. First at Hereford House, then at Portsmouth, where Jimmy, by now a Rear Admiral, was stationed and had his home, and then back to Hereford House until his departure for India.

He also found time when in London to visit the offices of *The Daily Mail* where the editor was Mr Frank Owen. Harry and he had worked together during the war when both were involved in the official SEAC Newspaper* for some years. Frank Owen embraced him with delight; more cries of "Harry, Harry welcome back." At that time Frank Owen was writing a column in his paper under the pseudonym of Ian Coster, and he devoted the greater part of that column to Harry on 27th October, which will be found set out in Appendix 3.

From Dorothy's point of view it was one of the most completely happy and successful periods of her life. She and Pat pulled out all the stops when Harry was with them. They gave him my bedroom, and made an office for him in the second, largely unused, surgery. All their old established friends, some of whom he knew from of old, some he did not, they invited to dinner. Not all together – the dining room would only take six in comfort, eight at a pinch – but on different evenings. Friends responded with invitations for them to bring Harry out and to meet others. He found himself the centre of attention and in interesting company, and he thoroughly enjoyed every minute of it.

There were two aspects of Bournemouth life which struck him particularly. The first was how hard the lady of the house – the Memsahib – had to work. Not a question of telling cook it would be eight for dinner and we'll have roast beef, and then enjoying yourself until the gong rang. He saw for himself the shopping, the fetching and carrying, the table laying and clearing away, the cooking and the washing up. He couldn't get over it. He must have heard about these things, from correspondence as well as from the papers, but it had not got through to his imagination. He was most impressed at the sight of so many ladies doing it all for themselves – even if their

---

* South-East Asia Command.

husbands did give some help, as most of them did.

The second thing which struck him was almost the opposite of their hard work. It was the comfort of their homes. Dorothy had found, and was later to find again, that his abode, at any rate, in India had little about it which gave any feeling of relaxing in comfort in an easy chair. Carpets and curtains were more or less non-existent. A bare bulb dangled from the central ceiling light. Many of the furnishings at Hereford House were quite old, but they had picked up one or two rather good pieces over the years and it made for pleasant surroundings. There was no central heating in the flat at all, so Pat made sure that the open hearth was put into use by the time Harry was staying there. He had always been going back to India when fires began at Chingri Khal. To sit in front of an open fire, in a softly padded chair with a newspaper or a book to read, or someone to whom he could talk, was almost a completely new experience for him, and he relished it.

As for his famous temper, that never manifested itself at Hereford House. Dorothy found that he had mellowed a great deal. He still liked to hold forth with everyone listening to him – both the intended and the unintended audience – and he often went off at a tangent with "That reminds me of a story" and to recount an experience, not infrequently one he had told us about before.

And then there was the piano in the lounge. By this time the upright had been moved downstairs into the large hall in the professional part and the grand was in its rightful place. He played it quite a lot. No longer set pieces. "No, no, I can only play what comes into my head now," he said to me when I asked for something, I forget what. He played by ear, with a firm, clear touch, tunes from the shows, popular songs, whatever came to mind as he sat there. The piano was well positioned, with a large window behind the player. To see him at the keyboard in the sunshine gave Dorothy much pleasure, as well as a bit of a lump in her throat.

He did not mention Jennie. Not once. Dorothy did, on one occasion, ask him if he wanted her to take him in the car to see Chingri Khal. His monosyllabic reply, "No," was as much of an indication of his feelings for the past as she ever got. It would probably have been a mistake for him to have gone there to see it, and certainly heartrending for Dorothy. She avoided Queen's Park Avenue if she could, and if she could not, she got past Chingri Khal as quickly as possible. It was but a shadow of its former self. The house had been converted into flats. Three houses had been built on the wood, two more on the rose garden and 'back' lawn, and others on the north encroached into what had been the kitchen garden. At that time the old name was retained, strangely, for it is awkward to spell, and meaningless outside the family. I am glad that it now has a different name. I hope it makes happy homes for those who live in it. If Harry had retained any feeling for "the beautiful place," it could only have been upsetting for him to see it. If he had not, then why go at all?

He had just under seven weeks in England. On Thursday, 3rd November, like an Old Campaigner he was packed and ready to leave in plenty of time. What more natural for him then, than to sit down at the piano; the piano he had designed and selected and given to Dorothy nearly forty years before? His heart was close to bursting at the prospect of leaving, but he launched himself into a cheerful selection of whatever came into his head. Tunes from the shows, popular songs, military songs. From time to time he would stop and ask, "Is the *gharry* here yet?" And when told, "No, not yet." he turned back to the keyboard and carried on. 'The Man that Broke the Bank at Monte Carlo,' 'Who were you with last night?' 'The Soldiers of the Queen' – they all came tumbling out.

But, inevitably, there came the answer "Yes, it's here, we'll start loading your things." Then the mood changed. 'Tipperary,' 'Pack up Your Troubles in Your Old Kit Bag,' 'There's no Place like Home,' 'Auld Lang Syne.' There was not a dry eye in the house, nor a throat without its lump by the time he rose from the stool and strode out to the taxi.

And so to London and on to the airport. Phyllis and Jimmy were there as well as Dorothy and Pat to see him off. You could see friends off properly at that time. "I saw him walking steadily across the tarmac," Dorothy wrote to me afterwards, "carrying a bag of fresh, ripe pears he had bought at the airport shop. He climbed the steps and at the top a stewardess held his arm and guided him in, and that was the last I shall ever see of my beloved father."

She was right. It was.

The great success of the whole trip from Harry's point of view is manifest from his letters home after he was back in Calcutta. The first of these, dated 10th November, shows that, however much he had been affected by the events surrounding his departure, he had lost nothing of his Hobbsian spirit in the process.

My darling Dorothy.

Well, here I am: after being 46 hours without lying down, tired with work and callers who keep me from doing what I ought to do.

I am not ashamed at showing my feelings when we parted. The tears come into my eyes now when I think of the loving kindnesses which overwhelmed me. There was too the feeling that we might never meet again – also I don't like travelling. Seated in my chair near the fire in your beautiful home was almost new to me, and I was ever so proud of you.

Miss B sent a chit to my room asking if her name would be on my cable or should she send a separate one. That was yesterday. I was too tired to go to dinner. This Thursday morning I began to feel like an insurable risk, but I was tired beyond words.

You and Pat were the 'Everest' of kindness and I didn't like going away – never have I been so upset, and "Farewell" is the saddest word in the English language. I have had to say that far too often. It was my intention to write a long story; bought airmail envelopes to hold it, but that is as far as it goes, so far.

Several men on the plane knew me. One curious happening. At Brussels two men were at a table. I sat down and eventually one man asked, "Are you Harry Hobbs?" Admitted that and he told the other, "This is the greatest man in India," leading to talk. Expressing my views about India led the second man to say, "I see that you believe 80% of what you say!" Sensing that that was a practised bit of dodging I retorted: "I don't say 20% of lies. When I express opinions they are 100% as near as I can express them I'm not trying to convert anybody, and I don't care a damn what anyone thinks."

Although seated in corresponding seats, we never spoke until he was disembarking at Delhi; he came over, shook hands. "I want to see you again." "Come to tiffin," said your loving father   H. Hobbs

And the following week he was still marvelling at his experiences in England, also referring to a short break Pat and Dorothy seem to have had – I do not recall being told about it.

> I haven't yet got over the parting. And when Jim wrote about my walking with martial tread to the plane – well that was just about the exact opposite to what I felt. You gave me a delightful time; every hour I compared the loving welcome with how I should have felt had I been even in the Club, to say nothing about a hotel. Well, I am everlastingly grateful for all you did only regretting that you had too much to do. You and Pat were not only ideal hosts, but excellent audiences. It was the most enjoyable time I have ever spent in England and never was I so sorry to say farewell…One pleasing thought was that you had one or two days without having to cook and wash up. What a change that must have been to you. Actually that was felt by me to be about the only real return for your loving kindness.

He still came back to the same theme on 27th November:

> …I understood that all your kindnesses meant work and was sympathetic while all the while feeling how miserable I would have been had I stayed in an hotel. Often out here when I read the menus I say how much you at home would enjoy the bounty and still further thought what a treat it would be to have everything done for you. I derived a lot of happiness to know [of] the few days of respite from washing up to say nothing about cooking. More than all the rushing around I enjoyed those quiet days with my comfy chair and the cheerful fire.

He was more perspicacious than he may have realised in his assessment of the work his visit had created for Dorothy. Not just the extra mouth to feed, of he who, inevitably, could not be expected to play any significant part in the domestic scene, but also the considerable extra entertaining that was undertaken for his benefit. Those twelve steps in all from kitchen to dining room and back, often when carrying heavy trays and loads of all descriptions, had taken their toll. During the war years to start with, and now this visit had been a pretty heavy additional burden.

I was home for a fortnight's Christmas leave and Dorothy was well enough then to my eyes. But I had not long returned to my unit in the New Year when Pat told me in a telephone call I made that Dorothy had had to go into a nursing home for a rest and treatment. A 'strained heart' the doctor called it. He gave the two of them a bit of a lecture. "It is not for me to tell you where to live, but this house could turn into a killer if you do not do something about the way the layout here makes extra physical work."

Any sort of change tended to be anathema to Pat, and the expense in addition of making a fundamental move away from Hereford House, whether to live, or to work, or both was not something he could contemplate. What they did do was relatively simple, and a pity they had not thought of it before. They got a carpenter to build a bridge, using half the width of the staircase, from the top step by the kitchen door to the fifth step on the final flight to the lounge and dining room. The number of steps between kitchen and dining room was thereby reduced from twelve to two. It was still quite a long walk, but it became more manageable. And Hereford House must have been one of the few homes in Bournemouth, or even in the country, which had two bridges, one outside and one inside.

The few days in a nursing home were followed by a few weeks in Meyrick Mansions Hotel, just at the end of Hinton Road and run by an old friend of hers, before Dorothy was thought fit to get back to the normal grind. For many years after that she was fearful of her heart, although I do not think it can have done anything other than make a full recovery: it was the strength of her heart which kept her alive for so long.

In mid to late April, 1950, my inglorious military career came to a welcome end, and all of us were very happy to be a threesome again. It was a little under six months before I was due to go up to Oxford. I cannot claim to have used the time very fruitfully, although I did try to do some preliminary reading. It was, perhaps, long enough to encourage laziness, not long enough to be useful in the way in which today a gap year may be useful. That summer, however, proved to be a grand opportunity to hear the Bournemouth Municipal Orchestra, as it was then still called, performing weekly in the new Winter

*Pat and Dorothy
at the end of the bridge
at the back of
Hereford House, 1948.*

*Outside Whitehall Court,
18th September, 1949.
(Left to right) Ian Collie, Toff Collie,
Jimmy Breaks (holding Keith Collie,
Harry's first great-grandchild, age 1)
Harry, Martin, Dorothy.*

Gardens. Dorothy was only too glad to come as well, and even Pat, who was not someone to whom music mattered very much, enjoyed many of our evenings there. This was interrupted at the end of May for seven frustrating weeks by the music strike, which came very close to killing off the Orchestra altogether. We had a very successful holiday at a hotel in Minehead, in Somerset where Holman, the former Head Waiter at the Royal Bath Hotel and later Manager of the Trossachs was now in charge. It was to be our last family holiday together.

That summer would have been an obvious time in which I could have learned to drive the car. In common, I suppose, with many young men and women, I had taken out a Provisional Licence in the first holidays in which I turned seventeen, that is in April, 1947, and followed it with a second, so lasting until the October. Pat paid for some professional lessons for me. But I did very little driving of the family car. Consequently, when I took the test towards the end of the summer holidays that year I was failed; quite correctly. I had had far too little experience. Why I did not insist on learning properly as soon as I was demobilised I find hard to understand now.

In the way parents can, Pat and Dorothy enjoyed my three years at Oxford, which started in October, 1950. There were no academic problems that they found themselves facing on my behalf. I made at any rate one important career decision in my first year, namely to opt for the Bar rather than for the Solicitors' branch of the legal profession. I did not ask their advice, they did not proffer any off their own bat. I think they were glad when I told them – both glad to be told, and glad I had decided that way. They expressed no regret that I had not consulted them beforehand. Again Pat was reluctant to be involved in that sort of decision making. Dorothy would have liked more social life than I was able to offer them when they came to Oxford. She had in mind parties and dances with Arthur and his friends, thirty years before, and was hankering after a repeat of those times. But life was very different. Quite apart from the rather short shoestring on which I was coping, food rationing continued throughout my time at The House, and entertaining in one's rooms, at any rate in any style, really never took place.

They rather went to town for my twenty-first birthday in April, 1951. First a family dinner party in Meyrick Mansions Hotel. A few days later they gave a cocktail party in our large hall for a considerable number of friends of all ages, followed by a dinner dance in the Royal Bath Hotel for a dozen or so of us youngsters. It was all a very generous spread on their part and a very happy time all round. Harry wrote in his usual vein, and I now much regret that his letter has been mislaid. Such of it as I recall has been set out in Chapter 1. The Festival of Britain that year almost continued the celebrations. They borrowed the flat of a friend, which was situated somewhere in the S.W. district of London, very convenient for the West End, shops, theatres and, of course, the Festival itself on the South Bank. For a week or so in June we had a busy time making the most of the fun.

A letter from Harry that month must have made Dorothy sit up for a moment. After saying how he had had food poisoning, he went on, 'Some days before I fell ill I met Bagnall who came out with you in 1925. He is now a Captain in the Indian Army Ordnance Corps working on one of the munition factories.' Nothing more. Nothing to say how he was, how he looked, whether he was married, whether he asked after Dorothy. Had Harry realised that she had called him her 'Devoted Slave,' and that he had been really very smitten with her? She must have been full of questions in her mind. The remark would have meant nothing to Pat when he read the letter; but it would surely have made her think back over twenty five years and pondered her luck.

That long vacation I realised I had to learn to drive, and rather demanded assistance in achieving that end. I think it was difficult for both of them, in different ways, to do what I wanted, but they did it. Pat's car was a bit like a child to him. He looked after it, washed it, polished it, and took great pride in it being kept very spick and span. It was a wrench for him to agree to my driving Dorothy in the car when she needed to take it around the town. And as far as she was concerned the very act of allowing herself to be driven by a complete – almost complete – beginner was, as Dorothy put it, a great 'Act' on her part. And so for several weeks I drove her shopping, parking the car, coping with a fair bit of traffic, and getting really used to handling the machine. A few professional lessons at the end to prepare me for the test and I got through all right. It was a relief to have that under my belt. Harry's laconic comment was 'So Martin has become a taxiwallah and it will do him no harm to learn a bit about cars.'

In the same letter Harry goes on 'Miss B. is determined to go to England next year and is almost packing up. It is likely too that I shall go too as I'm working but drawing no pay.' However nothing ever came of any such plans. One gets one clue as to his reasons – one of his reasons – for remaining in Calcutta from a collection of letters written by him to a M. Leon Petit. There is little to tell me who this gentleman was. Harry met him in about 1950, seemingly when M. Petit (it appears he was a Frenchman with a home in England) was working at Spence's, very possibly as a chef. Certainly he did some cooking for Harry, and for friends of Harry's in the early fifties. In addition he was a budding author, who sought Harry's help and advice, which were freely given, and also a keen amateur photographer, thanks to whom we have a record of Harry in extreme old age.

When M. Petit was in England on a home visit Harry wrote to him on 3rd January, 1951:

> I have not been inside Spence's since you left. They are striving hard to make the place pay but the fact is that splitting India into three – India proper, West Pakistan and East Pakistan – have raised constant hostility and trade barriers so that they drift farther apart. Yet after all the disorder and bloodshed we had Nehru in Calcutta. Estimates from half a million to a million gathered to meet him. As he doesn't know Bengali he had to talk in English, and not even half a brick was thrown. It might have been a parson's tea party. How he manages to get about making 8,000-word speeches five times a day, making long journeys, too, is amazing. He can't keep it up without a breakdown.
> I expect your mind comes back to our beautiful weather, with

bright sunshine and servants to wait upon one. I expect you feel like I did at Home. In India I'm a Sahib. In England nothing but a bally native.

Six months later he returns to the subject of Spence's Hotel.

> …You must understand the change (debasement) that has come over Spence's Hotel which had a character so different from what has been thrust upon it.
> 98% of the people who used to say Spence's was a home from home were apparently steady decent folk, staying 20 and more years to earn their living. The gradual, but steady descent to life such as can be found in parts of South America robs this Country, so far as British residents go, of its former respectability. (The more the World improves the worse it gets.)

So there we have his two reasons – or were they excuses? – for not retiring to England. The English weather (mainly the winter) and the lack of servants. Considering that he was treated like a Lord and waited on hand and foot on his visit home in 1949, and in addition managed to choose one of the longest and most pleasant summers of that time, one can only wonder if he was being entirely frank. But he comes back to the same theme six months later when M. Petit was again in England.

> …I fear the Hotel is going phut. Hardly anyone living there – few come to concerts, air conditioning blew up – no punkahs and bills to be paid…After your stay in India I don't think you will find the cold pleasant. I consider myself wise and lucky to be here. It is hot at times but 'it ain't cold.' Things are dear but you can buy them if you have the money
> My family want me to go home but I consider having a servant worth the advantages offered by England when the weather is good. Unfortunately for England conditions are often not what we liked.

The late summer of 1951 was saddened by the sudden death of Edith. She had given up her beautiful flat, I suppose because of perceived need to economise, and took herself first of all to her favourite Hydro in Derbyshire where she had often 'taken the waters.' While there she had fallen ill with appendicitis, strangely perhaps at her age of 75, and had been operated upon, apparently successfully. A day or two later, however, she had a sudden heart attack and died at once. Her funeral in Exeter was well attended. She had been much loved, and was greatly missed.

Harry's letter to Dorothy for her birthday in 1952 is very affectionate, and in reminiscent mood, and touches on the fear of every mother – especially a mother of an only son:

> In 1897 I had taken your mother to England and was in bad health through overwork. So far as I remember I had been back here three, maybe four weeks when the news of your arrival came. It was a pretty grim struggle for me but I had confidence and industry and stuck at it. Not until the £1,000 I won in the Calcutta Sweep did I make much headway, but that was no end of a lift up...
>
> I hope Martin will long be the apple of your eye and no other woman will obtain too strong a hold on him. To me, that seems the only risk outside health.
>
> You have a good home and Pat is real gold – a fine man...

I did not see that letter at the time.

By the summer of 1953 Oxford for me was drawing to a close. It all seemed to have gone well, but one took nothing for granted. Finals started the day after the Coronation, so I spent that great day swotting like mad. I only allowed myself to switch on in time to hear the actual moment of crowning on the wireless. (Cambridge was kinder to its Undergraduates: Finals there were brought forward so that most, if not all, had finished in time to join the London crowds if they so wished.) It seemed a good sign that I was asked to return for a *Viva Voce* exam, but it added to the tiresome wait. By the time the results came out I was in digs in London, having begun six months as a Bar Student at a fairly large firm of Solicitors. Both Pat and Dorothy telephoned to my digs. I forget who spoke first with the words "Good news," and I knew all was well.

The timing was good, too. It was just before Harry's birthday, and Dorothy was quick to send him a cable with the result. That produced a letter from Harry to me, which might be described as a piece of vintage Hobbs. It is Harry at his best, and I have dined out on it, and passed on his words to children, godchildren and anyone who will listen. It certainly caused much merriment at the time. The enclosure must have been a cheque: I regret that I do not recall the sum in which it was drawn.

23rd July 1953

My dear Martin,

A cable just to hand this morning that you had gained your B.A. with second-class honours and your Mother considers it a fine birthday present for me, which it is. I felt sure of it but after all there must be ever so many risks about it. Well, these subsections of the alphabet after one's name are real marks of distinction 'lifting a man above the common herd' and to those like me, seeing these decorations at a distance, are recognised as something worth having. I congratulate you but without something more to show the practical side the enclosed will, I feel sure, make you feel like the Village Blacksmith who 'And he looks the whole world in the face, for he owes not any man.'

What a difference it makes in life to be, if only for a short time, financially independent. The feeling, as a man of experience, is to be free from petty anxieties and I feel sure you will be a better man while the money lasts.

Have a number of cables and letters to acknowledge, so, with my hearty congratulations and wishes for future success, I'm glad to confess I am proud of you. Whatever you do don't make a fool of yourself over any woman. There is a hell of a lot of women and when you begin to feel that life without that particular one is unbearable, get busy with another one. Love is the most transient of our emotions. You can lose your heart and lose it over again even when it isn't yours to lose. As the worst vice is ADvice, I suppose you will do exactly what you like and I can say "I told you so!"

Your affectionate Grandpa   H. Hobbs

Merriment there certainly was, but I expect Dorothy hoped that I would realise that there was a serious point he was trying to make. I had not seen his earlier letter to her about 'the only risk.' The start of my time at Oxford more or less coincided with the first occasion on which I took a newly-met young girl to the cinema and brought her home for tea. From which small beginning the number of young ladies somewhat grew over the years. 'All very agreeable girls, and none were over the age of twenty-one.' Well, not much, if they were at all. Dorothy showed every sign of enjoying the increase in social activity and was in no way discouraging. She would have been right in thinking, "He's still only an undergraduate, nowhere near qualified, let alone earning a living, nothing can be really at all serious." And she occasionally repeated one of her favourite remarks "There's safety in numbers." She should know: we have seen the numbers attendant upon her – far more than I ever had in my purview.

And so it was that when, in 1954, shortly before I sat the Bar Final which took place in May, there was a very delectable addition to the number of young ladies coming to the house, very pretty, very slim, fair-haired and a highly talented pianist to boot, it did not cause any sort of further flutter in the maternal dovecote. "After all he won't be called until the summer at the earliest, and it will be a long time after that before he earns a living." She was always very good about inviting any one of them to stay for dinner, come on a picnic outing or some such family event, chatting and being very friendly. Pat took his lead from her. Socialising was more of an effort for him, especially after a long day in the surgery, but he, too, was always kind and welcoming and not in the least disapproving.

Bar Final is an examination the results of which are first gleaned from the pages of *The Times*. In 1954 it was on 23rd June. You scan the list from the bottom up, missing your name altogether the first couple of times. It is a nerve-racking business, but I was able to feel relief when I eventually found it. Happily the news was just two days after Pat and Dorothy's twenty-fifth wedding anniversary, so an added pleasure for them. Dorothy wrote a loving letter of congratulations.

She must have cabled her father immediately, for he, too, wrote on the very next day. Again it is vintage Hobbs, pulling no punches. I apologise for one of his final remarks: it surprises me to see it; by then he was regarded in India as pro-Indian if pro-anything. More realistically anti-cant and anti-humbug. He makes his views clear enough:

> Good news about the exam but it wasn't what the lady novelist said "an unexpected surprise."
>
> So now you are going to start among those whose ideas run on "And now, Gentlemen of the Jury, I hope you will hang this chap after giving him a fair trial."
>
> I wish you luck and, if I can get some money home, you will see that my wishes are genuine. Do what is fair and honourable – <u>don't do good</u>!! That is the surest way to make enemies. Take India. Take the U.S.A. – hated all over the world. Have nothing to do with coloured people. I make no charge for this good advice. My love and - good luck! Your affec. Grandpa   H. Hobbs

With Bar Final successfully behind me, I began my first six-month pupillage, before being called to the Bar in early July. Pat and Dorothy had not had a big party for their Silver Wedding. He took her to dinner at the Haven Hotel on the very day, with the old menu in his pocket. They had each signed it in 1929, and they signed it again in 1954. To celebrate they again borrowed a flat in London, a different one, from a different friend, and had about a week doing a few shows and enjoying a few nights on the town. They were able to include me in much of what they did. It was a happy time, but I was a bit anxious for them.

I knew very well that Pat was not making much of an income from his practice. I had encouraged them, ever since that last holiday *en famille* at Minehead in 1950, not to be bothered to include me if they wanted to go away. However, they never seemed to want to do more than spend a few days in Devon with distant relations. They were evidently trying to be economical. I see now why: after his 'good year' of 1949, and two not-too-bad ones after that, his gross profit slumped in 1952 to little over half that of 1951. Despite rallying somewhat in 1953, it never again got into four figures, and declined miserably from 1955 onwards. Furthermore, his mortgagee, although an understanding man, was asking for the mortgage to be redeemed, rather on a 'soon as convenient' basis. It wasn't really convenient, but in March, 1956, Pat was able to pay off a little over a quarter of the loan thanks to a couple of life policies maturing.

The truth was that Pat, despite his personal skill and popularity with his established patients, was becoming a very old fashioned dentist. His practice needed a massive injection of capital to introduce the modern equipment which people were coming to expect. High-speed drills are one example which comes to mind. And a younger partner to bring in new life, new ideas and new energy would have been a welcome boost as well.

Pat, however, had no funds with which to endow the practice with the former, nor energy nor enthusiasm to seek for the latter. In consequence new patients were becoming fewer, and overheads inevitably increased. It was beginning to cross my mind that there was more than a slight chance that they could find themselves looking to me for support in the not too distant future. But as Pat approached his sixtieth birthday he was still paying me a small living allowance. I had only just earned my very first fee, shortly before the end of my second six months of pupillage, namely two guineas for defending a postman in the Portsmouth Magistrates' Court on a careless driving summons. I was unsuccessful. But it was a start.

Harry became a nonagenarian in July of 1954. Although he had been able to put together some autobiographical details in *Scraps from my Diaries*, which was published at the end of that year, it became evident that he was now starting to show his age. His handwriting was less firm, his letters were more brief, and contained even more than usual about his ill health. In his Foreword to *Scraps* he says of it, 'Unfortunately, owing to two years of poor health the results of my labours have been to me disappointing, for which I hope to be forgiven.' One can understand why he was disappointed. At the risk of being accused of a cheap pun, it is too scrappy, as well as being less well produced than most of his previous books. To be able to do it at all at that age, however, must be regarded as no mean achievement.

It was good of him to write to me in the terms he did after Bar Final. He did not have much of an opinion of lawyers, and I expect my chosen profession was the last he would have selected if it had been up to him. But that very slight innuendo was the nearest he got to complaining. In truth, Dorothy understood, from some circuitous route, that he had once been worsted when cross-examined many years before in India, and had never really forgiven the profession which had brought that about. She kept him posted about some of my early Court appearances, in which he seemed to take quite an interest. He was also delighted to receive a copy of her booklet about the life of Reverend Mother Kelly 'told in excellent English and well printed.'

He had yet another book in preparation; quite a sizeable affair it sounds. He wrote in April, 1955, 'What I am most anxious about is my book mss. There must be 140,000 words. Good stuff. To get it out of the Country is the problem.' And again in October, 'I have an idea of sending one copy of some political matter for my book. Danger about getting matter home. If it gets through, more will follow. After a long illness, suddenly felt better. A week ago a heavy teak-wood box fell on my foot. Was crippled for a week. Boot on first time today.' Whatever they may have been about, there has never been any sign in this Country of any part of those 140,000 words.

By the end of January, 1956, I had been paid a little over £280 in the first eight months since I had started in practice. I had been lucky enough to be taken on by my pupillage Chambers, whose Head was John Scott Henderson, QC and where the Clerk was the legendary Sidney Newland, by far the longest serving Senior Clerk in the Temple. Having had the good fortune to find myself now as well placed to make a start on the Western Circuit as any young man could hope for, and with a bit of money coming in, I felt able to say to Pat, sometime that winter, that he could stop paying me the allowance. He was immensely grateful and, I think, surprised. I was very glad I had made the first move in that direction: the poor man would have found it horribly embarrassing to have had to have asked me if he could stop it. I had no doubt he needed the money himself.

It was getting close to the second anniversary of my being Called to the Bar. And even closer, therefore, to the second anniversary of the first time that the beautiful young pianist had started to be seen in the family circle. In the course of those two years Sheila Wateridge, for that was her name, had become more and more obviously the girl on whom I was most keen. Dorothy was as welcoming and kind to her as she always was to any others who had been – and sometimes still were – around. Indeed, at a time not more than a few months after we had first met, a friend had joked to Dorothy about my girlfriends and Dorothy had replied, "Martin has brought home some very nice girls over the years. I have liked all of them. But the present one he's seeing quite often, I think I like the best of all." The reference was plainly to Sheila; I was glad to hear it, and said so.

On 22nd February, 1956, Harry was able to summon up the energy to write in something like his old style and to fill an air letter with handwriting, if not always completing a sentence –

> It was disturbing to find from yours of (I forget the date) because you are my No. 1 correspondent. Part of the stoppage was due to expecting a letter from you; then Martin had a long letter – same as if to you, but mostly illness. I more than half hoped to die – there is little good about old age. Sight, hearing, walking, prostate, all below par – not that I am unappreciative but feel I've had enough.
>
> Of all those I write to you should have been the last to be neglected, but, although sick, I had to sign bank draft and dictate, and one page tires me out. Am never free from worry – probably that keeps me alive…After 14 days in the flat, came (drove, taxi, as usual) to office for 2 hours last Monday, 21st, and on Tuesday 22nd came again. Started this, when a Jewess, customer, spent 45 minutes telling me what a scoundrel her husband was. Drove home at 1.15 prostrate and in bed right on to evening the following day. Am back now, oh so tired.
>
> After being devoted to correspondence that has come to an end.

I wrote Martin about mesmerise. The Rose family,* 4 of 'em would concentrate together and hold the victim. To me that was easy by myself. I had the power. F.B. can bear that out from hotel incidents – scores of 'em.

To be able to manage men is a greater gift than painting or music. When a scoundrel has it – well, look out.

All those in the piety trade start wrongly by claiming that humanity is born good. They are all bad – have to be taught good from natural evil. Sentimentalists like traders in piety falsely believe that scoundrels can be reformed. The silly story of the Prodigal Son. After a feed on the fat-headed calf, the first girl with the glad eye gets. Another thing is how piety traders refrain from exposing scoundrels…Selah! Much love. Hope I may be able to write again. Your loving old father   H. Hobbs

A telegram on 7th March said 'Your father seriously ill anxious – Briscoe.' He recovered and wrote on the 12th 'Well, I'm still alive. No end of a shake-up; to grow weaker every day. My love. Pat may have to come out – later. I may write again. Doubtful. Love and my blessing.' While on the 20th his remarks make one have considerable sympathy for his Doctor. 'Am not dead yet. That's about all. Doctor said I'd "A touch of pneumonia." Told him not to make an ass of himself. He was trying to make a case. He packed in. Learnt my opinion of blood pressure. Bloody nonsense. There is no standard.'

He comments on the conditions at the end of a letter on 19th April, 'No more now. 107 and 108 too much for me. F.B. has a big lump of ice alongside my bed with a table fan blowing off it on to me, while the big fan overhead is on full speed. I don't expect to stick it for two more months.' And again on 8th May, 'With ther: up to 97 – sometimes higher – been up to 108 in Calcutta, it is rather trying, but I seem to be improving.'

In the early afternoon of 15th May there came a telegram. It said, 'Father very seriously ill please inform family = Briscoe.' This was followed almost immediately by a second, 'Your father passed away peacefully very grieved = Briscoe.'

---

* A reference to a case I had been in, which had received a lot of publicity.

CHAPTER 32

THE THIRD DECADE
(2)
THE END OF THE LOVE AFFAIR

THE DEATH OF almost any really old person, can usually be described as the end of an era. It was surely true in the case of the death of Harry Hobbs, both for his family in England and for many people in India. He had claimed for some time to be the oldest European working in Asia, and was probably the oldest European citizen of Calcutta. On the news of his death the Calcutta Corporation rose to observe a minute's silence and adjourned for a further ten minutes 'as a mark of respect to his memory.' Their Secretary wrote to Miss Briscoe:

> Madam,
>   I shall deem it a favour if you kindly convey the following resolution passed by the Corporation at their meeting held on the 18th May, 1956, at the death of Major Harry Hobbs, to the members of the bereaved family of the deceased:-
>   "That the Corporation place on record their deep sense of sorrow at the demise of Major Harry Hobbs, an ex-Municipal Commissioner and a distinguished citizen of Calcutta and desire that an expression of their sincere sympathy and condolences be conveyed to the members of the bereaved family."

Many Indian newspapers and journals carried obituaries of Harry. A selection of material published at that time will be found in Appendix 4. Miss Briscoe wrote a long letter to Dorothy setting out the last days and hours of 'The Boss' as she called Harry when writing about him. He had been getting more and more frail so that nurses had to be called in, but not until the day before he died. 'Every morning the Boss used to talk politics and slanged Nehru and the Indian Government for current events.' After a tiny supper of chicken jelly at 7.30 in the evening, he suddenly died at 8pm.

The funeral was late the following day, and he was buried in the Bhowanipore Military Cemetery in Calcutta at the request of Miss Briscoe, who had promised herself that she would try to have that arranged, and it did prove possible. She could not bring herself to go to the funeral, but 'the Office was closed for two days. I arranged that the entire staff, household servants and friends who did not have cars should go in taxis and attend the funeral. All were deeply grieved.'

Soon Dorothy also had a letter from a Mr Samuel Routh. Miss Briscoe described him as 'an Anglo-Indian and aged about 32 years of age [who] worked in the Hotel for us. The Boss was delighted to have him come in here and do his typing – for as the Boss revised so he typed – he too has been a great help – and while the Boss has been so ill Mr Routh has done day and night duty – taking his rest and sleep when he could. He never grumbles or complains and is always ready to tackle any job whatever it is.'

Even if his poetry hardly rises to the level of a classic panegyric, but belongs rather more to the realm of the greetings card, Mr Routh makes his feelings very clear, and his sentiments are sincere.

As an ex-staff of Spence's Hotel and lately personal staff of the late Major H. Hobbs M.B.E., V.D. may I please take this liberty of sending you and other members of the family my most deepest sympathy in your recent bereavement.

> So quickly and quietly was the call,
> His sudden death has broken us all,
> Only those who have lost can tell,
> The loss of a Boss without a fond farewell.

It was not only a pride but pleasure to work for such a fearless personality. The little I have learned from his vast experiences shall always cherish in my memory.

> For Memories are treasure no one can steal
> Though Death leaves a heartache no one can heal.

In due course Miss Briscoe caused a gravestone to be placed, covering the whole area of the grave. It does not contain the epitaph he had once suggested for himself. In addition to his name and dates being inscribed within a cross, there is an open book below the cross. On one page it says 'His Pen was His Sword;' and on the other, 'Greatly loved may He Rest in Peace.'

As when my exam results arrived I was not at home when the telegram containing the news of Harry's death came to Hereford House. I was in London, and not home until the week-end. Dorothy, of course, was upset at the news, but the event was hardly unexpected and the death of someone at that great age is not an event normally giving rise to prolonged grief. Much nostalgic talk and thoughts, of course, and also discussions about the future. Details about Harry's Will had started to be known. Pat was to be an Executor, together with Miss Briscoe. That was going to involve him in a good deal of work, starting more or less immediately, and ultimately requiring a visit to Calcutta.

Very soon the full contents of the Will were sent to Pat. It became clear that in all probability the amount Dorothy would receive from her father's estate would be adequate to keep the two of them in some degree of comfort and security on Pat's retirement. It was by no means a huge amount, but it would be enough. The feeling of relief for the two of them must have been considerable. Apart from an expected pension from the newly-fledged National Health Service, which was likely to be small (it proved, in fact, to be just over £100 a year) together with an even smaller disability pension from the Great War (£70 a year, tax free) Pat had been able to make no provision for his retirement at all. Such life policies as he had, had largely been used to pay off a portion of his mortgage. The remainder was still an ongoing liability. Their situation could soon have become very parlous indeed. Both of them must have felt a great weight off their shoulders.

With the exception of Toff, who was left a good deal more, understandably as she had three children by then, Harry gave all his grandchildren a legacy of £500. This instigated some quick and rather exciting thinking as far as I was concerned. Five hundred pounds went quite a long way in the mid fifties. One could live on it for about a year. Fees were starting to come in a bit more frequently. Growth was still slow, but it was there. Furthermore the prospect of being required now, in these new circumstances, to act as a significant support for my parents in the years to come had virtually disappeared.

I was becoming more and more convinced that I wanted to marry Sheila Wateridge – if she would have me. The indications were reasonably favourable although one takes nothing for granted. Furthermore most young barristers would probably agree that the start of the Long Vacation was a good time to get married. It only exists in an emasculated form these days, but in the fifties it was still very much a reality. The High Court rose at the end of July. Assizes had finished by the same date. Most mid-summer Quarter Sessions had finished, and Michaelmas Sessions would not be upon us until well into September. August was the month when many County Court Judges took their holidays. All-in-all August was a very quiet month, and you ran a smaller risk of losing a good brief by being away in August and early September than at any other time of the year.

Well, it was obvious that we were too close to the Long Vacation for it to be possible, even had I wanted it, for any wedding to be arranged for the year 1956. If I got engaged it could only be on the basis of a fairly long engagement until the summer of 1957. And, by then, my 'practice' (I certainly still thought of it in inverted commas at that stage) might have blossomed forth a little bit more.

I was rather keen to clear the air. Sheila and I had by now known each other for over two years and had spent a lot of time together and with each other's families. Optimistic I may have been as to the outcome of my bringing matters to a head, but after all there's many a slip…And if I delayed for another six months or a year who can tell what glamorous young gallant might not appear on the scene and sweep her off? How did the old song put it? 'Once aboard the Lugger and the Girl is Mine!' Not a bad idea to scramble on board while the going is good. And I recalled the Proverb Trio from *Iolanthe*:

Nothing venture, nothing win,
Blood is thick, but water's thin,
In for a penny, in for a pound,
It's love that makes the world go round.

It took a few weeks. When in Chambers I spoke to Sidney, my Clerk, in a quiet moment. Without telling him why I was asking, I enquired if he thought the prognosis looked not altogether too hopeless. "We are never satisfied, Sir," was his reply, "but it does look reasonably promising." For one 'who was, as many young barristers are, an impecunious party' I could not expect any more enthusiasm. But it seemed to me to be enough.

I was at home for the week-end on Saturday, 23rd June. Sheila was due home for a couple of nights that afternoon from Sherborne School for Girls, where she was on the music staff, and I had been asked to dinner that evening. This, I thought, is the moment. I felt I ought to warn Dorothy of what might be in the offing. I had a slight anxiety. I was concerned that the news, hardly surprising one would have thought, would not be too enthusiastically received. Nothing to do with the recent death of Harry. She was not in the least prostrated with grief. She treated that event in a proper Christian light as the end of a long life, well lived, with the hope of better to come. I was not completely explicit, but she could have been in no doubt what I had in mind. "Well, I should wait," was all she said, "I think you should wait." Maybe she thought back to that remark about twenty-one years and twenty-one minutes.

I could see no point in waiting, nor did she give any reason. The roller-coaster had started and I was in no mood to try and stop it. Sheila's home, Robinswood, was in Branksome Park, just over the border into Poole, but no more than a mile and a half, two miles at most from Hereford House. Her parents, Hugh and Kathleen Wateridge, had lived there since shortly after the War with Sheila and her younger sister, Bridget (later to become Mrs Christopher Dearnley.) I had the good fortune that evening to find myself being given the answer for which I had hoped, Hugh and Kathleen expressing gratifying pleasure at the news. At least they did when I could get a word in. It was not easy. There was a Test Match in progress and Hugh was listening to the commentary (they did not have television yet.) As soon as play ended I took a deep breath. "Shall we find out what's happening at Wimbledon?" he said, getting his word in first as he tuned in to another station. There was nothing for it but to stick it out, while Sheila, outside the room, wondered frantically what had gone wrong, and her mother could not understand why she kept rushing out of the kitchen to the front of the house and back. Patience, in the end, was rewarded, and very satisfactorily so. Thus by the time I left I was engaged.

And now back to Hereford House, to tell Dorothy and Pat. I put them in that order, for she was the one, I was quite sure, who would set the tone. I probably had to walk, as the last bus was on the early side, but that took not quite half an hour; they were late birds, and were still sitting either side of the fireplace when I got in. I was more apprehensive than I had been in the morning. The maternal suggestion – I could not put it as high as a request, even, let alone a command – had not been followed, it was an important decision, and I had made it entirely by myself. Another deep breath.

I told them briefly what had happened. It did not take long; they did not interrupt. When I had finished there was a short silence. "So, I suppose, you are engaged?" was Dorothy's comment. "Well, yes, I am," I replied, "and they are all very happy about it at Robinswood." After that – not a word. Complete silence. Dorothy continued with her sewing. Pat, as ever taking his cue from her, had put his newspaper down to his lap and I could see he was looking at her for a lead. But none came. Nothing. How long did I wait there, looking from one to the other? It seemed like a couple of hours, but was probably no more than a minute or two, when I broke the silence. "Well, I think I'll go to bed now, good night," and suited action to my words. When upstairs I heard their voices, particularly Pat's, but it was not possible to hear what was being said. I think he was remonstrating with her. But beyond that I have no idea what transpired.

Nor have I any really convincing idea as to why Dorothy acted as she did. She had had plenty of time in which to reconcile herself to my intended course of action. She had never shown any dislike of

Sheila – rather the reverse, as has been mentioned. The fact that Sheila was not a Catholic would have made no difference to her, in the light of her own and her parents' marriage. Did she want me to find a University educated wife? With two LRAM Diplomas (Performers and Teachers) Sheila had the next best thing to a degree, as well as five years experience teaching in prestigious Schools. I still find it puzzling quite how to understand what caused her strange and, it has to be said, at the time rather hurtful reaction.

To do her justice, Dorothy made a very big effort overnight. Whether because of what Pat may have said to her, or off her own bat, or, most probably, a combination of the two, she came round completely, outwardly, at any rate. She said she was "sorry about last night, but it had come as a bit of a surprise" (which I took as an excuse rather than a reason.) From then on she was as generous in her kindnesses to Sheila – and to me – as one could possibly wish. If I had had a more communicative nature, I expect I would have had it out with her, then or later, and demanded to know what it was all about. I did not do so, either then, or at any time in the many years that followed. What is the point, I thought, of opening up past moments of sadness, out of nothing really more than curiosity? It might only add to present day sadnesses, and is unlikely to be able in any circumstances to improve anyone's relationship with anyone else.

For the relationship between Dorothy and Sheila became very good indeed over the years, and Dorothy had good cause to be very grateful to her, as well as to her Parents. For this a great deal of the credit must go to Sheila herself. Of course I had to tell her what had happened on my return home that night. That could only have made her very concerned both as to what her reception would be when they met again, and determined not to show resentment but to work for a good and loving relationship. In this she succeeded from the first. And the first came pretty quickly.

Sheila came to Hereford House on the Sunday, and her parents followed later on the same day. Dorothy herself arranged it on the telephone. She produced some jewellery to see if there was a ring Sheila would like her to give me to give to Sheila as an engagement ring. And there was: Sheila was very delighted with it, despite many a bride-to-be wanting to go to a shop to choose. Pat produced a bottle of Champagne in the evening. Its label is on the first page of an album as evidence. When the others had gone he said to Dorothy and to me "The bottle has pupped" and produced a further half bottle for the three of us. I am sure he was now quietly enjoying the whole thing and would have been happier had it been like that from the outset. He had asked me in the morning if I was sure of myself for "We only want your happiness" but I suspect that was as much prompted by Dorothy urging him to say something. I replied that I was sure and thought she had a fine character. He said no more. I was right, too. And both of them came to agree in the fullness of time.

The nearest Dorothy got to making any express admission to me that her reservations, whatever may have been their basis, had been wrong was probably more than twenty-five years later when she remarked to me "Sheila has been a pretty marvellous wife to you all these years, hasn't she?" I was glad to agree, wholeheartedly. Perhaps this is the place to say that, just as the decision to send me to Downside was about the best decision made for me, the decision to ask Sheila to be my wife was far and away the best decision I have ever made for myself.

The announcement was in the papers the following Saturday and from then on it was a very jolly time for us both. From the point of view of Pat and Dorothy, however, there was a lot of work to be fitted in with sorting out Harry's estate. They had one or two trips to London to see Solicitors and others, for there was a very small amount of cash in a London Bank for which Probate had to be obtained in this Country as well as in India. It became clear that a visit to Calcutta could not be very long delayed. It would mean quite a long time away from the practice, but the personal legacy to Pat, doubtless intended for this purpose, should more than compensate for that absence.

Eventually they flew out to Calcutta on 19th January, 1957, and were back on 3rd March, just over six weeks later. Before departure Dorothy had said to me that if they found it could be arranged satisfactorily from out there (the money was there, and taking money out of England then was much restricted) they would let me know and I could go out too. I was rather keen to go and see some of the places I had heard about. I had not read as much about India in general nor Calcutta in particular – let alone about Harry – as I have now done, but still enough to whet my appetite for a personal visit to see for myself.

They found that Miss Briscoe had arranged for them to have Harry's flat – No. 11 Park Mansions. The lease was still running, and it was close to Miss Briscoe at No. 6. There was ample room to accommodate me, and so Dorothy wrote home almost at once to say, "If you can spare the time do come out." Well, I could easily spare the time. If ever there was another slack time of the year, apart from the Long Vacation it was February, at any rate for a young man working the eastern end of the Circuit. So I wrote back to say I would get ready to come.

The getting ready necessarily included a number of jabs from our Doctor. I forget how many. It was enough to make me feel thoroughly uncomfortable and out of sorts, unable to stand, sit, sleep or lie without some sort of twinge, or worse, to disturb my equanimity. But it was all in a good cause. And then, to my chagrin, there came a telegram. "All awful don't come." Without their co-operation from India, not least in matters of finance, there was no way I could get out there, and so my painful behind and other places had all been in vain.

The change of heart, I later came to learn, had been Pat's doing. Dorothy's letter had been written before they had seen much of Calcutta and was prompted by the reasonable (and virtually free) accommodation waiting there. But after a few days Pat had become utterly appalled by the poverty he saw in every street, on every pavement, wherever they went. He came to the conclusion that it "would upset Martin to come here and see all this." And he insisted on sending the telegram to stop me.

It was a strangely unenlightened attitude for him to adopt. Neither was prone to act in an unenlightened way where I was concerned. But there were times, not very often, once every few years, when Pat would get an impulsive idea, from which nothing would deter him.

Unfortunately this was one such impulse. "I must stop Martin coming out," and he got the telegram sent. Dorothy did not agree. She thought that I was quite old enough to be able to cope with some of the realities of life in other parts of the world. She was right, of course; she nearly always was. Ever since I have regretted missing the opportunity of seeing Calcutta with them, and before the business finally closed its doors. I would probably have wanted to get them to try to see Chingri Khal and the Chingri Khal Fort. They did not attempt to do so. Dorothy, indeed, was never there, neither as a child, nor in her 1925-6 visit, nor on this last trip. My pilgrimage there had to wait until 2003 as described in Chapter 6.

Pat kept a brief record of their movements. It is mostly one line entries, but he is a little more eloquent in relation to Friday, 25th January:

> 1030 a.m. Went to H. Hobbs & Co. Ltd., 21, Old Court House Street with Miss Briscoe. Whilst seated the whole staff of 25 was assembled, workmen, bearers and coolies. One by one they were called forward by name to salaam. Then two of them came forward with double garlands of most beautiful flowers and two posies. The garlands were draped over Dorothy and Self and posies put in our hands.
>
> All this done in silence but with dignity. All very touching.
>
> Thus bedecked we toured the establishment to see the men at work. They all assembled again as we left. The next day was a holiday and Dorothy gave Rs.25 to be distributed.
>
> As we finally left we were presented with a box of Indian sweets.
>
> A most memorable occasion.

Fortunately a photographer was present and a record of the 'memorable occasion,' both at Old Court House Street and at Miss Briscoe's flat, has thus been preserved

Of the many places which Dorothy frequented thirty years before only Spence's Hotel and Firpo's are mentioned in Pat's diary, and at that only once each. Perhaps she did not have the heart to insist on Pat taking her to them once again. How they compared with her memory of them is nowhere recorded. Most of the buildings remain even in 2003. They are in a very different condition from the days of her journey in 1926, when she wondered if she would ever return to the life she had experienced in those few weeks. Just about recognisable the places may be, but they are only ghosts of their former incarnations.

They gave themselves a taste of the tourist trail. They went to Delhi, where they saw old Delhi and the New Delhi of Lutyens, and Agra where they visited the Taj Mahal. A few days back in Calcutta and then it was on to Darjeeling, where they saw the famous view of the Himalayas in general and Kanchenjunga in particular, and much else. They were able to go to the Loreto Convent, where Dorothy had been to school more than fifty years before, and she met one of the Community, Mother Antoinette, who had been a friend of hers when they had both been pupils there together. And then again back to Calcutta for the last few business meetings.

Their homecoming in early March was an exciting and joyous time, with much news to exchange on both sides. Our wedding date had been fixed with the Church, that is the Sacred Heart in Bournemouth, for 17th August. I had told them in a letter of the proposed date. It was far enough ahead for it to pose no problems from their point of view.

Convention normally dictates that the wedding venue is the Church of the Bride, but neither Sheila nor I were known to or knew the Church of the Catholic parish in which she lived, so it made sense to look to my parish. Particularly as from soon after our engagement she had been regularly seeing the Rector and Parish Priest, at this time a rather wonderful man, Father Edmund Bassett, S.J. Not quite so charismatic as his better-known brother, Father Bernard Bassett, he was exactly the right man to whom Sheila could talk about her future as the wife of a Catholic man. Brought up in a churchgoing Anglican family, she had no ingrained prejudices against the Catholic Church. It was sensible to introduce her to Father Bassett soon after we became engaged. It was her decision to see him on a fairly regular basis from then on. It was a great delight to me when she told me that she had decided, with his encouragement, to ask to

Pat and Dorothy wearing their garlands at
H. Hobbs & Co., 21, Old Court House Street, Calcutta, 25th January, 1957.

Dorothy and Pat relaxing with Miss Briscoe at her flat in Park Mansions
after the ceremony at 21, Old Court House Street.

be received into the Church. The little ceremony was to be on the Tuesday in Holy Week, 16th April.

I told Dorothy very soon after Sheila told me. Her reaction was interesting. It was a mixture of pleasure, of some doubt, and, I feel fairly sure, also a hint of envy. Pleasure, obviously, as any Catholic feels when he hears of someone else being received into the Church. The doubt emanated from an assumption she made, which was false. It was very many years, probably thirty or more, before she made it known to me that she had assumed I had made it a condition of getting married to Sheila that she should take this step. I was glad to be able to disabuse her. Nothing of the sort took place. I had always thought of such a condition as the reverse of what conversion should be all about, and liable to produce a very unsatisfactory situation in the long term if not in the short. I left it to Sheila, with Father Bassett to help her if she wanted his help and, no doubt, a great deal of enthusiastic work by the Holy Spirit.

As for the touch of envy, this is only something that I might call a gut feeling. It had often seemed to me over the years from when I had first been at school, that Dorothy and I had something important in common which we could share, and which she did not share with Pat. Close as they were in so very many ways, there was no common ground between them on what, it must be acknowledged, is perhaps the most fundamental part of an individual's make-up. She, too, had never attempted to make any condition that he should become a Catholic. As far as I am aware after that first exchange about religion just after they became engaged, the topic was never mentioned. He never felt motivated to make any further enquiry. She never tried to press him to do so. She occasionally said to me that, if he ever did become a Catholic, she would want a Nuptial Mass. Not possible, in those days at any rate, in a mixed marriage, this solemn form of blessing is independent of the actual wedding ceremony, and can be celebrated at any time after that has taken place. Whether she ever said that to him I have no means of knowing. But it makes me believe that she had a certain sense of regret that their very loving relationship lacked that one feature which she would have valued so much. And here was I, about to gain just that benefit.

I had asked the Abbot of Downside, Abbot Christopher Butler, who had been my former Head Master (the first of two in my time there) if he would be willing to marry us. His letter agreeing to do so arrived a couple of days or so before Sheila was received. I had told him of what was impending as far as she was concerned. He had a fellow feeling for her, having gone to Downside first as an Anglican lay master. He wrote, "Tell her that my funk and misery at the corresponding time were unspeakable. Like going to a dentist...a spiritual dentist, if you can imagine such a horror." She had had many rather unpleasant experiences of dentists but she did not let that put her off. Her parents did not put any difficulties in her way and the event went off happily on a small scale, having a drink and lunch at Hereford House afterwards. Dorothy was very sincere in her congratulations. Pat, slightly embarrassed, joined in with congratulations. I expect he was wondering quite what he might be congratulating her for and generally how to approach the occasion. I think he was getting very fond of her in his quiet way.

Support, help and encouragement came from them both as the wedding approached. There was much to be done, including finding somewhere to live. We eventually hit upon the most tiny flat imaginable, much smaller than the flat at Hereford House, (it was not quite flat, either) in Winchester, very close to Winnie and Charles. After having tried London and various other places on the main line from Waterloo to Hampshire, we agreed to try our luck in the Ancient Capital. It was a little daring for a young practising barrister to settle so far away from his Chambers, and on the Circuit, but it seemed to be a good idea at the time. It proved very much to be so as time progressed. The flat was obviously a very temporary measure – we were in it for under a year – but it was an excellent start. And at least it was just big enough to take the Rachals upright piano, which Dorothy generously let us have on more or less permanent loan. That meant a great deal to Sheila.

The marquee for our wedding reception went up in the garden of Robinswood on the Wednesday in pouring rain. Dorothy was more than anxious. "I told the Saints," she said to me afterwards, "that if it was not a fine day on Saturday I would never speak to any of them again." Something did the trick: the day was dry and by lunchtime the sun was out for a perfect afternoon. Dorothy was in her element.

Both families had lived in Bournemouth for some time, she, of course, for much the longest of the four parents. There were many of her friends among the guests in addition to the relations, and it was all very lively and cheerful. Pat, sentimental as ever, had evidently bought her something. It was probably no more than a corsage for her wedding outfit, but the note he enclosed has been carefully preserved:

> For – The mother of the present from her erstwhile bridegroom with the same love as ever.   17th August, 1957

He almost seemed a little overcome at times during the reception, coming up and touching my arm, or Sheila's, especially as our departure drew near. Perhaps he was thinking of his own wedding in the same Church twenty-eight years earlier. He said nothing of any special note when he did so. I have no doubt he was quietly very contented. It was a happy day for all.

That Christmas was a little strange for Pat and Dorothy, since Sheila and I stayed at Robinswood. Although there was much visiting between the two homes, they would have felt my first absence from Hereford House at that time of year. Pat loved Christmas, and always wanted to make a big show of decorating a tree and the drawing room. He did not do very much of it that year. There were compensations. Their delight was very clear to see when Sheila was able to tell them at the end of January, during a week-end visit to Hereford House, that they were going to be grandparents. They took a great deal of interest in preparations for that event, particularly in our house-hunting which was imperative because our flat was far too small for more than the two of us.

In the event we found a house which was about to be built. One of four, the one which had not yet been started, and so we were able to have alterations made to the plans without extra cost. It was a time when mortgages were hard to come by, and I was no exception. "No prospects," they said when I approached various bodies for the purpose. Harry's estate was beginning to be realised. Pat was able to

17th August, 1957

A HAPPY DAY FOR ALL

Martin and Sheila.
"We've done it."

(Left to right) Pat, Kathleen,
Bridget, Sheila Wormald,
Dorothy, Hugh.
Winnie and Charles behind
in the doorway.

pay off the remainder of his mortgage in July, and Dorothy decided to be my mortgagee as she felt the investment secure. And so we were able to acquire our foothold on Sleepers Hill, and they were able to feel, at last, that their home was their own.

Their first grandchild, Adrian, was born on 5th September. He was the first of that generation for Hugh and Kathleen Wateridge as well. Pat and Dorothy were holidaying in Devon at the time. He arrived early, and at home, which had not been the intention. I telephoned their hotel and spoke to Pat. A little later they rang back for Dorothy to have a word. She had been a little overcome with tears, but was very thrilled. All was well. She kept the first letter Sheila wrote to her after the birth. They were the best of friends by now, although it was still "My dear Mrs Tucker" in the custom of that age. Christian names came much later. By their return from holiday Sheila was at Robinswood to which they came for the first sight of their new grandson.

Soon after that, Pat came to realise that he had a hernia. It was not serious, but, like all hernias, it had to be dealt with. That would involve him being off work for a few weeks and he took stock of his situation. The decline in his practice had accelerated, and in this last year he made a loss. So he decided to take the opportunity to retire altogether. Unlike Deane Webb thirty-two years before, he found he had no good will of value to sell. He came to an arrangement with a younger colleague that he would pay Pat £1 for every patient who transferred to him. Letters were sent to all who might be concerned, informing them of the closure of the surgeries. Pat was really taken aback by the number of letters he received from grateful patients lamenting his departure, wishing him well in his retirement and saying they would never find anyone else to look after their teeth like he had done. It helped to make him feel that his work had not all been in vain. He had always lacked self-confidence ("His only fault is too much humility," Dorothy had said to me more than once) and it was heart-warming for him to have so much spontaneous appreciation.

Retirement was not just the end of Pat's work as a dentist. It also marked the time when Hereford House became obviously far too big for them. Cramped they may have been in the flat. But now that the two surgeries, two offices, waiting room, reception hall and workshops were no longer needed as such, there was much more space than they needed.

Dorothy had hoped that retirement would result in Pat taking on a new lease of life. Freed from the daily round, which he had never enjoyed, and with now a degree of financial security, the two of them had much they could enjoy together. And first and foremost was choosing a new home. But Dorothy found that Pat was lethargic in his approach to the search. He did not seem to have the heart for it. Their names were with Agents, and, once he had recovered from the hernia operation, they did try to see a number of properties. It took very little to put Pat off, sometimes before they had even got out of the car. It was all very different from what she had imagined, and it made her anxious.

She was glad, therefore, when he spotted a plot of land which rather took his fancy in a pleasant residential road, Glenferness Avenue, where a speculative builder was due to erect three houses. After some thought they decided on the uppermost one. Pat assured me when I queried it, that the lower house would not interfere with their likely view across the Upper Gardens. He took the plans to our next-door neighbour, an architect, older than Pat, and of great experience. He took the view that the builder's intended house was 'cranky' and on much the same ground plan designed something quite different. It must have added greatly to the potential cost, and was not really what Dorothy wanted, but she was so glad that Pat had at last got enthusiastic about something, that she went along with it.

It was a step in the right direction, but there was a lot more to be done in the way of adapting to retirement. Answering the telephone for a start. There was no reason now why Pat should not pick up the receiver if he were the nearer of the two of them, but he was surprised, almost hurt, to be told so. More help from him in the house generally was expected, and not always forthcoming. Furthermore she wanted him to arrange a holiday for them in the early summer. They had had a week or so in the New Forest in November, nothing else since he retired. She wanted to go to Ireland, never having been there, and well aware of the family roots in that country through her mother. But Pat seemed full of lethargy, hummed and hawed, and got nothing done. "Whatever's the matter," she wondered, "is he ill? Or, almost worse, has he fallen out of love with me?" Eventually she had to get really cross. "You may have retired, but I am working just as hard as ever, and I need a holiday, you must get on and arrange it."

So he did. They were to be away for a little over a fortnight in June. In the meantime Sheila and I had managed to furnish a spare bedroom in Aspen House, our first proper home. It was ready in time for her parents to stay with us over Easter. When Whitsun came, with its Bank Holiday, it was the turn of Pat and Dorothy. Their stay, from Friday to Wednesday, in mid May was an unqualified success. Pat in particular enjoyed himself, doing a little work in the garden and enjoying his grandson, with whom he had quickly built up a considerable rapport, young as Adrian still was. There was more potential in that line as well. Sheila had become pregnant remarkably soon after Adrian's birth, and by this time was already six months on the way to her second delivery. It was a wonderful, mainly very hot summer, a joy to most people, but oh! so tiring for a very pregnant mother of a lively, not-quite-walking baby.

Their Irish holiday was a similar success to their Whitsun break, hiring a car there and driving to several beautiful places. They found Derry Fadda Farm and Larkin's Cross and met Matthew Larkin, Dorothy's cousin. They ended their stay at Parknasilla, in an excellent hotel in a particularly lovely situation on the Ring of Kerry. They loved it there. "For two pins, Dothie, I'd book our room here for next year," said Pat before they left. But the two pins were not forthcoming, and the reservation was not made. Maybe they remembered booking those rooms in Sark for 1940…

They were home in time for their thirtieth Wedding Anniversary, a Sunday, on which they came to Winchester for the day and we had dinner at a restaurant just outside the City on their way home. There was a great disappointment in store when they visited the site of the new house. It was getting on fairly well, but so also was the lower house. My query had been all too well founded. The roof of the lower house was now on, and it largely blocked out any aspect from theirs. Dorothy did not know which most upset her, the blocking of the view, or Pat's stunned look as he took in the reality. "Never mind," she said to him, "we need never live here if we don't like it, we can sell it and look elsewhere."

In the next two weeks I was in Court in or near Bournemouth quite a lot, and called in several times. Dorothy was plainly worried about Pat. His lethargy had returned, he was sleeping a great deal during the day and she could not understand why. There was so much to look forward to. Could he be seriously ill?

July saw first Dorset Quarter Sessions, followed by Winchester Assizes. I had no occasion to go to Bournemouth, but Dorothy telephoned quite often, her anxiety getting no less. On 24th July she telephoned to tell me that he had had some curious painful attack the night before, "a bit like a fit." He would have to go and see the doctor.

In the evening of 28th July the telephone rang. It was their family doctor. Doctor Eddie Grant had been our doctor since before the end of the war, and he and his wife and their two daughters had been friends for a good deal longer than that. He wanted to tell me first. He was not certain. He suspected cancer. Possibly operable, possibly not. Should he tell them? I said tell Dorothy first.

Fortunately, perhaps, I had to be in Bournemouth County Court on each of the two following days which enabled me to go to Hereford House when I had finished. It was harrowing. On the first day Dorothy got me on one side and completely broke down. She did not often shed tears in front of others (except, possibly, with Pat to comfort her) and she had plainly made up her mind that there was, realistically, no hope. The cancer was thought to be in the bronchus, with secondaries in the liver, "And you can't live without your liver." He did not look significantly different from normal at that time, but one could see he was not feeling himself.

On 4th August I had to be in Court in Bournemouth again. Pat had gone into hospital for an examination by bronchoscope. I saw him on the next two days. He seemed no worse. That Sunday, 9th, Hugh and Kathleen brought Pat and Dorothy to Winchester to see us. When they arrived Pat looked a very different man. He had suddenly become very jaundiced, and was a most peculiar and unhealthy colour. He looked a very sick man, whatever the result of the test. How long could this possibly go on? Dorothy looked like wanting me around as much as possible.

But Sheila was under a fortnight from her due date. She was very large and very exhausted, coping with her size, her lively eleven-month old baby and the great heat of that summer. A Home Help had been booked through Social Services to start with us from the birth. But at that time, apart from a dear old lady who came to clean for a couple of hours a week, we had no help in the house. A young Mother's Help had been engaged, but was not due to start until some time in September. The confinement was planned to be at home and for us all to go to Robinswood afterwards for a week or so once Sheila was ready to make the journey. Until then I was wanted at home even more than at Hereford House, and likely to be increasingly so as the days went by.

On that Wednesday, the result of the test came through: negative. It gave Dorothy a moment or two of almost delirious joy and relief to all of us. Perhaps he would soon show signs of getting better. We were able to enjoy our second Anniversary on 17th August without any great cloud in the sky over Bournemouth. But Dorothy watched, with growing concern as Pat, far from improving, showed less appetite, less energy and a greater degree of jaundice. He was starting to get thin. Through Eddie Grant she arranged for Pat to see a Consultant in London. An appointment was made for the end of the following week, Friday 28th August. On the Monday she allowed Hugh and Kathleen to be bring her to Winchester for tea, leaving Pat behind as he did not feel up to the journey. Sheila was already three days passed her expected date and was glad of the visit. The great heat made waiting rather a trial for her. Dorothy had left something for Pat's tea, but she found on her return that he had done nothing to help himself. She resolved not to leave him again until this crisis had been resolved.

The crisis, in fact, brought them even closer together. Pat had never been physically very demonstrative. But on the long summer evenings, when the light was fading, and so his unnatural colour was less likely to be seen, he liked to go out for a walk with Dorothy in the Central Gardens. These are only a step away from the front door of Hereford House, and he could manage that reasonably well. "He never used to like any physical contact when were out walking in the normal way," Dorothy told me afterwards, "not even for me to take his arm. But once we knew he was so ill, and we went out together in the evening he held my hand all the way."

On the Friday evening, after their return from the Consultation in London, Dorothy telephoned. The news was as bad as it could be: the original diagnosis was confirmed. "How long has he got?" she asked when Pat was dressing in an adjoining room after the examination. "With his current level of jaundice, I would think about six weeks," was the devastating reply. About then, in her distress she went to see Father Bassett who, but two years before, had guided the family through such a very happy time. He was a great help to her, encouraging and consoling her and promising prayers for them both. She was glad to have him so near.

The following day, 29th August, and more than a week late, Sheila went into labour. She was a little doubtful in the morning, but certain by mid-day. It was slow, and our first daughter was born quite late that evening. We called her Helen. Hugh and Kathleen came for the day on Sunday, and on Monday the Home Help arrived, a worthy lady, but a little uninspiring. She was better than no one. Dorothy managed to bring herself to write a kind letter to Sheila, enclosing a cheque, but it was really Pat who excelled himself. Ill as he was, indeed he must have known by then that he was dying, he was able to summon up both the nous and the energy to send Helen a telegram. At least, it was addressed, of course, to Sheila, but its contents were directed to Helen herself. It was a little gem, simply saying:

Congratulations Helen. Now for a thousand ships.

A telephone call from Dorothy made it clear that Pat was getting worse, and doing so rather fast. I felt very torn between the two.

573

Dorothy would have liked me there. Sheila, trying to establish her feeding of Helen needed as much help – physical and emotional – as she could get. New life seemed to me to have greater priority, but as a partial compromise I took Adrian to Bournemouth for the day on 2nd September. Pat and he had always got to so well together and Pat used to make him laugh talking nonsense to him. It might help to cheer them up. It only partially succeeded. Pat's jaundice was by now very marked and his voice had become affected, a little muffled and slightly hoarse. He was still up and dressed and he tried to amuse his grandson, but Adrian obviously could tell the difference in his grandfather. His only reaction was to cry.

I was able to visit again later in the week on my own after a short Court appearance. That week-end saw Adrian's first birthday – his sister was one week! – both Sheila's parents came, but neither of mine, understandably. Sheila was still very tired after the birth. Arrangements were made for all four of us to go to Robinswood at the end of the week, on Friday, 11th September. I was glad to think that, once there, I could leave Sheila in the care of her mother for much of the time while trying to support Dorothy.

But the news from Bournemouth was alarming. Sheila had her first outing on the Wednesday; we did a little shopping together. That evening it was plain that Pat was getting much worse, and quickly. To add sadness upon sadness we heard, too, that Father Bassett, of whom we were all so fond, had sustained a massive heart attack. He was in hospital, and likely to be there for a considerable time. In fact, he never fully recovered nor returned to his old parish. It was a great loss for Dorothy to be deprived of his counselling, just when she needed it the most.

I felt it necessary to go to Hereford House on Thursday. I was rather shocked by Pat's appearance. An even worse colour, and appearing distinctly emaciated, he was in his dressing gown and walking only a very little, and that only with difficulty. "I'm not in any pain," he assured me, but whether truthfully or not I don't know. Doctor Grant had given him morphia, and I know that that had helped him a lot at the time. Dorothy had got someone to bring a single bed into the drawing room. That night was to be the first they had slept apart for very many years. I stayed quite late, but had to be back for the family move the following day. "We shall all be down at Robinswood to-morrow," I told her, "probably about tea time. Once I've got Sheila installed there I shall come down here straight away." And so I left them.

It must have been a dreadful night for them both. He was plainly sinking. "Do you want me to get a clergyman for you?" she asked. "No," was the short reply. And then, a little later, he followed it up with a remark which showed the considerable mutual understanding between them. "I'm sorry for your sake that I'm not a Catholic." It certainly would have made it easier for her if they had been able to pray together. She must have felt desperately on her own. We often feel we need reassurance in moments of stress. Dorothy was no exception. "I do hope I have made you happy?" she said to him. He replied with a question of his own, "Do you imagine I could go through all this if you had not?" It was reassurance indeed.

Friday, 11th September was the day Sheila and I were due to travel to Bournemouth with our two babies. Our Morris Minor would only just hold us all, but it could be done. The Home Help had finished her time with us (we were quite glad of that.) Our dear old cleaning lady came to wash a few nappies and assist generally for an hour or two. At ten o'clock the telephone rang. I answered. It was Dorothy. "Oh, Martin..." was all she got out, before breaking down into sobs. I thought he had died. But no. Her stalwart thrice weekly help, a Mrs Long, had come that morning as usual, taken one look at Pat and told Dorothy that she must get me down at once or I would be too late, saying, "You would never forgive yourself if Martin did not get here before his father died."

She was right, of course, but it did require a lot of nimble footwork. Yes, Hugh Wateridge was free and could drive to Winchester, leaving very soon, to help Sheila pack and take her to her old home. "We'll get by all right," said the dear old thing, in an attempt to ease Sheila's rising panic. I threw a few of my things into a suitcase, which went into the boot of the car, kissed Sheila a quick good-bye, and rushed out, leaving her in tears and two youngsters clamouring for attention. I expect I was a danger on the road, with mind in a turmoil and trying to make the little car get through the miles as never before. More than halfway to Bournemouth I spotted

Hugh in his car, driving in the opposite direction. A comfort at least to know that he had been able to get away as promised.

I was in Hereford House soon after eleven. Pat was in the single bed in the drawing room. He was semi-conscious. If possible, his colour was even worse, and an unpleasant odour, which had been discernable the day before, was now very much in evidence.

Dorothy told him in a loud voice that I had arrived. He roused himself a little and thanked me for coming. A nurse had been sent by some Agency – I never asked at whose instigation. By chance she was a Catholic, which was a bit of an extra help to Dorothy. There was nothing much I could do except be there. We looked at him together, Dorothy and I. Her mind went back so many years, to the bridge party at Asenby, to the golden day in the Sacred Heart and at Chingri Khal, to many shared joys and sorrows. Only once did she give voice to her thoughts. Almost more to herself than to either of us, she murmured in rather a trembling voice, "He was so very sweet to me when my poor little baby died."

Pat was struggling for breath, and occasionally asked to sit on the edge of the bed, but soon sank back on to the pillows. Memory is fickle. Did we have any sort of food or drink? Probably not, but I am unsure. By the afternoon hot sunlight was flooding into the room, making a mockery of events within by its contrast with the brilliant holiday weather without. The struggle for breath, painful to observe, continued. Then came a change in a strange and unexpected way. Pat seemed to rouse himself a little. His eyes opened and he looked at the foot of the bed. Not one of the three of us in the room was in his line of vision. He found his voice. "There they are, there they are," he exclaimed, quite loudly and clearly, "they have come." Whom did he see? Or whom did he think he was seeing? The question you think right to ask will depend on your belief, or lack of it, in life after death. He had no such belief, none at all, yet he thought some people were there. Our belief was succoured by his disbelief. So who was it? His father and mother? His baby son? His stepmother? All four come to help him on his last journey? He said no more. After looking intently for a few seconds he lay back again.

The struggle grew weaker, the intakes of breath more widely separated. Quite spontaneously Dorothy and I began to say together the De Profundis – Psalm 129 (130 in the Anglican Psalm Book) which is closely associated in Catholic practice with prayers for the dead and dying.

> *"Out of the depths have I cried unto Thee, O Lord! Lord, hear my voice – and let Thine ears be attentive to the voice of my supplication…"*

The nurse was standing silently beside us. How long could this go on?

> *"…My soul hath relied on His Word, my soul hath hoped in the Lord - from the morning watch even until night let Israel hope in the Lord…"*

When we eventually finished the last slight sign of a gasp seemed a long time ago. The nurse went up to him, felt for a pulse or any other indication of life, but found none. Death had parted the two lovers.

The nurse began the task of preparing the body for burial while Dorothy, in a slightly old fashioned gesture, pulled down the blinds in the drawing room and the blazing, mocking sunlight was shut out.

CHAPTER 33

ON HER OWN

WHEN I EVENTUALLY got to Robinswood that evening it was doubtful whether Sheila or I was the more tired and shattered by the events of that day. I did at least feel that the worst was probably over. Certainly from Sheila's point of view that was so. Her parents, their domestic help, and the general facilities at Robinswood would see to her needs and those of the two very young children for the next few days, while I could give most of my time to helping Dorothy with the aftermath of Pat's death.

Her domestic help, Mrs Long, had been a perfect brick on the day Pat died. She realised that I would really have to go to Sheila before the end of the day and she told Dorothy that she would go home, get a few things, and return to spend the night at Hereford House. She was as good as her word, and had returned before I had to leave, so Dorothy was not on her own. The offices of our family solicitor were only next door but one. I informed him very quickly of Pat's death and he put in motion the necessary steps to arrange with undertakers, the church and the crematorium. Pat had wanted to be cremated and Dorothy had no objection to that. The service beforehand could have been awkward. A Catholic funeral would not have been appropriate or possible. The Parish Church of Bournemouth, St. Peter's, is only a hundred yards from the front door, but Pat had hardly ever been inside the place, and we were not known to the clergy there.

Mr Preston, our solicitor, made the necessary arrangements, and the Vicar was kindness itself and came to see Dorothy before the service. She had not wanted Pat's body to be removed from Hereford House prior to the service, so the undertaker laid the coffin on a low catafalque in the large hall downstairs, from where in due course it was carried to the Church. But not before one of those silly incidents which sometimes occur at solemn moments.

The Vicar, plainly knowing that Dorothy was a Catholic, and seeing the coffin lying there in state asked her if she would like it if they said the De Profundis together beside the coffin before he left. She gladly agreed. He then began the Psalm – but in Latin.

> *"De profundis clamavi ad te Domine…"*

Now Dorothy knew the standard Catholic English version very well indeed – both of us did – but she had never learned it in Latin. She tried to remember or guess.

> *"…Domine exaudi vocem meam…"*

Quick thinking got her thus far, but from then on she could only mumble.

> *"…Sustinuit anima mea in verbo eijus: speravit anima mea in Domino – A custodia matutina usque ad noctem speret Israel in Domino…"*

At last it came to an end. I am sure he thought he was making a friendly gesture to his 'Roman' parishioner. She had the greatest difficulty in stopping herself from breaking into hysterical giggles, and just managed to keep the mumbled contribution going. She kept her composure and was grateful for his kind thought.

Indeed, she kept her composure throughout. If she wept, as I expect she did, she wept on her own. The funeral was on the Tuesday. Sheila was able to come as well: we supported Dorothy on either side as she walked to St. Peter's behind the coffin, and again at the Crematorium at the Central Cemetery. There was a very small reception at Hereford House afterwards for close family. It is when all mourners depart and the bereaved spouse is first completely alone in the family home that the worst sense of loss will be felt. Dorothy was spared a good deal of that by the great generosity of Hugh and Kathleen who made a spare room available for her at Robinswood where she stayed for several days before returning to Hereford House to sleep, and later, on 7th November, coming to us in Winchester for a prolonged stay.

Even in those early days she was able to talk about Pat and his death in quite a detached way; it probably helped her to do so. "It was a very holy death, wasn't it?" she said to me during the first week, and I had to agree. I have no wish here to enter into any detailed consideration of proposals to permit euthanasia, but it has been plain to me since Pat died that the argument based on a principle of allowing someone to 'die with dignity' is not well founded. Pat's death was not pleasant to behold, and I do not suppose it was at all pleasant to endure it, despite the relief he was certainly given by the painkillers. But it was hugely, immensely dignified. The calm acceptance of what his end was to prove to be, without complaint and with anxiety only for Dorothy, displayed all the human dignity one could ever hope to see. And probably all the more so in the light of Pat's own hopeless belief that death was the absolute end.

However, Dorothy was not always correct in her assessment of the future. In that same week, she had been talking to me about her plans generally and she came out with the remark, "I have a feeling I am not going to live very long." She said it more than once in those first few weeks. I do not think she was simply seeking my attention; she believed that to be the case. But she could hardly have been more wrong: she had another third of her life still to live.

There were two main concerns for the future: her health and her home. It was not the potential damage to her heart, which had caused anxiety soon after Harry's last return to India, that was casting a shadow now. The problem was arthritis. She put it down to an accident she had had when a teenager and had fallen off her bicycle. "I sprained my knee," she told me. This had resulted over the years (this is how it was put to me: I do not vouch for medical accuracy) in uneven wear on her hip joints and the right hip was wearing out. She had first noticed the consequential pain in 1957. When she came to our wedding, having walked the quarter of a mile from Hereford House, she sat for a few moments at the back of the

Church so as not to be seen limping as she walked up the aisle with Pat.

In the following two years this had developed and her limping was quite noticeable by the time of Pat's funeral. It was to be a permanent and increasing disability for her over the many years she had left. Her condition generally was probably not helped by having the misfortune, when visiting friends in Holland in March, 1960, to fall over and break her right femur. She had to be flown home on a stretcher and spend some time in a Bournemouth nursing home. The orthopaedic surgeon who looked after her told her cheerfully that she had broken it in just the right place to help the arthritis in the hip. But this proved to be wishful thinking. She recovered from the fracture, but the hip continued to deteriorate.

The arthritis was not by any means confined to one hip. Many joints became affected, including her spine, in which she developed a considerable degree of curvature as the years passed by. Having been rather tall and straight she became more and more short and bent – a rather stark contrast to her younger self. She bore it with resignation, and was glad to have some mobility left, greatly helped by her disabled driver's badge for her car.

As for her home, complicated as the position appeared to be when Pat died, a most satisfactory solution was found. The house in Glenferness Avenue had never been to her liking. She determined to get rid of it. It was thought best to continue with the building contract, and only to seek a buyer on substantial completion of the works. Relationships with both architect and builder became somewhat fraught, but she got there in the end, and the place was ultimately sold at a price which at least did not see her out of pocket over the whole venture. But it had taken the better part of a year from the date of Pat's death.

Dorothy had been turning over in her mind what alternative she wanted. Hereford House as it was in 1959, unchanged in thirty years save for the removal of the dental furniture and equipment on Pat's retirement, was not a long-term option. But she was becoming convinced that it could be made a very satisfactory home for her if suitably converted. Her increasing disability was causing her trouble with stairs. A flat – a proper flat flat – would really suit her better than a conventional house. Why not convert the former professional part of Hereford House into a large flat for herself and let the old domestic part to tenants? The situation of the place was ideal; no more than two hundred yards almost level walk to the nearest excellent shops, parking space available for her car at both front and rear, and at least a tiny bit of garden in which she could potter about, without being under any pressure to do more than she wanted.

Two friends of hers had divided their family home into two separate units, and confidently recommended their firm of architects. So, after a good deal of discussion with Sheila and me, Dorothy decided to start the ball rolling. It all took quite a long time. By March, 1961, the plans had been drawn up, in more or less their final shape. The work did not begin until January, 1962. Dorothy had spent that Christmas with us. On her return to Bournemouth she did not go back to Hereford House, but stayed at Meyrick Mansions Hotel, where she had recuperated in 1949, and which was still run by the same friend. It was ideal for her to be able to keep an eye on the works, with a minimum of disruption of her social life, and at a reasonable cost.

The work was extensive. The first half of the old main staircase was removed, a floor inserted at first floor level, and the old residential part thus severed completely from the remainder of the building, with its own sole access at the rear, from Upper Hinton Road and over the outside bridge. While downstairs even more alterations were made. The front door was moved one bay to the west, that is, in through one of the surgeries. The old entrance hall was thrown into the waiting room, making a room virtually identical to her old lounge on the first floor. Her bedroom was made out of the second surgery, and the old dental workshop made a pleasant dining room. The only stairs remaining in what was now 'her part' of the building were those to the two former first floor offices, which now became two spare bedrooms. It made a convenient, spacious and well situated home. On 30th April, 1962, I helped her move back into Hereford House.

Life, of course, is more than health and home, important though these may be. There can be no doubt that, of the two of them, Dorothy was far better able to cope with widowhood than Pat would ever have been. She was just as capable as he of dealing with the business side of running a home, and she had the housekeeping ability which he almost completely lacked. Her social activities gradually resumed to the stage where they were as extensive as they had ever been. Her bridge circle continued for very many years, really only coming to an end when old age and death removed too many for it to continue. While entertaining, which she much enjoyed, and did very well, was much easier in the converted building. Kitchen and dining room were on the same level and quite close to each other, and laying on a dinner party for six or eight people held no terrors for her.

That is not to say that she did not miss Pat. I think she did miss him dreadfully. As once she pointed out to me, in the whole of their thirty years together the number of nights they had slept apart in total was probably no more than four to six weeks. Companionship which has lasted so long must leave a void when it comes to an end. That void was particularly felt by Dorothy in the lack of someone to consider her first in all activities. There is no doubt that Pat put her on a pedestal and took virtually no decisions without consulting her. He had few hobbies or activities which took him out of the home. The only exception was his occasional golfing outing with the Hazards, and Dorothy herself would often join in by coming with him, or coming later with a picnic, walking round the course and thereby making it a shared outing.

It was simply not possible for me to be an adequate substitute for Pat in that respect. We lived close enough for me to be able to see her quite frequently. If I happened to be in court in the Bournemouth area I might visit even daily. But obviously that came nowhere near to providing the companionship she had lost. My own family, with two very young children so close to each other in age, had to come first. Dorothy realised that, of course, but she did need a great deal of involvement with us to help her get used to the consequences of Pat's death.

Sheila's parents lived only a couple of miles from Dorothy, and we had to be careful, if we went to stay with them, to spend nearly as much time at Hereford House as we did at Robinswood. Dorothy would urge us to do likewise if we were based with her for a few nights, although Hugh and Kathleen were more relaxed about it. When she came to stay with us it was really easier. She simply joined in with what we were doing. The years 1960 and 1961 saw four weddings of our contemporaries, some family, some friends, to which Dorothy came with us, each time making a short holiday for us all out of the occasion. There were other holidays taken with her over the years – and very happy occasions they all were.

Quite understandably Sheila enjoyed the prospect of a break also with her parents. These would be of a very different sort. As a young family they had spent many summers on the Norfolk Broads in a sailing boat, or motor cruiser. I was keen to see the country which had featured so vividly in some of my favourite Arthur Ransome books. It was thus not surprising that Hugh and Kathleen came with us on several such holidays over the years. Dorothy would not have been capable of joining in, even if she would have enjoyed it, which she would not. It was unfortunate that Dorothy seemed to find difficulty in coming fully to terms with that situation.

The problem probably owed its origin to the second such holiday on the Broads in August, 1962. Our then two children were almost four and three years old, and they came too, making a very happy three generation boatload. The plan, which had been perfectly amicably agreed, was that Sheila and I would go to Scotland for a fortnight after returning from the Broads, and that Adrian and Helen would stay with Hugh and Kathleen for the first week and with Dorothy for the second.

The first thing to go wrong was when we were on the Broads. Dorothy did not like me being out of touch for more than a very few days so I would telephone her once or twice a week. When I did so on 21st August from Horning she was in quite a state. She had learned that her sister, Phyllis, had died. She had not been able to get in touch with me. She had not been able to go to the funeral, because she had heard the news too late. She was upset at the death, upset at her inability to be there, and upset that I was not on hand as a potential comforter.

Matters were made rather worse by the time her two grandchildren were with her. They had already had one week at Robinswood where there were several people to look after them, a large garden and frequent access to a beach hut at Sandbanks with all that that entails. They found life at Hereford House much less to their liking. Far too full of small delicate objects with a 'careful' or 'don't touch' aura, hardly any garden, no visits to the beach, and only one rather less than agile person to take care of them. Not surprisingly at their ages they had no sense of tact at all, and their comments and requests made it all too clear that they would much rather still be with their other Granny.

The result of all these factors combined was that we returned from Scotland to a very disgruntled Dorothy, hardly mollified at all by the news we were able to give her that Sheila was expecting our third child about the following Easter. While we were well able to understand what caused her upset and feelings of dissatisfaction, it was not quite so easy to come to terms with the apparent implication that most of it was my fault. Of course it all blew over in time, and all relationships were restored. Had Pat still been alive, he would have been able to give the necessary support, at both moments of difficulty. We came to recognise the need for special care when there was a risk of 'Dorothy taking umbrage' as we came to call these periodic problems. She was not a daughter of Harry Hobbs for nothing, and was developing into quite a Matriarch.

On 15th May, 1963, I received a telephone call which was ultimately to be of the greatest significance to the whole family. It had been recognised by both of us that, pleasant as our house was, it would probably not be big enough in the long term. The lack of a separate room for me to use as a study was becoming increasingly tiresome, our children were getting bigger, and there were more of them. Our third, Elizabeth, had been born on Maundy Thursday that year and we hoped for more. One option could have been to build on further rooms. However I had seen a vacant site, some two hundred yards further up Sleepers Hill which struck me as potentially a marvellous piece of land on which to build a house to meet our own wishes. It was very secluded, being surrounded by trees – mostly within its boundary, and so within the owner's control – and with potentially a splendid view to the Isle of Wight some thirty miles to the south. I found that it belonged to an elderly lady who lived in the house opposite, and it was thus really a view-preserver for her. I mentioned to one or two of our neighbours that if the land ever came on the market I should be very tempted to put in a bid.

The telephone call was from one of those neighbours to tell me. "Miss Blencowe is going to put that land on the market." The news caused much excitement and heartsearching. Could we afford it? Was it a good idea? What chance of persuading her to sell to us? It was to be sold as two plots; did we want to buy it all, or only half? Fortunately this was before the very rapid rise in the price of building land. In the five years since we had bought our first house land had about doubled in value. By the end of the next five years it had gone up tenfold. We were just in time.

It was a few weeks of much activity, consulting estate agent, bank manager, parents and friends, with our fingers crossed at every stage. On 6th July we learned that we had secured the whole site. Miss Blencowe evidently liked the idea of selling to a young couple who, as she put it, "were going to found a family." That may have tipped the scales. She accepted my offer, and we rejoiced but felt a little stunned.

Friends were able to recommend a local architect and we met him for our first consultation at the end of September. It was a good move. We had the happiest and most fruitful relationship with Charles Burford. He listened to what we wanted; advised us as necessary; and was glad when we took his advice. He smiled ruefully when we wanted something else and then did what we asked. In the event he realised our wishes as fully as anyone could have hoped. It took quite a long time. We made it plain we were not in a hurry. The new house was about a year in the planning. Work began in early December, 1964. It was a small builder who was successful in the tenders and in consequence building was a slow process. We moved into an incomplete house on 10th December, 1965, with much work still to be done. It was March, 1966, before the builders moved out.

There are no street numbers on Sleepers Hill. We had already had to name one house. We had then decided to use the tree which stood at the entrance as our cue. It was an aspen tree. 'Aspen House' sounded quite reasonable, and we adopted that name. We were not to know that, quite soon after we sold it, the tree in question would have to be felled – leaving its namesake appearing, perhaps, a bit of a botanical curiosity.

There was no obvious tree to adopt for the new house. In any case, I had other ideas. Here, it seemed to me, we had a house worthy of the old family name. True it was not as big as the house in Queen's Park Avenue, nor was the garden – in particular there was nothing remotely resembling the wood. But house and garden were a fair size nonetheless and it had the same potential for making a long-standing family home. I broached the possibility with Sheila. She agreed with enthusiasm. None of my cousins, nor anyone else as far as I knew, had used the name. It might well be unique. So the new house became the fourth Chingri Khal.

Sheila and I had decided on the name during the course of building, although we kept quiet about it until we were about to send out change of address cards. I was glad to find that the choice received a warm welcome from everyone. Dorothy was the first to be told, and she was delighted that I still remembered her old home with enough affection to want to keep the name. Arthur, with whom I had corresponded on an occasional basis from the time I went to Oxford, seemed equally pleased. And so did all my cousins. It was a happy choice of name, complementing the wise decision to build as we did and the house has proved to be indeed a worthy successor to the third Chingri Khal.

Moving into a house which is very far from complete is not an activity I would recommend to anyone. We undertook this otherwise rather silly exercise in order to try to speed up the work. It may have had the opposite effect. The feeling of impatience, after having been very relaxed about the timing, was due to Dorothy's operation. Arthritis in her right hip had got much worse. She was in a lot of pain and her mobility was greatly impaired. She was advised to have the new surgical technique of hip replacement. I took her to King's College Hospital in London on 16th November, 1965 for the operation two days later. The procedures were more lengthy in those days, and she was in hospital for over five weeks.

The design of Chingri Khal included a downstairs bedroom, which would have been ideal for Dorothy to use for a period of recuperation after her discharge. We had hoped that by moving in on top of the builders we would encourage them to get far enough advanced for that room to become available for her on her discharge. It very soon became clear that it was a hopeless quest. Other arrangements had to be made. I made enquiries of hotels in Winchester, but in the event good friends of hers in Bournemouth, whose home was a flat, in which they had a spare room, invited her to stay with them for Christmas. So when I went to fetch Dorothy from King's College Hospital on 23rd December, I was, sadly, not able to bring her to Chingri Khal as we had hoped. Instead I took her to Bournemouth. She was with her friends for Christmas itself, and then spent further recuperating time at Meyrick Mansions, where she had been several times before. She was in no condition to be able to manage stairs, and the downstairs bedroom was nowhere near ready. It was an arrangement which worked, but it was not how any of us had planned the Christmas period, and it left Dorothy rather depressed and feeling that she had been rather let down by all and sundry.

It was March before the builders moved out. On Easter Sunday afternoon the House was blessed in a short, simple service by our Curate, Father Pat Murphy-O'Connor (elder brother of the future Cardinal.) Apart from a party for our neighbours on the Hill, who were all agog to see inside this place they had witnessed rising up for well over a year, Chingri Khal first really came into its own that Easter. Our family was now six in all, Catharine having been born in September, 1964, and yet we were able to have Dorothy and Hugh and Kathleen to stay, without any feeling of overcrowding. The downstairs bedroom proved ideal for Dorothy in her still somewhat disabled state (although the operation had effected a considerable improvement,) while there was a more conventional upstairs spare room for Sheila's parents. It was a pattern of things to come. Many visits were paid by all three of them, sometimes together, sometimes separately. Dorothy in particular was with us on most public holiday occasions from then on. She was able to spend every Christmas left to her (and there were two dozen of them) at Chingri Khal, as well as many holidays with us at other times in the year.

The pattern thus set then continued in much the same general manner for the next two decades. Dorothy made many visits to Chingri Khal where she was able to enjoy her grandchildren to the full, their number increasing to five in May, 1968, with the birth of Philippa. Her social life in Bournemouth was as full as ever, and not only in Bournemouth. She had friends in many parts of the country and had no hesitation in driving herself to stay with them for a few days. Her considerable driving experience stood her in good stead and I do not believe she ever got lost. She had one car which proved unreliable and let her down, so that journeys were sometimes completed in an RAC van, or even once in the cab of a commercial lorry. But in the main her travels were without incident or mishap. Such was the extent of her activities at home, in Bournemouth and further afield that I often thought that she was having a fuller and more congenial lifestyle than would have been the case had Pat still been alive. But that was to forget the real companionship and bond between them. That was what she missed so greatly, and what she tried to replace by turning to me. But however hard I tried to be on hand as much as possible, I was never going to be able to fill the place my father's death had left vacant.

She rejoiced very much when, at Easter, 1975, I was successful in my application for Silk. She decided to throw quite a big party at a Bournemouth hotel, which took place in June. This was a very successful event and she was in great form. She was getting rather bent and was walking with a stick to help her, but her general health was very good for someone now approaching her seventy-eighth birthday. In the summer of 1973 her nephew, Harry Hobbs, as yet unmarried, had paid an extended visit to England, staying much of his time with Dorothy. That started her thinking about the long family separation from Arthur. She felt that, if she did not make the effort soon, one or other of them would be too old or too ill, or both, to make the journey possible or worthwhile. In the event it was not long after the 1975 party that she announced she was determined to go to Canada to see her brother.

So on 23rd September I took her to Heathrow to fly to Toronto from where Arthur and Pauline would pick her up. She had last seen him just before she set off for India in November, 1925, almost exactly fifty years before. She was away for a month, coming back tired, wiser and just a little saddened. It had not been altogether without incident, and she had found Arthur at times difficult to deal with. However she enjoyed the visit generally, the journey by car into Vermont to see the autumn colours, and making friends again with Pauline. This last was probably the most enduring outcome. Arthur did not live very long after that visit, but Pauline made several trips to England over the next few years. We were very glad to have the opportunity to get to know her. She was very agile, young at heart and a delightful companion.

It was in Novmber, 1981, that my appointment as a circuit judge was announced. These things do not happen in an instant: it had been brewing for many months. I had been glad to have had the offer, particularly as it entailed being based in Winchester and probably spending more of my time there than anywhere else. But in the time leading up to the announcement everything had to be kept highly confidential. You were only allowed to tell 'your clerk, your accountant and your wife.' Thus it was that I had to telephone Dorothy on the evening of Tuesday, 3rd November to give her the news and to invite her to be with us by Thursday evening ready to come to London for my swearing-in on the Friday.

She was completely taken aback, and took a moment or two to congratulate me. I could sense a slight hint of disappointment in her voice. In truth I do not think she ever entirely forgave me for taking the job. She was one of those parents who feel that their little darling is destined for the top of whatever tree he chooses to climb. Particularly is that so when the little darling in question was, when very young, an early developer. If you could read and recite your tables a year before the next child, then the sky's the limit. No matter that by the time you are in the sixth form you have sunk back to average, parental pride and hope remain doggedly in place. In later years she occasionally said, "You ought to have waited to be offered to become a High Court Judge." No use replying to that to the effect that I would have waited forever. Probably the last time she said it she added, "But perhaps you would not have been as happy as you are." And there, I feel, one can detect that reality had started to dawn.

But she did come on that Thursday and travelled on the Friday and was present when the Rubicon was crossed. She joined us at an uproarious family lunch at a smart restaurant (Adrian ordered champagne for our aperitif – a very kind touch) which completed a memorable day. Dorothy then went to stay with Toff and Ian Collie near Hampton Court for the week-end. Toff and Dorothy had always been close and were becoming more and more so as time went by. Toff was very good to her, visiting her in Bournemouth and having her to stay at her home, even at times going with her for a few days holiday at a hotel. It gave an added dimension to Dorothy's life, and one she valued greatly.

Whatever reservations she may have felt inwardly about my appointment, she was not one to miss the opportunity for a celebration. Sure enough, on 2nd January the following year she gave, in the same hotel, a similar party to that which we had all enjoyed so much on my taking Silk.

So she soldiered on at Hereford House. She never had the help of anyone living in the house. Mrs Long, who had been so kind to her at the time of Pat's death, had emigrated to Australia not long afterwards to be with one of her family. But Dorothy managed to find other devoted ladies who came in from time to time to help her with some aspects of keeping the place in a reasonable state. And there was always Beatrice. She had somehow never stopped coming. Habit dies hard, and she had been coming every weekday to Hereford House since the 1920s, so that neither Pat's retirement, nor his death, nor anything else seemed to break her routine. She and

Dorothy, in the early days, had had a somewhat tricky relationship. It seemed to Dorothy that Beatrice was suspicious of any influence Dorothy might have had on the professional side of the household. They never got on to terms of close affection, but that did not deter Beatrice in the least. Dorothy was glad to have her around, and she did continue very faithfully to come and do odds and ends until she felt she had to retire to her family in Worcester, not very long before Dorothy left Hereford House herself.

But it was becoming clear that Dorothy could not go on indefinitely managing on her own. She was getting physically slower and less confident. And while she was in most respects just as alert and sensible as ever, she herself recognised that she was getting forgetful. She laughed afterwards at herself for having walked, very slowly and lamely, almost home from the International Stores (they were about two hundred yards away) with their wire basket in her hand, full of greengroceries for which she had not paid. She slowly trudged her way back when she realised what she was doing, but did not find anyone there who thought it was funny. She paid a rather censorious till girl and trudged her way home again. Then losing her car keys (and so the front door key) became something of a drama which occurred every two or three weeks. There were many such events, little things warning her that she could not be on her own for much longer.

Chingri Khal plainly had the potential to provide enough room for a home for Dorothy when one was needed. We had made this clear over the years, from long before any question of moving had arisen. We all realised how much the elderly value their independence, and no one thought of any move until well after my appointment to the Bench. Dorothy had occasionally remarked that she had put her name down at a home for the elderly in Bournemouth, run by an order of nuns (not that of her former school) and I had said she would come to us, rather than to any such place. She would decline the prospect, inventing, as it seemed to me, rather silly excuses for doing so. One, for instance, was that she had always lived at sea level and we were 300 feet above it at Chingri Khal. Nothing was done; nothing was settled. She carried on in her old home where plenty of friends and relations would call to have a chat, to listen to her talking and reminiscing and to enjoy her – still excellent – cooking. She managed to have a full life at Hereford House.

In July, 1985, we had the first wedding in the family for many years. Elizabeth was married to Andrew Dickens, and the reception was in the garden of Chingri Khal. Dorothy, of course, was present. The house was too full of immediate participants for her to be able to stay in it; she, together with Hugh and Kathleen, stayed at a hotel in the city. But the party was a good one, and must have caused her to think back to earlier wedding receptions – Sheila's and mine at Robinswood and her own at the third Chingri Khal. The house really did come into its own for the occasion. She enjoyed seeing Hugh and Kathleen again. Some years earlier they had finally left Robinswood and gone to live with the Dearnley family at their home at Dovercourt, near Harwich. This move had meant something of a loss for Dorothy. Hugh and Kathleen had become good friends from even before Sheila and I were married, and that had developed still more after the death of Pat. Since then they had seen a great deal of each other, and entertained each other many time in their respective homes.

Dorothy went back to Bournemouth after the wedding, but returned for a fortnight's stay from mid August. After that visit, she was back in less than three weeks in order to join our celebrations for Catharine's twenty-first birthday. These various family occasions, together with the comforts and advantages of Chingri Khal and its garden brought home to Dorothy what a pleasant alternative to carrying on alone at Hereford House was available for her at Winchester. So on the last day of that visit she took the plunge and asked if she could move in with us. The answer, of course, was yes – and then a lot had to be done, but not before there was very nearly a major disaster.

The house was well suited to a visit by Dorothy for a few days, or even a few weeks. But if she were to be with us permanently, significant additions and alterations would be required. Enquiry had confirmed that Charles Burford, who had designed Chingri Khal so successfully twenty years before, was still in practice. He agreed to help us again and a first appointment was made for Friday, 4th October, at our home. I was due to be in court in Southampton, and may well only just get back in time for the meeting, which obviously had to fit in with the architect's convenience. While Dorothy was still driving her car in Bournemouth for shopping and similar short distances, she had not been at the wheel for longer journeys for some time. On this occasion, however, I asked her if she thought she could get herself to Winchester, as I would probably not have time to get to Bournemouth and back after Court before Mr Burford was due to arrive. "Could you manage that – we can take you home in the evening?" "Of course." "Are you sure?" "Yes, dear."

And so Dorothy set off that afternoon to make the journey she had driven probably hundreds of times before, and knew very well indeed. The motorway and dual carriageway which now exist were only partly built. She did not waste time, and was quite capable of overtaking heavy vehicles going slower than she was. As she was approaching the hill down into Cadnam at the northern end of the New Forest, she overtook a large commercial vehicle, whose driver saw that she was pulling back to her nearside before she had finally cleared the front of his truck. Although he braked and sounded his horn, Dorothy's car was given enough of a glancing blow to send it fast off the road to the left hand verge, which was fortunately unfenced, where it turned over one and a half times, leaving Dorothy suspended upside-down by her seat belt.

Fortunately again, a doctor happened to be passing in his car, and managed to extricate her. She seemed uninjured, but as someone, very sensibly, had sent for an ambulance, she was taken to Southampton General Hospital for a check-up. The police telephoned Sheila to tell her, and she telephoned the court where I was told. So, as soon as I could get away, I went to the hospital, in considerable anxiety as to what sort of a state I should find her in. I had only had a fairly garbled, third hand account as to what had happened. Would she be in bed? Conscious? Too ill to be moved?

I need not have worried. She was sitting up in a chair in casualty, as bright as a button. "How are you?" "I feel a little tired now, dear." "I'll go and get the car to the door." "How far away is it?" "It's in the car park, perhaps two hundred yards." "I think I'd like a little walk, dear." And so the two of us walked to my car and I drove her to Winchester. There we had a most helpful time with Charles Burford and the planning of the alterations was put well in hand. Sheila and I then took her back to Hereford House. We had a meal at a restaurant in Bournemouth, and saw she had all she needed before returning to Winchester. She seemed perfectly happy to be left.

I had my doubts, however, as to what she would be like the following morning after such a traumatic day, so I telephoned at the earliest reasonable opportunity. "How do you feel now, after all that happened yesterday?" "I feel a little bit stiff, dear." And that was her only comment. She was none the worse. Her car was a write-off, and the police only did not being any proceedings against her on my assuring them that I would see to it that she never drove again. She never did: but I think it upset her a bit that such a very long, and almost entirely incident free, driving career should have ended in that way.

It is, perhaps, in the nature of "events" that they are unpredictable in both their occurrence and their effect. Dorothy had survived, completely unscathed, an accident which could easily have killed her. All went well for the next few weeks. The planning of the alterations continued, with a good deal more urgency in the matter than in the original building operations. Likewise first steps had to be taken to find a purchaser for Hereford House. I fetched Dorothy for Christmas, and, soon after Christmas itself, I brought Hugh and Kathleen to stay as well. It was a bit hectic, but there were no real problems. By the middle of January Dorothy was back at Bournemouth. She now had to shop for herself by taxi. She was getting distinctly unsteady on her feet, and was taking very great care not to fall. She avoided, if she could, going out when the weather, either because of ice, or because of wind, might present an extra hazard in that respect.

The forecast for Tuesday, 14th January was not good, and the day lived up to it. Strong winds, blustery showers, just the sort of day to stay at home. But, for reasons she could never quite understand, Dorothy got a taxi to take her to the other side of Bournemouth Square to do some shopping. She was well wrapped against the elements. As soon as she got out of the taxi the wind whipped up into a sudden, violent gust, and got under her overcoat, which billowed up, lifted her off her feet, and threw her to the ground. She sustained several fractured bones, including a wrist and a part of her pelvis and one of her shoulders was dislocated. It was a very nasty accident. An ambulance was called and she was taken to hospital where she stayed for a couple of nights before transferring to a nursing home. There she remained until the end of February by which time she was just recovered enough for me to fetch her for the week-end, so that she could attend the wedding of her great niece (Phyllida's daughter) in Portsmouth. Even so, she was very frail and shaky, and very frightened of the icy conditions under foot. After the week-end she had to return to the nursing home where she stayed for just over a week, after which she moved into a hotel in Bournemouth (this time the Norfolk.) It was not until 4th May, after spending a couple of nights with us, that she felt strong enough to return to Hereford House. Even then her agility and her confidence were not fully recovered. The whole episode had set her back a lot, and she never fully made up the lost ground. We all thought what a good thing it was that fundamental change was now close at hand.

But there were still some weeks to go. Sheila and I had a long-booked holiday in Colonsay for a fortnight at the end of May and early June. Work had started before we left, although it was still in an early stage. It involved building on a new bedroom on the ground floor, beyond the children's old playroom, together with an adjoining bathroom. The playroom was converted into a drawing room for Dorothy. The old downstairs bedroom became 'the ante-room' and fortunately was able to house Dorothy's two rather large bookcases. By happy chance the playroom proved to be just big enough to accommodate Dorothy's drawing room furniture from Hereford House – lacking only the feature of the bay window to make the two rooms virtually the same size.

It was whilst we were away that the welcome news came through that a buyer had been found for Hereford House, at a very good price, and the deposit paid. Things really were happening. The work on the extension continued during June and July. I had to try to give my administration enough warning of when I wanted to take the necessary leave to enable me to help with the move. We all thought that it was bound to be a major operation, notwithstanding some clearing out during the alterations of 1962, and so it proved to be. The removals vans arrived at Hereford House on the Monday morning – just before Sheila and I got there. It was a long day, but only half the job was done. The same happened on the Tuesday. Dorothy was by now staying again at the Norfolk Hotel for these two nights.

And then there was quite a remarkable coincidence, and one entirely unappreciated by any of us at the time. Dorothy, perhaps, might have realised it, but she had more than enough to think about. I only came to realise it when looking at Pat's diary for 1929 – by which time the third millennium was well under way. Dorothy and Pat had moved out of the third Chingri Khal into Hereford House on 6th and 7th August, and here was Dorothy, fifty-seven years later to the day, moving out of Hereford House into the fourth Chingri Khal. It was early on the morning of 6th August, 1986, that the pantechnicons arrived in Winchester and unloading began. It was a bit chaotic, but Sheila and I were able to get her bed put in place and made it up for her, and there was some semblance of order by the time Dorothy herself arrived in the late morning. A kind friend drove her from Bournemouth with her small amount of overnight belongings, which were all that remained for her to bring. We welcomed her to her new home – back at Chingri Khal once more.

The fourth Chingri Khal, from 1965.
A photograph taken in 2002.

CHAPTER 34

RETURN TO
A FAMILIAR FOLD

WHEN THE REMOVALS MEN had departed on the Wednesday evening, the furniture was in place, and the main necessary boxes had been unpacked. But there remained no fewer than sixty-five packing cases stacked in the garage. It took three months for me to deal with them. It was amazing that a place was found for nearly everything, even though much unwanted stuff had been left behind for the house clearers to take away. Dorothy was, of course, free to come and go in any other part of the house, but her own two main rooms contained most of her familiar belongings from the two equivalent rooms at Hereford House.

There can be no doubt at all that the move was a tremendous success, despite having moments of difficulty. Inevitably there were problems, as we had realised that there would be. Sheila was under no illusions about the need to be as tactful as she could when dealing with Dorothy's likes and dislikes. Dorothy's niece, Toff, had kindly added a warning of her own – not that Sheila needed much warning. Fond as Toff was of Dorothy, she knew how powerful a character she was, and how she liked things done in her own way, and liked being at the centre of everything, just as Pat had put her. "So long as you know what you are taking on" was her final comment to Sheila after they had had a talk about the impending changes.

The incident of the key is an example. It was a silly slip on my part to forget to have a key cut for Dorothy. That could so easily have been done, and, had I thought of it, I would have had it ready to hand to her on her arrival, but it never occurred to me. That was probably because the number of times she would really need a front door key was small: she was usually in and out with one of us. Rather than asking for one cheerily soon after arrival, she allowed the oversight to fester in her mind, and to make her think that she was not regarded as being really in her own home. The result was that, a month or so on, she asked for one in very aggrieved terms – and tones. The omission, once pointed out, was repaired immediately – and we realised that we still had to be very alert to avoid causing possible umbrage.

But episodes like this were the exception. Our ability to provide a happy and comfortable home for Dorothy's declining years reflects the effort that was put into it by all three of us. But the lion's share of the credit must go to Sheila. First she had to cope with extra demands on her managerial and culinary skills. Even more important was the need for what she herself would call 'TLC' ('tender loving care') which she lavishly bestowed on Dorothy, the need for which increased steadily with time. She was still working about half time on the Music Staff at Winchester College, and keeping up her professional standard of playing. She had long got over the nervousness she had felt when first married at having to cook for and entertain Dorothy from time to time, but the general responsibility was considerably increased when Dorothy moved in with us.

There were many friends left behind in Bournemouth and elsewhere, as well as relations, close and distant, who she would like to visit her. I suggested we gave a party to invite a large number of those who would be glad to see where she was living. But no, she wanted a dinner party for each person, or couple, with our friends invited too. This was very enjoyable, but it meant a great deal of work, again especially for Sheila. And it took quite a long time to work through them all, probably even longer than coping with the sixty-five packing cases – and a good deal more hard work.

But these problems apart, it was a very happy and successful solution to what would otherwise have been a depressing situation for her. Particularly after her accident in being blown over, there was little chance of her being fit enough again to run her own show at Hereford House, or anywhere else, without a lot of help. She would not have enjoyed life in any sort of institution.

As it was, she found herself living again in a fairly large family house, much family coming and going, cuisine as good as anywhere you like to name, five grandchildren to talk to her and to take an interest in her and her reminiscences, a garden full of colour in spring, summer and autumn, and a view to the distant hills of the Isle of Wight. She knew she was very well off, and she was deeply grateful for it.

For our part we were glad to be able to achieve this result. We were also glad to be close at hand to deal with any emergency. The problems and disasters, some minor, some major, which had become an increasing feature of her life in Bournemouth, became fewer in number, and it was much easier to deal with those which did arise. It was also good for the family to have her around. Only our two youngest, Catharine and Philippa, were still at home, and at that only spasmodically. Catharine was at Cambridge and Philippa had just left school and was soon off to Nottingham. But all of her grandchildren came home frequently, and there was much benefit gained by them as well as by Dorothy from the mutual enjoyment of each other's company. It was good for our children to have frequent contact with their grandmother, and she was always glad to have an audience. Philippa, being the youngest, was at home more than the rest and in particular remembers the encouragement she had to persevere with singing – even though Dorothy often chided her for using her voice unwisely. Catharine, on the other hand, who went to live and work in Cairo in 1987 recalls how Dorothy made a point of a fond farewell every time she left to go back there after a holiday in England, as if to underline the possibility of it being the last time.

When she first came to live at Chingri Khal Dorothy was still fairly mobile. She had always liked shopping and would take herself into the town by taxi, enjoying thereby a measure of independence. Equally, Sheila and I were able to have our holidays much as usual, taking steps for Dorothy to be looked after at home or to stay somewhere else. Occasionally, too, all three of us went away together. She had a full life, if, inevitably, lacking the company of her old friends from Bournemouth, save on relatively rare occasions.

We have seen how Sheila's parents had been particularly good friends to her, from the time of Pat's death onwards, and how their move to the Dearnley home at Dovercourt had been rather a loss for Dorothy. They did, however, come to stay at Chingri Khal in January,

1987, when the Dearnleys were abroad, and were with us for three weeks. All rather like old times. It was to prove to be the last time that they and Dorothy saw each other.

Another occasion for seeing old friends, this time many of them, was Dorothy's ninetieth birthday party, just over a year after she came to Winchester. On the day itself, 12th November, 1987, a Thursday, we took her to the theatre. On the Saturday there was a large lunch party for her at Chingri Khal. We sat down thirty-seven people in our reception rooms, relations, old friends from Bournemouth and new ones from Winchester. One of the stars was Dorothy's first great-grandchild, Emily Dickens, who had been born in the September, two months before, brought, of course, by her parents, Elizabeth and Andrew, who lived in the city. Dorothy was in great form. Without my saying much more than "lift your glasses" we drank her health. To my astonishment Dorothy got slowly to her feet and delivered a speech, lasting quite a few minutes, mainly directed to thanking Sheila – to whom she referred throughout as "my daughter-in-law" – for giving her so much hospitality and help. It was a spirited effort, and won a warm round of applause for both of them.

Only three weeks later there was another, just as happy a party, albeit somewhat smaller, for Emily's christening in St. Peter's Catholic Church in Winchester. She wore the christening robe which Dorothy had made for me nearly sixty years before, and which had also been worn by all of Dorothy's grandchildren. She felt a very proud and contented great-grandmother holding the baby in the robe of her own making.

There was all too much evidence of the passing of time in 1988. Hugh and Kathleen celebrated their Diamond Wedding in April. Just as they had not been fit enough to come to Winchester for Dorothy's birthday, so Dorothy was not able to make the journey to Dovercourt. Hugh was now ninety-three, and getting very frail. Kathleen, at eighty-eight was not much more robust. It was sad for Sheila, but caused little surprise, when she received a telephone call in August to tell her that Hugh had died peacefully at the retirement home where they were then living. Sheila and I, of course, went to Dovercourt for the funeral, most of our children being there as well,

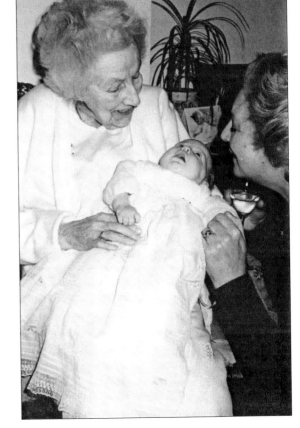

Dorothy with her grandchildren on the terrace of the fourth Chingri Khal, August 1972. (Left to right: Philippa, Adrian, Elizabeth, Dorothy, Helen, Catharine).

After the Christening. Dorothy, by now over 90, holds her first great grandchild, Emily Dickens, who wears the robe Dorothy made in 1930. Sheila looks on. 5th December, 1987.

but Dorothy was not up to the long journey

Just over two months after that came an awful blow for Dorothy. Toff had always been more than kind to her, and her move to Chingri Khal meant that she was that much closer to Toff's home near Hampton Court. So, quite apart from Dorothy's occasional stay with her, Toff made a point of coming, sometimes with Ian, more often on her own, for quite frequent visits to see Dorothy and chat with her, perhaps go into the city for lunch. Any opportunity for a talk, especially about old times, was greatly welcomed. On some of those visits I would see Toff myself, at others she would have left for home before I got back from Court.

I was home in time to see her in September, 1988. She had found Dorothy just a little trying during that afternoon, and as she got into the car she said to me, in a slightly exasperated tone, "I don't want to be old." I laughed and waved her off. She came again on the last day of October. I was too late back to see her. Sheila had had several commitments and was in and out of the house, being quite surprised to find Toff still there on her return from her final outing. Toff seemed to want to linger, Dorothy had wanted her around. But when she did leave she told Sheila what a wonderful job she thought she was doing in coping with and looking after Dorothy. It was typically kind of her to say so. And then she drove away just as usual.

It was, therefore, a great shock for us all to have a telephone call early the next morning. I took it in Dorothy's bedroom, where I had gone as usual to pull her curtains first thing. It was Toff's daughter: Toff had died suddenly in the night, could she speak to Dorothy? I simply handed over the telephone. I was very concerned as to how Dorothy would react to this devastating news. She had frequently referred to Toff as "the daughter I never had," and this was a grievous loss. In fact she coped with the situation very well, and was able to come with us to Toff's funeral the following week in Hampton. It was the first funeral in the family which she had been able to attend since that of Pat nearly thirty years earlier, and her memories of Toff went back even longer. She deeply mourned her, and sadly missed her lively visits.

A year of decline and loss was completed in mid December when Sheila, who had been preparing to visit Dovercourt to see her mother before Christmas, received another telephone call this time telling her that Kathleen had died that day very suddenly. We had always thought that Hugh and Kathleen had been keeping each other alive for some years, and so the death of one seemed likely to lead to the death of the other in quite a short time. The sadness for Sheila was no less on that account, and again we had the journey to Dovercourt for her funeral, attended by nearly all her family. But, as before, Dorothy was not able to come too.

So the year ended with Dorothy feeling that she had lost three persons who had meant a great deal to her, especially in the last twenty years or more. But all her grandchildren were around for Christmas, the house was full of cheerful people and she, along with the rest of us, was able to enjoy Christmas as of old.

But there was no escaping from the gradual decline in her health. She became more and more reliant upon the help of others, and more and more in need of the wheel chair. Matters were not helped by increasing problems with incontinence. There had been occasions of this from the time she first came to live at Chingri Khal, but it was making some aspects of life quite difficult. Especially as she was reluctant to acknowledge it as a problem at all. She still had her love of the theatre and still liked to be taken to it, particularly to the opera. The latter was available at the Mayflower Theatre in Southampton two or three times a year. Our theatrical outings in this period tended to be a considerable trial for Sheila who found herself having to cope with Dorothy for most of the intervals.

Her love of opera gave rise to a slight echo of Jennie's intervention when receiving the last sacraments. We had booked tickets many months before to see *Salome* by Richard Strauss on Tuesday, 26th April, 1988. Towards the end of the previous week Dorothy got rather worse, very frail and in a good deal of pain. The outing seemed to be in question. Without telling either Sheila or me (although we knew he was coming to see her) she telephoned our Parish Priest, Canon Nicholas France, to tell him she was dying and would he, please, come and give her the last sacraments. He clearly recalled the events when writing to me fifteen years later:

I went round and let myself in through the side door as I usually did.

You were in Court and Sheila was out. Your mother was sitting up in bed looking well though she insisted, quite cheerfully, that she was dying. So we talked of death, of Heaven and the last things without any fear or dismay. I then heard her confession, anointed her and gave her Holy Communion. I later made my farewells and as I was going out of the room she said, "I hope to be able to get up tomorrow in order to go to the opera."…What struck me about her was the very natural faith that she had which was integrated with the good things of life, something she must have inherited from her Irish mother in an age when the Irish didn't see a distinction between religion and life."

She did indeed get up – just – for the opera. She was very frail and shaky on that outing, but she made it. And slowly she got over the worst of that episode. Curiously she never told Sheila or me that she had been anointed. The first we knew that she had been was when Canon France told the story in his homily at her Requiem, more than two years later.

By the time 1990 dawned Dorothy was ninety-two years old and already four months older than her father had been when he died. This did not trouble her at all. But we all seemed to sense some unspoken portent in February. Our labrador, who was, at rather over twelve, not a very old dog, had to be put down by the vet. It happened before breakfast; Dorothy came out of her bedroom to see it done in a downstairs corridor. Although he was replaced quite quickly by a labrador puppy – a present from Dorothy – the old dog's sudden decline, and Dorothy's more gradual one, had a poignant complementary quality.

One of the things Dorothy enjoyed was being taken out in the car for a drive around the countryside near Winchester. I would do this if I had a short day in court, taking an hour to do some twenty or thirty miles, out along one compass point and back along another. She would keep up a running commentary on everything we passed – houses, gardens, woodlands, fields, animals, humans, in fact anything which came into sight. On the Monday in Holy Week I had just such an opportunity, and she was glad to come. But once in the car she was strangely silent. She hardly uttered a word during the whole of the drive, sometimes dozing, sometimes not. It seemed to me something was not quite right.

By Good Friday something was very clearly wrong, as the lady who came to help with her also found. She could hardly stand at all. By the next day she was worse, the doctor had to be called and he advised having her admitted to a nursing home quickly. This was done, not to the nursing home on Sleepers Hill which we would have chosen, for that was full, but to one adequate for the emergency. She was there for a little over a fortnight before returning home. But it proved impossible adequately to look after her in the domestic situation, even with much help coming to the house, including a nurse at times during the day, and a night nurse as well, After just over a week of trying to cope at Chingri Khal a vacancy had arisen at Westacre, the nursing home on Sleepers Hill, and we took her there on 9th May. It was never stated that this was to be a permanent move. Indeed, if she had recovered enough strength to return to Chingri Khal we should have been glad to bring her home. At least Westacre was near enough for me to be able to wheel her in her chair up the hill to have lunch at home and to sit in the garden.

Sheila and I had a long-standing holiday booked to begin on 26th July. We were to spend two weeks in Sark. Although Pat and Dorothy had never felt moved after the war to try to repeat the success of their first and only visit to that tiny island, for Sheila and myself it had become much the most popular destination for a break, both with and without our children. The number of times we had gone there had run well into double figures. So it was no great surprise to anyone that we were going there again. It had the advantage of not being too far away in the event of an emergency.

Dorothy had not shown much improvement in the time she had been in Westacre, but equally there had been little sign of getting worse. She could carry on a perfectly sensible conversation, although at other times she might appear a little *distrait.* Thus after a chat about the family, it was a little disconcerting to be asked as we were going out "What am I watching?" For the reply had to be "You are watching the tennis at Wimbledon," which one might have thought would have been obvious to almost anyone.

So at the end of July, when we said good-bye and see you in a fortnight, she showed no sign of any significant deterioration. We left her fully expecting to find her in much the same state on our return. She was reasonably happy there, and had often said how nice it was. Those of her grandchildren who were in Winchester came to see her from time to time, as well as other friends. On Sunday, 5th August, Elizabeth, by now very big with her second child who was due in two months time, called to see her, taking with her Emily, Dorothy's great-granddaughter, not quite three years old. They had a jolly time, which became almost uproarious when one of the nurses came in with a choc-ice for Emily. The next few minutes saw Emily transfer the greater part of the chocolate covering from the ice cream to her face and fingers – a typical filthy, but happy toddler. When the time came to go they had all had a lot of laughs, and had given Dorothy a very happy afternoon.

On the Monday morning the visiting hairdresser paid one of her regular calls. Dorothy had her hair shampooed and set. She was glad to have that done. It is good for the morale, and, after all, she had always tended to be fastidious about her appearance, especially if she were going to meet someone important. She coped perfectly well with that bustle of activity.

But in the afternoon she complained of feeling cold. She was given a shawl to put over her shoulders. But that did not seem to be enough to keep out the chill, despite it being a fine, warm summer's day. She seemed to be distinctly weaker. The staff became anxious and sent for her doctor. He came and took in the situation quite quickly. "Keep her as comfortable as you can. There is nothing more we can do: I think she is on her way."

Well she might be. Was it not the 6th August? On this day sixty-one years before, had she not started to move out of Chingri Khal, her much loved home, and into Hereford House? And on this day, just four years ago, had she not moved out of Hereford House and into a new, even more loved Chingri Khal? It was the right time of year for her to make a really significant change. Now was the time for moving on.

She got weaker, and slept most of the afternoon, her breathing shallow, her awareness very slight. As evening came she was plainly not interested in any food. Just dozing on and off. The night staff came on duty. They were told about her condition and were asked to keep an eye on her. Someone went in every twenty minutes during the night. She clung to life for the rest of that day. But at about four o'clock in the morning, as the first light of the new day began to brighten the sky behind St. Catherine's Hill, her breathing stopped and her soul slipped away to God.

EPILOGUE

INEVITABLY IT CAME as a shock to be awakened by our hostess bringing in a cordless telephone (there were no room telephones in our Sark hotel) an hour before tea had been due, and so being given the news of the death of Dorothy. It meant that there was much to do in a short period of time. Just as well that there was: I felt a curious detached air of unreality. From our point of view it was the severance of the last close link with an earlier generation, and it was hard to realise that Dorothy would not be there as expected on our return.

But there was no time for morbid contemplation. We were not due home for a couple of days. Arrangements were made for our return journey to be brought forward to that morning. We raced through our packing and were back in Winchester soon after midday, and began the necessary round of registering, organising and informing. She had timed it very well. I was still on leave the following week. Catharine, the only one of our children out of the country, was due home in two days' time. We were therefore able to muster a full turnout for the funeral on Thursday of the following week.

Following old Catholic custom, her coffin was received into the Church after the evening Mass of the Feast of the Assumption, 15th August, where it remained before the High Altar until the funeral Requiem Mass the following day. Sheila played the organ for the funeral. Catharine and Philippa sang a couple of duets. Most of her relations were able to attend, as well as a fair number of friends old and new, from Bournemouth and from Winchester. She was buried in St. James's Cemetery in Winchester, one of the few Catholic burial grounds in England which has been consecrated ground since before the Reformation. There followed a lunchtime reception at Chingri Khal – indeed, one could properly call it a party. The death of someone very old at the end of a life well lived, despite the inevitable sadness arising from the loss, is not an occasion for prolonged mourning. And then our guests departed and the family entered into its post-Dorothy era.

That, one might expect, would be the end of the story. But not quite. It was not only the letters in those promising-looking boxes which I found when I began the task of going through Dorothy's effects. There was a letter, written on very old Hereford House headed paper, addressed to me – just the one word 'Martin' on the envelope. It was undated, but it was quite obviously a letter written many years earlier. Although the occasion for writing letters had not arisen very often in the time Dorothy had been living at Chingri Khal, I had become accustomed to seeing her handwriting degenerating slowly into the shaky and hesitant script that is so typical of the very old. This, by contrast, was in the handwriting of the young Dorothy, really no different from the script in the letters from India and the rest of that journey.

It had plainly been written in the immediate aftermath of that disaster in her life which the death of Pat undoubtedly had been, in the first flush of her grief that she had so largely kept to herself. At that time she had thought she would not live very long, and so she probably expected that I would be reading what she wrote within a few months, or at most a year or two. As things turned out it had remained in her bureau for over thirty years, by which time I was almost as old as she had been when she wrote it, and, sadly, far too set in my ways to do much about obeying one of the injunctions she gave me. I had a most curious sensation as I read the words coming to me from so long ago in the past. There is no escaping the depth of her feelings when she wrote them.

My darling darling Martin,

You mustn't expect a long letter from me – I'm so inclined to cry.

I just want to send you my love & to tell you how happy Pat & I have been & how much we wanted you & loved you. I hope you will never forget this.

I also want you to try and be like your father and copy him as far as you are able.

Please pray for me & don't forget me.

Your loving,

Mummy

They were, in almost every way, a conventional couple. Despite their very different backgrounds and upbringing, and despite their widely differing beliefs in the meaning of life and death, in the reality of God and in the teaching of His Church, they shared the same approach as to how one should behave.

Except in the matter of observance of purely Church law or practice – Sunday Mass, fish on Friday, Lenten observance and the like, as to which Pat simply kept quiet and did not interfere – I was not conscious of any disagreement between them as to how men and women should try to live their lives. Keep your promises. Tell the truth. Act honestly and honourably. Own up if you get something wrong. Work hard. Be moderate in eating and drinking. Sex is for marriage and marriage is for life. All these, and more, were principles they held in common.

Differences were more superficial. Pat was one of the purest lipped men I have known. Even as mild an imprecation as 'damn' hardly ever passed his mouth. Dorothy, by contrast, was very inclined loudly to 'blast' as well as 'damn' – for instance, whenever she burnt the toast (which was frequently in the days before automatic toasters.) It rather pained Pat to hear it. "Your father has a non-conformist conscience" she used to say to me. And, for a devout Catholic, she had a strange superstitious streak. An example is the moon. She knew it was nonsense, but she still liked to greet the new moon, carefully avoiding seeing it first through glass, by curtseying nine times and turning her money over. When I was a small boy she would encourage me to do the same, only for a man it was three bows rather than nine curtseys, but I still felt rather stupid and self-conscious as I followed the ritual. Pat took it all with slightly amused indifference.

Conventional they may have been, but that did not make them an unattractive, forbidding couple. They were not frigid, censorious people, without joy in their lives and without love in their relationships. They made a very happy home, a relaxed home, a home full of love and understanding, of laughter, joy and contentment. They gave me a very happy childhood, not one without discipline, but one certainly without fear, frustration or cause to rebel.

That is not to say that I agreed then, or agree now, with everything they said or did. But the framework within which they ordered their lives, and tried to encourage me to do the same, was in no sense a recipe for the sort of disaster so often depicted as being the consequence of following a conventional Christian lifestyle. Rather is the opposite the truth. In common with many other couples, then and now, their confidently held convictions about the basic principles of behaviour, helped them to succeed in dealing with the many difficulties they faced over the years, and to give as fine a start as one could hope for the next generation.

APPENDIX 1

THE PUBLISHED WORKS OF HARRY HOBBS

Unless otherwise stated all books were published by H. Hobbs or H. Hobbs & Co. of Calcutta.

The Piano in India – how to keep it in order (Thacker, Spink & Co., Calcutta) (1899, 2nd edition, 1914)

It was like this! (Thacker, Spink & Co.) (1918)

Digressions of a Ditcher (1925)

The Romance of the Calcutta Sweep (1930)

Scoundrels and Scroungers (1933)

Spence's Hotel and its Times (1936)

Indian Dust Devils (1937)

Talkeetalkeewallahs and Others (1938)

Any Soldier to his Son (Thacker, Spink & Co.) (1941, 2 editions, 3rd edition 1944)

John Barleycorn Bahadur (1943)

The Glory Hole (1943)

Scraps from my Diaries (1954)

APPENDIX 2

HARRY HOBBS AND THE CALCUTTA SWEEP

WE HAVE SEEN in Chapter 5 (pages 92-93) Harry's account in *Scraps from my Diaries* as to how he came to be £1,000 better off as a result of good fortune in the Calcutta Sweep. He wrote that book when ninety years old. He was nearly that age when he wrote the letter to Dorothy set out in Chapter 31 (page 544) in which he refers to the same event. He had probably forgotten by then that, in giving the full account of his experiences in his book, published in 1930, *The Romance of the Calcutta Sweep*, he had concealed the fact that it was his own experience by creating a fictitious person whom he called 'Hart.' It must be the case that 'Hart' and Harry are one and the same person. Only one ticket holder can draw any particular horse, and the year and the name of the horse are the same in both the 1930 and the 1954 accounts. Then in both accounts Harry Norton – a very old friend of Harry Hobbs – is named as the purchaser of the quarter share. Finally, the use of the *nom-de-plume* 'Dorothy Dene' is a clear pointer to Harry. It is the title of a popular song of that time, which Harry often applied to his daughter Dorothy, and sang it to her as if it were 'her song.' The refrain was:

> *Oh Dorothy, Dorothy Dene!*
> *Oh Dorothy where have you been?*
> *You've travelled alone*
> *To regions unknown*
> *Along with the man in the flying machine.*

So what follows comes from pages 263 to 282 of *The Romance of the Calcutta Sweep*, set out as written. Remember that for 'Hart' read 'Harry Hobbs' and for 'Hart's business as a coach builder' read 'Harry Hobbs's business as a piano importer.'

In 1901 with but one ticket bearing the *nom-de-plume* of 'Dorothy Dene', a Calcutta man drew Handicapper, second favourite in the Derby, the winner of the Two Thousand Guineas, and for a few short days found himself really popular. Dan King of the Delhi and London Bank, acting for a syndicate, offered Rs. 22,000 for the chance. Hart was prepared to take that for a half share, but he was assured that the horse would be nowhere, that the syndicate was buying merely to hedge, and King's orders were to buy every starter at a price. Of course Hart didn't believe that, and friends encouraged him to stand by his luck, fortifying him with the old proverb that the fittest horse wins the Two Thousand Guineas, the luckiest horse wins the Derby and the best horse wins the St. Leger. Then Harry Norton bought a quarter share for Rs. 10,500. Those who believed in omens foretold a fortune for both, and in regard to Norton they were right for he eventually became a millionaire. When a very rich man he went to the war and did good service in France, while in his declining years he settled in Bournemouth, growing very charitable, and taking under his wing those whose sole inducement to longevity was an old age pension, or the alternative of a shelter in the local workhouse. If winners of Derby sweeps turn mean, losers like Harry Norton grow more generous.

When the news of Hart's good fortune was known, he sprang into something between a celebrity and a notoriety. Many called to tell him that nobody better deserved good fortune. Those who made a comfortable living out of charity thought it worthwhile to tell him that those who give to the poor lend to the Lord. Others, more practical, scornfully asserted that a fool and his money's soon parted. The number of aged parents who were not expected to live, and to whom a good doctor would mean so much, staggered Hart. So did their sons when they talked about the way they stinted and starved so as to send the old people something to make them happy. Women, "More pleased than if I'd won it myself" with unblushing modesty poked him in the ribs and tried to put a coy look into experienced eyes. When nothing happened they sadly explained that "You know I'm not like a lot of other women!" forgetting, poor souls, what a lot of other women there were about like them. High Court Judges were curious to see how Hart stood up to it. Men from upcountry called specifically to see if anything could be done to stop the winner from drinking himself to death. Hundred must have looked forward to agonising details of a martyrdom to delirium tremens, but the truth was that Hart was like a cocoa firm in war time – out to do more business than ever with friend or with foe. Perhaps all that can be said is that most of the callers, puddle-sellers, blue-sky merchants, opportunists and life-long scroungers were merely out for a bit of sentimental arithmetic.

It would be difficult to find one so little interested in racing as Hart, yet during that brief spell, he was consulted on Turf matters as though his life had been spent in watching the starts during the early mornings, or in tracking abandoned females to the totalisator, to see the number they were backing. That is said to be a far more reliable way of picking up tips than anything the barber is likely to give you. In those days it was more difficult to place bets on the Home races than it is now. The population of the world was not so near to being saturated with those who toil not, neither do they spin round anything but starting-price odds, and Hart found himself asked to take bets on that and other races. As he knew nothing about racing, he was easily persuaded to give starting-price odds, and with the luck of a novice, he won the lot. One sportsman came with a message of consolation, feeling sure that Handicapper would not win because: - "When I was a servin' of me time I knowed a bloke wot 'ad a dream as to how Spavin was agoin' to win a race, and he spent the whole day goin' round the pubs in Leeds and Oodersfield to find a bookie to put twenty quid on Spavin but nobody wouldn't take him on. And Spavin won at 100 to 1. My pal was agoin' to git married and he was so upset about it that 'e nearly broke 'is 'eart. Now I've 'ad a dream as to 'ow Revenoo is agoin' to win the Derby, and I'm in just the very same 'ole as my pal wot was in Oodersfield, because I can't find no bookie to take my bet. There's five of us in the chummery; the other four chaps knows about my pal, so they've joined in to make up four 'undred dibs. I lay awake 'arf the night wondering if I could get you to do it. So properly certin' was I that Revenoo will just romp 'ome that it give me a fever. I must be over a 'undred now, and I woke up with a 'ell of a 'eadache."

It was hardly worthwhile to tell him to take a couple of aspirates for it, but so easy to take his money, and the result was that, for him, Revenue was turned into expenditure.

Hart had just started business as a coachbuilder and the money gave him the opportunity for a short holiday in the hills. While he was in Darjeeling, two Mahommedans called with a staggering order. They wanted eighteen conveyances – dog carts, phaetons, landaus and barouches – for a new palace being built by the Nizam of Hyderabad. The news of this fine order was duly sent on and Hart naturally assumed that good fortune had not only knocked at the door, but had fallen into the passage.

As soon as the rains set in and the air cooled, Hart returned to Calcutta to find a shabby little fellow who said he came from the "Nawab" to fix up a meeting. The next day he took Hart to a house in Coolootollah Street, where, in a large, almost bare room, he was received by a magnificent old Persian garbed in snowy muslin, looking for all the world as if he had stepped out of one of Shah Jehan's picture galleries. With that mixture of courtesy, dignity, and deference which constituted so great a part of oriental politeness, he talked like a chapter in the Arabian Nights. Oriental expressions are fascinating, and Hart was much impressed to find himself listening to parables gilded with metaphor, taking no offence when the fine old man asked if the business was his own, whether he owed the bank any money, had he a wife, and were there any "issues." Among Indians it is not considered rude to ask questions; after all, questions are seldom indiscreet although answers may be. While they talked Mahommedans continually passed through the room, fraternising with the crowd lolling on the verandah, defiling floor and walls with *pan-supari*, or blatantly clearing their throats as though anxious to explain to a disgusted world how difficult they found it to bring up a family. They were the usual ill-mannered horde one sees hanging round *Mofussil* courts and railway stations, who use verandah rails and posts as pocket handkerchiefs, and force one to thank God a thousand times that necessity does not compel you to see them too often. All loudly bawled for the Nawab and swaggered round the room while Hart, tolerant but contemptuous, saw without a *punkah*, dripping with perspiration, wondering what was going to happen.

Haste forms no part of the mental equipment of Orientals – slowly slowly catchee monkey being one of their proverbs – but when they detected Hart growing tired of waiting, they explained that the Nawab had come a long journey and could not be interrupted, as he was saying his prayers. Why is it that Christians are always impressed with a statement like that? They seem to be unable to understand that a Mahommedan can pray five times a day and act as though he never prayed at all, but, of all humbug, that about prayers carries most weight. Hart was impressed, although it did not occur to him that they spelt it with an 'e' and, after a sticky wait of three hours, he was easily persuaded to come the next day. The shabby little fellow called punctually, and there were the same happenings. Mahommedans walked aimlessly in and out, squatted on the floor, shouted at the tops of their voices, kicked off their slippers, spat on the floor, or sat cross-legged on chairs to scratch themselves, evidently proud of their manners. Then a young, intelligent looking man, well, but unassumingly dressed, passed through the room, gazing at the European with something like inquisitive contempt. The old Persian deferentially explained. He sat down and talked, but was obviously suffering from drink or drugs, for his attention wandered. Then a new-comer, shouting for all to hear, suggested

619

a gamble. The dissipated fellow demurred. He had lost twenty thousand rupees yesterday, and gambling was off; he was tired of it. Chaffed for his timidity, he consented to play and went for some money. During his absence a pack of cards was arranged so that Hart could see how it was done. When the man returned he slammed a cash box on the table, opened it, casually showing thick bundles of notes.

In less than no time and in a most childish way, he lost two thousand rupees, showing a deal of irritation when paying up. Cursing his bad luck he staggered out of the room. The winner, all smiles, light-heartedly threw a few hundred-rupee notes to the men standing round the door, winked knowingly at Hart, and walked off triumphantly.

The old Persian, who had sat throughout the gamble in stolid helplessness, asked what Hart thought of it. Hart said it was barefaced swindling. The old man went on to say, "When the Nawab's father departed from this house of grief towards the mansions of immortality, he commended his soul to Allah and his son to me. Ever since then I have never slumbered in ease nor waked but in sorrow and anxiety. The wealth of the Nawab was so great that it placed him above the law. Like a pearl in the shell it was beyond the powers of estimation, yet his son, of whom it was hoped he would open the hand of charity to the poor, gave himself up to wine and pleasure. His offences are great, and the punishment Allah inflicts is just. It must come, for he who rides a tiger can never dismount. If you will call tomorrow this bud of friendship may ripen into a golden flower. May you never be tired."

The next morning, while Hart was waiting, a broker called to collect money for a house in the Mofussil. The Nawab made out a cheque for something over a *lakh* of rupees. When the broker left, the Nawab lost some more of his wealth at cards and than asked Hart to play. Hart explained that he had come for an order for gharries, not to play cards, and certainly not to swindle him as the other men had done. Ignoring this the Nawab again suggested a gamble, if only for nuts, stating that, "In my hand I hold a man who will give very large orders." The old Persian returned. Hart asked about business and was assured that the order was all right. There was no need to worry. The Nawab said his prayers at this time, but he will pay you tomorrow.

In gentle tones the old Persian added:- "I have been providing food for my children for fifty years in the family of the Nawab. His father was a worthy man who spread the carpet of justice smoothly upon the face of the earth, and now the fruit of two gardens is within his reach. The sin of ingratitude never darkened the face of his fortune, and had I cared to lengthen my hands on his possession I should not now be consumed with anxiety about the future, for I can see no way whereby I can receive even the mere mockery of my wants. You saw how he threw away a *lakh* on that house, He has six others, bought on impulse, and he has never seen them. To strangers he gives everything; he buys what he needs not, but to one who has long eaten his father's salt he is niggardly to the degree of shame. Now that I am old, the star of my fortune has reached the house of adversity, and before I drink the sherbet of dissolution I see the fruits of my care torn from me and I am to become a beggar. Calamity was destined for me a birth. The tempest of misfortune has overwhelmed me, and though the pure spring of loyalty should not be polluted with the ashes of indignity, necessity has turned my face. I have no one to look to but God and God is far off. I see the flames of ruin arising on every side, but when I saw your face I knew that I was blessed with one bright ray of fortune. An honourable Sahib could win some of this great wealth, so that, when all is lost, he could allow me eight or nine rupees a month to keep me from begging for a few grains of rice. Your honour, to whom everything is well known, is a *pucka Bilati* Sahib and if you will win ten thousand rupees from him I shall know that my life is safe in your hands."

Hart was much charmed and flattered, but again referred to business and said he would not mind risking a thousand rupees after the carriages were paid for.

"Ha! He is superstitious, and nothing will induce him to play with the money he has paid to anybody, but if you come here with three thousand rupees of you own money, I will borrow five hundred from the safe – at least two *lakhs* are there – you will win ten thousands and can return the five hundred. When ruin overwhelms the Nawab I shall know there is a *pucka* Sahib who will save an old man from appealing for charity with a mendicant's tin can. We are compelled to play the game of life according to the casts of fortune. *Rakshat!* May you be blessed by all who leave their shoes at your door!"

Full of sympathy for the venerable old man whose perfect silver beard compelled respect, and with a growing sense of avariciousness, Hart half condemned the drunken vagabond of a Nawab for spending his own money on himself. If that bazaar ragtag and bobtail could make thousands, why shouldn't he make a few for himself? Before he realised it, he had promised to call the next day with enough to help him double the Sweep money, and then, with that in hand, he could save the faithful old *Wazir* from that poverty which is the reward of loyalty and honesty.

Before Hart drove away *Wazir* blessed him, hoping that Allah would protect him against all evil, but once clear of the house, the magnetic influence of that old man seemed to fade. Hart began to think. Here he was, out to do business, and yet he was going to draw money out of the bank to play cards with a drunken Mahommedan. The thing was absurd, particularly so for Hart who hardly knew the difference between the tray of diamonds and a silver salver. And, knowing that, he was pitting himself against a crowd of Mahommedans who had probably revelled in scoundrelism from birth. At that moment he was passing Lall Bazaar Police Compound and thought he might as well go in an have a *bukh* with *Parawallah* Johnson, a prominent Superintendent of Police, who heard his story and cursed for all he was worth. "Of all the stupid fools in this world or any other, you're one!" was the first comment Hart heard. "Don't you understand that you've been watched day and night ever since you got back? Couldn't you grasp the idea that the *gharriwallah* is in their pay? Haven't you a notion that he will tell them all about your visit here and therefore you'll not see that bunch again? Not one of them! You are a first class fool if ever there was one! Why you weren't drowned when a pup beats me!"

Johnson began to reel off the names of Calcutta men who had been swindled by the same crowd, who originally came to Calcutta with the last King of Oudh and had never done an honest job of work in their lives. Not only did they operate in Calcutta, but they also worked all the large Indian cities, so that, if things became too hot in one, then went to another until things quietened down.

Several commercial travellers representing English firms had been induced to gamble and to lose their firm's money. They either disappeared or committed suicide. A livery-stable keeper was driven into bankruptcy court before he understood that he was being swindled. When he found it out, matters had been complicated by most of the money being lost in Chandernagore, which meant trouble over extradition.

Wealthy Indians were tackled in a different way. As most of them when young are sensualists, the bait was a girl who, if she wasn't good, was good-looking and once the victim was in the coils he had to pay or feel sorry for himself.

Then Hart mentioned the matter to R. N. Matthewson of No.1, Calcutta. He knew all about it. Thirty or more years before then he had been tackled in the same way by the same gang and in the same house. They let Matthewson win Rs. 800 before persuading him to draw Rs. 3,000 out of the bank. He drew a cheque, sent his *peon* to cash it, but before leaving the house to win the Nawab's money, he took the precaution to cut up newspapers to the size and bulk of ten rupee notes, then, placing a genuine note top and bottom, he left the good money behind. On all his previous visits Matthewson had been received on the ground floor; this time they took him upstairs where he found six men seated on the floor. He was asked, "Did your Honour bring the money?" In reply, he pressed his coat pocket to show what was there, when they rushed at him. Matthewson was a strong and parsimonious Scot, so he put up no end of a scrap while fighting his way to a sweepers' staircase, with the crowd hanging on to him trying to get at his pocket. On the outer wall of the staircase there happened to be a loose brick; he hit out with it which gave him a chance to run downstairs, while they yelled out to men in the courtyard to kill him. A *durwan* in the compound rushed at him brandishing a sword. Matthewson was a crank, and one of his idiosyncrasies was that he never wore a topee but always carried an umbrella. He lunged at the swordsman with that, and caught him in the eye, killing him on the spot. This gave Matthewson a chance to bolt into the street and to report what had happened.

In the subsequent proceedings, details of missing Europeans were brought to light. Matthewson said that their bodies were exhumed in the compound of the house. At any rate several of the gang were sent to the Andamans while Matthewson exulted over the fact that he had won eight hundred rupees and lost nothing. While boasting about this he so rubbed it into Hart for being a chump that they nearly came to blows.

Exactly as Parawallah Johnson had said, Hart saw no more of the Coolootollah mob. They faded out of sight. Then one day, six years later, a well dressed Mahommedan walked into Hart's yard – be was a prosperous business man then – followed by a sturdy fellow in ammunition boots, with a heavy stick such as a *zemindar's peon* carries.

There was the same story of a big order for Hyderabad. The Nawab who "in my hand I hold a man" was coming to Calcutta the next day. He was paying cash for twelve dogcarts for the Sahib logue, and six barouches for the Missi-baba logue. Hart, with old Matthewson's jibes and Parawallah Johnson's sneer still rankling in his mind, welcomed the man enthusiastically.

The goods were examined, pictures and drawings were approved, and then they went upstairs to smoke cigarettes and talk.

Hart laboriously wrote down details in the order book, and was amiably chatting, when something prompted the orderly, who was waiting outside the office door, to throw himself downstairs five at a time. As it happened, the cashier, who had been for the police, was walking up and the man, as he "fled away," knocked him flying. Hearing the commotion the

Mahommedan paused, listened, and looked round, while Hart thought he might as well have the name and address. Receiving no answer, he asked, "Is it No. 35, Coolootollah Street?"

Most embarrassed, the man made a pretext to leave, but a good grip of his ear helped him to examine the order book more closely, while Hart rubbed it in. "Your crowd made a fool of me six years ago. I was laughed at all over the place. It's my turn to laugh now. But I'll give you a chance. Write down which you prefer – a damned good hiding, or be run in?"

Seeing what he was in for the Mahommedan turned abusive, but a short arm jab or two checked any real flow of language, and the police called in time to save Hart from letting himself go.

The prisoner was first released on bail of Rs. 500 which, after the second hearing, was raised to Rs. 5,000. While proceedings were pending, Hart, who was in the Volunteers, was on guard of honour at Government House top receive the Viceroy, when he noticed his friend, the Nawab, driving in a barouche almost directly behind the Governor-General. It was evident that he went about in style when not on a swindling stunt.

Mr Donald Weston, ICS, one of those levelheaded, capable characters one only finds in Government service, and then far too seldom, was Chief Presidency Magistrate at the time. He accepted Hart's memoranda as *pucka* evidence.

On the last day of the hearing, the whole gang were assembled in the Police Court. Hart recognised the venerable old Persian, although he had dyed his snowy beard with henna and was dressed in dirty rags which made him look as if the long-feared destitution had already overwhelmed him. The Nawab Sahib, furtive as a sewer rat, sat uneasily on one of those wooden bug-garages in the body of the Court, while his friends who won thousands and gave away hundreds, looked like sweepers on half pay. The other confederates were there too, but they no longer affected muslin shirts, gold slashed waistcoats, and poll parrot caps. They looked more like those dirty *kazaks* who, late at night tout for female beguilers of darkness in crawling *ticca gharries* drawn by glandered horses.

Parawallah Johnson warned Hart to be careful, as they were sure to get even with him some dark night, so he thought it wise to carry the war right into their territory. Pointing them out in Court one at a time, he drew attention of the police to each one, while they, under the leadership of the Nawab, who probably thought it about time to ring up Mecca, sneaked out like sick jackals chased by crows through the bazaar.

When a sentence of four months rigorous was passed, Hart met the whole gang on the landing of the Police Court and, with a pungent fluency, cursed them in English and Hindustani, threatening that if he ever caught one of them near his place he'd murder him. Taken by surprise they made themselves scarce and Hart says he never saw one of them again.

Six weeks later the Chief Justice heard the appeal. He seemed to be prepared to act like the Irish mayor, who asserted that he was out to discharge his duties without partiality on the one hand or impartiality on the other, although he did not create the impression that Justice is the treatment of people according to their deserts. He said that in all his professional career he had never heard such a scandalous proposal as to ask a man which he preferred, "A damned good hiding or be run in?" and with a sturdy, fat-headed sense of British justice he ordered the prisoner to be released.

Of course there were many who considered the decision of the Chief Justice a nasty jar for Hart, but there was nothing to be gained by broadcasting other details.

When the culprit was taken to the Presidency Jail, Hart's old sergeant-major happened to be the jailer, and he felt sure that the sentence would be set aside by the High Court. He therefore thought it a good idea to make sure of giving him something to get on with while the lawyers were skinning the friends outside. Tobacco was found concealed on the prisoner's clothing, for which the punishment was automatic – a dozen on the triangle. The day before the appeal was heard, more tobacco was discovered, and as true discipline knows no exceptions, a Burmese life convict, encouraged by seven-octave yelps of appreciation, laid on a full ration of the very best. By that time the confidence trickster began to understand that the ways of transgressors can run on hard lines.

APPENDIX 3

FROM IAN COSTER'S COLUMN
IN *THE DAILY MAIL*

(Reprinted by kind permission of the Publishers of *The Daily Mail*)

SEE CHAPTER 31, page 533. 'Ian Coster' was the pen name used by the then Editor of *The Daily Mail*, Frank Owen, who had known Harry Hobbs when they both worked on the SEAC Newspaper during the war. He was delighted to meet Harry again, and subsequently wrote the following about him, which was published on 27th October, 1949:

A character has arrived from India to lessen the gloom. He is 86-year-old Major Harry Hobbs, MBE, VD, soldier, hotel-keeper, author, musician, businessman, raconteur, traveller, lecturer.

Hobbs has been in India for 65 years. In Calcutta, where he runs an hotel and a piano business, he is a prominent citizen and a legend.

Spare, grey-moustached, with twinkling blue eyes, he claims that he has based his life on three rules: "Never threaten, never promise, never apologise."

Age cannot tame him; he comes out fighting at the blink of an eyelid whether it is to attack the memory of Gandhi – one of his great hates – or bungling officialdom or sentimentality.

In a country which was largely run by managing agents he courted libel by addressing letters "Messrs. So-and-So, Mismanaging Agents."

A thorn in company meeting, he once leapt to his feet and said: "Mr. Chairman, this board had the same qualities as any other board, it is long, it is narrow and it is wooden."

I met him one afternoon in Calcutta as he walked out of a building filled with uproar. "A board meeting?" I asked. "Yes," he said. "After the chairman's statement I got up and simply said: 'I have read the balance-sheet, Ananias.'"

Ask him about the Indian Mutiny and he'll reply: "The story of the Mutiny can be told in four words: ignorance, arrogance, cowardice, panic."

Truculent, intolerant and merry, he has written ten books (published at his own expense), with provocative titled such as Scoundrels and Scroungers and Talkeetalkeewallahs and Others.

"Didn't you ever get any writs for libel?" I once asked him. "Certainly, he replied, "four in one day." "And what did you do about them?" "Took no notice."

His fund of stories is inexhaustible and over luncheon he reels them off with a Trinder routine. "The worst thing you can ask of a good story is 'Is it true?'" is one of his favourites.

Hobbsian epigrams are innumerable: "The ladder of success is full of splinters which hurt most when you're sliding down." "Marriage is like a besieged fort – those inside want to get out and those outside want to get in." "Strategy is that art of continuing to fire on the enemy after your ammunition had been expended."

Of all his merry stories I like the one of the Indian horse-coper who sold another a racehorse which had to be sent up-country. As the horse was being put into the railway box it fell dead. But it was sent on. The copers met months later. "How's the horse I sent you?" asked the seller. "He's dead," said the other, "he was dead when he arrived." "Oh, I am sorry. What did you do about it? Why didn't you let me know?" "It turned out alright said the buyer, "we raffled him at 100 chips a time." "But didn't the winner make a fuss?" "Oh no, we just gave him his money back."

The gallant major leaves for India in a few days; it's a pity he can't stay for the election.

APPENDIX 4

OBITUARIES
OF HARRY HOBBS

THE FOLLOWING OBITUARIES appeared in Calcutta newspapers a few days after the death of Harry. All three of these journals have ceased to publish and it is my regret that I have been unable to seek, let alone to obtain any permission for reproducing them here. If there is an avenue I should have explored which might have led to a copyright holder I can only apologise: I did all that I could think of to trace any such person.

From *Capital*
of 24th May, 1956, in
A Ditcher's Diary

So old Harry Hobbs is dead. When I last spoke to him three months ago he was still every inch Major Harry Hobbs, MBE, VD and looked good for many more years. His feet shuffled a little, but his eyes were bright and his tongue was as sharp as ever. His only complaint seemed to be a touch of deafness, but for one of such venerable years that is no great disaster because friends usually call to listen rather than to be listened to. Not that I can ever claim to have been a friend of Harry Hobbs. He had a particular contempt for journalists and their newspapers and, characteristically, never tired of saying so. His favourite name for the Press was the sup-Press, which must have been true enough so far as concerned some of the outrageous and unprintable – though frequently quite justified – things he has been known to say. His life-long hatred of the stingy and small-minded must have influenced his ideas about newspapers. He once wrote; "The meanness which pervades in newspaper offices is not found to that extent in other walks of life." He goes on: "For the hundreds of columns I have written for the Press I have not received a total of Rs. 200." That is a pity because Harry Hobbs had a fine virile style and what he wrote was always worth reading whether one approved of it or not. Calcutta owes him a debt as one of its greatest unofficial historians, and there must be a great deal of information still to be rooted out from those voluminous files of his. What will happen to his papers is something we have not yet heard; he used to claim that the Bodleian had asked for them. They should make interesting – if occasionally libellous – reading because there must be few personalities who have featured in the Indian scene during the last seventy years who are not also featured in these files. I am sure their doings are recorded with a thoroughness and precision the lack of which he once regretted in a newspaper report of his own interspersions at a company meeting "where the Chairman was a crook who had swindled people out of about a couple of millions," which read "Mr Hobbs made a few humorous remarks." Harry Hobbs lived to be the oldest European in India. He survived an age which had left little time or respect for the dull middle-class lives to which taxation and social change seem to have reduced the present generation of his fellow expatriates. He future is unlikely to give us – and India – another like him.

If I cannot claim to have been a friend of Harry Hobbs, there are many who were more fortunate. One of them, *Capital's* legal correspondent, writing to me of his recollections of this remarkable man, says: "He was unique. An Institution. Each generation produces about one such and then destroys the mould. Absolute independence, fearlessness, integrity. 'Can mix with kings nor lose the common touch. George Bernard Shaw, Dean Inge, Bertrand Russell, George Lansbury, Brougham (who threatened to topple the Throne and would have done it too for Queen Caroline), Edmund Burke, Dr Johnson and the rest, the lights of the world in their several generations. No one pretends that Harry Hobbs was of their stature. But he was of their clan. Plenty has been written about his searing sarcasm, his hatred of pomposity, hypocrisy and humbug; in that respect had his early years been different he might, I think, have been another Dean Swift. I want to emphasise another side, his innate kindliness and his courage. I met him first many years ago at a mutual friend's funeral. We were the first arrivals and chatted together. He spoke with quiet reverence about things that matter, this man supposed to be anti-religious but actually only anti-clerical, and later, upright as a ramrod, joined in every response with curt military precision. He was deeply moved. But there had to be a Hobbsian climax. After the service he complained bitterly of the callous, unfeeling, mechanical way in which the chaplain had conducted it and wanted

Geoffrey Tyson to lead us all back to the graveside and have a little service on our own. His complaint was justified and Tyson was in two minds about actually doing it, I think. Later when I knew that this quiet reverent man was the great iconoclast, Major Harry Hobbs, I could hardly believe it. I find myself marvelling at his composed courage at Journey's End. He knew it was a matter of days, and four days before his death he concluded our weekly correspondence with a farewell letter. Any one of us may well be proud if we can write such a letter when similarly placed. Shed were all the sharp invective, the biting criticism of men and things, but not in favour of gloomy resignation. Far from it. Written in his bold, clear writing it might have been the letter of a brilliant rising young man of thirty. After an admonitory lecture on literary style; – 'A book, essay, conversation or letter should be interesting, true (or read as if it were) and with a touch of humour...,' he tells three witty stories, including Sir J. M. Barrie's reminiscence of Ranji at a farewell dinner: – "I saw him bat twice; the first time he made one run; the second he was not so successful;' and ending with a delightfully *risqué* one about Spence's Hotel. Death was a casual thing. In this joyous happy letter, not a word about it except a hint at the end: 'Goodbye. My Blessing.' A good, brave, stout-hearted Englishman. There are many such and will be many more. But there will not be another Harry Hobbs – not in our lifetime.

From *The Calcutta Municipal Gazette* of 19th May, 1956

Death of a nineteenth century municipal commissioner

Death has snatched away from among us the oldest European resident in the city, the man who undertook a 45-day voyage to come to India from England. Major Harry Hobbs passed away on Tuesday night at the age of 92, after spending 72 years of his life in India.

As a satirist, journalist, author, a commercial old-stayer and above all a lovable man, Major Harry Hobbs does not, cannot die. Calcutta will ever remember him as its 'Bernard Shaw.'

Born in London in 1864, he started work at the age of 13. But the lure of India induced him to undertake a difficult voyage in those days.

His desire to know India led him to travel widely in India and Burma under the most strenuous condition. He tried to understand Oriental music and present it through European musical instruments.

An officer of the Calcutta Volunteer Rifles and a member of the Calcutta Port Defence Corps, the late Major Hobbs was a good marksman with the rifle.

As a Municipal Commissioner, the late Major Hobbs was connected with some of the early improvements of this city towards the close of the nineteenth century. He entered the Municipality in the year 1899. He also popularised himself by other social activities, such as organising concert parties and games.

After 20 years in India he gave up his musical career in preference for journalism. For some time he was a regular Correspondent of the 'Indian Daily News.' While earning appreciation from many quarters, he drew sharp criticism from others, but was regardless of either. To the last day his spirit never flagged. Among the multitude of people who met him, most of them remembered him for his remarkable gifts of humour and wit

The India he came to in 1883 is only a memory today. About those early days one of his sayings was that, while things were cheap, "nothing was cheaper than pay." And that is, perhaps, a clue to his development as a satirist.

Many people, in this country and abroad, will sorrow at his passing; know that they will not see his like again. His spirit rose above the harshness of this city to which he came in the eighties of the last century. People complain of the present uncleanliness of Calcutta, but in the eighties and nineties it seems to have been worse. Harry Hobbs could not conceal his disgust at the stench in some streets in those times. Nevertheless he enjoyed his long life despite all the asperities of the Calcutta that he had known.

The Corporation mourned his death at it weekly meeting on Friday, the 18th May, and adjourned its sitting for ten minutes as a mark of respect to his memory. Moving the condolence from the Chair, the Mayor, Shri Satis Chandra Ghosh, said the city has lost in him a distinguished citizen who gave is mind to its improvements even in the late nineteenth century.

From *Monthly Review*
(the official journal of the United Kingdom Citizen's Association) for June, 1956

Calcutta members will have seen in the press the death of our oldest member, Harry Hobbs. Those who do not know him will also have learnt something of the details of his quite out of the ordinary career. But then, Harry Hobbs was a man who was quite out of the ordinary himself. He was an individualist and an extremist to whom the normal British traits of compromise and "letting the dog see the rabbit" were quite unknown. He had a very complete integrity and a passionate belief in the rights of the individual. His make-up included a considerable amount of humour and wit, which, despite its caustic character, was far from unkindly.

In recent years he has not, for reasons of health, taken any active part in the community's affairs in Calcutta, and therefore was no longer known to many of our members. Our older members, however, will recall many lively meetings both of the UKCA and of individual companies in Clive Street, where Harry Hobbs's voice was often raised in defence of the individual as he saw it and castigating the official, and (dare it be said?) the slightly smug view that sometimes prevailed. At the same time he never let his opinion interfere with his friendship for many of those whom he had just severely criticised.

As an individual, in his long life in Calcutta, he has probably left as big a mark as any in the life of this city, and it would be well for our community if there were many more like him in their sense of patriotism and their duty to their fellow men.

NOTES

Chapter 1.
From London to Calcutta.
1. *Scraps from my Diaries* pp. 1–2
2. *ibid.* p. 3
3. *Talkeetalkeewallahs and Others* pp. 125-126
4. *Scoundrels and Scroungers* p. 92
5. *Scraps from my Diaries* pp. 3-4
6. *It was Like This!* pp. 3-4
7. *ibid.* pp. 6
8. *ibid.* pp. 4-5
9. *ibid.* pp. 5-6
10. *ibid.* p. 6 and *Scraps from my Diaries* p. 7
11. *Scraps from my Diaries* p. 8
12. *It was Like This!* p. 8
13. *Scraps from my Diaries* p. 8

Chapter 2. The first five years.
1. *Scraps from my Diaries* p. 93
2. *ibid.* p.9 and *It was Like This!* p. 1
3. *Indian Dust Devils* pp. 6-7
4. *ibid.* pp. 8-9
5. *ibid.* pp. 18-30
6. *Scraps from my Diaries* pp. 58-60
7. *It was Like This!* pp. 33-35
8. *Scraps from my Diaries* p. 93
9. *Indian Dust Devils* pp. 32-33
10. *Talkeetalkeewallahs and Others* pp. 141-142
11. *Indian Dust Devils* p. 33
12. *ibid.* pp. 33-34
13. *Scraps from my Diaries* pp. 15-16
14. *The Piano in India* p. 9
15. *Indian Dust Devils* pp. 35-37
16. *Scraps from my Diaries* p. 14
17. *It was Like This!* pp. 157-160
18. *ibid.* pp. 355-357
19. *ibid.* pp. 167-168
20. *ibid.* pp. 19-21
21. *Indian Dust Devils* pp. 37-44
22. *ibid.* pp. 44-46
23. *It was Like This!* pp. 179-186
24. *ibid.* pp. 351-354; *Scraps from my Diaries* pp. 16-17
25. *Scoundrels and Scroungers* pp. 53-56
26. *It was Like This!* p. 31
27. *Scraps from my Diaries* p. 61
28. *ibid.* pp. 62-63
29. *ibid.* p. 66
30. *It was Like This!* pp. 35-36
    a. *ibid.* p. 30

Chapter 4.
Return to India and beyond.
1. *Digressions of a Ditcher* p. 2
2. *It was Like This!* p. 259
3. *ibid.* pp. 259-264
4. *The Piano in India* p. 14
5. *ibid.* pp.14-15
6. *ibid.* p. 127
7. *ibid.* p. 193
8. *It was Like This!* pp. 70-73
9. *Talkeetalkeewallahs and Others* pp. 60-61
10. *Indian Dust Devils* pp. 129-131
11. *ibid.* pp. 98-99
12. *Romance of the Calcutta Sweep* pp. 200-201
13. *It was Like This!* pp. 218-221
14. *Scraps from my Diaries* p. 93
15. *ibid.* pp. 69-70
16. *ibid.* pp. 71-73
17. *ibid.* p. 76
18. *ibid.* pp. 60-61

GLOSSARY

Banchute	Literally 'sister-raper,' a particularly vile term of abuse.
Bihari	A native of the State of Bihar (N-E India).
Bilati	From abroad; foreign (i.e., to India); English.
Bukh	A chat.
Burra Mem	Short for Burra Memsahib; the wife of the headman in a firm or a family.
Chapatti	Small, flat, round, unleavened loaf of bread.
Charpoy	String used for stuffing a mattress.
Chota hazri	A light breakfast.
Chup	Silence; 'to keep chup' = to keep quiet.
Coop	Very, extremely, almost over the top.
Cutcha	Crude; shoddy.
Dacoit	Indian gang-robber.
Dak	A dak bungalow was a rest-house for the accommodation of travellers, maintained by the Government of India.
Dhurry	Indian cotton carpet.
Dib	Money.
Durwan	Doorkeeper.
Gharry	Carriage; taxi.
Gharriwallah	Carriage – or taxi-driver.
Ghat	A quay; steps leading down to a river.
Ghora	Ride (such as a horse would give).
Gubbrowed	Perturbed; confused; worried by.
Izzat	Honour; prestige.
Janiwala	Green, fresh, inexperienced.
Jemandar	Head servant.

Jhilmil	Venetian blind.
Khitmagar	Male servant; waiter.
Lakh	One hundred thousand.
Mistri	Foreman.
Mofussil	Rural; up-country.
Nawab	Muslim Governor; nobleman.
Nullah	Watercourse.
Pagri	Indian light turban; scarf or veil wound round a topi.
Pan-supari	The leaf of the plant betel, wrapped around chopped areca-nut, lime, cloves, tobacco, &c., and chewed as a masticatory. Often used as a form of ceremonial hospitality, particularly towards guests who are about to depart.
Parawallah	A para is the hog-deer of N. India. So literally a man who looks after them. Used by Harry as equivalent to policeman.
Palki	A covered box littler, carried on a pole by 4 or 6 men.
Peon	Footman; office-boy.
Pucka	Real; genuine; sound.
Punkah	A large swinging fan, suspended from the ceiling and worked by a man (punkah-wallah) pulling a rope.
Rajbari	Head office.
Rakshat	Something to be guarded against; a demon.
Sahib	Master, Sir.
Shaitan	The Devil; an evil spirit.
Syce	A groom.
Thannah	Police station.
Ticca gharry	Hired carriage.
Tonga	Light, small, two-wheeled, horse-drawn carriage.
Wazir	Member of a Pathan tribe in N-W India.
Zemindar	Landowner.